EISENHOWER

Also by Jim Newton

Justice for All:
Earl Warren and the Nation He Made

EISENHOWER

The White House Years

Jim Newton

DOUBLEDAY
New York   London   Toronto
Sydney   Auckland

DOUBLEDAY and the portrayal of an anchor with a dolphin
are registered trademarks of Random House, Inc.

Book design by Michael Collica
Jacket design by John Fontana
Jacket photograph courtesy of the Library of Congress
Frontispiece courtesy of White House Historical Association (White House Collection)

ISBN 978-0-385-52353-0

PRINTED IN THE UNITED STATES OF AMERICA

Book Club Edition

To Jack and Karlene, with love

CONTENTS

EISENHOWER

INTRODUCTION

May 1, 1958, was a fairly quiet day in the world. It was international Communism's traditional date of celebration, and Moscow marked the occasion with a peace-themed rally in Red Square, presided over by Nikita Khrushchev and provocatively attended by Gamal Abdel Nasser of the United Arab Republic, ostensibly a Cold War–neutral but often a flirtatious friend of Russia. In London, Labourites hoisted a red flag, while in Nazareth, Moscow's celebration of peace frayed a bit: eighty people were injured when fighting broke out after Communists heckled a group of labor demonstrators. At the level of diplomacy, the American secretary of state, John Foster Dulles, was pursuing an agreement with the Soviet Union to remove bombers and military bases from the Arctic; Vice President Richard Nixon was in Argentina for the inauguration of Arturo Frondizi, that nation's first freely elected president in twelve years.

Dwight David Eisenhower, thirty-fourth president of the United States, spent the day at the White House, all but invisible to the outside world. He woke to a cool, sunny morning in the capital and had breakfast with members of his staff at 7:45 a.m. in the White House mess. He arrived at his desk at 8:36 a.m. Looking over his schedule, the president saw that he had a short workday ahead, with just one meeting of consequence.

Five years into his presidency, Eisenhower was in a slump. His approval ratings, which generally hovered between 60 and 70 percent, had fallen below 50 for the first time as the American economy slogged through a mild recession. Knocked down by a heart attack in 1955 and a hospitalization for ileitis in 1956, he was perceived by many journalists and much of the nation's elite as ailing, ineffectual, and detached, surrounded by scheming, powerful cabinet members who carried out the nation's work while Ike served as its benign figurehead, devoted to golf and bridge, manipulated by a coterie of shrewd businessmen. The administration's response to the recession seemed to its critics lamentably typical. The House of Representatives that day passed a bill to extend jobless benefits, but the legislation represented a compromise—liberals had supported larger benefits for longer, while Eisenhower backed a more modest alternative. Eisenhower, one editorial opined, was confronting the nation's economic difficulties "by the device of wishful thinking."

Dissatisfaction with Ike was captured that year by Marquis Childs, an influential Washington journalist whose 1958 book, *Eisenhower: Captive Hero*, portrayed the president as indecisive and lazy, stodgy and limited by his military upbringing. "He is moved by forces," Childs wrote. "He does not undertake to move them himself." Ike, in Childs's view, had fallen woefully short of public expectations for his presidency and had failed to marshal the powers of his office. For that, Childs concluded, "Eisenhower . . . must be put down as a weak president."

That was Eisenhower as viewed by press and public—limited, captive, disappointing. But on this May Day of 1958, the President Eisenhower invisible to Childs, unappreciated by his critics, was at work offstage on matters of grave consequence. At 9:00 a.m., the president and thirty-four of his most senior and trusted advisers assembled for the 364th meeting of the National Security Council. The meeting opened, as it usually did, with a briefing on world events—updates on fighting in Indonesia and Yemen highlighted the report—then turned to a review of basic U.S. security policy, a matter that had been under constant consideration since Ike's election in 1952.

For months, Eisenhower's top aides had grown increasingly restive about the nation's reliance on massive retaliation as the centerpiece of its strategy to contain Soviet and Chinese Communism. The threat of annihilation had maintained an uneven peace since the end of World War II, and America's nuclear might had allowed Eisenhower to leverage advantage in conflicts from Berlin to Korea to Taiwan. But as the Soviets gained nuclear strength, America's allies—and its military leadership—worried that the threat of retaliation was growing hollow. Would the United States actually risk its own destruction to deter a Soviet advance on Austria, say, or Berlin or Vietnam?

On that Thursday morning, it was Secretary of Defense Neil McElroy who opened the argument, noting that his Turkish counterpart had three times during a recent NATO meeting raised questions about whether the United States was actually prepared to live up to its commitment to its allies—"to resist a Soviet attack on one member of the Alliance as an attack on all." General Maxwell Taylor, chief of staff of the Army, echoed those concerns, citing recent setbacks in Indonesia and the Middle East and warning that the Soviet Union was on the verge of achieving nuclear parity with the United States. Taylor and McElroy proposed to address what they saw as a dangerous trend by adjusting American security policy: rather than relying on the threat of massive retaliation, the United States, they argued, should develop a tactical nuclear capacity to fight limited wars. They acknowledged such a course would be expensive, especially if new, smaller nuclear weapons were to be developed even as the nation continued to arm itself with large deterrent forces. But Eisenhower's top military advisers insisted that the price was justified; the survival of the Western alliance and, with it, Western civilization itself depended on it.

Secretary of State Dulles, Ike's closest adviser, agreed with his military counterparts. So grave was the stress on American alliances, he said, that those nations who had bound their fates to that of the United States—many after long urging by Ike and Dulles themselves—would break away if they did not have better assurances that the United States would help protect them. It was thus "urgent for us to develop the tactical defensive capabilities inherent in small 'clean' nuclear weapons." Although Dulles himself was a principal architect of massive retaliation, that approach to deterring war, he now argued, "was running its course" and would soon be obsolete: "In short, the United States must be in a position to fight defensive wars which do not involve the total defeat of the enemy."

Eisenhower sat quietly as his top aides urgently pressed him to abandon the most fundamental security precept of his presidency, a policy deliberately arrived at beginning with a landmark, classified study in 1953 and patiently pursued in the years since. When Dulles finished, the president noted that he had a "couple of questions." In fact, they were more in the form of observations. Eisenhower challenged first the utility and then the plausibility of shifting from massive retaliation to flexible response. The nuclear option that his advisers recommended, Eisenhower pointed out, would transform weapons of deterrence into weapons of war, from an umbrella shielding allies to a "lightning rod" drawing fire to earth. Imagine a Soviet attack on Austria, the president said. American repulsion of that assault would never take the form of a "nice, sweet, World War II–type of war." It would be a fight to the finish. Tactical nuclear weapons would not change that; they would merely escalate conventional war to nuclear war and thus extinction. Massive retaliation, by contrast, was predicated on the premise that an all-out nuclear response was America's only retort to such an invasion; recognizing that, the Soviets would presumably refrain from courting their own destruction.

Moreover, Eisenhower added, creating a new force of tactical nuclear weapons could only be accomplished in one of two ways. The United States could switch from building deterrent weapons to building tactical ones, or it could attempt to do both. To cease building large nuclear weapons even as the Soviet Union galloped to catch up with the United States was almost too perilous to contemplate, but attempting both also came with profound implications. It would require a stupendous increase in military spending, an idea that Ike had fought his entire presidency as he strove for balance between national security and economic stability. To reverse now would require the focused expenditures and sacrifices possible only within a controlled economy, nothing short of a "garrison state."

Dulles fought back. America's European allies needed at least the illusion that they could resist a Soviet attack, a defensive capability short of global nuclear war. Ike was bewildered. What sort of defense would that be, he asked, when 175 Soviet divisions confronted 6 Western divisions? Dulles countered that the United States was, of course, encouraging the development of Western forces, but the imbalance remained and, with it, the instability of the alliance. Pressing his point, the secretary of state remarked that he was soon to depart for Berlin, where he would perform the "ritual act" of insisting that any Soviet attack on that city be treated as an attack on America itself. Eisenhower refused to let that pass. He did not consider America's pledge to the defense of Berlin shallow or illusory. Failure to respond with the full might of American forces in the event of a Berlin takeover, he reminded Dulles, would doom the city and then Western Europe. Western security depended on the existence of an American deterrent and the willingness to use it. Eisenhower dreaded the day that such a decision might be his, but he understood that to avoid it, he had to be prepared to order it.

Ike, whose temper could flare at times, this day chose to be gracious even as he was insistent. The discussion, he said, was one of the most important ever to come before the council. And the National Security Council's strategic paper, known as NSC 5810, was worth all the other policy papers he had read in the past six months. He acknowledged that he and Dulles were on opposite sides of this crucial question and said he expected to keep facing these questions in the future.

And yet there was no mistaking his resolve. Eisenhower's top command continued to debate details, but Ike had already prevailed. He would not, then or ever, reorient American forces so that they might more easily fight a nuclear war. He would pay a political price. Democrats, including Senator John Kennedy, positioned themselves as the more stalwart cold warriors, more serious than Eisenhower about investing in national security and fighting Communism. They baited him for allowing a "missile gap," for being too soft on defense. Ike refused to waver. He would check the Soviets where he could, roll back Communism when the opportunity arose, negotiate for arms reductions, fight relentlessly for peace, and construct an astonishing period of prosperity, stability, and freedom. Far from the caricature presented by Childs and others, Eisenhower was certain, resolute, and, though respectful of his advisers, commandingly their boss.

The NSC concluded its business at 11:18 a.m. Ike welcomed the mayor of Duluth and his wife and chatted with them for a few minutes. He conferred with his appointments secretary and a representative of the Secret Service. In the afternoon, he met with a representative of the United Nations on refugee matters, talked with a few aides, then hit a bucket of golf balls on the White House's South Lawn. At 5:40 p.m., he called it a day.

The next day's papers contained no hint of the NSC deliberations, barely any reference to Eisenhower at all. Publicly, he had conducted routine business during a quiet day at the White House. Privately, he had committed the United States to his precarious pursuit of peace.

PART ONE

MAKING IKE

By the time he declared his candidacy for president in 1952, Dwight Eisenhower was a formed man, exquisitely prepared for the burdens and the opportunities of the office. No person in the United States had greater experience in leadership, greater knowledge of America's most important allies, greater grasp of Washington's most essential institutions. And yet he developed all of those insights and skills outside the realm of politics. Ike constructed them from the lessons of his mother, the patience of his wife, the gallantry of George Patton, the patient tutoring of Fox Conner, the negative example of Douglas MacArthur, the serene leadership of George Marshall, and the wise political tutelage of Herbert Brownell.

Those seven women and men—and the experiences they bestowed upon Eisenhower—made him the person and the leader who would guide America through the 1950s, inheriting a nation at war and leaving one at peace. All of those men and women led lives of their own, some of great consequence, others of humility. Collectively, however, their greatest contribution was that they made Ike.

1

The Lessons of Family

I da Stover Eisenhower was a woman of special depth—cheerful and sunny, serious and devoted, a dedicated pacifist whose aversion to war was forged in the aftermath of the Civil War, into which Ida was born. Her memories of those days must have been dim—born in 1862, she barely experienced the war itself—but she came of age in Virginia, a land torn to pieces. Ida's mother died when she was five, her father when she was eleven, leaving her a small inheritance. She was raised by her mother's father, taught for a time, and then, in 1883, decamped for Kansas and college.

Ida's determination to get a college degree, so uncommon for a woman of her era, suggests her distinction. She was studious and religious, though hardly doctrinaire. She read Greek and consulted Greek texts of the Bible when she had questions about its commands. As a student at Lane University in Lecompton, Kansas, she met David Jacob Eisenhower, an aspiring engineer of German stock who had come west in 1878. Ida was a year older. They were married on September 23, 1885.

By 1890, David and Ida had two sons, as well as a burden and a grudge. Their wedding present from David's parents was a 160-acre farm and $2,000, but he had no interest in farming, so he mortgaged the land to his brother-in-law and used the money to open a store in Hope, Kansas. Hard times followed, and as farmers fell behind on their credit, the store suffered, then collapsed when Eisenhower's business partner stole what little cash there was left. The failure of that enterprise shadowed the Eisenhower family and impressed on David Eisenhower a devotion to frugality; never again would he go into debt or allow his family to borrow a dime.

The loss of his store wounded David, and those around him felt he never quite recovered. Ida was less rattled by the episode but no less resolute. So determined was she to see justice done that she taught herself the law, pining for a confrontation with the ex-partner that never came.

David took his family to Texas, where he secured work as a railroad engineer and tried to rebuild their lives. It was there, in a Texas thunderstorm on October 14, 1890, that Ida gave birth to her third son, David Dwight Eisenhower.

David may have been the family patriarch, but he was a brooding, remote presence, especially in his later years. He administered discipline and provided for his family, but he was serious to the point of being glum. Ida, by contrast, was the steadfast center of a boisterous home. Although she appears dark haired in some pictures, especially as she grew older, her children remembered her as blond and fair. She played the piano and often sang to herself. She was an accomplished baker who cooked as quickly as her sons could eat. She could whack the head off a chicken without remorse, impart gentle bits of wisdom, chuckle over mischief. "I have seldom seen an unsmiling photograph of her," recalled one of Ike's brothers.

Religion, too, was at the core of their lives. David Eisenhower was raised as a member of the River Brethren, a Pennsylvania Mennonite sect whose Kansas migration swept along the Eisenhower family. Of the nine River Brethren congregations that settled in Kansas in the 1880s, four were clustered in Dickinson County, where Abilene was located. They nevertheless remained a small sect, never numbering more than six hundred followers in the area. They practiced a firm, devotional faith, with emphasis on the moral value of work, the permanence of marriage, and an aversion to gambling, smoking, and drink. Dinner was followed by readings from the Bible; when members of the family fell ill, their fellow congregants prayed for their recovery. But if religion was central to the Eisenhower home, so was a spirit of inquiry. Though David grew up with the River Brethren, he and his wife dabbled with the Baptists and the Methodists and finally joined the Bible Students, a tiny Mennonite group devoted, as the name suggests, to biblical study.

Ida's force of will and David's financial distress combined to create, in some minds, the impression that David was a marginal figure in the Eisenhower home. Ida was indeed a source of great strength. She cared about her values and was entirely devoted to her sons. The slighting of David, however, does him an injustice. Ike recalled his father as a forceful parent, an occasional wielder of the hickory stick against his sons; he fought, usually successfully, to control a brooding temper. "He was not one to be trifled with," Ike wrote many years later, "unless you were prepared to take the consequences."

Their stay in Texas was brief. Soon after Dwight was born, the family returned to Kansas, where the Eisenhowers settled first into a small cottage, then into a modest home that they purchased from David's brother, Ike's uncle Abe. From that point on, David and Ida and their growing family of boys shared a two-story white clapboard ranch house, most of the boys sharing bedrooms in decidedly tight quarters: the home was 818 square feet, smaller than the office Dwight would eventually occupy as chief of staff of the Army.

Abilene was then, as it is today, a modest post on the Kansas plain, windswept in winter, blazing in summer. Wide porches shielded residents from the sun of the prairie, and dust gathered in the corners of every home. The sun beat down on the wheat that extended for miles in every direction. Shade trees shimmered in the evenings and supplied the switches used to discipline the Eisenhower boys. Floods enriched the soil and occasionally did damage. Cattle thundered through the rail yards, heading for eastern markets.

Though destined for a career of breathtaking consequence, Dwight gave bare indication of such potential in his early years. He jockeyed for position in a home of intense competition. Ida and David ran a formidable household where Ike was one of six brothers. Arthur was the oldest, followed by Edgar, then Ike; Earl, Roy, and Milton were younger. A seventh, Paul, died of diphtheria in infancy. Surrounded, Dwight had to wrestle for an identity. Even his nickname, Little Ike, was a nod to his brother Edgar, known in those years as Big Ike. Nor was school a source of distinction. He was a bright student but hardly a dazzling one. Ike's math teacher mildly recalled him as "a very capable and interesting boy." Ike himself recognized his limits. "Baseball, football, boxing were all I wanted to know," he confessed.

For Little Ike, Abilene was formative in ways both subtle and obvious. He fished and trapped and would remain comfortable sleeping in tents and wading in streams his whole life. He struggled with a powerful temper, once beating his fists until they were bloody because he was denied the right to trick-or-treat with his older brothers. He was fascinated by history, particularly military affairs and leaders. He took to sports and learned to play poker percentages with calculating skill. He assumed his share of responsibility in a working home where the boys made money raising and selling vegetables on a small plot near the house.

Ida rotated chores weekly to avoid fights. She was, among her many other characteristics, intensely devoted to fairness. Late in life, when her middle son had vanquished Hitler's Germany and earned the gratitude of the free world, Ida was asked what she thought of her "famous son." Her reply: "Which son do you mean?"

In addition to the family vegetable garden, the boys oversaw a small flock of chickens; they milked the family cow, tended the orchard, washed dishes, cleaned clothes. Among the chores as the boys grew older was cooking, and that, too, left a lasting impression on Ida's middle son. For the rest of his life, Eisenhower would cook to please family and friends—and to calm his nerves.

Ida would later describe Ike as the most difficult of her six boys, but she handled most flare-ups with equanimity. Problems that reached David were often solved with "the old leather strap," but Ida "would philosophize . . . As you thought it over years later, you realized what she had given you." That was no small feat with young Ike, for the boy manifested at least one outstanding trait: he was magnificently stubborn. One fistfight at age thirteen was destined for the history books not because he won it but because he and his combatant fought to exhaustion; by the time it was over, Ike "couldn't lift an arm." And when an infection overwhelmed him and threatened to cost him a leg, even in his delirium, Ike resisted. He enlisted Edgar, Big Ike, to fend off the doctor. Edgar stationed himself at the door to his brother's room, and Dwight, drifting in and out of consciousness, gritted his teeth and toughed it out. Finally, on what the doctor judged as the last opportunity to save him, they painted the young boy's body with carbolic acid. Ike screamed, but it stopped the creeping infection. The leg and the boy were saved.

Eisenhower in those years acquired an enduring and endearing folksiness, one that would ground his achievements in a solid sense of home. Take, for instance, the notes he appended to his final memoir. Among them: his stirring 1945 Guildhall address in London and his recipe for vegetable soup. And Abilene, too, supplied lessons and imagery of the Old West. In his later years, when Ike would visit home, he would often stop by the grave of Tom Smith, the town marshal in its wilder days, axed to death by local outlaws in 1870, just twenty years before Ike was born. Smith, his gravestone reads, was a "martyr to duty . . . who in cowboy chaos established the supremacy of law." Eisenhower extended a schoolboy fascination with Smith into a lifelong admiration. He loved the romance, the triumph of order, the paean to duty. From it was born, among other things, a devotion to Westerns.

An appreciation of history and the outdoors, self-reliance, and ruddy athleticism were among the traits Ike learned in Abilene—along with a fierce will and a clumsy way with women—but what may have most shaped him in those early years were his lessons in moderation, the skill he developed as a boy to navigate between powerful forces, to fight his way past school-yard bullies, and to claim a place in his crowded home of brothers. It is no coincidence that the architect of the "middle way" grew up smack in the middle of six strong boys, their passions channeled by a patient mother.

Two other memories of Abilene influenced Ike in fact and legend. A battle with a stubborn goose as a five-year-old ended when his uncle armed him with a broom handle. The lesson: "Never . . . negotiate with an adversary except from a position of strength." At school, meanwhile, Ike appreciated that students were summoned back from recess with a drum, a system that promoted "quiet, orderly movement . . . The drum communicates a message and calms as it warns. The siren is an assault on the senses." He would always favor steadiness and order and be repelled by the shrill or abrupt.

David and Ida Eisenhower wished for their sons to acquire an education and, with it, prosperous careers; David mercilessly beat Edgar one day when he discovered that Edgar had been skipping school to work in a local doctor's office. Despite occasional setbacks, however, the hopes of the Eisenhower parents were largely realized, as most of their sons pursued higher education. Arthur left home at fifteen and was one of two who did not attend college, but he became a successful banker anyway; Edgar went on to be a lawyer (that irritated his father, too; neither Ida nor David Eisenhower liked lawyers); Earl worked in journalism, radio, and newspapers; Milton, whom his brother liked to refer to as the brains of the family, compiled a distinguished career in academia, capped by the presidency of Johns Hopkins University. Roy also avoided college but worked as a druggist; he died young, too soon to see the crowning moments of Dwight's career in Europe and the United States.

The Eisenhower brothers differed in looks and dispositions: Arthur and Roy were dark haired, Edgar and Milton were slightly fairer, Ike was blond, and Earl was a redhead; Arthur, Roy, and Milton were easygoing; Edgar, Earl, and Ike were "hot-tempered and quarrelsome." Edgar was a cranky conservative and Milton an elegant liberal, and they often jostled for their middle brother's ear; Milton almost always prevailed.

If Ike's mother raised him and brothers enveloped him, still another source of sustenance was his friends. In those years and across the decades to come, one particularly meaningful chum was a strapping young man from Abilene, the imposing but shy son of a town doctor. Everett Hazlett, known to Ike as Swede, had gone off to military school and returned to

Abilene with a determination to win an appointment to the U.S. Naval Academy; Hazlett's signature contribution to the history of his nation was that he persuaded Ike to join him. Ike in those days was working nights and had concocted a plan with Edgar to spot each other through college: Little Ike worked for two years at a local creamery to help pay Big Ike's way, at which point Edgar was to take time off to subsidize Dwight. That promised, however, to be a protracted undertaking, and when Ike first learned of the military academies, he was especially drawn by the prospect of a free education.

Taken with the idea and prodded by Hazlett, he spent several hours each afternoon huddled with Swede studying for the entrance examination for Annapolis. He solicited letters of support from friends and neighbors—discovering in the process the great esteem with which many Abilene residents regarded his parents—but then was chagrined to learn that by the time he would be ready to enter the academy, he would be too old to be admitted. Fortunately, the examination for West Point was nearly identical to that for Annapolis, and when the tests were tallied, Ike finished first among the Annapolis candidates and second among those applying to West Point. The leading West Point contender failed the physical, and Ike secured his appointment.

His mother, who had stoically accepted this turn of events despite her steadfast pacifism, was now forced to acknowledge that her third son was embarked on a military life. On a June day in 1911, he boarded the train with a single suitcase and headed east. Ida and David saw him off, then returned home. Ida entered the bathroom and closed the door behind her. From outside, Milton listened as, for the first time in his life, he heard his mother cry.

It was a Sunday afternoon in October 1915 when Lieutenant Eisenhower, the officer of the day, was making his inspection of the base at Fort Sam Houston, in San Antonio, Texas. Eisenhower was on his first assignment since graduating that spring from West Point. He took his duties seriously.

He was nonplussed when the wife of a major interrupted his rounds and called him over to introduce him to a young woman. At first, Eisenhower brusquely declined. But she persisted, and within moments Ike was face-to-face with a sparkling brunette, still a teenager, daintily feminine in a pair of beige lace-up boots and equipped with what Eisenhower would later describe as "clear blue eyes that were full of impertinence." Despite her uncomfortable shoes and distaste for walking, Mamie Geneva Doud joined the strapping young officer on his rounds. The attraction was immediate for both. They had dinner that night and again about ten days later.

Dwight Eisenhower in 1915, the Eisenhower whom Mamie Doud met that fall, was at a juncture familiar to many young men. Newly graduated into the world, he was ambitious and alert to his potential. He craved adventure, imagined himself a leader, was groomed for command. And yet he also was a bit of a prankster, and having grown up with six brothers and been educated at West Point, he was barely accustomed to the company of women.

Ike had managed to be both average and memorable at West Point. He was a modest student, and his athletic career, highlighted by a briefly successful effort to shut down the great Jim Thorpe, ended with a knee injury suffered during a 1912 football game against Tufts. He was disconsolate after the injury, bored with his studies, lethargic. "The fellows that used to call me 'Sunny Jim' call me 'Gloomy Face' now," he wrote in 1913. He considered dropping out, but friends convinced him to stay. He took up smoking, to his later regret.

And his stubbornness cost him. Try as they might, Army bosses could never convince Ike of the importance of a tidy barracks. He racked up his share of demerits, more than his share in fact, as he qualified as one of the school's legendary "century men," so named because he spent more than a hundred hours marching off penalties for various infractions. They ranged from messy rooms to showing up late for parades or meals to "smiling in ranks at drill after being corrected" to violating Special Order 106, the section proscribing inappropriate dancing. Still, after his freshman year, he ranked fifty-seventh overall in his class under the "Order of General Merit," with an especially high ranking in his best subject, English, where he ranked tenth. That was a respectable showing in a class of 212. As the class dwindled, Ike's ranking fell, drawn down by his demerits—he finished sixty-sixth overall in a class of 168—and he managed to finish an unimpressive 125th in terms of conduct.

As his class standings made clear, Eisenhower was not preoccupied with his studies, nor was he committed to exemplary behavior. He was, however, a gregarious classmate, a solid athlete, and a joker. He developed a parlor trick that took advantage of his physical strength: he would bend his elbows and place his hands inches in front of his chest, then pitch face forward to the floor, stopping himself just before his nose crashed to the ground. Generations of soldiers would be treated to Ike's gag.

Ike completed his studies in early 1915, graduating as part of the "class the stars fell on," because so many of its graduates went on to become generals. His yearbook entry, prepared by a classmate, pokes fun at Eisenhower—weirdly, it calls him "the terrible Swedish-Jew" and teases him about his self-image as "the handsomest man in the Corps." In contrast to the serious encomiums to his classmates, Ike's entry reads as one playfully ribbing a man who can take it. On February 17, 1915, Eisenhower was commissioned a second lieutenant in the U.S. Army. He requested to be stationed in the Philippines, the only member of his class to ask for that exotic posting, but instead was assigned to Fort Sam Houston. Before shipping out, Ike detoured home for the summer.

Through his West Point years, Ike carried on a flirtation with one Abilene girl, Ruby Norman, swapping stories from school and home and occasionally complaining of homesickness. Home between assignments in 1915, however, he transferred his affections to Gladys Harding, who was something more than a playful pal. They attended a picture show and enjoyed a summer of shows and concerts, riding and swimming, the occasional beer. They saw *The Bawlerout* and *The Outcast*, and Ike dazzled Gladys by appearing one evening in his dress whites.

Other girls hovered, too. Ruby worried Gladys, but Ike reassured her that Ruby "never gives me a thought, except as a good friend." Infatuation turned to love, or at least what seemed like love to a young man and woman, especially as their summer drew to a close.

"Girl, I do love you," Ike wrote in August, "and I want you to *know* it—to be as certain of it as I am—and to believe in me and trust me as you would your dad." Ike was up late that night, smoking, wondering whether his feelings were reciprocated, dreading the moment when he had to ship out. "Sept. 1st seems so fearfully close tonight. This parting is going to be the hardest so far in my life."

But Gladys was determined to pursue a career in music, and Ike had his orders. The end of summer thus meant their separation, and both approached it with dread and longing. By the time Ike had to leave for his first Army posting, Gladys described their farewell as a "sad parting." It was, she sighed to her diary, "Love."

They corresponded emotionally through the fall, pining and moony. "Sweet girl of mine," Ike addressed her. But summer loves will fade. Their romance melted away as Eisenhower settled into his new life in Texas.

Mamie was another matter. From the start, Ike was smitten. Regarded as the prettiest of her four sisters, Mamie was well-off and slightly spoiled. Her father ran a meatpacking business so successful that he was believed to be a millionaire—he owned a car in 1904, the first man in Colorado Springs to be able to afford one. Birthdays and other holidays were extravagantly observed in the Doud home, money and jewelry lavishly bestowed. Although Mamie's father, John Sheldon Doud, was a rugged man, he and his wife, Elvira Carlson, gave birth to small, somewhat frail daughters. Mamie's older sister, Eleanor, was particularly weak and required nurses from the time she was eight; Mamie, though stronger, herself developed a rheumatic heart as a young girl. Worried for their health, John Doud moved his family from Colorado Springs to the lower elevation of Denver and annually shipped them to San Antonio for the warmer winter.

Mamie had expectations of her new beau, and Ike did his best. He courted her with martial doggedness and flashes of generosity and creativity. He was still in debt from borrowing to buy his first uniforms, so he subsidized his courtship by playing poker to boost his income and skimped where he could. He stopped buying premade cigarettes and returned to rolling his own. That freed up a little cash, and he tried to keep his outings with Mamie affordable, often taking her to a local Tex-Mex restaurant or vaudeville house (more than fifty years later, Ike could still recall the price of a tamale at the Original). Economies such as those allowed him to indulge Mamie now and again, notably with an engraved, heart-shaped silver jewelry box at Christmas, an extravagant gift from a man making $147 a month—and to a girl to whom he was not yet engaged.

The romance between Ike and Mamie moved swiftly as she dropped other suitors to concentrate on him, preferring his sturdy military bearing to the less serious rivals for her attention. By Valentine's Day 1916, he was bold enough to propose, giving her a copy of his West Point class ring, a bulky piece that she nevertheless happily wore on her delicate hand. Ike formally asked John Doud for permission to wed his daughter, and Doud, despite some reservations about Eisenhower's ability to support a family, consented, initially with the caveat that he wanted to postpone the wedding until the fall, when Mamie would be twenty. Instead, the brewing conflict with Mexico stirred anxiety that Ike might be deployed in combat, and the two were married at noon on July 1, 1916. Mamie's father escorted her down the stairs of the family home and to the fireplace altar. There were no attendants, and the service was brief. Afterward, Ike tried to commemorate the event by preserving Mamie's bouquet in wax; it melted.

The honeymoon was similarly modest. The couple spent a few days at a resort in Eldorado Springs, outside Denver. The newlyweds briefly returned to Denver before heading by train to Abilene, where they arrived at 3:00 a.m. and Mamie met Ike's family for the first time. She took an instant liking to Milton. "I've always wanted to have a brother!" she exclaimed, kissing him on the cheek. He was charmed.

The early years of Ike and Mamie's marriage were often difficult as they learned to support each other amid the rigors of Army life. Raised in his stern home and educated at West Point, Ike could be domineering, while Mamie, the product of her more voluble and emotional upbringing, was occasionally tempestuous. Soon after their wedding, the two experienced their first fight, and Mamie struck Ike's hand. Their rings collided, and Mamie's broke the amethyst stone in Ike's. "Well, young lady," he said coldly, "for that display of temper you will replace this stone with your own money." And yet Ike also could be a dedicated and thoughtful husband: at every wedding anniversary through the 1930s, he added one piece of silver to Mamie's tea set, eventually completing it; she displayed it with pride the rest of her life.

If Ike was sometimes bossy and Mamie could be prissy, well, they adjusted. Mamie had grown up wealthy and was now forced to cope with Army life, though the privations were eased somewhat by an allowance from her father. Ike had grown up with men and boys and now had to adjust himself to life with a woman. He showed affection with a gentle pinch more often than a warm embrace; he cooked but preferred to do so on a grill or over a fire. He enjoyed cards—he had long been a ferocious poker player and later developed into such a demanding bridge partner that many of his closest friends hated to be his partner—but found it difficult to play with Mamie because she would make mistakes and he could be witheringly critical. "Ike never had the slightest notion how to live with women," Mamie gently complained in retirement.

Fifteen months after Ike and Mamie were married, they were parents. Doud Dwight Eisenhower was born on September 24, 1917, his father a newly promoted captain. His parents called him Ikey at first, then Icky. He was a healthy boy, spirited and bright, openly adored by his father. When Ike and Mamie were transferred to Fort Meade, soldiers there nicknamed him "Mascot of the Corps." He loved to march about in his miniature Army uniform and was delighted by football and tanks, parades and pageantry. Ike's reserve melted in the presence of his son. "I was inclined to display Icky and his talents at the slightest excuse, or without one, for that matter," Eisenhower wrote many years later. "In his company, I'm sure I strutted a bit and Mamie was thoroughly happy that . . . her two men were with her."

As Christmas of 1920 approached, Ike splurged on his son. The house was decorated. A red tricycle shimmered beneath the tree. A few days before the holiday, Mamie went into town to do some shopping and returned to find that Icky was not feeling well. The base doctor looked at him but thought little of it, suggesting that perhaps he'd eaten something that did not agree with him. Then Icky began to run a fever, and the following morning the doctor advised that he be admitted to the hospital. As he was carried out of the house, Icky pointed at the tricycle and smiled.

His condition worsened, and it took a civilian doctor to realize that he had scarlet fever. Icky was quarantined. Ike took up a spot on the other side of the glass, talking to his son, comforting him but unable to hold or touch him. Scarlet fever turned to meningitis. Late one night, while Mamie teetered on the edge of pneumonia, Ike was allowed past the glass to hold his boy one more time. Icky died in his father's embrace. Ike never quite recovered. He and Mamie had difficulty sleeping, and Ike withdrew into his grief. On January 2 every year thereafter, he sent Mamie yellow roses. Icky loved yellow.

Nearly half a century later, as he reflected on a career filled with accomplishment and the crushingly serious duty of sending soldiers to their deaths, Ike described the loss of his son as "the greatest disappointment and disaster in my life." Even at the vantage of so many years and such ranging experience, he added: "Today when I think of it, even now as I write it, the keenness of our loss comes back to me as fresh and terrible as it was in that long dark day soon after Christmas, 1920."

Icky's death was the most tragic moment in Ike and Mamie's long marriage; it changed them both and for a time introduced a reserve between them. It was not, however, the only crisis they endured as a couple. They both struggled with their health: Mamie battled heart problems from her youth, as well as shaky balance brought on by an inner-ear affliction; Ike picked up an intestinal disorder that would flare up periodically over the years, sometimes causing nearly unbearable pain. Their marriage came closest to failing in the early 1920s, when Mamie left Ike for a time—driven from him by the hardships of a tropical posting and his devotion to duty, sometimes at the expense of his wife. And it was tested again twenty years after that, when Ike's affections for his wartime driver wounded Mamie.

The latter episode is the best-known friction in the Eisenhower marriage, one exhaustively, if delicately, examined in their lifetimes. It began with World War II raging, a time of nearly unimaginable pressure on Eisenhower as he assembled, trained, and planned for the moment that would chart the course of liberty and the future of his country, as well as the millions of lives placed at his disposal. Under the circumstances, one might be inclined to forgive him indiscretions; one might excuse an affair by a man so far from home, so immersed in the fate of his men and their cause. What we do not know, even these many decades later, is whether the rumors, gossip, and reports of his affection for his wartime driver, the strikingly beautiful Kay Summersby, were merely titillating innuendo or correctly recorded a betrayal of Mamie.

Summersby herself left conflicting accounts. She wrote one memoir soon after the war that Eisenhower and those close to him eyed nervously. It was fond and appreciative but in no way suggested a romantic relationship. Years later, after Eisenhower had died, Summersby wrote a second memoir; in it, she described, albeit in somewhat modest terms, a physical affair. Aides from the war years vehemently contested Summersby's account. It troubled Mamie, but she willfully declined to entertain the possibility that her husband had been unfaithful to her.

During the war, there were no such written reflections by the principals, but the speculation about a relationship between the two was probably inevitable and certainly widespread. Eisenhower was at the center of England's attention in the war years, and Summersby was a shapely associate. That was bound to wag tongues, and photographs of Summersby occasionally made their way into the American press, agitating Mamie, who was far away, lonely, and worried. Her correspondence with Ike in the early months of the war—when Summersby was pictured in *Life* magazine and later shown with Eisenhower in North Africa (her ship had been torpedoed en route, and she and other passengers were rescued after being plunged into the Mediterranean)—indicates Mamie's unhappiness at what she perceived as a close relationship between her husband and his driver.

In his letters to Mamie, Ike avoided mentioning Summersby by name. "There are also a couple of WAACS around the office," he wrote reassuringly, if misleadingly, in early 1943, "but I never use one unless Marshall [another aide] is so busy that I am forced to do so. He's cheery, efficient and always on the job." That apparently did not calm Mamie entirely, for a few weeks later Ike wrote again that she should not "go bothering your pretty head about WAACS." In the early stages of the war, Summersby was engaged to a soldier, and that helped placate Mamie until reports began to question her fiancé's fidelity and background, adding a tawdry side element to the rumors about Ike and Kay. When Kay's fiancé was killed by a mine, Ike used the occasion first to scold Mamie about her inquiries and then, still again, to reassure her, this time somewhat more thoughtfully:

> Your letters often give me some hint of your loneliness, your bewilderment and your worries in carrying your own part in this emergency. Don't ever think that I do not understand or that I am not truly sympathetic to the lost feeling you must so often have. Just please remem-

ber that no matter how short my notes I love you—I could never be
in love with anyone else—and that you fill my thoughts and hopes for
the future always. You never seem quite to comprehend how deeply I
depend upon you and need you. So when you're lonely, try to remember that I'd rather be by your side than anywhere else in the world.

Whether or not the relationship between Ike and Kay was romantic, it
was undeniably affectionate. She was a physical woman, an accomplished
rider, brave, and outgoing. For a man who connected with women through
"a pinch and a kick," as Mamie put it, Kay was a welcome companion.
Throughout the war and in its immediate aftermath, Kay was often by his
side; they even shared a dog, a rambunctious little Scottie named Telek,
which she bought for him as a present.

Upon arriving in England in 1942, Ike had vowed never to partake of
London's nightlife until Hitler was vanquished—it was, he believed, vulgar
to be seen celebrating while charged with the duty of deciding men's fates.
But when at last the war in Europe ended, Eisenhower treated himself to
a night on the town. "I wonder if you people realize what it means to me
to be back here among friends," Ike said as he stood to dance. Then he
reached for the hand of his partner. Eisenhower's first dance at the end of
the war was with Kay. Mamie must have been hurt; she forwarded a clip
with news of the dance to her parents.

After the war, other deputies from Ike's European headquarters helped
Kay to land jobs and persevere through crises. Just as important, those
aides studiously kept her away from Eisenhower himself, and he assumed
a guarded distance from her, a pose that could be interpreted as either cutting off a former lover or simply distancing himself from a potential liability at a time when his own political aspirations were hardening. Moreover,
Kay took advantage of her connection to Eisenhower; she tried to use it to
secure a job at the Pentagon, and her presumption irritated him. In either
case, Ike's distance was a source of obvious pain to Summersby, and Eisenhower inflicted it knowingly. When, for instance, Kay reached out to him
in 1948 with news that her sister had died and her mother had suffered
a breakdown as a result, she included in her note a plea. "When you have
some spare time, I should love to see you," Summersby wrote, "also want to
ask your advice regarding a number of things." Ike tersely turned aside her
attempt to meet, even though both were in New York at the time. "I can
scarcely estimate when there might arise an opportunity for you to come
past the office," he wrote. Kay never again made such a request.

It was his son John who understood their relationship best. He saw them together, enjoying their dog, playing bridge, working; he understood that their relationship soothed his father. "Americans are funny," he reflected more than sixty years later. "They don't understand that a rapport is much more serious than a roll in the hay. Kay and my dad had a rapport, of which I very much approved."

The marriage of Dwight and Mamie Eisenhower would endure its share of travails. They would weather separations and difficult, occasionally public challenges. Gossips would titter about her drinking (Mamie's ear disorder affected her balance, causing her sometimes to seem wobbly, as if drunk) and snicker over his alleged affair with Summersby. Even after his death, the publication of Summersby's second memoir profoundly agitated Mamie, especially when a television miniseries glamorized the relationship. Ike and Mamie would lose one son and raise another; they would suffer failings of health and moments of irritation. But their marriage survived. It nurtured both for all the rest of their days together.

The Mentoring of Soldiers

Geroge S. Patton Jr. was a colorful, charismatic, strange man—mercurial, romantic, profane, brash, and emotional. He was a native of Southern California, raised in a wealthy home by doting parents. As a boy, he struggled with dyslexia; he stayed out of school for years, afraid of the humiliation of not being able to read well. Nevertheless, he privately immersed himself in the classics and tales of chivalry; they bore deeply into him. Young George came to believe in reincarnation and imagined himself a reborn soldier from ancient times.

Guided by a father whom he worshipped, Patton overcame his limitations as a student and pursued the greatness he felt history had ordained for him. Along the way, he met Beatrice Banning Ayer, a well-to-do, refined, and startlingly pretty young woman, during a family sojourn to Catalina Island in 1902. The children put on a play. As one of Patton's many biographers records: "Beatrice Ayer was polished in the principal role. George Patton was overdramatic in his." Beatrice, or Bea, as she would become known, was from then on the object of Patton's fascination; she counseled him through Virginia Military Institute and then West Point, proofreading his papers, indulging his black moods and insecurities. Patton graduated, fought with heroism in World War I, and then, back in the United States, was fatefully assigned to Fort Meade.

When Ike moved to Fort Meade in 1919—freshly back from a sixty-one-day, cross-country tour intended to draw attention to the nation's threadbare road network—the base assigned him to run-down wooden barracks with one distinct advantage: his next-door neighbors were George and Bea Patton.

Eisenhower and Patton struck up a fast, if unlikely, friendship, genial Ike and stormy George. At its core was a common appreciation for tanks. Eisenhower and Patton experimented relentlessly with the still-developing tanks of their day, stripping them down and rebuilding them, scuttling across the countryside to test their mobility and firepower. They loved the work and plunged into it with childlike gusto. Ike and others who had not seen action in the war raptly absorbed Patton's descriptions of battles, then tested their tanks under the conditions that Patton suggested.

One day, a Mark VIII tank with its hefty Liberty engine, designed for an airplane but retrofitted for the tank, came straining over the top of a ravine, towing two smaller tanks with inch-thick steel cables. As Eisenhower and Patton watched the tank strain up the hill, they were startled by a ripping sound. They wheeled around just as a cable snapped, skimming the surface of the hillside "like a striking black snake," mowing down brush, and nearly decapitating the two soldiers. They both went pale. Later that night, Patton broached the subject. "Ike, were you as scared as I was?" Eisenhower admitted it. "I was afraid to bring the subject up," he answered.

Shared danger and common curiosity bound the two men. Together, they explored the range of their equipment and its tactical ability. Conventional military strategy of the day imagined limited use for tanks, as clunky vehicles attached to infantry units and primarily used to clear out machine-gun nests. But Patton and Eisenhower conceived of faster, more nimble tanks, massed for impact rather than merely intended as infantry support. They were both impressed by the work of an inventor named J. Walter Christie, who had put together a design for a much speedier machine. As they experimented, Eisenhower and Patton both wrote articles on the subject and published their works in *Infantry Journal*. In his, Eisenhower argued that the old style of tank would be replaced by a "speedy, reliable and efficient engine of destruction." Patton concluded that tanks should be given independence from infantry. Likening tanks to the air service, he said, "They are destined for a separate existence."

Those were provocative ideas, and they attracted unfavorable notice within the Army. Patton and Eisenhower were ordered to cease their advocacy of tanks or risk court-martial. Chastened and irritated, they backed down, but the sullen response from the Pentagon only drove the two closer together in their friendship, which now featured a mutual belligerence.

Patton did more than just ignite Eisenhower's military imagination. He supplied Ike with a model of loyalty, one that highlighted duty to service and country but not abject subservience. Patton could be absurd—grandiose in ways that Ike would never emulate—but he was forcefully his own man, utterly of the Army but not beholden to it. What's more, George and Bea Patton were the center of a sparse social community, and Patton absorbed the Eisenhowers into it. Patton hosted Sunday suppers, and Ike, grafting Patton's tradition onto an older one of Mamie's family, began a Sunday brunch buffet. It became known as "Club Eisenhower."

Those brunches and suppers were a mainstay of officer life on the base, with the Eisenhowers and Pattons regularly hosting each other as well as guests from Washington and elsewhere. Brigadier General Fox Conner was vacationing at the Adirondack camp that belonged to his wife's family in the fall of 1919, when he accepted Patton's invitation to dinner. Conner was a gentle Mississippi man with a soft accent and a stocky, imposing mien, a philosopher of sorts comfortable with Shakespeare and Tacitus, full of literary and experienced wisdom. He had served as chief of operations during the recently concluded war and was already acquiring a reputation as a mentor to promising young officers. Moreover, his background was in artillery, so the tank was especially intriguing to him for its firepower and mobility. Thus, unlike his more defensive counterparts, Conner was intrigued rather than threatened by the ideas Patton and Eisenhower were promulgating. He spent the afternoon closely questioning the two men. Ike, aware that Conner was not only one of the Army's most senior officers but also one of its most highly regarded intellectuals, answered carefully and sometimes at length. They talked until nightfall. Conner said little, but Ike had made an impression.

George and Bea Patton left Camp Meade in September 1920. Even after he'd gone, Patton remained a presence in Ike's life, infusing his friend with his episodically brilliant insights and aphorisms on war and courage. "What is it," Patton asked in a letter in 1926, "that makes the Poor S.O.B. who constitutes the casualtie lists fight[?]" Patton's answer: leadership.

Patton bolstered Eisenhower at every opportunity. When Ike was accepted to the Command and General Staff College at Fort Leavenworth, Patton sent his notes from his time there. Ike graduated first in his class— "One," as he called it—and graciously credited Patton. Later, Patton tried to recruit Ike to his command. Eisenhower hesitated, flattered but by then attracting wide attention and angling for something more significant.

Once the war began, they resumed their friendship in a new config- uration, with Eisenhower as a commander and Patton as a complicated subordinate. Despite his idiosyncrasies, Patton fought marvelously, first in North Africa, then in Italy.

Once Patton's friend, Eisenhower now was his boss, an unenviable position at times. In February 1943, Ike warned Patton to watch his mouth. "My advice is . . . (if you want it) merely the old saw to 'count to ten before you speak,' " Eisenhower wrote. "This applies not only to criticism of Allies, a subject on which I am adamant, but to many others. A man once gave to me an old proverb. It was this: 'Keep silent and appear stupid; open your mouth and remove all doubt.' I do not mean that this applies to you, as you damn well know, but I do mean that a certain sphinx-like quality upon occasion will do one hell of a lot toward enhancing one's reputation." One can feel Eisenhower laboring in that note, can appreciate his almost parental care with Patton's feelings, his determination to deliver important advice without offending his delicate colleague's pride. At one level, Patton appreciated it; two weeks later, he wrote to his wife of Ike's greatness. But Patton was incapable of restraint.

The Allied invasion of Sicily commenced on the night of July 9–10, 1943, as air forces dropped paratroopers and amphibious craft overcame stormy weather and seas. Within days, Patton's divisions were stampeding across the island, sealing up its western reaches, while General Bernard Montgomery, commander of the British troops, waged a more cautious and deliberate conquest of the island's eastern sections. Much of the fighting was brutal, as were conditions on the island, in particular rampant malaria across its central plains. Casualties were high, the stress on men profound.

Patton visited the Fifteenth Evacuation Hospital in Sicily on August 3. There, he commended men for their courage, comforted the wounded, tearfully praised the brave. As he made his inspection, however, he encountered a shaken young private, Charles H. Kuhl. Patton asked what Kuhl was suffering from. The private responded: "I guess I can't take it." Patton snapped. He called Kuhl a coward, slapped him with his gloves, then grabbed him by the neck and threw him from the tent. Not finished yet, Patton visited still another group of wounded men at the Ninety-third Evacuation Hospital a few days later. There, Patton bore in on Private Paul G. Bennett, a twenty-one-year-old soldier who served for four years in the Army without signs of trouble until a friend was wounded in the Italian campaign. Bennett was shivering. Patton demanded to know what ailed him. "It's my nerves," Bennett replied and began to sob. "Your nerves, hell, you are just a goddamned coward, you yellow son of a bitch," Patton bellowed. He slapped Bennett and continued: "Shut up that goddamned crying. I won't have these brave men here who have been shot seeing a yellow bastard sitting here crying." With that, Patton slapped him again, hitting him so hard that Bennett's helmet liner was knocked from his head and rolled out of the tent.

Before leaving the tent, Patton vowed to have Bennett sent back to the front lines, adding that if he would not fight, Patton would put him before a firing squad. Flashing his own famous ivory-handled revolver, Patton added: "I ought to shoot you myself, you goddamned whimpering coward."

Those shocking incidents were witnessed by reporters who did not immediately alert their readers but rather, concerned about the effect of the incident on morale and the campaign itself, reported the matter to Eisenhower. Ike asked the reporters to hold off on sending dispatches home; they agreed. He also received word through the chain of command. As one doctor reported: "The deleterious effects of such incidents upon the wellbeing of patients, upon the professional morale of hospital staffs and upon the relationship of patient to physician are incalculable."

Eisenhower could not stand by and let one of his commanding generals abuse troops. His letter to Patton surely stands with the most excoriating and unyielding missives ever delivered by a superior to a subordinate, bristling with purposeful rage. It was written in secret and delivered by hand, included in no official file at the time. It enclosed the physician's report that had been forwarded to Eisenhower, and it threatened the end of Patton's career:

> I am attaching a report which is shocking in its allegations against
> your personal conduct. I hope you can assure me that none of them is
> true, but the detailed circumstances communicated to me lead to the
> belief that some ground for the charges must exist. I am well aware
> of the necessity for hardness and toughness on the battlefield. I clearly
> understand that firm and drastic measures are at times necessary in
> order to secure desired objectives. But this does not excuse brutality,
> abuse of the sick, nor exhibition of uncontrollable temper in front of
> subordinates.

Concluding, Eisenhower reiterated his affection for his old friend. "But I assure you," his letter ended, "that conduct such as described in the accompanying report will *not* be tolerated in this theater no matter who the offender may be."

Eisenhower understood the moral equation before him: he could not sanction the abuse of his troops, nor could he sacrifice a general who might hasten the end of the war and thus save the lives of those same men. Moreover, Ike's own command was at stake. Should Patton embarrass or discredit the U.S. effort, Eisenhower's handling of the matter—one involving a friend—would certainly be subject to close scrutiny. He wrote to his boss, George Marshall, to explain himself—and protect himself—by fulsomely praising Patton's military skills and candidly acknowledging his inability to check his emotions, what Ike called "those unfortunate personal traits of which you and I have always known and which during this campaign caused me some most uncomfortable days." (Ike's reminder to Marshall that "you and I have always known" was another subtle but clear way to signal that he was not alone on this issue.) Eisenhower assured his commanding officer that he had rebuked Patton—"I have had to take the most drastic steps," he wrote—and had done what he could to keep this from happening again. "Personally," he said, "I believe that he is cured."

The charges against Patton eventually made their way to the United States, where they ignited a furor when the columnist Drew Pearson disclosed details of the affair. By then, however, Eisenhower had confronted Patton and laid the groundwork with Marshall. Patton had apologized to those involved. Faced with a crisis that could have cost him his most aggressive battlefield leader, Eisenhower steadied his command, reprimanded the culprit, refused to allow friendship to distract him, and, ultimately, protected the lives of his soldiers.

Patton tested him again before the war was over—at a tenuous stage of the alliance between the United States and the Soviet Union, he denigrated the Soviets—and afterward, when he contradicted American policy on de-Nazifying Germany, a reckless comment perhaps fueled by Patton's latent anti-Semitism, which seemed to flare once Germany was subdued and the new threat arose from the Soviet Union. The final episode was one too many for Ike, who telegraphed Patton to demand "a report from you to be completed as quickly as it is physically possible to do so." Dissatisfied, Ike yanked his old friend's command.

Patton dreamed of dying in glory, of concluding his grand life on a fabled battlefield, sword or ivory-handled pistols in hand. Peace left him without a mission, and he dreaded it. "Now the horrors of peace, pacafism [*sic*], and unions will have unlimited sway," he wrote to Bea. Bored, he climbed inside his chauffeur-driven car on Sunday, December 9, 1945, thinking he would pass the time by hunting pheasant. The car collided with a truck, and Patton was thrown upward and into the partition separating passenger from driver. His head was badly cut and, more seriously, his spine broken. Patton lay in the hospital for twelve days, struggling but fading. He died on December 21. Ike was informed immediately and cabled Bea his condolences and his heartfelt reflections on a friend who taught him much. Patton was, Eisenhower wrote, "a leader whose gallantry and skill contributed outstandingly to the completeness of our victory in Europe." And he was, to Ike, more than that: "I have lost one of my oldest and dearest friends."

In the months that followed Icky's death in 1921, Ike and Mamie knew no consolation, no relief from their woe. When a break finally did arrive, they had General Conner to thank. Conner, much impressed by the Eisenhower he met at Patton's Sunday supper, asked Ike to join him in Panama, where Conner was given command of the Twentieth Infantry Brigade. Eisenhower welcomed the opportunity—the chance to leave the site of Icky's death—but was blocked by his commanding officer at Fort Meade, in part because Eisenhower was coaching the camp football team and thus was considered indispensable. Now, however, Conner called upon his allies in Washington and sprung Ike loose. He wrote to an influential colonel, George Marshall, "asking him to steer the matter." With the gentle touch of an experienced officer, Conner suggested to Eisenhower: "It might be advisable for you to drop in on Col. Marshall . . . and tell him your desire to go."

First, however, Ike needed to address what could have become a dire threat to his career. When Icky was born, Eisenhower applied for a housing allowance; that was standard and accepted. But at the time, Icky was living with Mamie and her parents, not with his father or in military housing. That violated Army rules, but Eisenhower had made the application apparently unaware that the benefit only was available to children living in the care of the military officer. An audit turned up the violation and concluded that he owed the Army $250.67. The acting inspector general recommended that Eisenhower be court-martialed. Ike desperately tried to pay the money back, but the inspector general persisted until a higher officer intervened. Ike's savior yet again: General Conner. Conner backed the inspector general down; Ike repaid the money, and the crisis passed.

The opportunity to work for Fox Conner was one proffered only to the Army's most promising young officers, and Eisenhower well understood that he was being ushered into select company. In World War I, Conner designed the divisions that Pershing used to attack the German army. At the moment of the armistice, twenty-nine of the American divisions in the field were those that Conner had created. The German surrender caught Conner and Pershing by surprise, and they warned the political leadership against stopping too soon. "Complete victory," they argued, "can only be obtained by continuing the war until we force unconditional surrender from Germany." They were ignored, but history vindicated that advice and only added to Conner's reputation.

Ike accepted the assignment with enthusiasm; he and Mamie shipped out—as soon as football season was over. Before they did, they registered another monument toward moving on with life: Mamie became pregnant again.

The voyage to Panama was miserable. The ship was dirty, and bad weather made the passage rough. Mamie endured a double bout of morning sickness and seasickness. The Eisenhowers' car was damaged in transit. Arriving in Panama, the post was no better. Their house was dilapidated and nearly overrun by jungle. The roof leaked, and mildew permeated the home. Bed frames had to be doused in kerosene and burned once a week to kill bedbugs. There were crawling insects and flying ones. And there were bats. Mamie hated bats. As Christmas approached, Mamie wrote to her parents again, confessing that she felt far away and homesick.

Ike and Mamie had been married for more than five years, separated for long stretches of that period by Ike's assignments. Mamie had struggled with the difficulties of Army life, uprooting herself over and over and trying to make comfortable homes on Ike's meager salary and her allowance from her father. She had adjusted, but then, on that unforgettable morning in 1921, they had lost their son. As she surveyed the fetid jungle around the Panama Canal and imagined having another child there, Mamie surely could be forgiven for having doubts. At first, she made the best of it. She took on volunteer work and helped to establish a maternity clinic on the base. But she was unhappy, and Ike knew it. It was, he conceded drily, "not the best introduction to life beyond our borders." In the spring of 1922, with the birth of their second child approaching, Mamie left for home.

There, on August 3, Mamie gave birth to John Sheldon Doud Eisenhower. Ike arrived just in time. Mamie went into labor late at night, and Ike, trying not to wake the neighbors, rolled the car to the end of the driveway before starting it. Nervous and hurrying, he stepped on the gas, but the car would not move. "Ike," Mamie implored, "you have to start the ignition."

Nothing would ever erase the memory of Icky's short, loving life, but John would occupy his own place in his parents' hearts. He grew to be a clever boy, willful and headstrong, the spitting image of his older brother. There would always remain a shadow of grief—as well as a residue of distance between Ike and Mamie and a veiled sense that John would fulfill not only his own destiny but that of his departed brother. But now, too, there was joy and family. Mamie returned to Panama with their son.

It did not last long. Charged with raising a baby even as her husband was increasingly absorbed in his work and tutelage under Conner, Mamie lost weight and grew frantic. The jungle pressed in, the insects and bats hovered and intruded. She worried over John—surely, she could not survive the loss of a second son. She could not sleep. Conner's wife, Virginia, watched with concern as Ike and Mamie seemed to drift apart. Finally, Mamie announced that she was leaving. Ike begged her to reconsider, pleading so fervently that she never forgot—though never recorded—his desperate attempt to hold on to her.

Once home, she regained her strength and reconsidered. Mamie, with John, at last returned to Panama. This time, it stuck. She took to riding to have time with her husband, he gave her a tea set, and they hosted regular dinner parties. "Am finally getting Ike housebroken again," Mamie reported happily to her parents.

Panama thus marked a crisis and recovery in the Eisenhower marriage. It also brought Ike some of his greatest professional satisfaction. He and Conner explored the jungle and roamed the margins of the canal. As they rode and camped, Conner painstakingly broadened his charge's horizons, drawing out Ike with soft questions, posed in his Mississippi drawl. "He gave the appearance of being leisurely," Eisenhower recalled.

Conner kept a learned library, deep in military history and classics— Shakespeare, Clausewitz, Plato, Tacitus, Nietzsche, Generals Grant and Sheridan, and many other accounts of the Civil War. He doled his books out to Eisenhower. Ike devoured them and, with Conner's help, extrapolated their meanings. Conner advocated the integration of technology, emphasized intelligence and logistics, stressed readiness as a means of deterrence.

Conner made Ike read Clausewitz's *On War* three times, and the message finally stuck. Clausewitz's analysis of military conquest and integrated command and his emphasis on the need for tactical flexibility and the centrality of political calculations in military planning all found expression in the presidency of the young man who studied him between the wars. Decades later, President Eisenhower would quote Clausewitz to his national security advisers and note his significance at work in areas as far-flung as the continuity of civilian-military leadership and the implications of war fighting in a nuclear era, when, as Clausewitz observed, the decisive goal would be to defeat not an enemy's capacity to fight but rather his will to do so. Military historians tend to divide between those who admire Napoleon and those who follow Clausewitz. Eisenhower, his son observed later, was "Clausewitz all the way."

Conner was a uniquely gifted tutor, patient and prescient—and practical as well. He foresaw that Germany would not be held down forever, that another war would test Europe before long. To defeat a resurgent Germany, Conner understood, would require a new type of Allied response, a union of nations willing to fight under a unified command, an excruciatingly difficult undertaking for independent nations, even those fighting for their lives. Conner knew it would be difficult. "Dealing with the enemy is a simple and straightforward matter when contrasted with securing close cooperation with an ally," he wrote. "America should, if she ever indulges in the doubtful luxury of entering another coalition, advocate the establishment of a Supreme War Council, coincident with entering a war with allies."

It was in those long, pleasant sessions, a fire to warm them in Conner's quarters or beneath a tropical night sky, that Eisenhower made a leap of intellect, the refinement of a serious, intelligent officer into a wise one. Conner would leave soon, and Eisenhower was relieved to exit Panama as well once it no longer had the attraction of the general. But in their time together, Conner created the foundation for the officer and politician that Eisenhower would become. Conner received in Panama a grief-stricken, promising, but still somewhat shallow officer; he sent back to the United States a man who could lead an army.

Eisenhower never questioned the debt he owed. On July 4, 1942, two weeks after arriving in Britain, he surveyed the challenges of unifying the Allies for war with Germany and recalled Conner's lessons. "More and more in the last few days my mind has turned back to you and to the days when I was privileged to serve intimately under your wise counsel and leadership," Eisenhower wrote to his mentor. "I cannot tell you how much I would appreciate, at this moment, an opportunity for an hour's discussion with you."

The following year, with fighting fierce in Italy and along the eastern front, with D-day six months away, Ike paused briefly on the day after Christmas to write to Conner's wife. He inquired about the old general's health and reminisced about those formative days in Panama: "I still long for opportunities to sit down with him in front of a wood fire and discuss this damnable business of war." There was no doubt about the degree of Conner's mark upon his protégé. "Outside of my parents," Eisenhower reflected late in his life, "no one influenced me as much."

Of Eisenhower's military mentors, none would occupy such a complicated place in his life as General Douglas MacArthur. Like Conner, MacArthur was incisive. Like Patton, he was theatrical. But MacArthur's explosions of brilliance, his undeniable daring, reinforced a profound arrogance that made him not just arresting but dangerous. Conner was the mentor who enlightened young Eisenhower; MacArthur was the one who warned him, by example.

MacArthur was a gigantic personality, a renowned alumnus of West Point, overbearing, and commandingly self-assured. He had a stunning memory—Ike recalled that MacArthur could look over a speech or memorandum and immediately recite large portions of it from memory. MacArthur often spoke of himself in the third person and insisted that his headquarters, wherever they were located, bear his name.

MacArthur displayed his ego early in Ike's time with him. The occasion was an infamous confrontation, the Bonus March of 1932. With the Depression deepening and broadening that year, veterans of World War I demanded bonuses that had been promised them for their service. The terms of that bonus, approved by Congress in 1924 over the veto of President Coolidge, allowed payments to veterans of the war but deferred the full bonus until 1945, a condition that seemed punitive to those veterans cast out of work by the Depression. In protest, they descended on Washington that May, their gathering mass a source of fear and threat to the Hoover administration, which moved ambivalently: Hoover tried to protect the rights of the marchers and even secretly slipped them supplies, but he also resisted their entreaties for aid. As thousands of bedraggled men set up tents in and just outside of Washington, clashes with police produced a few casualties and, among those inclined to imagine anarchy, raised the specter of an ominous challenge to order.

After the Washington, D.C., police department forcibly evicted the protesters from an abandoned set of Washington office buildings, Hoover ordered the Army to push the marchers away from the Capitol but to refrain from following them across the river, where more were camped. Eisenhower urged MacArthur to delegate the matter—it was, Ike thought, unseemly for the chief of staff to move on ragged marchers. MacArthur ignored him. Instead, he donned his uniform and ordered Eisenhower to do so as well—Ike had to scurry home to get it.

The troops under MacArthur's command pushed the marchers out of the buildings and toward the bridges leading away from Washington. As they approached, an order arrived from the White House reiterating Hoover's message of restraint: "Don't allow any of our troops to go across the Anacostia bridge." Eisenhower hailed MacArthur, but the general refused to listen. "I don't want to hear them, and I don't want to see them," he said of the orders the messenger carried. "Get him away." Instead, MacArthur ordered his troops to follow the veterans across the bridge, and on the other side the encampments burst into flame. "It was a very pitiful scene," Eisenhower recalled, "these ragged, discouraged people burning their own little things." Eisenhower, having advised MacArthur not to lead the troops himself and having been ignored, now advised MacArthur to decline comment. He was ignored again. MacArthur met with the press and sealed his place as the symbol of the attack on the marchers.

"That mob was a very angry looking one," he told reporters that evening. "It was animated by the essence of revolution." The elimination of the marchers was necessary, he added, because "they came to the conclusion that they were about to take over in some way either direct control or indirect control of the Government." That was absurd: twenty thousand ratty veterans, even with a few radicals among them, stood no chance of overthrowing the U.S. government, even in 1932. But it accurately captured MacArthur's megalomania and his paranoia. MacArthur saw radicals in those shabby shanties on either side of the Potomac River. Eisenhower saw desperate men, veterans who had served their country and wanted promised compensation for it. In New York, the ambitious young governor, Franklin Delano Roosevelt, listened to the radio reports of the rout and came to his own conclusion: Hoover, FDR decided, had just lost the 1932 election.

Many of the nation's newspapers defended MacArthur, not just in big cities, but in small towns across the country. The *Indianapolis News* predicted it would instill "a new pride in [the] federal structure," and the *Santa Cruz Sentinel* faulted authorities only for waiting so long. Ike was not deceived, and press coverage gradually soured as details of the rout were revealed. Eisenhower knew better than to break publicly with his commanding officer, but he had seen what he had seen.

In 1935, as MacArthur concluded his tenure as chief of staff, Eisenhower looked forward to leaving the Pentagon and receiving a command of his own, a return to leading troops rather than aiding a great man. MacArthur, however, was invited to command the construction of the army for the newly independent Philippines. He accepted and insisted that Ike join him. Twenty years after requesting the Philippines upon graduation from West Point, Eisenhower now received the belated assignment. Reluctantly, he went.

By the time Eisenhower shipped out to the Philippines in the final days of 1935, he recognized that he was entering the higher ranks of history. He began to keep a journal, and though his attention to it was sporadic, it marks the first evidence of an emerging self-awareness, of a sense that his was a story worth recording. It also supplies a convincing counterargument to the later contention that Eisenhower was clumsy with words. It is a direct and graceful document, not exactly introspective, but self-critical and occasionally deep. It records his admiration for MacArthur's ability alongside his increasing skepticism of MacArthur's integrity. In May 1936, Ike remarked on a decision made "quite suddenly" with unexpected effects on their mission. A few months later, Eisenhower noted MacArthur's vacillation over the acceptance of a Filipino military title and observed the general's reaction to the offer: "He is tickled pink—and feels he's made a lot of 'face' locally." By the fall of 1936, bemusement had grown to outright critique, as Eisenhower complained of a "bawling out" over a difference of opinion with MacArthur regarding the coming presidential election, in which MacArthur had become convinced that Alf Landon was a shoo-in to defeat Roosevelt. When Ike and a colleague disagreed, MacArthur responded with an "almost hysterical condemnation of our stupidity." Eisenhower's diary entry for that day concludes with the universal lament of the subordinate in the service of an unworthy boss: "Oh hell."

The relationship between Eisenhower and MacArthur stretched over decades and defies glib synopsis. Their correspondence is a study in guardedness, with Eisenhower frequently writing to flatter his former boss and complain that reporters had fabricated enmity between them. Invariably, MacArthur shrugged off the suggestions of discord or jealousy as his former subordinate claimed an ever more prominent role in the life of the nation. No matter how much Ike disavowed those reports, however, they captured his essential view of MacArthur: he was, in Eisenhower's estimation, startlingly vain and alarmingly contemptuous of command. Eisenhower similarly was flabbergasted at MacArthur's willingness to casually blame his subordinates for his own mistakes. "He had an obsession that a high commander must protect his public image at all costs and must never admit his wrongs," Eisenhower said in 1967.

The Eisenhowers weathered the Philippine years together. John spent much of his youth in the islands. He was a successful Boy Scout and shared the unair-conditioned hotel suite with his parents, absorbing military culture and eventually finding his steps within his father's. Thus, by the time Washington summoned Ike home, he was a proud father and a seasoned senior officer. It was with his son that Eisenhower shared his most considered thoughts on leadership, those acquired from the likes of Conner, Patton, and MacArthur.

"The best leadership and the finest relationship with associates, superior[s] and subordinates does not demand theatrics," he wrote to John decades later, and one hears "MacArthur," though his name is unmentioned. "On the contrary, honest straight-forward bearing of responsibility both for self and for subordinate, complete self-control in spite of any circumstances that put a strain on moral or physical stamina, and a human or even humorous relationship with men—are the qualities on which an enduring value and reputation are founded."

MacArthur processed their time together somewhat differently. Asked years later what he thought of Ike, MacArthur replied: "Best clerk I ever had."

It was December 1941. Ike and Mamie had just returned from a few days' vacation in a cabin near Brownsville, Texas. They had enjoyed high-balls, dancing, and Mexican food at a club in Matamoros, just across the border. They returned to the base in San Antonio relaxed and looking ahead to the holidays. They thus were home when, on a quiet Sunday that no American of that generation would ever forget, men and women, boys and girls, reeled at the news from Pearl Harbor.

General George Catlett Marshall, chief of staff of the U.S. Army, summoned to Washington officers who "will solve their own problems and not bring them all to me." One of those to whom he turned was Mark Wayne Clark. Marshall asked Clark for the names of ten capable brigadier generals who might be able to serve as chief of war plans. Clark replied with the name of an old West Point schoolmate a few years older than himself: "I'll give you one name and nine dittos: Dwight D. Eisenhower."

Ike got the call on December 12, placed to him by Walter Bedell Smith, who, like Clark, was to become a central player in Eisenhower's war and beyond. "The Chief," Smith told Eisenhower, "said you get on a plane and get up here." Ike alerted his troops and hustled around the base preparing to leave. He returned home that evening. To settle his nerves, he cooked. He made vegetable soup.

Eisenhower arrived in Washington two days later. His brother Milton met his train at Union Station and offered to take him home to freshen up. Ike asked instead for a ride to the War Department, then housed in Washington's Munitions Building. He entered, was directed to Marshall's office, and was quickly ushered inside. (Mamie followed a few weeks after that, stopping to visit John at West Point and then arriving in Washington to supervise the family's hunt for a place to live.)

Ike and Marshall had met twice before. After graduating first in his class from the Command and General Staff School at Fort Leavenworth,

Eisenhower was offered the chance to help compose a guide to World War I battle monuments, a post without much inherent appeal but for one thing: it was supervised by the revered general John J. "Black Jack" Pershing, America's most worshipped military leader of his generation. Ike accepted the job, which also offered him and Mamie their first tour of Europe, a luxurious and romantic period in their marriage and in young John's life. In those treasured months of 1928 and 1929, Ike and John would rise together, John bathing while his father shaved; Ike took his boy to school. Mamie studied French. They traveled to Italy, sunbathed at the beach, and played cards with friends while John napped in the afternoon. They were, Mamie wrote to her parents, "spoiled rotten."

Late in his association with Pershing, Ike was asked to review a section of the old general's war diaries in preparation for their publication as a memoir. Eisenhower immersed himself in the notes and reported back to Pershing that he believed sections dealing with the war's crucial battles would be best written narratively, departing from the diary form, which he felt distracted from the story. Pershing seemed to appreciate the suggestion but said he wanted to confer with a trusted aide, Colonel George Marshall. Marshall, the same colonel who had helped Eisenhower land his spot on Conner's staff, read the passages and preferred Pershing's original approach. Eisenhower was so surprised that he nursed the insult for years and insisted that friends often told him they found Pershing's version hard to decipher. (Others disagreed. Pershing's memoir won the Pulitzer Prize in 1932.) What mattered most about the literary squabble between Eisenhower and Pershing, though, was that even in resolving it in Pershing's favor, Marshall recognized the talent behind Ike's work. As with Conner years earlier, a brilliant Army leader had just spotted the flash of excellence in a promising officer.

Their other encounter was passing, but Ike remembered it well. Eisenhower had just returned from the Philippines, and the two were observing military exercises on the West Coast. Remarking on Ike's recent posting, Marshall remembered the ease of life in the Philippines, where he too had served and where servants were supplied to senior officers in abundance. Now that he was back in the United States, Marshall asked Ike, was he relearning to tie his shoes? Eisenhower's reply: "Yes, sir."

So while it was not a complete stranger who greeted Eisenhower that morning in 1941, nor was it someone he knew well, other than by reputation. And yet what a reputation it was. George Marshall was terse, taciturn, exquisitely restrained. He was absentminded, often confusing the names of subordinates, but deeply dignified. Rarely did Marshall ever issue an order.

Instead, he suggested and selected. His work ethic was legendary, and his disapproval was feared. Once, when an officer apologized for having to delay his departure to Europe because his wife was out of town and their home needed to be packed, Marshall replied: "I'm sorry, too, but you will be retired tomorrow."

Marshall and Eisenhower had grown up differently, Ike in the modesty of his Kansas home, Marshall in the boom-and-bust household supplied by his father, a prosperous coal executive who suffered in the Depression of the 1890s. If anything, young Marshall had been an even more indifferent student than young Ike. Marshall eventually graduated respectably from Virginia Military Institute and secured his commission by passing the examination that West Point alumni were allowed to skip. From that point on, Marshall's military career bore some resemblance to that of his new aide. Both served in the Philippines; both were graduates of the staff college at Leavenworth (Marshall, too, graduated "One"); both had served under Pershing, though Marshall in wartime and Eisenhower during the peace between the wars; both were well acquainted with Conner, whom they greatly admired. Both were handsome men, Eisenhower an inch or two taller; both possessed striking blue eyes, Marshall's a shade deeper.

When Eisenhower entered Marshall's inner office that morning, the chief of staff barely looked up. Sitting behind his desk, he briefed Eisenhower on the crisis facing the Philippines. MacArthur had inexplicably allowed American planes to sit on their runways in the hours after Pearl Harbor, and as a result Japanese bombing had destroyed much of America's airpower in the region. An invasion seemed imminent, and the United States was frightfully overmatched. Marshall relayed those facts squarely, speaking for about twenty minutes, then suddenly stopped. "What," he asked his new aide, "should be our general line of action?"

Surprised to be asked such a direct question of such immense consequence on such short notice, Eisenhower smartly declined a glib answer. "Give me a couple of hours," he requested. "Of course," Marshall replied.

Eisenhower went to his office and worked. "I have never pondered in my life like I did then," he said later. He returned to Marshall that afternoon. The defense of the Philippines might prove impossible, Eisenhower acknowledged. If the Japanese were determined to invade, reinforcements might well not arrive in time. The garrison on the islands might be overrun, lives and prestige lost. And yet America must fight anyway, Ike insisted. If not, the world—and especially America's allies in the region—would lose heart and confidence. "They may excuse failure," he told Marshall, "but they will not excuse abandonment." It was "seemingly hopeless [but] we have got to do our best."

"I agree with you," Marshall replied. "Do whatever you can."

Eisenhower had grasped the larger strategic context of the question. It was not merely about arms and supplies but also about nations and confidence, the imperatives of leadership, the limitations of democratic governments in conflict with authoritarian regimes. He passed his most crucial test.

Ike knew he was privileged to land a spot on Marshall's senior staff, but he still was, in one sense, anxious. Here was his second war, and at its outset it appeared he would fight again from an office, not the field. Conner counseled patience and urged Ike to trust Marshall. "Here's the man who can fight the war because he understands it," Conner once told Ike. So Ike settled in and went about raising an army.

Eisenhower was well suited to the task—comfortable with detail, proficient in training, committed to planning but open to improvisation. He had proved himself during a national training exercise in 1941, when Clark had been just one of those impressed by his work. The columnist Drew Pearson remarked on Ike's "steel trap mind" at the conclusion of those exercises, and Eisenhower's performance was recognized for his "marked ability and conspicuous success." Now Eisenhower tended to preparations on a national scale.

Men who worked for Marshall were expected to devote their lives to the task, and Eisenhower did. On March 10, 1942, Ike received word that his father had died. He recorded the news with two sentences in his diary: "Father died this morning. Nothing I can do but send a wire." The next day, he allowed himself a few more moments to grieve, confessing, "I loved my Dad," and adding, "I think my Mother the finest person I've ever known." He quit early that night, leaving at 7:30, and the following day, while his father was buried, Ike closed the door to his office and spent half an hour reflecting. "He was a just man, well liked, well educated, a thinker. He was undemonstrative, quiet, modest, and of exemplary habits—he never used alcohol or tobacco." Ike admired his father's reputation in his community and appreciated the lessons of his youth. "My only regret," he concluded, "is that it was always so difficult to let him know the great depth of my affection for him." With that, Ike returned to work.

Marshall was meticulous in all things, but none more than the selection of subordinates, an area to which he "gave long and earnest attention," rejecting the importuning of others. He kept a book in which he listed names of promising men, adding some as he heard new information about them, striking those who disappointed him. He had plucked Eisenhower off that list at Mark Clark's suggestion in 1941. Now, as armies trained for Europe and men died in the Pacific, as American industry stepped up to its role as the "arsenal of democracy" and the Depression subsided, Marshall made a fateful decision: he dispatched Eisenhower to Britain. There, Eisenhower took charge of coordinating an invasion by two armies, thankfully of shared language but of different strategic traditions, intelligence capabilities, technological advancement, and even rank structures. The melding of such armies was of paramount necessity, and Ike, still a novice, relied heavily on his chief deputy, Bedell Smith, whose sour willingness to say no balanced and permitted Eisenhower's cheerier disposition.

On July 25, after what Ike described in his diary as "tense and wearing" days, the Allies chose North Africa as the site for the Allied landing against the Axis powers—in that decision, FDR overruled his military commanders, who wanted a more direct strike on Europe—and agreed that they would fight beneath an American leader. The following day, Marshall picked the leader for the attack, known as Operation Torch. He named Eisenhower. In his official diary, Ike recorded the moment with dispassion that almost, but not quite, masked his unmistakable pride. "According to General Marshall's understanding of the agreement," he wrote, "I am to be that . . . commander."

The last hours before American forces entered the European war were agonizing, and Eisenhower had few to whom he could confess his anxieties. He shared them with Marshall. "We are standing, of course, on the brink and must take the jump—whether the bottom contains a nice feather bed or a pile of brickbats," he wrote. Hours later, with Eisenhower commanding from a headquarters in Gibraltar, American and British forces landed along the coast of North Africa. It was November 8, 1942.

Tens of thousands of young men flopped onto beaches near Casablanca, Oran, and Algiers; many died in ports or sank with ships, burned in oil, drowned in surf, their bodies cast into the waters of the Mediterranean Sea and the Atlantic Ocean, drawn by currents across thousands of miles of African coast. Those who survived the landings pressed inland off the beaches and harbors and turned left to confront Rommel and his German forces, then being pursued from the east by the British Eighth Army.

As soldiers poured from landing craft, Eisenhower paced and smoked and allowed himself a brief moment of wonder. "I have operational command of Gibraltar," he wrote. "The symbol of the solidity of the British Empire, the hallmark of safety and security at home, the jealously guarded rock that has played a tremendous part in the trade development of the English race! An American is in charge, and I am he."

If the landings at last put Allied troops in combat under unified command, the initial efforts also demonstrated America's rustiness and the enormous complexity of the task at hand. Poorly packed supplies were hard to unload, landing craft failed and sank, tanks turned out to be too wide to ship on some North African rail lines. Ike displayed some rookie failings as a commander. He was distracted by politics; he sometimes dawdled when quick and decisive action might have sped along the Allied advance. General Alan Brooke, chief of the British Imperial General Staff, sized up Eisenhower early in the war and dismissed him with a sniff: "Deficient of experience and of limited ability." Marshall may have harbored private worries as well. Still, he stood behind Ike.

The campaign for control over North Africa intermingled military and political strategy as the Allied forces confronted the vexing problem of how to deal with the French armies in the region. French soldiers yearned for liberation by the Allies, but the Vichy government was expected by its German masters to fight those same Allies. To face French resistance while embarking on a campaign to liberate Europe—including France—exasperated Eisenhower, and occasionally he let his temper boil over. "If we had come here merely to whip this French Army, I would be registering nothing but complete satisfaction at this moment," he wrote to Marshall. But he conceded he was "irritated" at the thought that every bullet fired at a French soldier was one that could not be used against a German, every lost minute on the way to Tunis was time for Germany to regroup. "I find myself getting absolutely furious with these stupid frogs," he fumed.

The pressure on Eisenhower mounted, and he punished himself. Roaming the gloomy underground headquarters at Gibraltar, he shivered and suffered. He was querulous and unpleasant, complaining about the pressures of his job. Patton worried that he was "timid" and complained to his wife that the Allied forces comprised "many commanders but no leaders." Ike smoked. He was inhaling sixty cigarettes a day and had become so dependent on them that on one trip aboard a B-17, the crew warned him of the danger of smoking with gas fumes all around. Eisenhower lit up anyway.

Eisenhower and the Allied leadership had hoped Henri Giraud, an angular, frosty, proud French general, would take command of the French forces in the area and ally them with the Americans and British. To that end, Giraud was smuggled out of Vichy and delivered to Gibraltar by submarine. Giraud quickly became a headache, "temperamental, wants much in power, equipment, etc., but seems little disposed to do his part to stop fighting," Ike confided to his diary. Denied the opportunity to lead the invasion force, Giraud pouted, and Eisenhower turned to another option, as his top aides in North Africa instead recruited François Darlan, a senior French naval officer promoted to its highest ranks by the Vichy government. Darlan offered the opportunity to bring French troops under Allied control, but that opportunity was mixed at best, as Darlan also was a detestable collaborator and opportunist. Eisenhower grimaced and cut the deal.

Under the agreement negotiated and approved by Eisenhower, French forces were placed under the command of Admiral Darlan, and those forces agreed to "take up the fight against the Axis powers for the liberation of French territory." France maintained control over North Africa, and the Allies promised no permanent occupation; in return, they were granted access to French ports and facilities.

That halted the fighting between the Allies and the French, but the decision to unite forces with Darlan was intensely controversial, flaring opposition back home and, even more acutely, in Britain. Some critics called for Ike's job. Marshall defended him, and Eisenhower, defensive about his actions but appreciative that Marshall protected him, thanked his boss. "I am pleased that you and the President saw the thing in realistic terms and realize that we are making the best of a rather bad bargain," he wrote to Marshall on November 17. Still, it ruined no Christmases in London or Washington when Darlan was assassinated on December 24. Giraud took his place.

After delay and difficulty of every type—rains that turned North African roads to mud, overstretched lines that buckled under German counterattack, faulty intelligence estimates of German troop strength, weak fighting by French soldiers, an alarming setback at Kasserine Pass—the Allies in the spring of 1943 mounted their decisive assault toward Tunis, where they hoped to rout the remainder of Germany's forces in the region and secure a port for their invasion of Europe. Marshall, having chosen Eisenhower for this assignment and defended him when others questioned Ike's judgment, now watched proudly as America's men took ground and defeated enemies. "At the moment there seems nothing for me to say except to express deep satisfaction in the progress of affairs under your direction," he wrote to Ike. "My interest is to give you what you need, support you in every way possible, and protect you against the ravages of ideologies and special pleaders of democracies, to leave you free to go about the business of crushing the Germans and gaining us great victories."

Marshall's confidence in Ike was vindicated. Patton, who just months earlier had privately scorned Eisenhower's capacity as a leader, now praised him fulsomely. Eisenhower had "developed beyond belief," Patton reported to his wife, back home in Pasadena, California. He was, Patton added, "quite a great man."

On May 20, a victory parade through the streets of Tunis marked the end of Germany's North African occupation. The Allies turned now to Sicily and Sardinia.

Since the beginning of the war, it was anticipated that Operation Overlord, the main thrust into northern Europe, would represent the heart of the Allied response to Hitler. Marshall yearned to lead it. It was, as all knew, the preeminent contest of the war, the moment when the fruits of America's military buildup, of which Marshall was the chief architect, would confront its most heinous enemy. So even as Mark Clark fought up the Italian peninsula, Roosevelt was meeting with Allied leaders in Cairo and contemplating his choice for Overlord. He admired Marshall; virtually every senior official in the war did. But Roosevelt also was deeply impressed with Eisenhower's victories in Africa and his successful management of the landings there and in Italy. Perhaps more important, given Roosevelt's penchant for sizing up associates, he liked Ike (he would not be the last). He appreciated Eisenhower's upbeat disposition and his genial ability to command, to be decisive without being overbearing, and to exercise professional but warm leadership.

Roosevelt considered and then, on December 5, broke the news to Marshall that he was going with Eisenhower. Gracefully, he explained: "I didn't feel I could sleep at ease if you were out of Washington." It is testament to Marshall's dignity that he gave no sign of displeasure. He took Roosevelt's handwritten order appointing Ike and forwarded it to Eisenhower as a keepsake. It was, Eisenhower later wrote, one of "my most cherished mementos." The note was dated December 7, 1943, the second anniversary of the attack on Pearl Harbor.

Eisenhower's orders were succinct: "You will enter the continent of Europe and, in conjunction with the other Allied Nations, undertake operations aimed at the heart of Germany and the destruction of her Armed Forces." Through the spring, the Allies trained and feinted. Patton, fighting his way back to the action from still another public blunder—one in which he seemed to denigrate Russia's role in the war—was used as a decoy to draw German attention elsewhere. Ike fretted over weather reports and tidal charts, searching for the ideal day. The options were limited: Stalin was desperately pushing for an early date; anything past midsummer was further complicated by the coming fall and winter and the difficulties cold weather would impose on fighting into Germany. Tides, weather, and geopolitics suggested June, and those days approached with gathering anxiety.

On June 4, 1944, a fierce wind tore through Britain, and Ike hesitated; then, as it began to clear, he gave his approval, officially issuing the order at 4:15 a.m. on June 5. That night, Eisenhower visited with soldiers of the 101st Airborne Division. They lustily cheered his arrival. In closer quarters, they shrugged off any hint of nerves or danger. "Don't worry, General," one young man said to Ike. "We'll take care of this."

Eisenhower stayed with those young men, many destined to die that night, until the final airplane was aloft. As it departed, he turned back to his car, where Kay waited for him. He had tears in his eyes. "Well," he said. "It's on. No one can stop it now." Thousands of miles away, John Eisenhower slept his last night as a West Point cadet; his graduation was the following morning. Ike pondered the implications of the invasion's failure and resolved that he alone would take responsibility if the Allies were repulsed. To insure his accountability, he wrote a note, to be released in the event of calamity. It read:

> Our landings in the Cherbourg-Havre area have failed to gain a
> satisfactory foothold and I have withdrawn the troops. My decision
> to attack at this time and place was based upon the best information
> available. The troops, the air and the Navy did all that bravery and
> devotion to duty could do. If any blame or fault attaches to the attempt
> it is mine alone.

As Eisenhower waited and worried, twenty thousand paratroopers drifted into Normandy that night. Many died landing in the darkness. Scuba divers also led the way, sliding into the dark ocean from submarines to clear mines and obstacles strewn by Hitler's forces along the coast.

Then, in the early morning of June 6, 1944, Allied forces came ashore on the beaches whose names would be imprinted on a generation: Utah, Omaha, Gold, Juno, and Sword. At last, word came from the Continent. Fighting was heavy in some spots—Omaha Beach was particularly hard-won as landing forces there came under devastating machine-gun fire. But troops bravely moved up and off the beaches, aided by confusion and miscommunication in the German high command (Hitler's aide elected not to wake him at the early reports of the landing); by night, more than 150,000 British, Canadian, and American soldiers were on French soil.

Tens of thousands more would follow. Eisenhower commanded an army of 2.8 million men.

At 9:30 a.m. on June 6, the free world reveled in the word released from the Allied headquarters in Europe: "Under the command of General Eisenhower, Allied naval forces, supported by strong air forces, began landing Allied armies this morning on the northern coast of France." The Battle of Stalingrad had broken the German army in the East; now it would face a fight on its western front as well. It was, Kay reflected, "the beginning of the end of the war."

The enormous undertaking of D-day was followed, for Ike, by a brief emotional letdown, the natural falloff from the execution of such a complex and consequential mission. He moped about for a few days, aching to join his forces across the channel, desperately craving news from the front. "He would sit there and smoke and worry," Summersby recalled. "Every time the phone rang, he would grab it." Those anxious days were broken by the arrival of his son, the newly commissioned second lieutenant John Eisenhower. With Marshall's help and encouragement, John shipped out for London before heading on to Fort Benning, where he would complete his infantry training. He arrived on June 13, a week after the invasion, and greeted his father with a kiss. Ike, Kay remembered, "was just one big grin."

An eager, young West Point alumnus and newly commissioned officer, John was thrilled to accompany his father and wanted to observe the niceties of their relationship—both as father and son and as superior and junior officer. Soon after arriving, John asked his father how he should salute if they were approached by an officer who outranked him but was outranked by Ike. Eisenhower's reply reminded John who was who. "John," his father said, "there isn't an officer in this theater who doesn't rank above you and below me."

As that exchange suggests, Ike could be tough on the young man. He did not suffer his son's military theories when they challenged his own; he grumbled when John seemed not to appreciate the hardships of others fighting around them. For his part, John was willful as well, every bit his father's son. They butted heads, as they had throughout John's growing up. But Ike enjoyed the rare treat of seeing his son follow in his footsteps with honor to them both. And John, as Kay recalled it, took his father's negative comments in good stride. "No matter how sharply Ike criticized him, it was obvious that he adored this son of his," she wrote.

The next months of World War II were dangerous and often calamitous. Hitler's armies fought furiously, and his machinery of death continued its genocidal mission even as his armies fell back through Poland and out of France and the Low Countries. Steadily, Eisenhower's forces pressed eastward across a long front. The Germans staged a ferocious counterattack, and the line buckled at the Battle of the Bulge, but the Allies rallied, led by Patton's stunning drive to the rescue. As the war ground on, Churchill meddled—even Marshall's confidence ebbed on occasion, only to be revived—and de Gaulle preened. When Ike proposed to withdraw troops from Strasbourg during the Battle of the Bulge, de Gaulle threatened to pull French forces out of the alliance. John recalled his father's reaction: "Dad told him to go ahead, since the Americans and British could win the war anyway."

Within his command, Eisenhower oversaw similarly varied and demanding personalities. Omar Bradley, whom Ike regarded as the most capable general of the war, orchestrated a methodical destruction of German power. Montgomery dawdled, sometimes at the edge of insubordination, and bickered over Eisenhower's decision to press a broad front across Germany rather than pursue a more focused charge toward Berlin. Patton strained at the bit, stretching supply lines in his manic quest to chew up enemies and territory. Yet even the most tempestuous commanders took their direction from Ike. Unlike Patton or Monty, de Gaulle or even Hitler, Eisenhower refused to be distracted by the lure of tactical success; he relentlessly balanced his forces and concentrated all his energies on strategic victory. He was, Lieutenant General Hastings Ismay said later, the "only man who could have made things work."

Much would be made in later years over Eisenhower's willingness to let Russia take Berlin. There is something to be said for holding Eisenhower accountable for broad strategic and political decisions. As was the case in North Africa, Ike functioned as more than mere military commander. With communications strained by the technological limitations of the time, Eisenhower was placed in the role of political strategist, not simply military leader. Still, his mission was to destroy German military strength, not to capture its center of government. And though Soviet occupation of Berlin would have consequences for the Cold War to come, there was no avoiding it in the early months of 1945. Even the occupation zones agreed to by the political leaders of the Allied nations contemplated Soviet oversight of what was to become, for far too long, East Germany.

It is, in short, unfair to blame Eisenhower for allowing the Soviets to occupy Berlin when Ike's orders, as well as logistical demands and European geography, prevented any other outcome. Nevertheless, few criticisms stung Ike more woundingly or lastingly; he devoted much of his later years to fending off the charge—raised most annoyingly by Montgomery—that the British and Americans could have taken Berlin if permitted by Ike to do so. The so-called pencil thrust might have taken Berlin, but it risked disrupting Allied supply lines and offered little long-term gain, since the Allies had already settled on the partitioning of Germany, with Berlin inside the Soviet zone. Monty's proposal, Eisenhower insisted, was "impractical—in fact, slightly hair-brained."

The war wound to its conclusion. Eisenhower visited the forward areas under the control of the First and Third armies, then arrayed in central Germany near the town of Gotha under Patton's command. First Eisenhower was dazzled by a display of German treasures, stashed inside a salt mine—gold, paintings, sculptures, historic works of art buried deep beneath the earth's bomb-scarred surface. Then he was taken to Ohrdruf-Nord. It was Eisenhower's first visit to a concentration camp. Its memory would never leave him. "The things I saw," he reported to Marshall, "beggar description." Starvation was rampant, the "cruelty and bestiality were so overpowering as to leave me a bit sick." In one room, thirty naked bodies were piled on top of one another. Patton glanced inside but refused to enter for fear he would be overcome.

On April 12, FDR collapsed in Warm Springs, Georgia, with his mistress by his side. He was pronounced dead that afternoon. Two weeks later, Mussolini was executed in Italy. Two days after that, Hitler committed suicide.

After the fall of Berchtesgaden in May 1945, Eisenhower toured the famous Nazi redoubt. At the entrance to a tunnel hung a sign that read: "Off limits to all EM [enlisted men] beyond this point, by order M.P. Command." Eisenhower turned to the commanding officer of the police unit and asked: "Tell me, General, was it only officers who captured this area?" The flustered brigadier general responded that of course it was not. "Then suppose we get rid of that sign," Ike said.

On May 5, the Germans Admiral Hans-Georg von Friedeburg and General Alfred Jodl presented themselves to Eisenhower at Reims. They attempted to negotiate a qualified surrender but were rebuffed. Protesting, they played for time, hoping that negotiations would allow more of their soldiers and other Germans to flee the portions of the country hourly falling under Soviet control. Eisenhower threatened to shut down the western front unless they surrendered without condition. At 2:41 a.m. on May 7, Jodl signed the surrender. Eisenhower was brutally terse: "You will, officially and personally, be held responsible if the terms of the surrender are violated, including its provisions for German commanders to appear in

Berlin at the moment set by the Russian high command to accomplish formal surrender to that government. That is all."

The war in Europe ended at midnight the following day. Marshall cabled his congratulations to Eisenhower, the expression of a proud mentor to his most exemplary protégé. "You have completed your mission with the greatest victory in the history of warfare," he wrote. "You have made history, great history for the good of mankind and you have stood for all we hope for and admire in an officer of the United States Army. These are my tributes and my personal thanks."

For Eisenhower, Marshall would always be the greatest general of all.

3

Learning Politics

Early in the morning of March 24, 1952, a car pulled up to the Hotel George V in Paris. A man traveling under an assumed name got into the car and was whisked to NATO headquarters. Arriving, the man resumed his real identity. Herbert Brownell was greeted by NATO's supreme commander, Dwight Eisenhower. For the next ten hours, Brownell tutored Ike in American politics. The phone did not ring; no notes were taken. The two men were mutually respectful, but their conversation was anything but light. When Brownell remarked that he had been to see the Folies Bergère the previous evening, "that fell like a lead balloon." Except for one aide who entered with a tray of sandwiches at lunchtime, Eisenhower and Brownell were left entirely alone.

Brownell was a Nebraska native born on the banks of the Missouri River, a graduate of Yale Law School, and a successful securities lawyer at the firm of Lord, Day & Lord. He had managed the New York governor Tom Dewey's campaigns in 1944 and 1948, and though Dewey had lost both times, Eisenhower was impressed with the governor and with Brownell's unrivaled command of national politics, particularly in the subspecialty of what was required to secure the Republican nomination. Moreover, Brownell did not fit Ike's generally negative view of people in politics: he was neither cynical nor opportunistic. He was smart, dignified, genial, armed with a light touch and a firm resolve. On that spring morning in Paris, he was there to explain certain realities to Ike and to discern whether Eisenhower's politics, largely unknown despite his renown, were compatible with those of the Republican Party and the American people.

Brownell traveled to Europe that March as a committed Republican and an admirer of Eisenhower. He also did so as a representative of Ike's inner circle, an exceptionally devoted group of friends. During the war, Ike's closest advisers had acted as an official family, loyal and protective of their boss. In the years since, Eisenhower had kept up most of those friendships while also befriending captains of industry, sturdy, competitive men who provided him with a circle of intimates with whom he could relax. They were bridge players and golfers; they were at his summons and would, throughout his presidency, travel the nation over when Ike needed a break, whether in Augusta or Pebble Beach, Gettysburg, London, New York, or Washington.

At the center of this group was Bill Robinson. Burly, gregarious, powerful, and slightly secretive (only after Eisenhower's retirement did Robinson confess that he and his wife had been separated since the 1940s), and also a nimble, subtle writer, Robinson revered Eisenhower, imagined him a savior of the nation. Though Robinson pursued his own ambitions through the 1950s, he was always at Ike's service.

Robinson introduced Eisenhower to some of the nation's leading men, and they became known as the Gang: Bob Woodruff, chairman and CEO of Coca-Cola (a job Robinson himself would later inherit from Woodruff); Cliff Roberts, an investment banker and president of the Augusta National Golf Club; Pete Jones, a self-made oil executive who carried $10,000 in his wallet to remind himself of his prosperity and who, like Ike, fancied himself a farmer, in Jones's case as the owner of two thousand Maryland acres of cows and hogs; George Allen, bon vivant and friend of Truman's, a man so garrulous he titled his memoir *Presidents Who Have Known Me*; Ellis "Slats" Slater, a diffident executive who worried about tarnishing Ike with their friendship since Slater made his fortune as the head of a liquor company; Al Gruenther, a war colleague who followed Ike through Europe and to NATO, soon to head the International Red Cross. Ike considered Gruenther worthy of the presidency itself, and he enjoyed him, too: Gruenther kept a file of favorite jokes and taught himself bridge as a young officer. He was always welcome at Ike's table—indeed, he was somewhat indispensable, as Ike was so intolerant of poor play that only Gruenther was up to serving as his partner.

Those men shared moderate politics, a firm belief that the peace of the world required American leadership, and an unshakable conviction that only Dwight Eisenhower could guide the nation through that fragile peace. They vowed that Ike would be president and set out to persuade him of it as well. At a Christmas party in 1951, they pledged to finance his campaign, and they picked an emissary to reel in the general: Brownell.

Brownell understood that this was a candidate—or at least a potential candidate—like none other. Ike was a hero on a grand, historic scale—as adored in Paris and London as in Washington and New York. Slater, along with the rest of the Gang, realized that his friend was a man of unsurpassed esteem. Brownell grasped the political implications of that regard. Ike was nothing less, as Brownell correctly observed, than "the most highly respected man in the world."

He had returned from Europe a conquering hero, and then, as Marshall's successor as chief of staff, he had demobilized an American force for the second time in his career, this time with a vision of continued American presence and power in the world. Eisenhower was urged to write a memoir and, after long hesitation, agreed. He began on February 8, 1948, and for weeks worked diligently, almost punishingly, on the project, typically dictating, writing, and correcting drafts from 6:00 a.m. to 11:00 p.m. He was aided by three secretaries and Doubleday's editor in chief, Kenneth D. McCormick, who often dropped by at lunch, and by Robinson, who coordinated the project and the book's serialization. Eisenhower was new at this, of course, but he modeled his prose on that of Ulysses S. Grant, the greatest of all presidential memoirists and a general whose writing Ike admired for its "lack of pretension." Aided by Robinson and propelled to set down his account of the war before others solidified that history, Eisenhower met his deadline: he finished the manuscript on Friday, March 26. *Crusade in Europe* was published that fall.

The book was glowingly received for its objectivity and evenhandedness and for its appealing prose style: "orderly, objective, well-documented," as one reviewer put it. *Crusade in Europe* codified Eisenhower's version of events in the war—a useful counterpoint to more snippy accounts by other commanders—and also allowed him and Mamie to salt away some money. In that, they were substantially aided by a novel interpretation of the tax code under which he completed the work, then allowed it to sit for a period and claim its publication as a capital gain rather than income. The result: at a time when income over $200,000 was taxed at a marginal rate of 91 percent, Ike was paid $635,000 for *Crusade in Europe*, of which he paid just $158,750 in federal taxes. The arrangement was approved in advance by the Treasury Department and saved him hundreds of thousands of dollars.

The interregnum between the war and his candidacy provided Ike with yet another opportunity, this one in the form of a warning. The cause was a flare-up of his recurring intestinal troubles, one so severe that it knocked him off his feet for several days in 1949. Although some scholars have hypothesized that Eisenhower in fact suffered a heart attack—and that he later covered it up to avoid questions about his health—no medical evidence supports that theory. Instead, it is far more likely that Ike, whose stomach had troubled him off and on since Panama and who had been periodically hospitalized by pain from it, endured a particularly sharp attack in the spring of 1949. Among the evidence pointing in that direction is that Ike was playing golf and working within ten days of the episode—in an era when a heart attack was typically treated with at least a month of bed rest. Alarmed by the pain Ike was in, his doctor said the time had come for Eisenhower to quit smoking. The next day, he did. "The only way to stop is to stop, and I stopped," Ike told Sherman Adams years later.

"Didn't you have quite a lot of battle with yourself when you gave up a habit that you'd liked and lived with so long?" Adams asked.

"Put it out of your mind," Eisenhower replied. "If you have anything like that to disturb you, put it out of your mind. Don't think about it."

Ike coveted a university presidency, which suited his desire for an intellectually stimulating, dignified sinecure. He hoped for a rural, small college, but he was offered Columbia University instead, and accepted it, joking later that he assumed the trustees had meant to offer it to his brother Milton and were too embarrassed to withdraw it from him once they had made the mistake. His installation as president provided Ike and his brothers with the opportunity for a rare reunion, and they gathered on the day he was publicly given the post. It was a happy gathering of the boys, now all successful men, as they bantered together in Dwight's office before the ceremony. Just as they were to leave for the event, Milton tapped his brother's mortarboard: "Father would have liked this."

The Columbia presidency came with a residence on Morningside Drive, so Ike and Mamie, who had never owned a home, had no immediate need of one. They were, however, suddenly rich, at least by their modest standards, and flush with the proceeds of *Crusade in Europe* they set out to buy a place of their own (so flush were they, in fact, that the Eisenhowers splurged at Christmastime in 1948 and bought a favorite aunt and uncle of Mamie's a Chrysler sedan, spending $2,434 on the shiny blue vehicle). They settled on a farm at the edge of the Gettysburg battlefield, a location rich with significance for Eisenhower and for the couple as well, since they had lived nearby early in their marriage, when Ike was training troops for World War I. The house was in terrible shape, and they embarked on a long and expensive renovation: Eisenhower grumpily complained of the cost in his final memoir, noting that it had come to $215,000 and pointedly adding that he had refused to use non-union labor, even though it would have cost less.

Eisenhower's tenure at Columbia was not altogether a success. The faculty was not quite sure what to make of its military leader, a president conspicuously lacking a Ph.D. But Ike made the most of it: among other things, it was at Columbia that he took up painting. As in so many things, Churchill supplied an example. The prime minister relaxed by painting and encouraged Ike to take it up. Eisenhower did not at first, but then he stumbled upon paints and brushes that the artist Thomas Stephens was using to produce a portrait of Mamie. He tried them out and enjoyed it. It became a source of relaxation and concentration, akin to bridge or golf. Eisenhower's first attempt at a painting was to copy Stephens's portrait of Mamie. It was, Ike said, "weird and wonderful to behold."

Barely had Eisenhower settled into his Columbia post than duty commanded again, this time in the form of what he regarded as effectively an order from President Truman to take charge of forging the European mutual-defense agreements that would form the basis of NATO. He left Columbia on January 1, 1951, intending to resign his post but persuaded to accept a leave of absence. He stopped in Washington to pay his respects to a fallen colleague, then proceeded, once again, to Paris, returning this time with the responsibility of securing America's allies against Soviet Communism.

Through much of 1951, Ike closely monitored and subtly influenced the lobbying for him to become a candidate. Working through a trusted emissary and former military aide, General Lucius Clay, one of the rare men who could lecture his vaunted comrade, Ike tracked the calls for his candidacy and allowed Clay to encourage them. Though a military man, Clay intuited politics and recognized that Eisenhower's distance from partisan squabbles only enhanced his appeal. "You are," he said, "in an unassailable position."

As the urgency of Ike's supporters increased, so did the complexity of nurturing the campaign without committing the candidate. Again, Clay played the key role. He brokered understandings between Eisenhower's leading backers, settling disputes in Ike's name. By the middle of 1951, Eisenhower's support had become so broad—and the matter so delicate—that Clay devised a code to keep Ike abreast of developments. Each of the principals was assigned a letter: *A* was for the Pennsylvania senator James "Big Red" Duff, *B* for Brownell, and so on. The code grew increasingly elaborate until, in September, Eisenhower confessed to being unable to follow it.

His supporters visited him with increasing frequency and ardor through late 1951 and early 1952. And yet Eisenhower would not commit. He knew enough to know that he alone could disdain politics and remain at its center, so he took his time, gauged his choices.

Hoping to coax him with a demonstration of popular appeal, one group of enthusiasts scheduled a rally at Madison Square Garden at the conclusion of the Friday night fights in February. Expectations for the event were low: it was held late on a winter night, and the candidate, of course, refused to attend. Nevertheless, fifteen thousand people turned out in what was billed as a "Serenade to Ike." Veterans pleaded, so did children. A Truman impersonator drew big laughs. Irving Berlin and Ethel Merman sang. A group of Texans passed a saddlebag that they filled up with silver dollars. Over and over, the thousands chanted and sang: "I like Ike."

As soon as the event ended, a film of it was rushed to processing, and then Jacqueline Cochran, a pioneering aviator and friend of Eisenhower's—and one of the event's organizers—crammed into an upper berth of a transatlantic flight and headed for Paris.

She arrived at Eisenhower's home on an unseasonably warm evening in February, a mild breeze drifting across the channel and over the French countryside. Inside the Villa Saint-Pierre, where Napoleon II once resided in surprising modesty, above ordered gardens and a calm pond (which Ike had stocked with trout and where he practiced his fly casting), against the incongruous but portentous backdrop of a Communist-led general strike outside, Cochran arrived bearing the film canisters and loaded the projector.

Eisenhower's sense of duty cabined his response to flattery or strain—this was the same Ike who spent half an hour mourning the death of his father. But as he watched the yearning expressed by the Madison Square Garden crowd, his reserve was tested. So many Americans were worried and, he believed, with good cause. The Truman administration was exhausted, the war in Korea stalemated, the threat of Communism growing. America's problems, it seemed to Ike, were "nagging, persistent and almost terrifying." Its citizens were desperate. He watched with Mamie as those men and women cried out for him. Eisenhower was, he realized as the two-hour film rolled on, "the symbol of that longing and hope." "I've not been so upset in years," he confided to his diary.

When the film stopped, Cochran raised a glass: "To the President." Eisenhower was overwhelmed; tears ran down his cheeks.

Supporters kept up their pressure. A few days after he watched the film of the Madison Square Garden rally, nineteen leading, moderate Republicans—including Jacob Javits, Hugh Scott, Christian Herter, Norris Cotton, and Gerald Ford—beseeched him on behalf of the American people to seek their party's nomination. Those politicians reported that their constituents wanted Ike. "They want you to come home; they want you to declare yourself on the pressing issues of the day; they want the inspiration of your dynamic honesty and the forthrightness of your states-manship," the group wrote. "The demands of these patriotic Americans have a right to be heard, and we beg you to listen to them because we agree with them."

For Eisenhower, the essential call was always to duty. When leaders he respected urged him onward, when thousands called his name, his duty to those men and women overcame his doubts. "My attitude," he confided to Clay, "has undergone a quite significant change."

But it was one thing to consider accepting the presidency, another to actively seek it. With his permission but without any action on his part, supporters campaigned for him in New Hampshire, which was predictably billed as "the first big test of Eisenhower's voter appeal v. Taft's." Eisenhower won the March 11 primary handily, puncturing Robert Taft's command of the party loyalists. A week later, Ike finished second to the favorite-son candidate Harold Stassen in Minnesota, another stunning showing for a noncandidate. In some ways, Minnesota made an even bigger impression on him than New Hampshire did. Thousands returned ballots with the word "Ike" scrawled across them.

On March 20, two days after the Minnesota results, Ike announced that he was reconsidering his refusal to run for president but still declined to declare himself a candidate. It was at that juncture, hovering on the edge of a monumental decision for himself and the United States, that Herb Brownell arrived to seal the deal.

He was there by invitation. The day of the Minnesota primary, Ike wrote to Brownell to encourage the visit and to "assure you of a warm welcome." Arrangements were delicate: Brownell was so associated with politics gen-erally and Dewey specifically that his contact with Eisenhower would cer-tainly have signaled Ike's presidential ambitions. Brownell thus booked his tickets under another name, and Eisenhower made sure his visit was not included in the general's daily schedule, often reviewed by reporters.

Although Ike had been courted for the presidency since the end of the war—during a break in the Potsdam Conference in 1945, Truman startled Eisenhower by offering to secure him anything he wanted, adding, "That definitely and specifically includes the presidency in 1948"—his views of domestic politics were so vaguely known that both parties fancied he might belong to them. Now Brownell asked Eisenhower to clear up those myster-ies, quizzing him about his political beliefs so that Brownell might ascer-tain whether they could carry the electorate.

Responding to Brownell's questions, Ike revealed that he believed in limited federal government, favoring the private economy over government spending and states' rights over federal power—he sided with Texas, for instance, in its claims to offshore oil rights that the federal government asserted belonged to it. He felt strongly that the government should balance its budgets and was shocked at Truman's latest spending plan, which anticipated a $14 billion deficit. Unsurprisingly, he felt strongly that the United States had an obligation to provide a stalwart national defense.

He was, portentously, murkier on the emerging domestic issue of the day, civil rights. Brownell was an ardent supporter of the gathering call for elimination of American apartheid, and the issue had helped give moderate Republicans a broader appeal in an era when southern Democrats continued to restrain the ambitions of more liberal members of their party. But Ike was raised in Kansas, where segregation had been practiced, and he rose through a segregated military, so Brownell was concerned about where he might fall on this issue. "I was relieved that his views were generally in accord with the pro-civil rights stance of the moderate wing of the Republican Party," Brownell wrote. Still, Ike sent mixed signals. He noted that some of his supporters were southern Democrats who opposed civil rights legislation, an ambiguous remark that left Brownell convinced that though Ike's "heart was in the right place," he "would not lead the charge to change race relations fundamentally in the United States." Brownell was to be proved half-right in that prediction; to the extent that he was wrong, he himself would largely be the reason.

Having sized up Eisenhower's politics and concluded that they would fall comfortably within the moderate-to-liberal wing of the Republican Party, Brownell then moved to the other part of his presentation. He forcefully insisted that Eisenhower stop being coy. Neither the nomination nor the presidency would be handed to him, Brownell insisted in terms so adamant that he feared he was being brash. To gain the Republican nomination, Ike would have to return home and fight for it. Eisenhower, who had already fared well in two primaries without being a candidate, seemed surprised at that, but Brownell was expert where Ike was not, in the machinery of American politics. Ike had learned from Marshall to place faith in capable subordinates. He took heed. "It was," Brownell said later, "an important turning point in his thinking."

After ten hours, the two men parted. Brownell returned to his hotel and then headed home. Two weeks later, Eisenhower resigned his NATO position. On June 1, he returned home to campaign for the presidency.

PART TWO

THE FIRST TERM

4

From Candidate to President

I t is natural to think of landmark American elections as destined. In retrospect, George Washington seems to have ascended to the presidency rather than to have won it, and Abraham Lincoln's election is recalled as a matter of faith as much as politics. The thought of Roosevelt losing in 1932 seems preposterous given our memory of the New Deal and the war. So it was with Ike. His renown after World War II makes him seem, with hindsight, an insurmountable candidate, and his identification with the 1950s renders it difficult to imagine the era without him at its head. In fact, however, Ike fought hard to be president and stood a good chance to lose.

In June 1952, Eisenhower swiftly completed his transition from general to political candidate. Although his campaign had been under way for weeks, he gave his first official speech in Abilene, delivered at the conclusion of a drenching rainstorm—a "gully washer," as Ike recalled it. With it, he sketched the broad themes of his candidacy. "America must be spiritually, economically and militarily strong, for her own sake and for humanity," Eisenhower told a damp, sparse crowd. "She must guard her solvency as she does her physical frontiers." For a public waiting to hear more about his specific policies, the speech was as disappointing as the weather.

Henry Cabot Lodge, an old friend and early political supporter, tried to tutor Ike in politics. Soon after Eisenhower announced, Lodge sent him a list of sixty questions for him to be prepared to answer, as well as some general observations on how he might be viewed. "I think I have no quarrel with your general observations," Eisenhower wrote. "I merely want to make the point that I am wary of slogans, and if I have a real conviction I am not to be deterred from expressing it merely because I am afraid of how it will read in the headlines." Lodge had suggested no such thing, but Ike, sensitive at the outset to being above politics, insisted that he did not "intend to tailor my opinions and convictions to the one single measure of net vote appeal."

Those were the grumblings of a man new to campaigning for office. By contrast, Eisenhower's primary opponent was a seasoned, experienced politician with a deep, loyal base of supporters. Indeed, despite Ike's great appeal as an American hero and strong showings in the early primaries, smart political money that summer favored Robert Taft, who had a narrow lead in delegates and thorough command of the party apparatus. The son of a president and chief justice—William Howard Taft being the only man ever to hold both those offices—Robert Taft was a leader of the U.S. Senate and an ideological archetype, a sharp critic of labor unions and the New Deal, an isolationist so committed to American nonintervention that he opposed war against Nazi Germany until the United States was attacked at Pearl Harbor. Clever, vindictive, and tough, double chinned and yet curiously dapper, Taft possessed "the almost evangelical loyalty of his followers." His reach through the party ranks was unequaled. Taft allies picked the convention's key speakers and even controlled the seating, relegating rivals to distant corners of the hall. Not for nothing was he known as "Mr. Republican."

That gave Taft a strong advantage on an obscure rules matter that ultimately proved decisive: the seating of delegates from Louisiana, Texas, and Georgia, where competing slates of Eisenhower and Taft delegates were vying for voting slots at the convention. The conflict grew from the general's late entry into the campaign and the efforts by the Taft forces to impose caucus rules intended to favor their candidate. In Texas, for instance, the Taft-sponsored rules held that only Republicans who had been registered as Republicans in 1948 were permitted to participate in the 1952 delegate-selection process. That had the effect of excluding new party members drawn to Eisenhower's candidacy. The result was a strongly pro-Taft slate. Eisenhower's supporters responded by electing a slate of their own, and the two camps stomped into their respective corners. The question before the Republican Party was which delegation to seat—and whether the contested delegates would be allowed to vote on that contentious question.

Eisenhower had the support of an intelligent campaign apparatus, led by Brownell. Having helped persuade Ike to run—and convinced of his electability—Brownell now plotted the strategy to secure the nomination. His role was largely unappreciated at the time, as he stayed out of public view for most of the campaign, careful to avoid pricking the animus of those who blamed Dewey for letting the party down in 1944 and 1948, when Brownell managed his campaigns. This time, Brownell formulated his strategy from the stacks of the New York Public Library, poring over records from earlier Republican conventions, including the complete transcript of the 1912 contest that pitted Theodore Roosevelt against Taft's father in a debate over delegates.

Brownell emerged with a proposal that was part legal brief and part public relations strategy. Its central argument was that Taft's strength among Republican stalwarts might earn him the nomination but would almost surely fail in the general election. Republicans savored a return to power, and Brownell knew that the choice was between pragmatism and idealism: a vote for Taft was an opportunity to assert old values; one for Eisenhower was a chance for victory. Brownell wooed wavering delegates with the promise of the White House and simultaneously challenged Taft's tactics as suppressive and unfair. He wrote what he brilliantly branded the "Fair Play Amendment" and arranged for Governor Arthur B. Langlie of Washington, an Eisenhower supporter, to submit it to the convention.

Party rules at the time called for all delegates to be provisionally seated while rules matters were debated. The Fair Play Amendment, however, forbade contested delegates to vote on their own seating. Taft supporters argued it was unfair to change long-standing rules. Brownell countered that it was unfair to allow contested delegates to seat themselves. Taft controlled the relevant rules committee but hurt himself by refusing public and press access to the committee's hearings in the days leading up to the convention. When Brownell and Ike's supporters theatrically showed up outside the door, the newsman John Chancellor joined the group. He knocked on the door and was denied entrance, too. On July 2, with the convention's opening less than a week away, the committee voted to recommend the seating of Taft's Georgia delegates, a victory for Taft, of course, but one that reinforced the Eisenhower campaign's claims of "stolen" delegates and party secrecy. In Fraser, Colorado, where Eisenhower spent the day fishing (catching ten trout, the legal limit), he announced: "I'm going to roar out across the country for a clean, decent operation. The American people deserve it." In politics, as in war, he was a quick study.

That was where matters stood on the eve of the Republican convention. And with that technical debate the first order of business, the delegates began to assemble. They streamed to Chicago by car and train—a few lucky ones made the trip by plane—arriving to brass bands and banners. They swarmed bars and restaurants and filled the lobbies of the city's grand hotels, reuniting with old friends and trading rumors and strategies with journalists and colleagues. They presented their credentials at the counters of the Congress, the Blackstone, and the Conrad Hilton. At the Hilton, the Eisenhower forces had already pulled a fast one. Brownell realized at the last minute that the Eisenhower campaign had no place for its headquarters. Luckily, Brownell's clients included the American Hotel Association. He rang up two associates from the Hilton chain, and they found space. Although Ike and Mamie stayed at the Blackstone, their headquarters were two floors above Taft's—at the Hilton.

As the delegates arrived, they got the first whiff of the week—Chicago's convention hall was a little too close to its stockyards for many tastes. But to win the White House, the Republican Party would need the cattle states, which had defected to Truman in 1948. The rest of the map was tantalizing but murky. Could southern states committed to the Democratic Party since Lincoln be drawn across the aisle? Could California, which slipped away to the Democrats in 1948 despite Governor Earl Warren's place at the bottom of that ticket, be coaxed back into its traditional alignment? Delegates buzzed over those questions late into the night, seduced by the enormity of their opportunity. For decades, Republicans had gathered, often in Chicago, to pick a nominee. This year, they knew they had the chance to pick a president.

There were warnings and conflicting signals. In the week leading up to the convention, the *New York Times* editorial page featured a provocative series. The headline said it all: "Mr. Taft Can't Win," in parts 1, 2, and 3, no less. "We conclude this series," the paper's editorial board wrote on July 3, "with the argument that the Taft record and campaign are of such a character that the Senator is not likely to pick up the independent or Democratic votes which the Republicans must have to succeed. General Eisenhower, on the other hand, is in a position to attract precisely that additional support that can spell the difference between Republican victory and one more bitter, frustrating and ruinous Republican defeat."

In raw terms, however, Taft held the advantage. He came to Chicago with a lead in delegates: the Associated Press calculated that Taft had 530 of the 604 needed to win; Eisenhower had 427; Warren 76; Harold Stassen 25; and a few other candidates divided up the balance. Taft contested the AP's calculations; his campaign publicly insisted it had 600 delegates, on the verge of locking matters up.

To the attentive ear, however, there was a note of desperation in the Taft camp. On July 5, reeling from the charges that his campaign was stealing delegates, Taft complained of "libel" and "vituperation," shrill notes that hardly conveyed confidence. Even his rejection of the AP delegate count seemed fishy; no matter how often he insisted that the matter was all but won, the press refused to accept his analysis and continued to cover the race as a hot contest.

At 11:30 a.m. on Monday, July 7, the Republican national chairman, Guy Gabrielson, banged the convention to order and turned immediately to the issue of delegate seating. Brownell had laid the groundwork for this debate well, framing it as one of fairness and openness against secretive party bosses. When Taft forces sought to allow delegates to be provisionally seated and cast ballots for themselves, Langlie countered with the Fair Play Amendment, after which Taft allies parried with an amendment to Langlie's proposal. On the floor, there was bedlam as delegates argued over the intricacies of an issue that all understood could decide the nomination. Finally, the questions were put to votes, and on the key question Eisenhower won by 658 to 548. Taft's floor managers suddenly understood Eisenhower's strength and did not protest when the Fair Play Amendment itself was put before the convention. It was accepted on a voice vote. Although the full convention had yet to consider the seating of each of the contested delegations, the rules, which had once favored Taft, now gave the edge to Eisenhower.

Ike stayed away from the convention floor but monitored the roll call from his hotel suite, where he relaxed in a robe and slippers. He won a bet on the final vote and collected $1 from an aide. Mamie shrugged off a painful tooth infection for long enough to speak briefly with reporters. She too cheered the results, which she described as "encouraging," and promised she would campaign with her husband if he were nominated: "I go everyplace I can with him. I've been following him for 36 years."

Fights over procedure gave way to a less consequential but more histrionic event, Douglas MacArthur's keynote address. It had been arranged by Taft and was intended to stir conservatives who violently opposed his firing by Truman the year before. But MacArthur—he who spoke of himself in the third person—often misunderstood his effect on those around him, allowing his stentorian voice and self-regard to overwhelm his better sense. Thundering from the podium, he declaimed that the Truman administration had "brought us to fiscal instability, political insecurity and military weakness." The Democratic Party, MacArthur charged, had "become captive to the schemers and planners who have infiltrated its ranks of leadership to set the national course unerringly toward the socialistic regimentation of a totalitarian state." It was, one perceptive *New York Times* analyst noted, "a stirring oration for a lost cause." MacArthur's time was up.

That pattern—delegate fights on the floor that formed the convention's real business while odes to a bygone Republican philosophy emanated from the podium—continued the next day. Herbert Hoover recalled the party's history from the dais as Herbert Brownell molded its future on the floor. Hoover complained of Democratic misrule and urged the rapid buildup of the U.S. Air Force. Meanwhile, Brownell sold Eisenhower's case to delegates, concentrating on those pledged to other candidates on the first ballot but who would be up for grabs if there was a second. Ike did his part, meeting with two hundred delegates that day in his fifth-floor suite at the Blackstone; some wore their Taft buttons, but they came to meet the general anyway.

The following morning, the seating of the contested delegations finally came before the full convention. The results quickly established Ike as the front-runner. The Georgia slate that favored Eisenhower by fourteen to three was seated over the objections of Taft's managers; having lost that key test, they folded on Texas, where a slate favoring Ike by thirty-three to five was approved. For the first time, Eisenhower moved ahead of Taft in the AP poll. The general told Senator John Sherman Cooper of Kentucky, "I'm going to win." Supporters began speculating on the choice of a vice president. In Washington, Truman, who believed Taft the easier candidate for Democrats to beat in November, announced that he was "worried" about the turn of events in Chicago. "It looks like my candidate is going to get beat," he joked.

The seating issue ended all hopes for Taft. Illinois placed his name in nomination, California nominated Warren, Maryland did the honors for Eisenhower, Minnesota tapped Stassen, and then Oklahoma nominated MacArthur. At the end of the first ballot, Ike led with 595 votes, just 9 short of victory. Stassen then declared that Minnesota would switch to Eisenhower, and the race was over. The final tally was 845 for Eisenhower, 280 for Taft.

In the ensuing bedlam, Ike left his hotel to cross the street and see Taft personally, a thoughtful gesture intended to emphasize Republican unity. As he elbowed his way through the lobby of the Hilton, Eisenhower was surrounded by Taft supporters, many of them fighting tears. He mumbled sympathies and proceeded upstairs, where he found the defeated candidate staggered by the vote but willing to pose together for the press. It wasn't exactly a picture of a unified Republican Party, but it would do.

Ike wasted no time moving forward: he hired Tom Stephens to serve as his appointments secretary and James Hagerty to serve as press secretary. Both would remain at his side for the next eight years.

The convention's other piece of business was the selection, nomination, and confirmation of a vice president. Although the selection would prove immensely important, Eisenhower essentially turned it over to his top political aides. "He expressed surprise," Brownell later wrote, "that for all practical purposes he could select his running mate by letting the delegates know his personal choice." Learning this, Eisenhower ruled out several men in whom he had great confidence—his campaign manager, Henry Cabot Lodge, was running for the Senate; Brownell himself had no interest in the post, nor did Tom Dewey, who would have been a difficult sell to the convention in any case—but then wrote down the names of others who would be acceptable to him. They were Congressmen Charles Halleck and Walter Judd; Colorado's governor, Dan Thornton; Washington's governor, Arthur Langlie; and California senator Richard Nixon.

In 1952, Nixon was a fresh, up-and-coming senator, seasoned in the tricky politics of mid-century California. A native of Yorba Linda, a Navy veteran, and a lawyer, Nixon was a perennial outsider, a scrapper who worked hard for his achievements and resented those to whom they came more easily. He had established his national reputation in the prosecution of Alger Hiss, a debut that would stamp him to some as a brave and principled anti-Communist and to others as a snarling pugilist. He was young—Ike thought him forty-two, only to discover later that Nixon was just thirty-nine—with lovely daughters and a striking wife, whom he had courted in Nixon's dogged fashion, first by driving her on dates with rivals, eventually wearing down her resistance and winning her hand. And though he traveled with a chip forever on his shoulder, he could be charming in his fashion and politically savvy in the extreme.

Through the weeks leading up to the convention, he had done his best to assist Eisenhower while, as a delegate from California, formally pledged to support Warren. Nixon circulated a "poll" to constituents seeking their advice on what to do if and when Warren should fall short of his presidential ambitions. He worked the California delegation to woo its members to Eisenhower even as the Warren train sped to the convention. When the delegation arrived, the buses sent to pick them up were draped with "Eisenhower for President" banners. Those machinations would seal Warren's lifelong enmity, and Warren and Nixon would circle each other for the rest of their careers.

Ike knew of Warren's suspicions about Nixon. On July 8, the second day of the convention, Warren sent an emissary to the general's hotel room and asked for an audience. Admitted, the man reported that, according to Warren, "we have a traitor in our delegation. It's Nixon . . . He has not paid attention to his oath and immediately upon being elected, started working for Eisenhower and has been doing so ever since. I have word he is actively in touch with the Eisenhower people." Warren asked Eisenhower to rein Nixon in and to halt his interference in California's politics. Ike assured Warren's messenger that he was not behind any machinations, an assurance dutifully reported to an unconvinced Warren.

Nixon himself stewed over what to do if offered the vice presidency. Late into the night, he and his wife, Pat, sat up in their hotel room, debating whether he should accept. To do so, both realized, would derail his immediate plans for the Senate but establish him as a national figure. At 4:00 a.m., they phoned Murray Chotiner, Nixon's Machiavellian campaign manager, and summoned him to their hotel room. Chotiner urged him to accept. "There comes a time," he said, "when you have to go up or out." When Chotiner left an hour later, Richard and Pat Nixon were still debating.

Neither Nixon's ambivalence nor Warren's discomfort affected Eisenhower's appraisal of the young senator. He was impressed by Nixon's handling of the Hiss case and untroubled by Warren's allegations. Moreover, Nixon nicely balanced the Eisenhower ticket. His youth was a welcome contrast to Ike's age (at sixty-two, Eisenhower stood to become the oldest man ever elected to the presidency), and his California base represented an important addition to Ike's Midwest and eastern sources of support. So Eisenhower told Brownell that should top Republicans agree on Nixon, he would be happy to have him on the ticket.

Meeting in Brownell's office, the group considered first Taft and then William Knowland, the senior senator from California. They were "knocked down." Then Dewey, who saw early promise in Nixon, formally suggested the young senator. Paul Hoffman, the chief organizer of independents and Democrats for Ike, agreed: "Nixon fills all the requirements." With that, the group fell in line. Brownell reported the recommendation to a pleased Ike. The convention ratified the choice, and the Republican ticket for 1952 was formed.

Securing the nomination was the hard part of Eisenhower's work. His crossover appeal to Democrats was already well known. However bereft Taft's supporters were, it was unlikely that they would abandon their party in the general election. And whatever risk there might have been to the

Republican base ended a few weeks later when Democrats, also meeting in Chicago, chose a ticket topped by the elegant and eloquent Adlai Stevenson.

Stevenson's acceptance was delivered with the rhetorical gifts that endeared him to American liberals. The presidency, he declared, was vast in its burdens, inspiring in its possibility. "Its potential for good or evil, now and in the years of our lives, smothers exultation and converts vanity to prayer." His speech continued, rich and vivid, winding through scripture and policy toward a graceful conclusion. "Help me to do the job in these years of darkness," Stevenson told his audience. "And we will justify our glorious past and the loyalty of silent millions who look to us for compassion, for understanding, and for honest purpose."

Listening from Denver, Ike was among those "impressed by his speaking style and polish." Ike's friend George Allen was not so moved. "He's too accomplished an orator," Allen argued. "He will be easy to beat." What Allen sensed—and what the Eisenhower campaign then proceeded to exploit—was Stevenson's inexperience in the area of foreign affairs and his intellectual distance from America's working people. He was stirring, yes, but also aloof and cerebral. For Stevenson, the campaign was an opportunity to educate; for Eisenhower, it was a battle to win. So while Stevenson formed arguments and theses, Ike turned to short advertisements and jingles. It struck some as trite, but by Election Day no adult American had not heard "I like Ike." The 1952 campaign not only created a winner; it changed the character of American politics.

Stevenson, meanwhile, immediately compromised his appeal by choosing the Alabama senator John Sparkman as his vice president. Sparkman was a segregationist intended to shore up southern support (Ike's roots in Texas and Kansas made him a serious threat to Democratic dominance of the South), but his presence on the ticket undermined Stevenson's lofty liberalism and emphasized the profound Democratic split between its labor, intellectual, and segregationist bases.

Ike allowed himself the luxury of avoiding most public campaigning for the month of August, deciding that he could only hold up for eight or nine weeks. He spent August laying plans, venturing out on a light speaking schedule, and experimenting with television. The early efforts were unimpressive: Ike looked old on camera, and he struggled with the teleprompter. Aides advised more makeup and a sunlamp; the teleprompter was scrapped. Eisenhower took most of it in stride, marveling at the machinery of getting votes. Looking over one memo outlining arrangements for an upcoming trip, he arched an eyebrow: "Thirty-five pages to get me into Philadelphia. The invasion of Normandy was on five pages."

Truman's ascension to the presidency had been historically abrupt. He barely knew FDR, then had to step into Roosevelt's gigantic shoes with World War II still on. Wishing that on no man, Truman made what he considered a good-faith effort that summer to ease the transition for his successor. He cabled Eisenhower on August 12 in Denver, inviting Ike to join him at the White House for a briefing by the CIA and then lunch with the cabinet, a courtesy Truman was extending to both candidates so that they would be "entirely briefed." Truman's motives were sound, but he must have recognized that it would be difficult for Eisenhower to accept. Ike was running to end Democratic control of Washington, and his candidacy was predicated on his grasp of international affairs. To be briefed suggested that he needed briefing, and by those whose judgment he disparaged. Moreover, Ike had his own access to foreign policy information: the head of Central Intelligence, General Bedell Smith, was Ike's colleague during World War II.

So, to Truman's astonishment, Eisenhower turned him down. "It is my duty to remain free to analyze publicly the policies and acts of the present administration whenever it appears to me to be proper and in the country's interests," he wrote to Truman, releasing the letter to the press and public. Ike did, however, accept Truman's offer of regular CIA reports, stressing that he wanted it "understood that the possession of these reports will in no other way limit my freedom to discuss or analyze foreign programs as my judgment dictates."

Truman was furious. He responded by hand: "I am extremely sorry that you have allowed a bunch of screwballs to come between us. You have made a bad mistake and I'm hoping it won't injure this great Republic." A calmer exchange of notes soothed feelings somewhat, but the rupture was now there.

Ike moved quickly to make sure he would have the material that Truman offered without the strings that Truman's offer implied. He chastised Smith for briefing Stevenson: "To the political mind it looked like the outgoing Administration was canvassing all its resources in order to support Stevenson's election." Smith responded by making sure Ike received weekly briefings, some by Smith himself.

Once the campaign began, Eisenhower discovered what all generals, and most politicians, learn—that planning is essential but that plans rarely play out as intended. Two weeks after Labor Day, the Eisenhower-Nixon ticket confronted its first crisis. Rumors that Nixon's supporters had supplemented his government salary with a fund for political expenses murmured around the edges of the race, and Nixon addressed them quietly, discussing the matter with a friendly reporter, Peter Edson. Edson's report blandly described the money as an "extra expense account" and made clear that donors did not receive favorable treatment in return for their contributions. The *New York Post* took a far different approach. The headline on its September 18 story read: "Secret Rich Men's Trust Fund Keeps Nixon in Style Far Beyond His Salary." Traveling through California by train that day, Nixon tried to ignore the story and then to suggest that the allegations were the work of Communists. None of that succeeded. The bottom line—that he supervised $18,000 raised from donors for his benefit—was true. And it was particularly damning given that it undercut a principal theme of the Republican campaign: that lassitude in Washington had given rise to Democratic corruption.

Eisenhower was supportive but reserved. Carefully preserving his own options, he drafted a note to Nixon. "In the certainty that the whole affair comprises no violation of the highest standards of conduct, a critical question becomes the speed and completeness of your presentation of fact to the public," Ike wrote, dictating to an aide in the parlor car of their campaign train. As Nixon surely recognized, any hint that he had violated "the highest standards of conduct" would supply Ike with the excuse to dump him. Moreover, Eisenhower explained that he would be unable to speak to Nixon that day—their train schedules made it impossible. That, too, preserved Ike's distance.

Within twenty-four hours, many leading Republicans were insisting that Eisenhower drop Nixon from the ticket. Tom Dewey warned Nixon that his supporters were abandoning him; some suggested that he be replaced by Bill Knowland or Earl Warren. Warren, never a Nixon fan, declined to comment. Ike summoned Brownell from New York to meet his train in St. Louis; Brownell joined Adams, who counseled patience and urged Ike to wait until Nixon could explain himself.

Eisenhower, meanwhile, maintained his silence. When reporters probed for his reaction, he responded that while he generally had confidence in Nixon, he had not been able to reach him to discuss the revelations—a statement also well short of an endorsement. For two days, Eisenhower allowed Nixon to dangle. On September 20, the two finally spoke by phone. Eisenhower still refused to commit, insisting, "This is an awful hard thing for me to decide."

That was more than Nixon could take. Days of building anxiety exploded. "Well, General, I know how it is," Nixon said. "But there comes a time in matters like this when you've either got to shit or get off the pot."

Eisenhower absorbed that impertinence but still refused to give Nixon what he wanted. Instead, Ike proclaimed that Nixon would have to fight for himself. Eisenhower would not damage his candidacy even if it meant destroying Nixon's. Coolly, he said, "If the impression got around that you got off the ticket because I forced you to get off, it's going to be very bad. On the other hand, if I issue a statement in effect backing you up, people will accuse me of wrongdoing."

So Nixon booked television time for September 23, determined to make his best case for himself and to save his place on the ticket. The speech, which he delivered from the El Capitan Theatre in the heart of Hollywood, was maudlin yet masterful. "My fellow Americans," he began, faltering slightly at first, gaining confidence as he spoke. "I want to tell you my side of the case."

The fund was not a secret. It was not used to pay him directly, but rather for "political expenses that I did not think should be charged to the taxpayers of the United States." Its donors neither asked for nor received any special treatment. By modern standards, Nixon's fund was picayune; even by the laws of the day, it was commonplace and legal. Indeed, Stevenson himself helped pay for his political activities with a similar account. But Nixon did not wish to rest on mere legalities.

Instead, he explained that he'd declined to supplement his income by putting his wife, Pat, on the payroll, notwithstanding that Sparkman employed his wife—"That is his business, and I am not critical of him for doing that," Nixon hastened to add—and even though Pat was eminently qualified. "She is," he boasted, "a wonderful stenographer." He had submitted the records of his funds to an independent audit, which had come back clean. He was a poor kid, served his country, ran for Congress, and saved a little money. He laid out his mortgage debt and his insurance policies. Pat, he noted, did not have a mink coat, but she did have "a respectable Republican cloth coat."

He finished with the passage that would secure Nixon's speech in history:

> A man down in Texas heard Pat on the radio mention the fact that our two youngsters would like to have a dog, and, believe it or not, the day before we left on this campaign trip we got a message from Union Station in Baltimore, saying they had a package for us. We went down to get it. You know what it was?
>
> It was a little cocker spaniel dog, in a crate that he had sent all the way from Texas, black and white, spotted, and our little girl Tricia, the six year old, named it Checkers.
>
> And you know, the kids, like all kids, loved the dog, and I just want

to say this, right now, that regardless of what they say about it, we are going to keep it.

Nixon and his family were under assault by critics who would take their dog. He had volunteered his whole financial history, and he urged the other candidates to do the same. Eisenhower, whose tax treatment of his book income was sufficiently exotic to raise questions, jabbed his pencil into his pad when Nixon laid down that challenge.

Nixon's great strategic stroke was urging listeners to register their views with the Republican National Committee, effectively taking the matter out of Eisenhower's hands. And in overwhelming numbers, they did. Among those who urged Eisenhower to welcome Nixon back into his graces was Edgar, never shy about telling his little brother what to do. "If you don't unqualifiedly endorse Nixon after that talk last night," Edgar cabled, "you might as well fold your tent and fade away." Nixon had peered over the edge of the abyss. Exhausted and relieved, he crawled back.

Eisenhower asked Nixon to join him in Wheeling, West Virginia, and when Nixon's plane arrived, he was surprised to discover Ike waiting for him. "Why not?" Eisenhower asked. "You're my boy." If that was demeaning by design or merely by reflex, it was, at least, affirmation that Nixon's career survived. Speaking with reporters, Eisenhower expressed his confidence in the vice presidential nominee. A memorandum summarizing the campaign records the significance of Ike's comments: "This apparently settles the Nixon fund affair."

Ike's campaign strategy called for a sweep of the country. Over the objections of many advisers, he had vowed to campaign from coast to coast—reaching into areas such as the South, where Lucius Clay advised him to make an effort and where he felt an affinity with residents despite the region's wariness of Republicans that dated to Lincoln. He traveled 51,376 miles in total, 20,871 of that by rail. By the Republican National Committee's count, Eisenhower visited 232 towns in forty-five states. One day he was celebrating the dedication of an FM radio station; the next he was reassuring Westerners of his commitment to federal dam projects. He offered praise for postal workers, pledged to support Republican rejection of compulsory health care, and delivered strongly worded, if somewhat unfocused, criticism of the incumbent administration, which, he charged, had "bungled us perilously close to World War III."

During September, though, his speeches took on flourishes of elegance. He began quoting from Ecclesiastes. "There is a time to keep and a time to cast away," he said, first in Indianapolis on September 9, then more often and more prominently as he warmed to that remark. He spoke moderately to organized labor in New York City on September 17, refusing to overturn the Taft-Hartley Act, which set the terms of labor-management relations strongly in favor of management, but promising that he would consider amending it. He incisively addressed southern Democrats in Columbia, South Carolina, on the thirtieth: "My only appeal to you, my only appeal to America, is that of Governor Byrnes, to place loyalty to the country above loyalty to a political party."

Just as Eisenhower was becoming more nuanced in handling political affairs, he also began to master political debate. When Truman suggested that Eisenhower had been naive about the threat of Soviet Communism during the Potsdam Conference, Ike sharply retorted that Truman's mismanagement of foreign affairs was to blame for the Korean War, already by then responsible for 120,000 dead, wounded, or missing Americans. From early pledges of fidelity to a Republican platform he had done little to shape, he sketched a broader, more moderate template. He saw a limited role for the federal government in education and supported unemployment benefits, aid to widows, and help for children living in poverty. He belittled federal assistance that infantilized Americans—one favorite line of attack was to quote a federal manual that advised readers how to wash their dishes—but did not reject federal help for the needy or even some of the New Deal's hallmark programs. Speaking in Memphis on October 15, Eisenhower allowed that the Tennessee Valley Authority had done much good for that part of the country. He even gingerly waded into the topic of civil rights, noting that Democratic lip service to racial equality was undermined by the party's political factionalism; the hollowness of the Democrats' commitment to that idea, he emphasized, was illustrated by the persistence of segregation in the District of Columbia after twenty years of Democratic rule of Washington.

Rather than depleting Eisenhower, the campaign seemed to energize him. On October 14, he gave four speeches in a single day, canvassing much of Texas and celebrating his birthday in his home state. He was, he insisted, leading not just a political effort but a "crusade" intended to restore dignity to Americans and strength to those opposing Communism. The use of the word "crusade" also nicely reminded voters of his war record by adopting the title of his memoir. He was, Eisenhower said at the outset and throughout, committed to leading "us forward in the broad middle way toward prosperity without war for ourselves and our children."

The campaign's increasing confidence and the candidate's growing command of both country and idiom did not mean that the effort was without difficulties. Ike's determination to run nationally created problems in the South, where the candidate felt personally at home but overwhelmingly Democratic audiences were wary. More complicated even than that was Eisenhower's visit to Wisconsin in early October. There, the fall ballot included Senator Joseph McCarthy, Ike's fellow Republican and an incipient figure in the nation's politics and culture.

McCarthy's campaign of fear and innuendo was in its second year, broadening its reach as he discovered the ease with which he could smear opponents. It had begun, infamously, with his Wheeling, West Virginia, address on February 9, 1950. In it, McCarthy had claimed to have "here in my hand a list of 205 . . . names that were made known to the Secretary of State as being members of the Communist Party and who nevertheless are still working and shaping policy in the State Department." Two days later, in a letter to Truman, McCarthy appeared to amend that to 57 Communists, but added that he knew "absolutely" of another 300 "certified to the Secretary for discharge because of Communism."

Those charges were disconcertingly vague. But McCarthy could be specific, too. One of those he attacked was none other than Eisenhower's mentor General George Marshall, who had gone on to serve as secretary of state and then secretary of defense in the Truman administration. Among his assignments in the postwar years had been a mission to China, where Marshall attempted to negotiate an end to that country's civil war between the Communist forces commanded by Mao and Chiang Kai-shek's Nationalist army. That war ended in a failure of Marshall's mission. The Nationalist Party was defeated, and Chiang fled to Taiwan. McCarthy blamed Marshall. As usual, he did not charge directly, but his attack on Marshall was neither subtle nor fair. Addressing the Senate on March 14, 1951, McCarthy coyly declined the invitation to judge whether Marshall was an actual Communist ("I am not going to try to delve into George Marshall's mind"). He not only mischaracterized Marshall's efforts in China but also described his work as "the most weird and traitorous double deal that I believe any of us has ever heard of."

On June 14, 1951, McCarthy additionally alleged that Marshall had sent unprepared American troops to fight in North Africa during World War II—troops that Ike commanded—and that he had even collaborated with Stalin in the surrender of Eastern Europe and China. Even Marshall's refusal to write a memoir was viewed with suspicion by McCarthy, who suggested that the general was hiding his actions. To McCarthy, Marshall was "part of a conspiracy on a scale so immense . . . a conspiracy of infamy so black that, when it is finally exposed, its principals shall be forever deserving of the maledictions of all honest men."

Aside from Eisenhower's debt to Marshall, he owed his former boss a defense as a matter of decency. At a stop in Green Bay, he appeared with McCarthy after warning the senator that he would publicly remind the crowd of their disagreements. McCarthy predicted Ike would be booed, but Eisenhower's remarks were warmly received. McCarthy glowered afterward.

That night, Eisenhower was to deliver his major address of the day, a speech in Milwaukee. Unlike his earlier, oblique reference to occasional disagreements with McCarthy, his speech that night included a direct and specific mention of his support for Marshall. McCarthy and Wisconsin's governor, Walter Kohler, learned of his intentions, and the governor lobbied hard for him to drop the paragraph (McCarthy wisely kept silent). Kohler argued not that Marshall was unworthy of defending but rather that the passage, as written, seemed inappropriate to the rest of the address, which was focused on other topics. As the train rumbled along, Kohler pressed his case with Sherman Adams. Gabriel Hauge, Eisenhower's lead speechwriter and a man Adams described as a "high-minded and zealous stickler for principle," objected. But Adams sided with Kohler. "Some adjustments," he concluded, "had to be made for party harmony." When Adams made that recommendation to Eisenhower, he brusquely concurred. "Take it out," he growled.

Unbeknownst to Adams or Eisenhower, however, an early copy of the speech had already been released to reporters, who were all too eager to relay the news of such an open break between two leading Republicans. When Eisenhower delivered the address, attention riveted not on what he said but on what he deleted. Eisenhower's move emboldened McCarthy and wounded Marshall and naturally raised questions about both his politics and his character: Was he closer to McCarthy than it appeared? Was he willing to cast aside a trusted colleague for the sake of political expediency? The *New York Times* headlined its editorial "An Unhappy Day," capturing much of the press reaction. Eisenhower understood his error but responded to the torrent of criticism, much of it from friends, with a mixture of chagrin and defensiveness. After Harold Stassen weighed in, Ike conceded that he agreed "in principle . . . with the criticism you make on the revisions made in the Milwaukee talk." He went on, however, to defend the omission by asserting that his staff recommended it, that elsewhere in the talk he implicitly criticized the methods of the Communist hunters, and that there was some evidence that McCarthy's personal attacks on Marshall were overstated. That was disingenuous. Eisenhower knew he had let down a friend. No amount of hedging could undo the damage. "I am," the *New York Times* publisher, Arthur Hays Sulzberger, wrote to Eisenhower, "sick at heart."

It was, Hauge reflected two decades later, "as bad a moment as he went through in the whole campaign." John Eisenhower agreed. It was a "terrible mistake, the worst of my dad's life in politics." Ike's staff, perhaps responding to Eisenhower's disappointment, omitted any reference to the controversy in the file summary of the campaign's major addresses. According to the file, the speech was devoted to "good government—more specifically, communism and freedom." General George Marshall's name does not appear.

Eisenhower's performance was imperfect, as evidenced by the Slush Fund and Marshall controversies. But he was playing a strong hand, and Stevenson made that advantage even greater by so misplaying his. Through the crucial weeks of October, Stevenson chose to challenge Eisenhower on foreign policy and national security grounds. He accused Eisenhower of isolationism and of aiding Communism by his approach to international affairs. Bolstered by Truman, who emerged late in the campaign to lead the criticism of Eisenhower, the Democrats assailed the general for criticizing the war in Korea and for his skepticism about increases in defense spending. "All this," said Truman in a nationally broadcast address on October 22, "is the straight isolationist line."

Eisenhower was the nominee of a divided party. He had never held public office, never articulated a developed and coherent domestic policy. But the Democrats chose to confront him where he was strongest, in his command of international affairs. Predictably, the effort was a bust. Stevenson slid further behind in the polls, and Truman appeared more desperate.

Then, on Friday evening, October 24, Ike sealed the outcome. Speaking to an overflow crowd of some five thousand people at Detroit's Masonic Auditorium, he promised to forgo politics in "this anxious autumn for America." He vowed to deliver the "unvarnished truth" in examining America's place in the world, and he accused the Truman administration of failing to deter or repel Communist aggression. Eisenhower reminded his listeners: "I know something of the totalitarian mind." He then outlined his bill of particulars and insisted that the first task of the next president was to forgo all diversions and end the Korean War, saying: "That job requires a personal trip . . . Only in that way could I learn how best to serve the American people in the cause of peace.

"I shall go to Korea."

Democrats called it grandstanding. Stevenson said he would go, too.

But the prospect of America's supreme commander—the general who had accepted Germany's surrender—now personally taking charge of the Korean War was electrifying. Stevenson ended the campaign as he began, with eloquence but without effective counter to the appeal of a general who transcended his party and enjoyed the admiration of the world.

Swede Hazlett dropped Ike a note on the eve of the election. "If you win," he wrote, "I'll be bursting with pride; if you lose, I'll still be bursting with pride, tempered with a modicum of relief that you are to be spared a frightful four years of terrific responsibility."

On Election Day, Ike spent the afternoon at Columbia—the university lent him his old quarters for the campaign. He worked on a painting and chatted with supporters. He asked Brownell to drop by and, looking ahead, offered him the position of chief of staff, a new post that would carry enormous weight in the Eisenhower White House. Brownell thanked him for his confidence but said he was still enjoying his legal work. "So you want to remain a lawyer," Eisenhower replied. "Well, how about being attorney general?" After hastily reviewing his personal finances and huddling with his wife, Brownell accepted that evening.

As the returns poured in, the extent of Eisenhower's triumph became apparent. Turnout was astonishing. Two out of three American adults voted in 1952, and fully 80 percent of those registered cast ballots. Eisenhower received 33.9 million votes, over 11 million more than any previous Republican candidate. He carried every state outside the South and a few border states and made inroads even there, winning Texas, Florida, Tennessee, and Virginia and leaving just the core of the Confederacy to vote for Stevenson, a bitter result for the Illinois liberal. Sparkman arguably carried more seats for Stevenson than Stevenson did for himself.

At 2:05 a.m., Dwight Eisenhower addressed two thousand supporters in the grand ballroom of the Commodore Hotel in New York. He was subdued, humbled by the weight of the office he was to assume. He emphasized the importance of national unity and promised an energetic pursuit of a new direction. Dwight Eisenhower was now president-elect of the United States. Back in her hotel room, Mamie wept.

Changing America's Course

In the early hours of November 29, the streets of New York's Upper West Side dark and cold, two men in overcoats stood in the alcove of 60 Morningside Drive, at the time America's most closely watched private residence. A companion of theirs jumped from a waiting car and approached the police officer near the front door. He motioned for the officer to follow him, and when the policeman turned his back, Secret Service agent Ed Green and Dwight Eisenhower slipped out of the building and into the car. The door light had been removed, so they sped away under the cover of darkness. Ike's fabled trip to Korea was under way.

Ever since Election Day, plans for the trip had been hatched and honed, notwithstanding the terse skepticism of President Truman, whose congratulatory cable to Eisenhower on the election results offered Ike the presidential plane for the trip "if you still desire to go to Korea." Truman's gratuitous suggestion that Ike's pledge would be disregarded now that he had won the election was designed to irritate the president-elect, and it succeeded. Eisenhower responded coldly: "Any suitable transport plane that one of the services could make available will be satisfactory." Privately, he fumed to his son that Truman was accusing him of political gamesmanship. It was, John said, the "clincher" that ended their relationship.

As for logistics, security was, of course, paramount. Given an assassination attempt on South Korea's president, Syngman Rhee, months earlier, the prospect of Ike touring an area "crawling with Commies and other doubtful characters" made the military insist on elaborate precautions. Secretary of Defense Robert Lovett personally took charge of arrangements. "Secrecy of movement," he insisted, "is of cardinal importance." Ike's entourage would only stop at military bases, and he was strongly urged not to allow a press plane to accompany him. Weather planes and naval vessels were dispatched to track his progress. As it approached the Far East, Eisenhower's aircraft was shadowed by fighter planes; altogether, more than thirteen hundred escorted him along the way.

Ike could hardly disappear for almost a week without explanation, so the transition team announced that the president-elect was holding private meetings inside his residence. To dupe the press, two prominent officials, John Foster Dulles and Arthur Vandenberg, agreed to enter the house, stay a while, and then leave.

On that dark November morning, a handful of aides and cabinet members-in-waiting, a few lucky journalists, and the president-elect converged on Mitchel Field, which in 1952 was a rarely used airstrip on Long Island. Ike, in camel hair coat and brown hat, bounded from his car, shook hands with the waiting crew, and boarded his plane.

Awaiting Eisenhower nearly halfway around the world was a military and diplomatic morass that had sapped the energy of the American people and forced deep reconsideration of long-held principles of war, muddying strategic objectives and tactical pursuit of them. Was the enemy North Korea, China, or the Soviet Union? Was America's goal to repel North Korean invasion, to unify Korea under democratic rule, or to topple Chinese Communism? Was surrender required or merely the end of hostilities? Most important, was it possible to fight a war without using everything in a nation's arsenal to triumph? The United States, after all, was in sole possession of atomic bombs, yet it dispatched tens of thousands of American men, consigning many to their deaths, while withholding a weapon that could bring them home.

The Korean War had begun in treachery and was fought on grim terrain and wildly shifting fortunes. From the moment that Korea was divided in 1948, Kim Il Sung, Moscow's puppet leader of North Korea, pursued one obsessive quest: to unify the country under his rule. The idea appealed to Mao but was greeted cautiously by Stalin, without whose approval North Korea could not act. Dogged and ideologically blinded, Kim claimed North Korea could win a quick victory over what he viewed as lethargic capitalists. In April 1950, he visited Moscow, accompanied by a South Korean Communist leader who promised Stalin that Koreans south of the parallel would welcome an invasion as the opportunity to unite their country. Stalin still hesitated, worried about the implications of forcing a war with America, but Kim and Mao argued that the United States would not risk global confrontation over such a remote conflict.

Their belief was reinforced by actions and statements of the Truman administration. In June 1949, Truman withdrew American troops from Korea, and the following January, Secretary of State Dean Acheson delivered a speech in Washington in which he defined the American defense perimeter in Asia as excluding South Korea. Enticed by the possibility of Communist expansion and convinced that he could keep the Soviet Union out of direct hostilities, Stalin granted permission but warned Kim that "if you get kicked in the teeth, I shall not lift a finger." It was, for Stalin, a rare display of candor.

Although Stalin wanted to protect the Soviet Union from direct retaliation, he was happy to supply the North Koreans with equipment and strategic guidance. Soviet materials streamed into North Korea, and Kim massed his forces for invasion. On June 25, 1950, seven North Korean infantry divisions totaling more than ninety thousand men and an armored brigade made up of 120 Russian T-34 tanks stormed across the 38th parallel, capturing roads and railways and then moving nimbly south, crushing the surprised South Korean army—one force bound for Seoul, two others claiming the center and east coast. In Tokyo, General Douglas MacArthur, commander of the U.S. Far East Command, sank into depression. "All Korea," he warned, "is lost."

Truman was in Missouri, and the administration was scattered when the first reports reached America. To avoid showing alarm, the president completed his day's schedule before departing for Washington. He ordered MacArthur to rush supplies to South Korea and evacuate American civilians. There was no doubt that Truman meant to fight. "If we let Korea down," he told congressional leaders the next day, "the Soviets will keep right on going and swallow up one piece of Asia after another . . . If we were to let Asia go, the Near East would collapse and no telling what would happen in Europe." In light of that threat, Truman said he had "ordered our forces to support Korea as long as we could." Notes from the meeting record that when the president finished speaking, there were several moments of silence. The next day, armed with a UN Security Council resolution authorizing "every assistance" to the South Koreans (the Soviet Union elected to boycott the session and thus missed the opportunity to exercise its veto), Truman ordered MacArthur to use air and naval forces to strike south of the 38th parallel.

South Korea's small army was no match for its aggressive northern neighbor. Seoul quickly fell. U.S. forces tried to stiffen the South Korean resistance, but the Americans were unprepared to fight. Without proper training or equipment, U.S. troops were overrun and fell back.

At home, a stunned nation, less than a decade from victory in World War II, now winced as its forces ran from an army few had even considered a threat. By August, the South Korean and American armies had retreated to a small corner of the southeast. Contained within the so-called Pusan Perimeter, they fought heroically and desperately for time. Defeat suddenly was possible and possibly imminent.

It was then that Douglas MacArthur executed the boldest strike of his career. Over the reservations of some of the military's most senior officials, he led the landings at Inchon, west of Seoul, on September 15, 1950. It was an act of extraordinary daring: MacArthur committed virtually all his reserve forces to a landing at a port famous for its extreme tides, narrow channel, and daunting seawalls. His bravado was rewarded. Light defenses greeted the X Corps, which swept ashore with relative ease and then slogged its way to Seoul. North Korean forces in the area rallied but eventually succumbed to the newly energized invaders. On September 29, American forces recaptured the capital, ravaging it in the process. "Few people," one reporter wrote, "have suffered so terrible a liberation." Their suffering, however, was matched by that of the North Korean army: with the troops suddenly split, their supply lines fell apart and morale collapsed. The war turned decisively in favor of the United States.

If panache was MacArthur's signature in victory, hubris guided him afterward. He imagined a smashing victory over Communism and a unification of Korea—under the rule of the South. He dismissed those who cautioned that proceeding beyond the 38th parallel would invite Chinese entry into the war, and he capitalized on Washington's disarray. Already headstrong before Inchon, MacArthur was unassailable after it: he had defied the doubters and scored the most smashing victory of the war. "There is," Dean Acheson acknowledged after Inchon, "no stopping MacArthur now."

Sadly for the thousands who would give their lives, China's leaders did not share Americans' awe of MacArthur. Fueled by ideology and nervous about the approach of enemy soldiers to their border, China decided to commit its own troops if the United States crossed the 38th parallel. "If Korea were completely occupied by the Americans and the Korean revolutionary forces were substantially destroyed, the American invaders would be more rampant, and such a situation would be very unfavorable to the whole East," Mao wrote to Stalin on October 2, 1950, just three days after MacArthur received permission to head north with caution. The Chinese forces quietly moved toward the Yalu River, hundreds of thousands of poorly armed but driven men. There, they waited. On October 19, the U.S. Army captured Pyongyang, the first time in history that a Communist capital had fallen to Western troops. Victory stoked ego, and MacArthur, his force split, directed the advance to continue, further into the winter, plunging into a deadly trap.

He ignored every signal that China would unleash its armies. On October 24, two American planes were fired on by anti-aircraft guns, even though they were roughly three miles south of the Yalu River. Reconnaissance failed to detect Chinese camps in the area, and MacArthur disregarded the threat. Farther south, an American regiment uncovered weapons dumps that residents said were stashed for the Chinese. Even that failed to alarm MacArthur. On October 25, a South Korean division fifty miles from the Yalu was attacked in a fog by Chinese forces; again, MacArthur's headquarters ignored the warning.

MacArthur was hindered by his sycophantic inner circle and in particular by his intelligence officer, Major General Charles Willoughby. Born in Heidelberg and raised in Germany, Willoughby immigrated to the United States at age eighteen and enlisted in the Army. Upon graduation from Gettysburg College, he was commissioned as a second lieutenant. He was high-handed and vindictive and weirdly prim. He tailored his uniforms and wore a monocle. In MacArthur's service, he was best known for his frightening willingness to find intelligence data supporting the general's views. "Anything MacArthur wanted, Willoughby produced intelligence for," observed Lieutenant Colonel John H. Chiles. "He should have gone to jail."

In this case, Willoughby overlooked the presence of not merely several divisions but several *armies* of Chinese soldiers. Nearly 300,000 soldiers snuck across the Yalu at night over barely submerged bridges and lay in wait. MacArthur had assured Washington that this would never happen, so he trivialized any information that an assault was imminent. Then the Chinese struck. Despite their rudimentary weapons—rifles, grenades, satchels full of explosives—they attacked in darkness and unnerved exhausted UN troops with their haunting battle cries and whistles. The Allied forces beat a disorganized retreat, often abandoning gear in their haste. Then, as suddenly as it had begun, the attack ceased; MacArthur again allowed himself to believe that the Chinese threat was illusory. "The Chinese," he insisted against all reason on November 24, "are not coming in." Two days later, 200,000 Chinese troops attacked the U.S. Eighth Army.

By early December, Pyongyang had been abandoned, and American forces were fighting their way south. A month later, Seoul fell yet again, this time to China.

American troops fought back with bravery, especially once the Eighth Army came under the command of General Matthew Ridgway, a commander as modest as MacArthur was haughty. Ridgway, given the Eighth Army when his predecessor was killed in a car accident, refocused its energies from holding worthless pieces of Korean real estate to eliminating enemy fighters. Operation Killer, as it was inelegantly known, stemmed the Chinese advance and turned the war into a series of offensives and counteroffensives, as Chinese manpower met American technology. For MacArthur, however, the ignominy of having been so wrong encouraged a surly defensiveness and desperate need to blame others. He became increasingly contemptuous of Truman and frighteningly sure of himself. "MacArthur seemed at the time to have decided that his innate brilliance, so frequently illustrated by his military successes, rendered his judgment supreme, above that of all his peers and even of his duly constituted superiors," Ridgway wrote. When Truman emphatically ordered all his commanders to refrain from discussing diplomatic matters, MacArthur went ahead and publicly mocked China, threatening the administration's efforts to secure a negotiated peace. He was now in open defiance of the president. On April 11, 1951, Truman, after pausing over the political ramifications of censuring one of America's most revered generals, fired him.

The photograph of Eisenhower on learning of MacArthur's ouster is one of the most memorable and amusing images of the much-photographed Ike. In it, he is startled but hardly dismayed. His eyebrows are peaked, his curiosity piqued, but nothing about him appears angry. Indeed, one senses a suppressed smile as he avoids eye contact with the expectant men around him. It is a glimpse of the man who suffered MacArthur's theatrics and yet shared some of his mentor's frustrations with the president who fired him.

Lucius Clay, busy trying to organize support for Ike's presidential bid, urged Ike to keep quiet about MacArthur; Ike needed no prodding. "I am going to maintain silence in every language known to man," he replied.

Replacing MacArthur helped reassure leaders from Tokyo to Washington that the war might now be prosecuted effectively. A National Security Council memo from April 23 still anticipated that the war would end by December 31 of that year. Korea chewed up optimists: MacArthur had predicted it would be over by Thanksgiving 1950, only to then face the might of China, and then, delusionally, suggested it would be finished by Christmas of the same year. Through most of 1951 and all of 1952,

the conflict dragged on. American forces would advance up the peninsula, Chinese would barrel down. It appeared to many American civilians a
pointless struggle, a nauseatingly high price to pay for an uncertain reward.

That was the stalemate that Ike faced as he departed for his visit. Omar
Bradley—Eisenhower's West Point classmate, World War II commander,
and now chairman of the Joint Chiefs of Staff—was asleep when Ike boarded
the Constellation. He woke, greeted his old friend, and briefed him. As the
plane droned, the chairman and the president-elect and their various aides
interrupted their work now and again for rounds of bridge. There was a
brief layover at Iwo Jima. "I want to know about everything that happened
here," Ike said as he stood beside the memorial to the Marines who raised
the American flag.

At 7:57 p.m. on Tuesday, December 2, 1952, the Constellation arrived at
an airfield near Seoul; darkness hid the president-elect, and no top military
commanders greeted him so as to avoid attention. Once safely inside the
country, Ike conferred with commanders of the Eighth Army, inspected
troops and equipment, examined photographs of Chinese camps above
the Yalu River, and chatted with soldiers from across the UN command.
When he arrived at one post, a Marine band greeted him with ruffles and
flourishes. Just as the last note sounded, a UN unit fired a rocket fusillade
into a nearby hillside. "What are they dropping in here?" Ike snapped.
Officers explained that the rockets were aimed at a North Korean position
and that sound traveled fast in the cold air.

Asked whether the conflict was, as Truman described it, a "police action,"
one British commander boomed: "Police action, hell. It's warfare." Eisenhower visited an Army surgical hospital, where business was happily slow.
Most of those being treated were Korean children under the care of American doctors.

Throughout his visit, Ike was warmly greeted as a promise for peace. "If
anyone can end [the war], General Eisenhower can," said Sergeant Joseph
Killea. "He's the man to do it."

As he prepared to leave, President Rhee presented Ike with a Korean
flag for the White House. Major John Eisenhower carried it for the first
few hundred yards of its journey home, symbolizing his unique place in
his father's heart. Indeed, both father and son had an abiding sense of duty,
evidenced by a private pact: John Eisenhower promised his father he would
never allow the United States to be at risk of his being held hostage. "I
would," he wrote later, "take my life before being captured."

On December 5, Eisenhower began the long trip home aboard the USS
Helena, a heavy cruiser based in Long Beach, California. On the way, he

learned that MacArthur had boasted of having a secret plan to end the war. That agitated Truman, who demanded it, and intrigued Ike, who asked MacArthur to share it with him, too. MacArthur did so in a preposterous memo: Eisenhower should summon the Soviet Union to a conference and propose that both Korea and Germany be allowed to reunite their broken halves under elected governments; foreign troops could then be removed from Germany, Austria, Japan, and Korea. If the Soviets agreed, so be it. If not, the Soviets should be told of "our intention to clear North Korea of enemy forces." His plan then suggested the way to finally achieve the victory that had stymied him and his successors for two and a half years. "This could be accomplished through the atomic bombing of enemy military concentrations and installations in North Korea and the sowing of fields of suitable radio-active materials, the by-products of atomic manufacture, to close major lines of enemy supply." One last recommendation: "It would probably become necessary to neutralize Red China's capability to wage modern war." In short, MacArthur's solution to ending a protracted and difficult conflict, one that had cost him his job and thousands of Americans their lives, was to launch an all-out war against China while laying waste to the Korean peninsula and poison it for hundreds of years to come. There is no evidence of Eisenhower's reply.

Coverage of the Korea trip had been squelched by security and censorship, but once Eisenhower departed for home, the details flooded out. Truman derided the mission as "a piece of demagoguery." The press was more generous. Newspapers lauded Ike for seeing the combat up close, and Americans dared to hope that peace was possible.

Back in the United States, Eisenhower completed the more prosaic but meaningful work of building his staff. He was a shrewd judge of men, neither intimidated by excellence nor distracted by polish. His eye for character helped him construct a strong inner circle to manage the government and supplement his already formidable group of advisers, including his brothers, military friends, and political supporters, many of the latter successful businessmen.

Before appointing his cabinet, Eisenhower created a position that redefined the modern presidency and filled it with a man whose cold intellect had impressed him since the beginning of his campaign. Sherman Adams was the political mirror image of Eisenhower. Clipped, slight, famously taciturn, he was every bit the Yankee as Ike was the Midwesterner. Adams grew up in New Hampshire, graduated from Dartmouth, prospered in the region's timber industry, and then took to politics, rising through the ranks. In 1948, he was elected governor. New Hampshire was the perfect political stage for the ascent of a man who was admired by many but liked by few. He was an orderly and dedicated public servant, and he appealed to the voters of a state where the flinty held sway over the gregarious. In his role launching Ike's political career, Adams had demonstrated administrative skill. He ran Ike's campaign with efficiency and distaste for showmanship. (Typically, for instance, Adams dismissed the effect of the Madison Square Garden rally on shaping Eisenhower's decision to enter the race; it was, he sniffed, a "dog and pony act.") Adams could err—it was he who had abruptly pulled Ike's praise for Marshall from the infamous Wisconsin speech—but he was decisive, and Eisenhower admired his grit. Ike, without ever saying so, made it clear he expected Adams to stay on. Adams was mystified. "To the best of my recollection, he never told me that in so many words," Adams recalled in 1972, "but it was quite evident."

Ike naturally borrowed from his military experience. Efficient organization, he had learned, required unified command. He wanted a single person to manage his schedule and appointments, a hardheaded manager who could protect him from unscheduled visitors and say no to those the president would prefer not to offend. Bedell Smith had performed that function during the war, and his office was a model of efficiency. Now, as president, Eisenhower wanted a chief of staff. He avoided creating that title, for fear it would seem too military, but he insisted on the position. Adams was named "Assistant to the President" and was soon known as "the Assistant President." Having accepted, he said his farewells to New Hampshire and moved to Washington. Adams and Ike would never become intimate friends—Adams never joined Eisenhower at the bridge table or on the golf course, but Ike relied on him completely, and no one reciprocated his loyalty with greater ardor.

The most important position in the cabinet was secretary of state, and Eisenhower's pick exemplified his ability to recognize a man's flaws but not be overcome by them. John Foster Dulles was an austere and arrogant man, tall with sloped shoulders, mouth turned down at the corners, eyelids soft and puffy. Pious and imperious, he was prone to such deep concentration that guests would think he had forgotten they were in the room. His favorite exercise was a cold swim, sometimes in waters so frigid his staff feared for him. The son of a Presbyterian minister, and grandson and nephew of two different secretaries of state, Dulles was trained as a lawyer but drawn to the foreign service, as were two of his four siblings. By 1952, he had served presidents from Wilson to Truman, and was a leading member of the establishment, more suited to appointed than elected office. Named in 1949 to fill a vacancy in the U.S. Senate from New York, he took the job but lost his bid for reelection a few months later. No wonder, for if Dulles was indisputably brilliant, he also was undeniably cold. He was, in Churchill's arch observation, "Dull, Duller, Dulles."

The speechwriter Emmet Hughes, no fan of Dulles's, recalled the twitching impatience with which Ike would listen to his secretary of state—"the brisk nodding of the head, in a manner designed to nudge a slow voice faster . . . the restless rhythm of the pencil tapping his knee . . . the slow glaze across the blue eyes, signaling the end of all mental contact." Eisenhower chafed at Hughes's description (he regarded the Hughes memoir as a betrayal), but he too recognized Dulles's limitations. After noting in his diary that Dulles was dedicated, tireless, and devoted to service, he added: "He is not particularly persuasive in presentation and, at times, seems to have a curious lack of understanding as to how his words and manner may affect another personality." They occasionally disagreed. Ike watched his secretary closely at the outset and would forcefully overrule him in their later years together, but he never lost his admiration for Dulles's devotion or intellect. Eisenhower understood that Dulles brought depth and intelligence to the administration. Their relationship would form the core partnership of Eisenhower's administration.

Charles Wilson, Ike's pick for secretary of defense, was Dulles's exact opposite. Garrulous and outgoing, supremely confident and occasionally brash, the jowly, barrel-chested Wilson was tartly opinionated and outspoken. He came to Eisenhower from General Motors, and as such served as both cabinet officer and symbol of the administration's loyalties. Where FDR and Truman had found allegiance with labor, Eisenhower was more comfortable with executives, convinced that their expertise was required to restore fiscal soundness. During his confirmation hearings, Wilson initially resisted calls to divest himself of more than $2 million in General Motors stock. When one member of Congress asked whether he could make a decision that was adverse to GM's interests, he famously replied that he could but that he did not believe he'd be forced to "because for years I thought what was good for the country was good for General Motors and vice versa." (The comment is frequently misquoted as "What's good for General Motors is good for the country.") That nearly tanked Wilson's nomination and was just the first in a long line of inartful public statements that would mark his tenure. As with his assessment of Dulles, Eisenhower's appreciation for Wilson was nuanced. He understood Wilson's confidence was a source of strength and also a liability. "Mr. Wilson is prone to lecture," Eisenhower noted in his diary. "This not only annoys many members of Congress, but it gives them unlooked for opportunities to discover flaws in reasoning and argument."

Two more men would form the core of Ike's cabinet, Herbert Brownell as attorney general and George Humphrey as secretary of the Treasury. Eisenhower and Humphrey hit it off at their first meeting. Recommended by Lucius Clay, who knew him from their work on German reconstruction, Humphrey arrived at Ike's Commodore Hotel suite and introduced himself. Ike spotted Humphrey's bald head and exclaimed, "I see you part your hair the same way I do." A lawyer like so many of Eisenhower's top advisers, Humphrey had joined the M. A. Hanna Company steelworks in 1917 as a legal adviser. By 1952 he was serving as its chairman, having already spent decades as its president. Genial, capable, and modest—Midwestern in every good sense of that word—Humphrey was a counterpoint to Dulles's pomposity and Wilson's brashness, but he was every bit as forceful and effective on budget matters as Dulles was in foreign affairs. Thrift was his dominant concern. "If you're going to live a good life," Humphrey liked to say, "you've got to live within your income." Through his time in office, he insisted that the government do just that. He fought profligate spending, irritating liberals, and imprudent tax cuts, to the annoyance of conservatives. He exemplified Ike's "middle way" and was often the most persuasive member of the cabinet. "When George speaks," Eisenhower said, "we all listen." Eisenhower's initial fondness for the man never wavered; they hunted together at Humphrey's Thomasville, Georgia, estate and socialized with their wives, a rarity among Ike's professional associates. "He is," Eisenhower rightly observed, "a sound business type, possessed of a splendid personality, and truly interested in the welfare of the United States." In the Eisenhower cabinet, only Dulles would wield more influence.

Brownell was the cabinet member Eisenhower knew best upon taking office, their association dating to the 1952 campaign that Brownell had done so much to orchestrate. A piercingly intelligent and deeply principled lawyer, the soft-spoken, twinkly-eyed Brownell had counseled Ike in Paris and devised the Fair Play Amendment that secured his nomination. Brownell was shy but not retiring. He had an easy smile, and he filed away observations with the precision of a card counter. On Brownell's first day in Washington, he witnessed a Negro family being ejected from a restaurant whose owner was enforcing the city's Jim Crow laws. Brownell did not forget. He was deepest in the areas where Eisenhower was most lacking—domestic affairs and politics. As such, Ike might have regarded him with some suspicion. Eisenhower, usually wary of professional politicians, appreciated Brownell's subtle mind and marveled that one so steeped in politics could be so guileless. "It would be natural to suppose that he would become hardboiled, and that the code by which he lives could scarcely be classified as one of high moral quality. The contrary seems to be true . . . His reputation with others seems to match my own high opinion of his capabilities as a lawyer, his qualities as a leader, and his character as a man." Eisenhower then recorded a compliment reserved only for his brother Milton and very few others: "I am devoted to him and am perfectly confident that he would make an outstanding president of the United States."

Eisenhower's cabinet included two members whose mere presence represented breakthroughs. Oveta Culp Hobby was the second woman to serve in the cabinet and the first to do so in a Republican administration. And Ezra Benson, an apostle of the Mormon church, was the first clergyman of the twentieth century to hold a cabinet position. Benson's faith informed his service: austere, hardworking, and intense, Benson kept a cot, a wooden chair, and a desk in his basement, where he worked each morning before heading to the office. Benson, who would not work on Sundays, came to the cabinet with the conviction that farm price supports, adopted during World War II to stimulate food production, were economically inefficient and morally suspect. He became a lightning rod in farm-state politics, as his reductions of price supports invariably enraged those whose livelihoods were affected. Benson was unflappable. "Oh Lord," the motto on his desk read, "give us men with a mandate higher than the ballot box."

Initially, Ike placed Hobby at the head of the Federal Security Agency, but once the Department of Health, Education, and Welfare formally came into being, Hobby took charge of it. Hobby, a Democrat, was married to a former governor of Texas and was active in that state's journalism—she and her husband managed the *Houston Post*—and politics. During the war, she had deftly navigated Washington politics and overcame the discrimination of her day to forge a new force in the military, "an army of women," as she and others referred to the Women's Army Corps. She overcame resistance within the War Department and Congress to secure jobs for women and even redesigned the WAC uniform to make it more appealing. By the time she was through, the WACs were 200,000 strong, with three times that many applications. Hobby worked herself into exhaustion. When she resigned in 1945, her husband met her with a stretcher to take her to the hospital. She recovered and in 1952 spearheaded Democrats for Eisenhower. Eager to place a woman in a position of influence, Ike sought her out. It took some convincing, but she finally agreed. She would, again, work herself to a frazzle.

Once he had assembled his senior advisers, Ike recorded his thoughts about them in his diary. Brownell and Milton Eisenhower might make fine presidents. Dulles deserved to be regarded as a "wise man." Wilson and Humphrey were admired businessmen, well positioned for their new duties. Vice President Richard Nixon, by contrast, warranted not a mention.

Beyond the formal positions of power, Ike added three other loyalists before his inauguration. James Hagerty, a second-generation newsman who had signed up with Tom Dewey, was an early member of the Eisenhower campaign team. He was among the first to accept a post with the new president—Ike made him press secretary—and he remained in that position to turn out the lights.

C. D. Jackson, another media businessman, agreed to take a short leave from Time-Life to join the White House staff. He had served under Ike in Europe at the end of the war and later as a writer during the campaign. It was he who had first come up with the idea to have Eisenhower pledge, if elected, to "go to Korea." Given the consensus that the pledge sealed Eisenhower's victory, Ike turned to him not just for speechwriting but for strategic insights. Acknowledging Jackson's fierce anti-Communism and nuanced grasp of character, Eisenhower asked him to serve in the unusual position of director of psychological warfare. Jackson eagerly agreed, with the caveat that he would return to Time-Life after a short time in the White House.

As he filled positions in the first Republican administration in generations, Eisenhower bitterly disappointed one old friend. Bedell Smith had served him brilliantly in the war, acting as chief of staff and meticulously organizing the critical work of Ike's headquarters. In the years since, Truman had made him director of Central Intelligence. But Smith's loyalty was to Ike; during the campaign, he personally briefed Eisenhower on security matters and had repeated the favor just prior to Ike's trip to Korea. With Eisenhower's permission, Smith set up a small office at the Commodore Hotel during the transition, though Adams made sure he controlled Smith's access to the president. Given their long relationship, the director of intelligence imagined a vaunted position for himself in the new administration—perhaps secretary of state or defense or chairman of the Joint Chiefs of Staff. On December 19, he met with Adams and Eisenhower for an off-the-record discussion. Smith left visibly dejected. On the silent trip back to Washington, he muttered, "And I thought that it was going to be great."

Rather than slot Smith for one of the administration's visible positions,

Eisenhower placed him where he needed him, as undersecretary of state. That was a marked demotion from director of Central Intelligence, but Eisenhower was not handing out rewards. He was building an administration, and Smith served an invaluable purpose. As undersecretary, he would be in a position to watch not just Secretary of State John Foster Dulles but also Smith's own replacement at the CIA, Dulles's brother, Allen Dulles. Smith would prove invaluable to Ike, not just as an adviser, but as a counterpoint to the capable John Foster and the less reliable Allen.

One more associate would also shape Ike's presidency. Ann Whitman came to Eisenhower somewhat by chance. She had been working at Radio Free Europe, where she met C. D. Jackson, and Jackson suggested that she sign up with Eisenhower's campaign. She did and quickly became indispensable. When Eisenhower was preparing to leave for Denver that summer, the campaign needed a secretary to travel with him. Whitman offered to do the job for two weeks—what her husband would later describe as the longest two weeks in history. Described as "keen, sensitive, risible, youthful, chic and distinctly good looking," Whitman would be among the small group of aides who entered the White House with Eisenhower and stayed until the final day. Married to an executive for the United Fruit Company, Whitman kept a punishing schedule—usually at her desk by 7:30, often there until late at night, and always at the mercy of the president's travel plans. She could be irritable, especially when officials excluded her from meetings with the president. And she and Mamie clashed from time to time. Mamie was accustomed to managing Ike's private life, and Whitman assumed some of that responsibility during the presidency, to Mamie's irritation. But Whitman was careful to avoid direct conflict with the First Lady: One day in 1958, she was about to board the president's helicopter for Gettysburg when she learned at the last minute that Mamie would be meeting it at the other end. Whitman opted to drive.

And, of course, Ike brought with him the Gang. His friends worked hard for his election, but once it was won, they feared they might lose him to his new duties. They need not have worried. When Ike was inaugurated, Bill Robinson, the Gang's central figure, wrote to Ike of his joy and mixed feelings. "Your companionship shall be sorely missed," he said. "I can only hope to earn a continuation of a friendship which has become a precious possession." Ike would have none of that; he responded the same day, his first in office, to proclaim his dedication to their friendship and his determination to remain close with his friends, even as president.

Eisenhower's Gang formed a protective nucleus around the president for his entire tenure, giving him the outlet of focused relaxation that his temperament required. Whether at golf or bridge or even in relaxed conversation, Ike replenished his energy by immersing himself wholeheartedly in his distractions. The members of the Gang understood their importance. As Ellis Slater recorded in his diary in 1953: "This ability to segregate his thoughts—to relax—has been and will be the thing that will save him and make his life worth living."

Eisenhower rounded out his cabinet while still in New York. Although without formal position, the group gathered for a two-day meeting beginning January 12. At that session, Eisenhower shared his draft of his inaugural address. The members listened, then burst into applause. Ike scolded them lightly, saying he had "read it not for praise but for analysis and criticism." Privately, he was just as grumpy, complaining to his diary that his speechwriter was "no help—he is more enamored with words than with ideas."

Ike continued to fiddle with the draft as Inauguration Day approached. He wanted neither to lecture nor to preach as he tried to articulate the grounding principles of his administration. It was frustrating work, but telling: he was a careful draftsman, thoughtful and precise.

When the morning of the inaugural arrived, Eisenhower joined Truman at the White House for the short trip up Pennsylvania Avenue to the Capitol. Their meeting was frosty. The campaign had left scars on both, and the arrangements for the ceremony only exacerbated them. When Ike suggested that Truman pick him up at the hotel, Truman refused, believing protocol demanded that the president-elect present himself to the president. Eisenhower accepted that, but when he arrived at the White House, he discovered that the Trumans had planned a light lunch. Eisenhower declined. He and Mamie waited outside. Even Eisenhower's decision to wear a homburg rather than a top hat annoyed Truman, who felt it demeaned the ceremony.

The only warmth during their short trip up Capitol Hill came when Eisenhower asked who had ordered John Eisenhower home from Korea for the ceremony. "I did," Truman replied. Eisenhower thanked him, then resumed his silence for the balance of the ride.

All presidents save Washington are measured against their predecessors. As he ascended to the presidency that January morning, Eisenhower naturally was most compared to Truman, just as Truman had been so unfavorably, and unfairly, found wanting in the shadow of FDR. In fact, the president whose background and service most resembled those that Ike brought to the office was Washington himself. Both were military heroes of their country (their colonies, in Washington's case), and both commanded respect and regard that crossed party, regional, and sectarian divisions. They were presidents, of course; but more than that, they were cohesive forces for America, Washington at its outset, Ike as it entered a troubling phase of its history, a period of grave and vague danger, of war without war, of threat and bluff. But if Eisenhower's presidency echoed his distant predecessor's, so, too, did their difference speak to their times. Washington was the regal general, so removed from his colleagues that they feared to touch him; Eisenhower was bluff and warm, a hero of the Republic and yet also a man of its people, a natural politician as the nation turned to television. Even his famous gaffes spoke to that duality. In formal speeches, he was eloquent, precise, and equipped with a broad, deep vocabulary; informally, he bollixed words and mismatched verbs with nouns. His news conferences could be bafflingly hard to track, but when he prepared a text, it was polished.

His inaugural address evidenced the latter. It hinted at much of what would mark his years as president: the invocation of God; the resolute commitment to security that comprehended economic prudence. He asked the nation to place country over comfort and convenience, and he pledged to refrain from using American power to impress the nation's values on others. At its core were nine principles, ticked off by the president as he stood on the east steps of the Capitol, his head bare on a cool, breezy January day.

Eisenhower's prevailing argument was for balance: he abhorred war as well as appeasement; he trumpeted American strength as a source of international peace but insisted on restraint; he stressed the importance of economic well-being and human equality and expressed appreciation for the United Nations, "the living sign of all people's hope for peace." The speech was often lofty, laced with potent imagery. "The faith we hold belongs not to us alone but to the free of all the world," he said. "This common bond binds the grower of rice in Burma and the planter of wheat in Iowa, the shepherd in southern Italy and the mountaineer in the Andes. It confers a common dignity upon the French soldier who dies in Indo-China, the British soldier killed in Malaya, the American life given in Korea." Rejecting appeasement, he added: "Americans, indeed all free men, remember that in the final choice, a soldier's pack is not so heavy a burden as a prisoner's chains."

Eisenhower spoke for twenty minutes, shook the hands of the men around him as they offered their congratulations, and, in a touching note, kissed his First Lady, something no other American president had ever done at an inauguration. Then the exhaustion set in. After swearing in White House aides, presiding over the first official meeting of his cabinet, and bidding farewell to family and friends, Eisenhower fell ill with a cold and retired to his quarters, holing up there for two days.

This was a time of transition in American leadership, but also in the Eisenhower family. The brothers gathered, and their families bickered. As was often the case, it was Arthur's wife, Louise, who got under Ike's skin. During a rare moment when the family was alone, Louise caused a scene: she was angry with Ike for making it clear in his family tree that Arthur was divorced and Louise was his second wife. "I guess the old gal will never learn," Ike complained in a note to Edgar. "I do think it is really something on the order of a nervous disease rather than real intent."

Ike was pleased to see Louise off, and Mamie then began converting the White House from the Trumans' home to the Eisenhowers'. The White House had been renovated by the Trumans, so the residence now featured a movie theater and solarium, not to mention air-conditioning. A veteran of moving, Mamie decorated in pinks and greens—by then the Eisenhowers' trademark colors. She was forced to work with a limited budget, but she gamely improvised: for drapes, she purchased parachute silk and asked the White House seamstress to convert it. The Eisenhowers kept separate quarters but shared a bed, the first First Family in memory to do so. Mamie was delighted when the bed arrived; she could finally get a good night's sleep now that she could "reach over and pat Ike on his old bald head anytime I want to." Mamie also handled the family's personal accounts, supervising the renovation of the Gettysburg home and scrupulously seeing to it that family expenses did not appear on the government's bills.

Mamie's bangs and grandmotherly manners made her the object of much derision—particularly after Jackie Kennedy brought youth and vivacity to her position—but Mamie was a comfortable and gracious hostess, far more appreciated in her day than in history. Under her watch, military customs replaced the Trumans' frumpier entertainments. Formal protocol and dress brought style to the White House, and the Eisenhowers regularly hosted foreign leaders, many of whom were long known to Ike.

Mamie was proud of her style, even if it was not universally appreciated. Although she annually was named one of the world's twelve best-dressed women, some critics sneered at her charm bracelets and other middle-class affectations. She was superstitious and delicate, her health often frail. Rumors of her drinking, first whispered during the war, followed her to the White House. Though she drank, whispers of her drunkenness were exaggerated by the unsteadiness caused by her inner-ear disturbance. Her heart troubles as a little girl also worried her as an adult, and she took precautions to protect herself: Mamie disliked sleeping above an altitude of five thousand feet and hated to fly. She often worked in bed, propped up by pillows and surrounded by photographs and papers.

Mamie could be a rough boss—but she also tended to her staff and to those in trouble who beseeched the president for help. Year after year, Mamie answered thousands of letters, shook so many hands that hers sometimes ached, and pushed her sometimes-reluctant husband to rise to the social expectations of his office.

Through it all, Mamie was a dignified First Lady and a supportive, though hardly fawning, spouse for Ike. Like her husband, she enjoyed cards—canasta and Bolivia were favorite games—and she, like Ike, impressed friends with her concentration and memory. One story, perhaps apocryphal, though repeated by their granddaughter in her biography of Mamie, captures their partnership in full. One night, while Mamie was slow dressing, Ike became irritated. "You have kept the President of the United States waiting!" he is said to have complained. Legend has it that Mamie replied: "Oh, I thought I was dressing for my husband."

A few weeks after settling in, Eisenhower called a meeting of Republican legislative leaders and department heads to explain the efforts that the administration was making to trim Truman's budget. Eisenhower expected the meeting to be informational and uneventful—essentially a briefing intended to secure allies for a Republican campaign to reduce a Democratic deficit. All told, the measures under consideration would cut a projected $9.9 billion deficit to about $4 billion. Ike's hope for an easy consensus was quickly dashed. In the words of James Hagerty, Robert Taft "blew up." He complained on the one hand that the budget merely parroted Truman's approach—with minor cuts here and there—and on the other that it allowed for no tax cuts. Taft threatened to oppose the budget, predicted other congressional Republicans would as well, and suggested that it would doom the party in the 1954 elections. Eisenhower seemed stunned, and aides, seeing him struggle to control his temper, jumped in before he could respond.

When he did reply to Taft, his response crystallized the rifts in the Republican Party. Eisenhower stressed the financial obligations imposed by the continuing war in Korea and other security threats, and though he doubted Taft's prediction of dire political consequences, he was willing to risk them: "The nation's military security will take first priority in my calculations." With that, Taft's anger was defused, and he apologized—the beginning of a curious, though short-lived, friendship. It was "one of the worst days I have experienced since January 20," Eisenhower wrote in his diary, but the conclusion "was not quite as bad as some of the moments in its middle."

The tension between economy and security never disappeared for the eight years of Ike's presidency. But the administration's initial preoccupations were often directed toward accusations of treason and espionage, some emanating from Senator Joe McCarthy, some in the divisive case of Julius and Ethel Rosenberg.

Born in New York in 1918, the son of Polish Jewish immigrants, educated as an electrical engineer, idealistic, serious, and bighearted, Julius Rosenberg was hardly an extraordinary young man. As a teenager, he was drawn to an idealized vision of Communism and joined the Young Communist League. While studying at City College of New York, he attended a benefit for the International Seamen's Union where a pixieish young woman with a lovely face and a beautiful voice caught his eye and ear. She sang "Ciribiribin," and Julius fell in love. Julius Rosenberg and Ethel Greenglass courted for several years, and Ethel's younger brother, David, came to worship his sister's boyfriend; Julius shared his books and thoughts with the boy, who was less interested in politics than in pleasing Julius. Julius took an extra semester to graduate, receiving his bachelor of science in electrical engineering in early 1939. Four months later, Julius and Ethel were married, eventually giving birth to two sons, Robert and Michael.

Julius worked as a civilian employee of the Army Signal Corps, and David, then an Army sergeant, by chance secured a position with the atomic weapons lab at Los Alamos. The two men got those positions despite their Communist histories, in part by lying or evading government questions. For Julius, the lies caught up with him on March 26, 1945; government agents discovered his former membership in the Communist Party—and his lies to cover up that fact—and he was let go. David, meanwhile, continued his work at Los Alamos, an all-but-open Communist assigned to the most secret project of the war. He was hardly awed by those responsibilities. On the day that scientists exploded their bomb on the New Mexico plain, Greenglass slept in.

After the war, the two men tried their luck at running a small machine shop, but that, too, was a disappointment. They resumed their modest lives, giving no hint that they shared a terrifying secret.

Then, in 1950, a spy ring that had infiltrated Los Alamos began to unravel with the arrest, confession, and conviction of Klaus Fuchs, a German émigré who had worked on the Manhattan Project and now acknowledged sharing secrets with Soviet contacts. Authorities identified Greenglass as one of those associates, and he in turn fingered his brother-in-law. The evidence against Julius was strong. Questioned by the prosecutor Roy Cohn, Greenglass described Julius's efforts to recruit him and other scientists to supply information to the Soviet Union. He admitted that he had personally given Rosenberg drawings and other classified material. By contrast, the case against Ethel was notably weak; Greenglass said his sister had typed up notes of secret information in his presence, but that testimony was uncorroborated. FBI agents knew the case against Ethel was less compelling, but prosecutors pursued it to gain leverage over Julius, hoping he would confess and cooperate if Ethel faced prison. Neither she nor he gave in. "She called our bluff," William Rogers, then the deputy attorney general, said many years later.

The couple went to trial in early 1951, with the Korean War blazing and in a disquieting atmosphere of anti-Semitism and anti-Communism. On March 29, 1951, Julius and Ethel were convicted of violating the Espionage Act. One week later, Judge Irving Kaufman, ignoring the vastly different strengths of their cases, imposed identical sentences. His remarks at sentencing serve as a stark testament to the fear that espionage and subversion created in Cold War America:

> I consider your crime worse than murder. Plain deliberate contemplated murder is dwarfed in magnitude by comparison with the crime you have committed. In committing the act of murder, the criminal kills only his victim. The immediate family is brought to grief and when justice is meted out the chapter is closed. But in your case, I believe your conduct in putting into the hands of the Russians the A-bomb years before our best scientists predicted Russia would perfect the bomb has already caused, in my opinion, the Communist aggression in Korea, with the resultant casualties exceeding 50,000 and who knows but that millions more of innocent people may pay the price of your treason. Indeed, by your betrayal you undoubtedly have altered the course of history to the disadvantage of our country.

For his crimes, Greenglass was sentenced to fifteen years in prison, of which he served ten. A co-defendant, Morton Sobell, who had been a classmate of Julius's at City College, was sentenced to thirty years; he was freed in 1969. Julius and Ethel Rosenberg were condemned to die.

By the time Eisenhower was inaugurated, the Rosenbergs had been tried, convicted, and sentenced. Their appeals, however, continued, and as their executions drew closer, their supporters stepped up the intensity of their efforts to have the sentences commuted or overturned. From its earliest weeks, the new administration was immediately confronted with the question of whether to grant clemency to Julius and Ethel. Eisenhower raised the issue with his cabinet on February 13, 1953. He argued that there were no substantial issues raised by the trial record and no obvious national interest served by sparing their lives. He emphasized the seriousness of their crimes and worried that granting pardons to either or both would undermine the work of the Justice Department. Ike said he was denying their pardon applications but refusing to shut the door on their appeals. There was still time before their scheduled execution date, and "if anyone . . . believes by keeping them alive we can serve [the] interests of the country, we'll reverse."

Over the next four months, the White House was deluged with letters and telegrams, pleading for pardon, commutation, or execution. The pope asked for clemency. The Rosenberg children wrote begging the president to spare their parents. The foreign press overwhelmingly viewed them with sympathy; the opposition to their execution in France was so fierce that the ambassador there cabled his deep concern for the long-term effects on U.S.-French relations if the executions were carried out.

Still, Eisenhower and his top advisers never wavered from a central conclusion: they believed, without exception, that both Julius and Ethel were guilty of a heinous offense against the United States that had jeopardized lives and national security. They did not distinguish between their relative guilt. Indeed, Ike believed, if anything, that Ethel was the more significant traitor. He blanched at executing a woman but did not hesitate. "It is the woman who is [the] strong and recalcitrant character, the man is the weak one," Eisenhower wrote to his son, John. "She has obviously been the leader in everything they did in the spy ring."

On the same day that Ike wrote that note to his son, Ethel wrote to Eisenhower. Until then, she had refrained from appealing to him directly, inhibited, she said, by "a certain innate shyness, an embarrassment almost." With the hour of her death fast approaching, she abandoned her reserve. Written on Sing Sing stationery, her appeal was both cloying and angry. Ethel asserted her innocence and that of her husband but focused most intently on their sentences. To impose the death penalty, she argued, was an act of vengeance, not justice. "As Commander-in-Chief of the European theatre, you had ample opportunity to witness the wanton and hideous tortures that such a policy of vengeance has wreaked upon vast multitudes of guiltless victims. Today, while these ghastly mass butchers, these obscene racists, are graciously receiving the benefits of mercy and in many instances being reinstated in public office, the great democratic United States is proposing the savage destruction of a small, unoffending Jewish family, whose guilt is seriously doubted throughout the length and breadth of the civilized world." Eisenhower did not respond. The following day, Brownell once again recommended that he deny the Rosenbergs' final petition.

The Rosenbergs made one last appeal to the U.S. Supreme Court and, to the amazement of many observers, this time appeared to find purchase. William O. Douglas, the Court's cantankerous and iconoclastic liberal, agreed that there was a constitutional question raised by the death sentence (the Rosenbergs had been sentenced by Kaufman under the Espionage Act of 1917, but a subsequent statute, the Atomic Energy Act of 1946, required that a jury impose such a sentence. Since the Rosenbergs were indicted for violating the Espionage Act but tried after the enactment of the Atomic Energy Act, Douglas concluded that there was a question of whether the sentence had been properly imposed). He issued a stay just as the Court was concluding its term, then promptly left town to begin his annual summer vacation. Brownell, furious at the prospect of a long delay—Dulles described it as a "hell of a mess"—urged Chief Justice Fred Vinson to reconvene the Court. Vinson did. Over Douglas's protests, the justices vacated the stay.

Julius and Ethel Rosenberg were executed at Sing Sing prison on June 19, 1953. Before they were walked to the death chamber, a rabbi conveyed a message to each of them from Brownell: if they would supply names of co-conspirators, their executions would be stayed. Julius silently refused. Ethel replied: "No, I have no names to give. I am innocent." Julius was executed at 8:04 p.m.; Ethel survived the first jolt of electricity at 8:11 p.m. and was killed by two subsequent bursts, dying at 8:16 p.m. The Sabbath had begun at 8:13 p.m. The Dulles brothers and Brownell, scheduled to spend that evening at a Senators' game, decided it would be unseemly to be seen enjoying themselves while the Rosenbergs were put to death. They canceled those plans, and gathered instead for a quiet, private dinner.

Brownell and Eisenhower never had second thoughts about the executions; Brownell died believing that there was no "lingering doubt" about their guilt. Only half a century later would David Greenglass admit that he did not know whether his sister typed the notes, as he alleged on the stand; once freed from prison, he acknowledged that it could well have been his wife, not his sister. Long-withheld grand jury testimony reinforced Ethel's innocence. Today, history's verdict is far sounder than Justice's was in 1953:

Julius Rosenberg was a spy, a fact confirmed by Soviet intelligence cables and archives (his code name was Liberal, often shortened to Libi); Ethel was merely the wife of Julius, aware of his activities but not a participant. She died because her brother used her to deflect attention away from his wife and because the Justice Department was willing to sacrifice her in order to put pressure on her husband. By the time that verdict was rendered, however, she was long dead, her boys orphaned. They were six and ten when their parents were put to death.

Both the Rosenberg prosecution and Kaufman's sentence were influenced by the Korean War, which framed the charges as threats to American servicemen. The Rosenbergs almost lived long enough to see it end. Through the spring and summer, the administration, led by John Foster Dulles, blended threat and blandishment to try to end hostilities. The very nature of the conflict—a conventional war fought underneath the American nuclear umbrella—defied the essential assumption of nuclear deterrence. On February 9, Mark Clark, then the commanding general of the UN forces in Korea and the man who first recommended Ike to General Marshall, warned of a "strong possibility that any enemy offensive will be covered by large scale air action." He asked for permission to launch strikes against air bases in Manchuria. Two days later, the National Security Council considered Clark's warning, and Eisenhower raised the existential question of the conflict: UN and Communist forces were deadlocked, so should nuclear weapons be deployed?

Omar Bradley, now the chairman of the Joint Chiefs, advised against letting America's allies know that the United States was considering escalating the conflict, and Dulles grudgingly observed that the Soviets had succeeded in convincing the world that atomic weapons belonged "in a special category." It annoyed Ike to be boxed in by Soviet propaganda. If the Allies objected to dropping atomic bombs, he complained, they could cough up a few more divisions in order to drive out the Communist forces.

In March, Ike again raised the use of nuclear weapons with the reservation that their use be determined by military judgments as to their effectiveness against military targets. A meeting of the Joint Chiefs that same week made clear that the administration had "no unshakeable policy barrier to the use of atomic weapons"; rather, it was studying the diplomatic implications and military utility in the Korean terrain. At the end of that month, Eisenhower reiterated his willingness to pull the nuclear trigger. It would, he said, be "worth the cost" if it secured a substantial victory and captured the "waist of Korea," dividing that country to the West's strategic advantage.

As the UN, led by the United States, negotiated for an armistice—complicated by how to return prisoners of war held by each side, including the thorny issue of what to do with captured North Korean and Chinese soldiers who wanted to remain in South Korea—President Rhee proved a singularly unhelpful ally. He strenuously pressed for Korean unification under his rule and thwarted attempts at a peace that would leave the nation divided. When Chinese and North Korean officials proposed resuming peace talks in the spring, Rhee angrily threatened to expel American troops unless they were willing to fight on. If a peace agreement was reached that allowed Chinese troops to remain in Korea, Rhee informed Eisenhower, "we have to ask all the friendly nations whose armed forces are now fighting in Korea and who do not desire to join with us in our determination to defeat aggressive communism and drive up to the Yalu River, to withdraw from Korea."

Ike reined in his temper, reiterated the United States' "common cause with the Korean people," and reminded Rhee that UN forces had repelled the invasion and restored South Korea roughly to its prewar borders, though he conceded that he was "deeply disturbed" by Rhee's threat. Talks resumed, and exchanges of prisoners began, an important step toward an armistice. Then, in July, Rhee secretly authorized the release of twenty-five thousand North Korean prisoners; South Korea described it as a mass escape, but it was abundantly clear—and eventually admitted—that Rhee had set the prisoners free in order to undermine the negotiations. Livid, Eisenhower now threatened to abandon Rhee to fight the Chinese alone. "Unless you are prepared immediately and unequivocally to accept the authority of the UN Command to conduct the present hostilities and bring them to a close, it will be necessary to effect another arrangement," Eisenhower advised his Korean counterpart. John Eisenhower was blunter: "I guess Syngman Rhee pretty well scuttled the truce."

If Rhee did not succeed, it was not for lack of trying. He never gave up his dream of uniting the country under his rule, and his periodic demands of American support were a recurring theme throughout the 1950s. In the meantime, Eisenhower's anger had the desired effect. Rhee backed down, and negotiations went forward.

In addressing enemies, Eisenhower was no less firm. Administration officials quietly informed India's government, then acting as an intermediary to China, that the United States was prepared to use nuclear weapons to bring the Korean War to an end. Although it is difficult to know how seriously Mao regarded that threat, Eisenhower believed it had rattled his adversary. Asked years later by Sherman Adams what had motivated China to negotiate a truce, Ike answered without hesitation. "Danger of an atomic war," he said.

It did not end the war immediately. In late May 1953, the Chinese forces in Korea launched a final, withering assault. Howitzer and mortar fire rained down on South Korean positions, and along one stretch of the front Chinese soldiers fought in grueling hand-to-hand combat against Turkish adversaries. In early June, "the mightiest blow to fall upon our forces since the spring offensive in 1951" erupted with evening artillery attacks and built into a full-scale offensive along the Bukhan River.

While soldiers died on both sides, negotiators hammered out the final details of the armistice, their efforts hastened by the intensity of the fighting. Thousands lost their lives in the final weeks. At last, on July 27, General William K. Harrison signed the truce on behalf of the UN forces fighting in South Korea. In Washington, Eisenhower expressed his gratitude, mourning the fact that the conflict had caused such destruction, only to restore Korea to its former, divided self. "For this Nation the cost of repelling aggression has been high. In thousands of homes it has been incalculable. It has been paid in terms of tragedy," Ike said to the American people late that night. "We have won," Eisenhower stressed, "an armistice on a single battleground, not peace in the world."

Thousands of miles away, in muddy foxholes strung along windswept ridges, soldiers set down their rifles and toasted over jugs of whiskey and rice wine. "It was almost joy enough," Matthew Ridgway wrote, "just to be able to climb up out of a hole in the ground and look out over the countryside without getting shot at."

The administration—just six months old—had succeeded in fulfilling Eisenhower's "principal pledge." Ike ended America's most costly and protracted military engagement since World War II. With the Rosenbergs, he made it clear that if security required sacrifice, he would demand it. In Korea, he proved that peace was not merely an abstraction, nor was it defeat. Communism could be contained, and American men and women, dispatched to die in foreign lands, could come home alive.

Consequences

I n 1953, having been president for less than a year, Dwight Eisenhower made two decisions that shaped America's place in the world for decades to come. One ended up a source of irritation to Ike, even though it led to some of the most momentous changes under his leadership; the other was kept secret at the time, and though it delighted Eisenhower, it complicated history's view of his legacy. In 1953, Eisenhower nominated Earl Warren to the U.S. Supreme Court, less than four months after he authorized the covert action that toppled Mohammed Mossadegh from power in Iran.

Mossadegh was, by all accounts, an odd character. Eisenhower regarded him with derision. He was born to privilege, educated in Europe as a doctor of law (the first Iranian ever to receive such a degree), but steeped in the politics of Iran. He wobbled in and out of favor of the nation's rulers, alternately holding governorships and enduring banishments, winning elected offices and sweating out imprisonments. Theatrical, thin to the point of emaciation, Mossadegh had a "hawk-like face with the kind of tragic lines that are likely to win the sympathy of those with whom one talks, particularly when they are accompanied by an agreeable voice and friendly eyes," recalled Loy Henderson, the American ambassador who managed to resist the charms he so fulsomely enumerated. Dean Acheson described Mossadegh as birdlike and impish; the Iranian leader would tuck his legs beneath him in a chair and play his character for maximum benefit. Once, "suddenly looking old and pathetic," he had begged Truman to think kindly of his "poor country . . . just sand, a few camels, a few sheep." Acheson interrupted: "And with your oil, rather like Texas!" Caught, Mossadegh erupted in laughter. "No one," Acheson wrote, "was more amused than he." Before crowds, Mossadegh was a mesmerizing orator who could reduce an audience to tears, but he was physically and emotionally fragile. He often greeted visitors in bed, and he suffered from a condition that caused his throat to seize up under stress. Sometimes he stirred his audiences to rapture, only to faint dead away.

In 1951, Mossadegh campaigned for prime minister on a platform of nationalizing British oil operations in Iran, a mission that placed him squarely on a path of collision with the world's leading imperialist power. Mossadegh attracted zealous followers, and on March 15, 1951, the Iranian National Assembly, the Majlis, nationalized the company; five days later, the Iranian Senate unanimously approved the measure. In that fervid expression of nationalist identity, Mossadegh was elected prime minister and assumed the office on April 28. Britain's skepticism of Iran's new leader was thoroughly shared by its prime minister, Winston Churchill, who had returned to power in 1951 and who, like his Iranian counterpart, was no stranger to theatrics nor to greeting visitors in pajamas. Churchill viewed Mossadegh as a reckless demagogue intent on the theft of British property. In that, he was partly right, as Mossadegh deliberately provoked a diplomatic confrontation.

Animated by an abiding hatred for most things British, Mossadegh demanded new terms for the split between Iran and the Anglo-Iranian Oil Company of the revenue it derived from Iranian oil. The company refused even to provide an accounting, no doubt because an honest one later revealed that Iran was receiving less than 10 percent of the oil's value. Some of AIOC's profits were spent on bribes to secure the complicity of Iranian leaders. At first, British leaders, as well as other oil companies, were frustrated by AIOC's intransigence and encouraged the company to negotiate in good faith. AIOC's chairman—a stubborn, Victorian-era colonialist—refused. On July 31, 1951, the British oil company shut down the world's largest refinery, its facility in Abadan.

The company had backed Britain into a corner. British leaders tried to fight their way out. They moved to depose Mossadegh. That backfired when Mossadegh learned of the plot and publicly denounced it on September 6, threatening to expel all remaining British personnel from the refinery. The British dispatched naval forces off the Iranian coast. As the conflict intensified, an attempt at mediation by the American Averell Harriman fell apart. (Harriman's efforts were complicated by an intestinal disorder so aggravated by the heat that he cooled off by flying a private jet around the country and running its air conditioner.) The British government and other oil companies reluctantly rallied to AIOC's defense. AIOC launched a boycott of Iranian oil; American oil companies honored it, and the British fleet symbolically enforced it. Since British and American firms controlled three-quarters of the world's tankers, the boycott was devastatingly effective. Within months, Iran had effectively lost all of its oil production revenue.

Truman was under no illusions about the danger posed by an unstable Iran. He recognized that a Soviet incursion into Iran could leave America's most formidable enemy with an enlarged oil supply, strategic command over the Persian Gulf, and easy reach into the Middle East. Indeed, just after the North Korean invasion in 1950, Truman had turned to his aide George Elsey and pointed to Iran on a globe. "Here," Truman said, "is where they will start trouble if we aren't careful."

In those waning months of the Truman administration, American leaders balanced their condescension toward Mossadegh and their distaste for British imperialism against their fear of Soviet adventurism. They fretted a great deal but did very little. The U.S. government professed neutrality but quietly supported the boycott. The administration stood by its British allies—up to a point. Acheson tried to patch the situation together and received Truman's permission to attempt a last-minute negotiated settlement of the oil dispute. The secretary of state sent his proposal to London. "Back came a reply about two weeks later, related and relevant to our proposal . . . only by being expressed on paper by means of a typewriter," Acheson recorded in characteristically wry fashion. Failed talks led to more desperate proposals. Ambassador Henderson concluded that Mossadegh was deranged ("a sick leader," in Henderson's words) and that the oil crisis could only be solved by deposing him. But when British agents began to plot a coup and turned to the United States for help, Truman refused. In October 1952, Mossadegh learned of the British plans and responded by closing the British embassy and ejecting its officials, including the intelligence officials plotting the coup. Britain still wanted Mossadegh overthrown but needed American help more than ever. Truman continued to refuse.

The situation changed significantly when Eisenhower won the November election. Churchill had his old friend heading for the White House. Bedell Smith, the new undersecretary of state, was another valued Churchill acquaintance. Truman, who had resisted the English, was headed home to Independence, Missouri. Advocates of covert action recognized the opportunity and recalibrated their argument to appeal to the new president. No longer was the issue British oil or colonial rights; the central question for the new president was whether to stand by and allow a nation of undeniable strategic consequence to drift or plunge into the Soviet orbit. C. M. Woodhouse, delegated by the British government to sell the Eisenhower administration on overthrowing Mossadegh, realized what he had to do. "Not wishing to be accused of trying to use the Americans to pull British chestnuts out of the fire, I decided to emphasize the Communist threat to Iran rather than the need to recover control of the oil industry."

Those appeals had the desired effect. One week after Eisenhower's inauguration, Henderson cabled to say that events in Iran were "rapidly . . . approaching deadlock." The National Security Council took up the question of Iran's future on March 4, and Ike warmed to the idea of a coup. "We, not the Russians, must make the next move," the minutes show Nixon suggesting. Eisenhower agreed. "If I had $500 million of money to spend in secret, I would get $100 million of it to Iran right now."

Smith, too, became an impatient supporter of an overthrow, and by the spring of 1953, John Foster and Allen Dulles had made up their minds "that it was not in American interests for the Mossadegh government to remain in power." Left was the question of how to depose him. In humid conferences from Beirut to London to Washington, agents and officials of the American and British governments conspired to construct Mossadegh's downfall. On June 3, Henderson arrived in Washington to brief his superiors, while in Beirut and Nicosia, CIA officials worked through the details. Churchill approved the coup on July 1. Eisenhower gave his verbal approval on July 11. In his memoirs, Eisenhower presented a highly sanitized version of the exercise that relegated U.S. agents to a bit part. His only mention of America's role in the covert operation was an oblique acknowledgment that "the United States government had done everything it possibly could to back up the Shah."

In fact, he did far more. In authorizing the covert action against Mossadegh, Eisenhower also approved the expenditure of $1 million to drum up support for General Fazlollah Zahedi, a ranking member of the Iranian military and the Americans' chosen successor (British officials were uncomfortable with Zahedi, whom they had imprisoned during World War II for suspected Nazi ties, but they acceded to American wishes), and established a separate account specifically to bribe members of the Iranian Majlis. So armed with cash, American agents operating out of the embassy in Tehran launched an extraordinary three-week campaign in August 1953. After bribing, threatening, improvising, and nearly failing, they eventually achieved a historic triumph, at least on their terms.

Before rolling out their plans, the principals paused to check that they had appropriate authorization. John Foster Dulles asked his brother whether the plan was good to go. "It was cleared directly with the President," Allen Dulles responded, "and is still active."

The role of the United States during those August days is captured in two distinctly different accounts—a long-classified CIA history prepared in 1954 but not made public for almost fifty years, and a self-aggrandizing memoir by one of the participants, Kermit Roosevelt. Neither is entirely trustworthy, but both present the whirlwind nature of the coup. In Roosevelt's version, the Shah is depicted as cautious but capable—his leadership essential to the legitimacy of the American intervention. Roosevelt maintains throughout that he and his compatriots merely acted at the Shah's behest as the Shah fended off an attack on his throne. The CIA version portrays the Shah as dithering and weak. His more strong-willed twin sister is flown in to stiffen his spine, her cooperation bought in part by the gift of a mink coat. The Shah flees when the coup falters. He fears spies and microphones and insists on holding one meeting in the center of a large banquet room atop a table.

Documents from the period strongly support the CIA's characterization of the Shah. As the events gathered momentum that year, he was erratic and flighty, unwilling to challenge Mossadegh, afraid not to. In February, he complained he needed a vacation. On his return, he had meetings in his garden and complained of his humiliating treatment at the hands of his own army. His desired solution: a vacation out of his country.

The CIA had steadier nerves. Its operatives grindingly increased the pressure on Mossadegh and occasionally got lucky. The Shah, unsure of whether to cast his lot with the Americans and the British, stalled but was reassured that Eisenhower was supporting him. In an address to a Governors' Convention in Seattle on August 4, Eisenhower vowed not to let Iran fall behind the Iron Curtain. Roosevelt told the Shah that comment was meant as a signal. It was not, but it sufficed. Over the next few days, U.S. operatives planted highly critical stories about Mossadegh in the "controllable press" and, posing as members of the Iranian Communist Party, the Tudeh, unnerved religious leaders with ominous phone calls and threats to bomb homes. The Shah eventually capitulated and signed a pair of orders dismissing Mossadegh and replacing him with Zahedi. Trouble arose when the colonel assigned the job of serving Mossadegh with the papers—known as a firman—was arrested after presenting them to the prime minister's servant (Mossadegh was sleeping and had left word not to be awakened). Mossadegh then rallied forces loyal to him, and the Shah fled first for Baghdad and then for Italy, where he ran into the vacationing Allen Dulles in the lobby of the Excelsior Hotel in Rome. Ever the gracious spy, Dulles stepped aside: "After you, Your Majesty."

In Washington, officials were crestfallen. "The move failed," Smith wrote to Eisenhower, "because of three days of delay and vacillation by the Iranian generals concerned." The United States, Smith bleakly added, might now be forced to "snuggle up" to Mossadegh in order to salvage any strategic advantage from the failed effort.

Convinced that the danger had passed, Mossadegh relaxed his guard. Roosevelt and his cohorts were still frantically at work in the embassy compound, searching for Zahedi and other troops willing to stand with the now-absent Shah against the increasingly confident Mossadegh. CIA operatives distributed copies of the firman—collaborative newspapers published the document—along with a faked interview of Zahedi. The CIA paid demonstrators and capitalized on public revulsion at looting by Tudeh Party members. At dawn on August 19, the Shah's bands took their place in the streets and converged on Radio Tehran. Three people died defending the station. It fell at 2:12 p.m. Once inside, the Shah's supporters read aloud the firman. Sensing the government's imminent collapse, Roosevelt made it to Zahedi's hideout and persuaded the general that there was no time to wait. Zahedi donned his uniform, boarded a tank, and headed for the radio station. He spoke at 3:25 p.m. At 7:00 p.m., Mossadegh's home was ransacked and his belongings tossed in the street, sold off to anyone happening by. All that was left was mopping up, and that was done quickly. Even the CIA's official history, in its dry recitation of those events, conveys the agency's exuberance: "It was a day that . . . carried with it such a sense of excitement, of satisfaction, and of jubilation that it is doubtful whether any other can come up to it. Our trump card had prevailed and the Shah was victorious."

Eisenhower spent August 19 in New York. He lunched at the Waldorf Astoria with Nixon; the *New York Times* publisher, Arthur Hays Sulzberger; the president of Doubleday, Douglas Black; New York's governor, Tom Dewey; Secretary of Labor Martin Durkin; and his old friend Lucius Clay. Ike registered to vote that afternoon, then departed for Denver on the presidential plane. By the time he arrived, Iran had a new government, loyal and beholden to the United States. Ike cabled the Shah congratulations: "I offer you my sincere felicitations on the occasion of your happy return to your country."

American involvement in the overthrow of Mossadegh was long suspected in Iran and the Middle East—though only acknowledged decades later. Even today, Eisenhower's personal participation remains murky. But in his diary, Eisenhower made it clear that he enthusiastically approved. "The things we did were 'covert,' " he wrote in the entry, which was declassified at the request of the author in 2009. "If knowledge of them became public, we would not only be embarrassed in that region, but our chances to do anything of like nature in the future would almost totally disappear."

If exposure would have terminated such adventurism, success had the opposite effect. "When we realize that in the first hours of the attempted coup, all elements of surprise disappeared through betrayal, the Shah fled to Baghdad, and Mossadegh seemed to be more firmly entrenched in power than ever before, then we can understand exactly how courageous our agent was in staying right on the job and continuing to work until he reversed the entire situation," Eisenhower noted. "I listened to his detailed report and it seemed more like a dime novel than an historical fact." Eisenhower realized that Iran remained unstable, but if all went well, he hoped, "we may really give a serious defeat to Russian intentions and plans in that area."

Barely had Mossadegh been dislodged than Ike was confronted with a second decision that gave him the chance to shape history. On the night of September 7, 1953, Fred Vinson, chief justice of the United States, complained of indigestion as he nodded off to sleep. He awoke after midnight in breathless pain, then collapsed in his Washington apartment at 2:30 a.m. His son called for help, but Vinson, sixty-three, overweight, and a chronic smoker, died before the ambulance could arrive. His passing ended a disappointing Supreme Court tenure. Despite a lifetime of service to his nation in all three branches of government, the genial Kentucky moderate was outmatched at the Supreme Court by smart and willful colleagues, often bitterly at odds with one another and beyond Vinson's capacity to control. His final terms on the bench were marked by the deepening fractiousness of its leading justices, and at the time of his death the Court was facing the most divisive issue of the century: Did a Constitution that promised the "equal protection of the laws" mean what it said when those laws were applied to those whose ancestors were slaves, or had the Court, by its precedents, permitted something else?

Through a series of cases challenging separate educational facilities for black and white students, the Vinson Court overturned segregated graduate schools in Oklahoma and Texas, finding that the institutions in those states were not "equal" to those provided for white students. Those rulings in the so-called graduate school cases enforced the Fourteenth Amendment's prohibition against unequal treatment but allowed for the continuation of a practice endorsed by the Court in its infamous *Plessy v. Ferguson* ruling of 1896. The Court in *Plessy* had upheld segregated railcars as long as they were substantially "equal" in amenities, and thus had allowed the construction of American apartheid. Relying on that ruling, the South, and much of the North, had erected Jim Crow, the elaborate system of separate facilities for blacks and whites, insisting on the fiction that such separation implied no denigration and conformed to the Fourteenth Amendment's command of equality.

The graduate school cases were decided in favor of black plaintiffs because they were able to show that black universities were in no sense equal. At the University of Texas, for instance, the law school open to whites had sixteen professors and a library with sixty-five thousand books; that open to blacks, including the Houston mailman Herman Sweatt, had just four professors and ten thousand books on order. Texas courts had found no violation there, but Sweatt appealed his case to the U.S. Supreme Court and won. "We cannot conclude that the education offered [Sweatt] is substantially equal to that which he would receive if admitted to the University of Texas Law School," the Court found. However, the Vinson Court specifically and emphatically declined to take the next step of constitutional logic and acknowledge that separation in itself was inequality. It came close in *McLaurin v. Oklahoma State Regents*, where it recognized that restrictions on the plaintiff—he was cordoned off in the library and cafeteria, among other things—"impair and inhibit his ability to study, to engage in discussions and exchange views with other students and, in general, to learn his profession." But still the Court held firm. "Broader issues have been urged for our consideration," Vinson wrote in *Sweatt*. The Court avoided them.

In its refusal to address those broader issues, the Vinson Court had built a halfhearted record on segregation. It had ruled in favor of black plaintiffs seeking better educations, but it also had delayed reckoning with the real issue in favor of counting books and appraising the quality of librarians and accreditations. "Separate but equal" survived the Vinson Court.

By the time Vinson died, the Court had become divided and querulous. The Vinson Court consisted of four relatively undistinguished justices— Sherman Minton, Tom Clark, Stanley Reed, and Harold Burton—and four of the most brilliant jurists in the Court's history. Though all four were liberal in their politics and appointees of FDR, Justices Felix Frankfurter and Robert Jackson were the Court's fierce and principled advocates for a restrained judiciary, while Justices Hugo Black and William O. Douglas anchored the Court's activist wing.

Black was a courtly Alabamian and former senator whose gracious manners concealed a tenacious advocate and adventurous intellect. Since 1947, he had been developing a singular constitutional literalism and a sweeping view of the constitutional principle known as incorporation.

Where the First Amendment commands that Congress shall make "no law" abridging speech or religious practice, Black accepted those words as written, testament to his literalism. And he strenuously argued that the Fourteenth Amendment had imposed or "incorporated" the restrictions of the entire Bill of Rights onto the states. As originally adopted, the Bill of Rights only limited the federal government; states could, for instance, restrict speech or assembly or protection against self-incrimination in a way that the federal government could not. But the Fourteenth Amendment prohibits the states from making or enforcing any law "which shall abridge the privileges or immunities of citizens of the United States." It bars states from denying any person life, liberty, or due process, and it commands the equal protection of the laws. To Black, that meant that the states were fully bound by the protections it guaranteed. He never commanded a majority for those views, but his dogged pursuit of them won piecemeal what he could not win wholesale: the Court gradually extended the protections of the Bill of Rights one right at a time, with Black as a fervent advocate.

Black's most reliable ally was William Douglas, but he could be a difficult partner. Douglas—a self-styled western iconoclast, brilliant, rugged, irascible—practiced a fierce liberal libertarianism under which he resisted government encroachment in such disparate areas as speech, privacy, and travel. Douglas would, over his many decades on the Court, champion the rights of individuals against their government. Though he was an icon for liberals, at his core he was really something of a conservative, deeply wary of government intrusion, fiercely devoted to individual rights. "We have deemed it more costly to liberty to suppress a despised minority than to let them vent their spleen," he wrote in 1951. "We have above all else feared the political censor. We have wanted a land where our people can be exposed to all the diverse creeds and cultures of the world." Across his long career, Douglas would rarely waver from that conviction or miss an opportunity to express it.

At the other end of the Court's spectrum—defined by their view of the Court's role in society, not their politics—were Frankfurter and Jackson, no less liberal or gifted than Black and Douglas, but more concerned about the Court's reach. Like Black and Douglas, Jackson and Frankfurter were appointed by FDR and forged in the experience of the Court's initial resistance to his economic program. Frankfurter and Jackson extracted from that experience one of the core principles of that era's Progressive jurisprudence. In that view, judges were bound to operate with restraint, and courts were expected, in general, to defer to the elected branches. They rejected the judicial activism of their day for what it had long been—a conservative tool to blunt FDR's agenda.

Frankfurter and Jackson approached those ideas differently. Frankfurter was an esteemed Harvard law professor, mentor to generations of acolytes, and a Jew who had once found his path toward Wall Street blocked by discrimination. He had emigrated with his family to the United States from Austria as a young boy and grew up in the Progressive Era, imbibing its distrust of big business and its faith in democratic government. He feared the courts were "cumbersome and ineffective" in the pursuit of social change. He wrote and lectured on those topics with unrivaled genius. And yet, despite his brilliance, Frankfurter was a difficult colleague. He lectured and condescended to those around him and could barely disguise his contempt for those he viewed as lesser intellects, which included most men. When Vinson died, most of his colleagues released gracious statements; Frankfurter remarked that it was his first solid evidence of the existence of God.

Jackson was more personable and subtle, though also sensitive to slight. He elected to skip college and attended only one year of law school, but nevertheless apprenticed himself to a New York lawyer and passed the bar in 1913. He practiced as a small-town lawyer in rural New York, where he attracted the attention of Governor Franklin Roosevelt. Once elected president, Roosevelt tapped Jackson for a series of appointments, and Jackson served with distinction as counsel to the Internal Revenue Service, solicitor general, and attorney general. He was regarded by some as the country's most effective solicitor general, his arguments so eloquent and persuasive that he shaped many Supreme Court opinions even before joining the bench. He brought that eloquence with him to the Court, where his writing is among the greatest in the Court's history. In 1943, he broke with Frankfurter to uphold the right of Jehovah's Witnesses not to salute the American flag in school. His majority opinion is a classic of Supreme Court erudition. "The very purpose of a Bill of Rights was to withdraw certain subjects from the vicissitudes of political controversy, to place them beyond the reach of majorities and officials, and to establish them as legal principles to be applied by the courts," Jackson wrote. "If there is any fixed star in our constitutional constellation, it is that no official, high or petty, can prescribe what shall be orthodox in politics, nationalism, religion, or other matters of opinion, or force citizens to confess by word or act their faith therein." By 1953, Jackson had served for over a decade, with a notable break to act as the chief prosecutor in the Nuremberg trials. He was an advocate without peer.

Four such willful and brilliant men were bound to bicker, and they did. In 1945, Black and Jackson feuded over a recusal matter. Black voted in a labor case involving a former law partner and refused Jackson's suggestion that he step aside. Frankfurter joined Jackson, and both sides went away bruised. By the early 1950s, they were barely on speaking terms. Jackson contemplated resigning when Truman named Vinson as chief justice, believing he had been passed over in part because of his public squabbles with Black. Meanwhile, the prickly Frankfurter grew increasingly fed up. He called Black and Douglas "the Axis" and mocked their constitutional scholarship. Douglas returned the favor by ignoring Frankfurter altogether, sometimes leaving the justices' conference table until Frankfurter finished expounding on a case.

Vinson was unable to corral the difficult personalities and equally failed in bringing the Court to terms with the full meaning of the Fourteenth Amendment. As a result, his death in 1953 gave Eisenhower the opportunity to energize the Court with a leader.

Vinson and Ike had been friends, bridge partners, and mutual admirers. News of his sudden death startled Eisenhower, then vacationing in Denver. He released a statement lauding Vinson's "efficiency, dignity and integrity." At the funeral, held at the National Cathedral in Washington, Ike paid his respects quietly, stone-faced and grave. A few seats away, Truman, another friend and confidant of the chief justice's—their shared card game was poker—fought tears.

With Vinson buried, Eisenhower quickly turned to the question of his successor. He relied on Brownell, whose combination of legal and political acumen made him an extraordinarily capable judge of judges. In Ike's first and most important appointment, however, the president had already made a commitment, albeit a nonbinding one. After winning the 1952 nomination, Eisenhower had spent time with the governor of California, Earl Warren. When California conservatives floated the idea of placing MacArthur's name on the state's November ballot, some aides worried that it could hurt Ike's prospects by splitting Republican votes and tipping the election to Stevenson (Truman had carried California in 1948). Warren, then in his third term as governor, reassured Eisenhower that a MacArthur candidacy would go nowhere. No one knew California politics better than Warren, and his "advice was on the mark," Brownell recalled.

In those early meetings, Ike grew to like Warren. Both were hearty men, comfortable in the outdoors, strong, straightforward, and likable. Both were veterans, though Warren's service hardly compared with Ike's. Both were patriots, devoted to the service of their nation. As moderate Republicans with opponents on both left and right, they had common enemies, though their stiffest challenges tended to come from conservatives. And though Warren was more proficient in domestic affairs and Ike in international relations, both believed strongly that America needed to be engaged in the world, and both regarded the nation's isolationists as provincial. Even their backgrounds bore some similarities. Like Eisenhower, Warren was raised in modest circumstances: his father was a railroad man blackballed by the Southern Pacific in Los Angeles who then moved his family to rural Bakersfield and raised Warren and his sister there. And, perhaps most important, both were practical and largely nonideological. Ike championed the middle way; Warren eschewed partisanship, refusing to endorse candidates in most partisan races (one of those annoyed by that practice was Nixon, who asked for Warren's support in his first congressional campaign but did not receive it).

Eisenhower had considered appointing Warren to the cabinet, most seriously weighing him as a candidate for secretary of the interior. Then, before leaving for Korea, he phoned Warren to tell him he regretted not offering him a cabinet post but pledging to find an appropriate role for him later. In that conversation, Eisenhower told Warren—how firmly was later debated—that he would give him the "first vacancy" on the Supreme Court. In the meantime, the administration would keep Warren in mind for other openings. Brownell lit upon the idea of making him solicitor general, where Warren—who had not practiced law since moving from state attorney general to governor in 1943—could freshen his legal skills while waiting for a vacancy. Warren pondered the offer, then accepted on August 3, 1953, in a coded cable from Europe.

Returning home later that month, Warren quietly began to wrap up his governorship, announcing on September 3 that he would not seek a fourth term. Then, before the White House had a chance to announce his appointment, Vinson died. Warren assumed the position was his since Ike had promised him the "first vacancy." To Eisenhower, however, the promise had been offered for an associate justice seat, not for that of chief justice, and he did not feel bound to deliver that position to Warren.

Rather than tap Warren, Ike weighed possible candidates: he considered

John W. Davis, a Democrat and the lawyer representing South Carolina in its campaign to maintain school segregation; several leading circuit court judges; and Arthur Vanderbilt, chief justice of the New Jersey Supreme Court. Brownell admired Justice Jackson and briefly considered elevating him to chief justice and appointing a new associate justice, but Jackson's squabbles with Black had sullied his reputation, and as a New Deal Democrat, Jackson was hardly right for Ike's first nomination to the Court. Further proving that he did not consider himself bound to Warren, Eisenhower sounded John Foster Dulles out regarding the secretary of state's interest in the position, but Dulles declined, saying he was "highly complimented" but more interested in continuing in his "present post." Eisenhower never mentioned that offer to his attorney general.

Warren, meanwhile, played what cards he had. He called on friends with ties to the White House and then departed for Santa Rosa Island, off the California coast, where he made himself hard to reach while letting Eisenhower stew in the prospects of breaking his word. Warren announced that he was hunting deer with his sons, but really he was trying to make himself unavailable. "It was kind of a hideout," he conceded later.

As Brownell and Eisenhower sifted through their options, they decided they needed to be back in touch with Warren to clarify his understanding of the president's promise. A Coast Guard vessel was dispatched to fetch Warren from Santa Rosa. Back onshore, he conferred with Brownell by telephone. As Brownell attempted to explain that Eisenhower did not feel bound by his earlier pledge, Warren was adamant. "First vacancy," he insisted, "means first vacancy."

Sensing that they were making no progress, Brownell proposed a face-to-face meeting. Two days later, the two men met privately at McClellan Air Force Base, outside Sacramento. Warren came in his hunting clothes. They retired to a hangar, where they talked for several hours and Warren continued to insist that Ike honor his word. Brownell flew home, and Warren boasted to a friend that the job was his. Brownell leaked the idea to a few friendly reporters in Washington. Their reports were well received. Finally, Ike made it official the next week, naming Earl Warren as the fourteenth chief justice of the United States.

After confirming Warren's appointment on September 30, Ike explained the reasons for his choice:

> From the very beginning, from the moment of the unfortunate
> death of my great friend, Mr. Vinson, I have been thinking over this
> whole thing. I certainly wanted a man whose reputation for integrity,

honesty, middle-of-the-road philosophy, experience in Government, experience in the law, were all such as to convince the United States that here was a man who had no ends to serve except the United States, and nothing else. Naturally, I wanted a man who was healthy, strong, who had not had any serious illnesses, and who was relatively young—if you can call a man of approximately my age relatively young—relatively young with respect to some others that I was thinking of.

The press corps was so unsurprised by Eisenhower's announcement that reporters barely asked about it. Instead, they focused on how the leak had been orchestrated and largely ignored the qualifications of the chief justice designate. Warren, meanwhile, assumed his new duties with alacrity. Because Eisenhower made the appointment while Congress was in recess, Warren took his seat immediately. He left California on the weekend of October 2 and was sworn in on October 5. He arrived without even a robe and had to borrow one. It was a bit long, and he stumbled over the hem on his first trip to the bench. Ike and Mamie traveled up the Hill for the event, sitting in the front row as Warren was administered the oath.

From those who praised the appointment, including his brother Milton, Eisenhower accepted compliments. To those who criticized his selection, including his brother Edgar, Ike was brusque. "To my mind, he is a statesman," Ike lectured his older brother. "We have too few of these . . . Here is a man of national stature (and I ask you when we have had any man of national stature appointed to the Supreme Court), of unimpeachable integrity, of middle-of-the-road views, and with a splendid record during his years in active law work." When Senator William Langer, North Dakota's slightly wacky representative, held up Warren's nomination and subjected the chief justice to a bevy of false and salacious charges, Eisenhower fumed at the attack on "one of the finest public servants this country has produced."

Once Warren was seated, contacts between Eisenhower and him were rare but friendly. Ike invited Warren to a dinner and apologized when he was forced to miss a Court reception for Justice Burton. When Warren was confirmed, he thanked Eisenhower profusely. "No greater honor, responsibility, or opportunity in life could possibly come to me," he wrote. "I want to say to you that the remaining useful years of my life will be dedicated to serving the cause of justice in a manner justifying the confidence you have reposed in me."

And yet, even in those early months, there were hints of future conflicts. Eisenhower knew that the Court would soon face the question of

whether the Fourteenth Amendment prohibited the maintenance of separate schools for black students, no matter how "equal" their facilities. He
also knew that Warren's record in that area, though by no means fully
developed, suggested he would be unlikely to uphold segregation.

Eisenhower's own musings on that topic suggested he remained ambivalent, just as Brownell had sensed when they first discussed the matter a
year earlier. On July 20, Eisenhower lunched with "my great friend" Governor James Byrnes of South Carolina. Byrnes warned the president of the
South's fear of desegregated schools and its determination to resist. One
of the four cases consolidated under *Brown v. Board of Education* arose in
South Carolina, and Byrnes hinted that the wrong ruling could trigger
riots. His graver fear, however, was the same one that troubled Eisenhower:
What if school districts, ordered to integrate, simply closed, denying black
and white children alike the benefits of a public education? A few days
later, Eisenhower wrote in his diary: "Improvement in race relations is one
of those things that will be healthy and sound only if it starts locally. I do
not believe that prejudices, even palpably unjustified prejudices, will suc-
cumb to compulsion." Eisenhower worried that a Supreme Court ruling
that failed to acknowledge those truisms was doomed to produce defiance
of the Court. "I believe that federal law imposed upon our states in such
a way as to bring about a conflict of the police powers of the states and of
the nation, would set back the cause of progress in race relations for a long,
long time."

All through late 1953 and early 1954, Eisenhower fretted to Brownell
about Supreme Court action that would invite southern backlash. In
November, with Governor Byrnes coming for dinner the next day, Eisenhower shared his fears about schools closing. Brownell offered to reassure
Byrnes, suggesting that desegregation could proceed gradually: "Under
our doctrine, it would be a period of years." Still, Eisenhower wondered
whether the federal government would be forced to take over schools. As
the Supreme Court deliberated over *Brown*, Ike became more and more
worried. In January 1954, Brownell, undoubtedly tipped off by Warren,
informed Eisenhower that the Court was inclined to rule on the constitutionality of segregation first, then return later to a discussion of how
to remedy any constitutional violation that it found. "I don't know where
I stand," Eisenhower replied, "but I think the best interests of the U.S.
demand an answer in keep[ing] with past decisions."

That remark leaves Ike's ultimate view unclear but strongly suggests
he would have been most comfortable with a ruling that preserved existing institutions—and thus segregation. When Brownell told him that the

Court apparently wanted to defer issuing an order for as long as possible, Eisenhower laughingly said he hoped they could put it off until the next administration.

In spite of those remarks, there is no evidence in Eisenhower's diaries, directives, or actions as president that he was racist or that he was indifferent to the suffering of black Americans. But his instinct for the middle way, so useful in matters of military and budget, was inhibiting in the area of civil rights, as was his appreciation for order. Eisenhower was a Texan by birth and a Kansan by upbringing. Many of his friends were Southerners. He sympathized with them, with their fears of letting their children share classrooms with black children, with their discomfort at upending a fragile social order.

Eisenhower described his "middle way," as he put it to one confidant, as a rejection of extremism: "Anything that affects or is proposed for masses of humans is wrong if the position it seeks is at either end of possible argument." That was shrewdly put, though hard to apply in civil rights. Indeed, Ike explicitly exempted "the field of moral values" from his advocacy of centrism; there, he conceded, compromise was sometimes undesirable. Blinkered by his upbringing and friendships, however, Ike ignored his own wise recognition that moral undertakings generally and civil rights specifically warranted unambiguous support rather than compromise.

And yet Ike's record on civil rights, commencing with the nomination of Warren, helped propel the very movement that discomfited him. He relied heavily on Brownell in making judicial appointments, knowing well that the attorney general was a leading advocate of civil rights. Eisenhower appointed Elbert Parr Tuttle, John Brown, and John Minor Wisdom to the Fifth Circuit, which oversaw the Deep South, and Frank Johnson to the district court in Alabama. Those were inspired choices, and together they enforced federal protections of civil rights with great courage and fortitude. He demanded that the military fulfill its order to desegregate, announced but not enforced under Truman. He ended segregation in the nation's capital and included a smattering of blacks in appointments to subcabinet positions, sometimes with great symbolic significance. On August 16, 1954, Ernest Wilkins, an assistant secretary of labor, was filling in for the secretary and attended that day's cabinet meeting. It was the first time an African-American ever attended a meeting of a president's cabinet.

History has tended to judge Eisenhower harshly in this area—perhaps too harshly. Ike's life before the presidency gave him no history of regarding blacks as equals: he did not go to school with black classmates; his peers in the military were white; he never reported to a black man or woman.

As Brownell recognized from their first conversation on the topic, Ike was uncomfortable leading in this area. He was a man at ease with force, subtle in its use, conscious of its power to deter. He was less sure-footed in matters of moral suasion. John Eisenhower, so often the shrewdest analyst of his father, said it best: "My dad was not a social reformer. He was a commander in chief."

Eisenhower's achievement in civil rights, then, is not that he was moved by its morality but that he overcame his own limitations. He gave Brownell wide latitude to press civil rights from the Justice Department and to pick judges and justices who would advance the movement and protect its advocates. And when, in the end, force was required, Ike used it. It is no accident that his greatest personal contribution to the movement came in response to defiance. Then, his options exhausted, Eisenhower became the first president since Lincoln to dispatch American troops to quell rebellion in the South.

Some of the same—and some of the opposite—could be said for Eisenhower's role in toppling Mossadegh. There, Ike moved boldly. But, as with his nomination of Warren, the consequences of American action in Iran were only vaguely imaginable in 1953. In one sense, the coup was alarmingly easy to execute, despite a fundamental error in the intelligence that produced it. One common thread throughout the CIA report, Roosevelt's firsthand account, the original documents of the era, and Eisenhower's later reflection is the unswerving conviction that Mossadegh was moving the nation into the Communist orbit and that he would have delivered it to the Soviet Union—either by design or by inadvertence—had the United States not intervened. The evidence for that premise remains shaky at best.

Moreover, success in Iran sweetened Eisenhower's taste for covert action, with complex consequences. In Iran—and later, Guatemala, Indonesia, and the Congo, among other places—covert action offered a way to check Communism while avoiding a frontal confrontation with the Soviets or Chinese. In Cold War terms, that could seem prudent as it checked a menace without resort to ultimate force. But it substituted one version of colonialism with another, more subtle variant, relying as it did on the notion the U.S. reserved the right to chart the courses of smaller nations. The resulting resentments haunt international relations even today.

What was true and apparent at the time, however, was that Mossadegh was careering toward a calamity with no sure sense of direction or purpose. It was the United States—at Eisenhower's specific instruction—that pushed him over the precipice, but his escalating conflict with the Shah could just as easily have presented the Soviet Union with its pretext for invasion or coup. The long-view consequences of the CIA's work in Iran have been profound and unsettling: in the crowds that swirled through Tehran that summer was a cleric by the name of Ruhollah Khomeini, then fifty years old, whose enmity toward the United States ripened during the Shah's long reign. Viewed through our contemporary prism, then, the insult to the Iranian people and their faith inflicted by American intelligence agents in 1953 seems a deep and costly one. But so, too, could the alternatives have shadowed the twentieth and twenty-first centuries, if the Soviet Union controlled Iran and the Persian Gulf through the heart of the Cold War. Instead, Iran lay safely nestled within the American orbit for the balance of Eisenhower's tenure, indeed, for the rest of his life. When Ike finished *Mandate for Change* in 1963, he was able to write, with evident satisfaction, of Mossadegh's surrender—"in pajamas," Eisenhower added, vindictively—and to conclude that the coup's success was self-evident: "For the first time in three years, Iran was quiet—and still free."

Security

F   ew events in politics are genuinely inevitable. Too much rides on the
    decisions of calculating men and women. Sloppy thinking and writ-
    ers postulating the inevitable in retrospect merely prove the power
of cliché rather than destiny. Certainly, the break between President Eisenhower and Senator McCarthy was hardly inevitable; to the contrary, it was
eminently avoidable. They shared, after all, two common foes: President
Truman and the threat of domestic subversion. Eisenhower was disgusted
by McCarthy's methods, but he never doubted that there were Communists working in the United States and that party members and their allies
were actively trying to undermine American security.

Joe McCarthy could have given Ike a wide berth, could have cooled his
zeal once Truman left office. But he so enjoyed the limelight that he was
unwilling to drop the one cause that had brought him national attention.
And Ike found McCarthy, in the end, impossible to ignore. So they collided,
and the ramifications of that collision reverberated long and loud.

General Eisenhower and Tail-Gunner Joe had sparred during the 1952
campaign, when McCarthy's supporters baited Ike into his worst blunder
of that season, his refusal to give Marshall the full support he deserved.
Eisenhower later insisted that he had not "capitulated" to McCarthy, but he
knew he had let his mentor down. "If I could have foreseen this distortion
of the facts, a distortion that even led some to question my loyalty to General Marshall, I would never have acceded to the staff's arguments, logical
as they sounded at the time," he wrote. That was defensive. The error was
his, and he knew it.

By the time of Ike's election, McCarthy was well along on his rampage. After his broad assertions of Soviet spies at work in the U.S. government, he needed to produce names. First, he coyly announced that he had the identity of the "top Russian espionage agent in the United States" but declined to reveal it. Then he disclosed it to senators in a closed meeting and held an off-the-record meeting with reporters where he also divulged it, but since he refused to be quoted, the alleged agent's identity became the source of fiery rumor. McCarthy's unlikely target, as it was eventually revealed, was Owen Lattimore, a mild Asia specialist traveling in Afghanistan. Told of the accusations against him, Lattimore cabled back that the senator's "rantings [were] pure moonshine." He finished up his UN work in Kabul and headed home.

McCarthy had opened with explosive charges, delivered behind the safe veil of leaked remarks or congressional immunity. Now confronted with Lattimore himself, McCarthy retreated to safer ground, downgrading his attack to suggest that Lattimore was merely a "bad policy risk." He pooh-poohed his own earlier assessment by saying he had perhaps "placed too much stress on the question of whether or not he has been an espionage agent." Lattimore thus confronted shifting allegations, and unlike those who would follow him, he had no example of how to respond. With the help of his brilliant counsel, Abe Fortas, Lattimore elected to take on McCarthy directly. He testified in an open Senate session and blisteringly condemned the campaign against him. He even wrote a book about the experience while it was still under way. *Ordeal by Slander* was a thorough, steadfast, and principled defense of an individual against an unprincipled government adversary.

"We are in one of those national crises in which the fundamental cause of liberty will either be seriously impaired or renewed and strengthened, depending on what we do," Lattimore argued and warned. "To break the grip of fear we must revive both the letter and the spirit of the Bill of Rights."

McCarthy was unmoved. The FBI had compiled a flimsy collection of innuendo and suspicion. Lattimore was said to have denigrated Chiang Kai-shek in 1948, to have employed a Chinese economist who was "without a doubt a member of the Communist Party," and to have spoken to groups of a "questionable nature." The bureau's files did include one more troubling, if uncorroborated, allegation: a confidential informant told agents on December 14, 1948, that the head of Soviet military intelligence named Lattimore as a Soviet operative, one of two working in Asia. Other informants questioned that information, but it supplied grist for McCarthy.

The senator cherry-picked the FBI report and pressed forward, punishing Lattimore for his defiance. Lattimore fought off one inquiry after another and was charged with perjury. Ultimately, he was exonerated, but only after many years and much pillory. In the meantime, McCarthy was emboldened. Having tasted fame, he was unwilling to cease, notwithstanding the election of a Republican president.

His first overtures were tentative, as Eisenhower and McCarthy measured each other. Ike congratulated McCarthy on his Senate victory and referred cautiously to the nation's vote of confidence in "our crusade." Before Inauguration Day, McCarthy warned John Foster Dulles that his committee intended to investigate the State Department's filing system. Dulles welcomed the notice and the investigation, saying he "wanted all the help he could get."

Encouraged, McCarthy ventured a bit further. He conveyed through a close friend, the crusading journalist George Sokolsky, that he intended to press the case against the Voice of America, supposedly a safe haven for Communist infiltrators. Again, the message was delivered gently: Sokolsky was an old friend of Dulles's, having counseled him during Dulles's brief Senate tenure. Moreover, the new secretary of state was an icon of American anti-Communism, convinced that Communist infiltration in government posed a genuine threat to national security. Though he declined, for instance, to cast aspersions on the loyalty of American socialists, he refused to employ them in State Department policy-making positions.

Those initial parries, however, were followed by something far more ominous. McCarthy wheeled against Charles E. Bohlen, the administration's nominee to serve as American ambassador to the Soviet Union. There were warning signs from the beginning that his nomination would run into trouble. Bohlen had served as a translator at Yalta, long a bane of anti-Communist conservatives who accused FDR of betraying Western interests to Stalin in the 1945 talks. Though Bohlen was a peripheral actor in those negotiations, his mere presence made him vulnerable, as Lattimore's experience demonstrated. Eisenhower recognized that Bohlen's Yalta connection could create controversy, but he worked to head it off, securing Senator Robert Taft's promise to support the nomination by insisting that if Republicans defied their party's leader on a matter this public and this early, "it would be a serious blow to the President's prestige," as Adams put it. The warning deterred Taft, but not McCarthy.

Ike submitted the nomination and soon realized there would be trouble. On March 13, Sherman Adams warned John Foster Dulles that "perhaps we are on very shaky grounds." Publicly, the debate swirled around Bohlen's unwillingness to denounce Yalta as a failure. Privately, however, the controversy centered on other matters. Adams warned Dulles that "moral charges" had been brought against the would-be ambassador. Although Adams dismissed those as "unsubstantiated and speculative," they were rattling for the new administration. If anything, however, they steeled Eisenhower's resolve. Discussing Bohlen with Dulles a few days later, Eisenhower described the allegations as "incredible" and observed that Bohlen "has a normal family life." Ike insisted he had "not the slightest intention of withdrawing" his candidate's name.

As the matter came to a head, it was jolted by a careless remark from one of the administration's most conservative operatives. Scott McLeod, hired as the State Department's security officer to appease McCarthy, told McCarthy, through an intermediary, that he had not cleared Bohlen's nomination because of information contained in the FBI's background check. That implied that Bohlen's loyalty was under examination when, as McCarthy and McLeod both well knew, it was not. As Ike contemplated firing McLeod, Dulles publicly vouched for Bohlen, and McCarthy demanded that Dulles testify under oath while insisting that Bohlen was "part of the Acheson betrayal team . . . a very willing and enthusiastic part and parcel of the Acheson-Vincent-Lattimore-Service clique." Eisenhower fumed right through the final vote, in which Bohlen was confirmed despite the defections of eleven Republican senators. He went on to serve with distinction.

The incident highlighted the full danger of McCarthy and his methods. Innuendo offered under the protection of congressional immunity delivered McCarthy headlines and political opportunity while insulating him from either legal or political retaliation. Since attention was what McCarthy most craved, Ike decided to deny the senator that which he wanted. Eisenhower's approach, then, would be to shun McCarthy. On March 27, Eisenhower told his cabinet that he would refuse to "attack an individual." A few days later, he confided to his diary: "Senator McCarthy is . . . so anxious for the headlines that he is prepared to go to any extremes in order to secure some mention of his name in the public press . . . I really believe that nothing will be so effective in combating his particular kind of troublemaking as to ignore him. This he cannot stand." Ike complained to Leonard Hall, chairman of the Republican National Committee, that McCarthy was "a pimple on the path of progress." The following day, Eisenhower said of McCarthy's methods: "I despise them." Still, he added, "I am quite sure that the people who want me to stand up and publicly label McCarthy with derogatory titles are the most mistaken people that are dealing with this whole problem." To a sympathetic newspaper editor, he confidentially described McCarthy as a source of "embarrassment for the administration." Through much of 1953 and 1954, Eisenhower was counseled to take on McCarthy directly. He steadfastly refused.

There was one moment in 1953 when it appeared that Eisenhower might be preparing to change his approach. That spring, two of McCarthy's aides, Roy Cohn (one of the Rosenberg prosecutors) and David Schine, made a highly publicized tour of European embassy libraries, ferreting out works by Communists, fellow travelers, or otherwise suspect liberals. They returned with a list of 418 such disreputable scholars as John Dewey and Foster Rhea Dulles (John Foster Dulles's cousin), whose books shamed the shelves of American institutions abroad. Some of them were burned. Works by Jean-Paul Sartre and Langston Hughes, among many others, were stripped from the shelves of American libraries abroad. Amid international uproar, Eisenhower's friends again demanded that he intercede and confront McCarthy.

At the height of the controversy, Eisenhower delivered the commencement address at Dartmouth College. He was accompanied that afternoon by John McCloy, one of those infuriated by McCarthy's attack on books, and Judge Joseph M. Proskauer, a leading liberal jurist and partner in one of New York's preeminent law firms. The three men sat together on the dais before Ike began to speak, and Proskauer remarked that he was upset by reports of American libraries in Germany getting rid of books. At first, Eisenhower laughed, saying it could not be true since McCloy had personally informed him that the libraries carried books critical of him. Proskauer then asked McCloy whether some books were being dropped because of their authors' politics. McCloy acknowledged that it was true, and the judge then confronted Ike: "Mr. President, I think you are wrong about that." Books were in fact being removed, and the State Department was behind it. Ike listened quietly, and Proskauer concluded with a suggestion: "Mr. President, if you have anything to say about book burning, there is no better time than now and no better place than the campus of Dartmouth College."

Eisenhower's remarks were scripted. He urged the graduates to find meaningful joy in life, to pursue that joy with courage and conviction, to challenge prejudice and injustice as matters of patriotism. Near the end of his speech, however, Eisenhower departed from his text. "Don't join the book burners," he urged. "Don't think you are going to conceal faults by concealing evidence that they ever existed. Don't be afraid to go in your library and read every book as long as any document does not offend your sense of decency. That should be the only censorship."

Ike returned to his seat. Proskauer congratulated him: "You have double thanks for what you said, from Mr. McCloy and me."

Those who had urged Eisenhower to challenge McCarthy were thrilled. The *New York Herald Tribune*, Eisenhower's favorite paper, hailed the gesture that could "rally the nation to a defense of the right to know." The *New York Times* welcomed the president's "faith in the inquiring and open mind." The *St. Louis Post-Dispatch* characterized the speech as "the finest expression on the spirit and practice of Americanism to come from Dwight D. Eisenhower, not only since he entered the White House, but since he entered public life."

But no sooner had the president uttered those remarks than he began to back away from their implications. He publicly insisted he was still unwilling to tangle with McCarthy—to dwell on "personalities," as he put it. He assured Dulles that his comments had been directed not at the State Department "but to the general proposition of freedom of thought." Even while he denounced book burning, Ike recognized that federal money should not be used to "buy or handle books which were persuasive of Communism." The direct confrontation hoped for by so many was once again avoided. McCarthy's critics worried that Ike had lost his nerve.

Fencing with McCarthy over book burning was tedious business and distracted from the Cold War moment of genuine consequence during those same months. On March 5, 1953, Joseph Stalin, after a lifetime of high blood pressure and weeks of deteriorating health, at last relinquished his hold on life and cruel dominion over his nation. Stalin's death was among the most anticipated moments of mid-century American foreign policy. Nevertheless, it caught U.S. diplomats and intelligence officers flat-footed. Allen Dulles told Ike that Stalin was on his deathbed just after 6:00 a.m. on March 4 (Washington time), and Eisenhower summoned Dulles, C. D. Jackson, and James Hagerty to discuss a public statement. It was, they recognized, a moment of profound but uncertain possibility. They labored over the draft, then presented it to the members of the National Security Council.

The meeting opened at 10:30 a.m. Eisenhower explained that he saw this as a "propitious" moment "for introducing the right word into the Soviet Union," an opportunity, more psychological than diplomatic, to speak directly to the Soviet people. George Humphrey seconded the text as written, but Charlie Wilson then worried about the Soviet government's reaction; Dulles reserved comment on the statement but warned that these were treacherous waters. "It was certainly a gamble" to suggest that the Soviet people should contest their leadership in a time of mourning, Dulles cautioned.

They argued for nearly half an hour, but Eisenhower would not be talked out of saying something. The full council edited the statement a line at a time, issuing it just before the Soviet embassy notified the press. Official word of Stalin's death had yet to be released, so Ike's comments were crafted as a message of sympathy to Soviet citizens worried over Stalin's health. "The thoughts of America," the statement noted, "go out to all the peoples of the U.S.S.R." Ike's words, sent to a land of official atheism, dwelled on the common faiths of people split by ideology and statecraft:

> They [the Russian people] are the children of the same God who is the Father of all peoples everywhere. And like all peoples, Russia's millions share our longing for a friendly and peaceful world. Regardless of the identity of government personalities, the prayer of us Americans continues to be that the Almighty will watch over the people of that vast country and bring them, in His wisdom, opportunity to live their lives in a world where all men and women and children dwell in peace and comradeship.

The statement confirmed that the Eisenhower White House could work quickly and eloquently (the phrase "us Americans" notwithstanding) and that it could appeal to a common humanity. And yet Eisenhower was astonished to discover that there was no plan for responding to Stalin's death. "Ever since 1946 . . . all the so-called experts have been yapping about what would happen when Stalin dies," he fumed to the cabinet later that week. "Well, he's dead . . . We have no plan. We are not even sure what difference his death makes."

The NSC directed the CIA to assess the Soviet situation. On March 31, the agency returned with its findings: "We have no reliable inside intelligence on thinking in the Kremlin. Our estimates of Soviet long range plans and intentions are speculations drawn from inadequate evidence." The Cold War had entered a much-anticipated new phase, but the administration had no idea what it meant.

Those who hoped for diminished tension were to be disappointed. Soviet belligerence and jockeying for advantage continued without interruption. In August, the Soviets announced that they had exploded a hydrogen bomb. Although the weapon was a hybrid, combining elements of a fission and a fusion bomb, it nevertheless convincingly established that the post-Stalin Soviet Union remained bent on escalating the Cold War. More threatening, the Soviet tests revealed that it not only had a fusion weapon but could deliver it as a bomb; American cities, once protected behind the nation's nuclear hegemony, were now at risk. The steadiness of Soviet intentions was hardly a surprise to Eisenhower or Dulles—neither was under any illusion about Soviet aspirations—but it forced a bracing debate within the administration: Should the United States act while it still held the preponderance of power? The Soviet advances made it clear that America's advantage was diminishing, but to wage a preemptive nuclear war was a staggering option.

It was Eisenhower himself who posed the question many feared to raise. Addressing the NSC, he said that it looked to him "as though the hour of decision were at hand," the keeper of the minutes recorded. "We should presently have to really face the question of whether or not we would have to throw everything at once against the enemy." Eisenhower had long pondered this foreboding question—a scrap of notepaper jotted in July hinted at it: "Global war as a defense of freedom—almost contradiction in terms." Today, Eisenhower's message was dark and somber. He was raising "this terrible question" because ignorance and denial were no strategy at all. It was important to face the world as it was, "to determine our own course of action in the light of this capability."

The NSC did not act that day, did not recommend the war of devastation that Ike posed for consideration, did not leap at the chance to destroy an enemy before it was too strong to fight back. But rarely in the years since Einstein's haunting 1950 warning of the imminent threat of "general annihilation" had that threat ever beckoned quite so forcefully. Eisenhower faced it squarely and demanded that his aides do so as well. Having grasped the twin dangers of Communist advance and nuclear war, Eisenhower settled on a sophisticated strategy of containment, arms control, economic growth, covert action, and perseverance—always with annihilation at the door. The application of that strategy varied from flash point to flash point, but its core principles remained sturdy and largely unchanged. That September morning, Ike firmly asserted that the nation was charged "not only in saving our money or defending our persons from attack; we were engaged in the defense of a way of life, and the great danger was that in defending this way of life, we would find ourselves resorting to methods that endangered this way of life." That was the paradox of the Cold War. Ike never shrank from it.

Faced with those grave and complex problems, Ike in the summer of 1953 convened an extraordinary group of advisers to give shape to his security policy. Known as Project Solarium because it was hatched in the White House's Solarium Room, the group was divided into three advisory panels to assess Truman's national security policy and to make recommendations for confronting the threat of Communism around the world. Three esteemed experts—the Sovietologist George Kennan, a leading architect of Truman's containment policy, Vice Admiral Richard Conolly, and Major General James McCormack—were tapped to head panels consisting of ten members. Each of the groups was assigned to a different aspect of defense and diplomatic strategy. Once picked, the teams spent sixteen weeks honing recommendations in the basement of the National War College. Certain conclusions were consistent: all three groups viewed the Soviet Union as an obdurate enemy (though one worth negotiating with) and suggested a blend of conventional and nuclear weapons to deter Soviet aggression. Where they diverged was in assessing the immediacy of the threat and in proposing ways to check it. Task Force A argued for a continuation of Truman's containment policy. Task Force B relied heavily on America's nuclear deterrent. And Task Force C, whose records were sealed for decades, suggested a more aggressive course for rolling back Communist advances. "Time has been working against us," Task Force C concluded. "The only way to end the cold war is to win it."

The members of the panel proposed a relentless and multifaceted challenge to the Soviet Union and China. Nuclear weapons were to deter attack and to be put in the hands of field commanders so they could retaliate if attacked. Negotiations were desirable but chiefly to achieve strategic advantage. The United States would negotiate to diminish tensions and keep the Soviets in check. American nuclear weapons would deter the spread of Communism. Covert action would push it back. "A national program of deception and concealment" would cloak covert actions intended to roll back Communist influence. Allies were to be trusted, but only to a point: "They would undoubtedly oppose such an aggressive policy. Therefore, the full scope of the plan would be revealed to them only gradually as successes were won." Adoption of Task Force C's recommendations, the panel argued, represented not only a robust reply to Soviet Communism but the embarkment on "a true American Crusade."

Ike received all three reports on July 16, 1953. He listened intently and then summarized the work with precision. Kennan, for one, was dazzled by Eisenhower's synthesis of the information. Although frustrated that the groups could not agree on a single plan, Eisenhower forged ahead, asking the NSC to meld the key elements of each into a new security strategy. The result, known internally as NSC 162 and externally as Eisenhower's

New Look, refocused America's Cold War efforts, recalibrating Truman's hurried defense buildup and containment policy to deal with the long, persistent struggle that Eisenhower foresaw. It relied on three principles: the United States would not bankrupt itself to finance its military; America would save money without sacrifice to security by reducing military manpower and relying instead on the threat of nuclear weapons; and America would seek not only to contain Communism but to roll it back with the full panoply of tactical devices, from propaganda to covert action.

New Look had critics from the start. Chief among them were influential members of the military, who understood the implications of force reductions and who fought against New Look to the final hours of Ike's presidency. But the new strategy achieved balance, an overriding Eisenhower imperative.

Critics aside, New Look was now American policy. Eisenhower was satisfied that he had located a middle way on national security. His new approach rejected undisciplined defense spending as well as dangerous defense cuts. It recognized that the Cold War could only be won over time. It was a struggle of attrition and of competitive advantage. It did not aim for victory in a traditional sense, but rather required patient managing of conflict. It meant that America could not, at least in the foreseeable future, live in a genuine state of peace. New Look thus expressed essential aspects of Ike's leadership—compromise, patience, and conviction that time was on America's side.

Having embraced a broad approach to rebuffing Communism, Eisenhower committed to lessening tensions where he could, part of a delicate calculus in which the Soviets were the enemy, to be checked by nuclear weapons, but also in which nuclear weapons were an enemy in their own right, their threat to be limited by negotiations with the Soviets. Peace and victory coexisted in that equation, though neither could be attained at the expense of the other. Instead, peace was to be maintained until victory could be achieved through covert action and nuclear deterrence. Executing New Look would require exquisite subtlety and control.

As he developed this extraordinary strategy, Eisenhower knew he needed the support of the American people, even though much of his program demanded secrecy and subversion. So he shared what he could, sought advantage against his enemy, and tried to find a way toward peace.

Those competing and reinforcing impulses expressed themselves in three speeches during his first year in office. His inaugural address launched his presidency, of course, and established both its tone and its aspiration. The third address was delivered in December before the United Nations. And in between, soon after Stalin's death, Ike presented the American people with a stirring examination of the arms race and its implications.

The occasion was an April address to the American Society of Newspaper Editors. It was one of his first major speeches as president, and he prepared diligently. Two weeks after Stalin's death, he asked the speechwriter Emmet Hughes what the United States could constructively propose to reduce the danger of war. Hughes recalled that Eisenhower spoke "with the air of a man whose thoughts, after a permissive spell of meandering, were fast veering toward a conclusion." Pacing around his office, Ike abruptly turned to face Hughes: "Here is what I would like to say. The jet plane that roars over your head costs three-quarters of a million dollars. That is more money than a man earning ten thousand dollars a year is going to make in his lifetime. What world can afford this sort of thing for long?" Eisenhower continued that afternoon, sketching the vision and language of an address that would establish one of the moral underpinnings of his years in office—the commitment to peace through negotiation, his vision of engaging the Soviets in the common quest for coexistence while simultaneously seeking competitive advantage and ultimate victory.

Over the next few days, Eisenhower and Hughes circulated their draft among Ike's leading advisers and America's most important allies. Dulles was skeptical, worried about any proposed engagement with the Soviets; Churchill applauded the "grave and formidable" tone of the address but expressed a concern precisely opposite that of the secretary of state: he spied new hope for collaboration with the Soviet leadership and was nervous that the speech might be considered a challenge at a time when conciliation was more desirable. Milton Eisenhower weighed in, too: he proposed striking the language that might threaten the Soviet leadership and focusing instead on America's intentions. Grueling debates tested Hughes's patience and eventually Ike's as well. Eisenhower gruffly dismissed Dulles's objections: "I know how he feels, but sometimes Foster is just too worried about being accused of sounding like Truman and Acheson." He directed Hughes to complete the draft as they envisioned it.

Then, just before he was scheduled to deliver the speech, Ike fell ill. Interrupting a golf vacation in Augusta, Georgia, the president arrived at the White House at 11:00 a.m. and then departed for the Statler Hotel just after noon. He was suddenly overcome by abdominal pains—a resurgence of the ailment that had long haunted him—and as he approached the lectern, he was shaking and perspiring, beads of sweat visible on his forehead. "Those sitting close to him could see . . . that something was wrong," one journalist wrote later.

Gamely, Eisenhower began: "Today the hope of free men remains stubborn and brave, but it is sternly disciplined by experience. It shuns not only all crude counsel of despair but also the self-deceit of easy illusion." Those dualities—hope disciplined by experience, despair checked by illusion—framed the core of the address. But when it came to the Soviets, Eisenhower was singularly direct. In 1945, when Western Allies and Soviet troops met on the plains of Europe, hope had flickered. Now it was nearly extinguished. "This," he noted, "has been the way of life forged by eight years of fear and force." Continued passage along this road, "this dread road," led to awful alternatives, to atomic war or to "a life of perpetual fear and tension; a burden of arms draining the wealth and the labor of all peoples."

Eisenhower then moved to the imagery that thankfully survived the tinkering of others:

Every gun that is made, every warship launched, every rocket fired signifies, in the final sense, a theft from those who hunger and are not fed, those who are cold and are not clothed.

This world in arms is not spending money alone. It is spending the sweat of its laborers, the genius of its scientists, the hopes of its children. The cost of one modern heavy bomber is this: a modern brick school in more than 30 cities. It is two electric power plants, each serving a town of 60,000 population. It is two fine, fully equipped hospitals.

It is some 50 miles of concrete highway. We pay for a single fighter plane with a half million bushels of wheat. We pay for a single destroyer with new homes that could have housed more than 8,000 people.

There was the cost of the Cold War, in all its draining and dispiriting reality. And that was, as Ike emphasized, the best to be hoped for: "This is not a way of life at all, in any true sense. Under the cloud of threatening war, it is humanity hanging from a cross of iron."

Eisenhower proposed an alternative. He urged the Soviets to make a gesture of "sincere intent," to sign a treaty preserving the future of Austria, say, or to release prisoners still in its custody from World War II, or to conclude a lasting armistice in Korea and cease hostilities in Indochina and Malaysia. Concessions in those areas would allow the United States to negotiate limits on military forces and production of atomic weapons enforced by international inspections. Eisenhower invited the Soviet leadership to join America in a "new kind of war . . . [a] total war, not upon any human enemy but upon the brute forces of poverty and need." He was prepared to meet the Soviets in negotiation, but the Soviet leadership needed to demonstrate its sincerity as well. "I know of only one question upon which progress waits," Eisenhower said near the end of his speech. "It is this: What is the Soviet Union ready to do?"

Ike spoke for twenty-seven minutes, interrupted five times by applause when he expressed Western resolve or condemnation over specific Soviet provocations. He finished still in pain. It was, the journalist Marquis Childs recalled, "a remarkable effort of will."

In the years after Eisenhower concluded his presidency, generations of Americans would ponder the meaning of his Farewell Address, with its solemn warning of the "military-industrial complex." Some professed surprise that a great general would sound such alarm in the final days of his presidency. But that theme was there throughout, discernible to anyone who wished to listen.

Sadly, the Soviet leadership was among those who failed to fully grasp the import of Eisenhower's speech that April. In answer to his question of what they were prepared to do, the honest reply was very little. *Pravda* dismissed his proposals as so general that they "cannot in the least contribute to the urgent task of reducing armaments." Eisenhower had offered a chance for peace; the Soviets elected not to grasp it. He would try again.

If Eisenhower's April address marked the public opening of the strategy he would develop through Project Solarium and the National Security Council during 1953, the culminating speech came near the year's close and reflected even greater deliberation and nuance. Hatched in the spring as Operation Candor, Eisenhower's address grew out of varied impulses: a desire to be candid, up to a point, with the American people about the threat of nuclear war and his desire to engage the Soviet Union in serious negotiations to avoid it. Failing that, he wished to demonstrate American magnanimity. Eisenhower's interest in those contradictory themes was sparked by Robert Oppenheimer, who in the late months of the Truman administration chaired a special panel on disarmament. The Oppenheimer panel's classified report, delivered to Eisenhower in February 1953, observed that nuclear weapons had become a menace in and of themselves. As a result, America's two chief foreign policy objectives—the containment of Soviet Communism and the "defense of the free world"—now were joined by a third: avoidance of nuclear war. To respond to that evolving threat to civilization, the panel's first recommendation was to adopt a new policy of openness, of disclosing to the American people the risks and costs of deterring Soviet adventurism by atomic threat. Only with such candor, Oppenheimer and his colleagues argued, could the public comprehend the dangers ahead and the sacrifices necessary to avoid them. It was essential, the panel concluded, to encourage "wider public discussion based upon wider understanding of the meaning of a nuclear holocaust."

Eisenhower was impressed, but he adopted the recommendations selectively. He grasped the wisdom of alerting the American people in straightforward terms to the threat of nuclear war and understood that cultivating a measure of alarm—somewhere short of panic—would encourage support for spending on weapons he viewed as essential to maintaining peace. Eisenhower, however, never seriously entertained the report's more dramatic recommendations: that the United States should, for instance, make public "the rate and impact of atomic production." His strategy implicitly rejected the group's hope for reduced reliance on nuclear weapons. But he directed C. D. Jackson to work on a speech that would alert Americans to the danger and propose new, peaceful applications of nuclear technology.

From the start, the speech and the ideas it presented encountered stiff opposition within the administration. Dulles was wary, and Charlie Wilson warned that the fear of war would undermine the deterrent value of U.S. nuclear forces. As with previous doubters, Ike shrugged and pushed the project forward.

Jackson labored over scores of drafts. Officials weighed in, Ike mulled new ideas. By September, a clearly tiring Jackson confided to his diary that he believed the speech was "slowly dying from a severe attack of Committeeitis." Admiral Lewis Strauss, Oppenheimer's nemesis, became increasingly engaged in the project while falsely denying to Jackson that he and Oppenheimer were at odds. Strauss and Jackson labored over drafts in a series of breakfast meetings—Strauss privately regarded the entire effort as "foolish" even as Jackson viewed him as an ally—and whimsically rechristened the project from Operation Candor to Operation Wheaties. Candor, always a hedged ambition of the address, slipped now even from its code name.

Nevertheless, Jackson persisted, with Ike's encouragement. And despite several close calls, including a November 17 meeting at which John Foster Dulles vigorously denounced the entire undertaking, Wheaties took shape, with the speech now aimed at delivery before the United Nations, where Eisenhower was scheduled to speak in early December. After a tumultuous Thanksgiving weekend punctuated by an obnoxious McCarthy speech—the senator accused the Eisenhower administration of protecting John Paton Davies, a well-regarded American diplomat and "China

Hand" whom McCarthy falsely alleged was a Communist—the senator
now accused his government of permitting "twenty-one years of treason."
The internal debate crested on November 30, when skeptics mounted their
last furious objections. Charlie Wilson suggested simply doing nothing
and trusting that rising levels of Soviet education would eventually doom
that country's leadership ("an educated youth would overthrow the Soviets," he said), John Foster Dulles struck a neutral pose, and others offered
substitute ideas. As the session concluded, Eisenhower promised to reread
the address that night. Ike admired and appreciated his deputies, but he
refused to let their doubts deter him. When he returned the following
morning, it was with an edited, improved draft and a renewed commitment to deliver it.

There were more setbacks in the coming days. Eisenhower traveled to
Bermuda during the first week of December to meet with Churchill and
the French prime minister, Joseph Laniel, for a largely ceremonial meeting,
and Churchill took it upon himself to make suggestions. The drafting
came down to the final moments before Eisenhower's scheduled appearance at the UN. In fact, as Ike and his top aides flew from Bermuda to New
York, Jackson rushed last-minute suggestions to Eisenhower and Dulles,
who inserted the editorial changes and handed them back to Jackson. Ann
Whitman typed furiously, and other aides threw pages on a mimeograph
machine. Jackson's diary captures the intensity of the final push: "President
changed clothes, re-read Jumbo copy, underscored for emphasis, and as
wheels touched La Guardia, everything done. But not one minute before."

Eisenhower was whisked to the UN General Assembly. Although the
speech was far from what Oppenheimer and his colleagues initially imagined, it contained traces of the original commitment to candor. Eisenhower recited the history of atomic testing and development—forty-two
atomic tests since the end of World War II and the development of vastly
more powerful and versatile weapons with staggering destructive capacity: "A single air group, whether afloat or land-based, can now deliver to
any reachable target a destructive cargo exceeding in power all the bombs
that fell on Britain in all of World War II." The secret of such weapons—
"the dread secret," as Eisenhower called it—was possessed by the United
States, Britain, Canada, and the Soviet Union, meaning that the American
monopoly on atomic weaponry was long over. Those bracing acknowledg-
ments were followed by one additional fact "at least dimly" recognized
by the nations of the free world: there was no safety from such weapons.
"Even against the most powerful defense, an aggressor in possession of the
effective minimum number of atomic bombs for a surprise attack could

probably place a sufficient number of his bombs on the chosen targets to cause hideous damage."

The sober passages were delivered in Ike's familiar tone, inflected with his occasionally amusing diction: he palpably worked to pronounce the name of the secretary-general, "Hammarskjöld," fairly spat out his denunciation of "pious platitudes," growled over the phrase "hideous damage." Presenting those warnings candidly to the world fulfilled part of his mission. But Eisenhower was determined to do more than warn of catastrophe. "I do not wish to rest either upon the reiteration of past proposals or the restatement of past deeds," he said. "The gravity of the time is such that every new avenue of peace, no matter how dimly discernible, should be explored." And so Eisenhower presented his proposal. The nuclear nations, he suggested, should each make contributions of uranium and fissionable material to a UN agency, which would then apply that material to problems of "agriculture, medicine and other peaceful activities." The argument for such a sharing of material was twofold: it would apply the fruits of development to peaceful purposes, and it would shrink the global supply of fissionable material available for destruction. It was a genuinely new idea in the still-nascent politics of the Cold War, through which Eisenhower was improvising a fragile peace. Moreover, it reflected Ike's delicate triangulation of the conflict's forces: American defense, Soviet containment, and the threat of nuclear war.

There is no way to know how the world might have changed had the Soviet Union joined in Eisenhower's proposal, whether common cause in peaceful development of the atom might have dimmed mutual suspicions of the era's great adversaries. All that is knowable is that those suspicions ran too deep in 1953 for the Soviet Union to see the potential of what became known as "Atoms for Peace." And yet while one path toward peace was blocked, another opened. Though the central proposal of the speech never materialized, the attempt itself helped establish that Eisenhower would search for ways to lessen tension and signaled that there was a difference between the Cold War leaders in Washington and their brutish counterparts in Moscow. "Atoms for Peace" did not lead directly to peace, but it indirectly contributed to victory.

The speech capped an extraordinarily eventful year in the life of America and its new president. In his first twelve months, Eisenhower ended the Korean War, overthrew the government of Mohammed Mossadegh, appointed Earl Warren as chief justice of the United States, fought Senator Joe McCarthy, reimagined America's national security and defense posture, and laid out markers for future relations with the Soviet Union. At times, the administration's actions could seem inconsistent: Ike spoke passionately about the immorality of nations tampering in the affairs of others, only to authorize Kermit Roosevelt to topple Iran's prime minister; he summoned great eloquence on the common lot of all peoples and yet could be hamstrung in addressing inequality in his own country. Eisenhower and his advisers—his cabinet, his brothers, his "Gang" of bridge and golfing friends—believed America was a force of moral leadership in the world and that its strength was indispensable to the cause of freedom. He was occasionally wrong in the application of those principles, but he was consistently right about the ideals themselves.

Ike governed in those months determined to project calm. In private, he could be grumpy and short-tempered. But he marshaled his public persona—the optimism that he had appreciated in Marshall and Churchill—to deliberate effect. Worried that Washington's crisis addiction deprived Americans of their right to tranquil lives, Ike conspicuously vacationed, intentionally was photographed at ease. He believed in the opportunity that freedom afforded Americans to choose lives of fulfillment, and he led by quiet example.

His nation, however, was restless. Civil rights stirred in the South, Hugh Hefner launched *Playboy* magazine in December with Marilyn Monroe on its cover. The feminist revolution was nascent, sexual freedom rising, vindictive politics heightened by McCarthy.

In fact, even as Eisenhower rounded out 1953, he was in for one more brutal surprise. Having spent much time fending off McCarthy's charges of Communist infiltration of government and many months building "Atoms for Peace," Eisenhower received shocking news about Oppenheimer. On the night of December 2, he called Charlie Wilson to discuss ways to reduce American armed forces. As they were talking, Wilson asked whether the president had seen a new FBI report on Oppenheimer (in fact, the document was a letter sent to the bureau, not a report by it). Ike had not yet received it, so he asked Wilson what it contained. The material, Wilson said, included "very grave" allegations against the scientist. In addition to old charges that Oppenheimer's wife and brother were former Communist Party members, there were new suspicions about Oppenheimer himself. "Some of his accusers," Eisenhower wrote in his diary, "seem to go so far as to accuse him of having been an actual agent of the Communists."

The implications of Oppenheimer spying for the Soviet Union were mind-boggling. Over the past decade, no man had greater access to America's most delicate national security secrets. He had overseen construction of the most secretive and important undertaking of the war and knew more about the atom bomb and the science behind it than Ike himself. If Oppenheimer was a spy—had been a spy through the war—no American nuclear secret was safe, and no damage he could do now, as a mere government consultant, could compare to that which he had already done. "It would not be a case of merely locking the stable door after the horse is gone," Eisenhower wrote in his diary. "It would be more like trying to find a door for a burned-down stable."

Eisenhower was under no illusion about the threat posed by these allegations. For months, McCarthy had been pounding about the presence of Communists in government, and the best he had been able to come up with was an obscure Asia specialist working on the margins of the State Department. This was an accusation of an entirely different order. If McCarthy seized the case before Eisenhower could act to contain it, Ike would join Truman as a dupe of Communist infiltration at the highest level of government. In fact, unbeknownst to Eisenhower, McCarthy had already caught wind of questions about Oppenheimer, but J. Edgar Hoover, again for reasons of which Ike was unaware, had succeeded in persuading McCarthy to tread lightly, at least for the moment.

At the same time, once the FBI "report" caught up with Eisenhower, he recognized that the case against Oppenheimer was far less damning than it first seemed. The information was not a new FBI analysis but rather a letter written to the bureau by William Liscum Borden, a thirty-three-year-old Democrat who had recently lost his post as executive director of the Joint Committee on Atomic Energy under the new Congress. He and Oppenheimer had charted sharply different views on the preeminent nuclear weapons issue of the day, whether or not the United States should build a hydrogen bomb. So fervently did Borden believe in the necessity for the weapon that he concluded that Oppenheimer's resistance signaled a larger disloyalty. Borden undertook his own investigation of Oppenheimer's history, and "based upon years of study of the available classified evidence," he determined that "more probably than not J. Robert Oppenheimer is an agent of the Soviet Union."

Borden's letter checked off a long list of reasons for suspecting Oppenheimer, but the majority had already been investigated when Oppenheimer was cleared for work at Los Alamos. Yes, his wife had been a party member, as had his brother and his onetime mistress; yes, he had supported Communist causes and affiliated with Communists before entering top secret service in construction of the bomb. By 1953, however, all those ties had been long broken. Borden's evidence of Communist involvement in the postwar period was fresher, but far weaker. Indeed, his entire litany of suspicious acts by Oppenheimer from 1946 on consisted of Oppenheimer's attempts to discourage development of the hydrogen bomb and other atomic projects. That Oppenheimer's objections to nuclear proliferation might have been professional and principled seems not to have occurred to Borden. Instead, Borden transformed policy disagreement into suspicion of treason.

What was hidden from Eisenhower, however, was the real reason that these issues were returning to the surface ten years after they had first been examined by the U.S. government. The truth was that Borden was not acting alone; his chief but silent collaborator was Eisenhower's friend whom he had recently appointed to head the Atomic Energy Commission, Lewis Strauss.

Owlish, combative, and piercingly intelligent, Strauss was the son of a shoe wholesaler who grew up in South Carolina. His plans to attend college were derailed, first by a bout with typhoid fever, and then by his family's need for him to help their business through a downturn. He was a gifted shoe salesman, and he helped restore the family business. That duty accomplished, Strauss chanced upon a report of Herbert Hoover's famine relief efforts in Belgium and offered his services to Hoover as his assistant. Thus began a long and contentious career in which Strauss oscillated between public and private service—his private years characterized by a genius for investment; his public service by a ferocious belief in the secret development of American nuclear weapons.

Oppenheimer consistently foiled that effort, particularly with his opposition to the development of the hydrogen bomb. Though Strauss prevailed when Truman gave approval to the weapon, the salesman remained convinced that the scientist was untrustworthy. Strauss had watched with horror as Oppenheimer's call for "candor" had initially found favor with Eisenhower. Strauss, denying all along that he was at odds with Oppenheimer, had tried to scuttle "Atoms for Peace" and had succeeded in dampening that aspect of the address.

Named by Ike to head the Atomic Energy Commission in May 1953, Strauss made classified material in the AEC's files available to Borden. Strauss also moved to head off any investigation by McCarthy—not to protect Oppenheimer, but rather to preserve his own line of attack. Strauss feared that if McCarthy attacked Oppenheimer, the senator's flamboyance would ruin the case and turn Oppenheimer into a martyr. Unwilling to risk that, Strauss took great pains, legal and illegal, to insure that he would be the one to destroy his adversary. At Strauss's request, the FBI bugged the office of Oppenheimer's lawyer and, later, his home in Princeton. Through those illegal wiretaps, Strauss monitored Oppenheimer's consultations with his lawyers and insisted on leaving the taps in place even when the FBI suggested removing them.

While Strauss hemmed in Oppenheimer, Ike's first concern was to contain any possible damage should the worst fears about the scientist be realized. Though skeptical of the charges—"they consist of nothing more than the receipt of a letter from a man named Borden," Ike recorded in his diary—Eisenhower was not inclined to entertain any risk of espionage under any circumstances. Less than twenty-four hours after receiving Wilson's warning, and now having read Borden's letter, Ike instructed Brownell "to place a blank wall between the subject of the communication and all areas of our government operations, whether in research projects of a sensitive nature or otherwise."

Although he did not know it yet, Oppenheimer was cut off. Over the next three weeks, Strauss prepared his response to the allegations he had helped to generate. Meeting with top White House officials on December 18, he proposed creating a special panel of the AEC to consider whether to renew Oppenheimer's security clearance. The group agreed and suggested that Oppenheimer be offered a choice: he could resign and avoid the hearing, or he could fight and risk public as well as private humiliation. Three days later, Strauss presented Oppenheimer with his options and demanded a swift answer. Oppenheimer agonized—"I can't believe this is happening to me," he muttered after his meeting with Strauss—but elected to fight. Having made that decision, he collapsed on the floor of his lawyer's bathroom. The hearing was set for 1954.

Ike was worn out, too. Oppenheimer, Bermuda, and "Atoms for Peace" unfolded within a single month. He pushed himself almost to "the point of exhaustion," but he ended the year in an upbeat mood. Looking back, he confided in a Christmas note to Swede Hazlett, he found "moments of real satisfaction that have made all the rest of it seem worthwhile."

The year closed out with the normal press of business. The cabinet and the NSC held their regular sessions. Eisenhower met with legislative leaders to discuss the St. Lawrence Seaway, statehood for Alaska and Hawaii, public works and farm programs, and the coming budget. He shuffled ideas and drafts for the State of the Union and happily embraced one piece of advice. He would deliver a "message of hope," a reminder that despite difficulties for some, "there is a clear prospect of encouraging opportunity for the betterment of all groups, classes and individuals."

The holidays offered a few moments of respite, and Ike enjoyed them. Tom Stephens arranged a series of performances at the White House Christmas party—though it was meant for the staff, Ike and Mamie dropped in—and the president was delighted. Even irritations seemed more amusing than disabling. France elected a new president, and Eisenhower cabled his congratulations to the winner, René Coty. He then wrote to Al Gruenther, stationed in Paris. "In view of the number of people I have known in the various French governments, it is exasperating to find out that they picked the one I cannot remember meeting." Ike added: "That's the French of it."

On Christmas Day, Ike and Mamie departed for Augusta. The year ended quietly on the golf links and with cheerful gatherings of staff and friends. For a few days, Oppenheimer and McCarthy, covert action, nuclear weapons, civil rights, economic recovery, and the mysteries of the Soviet Union all receded. Though not for long.

"McCarthywasm"

Brothers can argue about almost anything, and Little Ike and Big Ike were no exception. Through the first year of Little Ike's presidency, his brother Edgar badgered him over a deeply divisive proposal to amend the Constitution. Sponsored by Senator John Bricker of Ohio, the measure tapped a vein of Republican dogma left over from the party's long ostracism during the FDR presidency. There lingered an abiding suspicion from the Yalta Conference that the president would abuse his power to make foreign treaties and might straitjacket domestic policy or overwhelm states' rights. An agreement, for instance, to honor human rights abroad might constrain the criminal sentencing systems adopted in various American states.

To remedy that, Bricker introduced an amendment intended to circumscribe the reach of foreign entanglement. If approved by two-thirds of the Senate and three-fourths of the state legislatures—the president himself has no role in amending the Constitution—the Bricker Amendment would block any treaty that conflicted with the Constitution; Congress would acquire the power to regulate all treaties and other executive agreements. Treaties would only affect "internal law in the United States" if their provisions were specifically enacted by separate legislation. The proposed amendment was first introduced in 1952, during the final year of the Truman administration; the Senate failed to enact it, and Bricker reintroduced a slightly rewritten version as Senate Joint Resolution 1 at the beginning of the 1953 session.

There was room for honest disagreement, but the debate surrounding it was soon swamped in emotional dispute over distrust of the presidency and the right of states to resist federal preeminence. Among those who felt most strongly—and who lobbied Eisenhower most avidly—was his brother Edgar. In March 1953, having just returned from Ike's inauguration, Edgar wrote two letters, four days apart, vigorously championing the Bricker Amendment. Without it, he said, the states would be at the mercy of foolish foreign agreements. Imagine, Edgar argued, if the United States' ratification of a human rights treaty pending at the United Nations stipulated certain protections for new mothers. That could require states to pay for milk for mothers who could not breast-feed and compensate mothers who could the same amount in order to prevent unequal treatment. "Just how silly can you get?" Edgar asked. The same week, he wrote again, this time quoting John Foster Dulles on the power of treaties—Dulles had since recanted a statement in which he suggested that treaty law could override the Constitution. Edgar complained that his nonlawyer brother was not heeding his recommendation: "I think that someone is giving you bad advice."

Ike was used to his brother lecturing him, but his patience with the issue—and with Edgar's presumptuousness—wore thin. "You seem to fear that I am just a poor little soul here who is being confused and misled by a lot of vicious advisers," Ike sarcastically replied, adding that while Bricker might marshal some legal support for his arguments, the counterarguments were stronger. Moreover, he pointedly reminded his big brother that neither Bricker nor Edgar "has had any experience in conducting difficult negotiations looking toward the necessary and essential Executive agreements." That still didn't silence Edgar. As they continued to spar, they also argued over Earl Warren's appointment to the Court and Edgar's general concern that his brother was leading the nation toward socialism.

With the Bricker Amendment still on the table in early 1954, Edgar warned that he was hearing more and more reports that Ike had become enamored of the New Deal policies he had once deplored—Social Security, farm subsidies, and an internationalist foreign policy—and that he had fallen into the company of old Dewey supporters, the last a snarling accusation from a conservative Republican. Ike responded sternly, saying that normally he would shrug off "a communication which contains all the hackneyed criticisms and accusations palpably based on misinformation and deliberate distortion." He was replying only, he said, because he was annoyed to have "one brother that seems always ready to believe that I am a . . . helpless, ignorant, uninformed individual, thrust to dizzy heights of governmental responsibility and authority, who has been captured by a band of conniving 'internationalists.' " Even that didn't shut Edgar up, but it did make the point.

If anything, Edgar's lobbying seemed to harden Ike's opposition to the amendment, which he became increasingly convinced would handcuff the president and undermine America's ability to enter into alliances and treaties—a threat to Ike's existential internationalism. It was tiresome, he acknowledged. "Never have I in my life been so weary of any one subject or proposition," he told Edgar in February. The amendment itself wound its way through a complicated series of votes and amendments. One was intended to soften the language to make clear that it would only bar treaties that conflicted with the Constitution. For a time, it seemed that might resolve the matter, as supporters had argued that such a clarification was all they sought. When Bricker refused to back that change, however, the lines were drawn. The Bricker Amendment failed a series of close votes in early 1954. Finally, on February 25, it was defeated. A proposal that Ike warned "would have spelled tragedy for the future of America" never again resurfaced as a serious notion. What's more, Ike won his argument with his brother. When Edgar wrote after the vote to complain that someone in the White House had tried to suggest a break between them on the issue, Ike refused to give in. He had never made a secret of their difference on the amendment, Ike explained, and had said so publicly. "I'm sorry you are upset about it," Eisenhower wrote, "but the explanation is as simple as that."

The Bricker Amendment was only one bit of carryover business from 1953. There were others, none more closely watched than Ike's duel with McCarthy. In June, the two had almost reached a breaking point, when Eisenhower responded to McCarthy's campaign to rid American libraries abroad of suspicious books by urging Dartmouth students not to join the book burners. Eisenhower's subsequent silence made it seem as though he had returned to ignoring McCarthy; in fact, he was quietly but methodically isolating the senator.

In early 1954, McCarthy appeared to be gaining, not losing, steam. He had ended 1953 with his renewed attack on the State Department and Davies, hardly new terrain but worrisome in that it was now Eisenhower's leadership, not Truman's record, that captured the senator's attention. Moreover, the still-secret investigation of Oppenheimer hovered over the administration, threatening to become public at any moment and offering McCarthy a chillingly rich target. Eisenhower publicly expressed the hope that Communists in government would not dominate the 1954 campaign, but taking that issue out of the debate would deprive McCarthy of his reason for being; neither he nor his allies could tolerate that. The *Wall Street Journal* captured the issue's threat to Eisenhower with the headline of its lead editorial on November 23: "Accessory After the Fact." The paper's editorial board warned Eisenhower not to minimize the serious and continuing issue of subversion. "The answer," the *Journal* editorialized, "is not to hush the whole matter up and forget it." Two days later, McCarthy pointedly rejected Eisenhower's attempt to talk down the threat of subversion and its relevance to the campaign. "The raw, harsh, unpleasant fact is that Communism is an issue and will be an issue in 1954," McCarthy said.

Then he pivoted ominously on the institution closest to Eisenhower, the U.S. Army. McCarthy's inquiries had revealed that an Army dentist, Irving Peress, had refused to sign a loyalty oath and yet been promoted during his time at Camp Kilmer, New Jersey. In high dudgeon, McCarthy summoned Peress, who refused to answer questions and was then honorably discharged from the service. McCarthy moved up the chain of command and hauled into the hearings General Ralph Zwicker, a former colleague of Eisenhower's from the war years and currently the commander at Camp Kilmer. In one ill-tempered hearing after another, McCarthy bludgeoned Zwicker with the repeated question: "Who promoted Peress?" When Zwicker tried to deflect the inquiry, McCarthy sneered: "Anyone with the brains of a five-year-old child can understand the question." Still, Zwicker refused to hand over names to the senator, prompting the furious McCarthy to exclaim: "Then, General, you should be removed from any command." Fed up with McCarthy's mistreatment of his subordinate, Robert T. Stevens, the secretary of the Army, ordered Zwicker to cease cooperation with the committee and said he would testify instead.

With that, the political leanings of a now-discharged Army dentist vaulted to the top of the nation's agenda and threatened a full-blown test of the separation of powers. Stevens, in good faith, accepted an invitation from McCarthy to head off that confrontation. They talked over lunch in the Capitol on February 24 and cut a deal: McCarthy would stop badgering witnesses, and Stevens would permit Zwicker to return to the stand and provide the committee with the names of those involved in Peress's promotion. Although McCarthy feigned friendship with Stevens—he once told the secretary that it would be easier to investigate the Army if he weren't so fond of Stevens—the senator promptly double-crossed him. They emerged from the allegedly private lunch to a klatch of alerted reporters, and McCarthy announced that Stevens had relented and allowed Zwicker to return. He never mentioned that he, too, had made concessions.

"Stevens Bows to McCarthy at Administration Behest," the *New York Times* trumpeted the next day: "What Secretary Stevens agreed to was precisely what Senator McCarthy had demanded." "My own reaction," Ike wrote years later, "was not pleasant." At the time, he described himself as "astonished." Stevens, meanwhile, was apoplectic, "in a state of shock and near hysteria," as Eisenhower put it to Lucius Clay. It was, Adams recalled, the moment that "blew the lid off the teakettle." Distraught, the secretary called Jim Hagerty and said he wanted to release a statement and then resign (a fact that also made its way into the *Times*). Ike's long simmer now heated to a boil as he contemplated his obligation to Stevens and Zwicker and those upon whom he relied for counsel. Eisenhower released a statement backing Stevens, and congressional leaders supported the secretary's version of events. Still, Clay advised caution in tangling directly with McCarthy. "Don't think you can lock horns on this one," notes of his February 25 conversation with Eisenhower record. "He has made fight impossible."

Eisenhower was in fact prepared to fight, but on ground of his choosing. On March 2, he called Herb Brownell for some legal advice. What authority did the president have, Ike asked, to protect his own people? "Suppose I made up my mind that McCarthy is abusing someone," he asked, hardly a vague hypothetical. "What is constitutional for me to do in this regard?"

While Brownell studied that question, Eisenhower laid the groundwork with important congressional leaders, asking their help to "get a better handling of things" and specifically urging Bill Knowland to keep a lid on McCarthy. He received their assurances and quietly telegraphed his mounting impatience to other key opinion leaders. "A lot of people are genuinely alarmed by what they consider to be his potential capacity for harm," Ike said of McCarthy in a note to the chairman of the board of General Electric. To Bill Robinson, then settling into his new job as chief executive officer of Coca-Cola (succeeding another member of Ike's Gang, Bob Woodruff), Eisenhower complained that the same media that had built McCarthy up now clamored for Ike to take him down, but he steadfastly refused to make the presidency "ridiculous" by tangling with him publicly. Worried that McCarthy was gaming for the presidency, Eisenhower vowed to deny him the chance: "He's the last guy in the world who'll ever get there, if I have anything to say."

Publicly, Eisenhower continued to avoid using McCarthy's name but signaled his displeasure with veiled—and well-received—swipes at the proceedings. His denunciation of book burning still heartened McCarthy's critics, and he telegraphed his sympathies in other ways, too. In September 1953, investigators for the House Un-American Activities Committee uncovered a 1936 voter registration card bearing the name Lucille Ball and claiming Communist affiliation. Ball was questioned about the card in a private session and admitted that it was hers but noted that she was young at the time and had registered as a Communist to gratify her grandfather Fred Hunt, who helped to raise her. "We just did something to please him," she insisted. The committee was satisfied with Ball's responses, but Walter Winchell, the radio commentator, later that week broadcast the news that "the top television comedienne has been confronted with her membership in the Communist Party."

Winchell's accusation was false and reckless. Other than to fill out that registration card, Ball had done nothing to cement a relationship with the party and certainly was not a member in 1953. Ball and her husband, Desi Arnaz, vigorously and persuasively rebutted Winchell's implications; Arnaz got off the best line of the affair, introducing Lucy as "my favorite redhead, in fact, that's the only thing Red about her, and even that's not legitimate." The matter blew over quickly, aided by America's affection for Ball. More people watched the episode of Lucy delivering her baby than tuned in for Ike's inaugural.

Still, in those days, even the taint of Communism was enough to cast a shadow across those touched by it. Friends of Ball and Arnaz mysteriously canceled social engagements, and Lucy and Desi worried that her career would suffer. To that, Ike and Mamie supplied a welcome antidote: the couple was invited to a White House dinner to celebrate Ike's birthday. They entertained the audience and then were asked to sit next to Ike and Mamie. Desi Arnaz well understood the blessing he and Lucy were being offered. "God Bless America!" he exclaimed.

Having worked to cut McCarthy off with colleagues and opinion leaders—and having signaled his distaste for the whole ugly business—Ike now analyzed his options under the Constitution. The key question was whether the president could refuse to make his aides available to Congress if they were subpoenaed to appear. The short answer, as Brownell soon reported, was that there was no legal precedent for such an action. But there was not necessarily a bar, either, and Ike's friends now pressed him to take the action he was contemplating. "Sooner or later—and probably sooner—Senator McCarthy will again summon . . . some member of the Executive Branch of the Government who should not be summoned," wrote Paul Hoffman. "Then and there, I suggest that you issue instructions to this person to refuse the summons from Senator McCarthy and give the reasons for so doing."

Easily said, not so easily done. Although defying McCarthy on this ground appealed to Eisenhower, it also was sure to provoke a political and constitutional confrontation with an uncertain outcome. It threatened Republican unity on the eve of the midterm elections, and it risked providing McCarthy with the stage that Eisenhower had worked so steadfastly to deny him. Eisenhower considered options: perhaps, one aide suggested, the Justice Department could supply government witnesses with lawyers to accompany them; perhaps there were other protections to give subordinates. Ike bided his time.

The Army positioned, too. Rather than defensively debate their handling of Peress, Army officials prepared a counterattack. They accused McCarthy's aide Roy Cohn of attempting to use his influence to secure favorable treatment for his friend David Schine, who had recently been drafted (it was widely assumed that Cohn and Schine were homosexual, so that inquiry posed a special threat to McCarthy and his aide). They would still have to answer for Peress, but now the Army leadership had McCarthy on the defensive. There was yet another piece of deft footwork as the committee prepared to reconvene. With Ike's encouragement, the Senate decided to televise the hearings. McCarthy readily agreed, imagining that television would deliver a national platform to him and fantasizing that he was about to vastly expand his reach and power. Eisenhower better understood the implications of that openness. Now the country would see McCarthy as he really was.

First, however, it received the stunning news that America's preeminent nuclear scientist, surpassed only by Einstein himself, was under suspicion. While McCarthy preened before the public, serious forces had quietly gathered to deliberate the fate of Robert Oppenheimer. The hearing began on April 12, the public still unaware that anything was afoot. The cards were decidedly stacked against the scientist: Strauss had handpicked the three-man committee to hear the charges and had picked the prosecutor to bring them. He had bugged Oppenheimer's home, his phone, and his lawyers' offices to keep abreast of their strategy. The prosecutor was permitted to meet with the panel to review the FBI's extensive file on Oppenheimer, while Oppenheimer's lawyers were excluded from those sessions. When the hearing began, the members of the board had before them large briefing books, all prepared by Oppenheimer's pursuers, none available for the defense to review.

The hearing was scheduled to open at 10:00 a.m., but Oppenheimer and his lawyers were late. Once it began, the first order of business was to read the allegations against Oppenheimer. The hearing was not styled as a criminal proceeding; Oppenheimer's liberty was not at stake, merely his access to classified and top secret material. Though essential for his work as a government consultant, denial of access to such material would not necessarily imply disloyalty, much less espionage. Rather, the case against Oppenheimer would turn on whether the panel believed he could be trusted with secrets. In 1942, despite his flirtations with Communism and Communists, the government had cleared him for service at Los Alamos; now those same old affiliations would come under the scrutiny of a Cold War government, one implacably at odds with Communism, again in contrast to the World War II years, when the Soviets were American allies.

When the hearing convened the following morning, the entire controversy had changed. The front page of the *New York Times* carried a dazzling exclusive. James Reston, the paper's premier Washington reporter and its recently named Washington bureau chief, broke the news that Oppenheimer was under investigation. Reston had known of the inquiry for weeks but had agreed to hold off reporting it at Oppenheimer's request. With the hearings now commenced in secret, Oppenheimer released him to report what he knew. Strauss, informed that a story was in the works, gave his blessing as well. The next morning's *Times* led with the Oppenheimer scoop: "Dr. Oppenheimer Suspended by A.E.C. in Security Review; Scientist Defends Record." The subhead was even more shocking: "Access to Secret Data Denied Nuclear Expert—Red Ties Alleged." Beneath those headlines was a pensive picture of Oppenheimer, chin in his hand, staring blankly downward. Accompanying the article were the letter of accusations against Oppenheimer and his formal reply.

It was a world exclusive, and the members of the board—all of whom were prominently named near the top of the story—were mightily displeased. As the hearing opened that morning, Chairman Gordon Gray grilled Oppenheimer's lawyer about who had spoken to Reston and provided him the material. "I think it only fair to say for the record," the chairman declared, "that the board is very much concerned." The lawyer, Lloyd Garrison, began an involved story of Reston's inquiries and his own entry into the case when Oppenheimer himself interrupted him. "May I correct that," he said. "I believe the initial conversation was with me." If anything, Eisenhower was even more angry than the commissioners. "This fellow Oppenheimer is sure acting like a Communist," he complained to Hagerty. "He is using all the rules that they use to try to get public sentiment in their corner."

Ike fulminated in private; publicly, he said nothing. That afternoon, he threw out the first pitch at the Washington Senators' game and stayed to watch them beaten by his favorite team, the Yankees, 5–3, in a three-hour game; in New York, the day's most closely watched matchup, the Giants and the Dodgers, ended in a 4–3 Giants victory, with Willie Mays clobbering the winning home run.

If Oppenheimer assumed that the public would back him once it knew the facts, he guessed wrong. As Americans became aware of his connections to Communism, some naturally sympathized with the scientist. But in the inclement climate of the Cold War, Oppenheimer's casual and continuing friendships with Communists struck many Americans as at best naive. Through that prism, Oppenheimer's opposition to the hydrogen bomb could appear to some as treason. Strauss and Borden, most importantly, but also more reasonable critics came to see Oppenheimer as sinister. Nor did he do much to help his case. Oppenheimer's cold manner—his curious blend of what McGeorge Bundy described as "charm and arrogance, intelligence and blindness, awareness and insensitivity"—made him an unlikely receptacle of public sympathy. He suffered through a long, aggressive cross-examination, his strength slowly ebbing away as he endured questions about his mistress and gave up names—all of them already known to authorities—of Communists he had known. Oppenheimer's sharp descent, from America's most respected military scientist to a haggard and broken suspect, took just three weeks.

Reston brought the Oppenheimer story to public view, but it just as quickly retreated into the closed hearing room. From April 12 through May 6, the commissioners took testimony behind closed doors. Much mischief had already been concealed by secrecy.

By contrast, the McCarthy hearings went live on the morning of April 22. And unlike the conclusions about Oppenheimer that the public was forced to reach by his absence, its understanding of McCarthy would be enriched by observation. The senator wasted no time in making his mark. As the *New York Times* put it, "New and special rules failed to restrain Senator McCarthy from interrupting witnesses and other Senators whenever he wished on what he called points of order."

General Miles Reber was the first to feel his lash as McCarthy insinuated that Reber was fashioning his testimony in order to retaliate for the committee's investigation of his brother, who had resigned his Army commission a year earlier. There was no connection between Samuel Reber's retirement and the McCarthy proceedings, but McCarthy asserted that the State Department had deemed him a "bad security risk," then withdrew the question when its relevance was challenged. General Reber demanded the right to reply and vigorously denied both that his brother was such a risk and that his retirement in any way influenced the general's testimony. Having warmed up on one general, McCarthy then proceeded to turn his fire against Secretary Stevens, the second witness to take the stand. Sarcastic, insulting, and rude, McCarthy browbeat Stevens for more than a week as millions of viewers looked on, many increasingly appalled by the senator's behavior. The senator, who often stayed up all night drinking, was heavy lidded as well as heavy-handed, his speech thick and slow and seething. All of that was picked up by the cameras, and McCarthy's downfall accelerated. It was, Ike confided to his friend Swede Hazlett, "close to disgusting."

Emphasizing McCarthy's defects were the characters of those arrayed against him. Stevens was mild, almost demure. Joseph Welch, the lawyer representing the Army, was incisive and witty. McCarthy introduced a photograph of Stevens smiling at Schine—suggesting that influence was not required to secure his special treatment—but Welch deftly demonstrated that the photograph had been cropped to excise the image of General Bradley, at whom Stevens actually was smiling. When a McCarthy aide tried to suggest that there was something unseemly about how Welch acquired the photograph, Welch baited his trap: "Did you think it came from a pixie?" McCarthy fell into it: "Will counsel for my benefit define—I think he might be an expert on that—what a pixie is?"

Welch happily answered: "I would say, senator, that a pixie is a close relative of a fairy." Gay-baiting was hardly an attractive response to red-baiting, but this was powerful theater, and Welch was the better actor.

A few blocks away, the Oppenheimer panel wrapped up testimony and took a ten-day break after hearing from its last witness. Oppenheimer waited nervously at home, Strauss eagerly in Washington.

Back up on Capitol Hill, the sparring continued into May, when Eisenhower finally played the card he had held so closely for weeks. The witness was John Adams, the Army's lawyer, who took the stand to corroborate Stevens's account of the pressure brought by Roy Cohn to secure desirable assignments for Schine. In the course of testifying, he was asked about a meeting on January 21 at the office of Herbert Brownell, the attorney general, at which strategy for the hearings was discussed. Senator Stuart Symington inquired about the role played in it by Henry Cabot Lodge, the U.S. ambassador to the United Nations. But Adams refused to answer, saying he had been instructed by Robert Anderson, the deputy secretary of defense, not to reveal details of that meeting. Adams said he believed Anderson was acting under instructions to deliver that message, but he did not know who issued the original order. He was asked to inquire during the lunch break but returned without an answer. The hearings then ended for the week.

That night, Eisenhower addressed the fifth annual Armed Forces Day dinner at Washington's Statler Hotel. Departing from his text, he spoke of the nation's inner strength and virtue: "We know we value the right to worship as we please, to choose our own occupation. We know the value we place on those things. If at times we are torn by doubts by unworthy scenes in our national capital . . ." At that reference to the McCarthy hearings, the audience began to clap and shout approval. Ike stood without speaking for a full half minute. Then he continued: "We know that we are Americans," he said. "The heart of America is sound."

When the hearings reconvened on Monday, May 17, Adams carried a letter, addressed to Secretary Stevens, dated that same day and signed by Eisenhower himself. After acknowledging the right of Congress to convene hearings and pledging to supply information to such inquiries, Stevens read the heart of Eisenhower's order: "Because it is essential to efficient and effective administration that employees of the Executive Branch be in a position to be completely candid in advising with each other on official matters, and because it is not in the public interest that any of their conversations or communications, or any documents or reproductions, concerning such advice be disclosed, you will instruct employees of your Department that in all of their appearances before the Subcommittee of the Senate Committee on Operations regarding the inquiry now before it, they are not to testify to any such conversations or communications or to produce any such documents or reproductions." In short, no one who counseled Eisenhower was to divulge those conversations. Or, as he bluntly put it: "Any man who testifies as to the advice he gave me won't be working for me that night."

That was a bald assertion of a power that Ike may not actually have possessed, but it served its purpose. The committee hearings were canceled for a week, and McCarthy was confronted at last by public presidential opposition. It was, McCarthy said, an "Iron Curtain" that blocked further inquiry. Others welcomed it as overdue. "By his statement of yesterday the President has finally recognized [his] responsibility in unmistakable terms," the *Times* editorial board wrote. Eisenhower's claim of executive privilege did not shut down McCarthy completely—when the session resumed, he attempted to enlist government workers to report subversives directly to him, angering Ike further—but the senator's investigation was now no longer ignored but actively opposed by his president.

During the recess forced by Eisenhower's invocation of presidential privilege, the Oppenheimer board returned its verdict. To the surprise of few—certainly not Oppenheimer—the panel recommended that he lose his security clearance. By a vote of 2–1, it concluded that the inventor of the American atomic bomb could not be trusted with American secrets. That vote, like the rest of the hearing, was taken in secret. A month later, the full Atomic Energy Commission convened in public and reviewed the findings. The full commission voted 4–1 to uphold the board. Oppenheimer lost. The *New York Times* had warned at the outset against any "implication of disloyalty because a scientist (or anyone else, for that matter) expressed his honest opinion, which later turned out to be unpopular or erroneous." Now, however, the paper weighed the evidence and applauded the commission for having uncovered "substantial defects of character." The board's work, according to the *Times*, was performed by "four experienced and able commissioners."

Oppenheimer had been, in some respects, the cause of his own undoing. Lesser men understood in the 1950s that those entrusted with secrets needed to watch their friends. Oppenheimer's most sturdy connections to Communism were long behind him by 1954; his wife no longer was a party member, nor his brother. His mistress was dead. True, he had recently visited in Paris with a Communist who had once raised the idea of Oppenheimer divulging secrets from the Los Alamos project, but there was no evidence that Oppenheimer had done any such thing. Instead, his censure was the result of naïveté and unwillingness to accept what eventually became an American consensus: that the hydrogen bomb was an essential instrument of national security. Never again, after 1954, would Oppenheimer lift a hand to help the government to which he had once devoted his life. Reston would long wonder about his role in the tragedy, whether his report had antagonized the board and turned it against the scientist. Garrison assured him that it had not, that the board was set to vote against Oppenheimer from the beginning. Still, the episode echoed into history, leaving behind many troubled participants. As Reston wrote late in life, "Many . . . intelligent men, including Eisenhower, Strauss, and Oppenheimer himself, contributed to the tragedy."

Meanwhile, McCarthy's hearings approached their climax. By June, the senator's desperation, fueled by his alcoholism and raw nerves, carried his intensity to new heights, with Welch acting as the principal adversary. As usual, McCarthy's weapon of choice was the smear. This time, he turned on a young associate in Welch's Boston law firm. Frederick G. Fisher had worked for the National Lawyers Guild and had briefly assisted Welch in preparing for the hearings. Once he disclosed his work with the lawyers' guild, Welch recommended that he drop off the case, fearful that McCarthy would suggest something untoward about Fisher's past association. (The guild, a progressive legal organization that still exists today, refused to administer loyalty oaths, and members of the organization had represented clients accused of Communist affiliations, including the Rosenbergs. To some fervid anti-Communists, including McCarthy, that made the guild a Communist or "communist-front" organization.)

On June 9, after Welch had questioned Cohn, McCarthy raised the issue of Fisher's association and suggested that Welch had tried to "foist" Fisher on the committee and allow him access to its files. Because Welch anticipated that McCarthy might make an issue of Fisher, he was ready with a reply. At first Welch struggled to get the senator's attention, as McCarthy commented that he could listen with "one ear" while summoning the attention of an aide.

"I want you to listen with both," Welch demanded. Once McCarthy focused, Welch shook his head and spoke with deep resignation: "Until this moment, Senator, I think I never really gauged your cruelty, or your recklessness." Welch explained the circumstances of Fisher's background and his work on the hearings, as well as Welch's decision to drop him from the group in order to prevent him from being damaged in precisely the way McCarthy had just done.

"Little did I dream you could be so reckless and so cruel as to do an injury to that lad," Welch continued. "It is, I regret to say, equally true that I fear he shall always bear a scar needlessly inflicted by you. If it were in my power to forgive you for your reckless cruelty, I would do so. I like to think I'm a gentle man, but your forgiveness will have to come from someone other than me."

McCarthy, undeterred, retorted that he was only responding to Welch's personal attacks on Cohn. Welch then looked at Cohn and asked whether his questioning had inflicted any such injury.

"No, sir," Cohn replied.

"And if I did," Welch added, "I beg your pardon. Let's not assassinate this lad further, Senator."

Still McCarthy persisted. "Let's, let's . . ." he began. But before he could complete his sentence, Welch interrupted cuttingly.

"You've done enough," he said, staring directly at McCarthy. "Have you no sense of decency, sir, at long last? Have you left no sense of decency?"

McCarthy attempted one last recovery. He argued he was merely laying "the truth on the table" and disparaged his adversary as "the completely phony Mr. Welch." He tried once more to contend that Welch had foisted

Fisher, with his suspicious background, into the work of the committee, but Welch was not about to yield. His air of sadness moved now to fury:

> Mr. McCarthy, I will not discuss this further with you. You have sat within six feet of me and could ask—could have asked me about Fred Fisher. You have seen fit to bring it out, and if there is a God in heaven, it will do neither you nor your cause any good. I will not discuss it further. I will not ask, Mr. Cohn, any more witnesses. You, Mr. Chairman, may, if you will, call the next witness.

The audience sat silent for a moment. And then they began to clap. McCarthy seemed confused. He fingered his glasses, considered the applause, stared blankly.

The hearings continued, but from that moment on McCarthy's arc was descendant. Americans, once transfixed by his charges, had now seen for themselves a triumph of public democracy. Millions were appalled and embarrassed. Within the year, the senator had ceased to play a meaningful role in American life.

For decades, historians have debated whether Eisenhower's strategy was the right one, and opinion remains divided. Refusing to confront McCarthy openly was canny politics. Truman had openly opposed the senator and had only raised his profile. Moreover, the risks were greater for Eisenhower, whose party included conservatives who supported some of McCarthy's goals, if not his methods. But Ike's reticence came at a cost: it allowed the senator to grill, harass, and defame Americans guilty of no offense—even the Communists who appeared before his committee had a legal right to their membership in what was, after all, a legal political organization.

That analysis obscures the real choice that Eisenhower faced. His option was not to sanction McCarthy or to stop him. It was how best to silence an independently elected official over whom Eisenhower had no legal authority. Eisenhower refused to name him publicly but shared his disgust with captains of industry and newspaper publishers, members of his staff and Congress, academic leaders and foundation presidents. By spreading word among those influential leaders, Eisenhower made it widely known that he deplored McCarthy without ever granting McCarthy the satisfaction of a direct retort. And by neither confronting McCarthy nor allowing any doubt about his own abhorrence of the senator, Ike quietly cut off McCarthy from sources of support. He isolated McCarthy from his colleagues, the media, and the mainstream of the Republican Party, then exposed him to the American people. After slowly drawing the senator into a blind created by his own hubris, Eisenhower sprang the trap. It was almost military in nature and, like so many aspects of the Eisenhower administration, deceptively deliberate.

When Eisenhower was elected, McCarthy was a formidable force in American politics. His influence was on the rise, and his opponents were terrified to challenge him. Conservatives, deprived of Taft by his sudden death, were hungry for a champion and might have dropped Eisenhower for a leader more faithful to their views and more willing to force military confrontation with China and even the Soviet Union. McCarthy could well have been that standard-bearer if Eisenhower had made McCarthy's Republicanism an alternative to Ike's. Within two years, McCarthy and his crusade already seemed a joke. History may continue to debate Ike's strategy, but as the president boasted to his aides: "It's no longer McCarthyism. It's McCarthywasm."

While the McCarthy and Oppenheimer hearings dominated the domestic Cold War, the international conflict posed far more worrisome threats to American security. In the spring of 1954, the United States set out to conduct what were, by then, routine nuclear weapons tests in the South Pacific. But on March 1, events went frighteningly out of control. A hydrogen bomb that scientists had expected to produce a yield of roughly six megatons instead detonated at a staggering fifteen megatons. That made it the largest explosion in human history, and it vaporized the Bikini atoll where it was staged. The unexpected yield of the weapon, combined with unfavorable weather conditions, spread fallout across hundreds of miles, with radioactive dust falling on nearby islands before residents could be evacuated and drifting onto the decks of U.S. ships as servicemen huddled below. A Japanese fishing boat, the inaptly named *Lucky Dragon 5*, unsuspectingly went about its work as ash from the explosion fell on the vessel. Twenty-three crew members continued fishing as the flakes drifted down and clung to their skin. Some soon felt nausea and many broke out in rashes, but it was not until they returned to port later that month that they connected their disorders with the explosion. Once a Japanese reporter pieced together the events, outrage ricocheted around the world—the spectacle of innocent Japanese suffering from American nuclear fallout being too redolent to escape international fury. Eventually, one crewman, a radio operator named Aikichi Kuboyama, died. The episode continued to roil relations between the United States and Japan for months.

As if that weren't enough to suggest the fragility of the peace in that turbulent spring of 1954, violence was visited upon the U.S. leadership just hours after the bomb went off. Half a world away, Congress was meeting to debate an immigration bill. Some time after 2:00 p.m., four Puerto Rican nationalists took their seats in a visitors' area then known as the Ladies' Gallery. Lolita Lebrón gave the order, her colleagues muttered the Lord's Prayer, then jumped to their feet and waved a Puerto Rican flag, struggling to unfurl it. Lebrón shouted "Viva Puerto Rico," and she and her colleagues began to unload their automatic pistols into the well of the House, where 243 members were gathering to vote. The protesters emptied their guns, reloaded, and kept firing. "Hit the deck," shouted Representative James E. Van Zandt of Pennsylvania, one of the first to realize what was happening. He dashed upstairs to help apprehend the shooters, jostling with police and spectators confused and then terrified by the violence. Five congressmen were hit, one through a lung, another in the back. Police captured the shooters quickly, while on the floor pages rushed to help the wounded. One congressman stripped off his tie and used it as a tourniquet to stanch the bleeding of a colleague. Another staggered into the cloakroom and collapsed.

Eisenhower heard of the shooting soon after it occurred. He called the rattled Speaker of the House, Joseph Martin, who was still dissecting rumors about what had prompted the attack. Martin was concerned that some of the assailants had escaped—none did—and told the president that the shooting might have been motivated by anger over the immigration bill, the wetback bill, as he indelicately described it.

"These people just shoot wildly, just shoot into a crowd," Eisenhower grumbled. "Probably blindly insane."

The Korean War had halted by 1954, but Korea remained a quarrelsome ally. Rhee would never be satisfied with the partition of his country, and he continued to harangue Eisenhower to support a war of reunification. In March, he delivered an impassioned appeal for help. His "hysterical" letter first was refused by Bedell Smith. Finally, Eisenhower replied: "I cannot comply with your request for support in military action to unify your country."

China was finished probing in Korea, but it yearned for conflict elsewhere and aggressively challenged the core principle of Eisenhower's New Look defense policy, the assumption that America's dominance in nuclear weapons would deter Communist aggression. In Indochina and in the straits that separated mainland China from the redoubts occupied by Chiang Kai-shek, armies refused to submit to the nuclear threat. In addition to Taiwan itself, Nationalist China claimed three sets of islands, each a few miles off the mainland. The northernmost, which included the Tachen Islands, was protected by thirteen thousand Nationalist troops; a center group including Matsu by about five thousand; and a southern batch including Quemoy by another forty-three thousand soldiers. Eisenhower considered the islands remote and nearly indefensible, but Chiang, deprived of all but these scraps of land, insisted that they were essential to the protection of his people and government.

As a result, the islands weighed heavily on Communists and Nationalists alike: Communist China saw Nationalist occupation as provocation, a garrison of tens of thousands of hostile soldiers less than ten miles from the Chinese mainland; Chiang Kai-shek imagined them as stepping-stones to his reconquest of mainland China, a mission to which his life was dedicated. An American observer of Chiang remarked in early 1958 that it was "his destiny, his responsibility, to liberate his shackled people and to rehabilitate his own prestige and reputation before he dies."

In the spring of 1954, China began massing forces on the mainland near the islands, escalating that provocation just as the McCarthy hearings were reaching their feverish peak. Eisenhower calculated the American response: Would an attack on the islands constitute an act of international aggression or a battle in the continuing Chinese civil war; more important, would it be of sufficient gravity that it warranted a nuclear response? It seemed frightfully provocative to meet the shelling of lightly defended islands of questionable strategic value with a nuclear attack on China, but the theory of American deterrence rested on the idea that the U.S. nuclear arsenal existed precisely to discourage aggression by threatening devastation in reply. Eisenhower took counsel of the military and diplomatic stakes and ordered the U.S. Seventh Fleet to pay "friendly visits" to the embattled islands, initially with instructions not to fire even if fired upon. For weeks, that uneasy stability held, thanks to the restraint of disciplined men on both sides of a perilous divide.

Meanwhile, the French in Indochina were confronting the liberation campaign of Ho Chi Minh. After years of frittering away their strength in Indochina, the French determined in 1953 and 1954 to build their forces to 250,000 and train another 300,000 Vietnamese soldiers, with the idea that the combined presence would be enough to defeat the North Vietnamese by the end of 1955. The United States supplied aid but not troops, and in the fall of 1953 the French occupied an outpost near the Laotian border, a strategically located stretch of plain known as Dien Bien Phu. At the time, holding Dien Bien Phu seemed to the French to offer a chance to contain guerrilla access to the Red River delta; in retrospect, the occupation of an isolated post, accessible only by air and surrounded by wooded hills, would reveal itself as military folly. Ike spied the danger early and asked State and Defense to relay his concerns to the French, but they ignored him.

The French were confident that their enemy neither possessed nor would acquire artillery to mount in the surrounding hills. They also imagined themselves superior fighters with superior numbers. All those assumptions toppled in the spring of 1954. On March 13, North Vietnamese troops attacked the French garrison at Dien Bien Phu, firing down on the isolated fortress from the hills with artillery supplied by the Soviet Union (and ferried through China). The immediate assault was repulsed, but, again with Chinese help, though not Chinese ground troops, the North Vietnamese regrouped and resupplied. Two weeks later, they attacked again, shelling the airstrip where French forces were resupplied. Dulles told the cabinet that American support for the French was vital. If not, he warned, "Reds would win that part of world and 'cut our defense line in half,' " Hagerty recalled. For Eisenhower, the moment of decision was at hand. The French begged for air support and more, while Ike weighed the merits of attaching American prestige to a European effort to maintain a colonial empire. "Air power might be temporarily beneficial to French morale," he reflected in his memoirs. But, he recorded fatefully, "I had no intention of using United States forces in any limited action when the force employed would probably not be decisively effective." Privately, Ike, who got his fill of French military misdirection during the North Africa campaign, was maddened by the position they placed him in now. For years, he complained, he had been urging France to internationalize the conflict in Indochina. Now the "frantic desire of the French to remain a world power" was undercut by that nation's "deep divisions and consequent indecisiveness." Strong action and clear purpose were required, but France resorted to "weasel words" and consequently "suffered reverses that have been really inexcusable."

Ike surveyed the military balance, braced for the political backlash, and withheld the support the French desired. On May 7, Dien Bien Phu fell.

American leaders feared for the wholesale collapse of the region and again contemplated nuclear war. Just before lunch on June 2, Eisenhower's top military and diplomatic advisers came to him to discuss American action should China advance on Vietnam or the rest of Indochina. Even read a half century later, their contingency plan trembles: "Congress would be asked immediately to declare that a state of war existed with Communist China, and the U.S. should then launch large-scale air and naval attacks on ports, airfields, and other military targets in mainland China, using as militarily appropriate 'new weapons.' "

The French and the North Vietnamese signed a partition pact later that summer, and the Republican right wing again rebelled, with Bill Knowland decrying it as "the greatest victory the Communists have won in 20 years." Ike was incensed at the recurring broadsides from the Republican Senate leader. He grumbled to Hagerty, "The more I see of Knowland, the more I wonder whether he is a Republican leader or not." Eisenhower and Hagerty assigned a more sympathetic senator to challenge any colleagues who criticized the settlement to ask whether they were prepared to send "American boys to fight in Indochina." The silence spoke loudly. Despite the pleadings of his own party and the desperation of an ally, Eisenhower refused to budge. He would not wage war in Vietnam.

Those were trying and often exhausting months. Eisenhower tried to relax with his golf clubs and family. One rainy day he moped around the White House, then brightened when it cleared just in time for him to take his grandchildren on a trip down the Potomac.

Ike's grandchildren were a source of joy and comfort. Failing to reach John and his wife, Barbara, one day to wish them a happy anniversary—they celebrated their seventh anniversary in June—Eisenhower instead dropped them a note of congratulations. "I couldn't possibly be prouder of you both," he wrote, "unless possibly if I had another grandchild!" He would get his wish: Ike's three grandchildren—David, Barbara Anne, and Susan—would be joined by a fourth, Mary Jean, in 1955. He took delight in the young ones, at ease with them in a way that had sometimes been difficult for him when John was growing up. As Eisenhower came upon David and Anne one day in the White House's Lincoln Bedroom, he overheard a snippet of their conversation. "This," David lectured his younger sister, "is President Lincoln's bed."

"That can't be," Anne replied. "That man isn't President. Ike is President!"

Eisenhower cheerfully relayed that exchange to Edgar, with the comment that "by the time they are eight, they will probably be candidates for their Ph.D.'s."

But family could also provide tragedy, none more shocking or heartbreaking than the news that Milton's beloved wife, Helen, was diagnosed with cancer in early 1954. She initially responded to treatment but then suddenly died at home of a blood clot on June 10. She was forty-nine years old. Milton and their son, Milton Jr., were by her side. A shocked Ike and Mamie canceled their plans for the coming week—Eisenhower had been scheduled to address a gathering of governors—to rush to Milton's home in University Park, where he served as the president of Pennsylvania State University. For months thereafter, Ike treated his little brother with delicacy, calling on him for advice and service but taking care not to over-burden him.

Dwight Eisenhower was a profoundly conservative man, dedicated to the conviction that government served society best by safeguarding the individualism of the governed and allowing maximum liberty within those limits. His "middle way," as he shaped and explained that idea, explicitly rejected the notion that government should control the lives of citizens or eliminate all fear or want. But he also stood firmly apart from those who would, as a matter of principle, reject the useful services of a government that could advance the economy or protect its people. As he wrote to a much more conservative friend in 1954:

> When I refer to the Middle Way, I merely mean the middle way
> as it represents a practical working basis between extremists, both of
> whose doctrines I flatly reject. It seems to me that no great intelligence
> is required in order to discern the practical necessity of establish-
> ing some kind of security for individuals in a specialized and highly
> industrialized age. At one time such security was provided by the exis-
> tence of free land and a great mass of untouched and valuable natural
> resources throughout our country. These are no longer to be had for
> the asking; we have had the experience of millions of people—devoted,
> fine Americans, who have walked the streets unable to find work or
> any kind of sustenance for themselves and their families.
>
> On the other hand, for us to push further and further into the
> socialistic experiment is to deny the validity of all those convictions
> we have held as the cumulative power of free citizens, exercising their
> own initiative, inventiveness and desires to provide a better living for
> themselves and their children.

That quest for balance, a defining feature of Eisenhower's life and presi-dency, found expression in the summer of 1954 with the completion of a long-sought deal to open the middle of the United States to oceangoing goods through the construction of a system of locks linking the Great Lakes to the Atlantic Ocean. The opportunity for that project, known as the St. Lawrence Seaway, had long fascinated engineers, but it was mired in complexity and cost, not to mention considerable opposition from rail companies that worried it would break their lock on trade through the region.

In this case, Eisenhower saw a constructive opportunity for government action. He urged Congress to create a public corporation that would issue bonds to build the seaway and then recoup the money through tolls from the ships that used it. Using the same logic that would later prevail in his support for a national highway system, he argued that the economic benefits were vast and that no blind fidelity to limited government should deter thoughtful progress. Congress passed the St. Lawrence Seaway Act, and construction began in the fall of 1954. When it opened, Eisenhower, joined by Canada's prime minister and Queen Elizabeth, proclaimed it "a magnificent symbol . . . of the achievements possible to democratic nations peacefully working together for the common good." It was also, he hardly needed to note, a triumph of the middle way—of government making possible private sector investment in order to advance a public good.

With McCarthy vanquished and the seaway approved by Congress, Eisenhower looked forward to a summer rest, only to have it delayed in July when the Chinese shot down British and American planes performing rescue missions in the South China Sea. Peace, it seemed, was always tested.

At last he escaped to Denver, where his staff worried about him. "Eisenhower had spells of depression that summer, and the reason was not easy to pin down," Sherman Adams wrote. He and Ike's secretary, Ann Whitman, feared that it was the result of too many problems that defied easy solution—long, deep questions that had perplexed and angered him all year. The stresses of the presidency were hard to bear and impossible for aides to ease.

Revolutions

Deterrence was one prong of New Look, but Eisenhower and Dulles promised to do more than merely contain Communism; that was the essence of Truman's foreign policy, which they rejected as too timid and defensive. Ike wanted to challenge Communism, to roll it back where he could and liberate its captive populations. Full-scale confrontation was out of the question—the expense far too great, the threat to humanity too horrifying—but so was passivity. The ease with which Mossadegh was bumped from office in Iran whetted Eisenhower's appetite for covert action, and Project Solarium had specifically identified subversion as a useful tactical device. The CIA hardly needed encouragement when, in the early weeks of 1954, it became increasingly uncomfortable with the direction of the Guatemalan government and its president, the former Army captain Jacobo Arbenz Guzmán. Indeed, Project Solarium's Task Force C had been shockingly unambiguous in its proposal for how to deal with this turn of events in the Western Hemisphere. Under recommendations for Latin America, the report suggested: "Coup d'etat in Guatemala."

For Truman, Guatemala had been a source of anxiety and ambivalence. Under the histrionic rule of Jorge Ubico—who fancied himself Latin America's Napoleon and liked to pose in the image of his idol—Guatemalans enjoyed no right of dissent, and the nation's large Mayan population was relegated to impotent poverty. But Ubico opened the country to foreign investment, and American firms, most notably the United Fruit Company, established large and prosperous operations. Still, suppression has its limits, and university unrest in 1944 spread to the middle classes. Together, students, teachers, and the Guatemalan bourgeoisie overthrew Ubico. Arbenz was among the military officers who deposed Ubico's junta; the officers then ceded power back to civilian authorities, and Juan José Arévalo was elected president in December 1944. Arévalo, a university professor educated in Argentina, launched the nation on an ambitious program of social and economic reform that placed him at odds with the interests of American corporations. In 1947, the Guatemalan National Assembly, with the encouragement of Arévalo, approved new labor rules permitting unionization of large industries, including United Fruit. The company appealed to the U.S. government for help and received it. "If the Guatemalans want to handle a Guatemalan company roughly that is none of our business," an American official explained, "but if they handle an American company roughly it is our business."

American support for United Fruit placed the U.S. government, first under Truman and then under Eisenhower, in lockstep with the repressive forces in the region. That connection was reinforced by John Foster Dulles, whose law firm represented United Fruit, and by other American representatives of the company, including the famous fixer Tommy Corcoran and General Robert Cutler, an old friend of Ike's who headed the president's NSC Planning Board. Even Ann Whitman's husband served as a public relations executive at United Fruit.

The objections of the American firms in Guatemala crested after Arévalo's historic transfer of power in 1951—he was the first civilian president of Guatemala to yield office voluntarily. Arbenz's chief opponent in that campaign was Francisco Arana, a fellow military officer who had joined him in the 1944 coup but had since tacked to the right and was supported by Guatemala's upper class. Arbenz was the strong favorite to win, but Arana tried to force an early election; his campaign ended in a shoot-out on a bridge outside of Guatemala City. Blame for Arana's murder was never fixed, but the shadow of culpability would hover over Arbenz and taint the CIA's later appraisal of his administration.

Arbenz's early moves as president troubled American officials and United Fruit. On June 17, 1952, just six months after taking office, Arbenz signed Decree 900, a land reform act that appropriated uncultivated land from large landowners and distributed it in eight- to thirty-three-acre plots to farmers who could pay back the government over time. Landowners whose property was taken were to be compensated for their loss based on the property's assessed value for tax purposes. Although all large landholdings were affected by Decree 900, United Fruit's properties were especially burdened by it since the company was Guatemala's largest landowner. Moreover, it had systematically avoided paying its share of Guatemalan taxes in part by securing absurdly low valuations for its land, which stung now that compensation was to be based on those same fraudulently low estimates. Over the next several months, the government moved to acquire large portions of United Fruit's property and proposed to pay the company $1,185,000; the company, with the support of the Truman administration, countered with a bill for $15,854,849.

As tension mounted, American officials increasingly came to see the Arbenz reform efforts as the work of a reckless administration, infected by Communists. With reference to Eisenhower, two things must be noted: First, his administration did not set out to put the might of the U.S. military behind United Fruit; rather, the challenge to United Fruit seemed, to Eisenhower as it did to Truman, to be part of a larger rejection of American influence in Guatemala. Second, Eisenhower was not wrong to spy Communist influence in Guatemala, but he misapprehended both its extent and its relationship to Moscow.

The National Intelligence Estimates for 1952 and 1953 highlighted the presence of Guatemalan Communists. In 1953, with Eisenhower freshly in the White House, the estimate reflected a gathering pessimism: "As long as President Arbenz remains in power the Arbenz-Communist alliance will probably continue to dominate Guatemalan politics." Arbenz did count among his supporters some Guatemalan Communists, especially in the nation's labor movement, which strongly backed the Arévalo and Arbenz reforms to strengthen labor's position in Guatemalan society (prior to Arévalo, it was a capital offense in Guatemala to join a union). Nevertheless, Guatemalan Communists never held high-ranking positions in the government, nor did they capture more than a handful of seats in the National Assembly. American intelligence officers searched enthusiastically for evidence of contact between Guatemalan Communists and Moscow—examining travel records and investigating allegations of a courier network—but never produced any evidence of such connections. Nor was Guatemalan Communism a dominant force in that country's politics. When Bill Allen, a friend of Eisenhower's, visited the country in 1954, he cabled back that there were indeed Communists in the country but, he noted, "not as many as [in] San Francisco."

From Washington, however, the possibility of Communism in Guatemala seemed real. Eisenhower would not have it. The U.S. analysis was in many respects flawed—Arbenz's reform plan more closely resembled the New Deal than Stalinist collectivization—but Communists operated in secret, so estimates of their strength were invariably regarded as conservative. There was, in fact, an international Communist movement directed by Moscow, and though Soviet leaders in practice were far more conservative in their foreign policy than Washington believed, their occasional aggressiveness made it easy to overestimate the danger they posed. As a result, the overarching threat of international Communism repeatedly caused American officials, including Eisenhower, to overlook or underestimate nationalist or regional impulses.

Those intelligence and analytical failings would become clearer over time, but in 1954 they were overwhelmed by the urgency for action, supported by Ike himself. In March, the Organization of American States met in Caracas, and the United States, led by John Foster Dulles, demanded an uncompromising resolution pledging member states to "take the necessary measures to protect" against Communist incursions into the Americas, language clearly intended to put Guatemala on the defensive. Even Ike conceded that the "draft resolution was harsh," adding, "It was meant to be." Arbenz stood his ground, accusing United Fruit of fomenting the false allegation regarding Communist subversion and pointing out that forces allied with the company had complained of Guatemalan Communism even before the party existed. "How could they invent an umbrella before it rained?" he asked plaintively. Still, after an acrimonious debate, the member states voted 17–1 to approve the resolution, with Guatemala voting no and Mexico and Argentina abstaining.

Eisenhower had already moved beyond resolutions. As early as August 1953, the CIA categorized Guatemala as its "number one priority," and Eisenhower authorized the agency to move against Arbenz. With some reluctance, the United States settled on Carlos Castillo Armas for its leader. A diminutive, mustachioed army officer with a small force of loyalists and an ill-defined political philosophy that barely extended beyond reversing the "Sovietization" of his country, Castillo Armas enjoyed the backing of neighboring Central American dictators. With American help, he assembled a small force of rebels just outside Guatemala's borders. There he waited as CIA operatives inside Guatemala worked to soften up the public and rattle Arbenz. Eisenhower imposed an arms embargo, covertly shipping weapons to the rebels while overtly cutting them off from the government. In the spring, a clandestine radio station began taunting the government. The Guatemalan leaders were so weak, the announcers claimed, that they could not even find and shut down one local radio station (it was, in fact, based in Miami). Forces loyal to Castillo Armas used U.S.-supplied airplanes to drop leaflets on the capital, and Arbenz responded by curtailing free speech and protest, "making Guatemala into the type of repressive regime the United States liked to portray it as," according to the CIA's classified history of the operation.

On September 11, the CIA completed its budget for overthrowing the Guatemalan government. A timely sprinkling of cash had helped in Iran, and agents now proceeded to draw on that experience. The money covered "subversion," payments to a cadre of five hundred men, and weapons—the total came to $2.735 million. Allen Dulles approved $3 million three months later.

Through those weeks, there was significant criticism of Eisenhower's policy, but not of the type that one might expect. Rather than reacting to Arbenz's appeals for international assistance, American opinion leaders were angered by what they perceived as Ike's inaction. A Communist threat had been detected in the hemisphere, and it appeared to many in Congress and the press that Eisenhower was tolerating it. NBC News aired a documentary that spring called *Red Rule in Guatemala*, Walter Winchell reported that Guatemalan spies had infiltrated neighboring countries, and newspaper editorials castigated Eisenhower for sitting idly by while Latin America succumbed to Communist influence. As was so often the case, Eisenhower's style of leadership cloaked fervid maneuvering behind what seemed to be inaction. Critics yearned for brash statements and confrontations—in scenarios as diverse as the McCarthy hearings and the threat to Dien Bien Phu. Receiving none, they assumed Ike was disinterested when, in fact, he was actively but covertly pursuing his objectives.

Certainly, no one in the Arbenz government believed that Ike was dragging his feet. To the contrary, Arbenz felt cornered. He then made a fatal mistake: he sent a trusted emissary behind the Iron Curtain to arrange an arms purchase. CIA agents learned of the deal and tracked a Swedish vessel as it traveled from Poland to Guatemala with two hundred tons of small arms stashed in its hold. It arrived on May 17. The U.S. ambassador to Guatemala stood on a dock in Puerto Barrios and waited for the cargo to be unloaded. The news of Communist weapons being unloaded on Guatemalan docks ignited the American press and Congress.

"Communist Arms Unloaded in Guatemala by Vessel from Polish Port, U.S. Learns," read the headline in the *New York Times*, directly abutting an article announcing that Eisenhower had invoked executive privilege in the McCarthy hearings. "This is a development of gravity," the State Department announced. The *Times* agreed: "The Guatemalan regime has been frequently accused of being influenced by Communists." American anxiety over Guatemala now liberated the Eisenhower administration to move more forcefully on the one hand while subjecting it to heightened scrutiny on the other. At his press conference two days later, Eisenhower responded with a carefully drafted statement; he could not deny the right of the Guatemalan government to secure weapons, especially given that he was well aware the United States was itself supplying rebels. "It is disturbing," he said of the situation, adding that it reinforced the American insistence on language at a recent conference deploring the presence of Communism in the Americas. To legislative leaders, he went further and announced on May 21 that the United States would stop and search suspicious vessels bound for Guatemala.

The United States had no right to police Guatemalan trade, but Eisenhower was playing for psychological advantage. And the stakes were high. The CIA station chief warned that the introduction of Soviet weapons might upend the balance of power in Latin America. "Should this ammo ship arrive and its cargo be dispatched nothing short of direct military intervention will succeed," he wrote. "I want you to know above is written not in panic but with cool, deadly determination that freedom shall not perish in this country."

Meanwhile, the clandestine radio broadcasts and the government's fruitless attempts to shut them down were squeezing Arbenz as intended. Arbenz begged Eisenhower for a meeting; Eisenhower did not respond. On June 8, Arbenz suspended constitutional freedoms, and two days later he rounded up suspected subversives, some of whom were tortured, continuing his descent into the repressive regime the United States imagined him to lead. On June 18, the invasion began.

"Even before H-hour," the CIA history records, "the invasion degenerated from an ambitious plan to tragicomedy." Castillo Armas's army consisted of three hundred to five hundred rebels, well armed by the United States but no match for the Guatemalan regular army, which was Latin America's largest fighting force. The army was still loyal to Arbenz, though nervous about his purchase of Eastern bloc weapons. The U.S. plan was for Castillo Armas to avoid direct conflict and instead to engage small firefights en route to the capital, destabilizing Arbenz without attempting to defeat his army. The military operation was supplemented by radio broadcasts trumpeting the success of the campaign and exaggerating the size and effectiveness of Castillo Armas's forces. Although the psychological aspects of the plan worked brilliantly, Castillo Armas was a singularly ineffective commander. By June 20, his band of followers had penetrated only a few miles into Guatemala. That day, 122 rebels met up with 30 Guatemalan soldiers and, despite orders to avoid conflict with the army, engaged in a long battle. The result: all but 30 of the rebels were killed or captured. Another fight the following day saw the rebels defeated at Puerto Barrios.

Desperate, Castillo Armas begged for American air support, but Eisenhower hesitated. Authorizing such a strike would risk exposing the U.S. role and antagonize other Latin American nations. But withholding planes might doom the coup to failure. On the afternoon of June 22, Allen Dulles, John Foster Dulles, and Assistant Secretary of State Henry F. Holland met with Eisenhower at the White House. Holland opposed supplying Castillo Armas with aircraft, while the Dulles brothers, or at least Allen Dulles, favored it. What, Eisenhower asked, were the chances of the rebels succeeding without the air support? Allen Dulles replied: "About zero."

"Suppose we supply the aircraft. What would be the chances then?" Eisenhower asked.

"About 20 percent," Dulles answered. That was good enough for Ike. He authorized two fighters to be sent into the battle.

Later, Eisenhower told Dulles he was impressed by the director's realism and said he might have rejected the request if Dulles had rated its chances of success at 90 percent.

Two planes were hardly enough to tip the military balance, but they contributed mightily to the psychological campaign against Arbenz. His army, though not challenged by a serious fighting force, was increasingly alarmed that the United States stood behind the rebels. The Guatemalan military could only wonder what might happen if the U.S. Army was committed to the fight. The day after Eisenhower authorized the two planes to the region, one of Arbenz's allies found officers "cowering in their barracks, terrified and unwilling to fight." Arbenz's support was fading. The American pilots were given free rein to hurl explosives out the windows, so they began a rudimentary bombing campaign in Guatemala City (one improvised bomb hit a British freighter in the harbor; the United States later paid $1 million to settle that embarrassing mishap). The ensuing mayhem reinforced the public sense that Arbenz was unable to defend the nation. The CIA radio station, meanwhile, broadcast that Castillo Armas's forces were converging on the capital, another falsehood but one easily believed in a city where bombs were exploding.

With his army frightened, his allies restless, and his public convinced that his leadership had failed, Arbenz gave up. At 8:00 p.m. on June 27, he announced his resignation, eventually leaving the country for Mexico. "Our first victory has been won," the CIA wired from Guatemala. Dulles disingenuously told congressional leaders the next day that it was a great triumph for American diplomacy. (It was anything but. Diplomacy had failed; victory had been achieved through subversion.) A series of juntas briefly held power after Arbenz's abdication, but Castillo Armas eventually received the position he coveted: command of his country. Briefed on the events of that month, Eisenhower listened in amazement as the CIA's representative Rip Robertson described a scrubbed version of what had actually taken place. How many men, Ike asked, had Castillo Armas lost?

"Only one," Robertson lied. The CIA's own files had identified twenty-seven dead at Puerto Barrios and sixteen at Gualán, not to mention the scores who were killed in Arbenz's final crackdown. The coup hatched in delusions of Soviet adventurism rather than nationalist aspirations ended with an intelligence community so emboldened by its covert capacities that it was willing to lie to the president of the United States. The CIA could truthfully boast of only two facts: it had overthrown an enemy and had done so within its budget. The entire coup cost precisely $3 million.

There was one other notable aftermath in Guatemala. Just as the overthrow of Mossadegh had left a deep mark on one of those who witnessed it, the cleric then known as Ruhollah Mousavi Khomeini, so, too, did the coup against Arbenz burrow itself into the consciousness of one of its observers, a young Argentine named Ernesto Guevara. He yearned for a political affiliation worthy of his intellect and passion; he found it in the Arbenz reforms. "Guatemala right now is the most interesting country in America and must be defended with all possible means," he wrote as the U.S. campaign gathered momentum. When the fall came, Guevara blamed Arbenz. To Guevara, the agents of Guatemala's downfall were a weak government, a reactionary press, a complicit Catholic Church, and a failure to "arm the people" to resist the invasion. Of Eisenhower, he wrote to his father: "Politically, things aren't going so well because at any moment a coup is suspected under the patronage of your friend Ike." Those notions, impressed upon the twenty-six-year-old Guevara, would return to haunt the United States when he resurfaced as Che.

Subduing McCarthy and overthrowing Arbenz represented Cold War victories of different types. But the period's most significant such triumph was only indirectly Eisenhower's work. At 12:52 p.m., May 17, 1954, Earl Warren, Ike's first appointment to the U.S. Supreme Court, startled lawyers and reporters by turning to the case they had been waiting for. "I have for announcement," he said, "the judgment and opinion of the Court in Number 1: *Oliver Brown et al. v. Board of Education of Topeka.*"

This was the long-awaited, much-postponed work of the Court in the most difficult area before it. It had flummoxed the Vinson Court and pre-occupied Warren since his arrival the previous fall. Those early months had been difficult for Warren. He had to leave his wife, Nina, behind in California to finish up their business there. The Warrens had six children—five together and one by Nina's previous marriage—and had spent a dozen years in the California governor's mansion. Eisenhower's appointment had sent Warren to Washington, and it fell to Nina to organize the move east. Warren himself was accustomed to presiding over a large staff and now had just two secretaries and his clerks. He was lonely and out of sorts.

But he also was busy. From the start, Warren charmed his brethren. Harold Burton buried any regret over being passed over and commended Eisenhower for the selection, remarking that Warren "will meet the opportunity admirably," praise that Ike gracefully acknowledged the next day. At the Court, Warren asked Hugo Black, the senior associate justice, for advice on what to read that would help him with crafting opinions. Black suggested Aristotle's *Rhetoric*, and Warren quickly picked up a copy. "The new Chief Justice is a very attractive, fine man," Black wrote to his sons approvingly. For the first few weeks, Warren asked Black to chair the Court's weekly conferences, but by the end of the year he felt comfortable doing so himself.

On December 12, 1953, Warren presided over his first conference on the subject of school segregation. Warren was chief justice, so, by tradition, he spoke first. As the other justices well knew, the matter had divided the Court in Vinson's final term, with at least three—and perhaps five—members of the Court prepared to uphold school segregation. Vinson, along with Justices Stanley Reed and Tom Clark, had clearly signaled his willingness to tolerate "separate but equal" schools for black children. Justices Jackson and Frankfurter flinched at such a prospect, but they, too, had reservations about the Court striking down segregation after specifically upholding the principle through decades of precedent. In his conference notes, Justice Douglas recorded Jackson and Frankfurter as likely to uphold those precedents, dating to the infamous *Plessy v. Ferguson*, which legitimized the practice of "separate but equal," in effect American apartheid. Though Douglas's observations must be regarded skeptically, no doubt colored by his deep dislike for Frankfurter and Jackson, there was at least the possibility that the Vinson Court could have, had Vinson lived, voted to uphold the constitutionality of Jim Crow.

What all the justices also knew, however, was that Warren's view would decide the matter. With Vinson gone, even if Jackson and Frankfurter continued to harbor reservations about the propriety of striking segregation by judicial fiat, only four justices remained in that column. So, as Warren began to speak that morning, he chose his words and tone carefully. The men around him were smart, successful jurists, but no one at the table was Warren's equal as a politician. He understood that his vote would decide the matter, but he was after something more than victory. He wanted a decisive ruling that would send a unifying national message.

The time had come, Warren said, to decide this matter. And in his view there was only one way the Court could continue to sanction separate-but-equal schools: it would have to rely on the "basic premise that the Negro race is inferior." That was a startling assertion, and it forced Jackson and especially Frankfurter into an awkward bind. Both had reservations about overturning decades of precedent in order to reach the result that Warren was proposing, but Frankfurter in particular had a long record of enlightened views on race (among other things, he had represented civil rights organizations and had hired the Supreme Court's first black law clerk). To be allied with such naked racism would deeply offend him, and Jackson too, even if it were in defense of a judicial principle.

And yet as Warren staked a hard position on the substance of the ruling, he also offered a gentle approach to presenting and implementing it. He did not blame the South for its construction of separate institutions—that system had, after all, been sanctioned by the Court itself. He did not propose to overturn all segregation in a single opinion, but rather offered to confine the Court's attention to public schools. And he did not suggest a sweeping or immediate order. He was open to remedies that would give the South time to adjust. Finally, he made a crucial tactical decision: contrary to custom, Warren asked that the justices not record their tentative votes that day. Doing so, he feared, would lock them into positions rather than allow them to consider the issue openly.

Then it was time for the other justices to offer their views. Black was absent, but all the justices knew he favored desegregation. Stanley Reed, who had declined to attend a Court Christmas party a few years earlier if blacks were invited, offered a thin defense of segregation as preserving differences, not establishing superiority or inferiority; he was inclined to uphold *Plessy* and segregated schools. Frankfurter then delivered ambiguous observations about the applicability of *Plessy* and the language of the Fourteenth Amendment. Douglas said he would strike down school segregation. Jackson followed Frankfurter's ambivalent lead, seeming to say that the Court should eliminate segregation and simply admit that it was doing so despite questionable legal authority. Burton fell in with Douglas,

Clark worried about how any desegregation order would be received in places such as his native Texas. Minton joined Burton and Douglas. The tally then, on December 12, 1953, stood as follows: Five justices—Warren, Black, Douglas, Burton, and Minton—solidly favored the end to public school segregation. Two, Frankfurter and Jackson, wanted to agree but were struggling with the law. Two more, Reed and Clark, were inclined to uphold segregation but were painfully aware that they were in the minority.

For the next three months, Warren methodically worked his colleagues. He lunched with wavering justices, drew out their concerns, paired them in congenial combinations. On January 15, he treated his colleagues to a duck and pheasant lunch (eight justices chose duck; Frankfurter preferred pheasant). In those conversations, Warren subtly shifted the discussion from whether to strike down segregation to how to do it. One at a time, the justices fell in line behind their new chief as he patiently guided them away from the tangle of the Vinson Court.

The Court's work occurs in splendid remove from daily politics, and Warren's leadership was invisible to the public in those months. That was fortunate since Warren had good reason for moving cautiously: as a recess appointment to the Court, he still had not received his Senate confirmation and would not until after first enduring a nasty committee investigation overseen by the irascible William Langer. Finally, on February 24, the committee voted out Warren's confirmation on a 12–3 vote, with Langer oddly voting in favor of Warren. Eisenhower lobbied hard for Warren's confirmation—notwithstanding his brother Edgar's disdain for the chief justice. Ike tracked the *Brown* deliberations, meanwhile, from a discreet distance, receiving Brownell's tip early in the year that a decision was likely in the spring.

The president did not cut off all contact with Warren. Indeed, their most significant encounter, that February, left a permanent scar on their relationship. Eisenhower established in his first year as president a tradition of hosting stag dinners at the White House—black-tie affairs at which a dozen or two leading men of politics, business, and culture gathered at the presidential mansion to discuss significant world matters. On February 8, 1954, the guest list was typically illustrious: Erwin Griswold, dean of Harvard Law School, and Franklin Murphy, chancellor of the University of Kansas, were among the prominent academics; the executives Ernest Breech of Ford Motor Company and M. M. Anderson of Alcoa represented big business, as did Lucius Clay and Alton Jones, two longtime friends of Ike's who now headed corporations; Attorney General Herb Brownell and Undersecretary of State Bedell Smith represented the administration. But two of the guests were especially notable for their presence there together. One was Warren, still the acting chief justice; the other was John W. Davis, one of the nation's most prominent lawyers, who was representing the state of South Carolina in *Brown v. Board of Education.*

Warren, a stern and somewhat prickly man, immediately took offense at Davis's presence. The two were seated within speaking distance, adding to Warren's unease. Then, as the men rose from the table and ambled into an adjoining room for after-dinner drinks, Eisenhower took Warren by the arm and nodded at the Southerners. "These are not bad people," Eisenhower said. "All they are concerned about is to see that their sweet little girls are not required to sit in school alongside some big overgrown Negroes."

Warren was appalled. He made sure to record Eisenhower's words in his own memoirs, revealing the exchange to make the point that Ike instinctively sympathized with those committed to segregation rather than with those suffering by its conditions (it hardly needs saying that the stag dinner at which this offense occurred was an all-white gathering). Ike's defenders have tried to explain away his damaging remark. David Nichols, in his elegantly argued *A Matter of Justice*, suggests that it may not have occurred at all, noting that Warren "alleges" the remark in his memoirs and "is the only source for the story. There are no corroborating witnesses." Nichols argues that Warren related the story out of resentment toward "the war hero who had destroyed his chance to be president." But, as Nichols acknowledges, others recalled Eisenhower making similar comments, and Herb Brownell, when he learned of the incident, attempted to reconstruct the evening and concluded that Eisenhower spoke clumsily and was angry with Warren for betraying the confidentiality that was supposed to govern the dinners—not that Warren made up the exchange.

Warren returned to his business, suspecting that he would not have the vigorous support of the White House should the Court strike down school segregation. Nevertheless, on the May afternoon that he announced the Court's opinion, he spoke evenly and deliberately, reading as reporters, scrambling into the chambers, slipped into their seats and flipped open notepads. For the first few minutes, Warren's recitation was factual, reviewing the circumstances of the case and the issues the Court had considered. Then he reached the decision's pivotal passage, and he departed briefly and momentously from the text. "We conclude that in the field of public education the doctrine of 'separate but equal' has no place," the decision read. But Warren interposed a word: "We *unanimously* conclude." Justice Reed, the Court's last holdout in *Brown*, wiped a tear from his cheek. Thurgood Marshall, lawyer for the plaintiffs, stood in amazement. Warren himself sensed the power of the moment: "When the word 'unanimously' was spoken, a wave of emotion swept the room, no words or intentional movement, yet a distinct emotional manifestation that defies description."

Troubled by the ruling's demands and the threat of rebellion from the South—and ever in search of a middle way—Eisenhower elected to regard *Brown* as an order from the Court rather than as a moral imperative to be joined. At a press conference two days after the Court's historic announcement, Ike conspicuously declined to embrace the rulings (*Brown* was accompanied by *Bolling v. Sharpe*, which desegregated schools in the District of Columbia, outside the reach of the Fourteenth Amendment, since that amendment applies only to the states). Eisenhower formally received the Court's decisions with studied neutrality. "The Supreme Court has spoken," he said at a press conference two days after the ruling was handed down. "And I am sworn to uphold their—the constitutional processes in this country, and I am trying. I will obey." Eisenhower's discomfort with *Brown* would become more, not less, severe, as southern resistance stiffened and he felt torn between the aspirations of American blacks, few of whom he knew, and the uneasiness of southern whites, many of whom were his closest friends. Seeking his "middle way," Eisenhower routinely deplored "foolish extremists on both sides of the question," suggesting moral equivalence between those who sought equality and those who denied it.

In 1955, Eisenhower was gratified when the Court issued its desegregation order (so-called *Brown II* allowed states to integrate schools with "all deliberate speed," a formula that permitted much deliberation and demanded very little speed). That announcement was well received in the South, and Brownell remarked to Eisenhower that it "followed the President's formula almost exactly." Nevertheless, school integration dominated the civil rights agenda through Eisenhower's tenure and provided recurring sources of conflict throughout the South. The issue brought out the worst in Eisenhower, making him churlish and defensive. By 1956, his patience was so exhausted on the question that he threatened to boycott his own nominating convention in San Francisco if the GOP leadership insisted on inserting platform language stating that "the Eisenhower Administration" supported the Court's ruling in *Brown*.

Civil rights confounded and annoyed Eisenhower as a domestic obligation, but it spoke clearly to him as Cold War advantage. Barely had *Brown* been announced than the Voice of America was broadcasting the news around the world. As Eisenhower recognized, *Brown* supplied a powerful counterweight to a mainstay of Soviet propaganda—that democratic capitalism, as practiced by the United States, upheld racist oppression. American apartheid validated that theory, and the Soviet Union exploited it throughout the Third World as it trumpeted the moral superiority of Communism. *Brown* undermined that argument, and the Voice of America made sure the world knew it. International reaction was overwhelmingly positive, especially in Africa (a notable exception being South Africa) and other areas of the Third World. In São Paulo, Brazil, the local municipal council passed a resolution expressing "satisfaction" with the ruling, and in Dakar, West Africa, a local paper proclaimed, "At last! Whites and Blacks in the United States on the same school benches." The stain of American racism was lightened by *Brown*, and America consequently gained strength in the long battle for international appreciation vis-à-vis the Soviets.

Brown capped a monumental spring, but as Eisenhower's unwillingness to associate himself with the decision suggests, it contributed to a trying period for the Republican Party, which was already riven by McCarthy. The controversy over *Brown* now threatened to erode the party's attempts to gain voters in the South, where Eisenhower believed there was room for political growth. Instead, many Southerners associated the Warren Court with the GOP, and the most ardent anti-Communists regarded Eisenhower with renewed suspicion. Swede Hazlett wrote from Chapel Hill, North Carolina, to convey his concern and express precisely the fears that Eisenhower himself harbored regarding *Brown*. "I'm afraid we'll have plenty of trouble," Hazlett wrote, "and some bloodshed, if the issue is forced too fast."

International developments offered no respite. China resumed its episodic aggression toward Quemoy and Matsu during September, and the Joint Chiefs itched for a fight. On September 6, they approved a proposal to allow Chiang to bomb bases inside China and, if that provoked a Chinese attack on Quemoy, to wage all-out war. Six days later, the Joint Chiefs presented their idea to the NSC, meeting in the Williamsburg Room of the Officers' Club at Lowry Air Force Base in Denver, where Ike was relaxing with the Gang.

After a brief presentation of the current situation and a display of maps of the region by the CIA's Allen Dulles, Admiral Arthur Radford opened the discussion that afternoon, urging support for the more aggressive policy. Bedell Smith objected. John Foster Dulles equivocated but warned that Taiwanese withdrawal from the islands would have implications for Korea, Japan, Formosa, and the Philippines. On the other hand, use of nuclear weapons to defend those same islands would invite the condemnation of the world. But it was Eisenhower himself who spotted the full implications of Radford's suggestion. The council, he said, needed to be clear about one thing: it was contemplating not a limited war but an all-out attack on China, a conflict in which there would be none of the restraint practiced in Korea. Moreover, he added, the war that Radford proposed, one to defend islands of remote consequence, would grow quickly into one of unimaginable violence. "If we are to have general war," Eisenhower said, it would not be against just China. The United States would "want to go to the head of the snake" and strike the Soviet Union itself.

Those ramifications were far more than Eisenhower was willing to wager. However much Radford and the generals might crave such a showdown, Ike would not authorize it. He said no.

On November 1, Chinese planes bombed the Tachen Islands, and three weeks later thirteen American pilots—eleven uniformed Air Force pilots shot down during the Korean War, as well as two CIA operatives—were sentenced by a Chinese court to prison terms for espionage. Bill Knowland urged a blockade of China even after Ike had counseled gentler action. "The hard way is to have the courage to be patient," Ike lectured the senator. Knowland did not listen; he rarely did.

Under pressure from the right to respond to Chinese provocation, Eisenhower agreed to a mutual-defense pact with Taiwan. The treaty's careful language reflected a delicate balance of factors as well as Dulles's gift for legalistic formulations in the conduct of foreign affairs. It pledged the United States and Taiwan to each other's defense in the event of any "armed attack in the West Pacific Area directed against the territories of either of the Parties." That was the warning to China and the bone to Knowland and the China-first lobby in Congress. But the treaty was vague as to what constituted the "territories of either of the Parties." It specifically mentioned the Pescadores, but did it include Quemoy and Matsu? If so, what about the Tachens? The treaty could be extended to protect "such other territories as may be determined by mutual agreement." The vagueness was intended to create uncertainty in China without committing the United States to wage a major war over a minor outpost. In case his point was missed, Eisenhower reinforced it a few months later, responding to a question at a press conference by acknowledging his willingness to use nuclear weapons to enforce the treaty. "In any combat where these things can be used on strictly military targets and for strictly military purposes," he said, "I see no reason why they shouldn't be used just exactly as you would use a bullet or anything else."

Mao did not take Eisenhower's threat lightly: China had negotiated an end to the Korean War after Ike passed word that he would consider using nuclear weapons to resolve that stalemate. Now the Chinese kept up their assaults on the remote Taiwanese positions but refrained from an attack on Taiwan itself. Ambiguity prevailed.

Finally, the year wound down. Ike wavered between testy and reflective, snapping occasionally at aides, lecturing, sometimes complaining. His family was annoying as well: Arthur lobbied for an invitation to a stag dinner and asked to bring Louise; Ike agreed but reminded his brother that Louise would not be allowed to attend the dinner itself. "I am afraid," he wrote, "there will be nothing for Louise to do unless she and Mamie go downstairs to a movie."

Eisenhower's frustrations were understandable. He knew he had done more than the American people were aware of, but he could not tout the victories that had resulted from covert action. In late November, Eisenhower turned on Knowland, who had been irritating all year, especially with his grandstanding over China. It was Thanksgiving week, and the China standoff was particularly tense. To Knowland, Eisenhower condescendingly explained the rigors of the Cold War. "I know so many things that I am almost afraid to speak to my wife," said Eisenhower, who by then had authorized the overthrow of not one but two foreign leaders. "You apparently think we are just sitting supinely and letting the people do as they please. Here's the thing to remember: Suppose one day we do get in war. If too many people knew we had done anything provocative . . ." Eisenhower trailed off, but his insinuation was clear: that Knowland should not know too much, probe too deeply, or complain too loudly. Knowland mumbled an incoherent reply—"indistinct" was how the note taker regarded it—and departed.

Ike's next guest that day was Field Marshal Bernard Montgomery. Monty and Ike—once rivals, then friends, bound by victory despite their differences—relaxed for a few minutes in the Oval Office, reflecting on their long association as well as fresh challenges facing their nations. To Monty, Ike could afford to gripe. "No man on earth knows what this job is all about," Eisenhower said. "It's pound, pound, pound. Not only is your intellectual capacity taxed to the utmost, but your physical stamina."

Nor did the problems let up. After Eisenhower cut off McCarthy, the senator slipped out of the national mainstream but remained skulking on the margins. Once the elections were over, the Senate moved to discipline him. A special Senate committee chaired by Arthur Watkins, a Republican from Utah, sifted through dozens of charges. Watkins, a devout Mormon who was as methodical and even-tempered as McCarthy was brash and inconsistent, carefully waded through the voluminous record and eventually settled on two counts: McCarthy's efforts to obstruct a committee investigating him in 1951 and 1952 and his abuse of Ralph Zwicker during the general's testimony earlier that year. The Senate, meeting between the election and the seating of the new Congress in January, pressed toward a vote, with Republicans dominating the debate (Lyndon Johnson, the Senate Democratic leader, urged liberals to hold their fire for fear of alienating moderate Republicans). McCarthy responded in predictable fashion, charging that the committee was the "unwitting handmaiden of the Communist Party" and specifically attacking Watkins as a coward. McCarthy's abuse of the Watkins Committee was so zealous that the Senate voted to add a new count for his conduct toward Watkins and his colleagues. The Senate was less convinced about the impropriety of McCarthy's attack on Zwicker. Watkins tried but came up short on the votes relating to the Zwicker count. He later told Eisenhower that he would "regret to his dying day" that he could not rally the Senate on that charge. Still, once the Zwicker charge was dropped, the Senate voted, 67–22, to condemn McCarthy on two counts of noncooperation and abuse of his colleagues. Democrats unanimously supported the motions, joined by twenty-two Republicans and the Senate's lone independent, Wayne Morse of Oregon. Knowland, the Republican leader, voted against McCarthy's censure, annoying Eisenhower.

Eisenhower gave the hearings wide berth, but once the Senate had voted, he signaled his pleasure at the outcome. On December 4, two days after McCarthy was condemned, Ike summoned Watkins to the White House. "I wanted to see you," he said as Watkins entered the office. "You handled a tough job like a champion." The two spoke for forty-five minutes as Eisenhower reviewed his misgivings about McCarthy and even indulged in a rare reminiscence about his years working under MacArthur. Their meeting had been convened privately—Watkins entered through a basement door to escape public notice—but reporters at the White House inquired about the president's schedule that morning and discovered the meeting. James Hagerty, Ike's erstwhile press secretary, afterward reported that Eisenhower told Watkins he had "done a very splendid job." Eisenhower was startled that Hagerty was so frank after the measures the White House had taken to keep the session off the record, but he was pleased anyway. "Confidentially," he told Hagerty, "I thought the stories were just exactly what I wanted to see in the paper, and I don't particularly care what the Old Guard thinks about it."

McCarthy used the meeting to declare his "break" from Eisenhower. "Why it was called such at that late date I could not fathom," Ike grumbled in his memoirs. Theatrically, McCarthy apologized to the American people for having supported Eisenhower in 1952. But McCarthy no longer struck fear. Ignored, he disintegrated into alcohol and irrelevance. He remained in the Senate, a lonely and shunned figure, shambling the halls, pleading for attention. He died three years later.

While the Senate belatedly rid itself of McCarthy, Eisenhower was busy fighting more dangerous enemies with more powerful weapons. In the fall of 1954, CIA officials, led by Allen Dulles, brought to him a proposal for a new addition to the nation's Cold War arsenal—a high-altitude surveillance plane, equipped with the most modern and sensitive camera equipment.

The meeting was attended by John Foster Dulles from State, Charlie Wilson from Defense, and leaders of the Air Force and was conducted, of course, in utmost secrecy. Eisenhower approved the project verbally but signed no written authorization. Worried that the Soviets would consider it an act of war if military planes were to fly over their territory, Ike directed that the program be run by the CIA and later indicated that he would prefer the agency hire non-U.S. citizens to fly the craft. With that, the U-2 program was launched.

The Senate vote cleared the nation's political landscape of McCarthy, but the November midterm elections highlighted the divisions in the Republican Party, as well as the gap between voters' affection for Eisenhower and their support for the GOP. Without Ike on the ticket, Republican candidates tanked. Congress slipped back into Democratic control, where it would remain for the balance of Eisenhower's presidency. He would govern by the strength of his arguments, his commitment to centrist bipartisanship, and his personal popularity, but never again would he enjoy the luxury of carrying a party-line vote.

Republican leaders naturally wasted no time after the elections before courting Eisenhower to consider a second term. Just two weeks after the results of the midterms were tallied, Lucius Clay came calling again. He arrived at the end of a busy day—the French premier, Pierre Mendès-France, was in town, so Ike had hosted a stag luncheon. Afterward, Eisenhower cleared most of his day for Clay. At first, Clay beat around the topic, then "once he got on to the real purpose of his visit, he pursued his usual tactics—aimed at overpowering all opposition and at settling the matter without further question." Eisenhower's reaction, recorded in his diary two days later, mirrored his initial response to the first draft-Ike movement: he was flattered but realistic about the suggestion that he was indispensable.

Clay received no answer the day of his visit, but he had placed the idea where he wanted it. Eisenhower began to mull the question of his own presidency. His thoughts turned to history and leadership, to the defining qualities of great men and great challenges. As was his habit, he found expression for those ideas by sharing them with Swede Hazlett. Rambling and digressive, his letter represented the unguarded musings of a friend, not the considered comments of a president. Nevertheless—or as a result—the letter revealed Ike's unguarded sense of himself and his place in history. "No man," Eisenhower wrote, "can be classed as great unless" he either is preeminent in a "broad field of human thought" or has, "in some position of great responsibility, so discharged his duties as to have left a marked and favorable imprint upon the future of the society or civilization of which he is a part." By his criteria, Plato was a great man. So were George Washington, Martin Luther, and Napoleon (though Napoleon, Ike emphasized, also had "obvious and glaring defects"). Of Churchill, Eisenhower wrote: "I think I would say that he comes nearest to fulfilling the requirements of greatness in any individual that I have met in my lifetime." Among Americans, Washington, Lincoln, and Robert E. Lee topped Eisenhower's list; he named George Marshall as the greatest American he knew personally and listed Henry L. Stimson and John Quincy Adams as men who left great legacies. Arthur Vandenberg and Senator Walter George, a Georgia Democrat who broke ranks to support Ike on important congressional matters, according to Eisenhower, "came close."

Amid those ruminations, Eisenhower sketched one short paragraph of special note. "The qualities we seek in a great man," he wrote, "would be vision, integrity, courage, understanding, the power of articulation either in the spoken or the written form, and what we might call profundity of character."

Eisenhower would not presume to consider himself alongside his idols, but his contemporaries were pleading for his continued leadership and appealing particularly to his sense of duty. By his own standards—vision, integrity, courage, understanding, and rhetorical power, not to mention leaving a mark on his time—Ike's early presidency qualified as great.

He was a man who knew the difference between greatness and lesser achievement. As his comments to Knowland a few weeks earlier showed, Eisenhower appreciated the gravity of the presidency and the extent of danger in the world. He had, over the space of two years, built a distinguished cabinet, ended a war, authorized the overthrow of two leaders, appointed a consequential chief justice, and ended the rampage of Senator McCarthy. Just as important, he had refused to act heedlessly when others clamored for action: time and again, advisers urged the use of nuclear weapons against America's enemies; Ike would not do it. When the French begged for assistance in holding their colonial outpost in Indochina, Eisenhower refused, judging that America's interests did not reside with colonialism. Weaker or more arrogant men might have escalated the war in Korea or entered one in Indochina. More cautious men might have flinched at action in Iran or Guatemala. Small men might have passed over Warren for the Court, choosing a safer pick, one with a judicial record that would make his tenure more predictable. Cautious men might have embraced McCarthy.

Ike was none of those. He was a great man at the height of his power, and as much as he resisted the idea of a second term, he was tempted and enjoyed the prospect of changing history. Eisenhower knew the challenges and difficulties, the toll that the presidency took on any man who occupied it. He ended the year contemplating politics past and future. He was determined to meet his own standard of greatness, but more pounding lay ahead.

10

Heartache

For Eisenhower, 1955 opened beneath portentous skies. He and Mamie were in Augusta to golf and relax, but he woke on New Year's Day to rain and wind across his favorite course. He shuffled all day between the residence and the office, hoping for a break in the weather, getting none.

The coming weeks would deepen the foreboding of New Year's Day. Churchill resigned the prime ministership. Einstein died in April. Ike wrote movingly of Einstein's contribution to the modern world, but losing Churchill as a colleague was especially sad. Eisenhower had known Churchill first from the perspective of a subordinate and later as a peer, had chuckled over his idiosyncrasies, and had been awed by his command of language and his bellowing truculence. The prime minister's departure from high office left Eisenhower as the last of the world's great leaders during the war that formed them all. When Churchill warned Ike that he was preparing to step down, Eisenhower's reply brimmed with shared memories and common affections: Churchill had taught Ike the quiet satisfaction of painting, as Ike recalled. Admitting to a wave of nostalgia, Eisenhower reminisced about the early, perilous weeks of the war and recalled the effect Churchill had on him: "I still remember with great admiration the fact that never once did you quail at the grim prospect ahead of us; never did I hear you utter a discouraged word nor a doubt as to the final and certain outcome."

Churchill's departure was especially poignant because it emphasized the contrast between leaders of his stature and those surrounding Ike in 1955.

Knowland, in particular, continued to irritate the president, even though the latest triggering event was relatively minor. The Senate Republican leader had annoyed Eisenhower in late 1954 with his vote not to condemn McCarthy (he voted, he said, as a member of the Senate, not as its Republican leader, a distinction that mattered to no one but Knowland). "In his case," Ike wrote of Knowland in January when the senator angered him again, "there seems to be no final answer to the question, 'How stupid can you get?' "

Ike could joke about the senator but not about China, which was again stirring. The latest eruption in that relationship occurred in the early hours of January 18, when the White House awoke to the news that China had launched a full-scale invasion of Yichang, a volcanic rock near the Tachens and under Nationalist control. Russian jets provided air support, and Chinese forces scaled cliffs as the Nationalist defenders broke ranks. Andy Goodpaster, a trusted adviser on national security matters, glumly observed that the Chinese were "growing up and getting tougher." And more strategic, too. The remoteness of the island—and the nature of the conflict between Chinese Communists and Nationalists—were enough to give China confidence that it could engage in aggression without fear of American nuclear retaliation. The Communists believed those factors would protect them from what Ike described just weeks earlier to Republican leaders as "the ability to blow hell out of them [any American enemy] in a hurry if they start anything."

The Chinese invasion was deliberately provocative, timed just as Eisenhower was attempting to build public and political support for a reduction in American armed forces—part of the New Look strategy that envisioned a long struggle against Communism, not a short and decisive war. That approach was integral to the administration's strategic planning and an outgrowth of the Solarium Project—with its multifaceted approach to containing and rolling back international Communism through nuclear deterrence, sound budgets, and covert action. But Ike continued to encounter resistance to New Look, particularly from defense hawks, including some leading Republicans, who were suspicious that its emphasis on reduced conventional forces marked a retreat from confronting Communism. Some military leaders accepted the change in course reluctantly, mindful of its implications for their turfs and budgets. The Army's chief of staff, Matthew Ridgway, who had earned Eisenhower's admiration during the Korean War—and especially as a welcome relief from MacArthur's megalomania—now emerged as an outspoken critic of the president's strategy. Ridgway complained that he was being asked to make irresponsible cuts—"I felt I was being called upon to tear down, rather than build up," the nation's fighting capacity, Ridgway wrote later—and warned that the Chinese action in the Taiwan Strait was proof of his fear. Only American ground forces, he insisted, could defend the Nationalist Chinese islands. Eisenhower was incensed and considered sacking Ridgway, only to be talked out of that idea by Dulles, though Dulles too complained of subordinates who "carry their dissents beyond privileged boundaries." Ike relented for the moment about firing Ridgway but stood fast on New Look and Taiwan. "I have no intention of putting American foot soldiers on Quemoy," he told Admiral Arthur Radford, the chairman of the Joint Chiefs of Staff. "A division of soldiers would not make any difference."

But if threatening the use of nuclear weapons would not deter Chinese adventurism, and Eisenhower was unwilling to commit American troops, what response was left? Ike knew that America's nuclear arsenal offered an option, not merely as deterrent, but as weapon of retaliation. Indeed, use might enhance deterrence, as it would prove the seriousness of the threat, precisely the argument advanced on behalf of a nuclear strike against North Korea in 1953. Eisenhower was unwilling to fight for remote volcanic rocks, but if China determined to take islands of greater consequence, including Quemoy and Matsu, Ike was ready to go to war. On March 6, Dulles reported from a trip to the region: "I said I did not think that as things now stood we could sit by and watch the Nationalist forces there be crushed by the Communists." Ike accepted that and acknowledged, too, the grave implications of such a commitment. According to Dulles, "I said that this would require the use of atomic missiles. The President said he thoroughly agreed with this." So, yet again, the administration faced the abyss, determined to deter by its willingness to engage. Eisenhower authorized American assistance in evacuating Yichang, then turned to the islands of Quemoy and Matsu. Would China now force the next move?

War seemed so imminent that Admiral Robert Carney, whom Ike had appointed as chief of naval operations in 1953, blurted an off-the-record comment at a dinner with reporters, saying he believed that China would attack within weeks—specifically, he predicted China would invade Quemoy and Matsu by April 15. Such a bald prediction from a senior member of the military was reckless, and it compounded Eisenhower's frustration. "By God, this has got to stop," he exclaimed to Hagerty. Ike recognized that Carney expressed a widely held view within the administration, but it was one thing to discuss that fear among colleagues, another to say it to a room full of reporters. Moreover, Charlie Wilson, Eisenhower's malaprop-prone secretary of defense, was publicly suggesting that the loss of Matsu or Quemoy would not significantly alter the international equation. Ike pulled Wilson aside after an NSC meeting to urge him to watch his tongue. Later, Eisenhower marveled in his diary at how Wilson "seems to have no comprehension at all of what embarrassment such remarks can cause."

Amid such confusion, Eisenhower was immediately forced to answer for Carney's prediction. A reporter opened Ike's news conference on March 30 with a question about the admiral's comments. Eisenhower roundly disavowed them. "I do not believe that the peace of the world, the tranquility of the world, is being served at this moment by talking too much in terms of speculation about such things," he said. Then, trying to end the matter, he added: "I think that is all I have to say about it." Reporters kept pressing him, asking whether Carney was irresponsible to discuss the enemy's plans so openly. Ike almost delivered a more direct rebuke, then pulled back when asked if Carney would be reprimanded for his comments. "Not by me," he replied brusquely. That ended the matter publicly, but by the rules in those days the White House cleared comments for publication. The president's remarks in the section of the conference that were not approved for quotation were even sharper. "I want to make clear that he does have a right to his personal convictions," Eisenhower said. "But he cannot utter them properly, in my opinion, if he is going to create difficulty for his administration . . . because then he doesn't belong as a member of the team." Carney knew he was in trouble. He halfheartedly expressed his regret to Eisenhower—Ann Whitman said the admiral had "apologized," which she put in quotation marks—and then all concerned waited anxiously as Carney's predicted date approached. The strain on Eisenhower was unmistakable. "Foster and I live 24 hours a day with that one," he told the Speaker of the House, Sam Rayburn. "That is the most difficult problem I have had to face since I took office."

April 15 came and went, and the islands remained in Nationalist hands. Strategic clarity, tactical ambiguity, military strength, and nuclear capacity succeeded where Truman's uncertain commitment toward Korea had failed. Ike deterred aggression and avoided war. Once the crisis had passed, Ridgway retired in June, followed by Carney in August. Wilson remained. Dulles was ebullient. "Of all the things I have done, I think the most brilliant of all has been to save Quemoy and Matsu," he confided to Emmet Hughes in 1956. Hughes was repelled: "I felt an almost physical reaction before the icy breath of his self-esteem."

Even as events roiled Asia and kept rival ideologies in the region at sword's point, the Cold War's dynamic—in which capitalism and Communism dispatched soldiers to one region and diplomats to another, where threats of obliteration were accompanied by pledges of cooperation and common pursuit—simultaneously encouraged conflict and negotiation. In 1955, those forces produced a growing public and political clamor for a four-power conference that would include Britain, France, the Soviet Union, and the United States. The initial impetus came from Britain, where Churchill's former foreign secretary, Anthony Eden, now served as prime minister. Eager to demonstrate his new position and convinced that a summit could help reduce international tensions, Eden wrote to Eisenhower in early May proposing the meeting. "I do hope you will be willing to try this," Eden continued, almost pleadingly. "The hopes of so many people, on both sides of the Iron Curtain, have been raised and a kind of mystique surrounds the idea. This may be foolish, but it is human."

As Eden suspected, Eisenhower was skeptical, not to mention slightly nonplussed to discover that Eden had hatched the proposal without first discussing it with his American counterparts (Ike was miffed when reports of the British intention to propose a summit leaked in London and reached him through the press before Eden's formal note). But Churchill urged Ike to go along, and Eisenhower responded with an open mind, suggesting that if such a summit were to take place, it should neither revolve around a detailed agenda nor be an entirely open and unstructured conversation. Rather, Eisenhower proposed that a summit should tackle three general subjects: nuclear arms reduction, limitation of forces and arms in Europe, and reunification of Germany. Although mindful of domestic opinion and concerned about angering "die-hard opponents of any contact with the Communists," Eisenhower clearly signaled that he was open to a summit under the right conditions.

Over the next several days, Dulles, checking in frequently with Eisenhower, met with British and French officials in Paris and then Vienna to draft language inviting the Soviet Union. The allied governments circulated a draft on May 10 that read, "Believe that the time has now come for a new effort to resolve the great problems which confront us. We, therefore, invite the Soviet government to join with us in an effort to remove sources of conflict between us."

Addressing reporters the following day, Eisenhower described the plans as exploratory but acknowledged that his initial resistance to a gathering had softened. His answer was not a model of clarity—it was one of those circumlocutions that earned him a reputation for rambling—but it did capture his hopes for the gathering. "This business of trying to reach a clarification of issues," he said, "if such a thing is possible, is so important that you can't stand on any other principle except, 'Do your utmost,' as you preserve your own position of strength, as long as you are not sacrificing it, as long as you are not expecting too much. Don't be just stubborn in your refusal to expect anything, but go ahead and see what you can find out about it." If it seemed Eisenhower was talking to himself, well, perhaps he was.

Two days later, in Vienna, foreign ministers of the four powers met over a Saturday evening dinner. Dulles pressed his Soviet counterpart, Vyacheslav Molotov, a scheming old Stalinist and survivor of many intrigues, to lay down rules for a summit. Molotov was receptive, yielding on what Dulles thought would be an insistence that China attend as well. The Russian proposed Vienna as the site for the gathering, but Dulles resisted, worried that holding the affair there would seem to reward Austria for adopting a position of Cold War neutrality in exchange for casting off Soviet occupation. Such a signal might encourage Germany to try to do the same. Instead, Dulles suggested Switzerland; Molotov warned Dulles privately that anything but Vienna might encounter resistance from the Soviet leadership—the Soviets favored Vienna for all the same reasons that the U.S. resisted it—but added that if the conference were held in Switzerland, the Soviets would prefer Geneva, where they had a consulate, to Lausanne. And so the principals circled in on a place. As for a date, Eisenhower preferred to wait until Congress adjourned for the summer. Molotov seemed flexible.

With plans coalescing for the summit, Eisenhower enjoyed strong popular support for his participation. Through 1955, his job approval rating rarely dipped below 70 percent, extraordinary numbers for a president moving into the second half of his term. Nearly eight out of ten Americans trusted him to lead a successful conference with the Soviets. Support was similarly strong in Germany and Italy, though the United States was generally viewed far more skeptically by the French and the British—indeed, in Britain, more of those surveyed expressed warmth toward the Soviet Union than toward the United States. Reviewing the data, Nelson Rockefeller, acting as a special assistant to Ike, concluded that the conference "is regarded as beginning a long process of easing world tensions."

Rockefeller in 1955 was a forty-seven-year-old comer, a pointy-elbowed, cocksure politician in training, heir to a family name synonymous with power and fortune. Rockefeller joined the administration early, initially at the Department of Health, Education, and Welfare, but moved to the position of special adviser for foreign affairs when C. D. Jackson returned to *Time* magazine. Dulles was suspicious from the start. Rockefeller's position encroached on Dulles's turf, and Rockefeller lacked Jackson's subtlety for internal politics. Although Rockefeller could count on Sherman Adams for some protection—the two Dartmouth alumni were fond of each other—Dulles eyed Rockefeller's moves warily, and Rockefeller responded by removing himself almost entirely from Dulles's scrutiny, an awkward position given that Rockefeller's mandate was foreign affairs. Dulles and his brother viewed Rockefeller as brash and shallow; when, for instance, Rockefeller offered up an idea for a political warfare school, the Dulles brothers chortled. Out of his earshot, they derided it as "amateurish" and "dangerous."

Dulles was wary of the summit to begin with but had reluctantly come to advocate it. Rockefeller, by contrast, was a full-bore enthusiast. He gathered advisers and experts at the Quantico Marine Corps Base to draft what he hoped would be a dramatic peace proposal to unveil at the conference. They worked in secret, to Dulles's consternation. "He's got them down at Quantico," Dulles groused to Adams one day. "And nobody knows what they're doing." By late May, Dulles and Rockefeller were feuding openly. Dulles told the president he had heard that Rockefeller was trying to chart policy for the summit; Rockefeller complained that he was so frustrated working with the State Department that he was considering a transfer to Defense. Ike saw the strengths in both men and refused to intervene.

Meanwhile, Dulles fenced with Molotov over the summit's arrangements. They met in Vienna and outside San Francisco. They jousted over Molotov's address to the United Nations and his planned appearance on American television; Dulles advised him to keep his speech short, Molotov agreed. They sounded each other out regarding progress over the release of the American airmen. They reached no agreement. Regarding the summit, now definitely set for Geneva, Molotov indicated that the Soviet leadership would want to discuss disarmament, European security, and economic cooperation. Dulles countered with disarmament and German reunification. The two agreed that Germany and European security were "interconnected," and they chalked that up to progress. But when Dulles suggested that the United States might also raise "the status of Eastern European nations," Molotov huffily replied that "the position of the Soviet Union had been made abundantly clear."

The American agenda firmed up over those weeks, guided by Dulles and Eisenhower as they assembled a list of American ambitions and tallied where they enjoyed French or British support. As late as July 6, just nine days before Eisenhower was scheduled to depart, Dulles's list of goals for the summit included no reference to the work of Rockefeller's group.

Before leaving, Ike had to tend to a sad duty: on July 13, he accepted the resignation of Oveta Culp Hobby. Over her thirty months in the Eisenhower cabinet, Hobby had resumed the work habits that drove her to exhaustion during World War II. Ike tried to persuade her to ease up. He gently urged her to take a long weekend at Thanksgiving in 1953. "I would deem it a very great personal favor," he implored after informing her that he himself was heading for Augusta. She declined. After meeting with her two months later, Eisenhower worried that Hobby was "nearing the end of her rope."

The demands on Hobby had grown more intense, not less. Her husband, the former Texas governor, was fighting ill health, and she was frantically overseeing the completion of the Salk vaccine for polio and its promise to halt the terrifying disease. Once known as infantile paralysis, polio was a global scourge that first devastated the United States in 1916, when twenty-seven thousand people were paralyzed after being felled by the virus; six thousand died. Year after year, the virus spread and grew in alarming epidemics. In 1952, the year Eisenhower was elected, more than fifty-seven thousand Americans were infected. Parents kept children out of school, forbade them to swim in public pools, prohibited them from mingling in public places.

Jonas Salk's breakthrough vaccine was subjected to an extraordinary field test during the early 1950s. On April 12, 1955, the tenth anniversary of the death of FDR—himself a victim of polio—scientists confirmed its efficacy. Americans flocked to get the vaccine. Hobby's department, HEW, oversaw its distribution and early release, thrusting Hobby into the middle of an experiment of nearly unimaginable promise.

With the announcement of the vaccine's successful field test, families pleaded for access to it. HEW selected six manufacturers that produced the vaccine under provisional rules and then were granted licenses. Distribution began immediately, but on April 26 six children who had been vaccinated were diagnosed with polio. Cutter Laboratories, which had produced those vaccines, recalled its product from the market, but by early May the number of infected children had grown to fifty-two. Although that must be considered in light of the five million who had been vaccinated over those weeks, the whipsawing of public hope and fear was agonizing to the administration and Hobby. HEW called for a halt to vaccinations on May 6 and intensively examined the vaccine and the labs producing it; the interruption was brief, and vaccines soon resumed.

But the stress of that episode, added to her worry for her husband, pushed Hobby to her limit. On July 13, she submitted her resignation, citing "personal reasons of a high order" and explaining that nothing less "could persuade me to leave your Administration." Eisenhower knew this was coming, but he was saddened nonetheless. "All who knew you as a dedicated, inspired American leader will miss your voice and counsel in Government," he wrote back the same day, in what he described as "one of the hardest letters I have ever had to write." "None will miss you more," he added, "than Mrs. Eisenhower and myself." When Hobby's resignation was made public, it was George Humphrey who most memorably captured the administration's loss. "She is," Humphrey said, "the best man in the Cabinet."

It was at that sad instant that Ike packed his bags for Geneva. Before leaving, he spoke briefly to the American people. He was going, the president explained, because no effort in the service of peace could be wasted. "We want peace," he said. "We cannot look at this whole situation without realizing, first, that pessimism never won any battles, whether in peace or in war." He was going not to compromise with Communism but rather to exercise tolerance, "to try to see the other fellow's viewpoint as well as we see our own." He did not guarantee success but promised to try to change the tone of international relations. "I say to you, if we can change the spirit in which these conferences are conducted we will have taken the greatest step toward peace, toward future prosperity and tranquility that has ever been taken in the history of mankind." Closing, Eisenhower asked his 165 million fellow Americans to pray for peace that coming Sabbath, to demonstrate to the world that America was a nation not of conquest but of sincerity. "That," he said, "would be a mighty force."

The Eisenhower family watched from the second floor of the White House, as did several close friends—Bill Robinson, Bob Woodruff, George Humphrey and his wife, Gordon Moore and his. Ike joined them immediately after his address and could see in their faces, some streaked with tears, the anticipation and hope that surrounded Geneva. Less than an hour later, Ike, Mamie, and John departed for Europe. They stopped in Iceland to refuel and were given an elaborate luncheon; although it was just 7:00 a.m. Washington time, the guests opened the affair with martinis. Mamie and John passed the flight playing Scrabble; Mamie won. As they neared their destination, she fretted about spending the nights at a high altitude, but John checked and discovered, to their surprise, that Geneva was only twelve hundred feet above sea level.

Their stay was a blur of administrative details and important conversation, set in the elegant, ordered streets and plazas of the pleasant Swiss city. As the summit drew near, Eisenhower met with his British and French counterparts for a two-hour discussion at the American headquarters, the "Geneva White House," as it was known. The European delegations had made their reservations earlier and snapped up all available hotel space in Geneva; the Americans were extricated from an embarrassing homelessness by a Swiss-Scottish couple who agreed to rent their fifteen-room lakeside château to the delegation because "we could hardly refuse to offer it to the President."

The conversation that Sunday morning featured Eisenhower at his most commanding, conversant on a wide range of details, relaxed but guarded, thoroughly in control. Ike urged the French prime minister, Edgar Faure, to edit his remarks to emphasize the importance of German unity, and the leaders reviewed such mundane details as the seating chart for the discussions. A French proposal to cut military expenditures and devote some portion of the savings to an international development fund received exhaustive attention, despite Eisenhower's clear skepticism. Ike then countered with his thoughts on weapons inspection. The meeting segued into lunch, followed by smaller conversations between various leaders and, finally, a private conclave with an old friend, Sir James Gault. Ike and Gault talked about the war, golf, and fishing as Eisenhower permitted himself a moment of quiet before the rush of the summit; the two retired to dinner alone.

The following morning, quiet Swiss crowds welcomed the delegates as the sun glinted through haze across the blue waters of Lake Geneva. Inside the hall, the participants took their places beneath high ceilings that once sheltered the League of Nations. The Western nations had agreed that Eisenhower would chair the gathering, so he spoke first. His remarks revealed little but stressed both his skepticism of past conferences and his flickering hope that this might be different. "I trust that we are not here merely to catalogue our differences," he said. "We are not here to repeat the same dreary exercises that have characterized most of our negotiations of the past ten years. We are here in response to the peaceful aspirations of mankind to start the kind of discussions which will inject a new spirit into our diplomacy; and to launch fresh negotiations under conditions of good augury."

The American delegation regarded the opening remarks as a prelude to the day's main event, a supper for the six-member Soviet delegation—Nikolai Bulganin, Nikita Khrushchev, Molotov, Georgy Zhukov, Andrei Gromyko, and an interpreter—at the Geneva White House. Eisenhower hosted and surrounded himself with his most trusted aides: Dulles, Hagerty, John Eisenhower, and Douglas MacArthur (Dulles's aide, not the general), along with Ambassador Bohlen and a few others. Mamie joined the group for a drink, then, by prearrangement, slipped out. For the Americans, the evening's chief fascination was to lay eyes on a mysterious enemy, one whose rhetoric and actions suggested obdurate hatred for American government and society. There was profound uncertainty about this enemy; two years earlier, Stalin was the sole recognized force in Soviet life. With his death, power had dissipated into shadowy corners. Who, Ike wondered, was his genuine counterpart that evening?

Deprived of any meaningful intelligence into the workings of the Soviet government, Eisenhower naturally imagined that Zhukov held power. Ike and Zhukov had met in the rubble of Berlin, and Zhukov in those years occupied a place of stature in Soviet society not unlike that which Eisenhower held in the West: both victors carried the gratitude of a triumphant people. But Ike had returned to a free nation, while Zhukov returned to Stalin's yoke. Ike had risen to his nation's presidency, while Zhukov for a time disappeared. Many in the West, including Ike, feared him dead.

When the Russians arrived, they were pleasant but notably careful and somewhat nervous. "They were jumpy as hell," John Eisenhower remembered. They drank "very, very little indeed," he added. Zhukov had only orange juice, Khrushchev was "most abstemious and proper." The Soviets exuded, if not exactly warmth, at least manners: "Even Gromyko managed by dint of much effort to smile a couple of times."

Sizing up the Soviet leaders, John Eisenhower demonstrated the acuity that made him such a valuable adviser to his father. Zhukov, he quickly surmised, "appears frightened and worried." So depleted did he seem that John Eisenhower wondered if he had been tortured: "Whether he was the physical receiver of actual rubber hose or whether he was only put in fear is, of course, not known." But Zhukov's presence was mandatory, so much so that he was forced to miss his daughter's wedding. He was the icebreaker with Ike and wasted no time reminding Eisenhower of their common history, "the bond of truthfulness between soldiers." John Eisenhower summed up the rest of the Soviet delegation: Bulganin appeared genial but restrained, "being driven and used principally by someone else"; Molotov as opinionated but stifled; Gromyko, notwithstanding his attempts at a smile, as "sour and fanatic." It was Khrushchev whom Eisenhower's son spotted as different, "extroverted and on this occasion pleasant. To the casual observer he is unimpressive, but to underestimate this man would be the gravest of errors."

The evening passed mainly with small talk. Toasts were exchanged, along with pleasantries and compliments to Mamie. The Soviets "left most decorously at approximately eleven o'clock," and John Eisenhower eagerly sought out Goodpaster to compare notes on the evening. Shrewdly, the young major spied humanity in his country's adversaries while recognizing the solid, imposing front that the Soviet leaders presented. "I think the fact of contact does serve to remind each side that the other side has problems," he added. And of his father, John noted: "Unquestionably Dad dominates a meeting between them."

Appraising the Soviets was an essential aspect of the summit, but the underlying purpose was to intimidate or cajole them into easing world tensions. Eisenhower believed that the best chance lay in the unveiling of a bold proposal—one sufficiently imaginative to capture the world's interest and sufficiently inoffensive to coax Soviet agreement or, at a minimum, to expose Soviet intransigence. Rockefeller's secret group had been at work on such a stroke for weeks. Now, as the summit participants parried ideas, the young aide rushed to Geneva, arriving on July 20.

Ike met that morning over breakfast with Harold Macmillan and Anthony Eden and lunched with Zhukov. Remembering that the conference had forced Zhukov to miss his daughter's wedding, Ike and Mamie presented him with a pen set and a portable radio, to be given to his daughter in honor of her marriage. "Zhukov was visibly and I am sure genuinely moved," recalled John, who attended as well. As for the proposal he was now prepared to present to the summit, Ike still said nothing.

The moment arrived at the afternoon session on July 21. Ike was at ease, relaxed from hitting golf balls that morning with John. He was well briefed by Goodpaster and Radford, among others. The Soviet representatives cycled through their proposal on disarmament, a suggestion that all nations renounce the use of nuclear weapons, knowing that the United States would never agree, both because Americans were convinced the Soviets would break any such agreement at will and, more important, because nuclear deterrence was the cornerstone of Eisenhower's New Look defense strategy. To renounce that threat was to concede Cold War defeat. The Americans listened patiently but without enthusiasm. Finally, it was Eisenhower's turn.

Ike spoke not from a prepared speech but from notes. He ticked off general topics for a few minutes, then paused. "Gentlemen," he began again, "since I have been working on this memorandum to present to this Conference, I have been searching my heart and mind for something that I could say here that could convince everyone of the great sincerity of the United States in approaching this problem of disarmament."

Now Eisenhower presented Rockefeller's grand idea: the United States would give to the Soviet Union complete blueprints of all American defense facilities and would open its airspace for reconnaissance photography. "You can make all the pictures you choose and take them to your own country to study." In return, the United States demanded the same access to Soviet defense facilities. This approach, he predicted, "will open wide the avenues of progress for all our peoples."

The proposal was simple and simply presented. Having placed it before the delegates, Eisenhower concluded: "A sound peace—with security, justice, wellbeing and freedom for the people of the world—can be achieved, but only by patiently and thoughtfully following a hard and sure and tested road."

Those final words still hung in the air when a clap of thunder exploded outside the room. The boom was deafening, and the lights blinked off. In the dark and sudden stillness, Eisenhower quipped: "I didn't know I would put the lights out with that speech." Ike's easy humor tickled the Soviet delegation immensely; its burly leadership burst into laughter, roaring as the lights came back up.

For a moment, annihilation receded, and peace seemed possible. The British and the French responded eagerly to Eisenhower's proposal, which was quickly dubbed "Open Skies." "I wish the people of the world could have been in this conference room to hear the voice of a man speaking from great military experience," Premier Faure of France said later. "They would have believed that something had changed in the world." Even the Soviets seemed receptive. Bulganin agreed that the idea had potential and suggested that the foreign ministers of the four nations convene to work on details. All four nations joined in that proposal. "I thought we had the makings of a breakthrough," John Eisenhower recalled.

At the conclusion of that afternoon's talks, Eisenhower mingled with the Soviet leaders over cocktails and in the buffet line. Khrushchev was among those milling about the room, and Ike sought him out. He seemed amiable, but, as Eisenhower recalled later, "there was no smile in his voice." "I don't agree with the chairman," Khrushchev said, bluntly dismissing the endorsement of Open Skies that Bulganin had just offered. Such open disagreement among the Soviet leadership was remarkable, and Eisenhower recognized what it signaled about the relationships between his counterparts. "From that moment until the final adjournment of the conference, I wasted no more time probing Mr. Bulganin," he wrote. Instead, Eisenhower lobbied Khrushchev, the beginning of their long and infuriating association.

Eisenhower at first imagined that Open Skies might capture Soviet support—the proposal seemed so transparently balanced, so genuinely innovative—and Bulganin's initial enthusiasm seemed to portend a "breakthrough," as John Eisenhower put it. But the follow-up meeting of the foreign ministers confirmed Dulles's skepticism and dashed Ike's hopes. Later, Ike would recall the missed opportunity with bitterness. "Khrushchev," Eisenhower wrote in retirement, "does not want peace, save on his own terms and in ways that will aggrandize his own power. He is blinded by his dedication to the Marxist theory of world revolution and Communist domination. He cares nothing for the future happiness of the peoples of the world . . . In our use of the word, he is not, therefore, a statesman, but rather a powerful, skillful, ruthless, and highly ambitious politician."

It mattered little that Eisenhower was right. Open Skies threatened Khrushchev, and so it failed.

In later years, Eisenhower would come to regard Geneva as a tragic disappointment, but the immediate public reaction was overwhelmingly positive, particularly toward him. Eisenhower's ever-impressive approval rating jumped notably, increasing five points on the eve of the conference and another three in its aftermath. By August 1955, 75 percent of Americans approved of Eisenhower's performance, compared with just 11 percent who disapproved. As those numbers suggested, Ike was suffused with goodwill. Back home, he met with legislative leaders, greeted the annual Boys Nation event, commemorated a new "Atoms for Peace" stamp, and took in a few rounds of golf at Burning Tree, in Bethesda, Maryland. He replaced Oveta Culp Hobby with Marion B. Folsom, who was confirmed without incident.

He tended to ceremonial functions, posed for a portrait, and bade a happy farewell to the nettlesome Admiral Carney. In August, he decamped for a few days at Gettysburg, where he took the Reverend Billy Graham on a tour of the farm, hunted, played golf, and tended to his cattle. It was, by the standards of the presidency, a quiet few weeks, interrupted only by meetings of the cabinet and the National Security Council as well as the unending parade of visitors, but free from crisis. When Ike arrived in Denver on August 14, he had every reason to expect a relaxing break.

So it was at first—golf at Cherry Hills, fishing with his old friend Aksel Nielsen at Nielsen's Colorado ranch. Ike was joined there by his grandson, David, always a delight to his granddad. Ike and Nielsen fished in the mornings and evenings, toured the ranch with David by Jeep in the afternoon, and practiced on a casting pond when time permitted. Back in Denver the next week, Ike and his grandson continued to enjoy their summer freedom—David was allowed to invite friends to join them, and they all lunched together after Ike finished a round of golf. Eisenhower flew off to New England to inspect flooding damage, spent a few days in the White House catching up on work, and delivered an address in Philadelphia, where he was followed to the podium by Chief Justice Warren, their relations now confined to pleasantries and little else. But that brief spell of business was followed by a return to Denver and time with family, lunches at the golf course, painting, and manageable public appearances.

On September 19, Ike ventured into the stream at Nielsen's ranch and emerged with seven trout. He reluctantly left the ranch four days later, celebrating a successful vacation by cooking a final breakfast: corn cakes, eggs, sausage, ham, black-eyed peas, and redeye gravy, then heading back down the eastern slope of the Rockies to Denver.

Once there, he was briefed on world affairs at Lowry Air Force Base, where he kept an office. At the United Nations, Molotov pledged "utmost consideration" of U.S. disarmament overtures, though his comments were undermined by the administration's release of a letter from Bulganin setting Soviet conditions on the Open Skies proposal. In Mississippi, meanwhile, a Tallahatchie County jury took sixty-five minutes to acquit the alleged murderers of fourteen-year-old Emmett Till, who had insulted the wife of one defendant and four days later been abducted from his grandmother's house. In New York, the Yankees clinched the pennant with a win over the Red Sox; Don Larsen got the victory, and the Yankees secured their sixth banner in seven years, the twenty-first in their history.

After briefly catching up on business, Ike departed for Cherry Hills, where, after some practice swings, he set off on the course at noon. He was interrupted twice by calls from Dulles but finished his eighteen holes at 2:00 p.m. He shot an 84, about average for Ike in those days, and enjoyed lunch with his foursome. He ate a sizable hamburger, adorned with thick slices of Bermuda onions, and sipped from a pot of coffee. By 2:15, the group was on the course again, trying to sneak in an additional eighteen holes.

It was then that Ike, so cool in the face of genuine emergency and yet so susceptible to petty annoyances, began to grow anxious. He complained to the club pro about an upset stomach, blaming it on the onions, and fumed when called back to the clubhouse to take another call from Dulles, only to find that the operator had put the call through by mistake and that Dulles no longer needed him. "The veins stood out on his forehead like whipcords," his friend and doctor Howard Snyder recalled. The group completed just nine holes that afternoon, and Eisenhower returned to his in-laws' home in Denver cranky and uncomfortable.

At home, Eisenhower and George Allen played a round of billiards, passed on an evening cocktail, and took a walk after dinner to settle Allen's stomach, which also was bothering him. Afterward, Allen and his wife returned to their hotel, and Ike and Mamie turned in for bed around 10:00 p.m., retiring to their separate rooms. A few hours later, Ike awoke with pain in his chest. He groped for milk of magnesia, and Mamie, who heard him stirring as she returned from the bathroom, got it for him. She could sense that there was something seriously wrong. At 2:54 a.m., she urgently called Snyder, who rushed to the president's side, arriving at 3:11 a.m.

Snyder's patient was agitated and at times incoherent, complaining of pain across his chest and shrugging off an oxygen mask. He was sixty-four years old and had a history of ailments, including his health scare in 1949 that prompted him to quit cigarettes after decades of heavy smoking. He was prone to irritation, and he was, after all, president of the United States; to say that he was subjected to stress would be hyperbolic understatement.

Under Mamie's anxious eye, the doctor said later, Snyder broke a pearl of amyl nitrite and injected Ike with papaverine hydrochloride, which seemed to have no effect. He then injected Eisenhower with heparin, an anticoagulant that would have been called for in the event of a serious heart attack. Eisenhower's pain was undiminished, and Snyder's notes indicate that he gave the president two injections of morphine, one soon after arriving and another at 3:45 a.m. Ike's blood pressure was falling, his pulse was rising, and his skin was turning clammy. A rubdown with warm alcohol did not help, nor did hot water bottles. His blood pressure then "collapsed," and Ike fell into shock, according to Snyder. Desperate to revive her husband, Mamie got into her husband's bed at 4:30 a.m. and wrapped herself around him. Ike responded immediately, calming to her touch. He fell asleep, and Mamie remained with him until 7:00 a.m., when she quietly slipped out of his bed.

Snyder let his patient sleep until 11:30 a.m., monitoring his blood pressure and respiration but, curiously, not alerting a cardiologist or the nearby hospital. Not until shortly after noon did the doctor call Fitzsimons Army Hospital, which dispatched its commanding general, Martin E. Griffin, to the president's bedside (Snyder specifically requested that the general dress in civilian clothes). Griffin administered a cardiogram and immediately concluded that Eisenhower had suffered a major heart attack.

Snyder's actions during that troubled night were puzzling. If his reconstruction of events is to be regarded as truthful, his eight-hour delay in summoning a cardiac expert to Eisenhower's side was inexplicably reckless, and his initial comment to Ike's traveling press secretary that the president had suffered a bout of indigestion was cavalierly deceptive (Snyder justified it later by saying that Ike had in fact suffered from indigestion the day before). There is, however, another explanation, one that emerges from a remarkable reexamination of the episode in 1997. In it, the author Clarence Lasby argued that Snyder doctored his notes in order to cover up the humiliating truth: that he mistook Eisenhower's heart attack for indigestion. Lasby's analysis explained much: why Snyder had not immediately summoned expert help, why he misled the press secretary, why he failed to follow up his initial heparin injection (the medication wears off after about six hours, but Snyder did not indicate that he gave the president a second shot), why he failed to tell other doctors about the heparin and papaverine injections, and why Eisenhower's shock is not reflected in any other notes of the episode. In fact, a second doctor who treated Eisenhower specifically noted after consulting with Snyder that "there has been no period of shock," adding that "pulse and blood pressure have remained stable." Those notations directly contradict Snyder's later recitation of the events. It is possible that Snyder misremembered or simply failed to inform other doctors of the care he had given his patient; it is, however, far more likely that he retroactively adjusted his notes in order to conform to the story that he wanted others to believe—that he had promptly diagnosed Eisenhower's difficulties and heroically tended to them.

Snyder's account presented the reassuring image of a president felled by a heart attack but saved by his attentive and responsive doctor and his caring wife. "The hours he slept during that period from early morning until 12 noon were more responsible for the ultimate recovery of the President than the entire remaining course of hospital treatment," Snyder boasted later. The probable truth was far more unsettling: in the early hours of September 24, 1955, the president of the United States suffered a devastating heart attack and lay for eight hours in the care of a physician who misdiagnosed the event and then lied to cover up his near-calamitous mistake.

Snyder himself did everything he could to discourage inquiry into that possibility. He wrote scores of unsolicited letters to friends and acquaintances—his own and those of the president—explaining that he diagnosed a heart attack and responded appropriately, thereby saving Eisenhower's life. Those letters themselves are curious documents, invasive of his patient's privacy, but they helped to squelch second-guessing of Snyder's actions. Press inquiries were similarly blunted. When a reporter months later gingerly raised the issue of the long delay in summoning a cardiologist, Eisenhower brushed it off. "I understood it was as much as 10 hours," she persisted.

"It may have been," Eisenhower responded. "But it probably may take some 10 hours to determine whether a person is suffering from having eaten some bad food or some other cause, I am not sure. I am not a doctor, you are sure of that."

Of course, Eisenhower's answer did not conform to Snyder's own account—that, soon after arriving, he had ascertained that the president had suffered a heart attack—but the discrepancy was lost in the relief at Ike's recovery.

The administration was scattered when Ike was hospitalized—Adams was returning from Europe; John Eisenhower was on a golf course in Virginia; Brownell was in Spain on vacation; other members of the cabinet were in Washington or traveling. John rushed to his father's side and found Mamie deeply worried. "I just can't believe that Ike's work is finished," she told her son. Her worry was haunted by an eerie coincidence: Ike suffered his heart attack on Icky's birthday.

The members of the administration, meanwhile, returned to the White House and sorted out their duties. The National Security Council met on Thursday and the cabinet on Friday, as scheduled, with Nixon presiding from his own chair, leaving Ike's seat vacant. Adams, meanwhile, decamped for Denver, taking his place at the president's side. Hagerty was so grateful to see Adams arrive that he kissed him, undoubtedly shocking the dour Adams.

Woodrow Wilson's incapacitation offered the only guidance American leaders had for grappling with the inability of a sitting president to fulfill the duties of his office, and Wilson's was a frightening primer in mismanagement. But Eisenhower's cabinet was blessed by both ability and luck. Luck that Ike's illness struck at a calm moment in domestic and international affairs: Congress was in recess; it was an off year politically; the glow of Geneva helped insure a tranquil summer abroad. And ability forged by two years of common effort and by Ike's selection of his top deputies. An informal committee assumed temporary control of the government: Adams served as the personal conduit to the president; Dulles took charge of international relations; Brownell supervised domestic and constitutional questions; and Nixon, assiduously deferential, coordinated the cabinet and directed the administration.

Nixon and Eisenhower in 1955 were closely associated but had never been friends. Barely acquainted when they were united on the Republican ticket in 1952, they found their early association strained by the Checkers debacle. Eisenhower recognized the younger man's talents and deep intelligence, but Ike also patronized his vice president, who seemed too young and too political to be trusted entirely. Eisenhower's contradictory impressions of Nixon—as capable but limited, intelligent but ambitious—persisted through their early years together but were abruptly challenged in the weeks after Eisenhower's heart attack.

Nixon calibrated leadership and modesty through those tense weeks, taking command but not power, deferring to Ike's position even when Ike was confined to an oxygen tent or barely allowed to sit up. Eisenhower recognized the sturdy job that Nixon was performing, and he appreciated it, though, as ever, he viewed Nixon as a capable understudy, not a peer. "He is a darn good young man," Eisenhower told Adams. He believed the country still regarded Nixon as "a bit immature," and though Eisenhower himself did not, he understood why others, including Adams, perceived a lack of readiness. "He has not quite reached a maturity of intellect," Adams said.

To the immense relief of an anxious world, Eisenhower recovered. Just a few days after the episode, he announced to Snyder: "If I didn't think you knew what you were doing, I would suspect you of having the wrong patient in bed." He was ordered not to work from the day of his heart attack until October 1, but on that afternoon Adams spent twenty minutes with him, catching him up on official business. From then on, Adams was a regular visitor, at first for short conversations, then for more serious matters. Ike signed appointments, reviewed classified material, approved promotions, named an ambassador, drafted a letter to Bulganin. Nixon came with Adams on October 9, Dulles spent half an hour with Ike on October 11.

On October 14, the president celebrated his birthday in the hospital, by then chafing at the restrictions imposed by his doctors and eager to handle an increased load; he grumbled about being tended to by too many physicians and was irritated by what he perceived as conflicting medical advice. Eleven days later, Eisenhower took his first unaided steps and was allowed to meet with reporters on the hospital rooftop. For the occasion, he dressed in a gift the press corps had presented him soon after he was hospitalized: a set of red pajamas with gold stars on the collar tabs and the words "Much Better, Thanks" embroidered over the breast pocket. Through those weeks, Ike's spirits also were raised by the thousands who wrote to wish him well. Mamie wore out her hand responding, grateful to have a way to contribute. Some admirers mailed records, which Ike happily played on a phonograph in his room.

Five weeks after the heart attack, Robert Cutler visited. He met Mamie at her parents' house, spent an hour talking and drinking old-fashioneds, then headed to the hospital. Mamie was tense and scared, "speaking rapidly and decisively, sometimes with tears." Cutler held her hand and comforted her. At the hospital over the next few days, Cutler assessed Eisenhower's condition and left reassured. It was strange to see Ike, so enduringly vital, forced to sit still and quiet, but he was, Cutler thought, "a wonderful patient."

Eisenhower's chief cardiologist, the internationally renowned Paul Dudley White, predicted that Ike would be able to leave the hospital between November 5 and November 12, and on November 11 he did. Eisenhower might have left even sooner, but he waited that long so that he would not be taken from Fitzsimons in a wheelchair. He wanted to be able to walk up the stairs to the airplane. Finally, he bade an emotional farewell to the medical staff before flying on to Washington. Thousands waited for him at National Airport and along the route from there to the White House. Ike did his best to stay calm, but he was jumpy and cross. Although he had asked for an open car to wave to crowds, a limousine was substituted at the last minute because the day was brisk. As a result, he squirmed back and forth to acknowledge well-wishers on either side of the car. "I was tired and annoyed by this inconvenience," he complained decades later in his memoirs.

Ike stopped briefly at the White House, where his staff monitored him closely. "Every one of us took a deep breath," Adams recalled. Ike and Mamie then proceeded on to Gettysburg to complete his convalescence, with Mamie zealously attempting to protect their home from being converted into an office, a mission in which she enlisted the help of the Gang (Robinson told Snyder he feared that possibility "more than any other possible development"). A local Catholic girls' school turned out to welcome the Eisenhowers home, and they arrived in time to mark Mamie's birthday, November 14. After the events of recent weeks, Mamie felt strongly that they should bless their home, and Ike invited the Reverend Edward Elson, the minister at the National Presbyterian Church, which the Eisenhowers had selected upon arriving in the city, to perform the ceremony. Elson bestowed that blessing in the home's living room, asking that "it may henceforth be a place of health and healing, a haven of tranquility, an abode of love, and a sanctuary of worship. Bless all who call it home, and all the loved ones and friends who are encompassed by it in abiding love and devotion to Thee."

Mamie pulled herself together after the heart attack, but Ike still suffered. He was, like many heart-attack survivors, morose and ill-tempered, and he fretted over his ability to recover sufficiently to resume shouldering the burdens of his office. Adams was reassured by his alertness, though he noted that Ike had lost weight and color.

Eisenhower shared his misgivings with Swede Hazlett, himself a victim of a heart attack. Ike described his rest and exercise regimen in some detail—a brief rest before lunch, daily swims and walks, eating slowly—and then allowed himself a moment of annoyance with his doctors. "I am to avoid all situations that tend to bring about such reactions as irritation, frustration, anxiety, fear and, above all anger," Ike wrote. "When doctors give me such instructions, I say to them, 'Just what do you think the Presidency is?' "

Though the fall of 1955 was a tranquil time in international affairs, there were rising confrontations at home, at first subtle and then increasingly intense. The *Brown* decision in 1954 had done more than place the Supreme Court's stamp of disapproval on segregation in public schools; it had supplied moral impetus to the growing demand for civil rights in all walks of life. If, as the Court ruled in *Brown*, "separate but equal" had no place in education, then what about restrooms or restaurants, beaches, golf courses, or buses?

On December 1, 1955, a Montgomery Fair department store worker, Rosa Parks, posed that question to the nation's conscience by refusing to yield her bus seat to a white passenger. J. F. Blake, the bus driver, ordered her and three other black passengers to move to the back; no one moved. He got up from his seat and ordered them again: "You better make it light on yourself and let me have those seats." This time, three of the passengers moved to the back, but Parks still refused. Blake warned her that he had the power to enforce segregation laws himself. Parks replied that he could do what he had to. She was not getting up. Blake arrested Parks.

After a short but harrowing stay in the Montgomery, Alabama, jail—no place for a black woman in 1955—Rosa Parks defied her family's objections and agreed to serve as a test case for the segregation of Montgomery buses. That was Thursday night. On Monday morning, the Montgomery bus boycott began.

While Parks and her neighbors launched their crusade, Ike was still regaining his strength. He shuttled from his Gettysburg home to Camp David and back in early December, presiding over the National Security Council and eventually the cabinet. He entertained close friends and family, though his commitments were kept to a minimum. George Allen dropped in often, Ellis Slater came early in December, Dr. Snyder stayed close by. Slowly, Ike built up his workday.

Eisenhower's heart attack reframed for him the essential question of those weeks, one that he had pondered almost since he became president: Should he run again? The question had been on his mind for months. As early as February 1955, he volunteered to Len Hall that the GOP should search for a host city for its convention other than Chicago, where Eisenhower argued that the "reactionary fringe" would coalesce around that city's notorious newspaper. Now, with election year at hand, Ike had no choice but to focus on his own candidacy.

Oddly, the heart attack did not discourage him from seeking a second term; indeed, it caused him to consider the question in a new light. Eisenhower now was less inclined to think of whether he wanted to serve a second term and more prone to debating whether he could. As his health improved, he began to debate the idea more seriously. Just a few months earlier, prior to his heart attack, he had often seemed drawn to retirement. Now he worried that no one was well suited to succeed him. The possible Democratic candidates struck Eisenhower as astonishingly unworthy, and he was frustrated that Republican contenders had not developed during his term. He wondered whether New York's Tom Dewey might at last be acceptable, but Jim Hagerty warned him that a Dewey candidacy would badly split the party. All the other possibilities also posed problems for Ike: Cabot Lodge needed steadying; Bob Anderson was little known outside Washington (not to mention a former Democrat); Sherman Adams and Herb Brownell lacked a political base; Milton Eisenhower had Ike's thorough approval, but the prospect of one brother succeeding another was too dynastic to fly. Earl Warren was renowned because of *Brown*, but Eisenhower disapproved of Warren stepping off the Court to pursue the presidency and felt Warren better suited to the Court in any event.

Nixon, the most obvious choice, still presented a question for Ike and his advisers. As Adams faintly put it: "On the whole, he felt that Nixon had made good progress." Although Eisenhower admired Nixon and considered him a capable vice president by late 1955, he remained convinced that Nixon was unelectable. He searched for a way to ease Nixon off the ticket, weighed the possibility of placing him in the cabinet, and definitely doubted his viability as a candidate for president in his own right.

Ike was growing stronger, tugged as always by his sense of duty. Now another December quietly drew to a close, and after Christmas at the White House, Ike and Mamie flew to Florida to mark the New Year. Ike golfed and walked the beaches. He, along with Mamie and the Snyders—sometimes joined by Milton Eisenhower, Hagerty, or others—ended each evening with a movie. They watched *Wichita* on December 29 and *Angels in the Outfield* (Ike's favorite movie) on December 30, and ended the year with *Tall Man Riding* on New Year's Eve. The president retired just after 10:00 p.m.

11

Crisis and Revival

As Eisenhower turned from pondering whether he desired four more years in office to asking whether he was up to it, his family and friends meditated on his stamina. Mamie, once determined to see her husband retire after the first term, now wondered how he would respond to being forced out by illness. She was afraid, as he put it, that "idleness would be fatal for my temperament." On the other hand, Sherman Adams wondered: "After a close brush with death, would Eisenhower have the courage to face four more years of punishing physical strain in the White House?" Put that way, the question nearly answered itself.

Nearly, but not quite. In early January, while still in Key West, Eisenhower prepared for his annual address to Congress, an exercise that gave him reason to review his record and potential legacy. He took justifiable pride in his achievements. The nation was at peace. Taxes had been reduced. Standards of living were rising. The federal budget, after years of deficits, was balanced. There was, to be sure, work to do—some areas of the country lagged in prosperity, farmers were struggling, the Soviet leaders were forever fomenting trouble—but progress was evident.

Against that backdrop, Eisenhower returned to "the full duties of the presidency" on January 9 and quietly convened his closest confidants and advisers to discuss his future. The gathering was to be kept quiet. Initially scheduled for January 11, it was called off when reporters got wind of it—Hagerty blamed Nixon for the leak—then rescheduled for Friday, January 13. Because Ike did not want anyone to know who was attending, he even took the extra precaution of preparing the place cards himself. Meticulously, he chose the seats for the men whom he most trusted with a matter of such grave personal and political consequence: John Foster Dulles; George Humphrey; Herb Brownell; Arthur Summerfield; Len Hall; Sherman Adams; Jim Hagerty; Howard Pyle, Ike's deputy assistant for intergovernmental relations; Tom Stephens, his special counsel and appointments secretary; Henry Cabot Lodge; Jerry Persons; and, of course, Milton Eisenhower. Before they talked, they dined. Mamie joined them for dinner, then excused herself, and the men took their places around a table in the president's second-floor sitting room.

Invited by Eisenhower, Dulles spoke first. He complimented the president's wisdom and dedication to service and pledged that all those present would "gladly" accept whatever decision he reached. After the meeting, Dulles recorded his comments, drafting a special memo detailing the affair: "As I saw the situation, there was no one person in the world, and perhaps there never had been any person in the world, who commanded the respect of as many people as did the President . . . I consider this an enormous asset at a time when humanity faces the greatest physical danger through the development of nuclear weapons which could destroy life on this globe." The work of the administration, Dulles hardly needed to add, was unfinished. "We were groping our way toward some solution of this problem, but had not yet found it. I felt that the President could be a decisive factor at some time within the next two or three years in really making atomic power a servant of humanity, not a threat to its existence."

There was a pause after Dulles finished speaking, and Tom Stephens piped up. "Well," he said to Eisenhower, "you ought to make up your mind because I want to be a candidate if you're not." That won a grin from Eisenhower and laughter from the others.

When it subsided, Eisenhower randomly called on his other guests. To a man, they reflected on his influence, on the mission still to be undertaken. They wanted him to run, with one lone exception: Milton urged his brother to retire. Still saddened by his wife's death the year before, Milton was "fearful of the strain that was on" his brother and "deeply concerned about his personal welfare." Moreover, there was always the chance that his brother might run and lose, tarnishing his legacy. If he retired now, Milton argued, Ike might be able to continue to wield a constructive influence even after leaving the presidency.

On that note, Ike then spoke himself. He too alluded to the dark possibilities created by his heart attack: he brooded on the "disturbing effect of any change in the presidency at other than the appointed four-year intervals" and warned his colleagues that he could not conduct a rigorous campaign as he had in 1952. Still, Eisenhower was impressed by the near unanimity of his advisers, and he promised to consider their advice carefully. "Thank you, gentlemen," Ike said. He stood up. The others followed.

At 11:15 p.m., the president's men retired into the night, cold and still in the Washington winter, the burdens of their counsel weighty upon each.

If Ike made up his mind that night—or if he had decided even before summoning that group of advisers—he kept the decision to himself. Questions about his future peppered his press conference on January 19, but he continued to dodge, reporting that he felt fit and up to the job but declining to say whether he was a candidate. He needed time to reflect, he explained, "in order that I may reach a logical decision. I will do it as soon as I can."

Ike was, however, already contemplating the implications for the rest of his administration. Most pointedly, he recognized the gravity of the position of vice president in the second term of a president whose health was suspect. The consideration that he might die brought to the surface all of Ike's ambivalence toward his vice president. Asked on January 25 whether he would keep Nixon on the ticket if he ran, Eisenhower professed his "admiration, respect and deep affection" for his vice president but demurred on his role in a second term, saying they had yet to discuss it. Three days later, he had an amiable conversation with Frank Lausche, the Ohio governor who was a Catholic Democrat; the two hit it off, and Ike began to ponder the possibility of a bipartisan ticket for 1956.

That, of course, depended on the sitting vice president vacating the post. Describing it to associates a few days later, Eisenhower said he had summoned Richard Nixon in early February and put the question to him: "If we can count on me living five years, your [best] place is not serving eight years as vice president because people get the idea the vice president does nothing, but to take one of the big departments—HEW, Defense, Interior—any one of which is entirely possible." If, however, Nixon bet that Ike was likely to die, "of course that is different." The decision, Eisenhower added, was up to Nixon.

The proposal put Nixon in an excruciating bind: To leave the vice presidency, as Eisenhower surely knew, would be interpreted as a political demotion and would damage Nixon's ambition to succeed Ike. But to accept it under conditions that suggested Nixon believed Eisenhower would die before completing his second term cast Nixon's ambitions in the most ghoulish light. Nixon recognized the dilemma and froze. He sullenly responded that he would do whatever Eisenhower asked him to.

Ike was torn: he believed Lausche would be a more exciting running mate and Bob Anderson a more capable vice president, but he was reluctant to dump Nixon against his will. He dispatched Len Hall to talk the matter over with Nixon, urging him to be "very, very gentle."

Ike's mood lightened as he moved past his indecision. Neither a jumpy pulse nor a brief bout of indigestion dampened his ebullience, and those early days of February found him in "radiant spirits," according to Ann Whitman. A checkup in mid-February pronounced him in good health—his doctor announced that if Ike ran again, he would vote for him. He teased his cabinet with hints that he was a candidate. "Don't any of you fellows come to me January 1st, saying you have something else you've got to do," he joked on February 13; the group burst into applause. Two weeks later, he told Dulles he was inclined to run, and Dulles urged him to do so. "The state of the world," Dulles recalled, "was such as to require the President to serve if he felt up to it." Ike tentatively agreed, though he worried about the chaos that would ensue if he died between the nominating convention and the election. Dulles downplayed that possibility. There was always some risk, he noted, "and that seemed a normal risk to accept."

Once again, Ike's reflections turned to Nixon. He told Dulles he was thinking of dropping Nixon from the ticket and replacing him with either Humphrey or Dulles himself. Dulles immediately withdrew his own name, saying he was too old. Ike then suggested Brownell but worried that he lacked popular appeal. As for Nixon, Ike noted that polls suggested he would lose if he ran on his own for the presidency and that he was not sure it was in Nixon's own interests to remain as vice president. Eisenhower again thought about installing Nixon as secretary of commerce or in another cabinet post, to which Dulles joked that he was angling for a way to replace him, Dulles, as secretary of state. Eisenhower laughed. No, he said, Dulles could not get out of his job that easily. In any case, Ike added that he doubted whether Nixon was qualified for that job. The meeting ended on that inconclusive note, but Dulles was now sure his boss was running. As a result, he "was leaving the room a much happier man than when I came in."

Having built suspense around his candidacy for so long, Eisenhower milked it a bit more. Appearing before the White House press corps on February 29, he first announced the opening of the annual campaign for the Red Cross, then expressed his pleasure at the visit of Italy's president, then urged Congress to act quickly on two bills, one to assist farmers, another to capture more water in the Colorado River basin. "My next announcement," he added, feigning afterthought, "involves something more personal, but I think it will be of interest to you because you have asked me so many questions about it." After all the consulting and considering, Eisenhower never-theless managed to mangle his revelation. He couldn't be sure, he said, that the Republican Party would nominate him or that the American people would elect him, but he asked for television and radio time to explain his decision, and "my answer within the limits I have so sketchily observed, but which I will explain in detail tonight so as to get the story out in one continuous narrative, my answer will be positive, that is, affirmative." It took a moment for that to sink in, but the reporters recovered and pounced on what Eisenhower had clearly not said: Would he run with Nixon? Eisenhower evaded, proclaiming his deep admiration for his vice president but insisting that it would be improper for him to express his desire to have Nixon on the ticket before the Republican convention. Pressed to say whether he would like Nixon to be that nominee, Eisenhower turned testy. "I will say nothing more about it," he snapped. "I have said that my admira-tion and my respect for Vice President Nixon is unbounded. He has been for me a loyal and dedicated associate, and a successful one. I am very fond of him, but I am going to say no more about it." Nixon would remain in suspense, embarrassed and imperiled, for months.

Eisenhower, on the other hand, slept soundly after announcing his deci-sion. Indeed, ending his deliberations seemed to energize both the presi-dent and his administration. He chased a full agenda in 1956, undeterred by those who warned that Congress would resist bold action in an elec-tion year. His State of the Union message in January reflected Ike's abid-ing insistence on balance: lowered budget deficits in tandem with steps to improve American military security; attempts to strike neutrality in relations between management and workers; the vigorous pursuit of peace by the spread of American ideas (Eisenhower proposed sharply increased funding for the U.S. Information Agency) but also the increased invest-ment in nuclear weapons.

Of the proposals Eisenhower offered in the final year of his first term, however, few would transform the nation more remarkably than one that Congress had ignored the previous year. "If we are ever to solve our mount-ing traffic problem, the whole interstate [highway] system must be autho-rized as one project, to be completed approximately within the specified time," Eisenhower stated. Congress had rejected this appeal in 1955, but Eisenhower made it again and dared Congress to oppose him.

The highway bill offered persuasive evidence of Eisenhower's remove from partisan orthodoxy. It was the largest public works project in Ameri-can history, a grand government investment with ramifications that would change the nation's future. Many of the proposal's specifics were the work of General Lucius Clay, whom Ike tapped to study the idea. Like Eisenhower's, Clay's experience in Germany—he served as commissioner there after the war—exposed him to that nation's famous autobahn, and he returned with a strong sense of its utility in moving goods as well as troops. Clay had reported back to Ike on January 11, 1955, setting out the broad parameters of a thirty-year plan to upgrade American highways. Ike had been instantly persuaded, expressing his "tremendous enthusiasm" for the Clay Committee's recommendations.

For a president committed to balanced budgets and private enterprise, the idea was startlingly expansive. Eisenhower, whose 1919 trip across country had left him with a lasting worry about the state of the nation's highways—and whose contrary experience in Germany during the war had impressed him as it had Clay—set out to construct forty-one thousand miles of American highways, principally to link major cities. It was the "largest public works and engineering task ever conceived as a peacetime operation," reaching every state and territory of the United States. Or, as Eisenhower observed, enough concrete to build "six sidewalks to the moon." The benefits were most obviously economic: an open system of roads expedited commerce and tourism. To sell the idea, however, Eisenhower also emphasized the military and civil defense implications of such a system. Troops, of course, could be moved more quickly on highways in the event of attack, as could emergency response crews.

Mindful of the cost—initial estimates put the program's expense at $27 billion, and it quickly exceeded that—Eisenhower insisted that the project not add to the national debt. To do so would countermand his fiscal efforts, so he initially favored a toll system. He dropped that idea after concluding that tolls would not generate enough revenue and instead proposed a tax on gasoline and oil (Earl Warren, while governor of California, had launched that state's epic highway system using such a tax). As it debated in early 1956, Congress modified Eisenhower's proposal but left the financing mechanism substantially intact. Highway user fees, including gas and oil taxes, paid for construction under a system in which states authorized the projects and paid the initial costs of construction, after which they were reimbursed for 90 percent of their costs by the federal government.

Ike's secretary of commerce, Sinclair Weeks—known to Eisenhower and others as Sinny—steered the lobbying on the bill and patiently guided it to fruition despite a partisan Congress in an election year. The endless debates over financing bored Eisenhower, and he pressed for a conclusion. "I wanted the job done," he wrote irascibly. Finally, Congress agreed and sent Eisenhower a bill. He signed it on June 29 while at Walter Reed for a checkup. The first project launched under its authority, a stretch of Route 40 in Missouri, started just weeks later. Elsewhere, work also began immediately—indeed, even before the bill took effect, as state governments received word of the money they would be getting and launched projects in anticipation of it.

Ike was forever proud of the highway system and justifiably claimed credit for having modernized the nation with it. "More than any single action by the government since the end of the war, this one would change the face of America," he wrote. "Its impact on the American economy—the jobs it would produce in manufacturing and construction, the rural areas it would open up—was beyond calculation." Indeed, its influence would traverse American society in ways even its creators did not imagine, giving rise to modern suburban life by connecting those residential communities to urban jobs. As an engine of economic and social development, it was rivaled only by the GI Bill; as a physical manifestation of the government's ability to make change, it had no peer.

For Eisenhower, the highway act was a welcome respite from politics in 1956. For Nixon, the year would bring no such relief. In fact, his tribulations were largely inflicted by Eisenhower himself. After receiving the president's suggestion that Nixon consider accepting a cabinet position, Nixon pouted, convinced that Ike was trying to bump him off the ticket and unsure about how to respond. As winter became spring, his mood was blackened by press reports that there was a move afoot to "dump Nixon." Eisenhower defended Nixon time and again to the press but adamantly declined to say whether he wanted him on the fall ticket. Eisenhower's refusal was, he and others insisted, merely a matter of form: Ike considered it improper for a candidate who had yet to receive his party's nomination to announce his selection of a vice president. He had to know, however, that his own nomination was a foregone conclusion and his reticence regarding Nixon was naturally viewed as caginess at the vice president's expense. Later, Eisenhower professed to be surprised that Nixon had ever felt uncomfortable. Though it is hard to believe, Ike said he only learned of his vice president's anxiety when he read *Six Crises*, Nixon's memoir published in 1962.

All through the spring, Ike and his advisers debated how best to deal with the vice president. In March, Ike reiterated his friendship with Nixon but also emphasized that neither friendship nor admiration "make[s] him vice president." Nixon "has serious problems," Eisenhower said to his secretary of the interior, Fred Seaton. "He has his own way to make . . . I am not going to say he is the only individual I would have for vice president.

There is nothing to be gained politically by ditching him [but] . . . Nixon can't always be the understudy to the star." Six days later, Hagerty returned from a trip through the South and told Eisenhower that "not one person was for Nixon for Vice President for a second term." Those who opposed him had a hard time saying why—some thought he was too immature or connected to "the Negro difficulty"—but they were uniformly opposed.

Finally, the matter wound to a conclusion. At a news conference on April 25, Ike—after first championing the highway bill then under consideration by the House—confronted what was becoming a customary query about Nixon's status. "Some time ago, Mr. President," began Bill Lawrence of the *New York Times*, "you told us that you had asked Vice President Nixon to chart his own course and then report back to you. Has he done this?"

Eisenhower replied: "Well, he hasn't reported back in the terms in which I used the expression that morning, no."

After months of waiting for Eisenhower to release him from his misery, Nixon now seized on the opportunity to do so himself. He called that morning to ask for time to meet with Ike, and the two sat down the same afternoon. Nixon assured Eisenhower that he was eager to remain as vice president, and Eisenhower accepted his decision. Hagerty quickly arranged a press conference, where Nixon announced his plans, and Hagerty informed reporters that Eisenhower was "delighted to hear of the Vice President's decision." Sadly for Nixon, the movement to dump him was not quite through, but he at least now officially enjoyed the president's support.

In the meantime, Ike knocked off victories on his legislative agenda, including approval of an ambitious proposal to overhaul America's national parks. That bill added 500,000 acres to the nation's total, including a new park in the Virgin Islands, and built dozens of visitors' centers and other amenities to accommodate the swelling demand for the nation's most treasured outdoor spaces. For Ike, ever enamored of the outdoors and rarely more comfortable than with a fishing rod in hand, the approval was a source of special satisfaction. "For increasing millions of Americans, this undertaking," he reflected later, "would bring benefits and enjoyment in great measure over the years."

On the final day of the Twentieth Party Congress, Nikita Khrushchev ascended the dais in Moscow's Great Kremlin Palace. Before him, fourteen hundred delegates nervously awaited the address from their preeminent official. These were hard men, toughened by revolutionary struggle, at ease with violence, ideologically committed. Lenin's statue greeted them. Stalin,

Second Lieutenant Dwight D. Eisenhower. Ike's West Point yearbook, the *Howitzer*, joked that he viewed himself as "the handsomest man in the Corps." *Courtesy of the Eisenhower Library*

Ike and Mamie on their wedding day, July 1, 1916. *Courtesy of the Eisenhower Library*

The Eisenhower family, circa 1926.
Courtesy of the Eisenhower Library

Eisenhower and George Marshall, June 19, 1943. *Bettmann/CORBIS*

Eisenhower and Kay Summersby. *Courtesy of the Eisenhower Library*

Eisenhower meets with soldiers from the 101st Airborne Division on the eve of D-day. *Courtesy of the Eisenhower Library*

Ike and Mamie walk outside Low Memorial Library at Columbia during the 1952 campaign. They are accompanied by John A. Krout (left), dean of the Columbia Graduate Faculties. *Courtesy of the Eisenhower Library*

Eisenhower receives the news that Harry Truman has fired Douglas MacArthur, 1951. *Courtesy of the Eisenhower Library*

Ike teaches Richard Nixon, his vice presidential running mate, how to fly-fish, 1952. *Courtesy of the Eisenhower Library*

Eisenhower greets the Republican National Convention, 1952. *Courtesy of the Eisenhower Library*

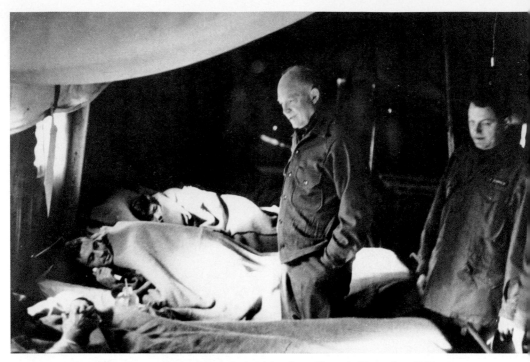

Eisenhower visits soldiers during his trip to Korea in December 1952.
Courtesy of the Eisenhower Library

The first Eisenhower cabinet. Fred Vinson, chief justice of the United States,
stands at the center, in robes. *Abbie Rowe, National Park Service*

On October 25, 1955, Eisenhower makes his first public appearance, on the roof of Fitzsimons Army Hospital, after his heart attack. *Courtesy of the Eisenhower Library*

Eisenhower and Earl Warren, joined by Attorney General Herbert Brownell, welcome a group of newly naturalized American citizens, November 10, 1954. *Bettmann/CORBIS*

John Foster Dulles and Eisenhower confer on August 14, 1956, as the Suez crisis builds to a boil. *Courtesy of the Eisenhower Library*

Richard Nixon at the Republican National Convention, 1956. *Courtesy of the Eisenhower Library*

Ike and Mamie, joined by John and Barbara, on the dais of the Republican National Convention, 1956. *Courtesy of the Eisenhower Library*

Orval Faubus arrives at Newport to meet with Eisenhower during the Little Rock school integration crisis, September 14, 1957. Sherman Adams accompanies him. *Courtesy of the Eisenhower Library*

Members of the 101st Airborne Division escort black students into Little Rock Central High School, September 26, 1957. *Bettmann/CORBIS*

The Eisenhower family—John and Barbara with their children, as well as Ike and Mamie—leave church on Easter Sunday, 1958. *Courtesy of the Eisenhower Library*

Eisenhower meets with civil rights leaders at the White House, June 23, 1958. *Courtesy of the Eisenhower Library*

Eisenhower and Khrushchev prepare to board a helicopter for Camp David.
Courtesy of the Eisenhower Library

Eisenhower and Khrushchev at Camp David,
standing outside the Aspen Lodge, where they
stayed. *Courtesy of the Eisenhower Library*

Khrushchev and Castro, September 20, 1960.
Bettmann/CORBIS

Eisenhower throws out the first pitch of the 1960 American League season.
Nixon (seated) accompanies him. *Courtesy of the Eisenhower Library*

Ike and Mamie enjoy a relaxed moment at their Gettysburg
home in July of 1966. *Courtesy of the Eisenhower Library*

who had died between the Nineteenth and the Twentieth congresses, was not pictured. Nikita Khrushchev spoke that day for four hours. It was the most important and brave address of his life.

His attack on the memory of Communism's heralded leader shocked the delegates and reverberated around the world. Stalin, his successor announced, had committed ghastly atrocities, "a grave abuse of power . . . which caused untold harm to our party." Possessed of a "capricious and despotic character," Stalin had authorized mass arrests and executions, forced false confessions, and directed torture, "extreme methods and mass repressions." To those who threatened or upset him, he practiced "physical annihilation, not only against actual enemies, but also against individuals who had not committed any crimes against the party and the Soviet Government." Stalin's "cult of personality" was insidious, vile, destructive, wanton, and cruel. Many in the hall that day knew it, but only Khrushchev dared to say it. The room was stonily silent.

Khrushchev's stunning attack on his predecessor was delivered to a closed session of the Congress—hence its reputation as the "secret speech"—but it was widely reproduced in the aftermath, as copies were distributed to party cells and headquarters in Eastern Europe and around the world. In June, the CIA supplied a copy to the *New York Times*, which published the text. The effect was electrifying, but the impact difficult to predict. Did repudiation of Stalin's crimes suggest a new attitude on the part of the Soviet leadership toward war with the West? Did it suggest liberalization of the press or religious practice under Communism? Most beguilingly, did the speech and the Congress's endorsement of "peaceful coexistence" and the pursuit of Communism by varying national paths suggest a new relationship between Moscow and its satellites throughout Eastern Europe?

For the Eisenhower administration, this was a moment of wondrous possibility. Ike had run on a platform of liberating the Soviet satellites, but the foreign policy that constituted the Solarium Project and New Look made no such promises; instead, the administration had settled for deterrence on a grand scale, combined with covert action at the margins of the Soviet empire. That was a sound—if morally debatable—approach to containing and rolling back Communism in the Third World. It offered no realistic solutions for the satellite nations of Eastern Europe, and it was nearly inconceivable that the United States could do anything to accelerate the liberation of those stranded nations without engaging the Soviet Union in a frontal confrontation—almost certainly with nuclear ramifications. Khrushchev's speech, however, raised the possibility that the Soviet Union would allow liberalization without American interference.

The CIA, despite its history of misapprehending developments in the Soviet Union, was appropriately skeptical that a new day was at hand. "The Soviet leaders are as unwilling now as they have ever been—and will be in the foreseeable future—to democratize their system and to permit public discussion of political problems," read an internal analysis prepared in 1956 and not released until 1999. CIA analysts, while doubtful about Soviet liberalization, did imagine that the speech and its ramifications might force "many communists throughout the world to make difficult adjustments" and specifically predicted that it would "create increasing demands from the satellites to follow their own path to 'socialism.' "

Poland was among the first to test that prediction. Protesters demanded higher wages and better food. The government hesitated in response until Soviet tanks restored order. Even then, however, Moscow allowed strikers to receive wage hikes and stood by as the dour Wladyslaw Gomulka, nearly executed by Stalin but saved by the dictator's death in 1953, was rehabilitated and returned to public leadership. Poland did not win anything approaching independence in those early months of 1956, but Khrushchev's response nursed the hopes of captive people from Warsaw to, most important, Budapest.

In the months following the announcement of his candidacy, Eisenhower's approval rating hovered near 70 percent, while less than 20 percent of Americans disapproved of his performance as president. With such strong sentiment to buoy him, Ike knew that his reelection was a near certainty.

Still, he had his critics. Edgar continued to needle his sibling about what Big Ike saw as Little Ike's drift to the left. Having vigorously protested Warren's appointment to the Court and irritated his brother over the Bricker Amendment, Edgar now tweaked Ike over his administration's liberalism. Quoted by a newspaper reporter as describing himself as "the only real Republican in the family" and calling Ike "a little bit socialistic," Edgar wrote to Ike to blame the reporter while reinforcing his point. "I never have thought you were socialistic," he explained, "although I do think and have said so to you, that the Government is rapidly drifting into a socialistic state." No pronouncement was too small or silly for the president to ignore when it came from his big brother. Ike's response was slightly condescending. He noted that while his brother worried about socialism, Adlai Stevenson was charging that Eisenhower was the agent of big money and monopoly. Both charges, Ike insisted, were ludicrous: his administration managed parts of the economy to stabilize it and allowed the private sector wide latitude to generate growth. "You cannot return to the days of 1860," Eisenhower lectured. It was not the last time an American president would have to fend off suggestions of socialist inclination, but it's one of the rare times the charge came from the president's brother.

Charges of socialism were hardly a threat to Eisenhower's reelection. As he realized, only two obstacles stood between him and a second term: a political crisis that might upend public confidence in his leadership and a health setback that might raise questions about his stamina. Over the next few months, he confronted both.

Thursday, June 7, was the occasion for the annual White House News Photographers Association dinner. Held at the Sheraton Park Hotel, not far from the National Zoo, it was a jovial occasion, and Eisenhower readily accepted the group's invitation. Before leaving, Ike hit a few golf balls with a friend and managed to lie down for an hour. The dinner was, as such things go, a pleasant evening, a clubby gathering of the nation's leadership and those who chronicle it. Most of the Supreme Court—though not Warren, even though he lived in the building—was on hand; seven cabinet members were there. Bob Hope performed. In short, "everyone and his uncle" attended. Eisenhower stayed until 11:00 p.m., then returned to the White House.

Later that night, he complained to Mamie of an upset stomach, and Mamie briskly summoned Dr. Snyder. Arriving, Snyder confronted a set of symptoms eerily familiar and yet reassuringly less severe than those presented to him in Denver. This time, he diagnosed a recurrence of Ike's long-running intestinal distress and ascertained that the president had wolfed down a Waldorf salad for lunch. No matter how often doctors urged Ike to slow down and chew his food thoroughly, the childhood habits of a boy racing his brothers for dinner died hard.

Now that lifelong habit cost him, as a piece of partially digested celery lodged in his intestine. Snyder sat with the president for several hours. Just before 8:00 a.m., he notified Ann Whitman that Eisenhower had a headache and was feeling sick to his stomach. He recommended that the president's appointments, including that morning's cabinet meeting, be canceled or postponed. Whitman and Adams began calling cabinet members, who received the news as routine. It was not until Hagerty ventured to see Ike himself that the staff realized how serious Eisenhower's condition was. At 11:00 a.m., Ike was taken by ambulance to Walter Reed.

A team of doctors examined the president, and all but one favored surgery. The holdout worried about whether the president, so recently recovered from his heart attack, could stand the strain of the operation. The others then hesitated as well, resisting operating without unanimous consent that it was the right course. Eisenhower continued to suffer until, just after midnight, one physician, Walter Tkach, warned that without quick action Ike might die. The holdout then relented, but the team hit another snag: Mamie, desperate to avoid a surgery she feared might kill her husband, refused to authorize the procedure. John Eisenhower did so in her stead, and Ike was sedated and wheeled into the operating room at 2:07 a.m. Informed of the medical consensus and his son's approval, the president concurred. "Well," he said, "let's go."

He awoke around 8:00 the next morning, but he was groggy. His staff and family nervously awaited his emergence from the anesthesia. At last, after forty-eight hours, he shook off the last remnants of sedation. His color was good, he was alert and responsive, if still somewhat uncomfortable. For a time, he confided to a friend, "I doubted seriously that I would ever feel like myself again." By July 1, he had recovered enough to resume his campaign and told Milton that he was "slowly but steadily . . . regaining some strength." The White House took special pains to telegraph the president's recovery. In August, for instance, Ike invited Tom Dewey to the White House; they spent forty minutes together for no other reason than that Dewey could then, in speaking engagements, say that he had seen Ike and that the president was well.

The health crisis passed, but it resuscitated questions about keeping Nixon on the ticket. If there was a reasonable chance that Eisenhower might not live out the term, Nixon might well become president, a possibility that unnerved many stalwart Eisenhower supporters, especially liberal Republicans, independents, and crossover Democrats (Eisenhower liked to refer to the last group as "discerning Democrats") who supported the president in great numbers. Just before Ike departed on a goodwill mission to Latin America, one of those GOP liberals, Harold Stassen, came to the White House to inform Eisenhower that he had lost confidence in Nixon and was prepared to lead a campaign to drop him from the ticket. Stassen, then serving as Eisenhower's special assistant for disarmament, spoke for twenty-four minutes; Ike listened in silence. When Stassen announced his position publicly, Ike released a statement saying that Stassen could support whomever he liked, but not as a member of the administration; Stassen went on leave.

If confusion about Nixon's role threatened Republican unity as the GOP convention approached, the Democrats helped even the score. Adlai Stevenson began sniping at the administration that spring, and Ike infuriated his adversary by laughing off the criticism. In the end, the Democratic Party nominated arguably its worst ticket—tapping Stevenson, who had already lost once to Eisenhower, and Estes Kefauver, a Tennessee senator known for his national crusade against organized crime. Stevenson and Kefauver were articulate, intelligent men, each with a base and a national reputation. But they were vastly overshadowed by Eisenhower's deep connection to the American people. The Democratic ticket lacked spark, imagination, and any strategic plan for undermining Ike's popularity. Stevenson tried attacking Eisenhower directly but found little purchase. He then suggested that Eisenhower was a good man surrounded by conniving cabinet officers: "The Republican campaign, 'Trust Ike and ask no questions,' really means something else. It means trust the men around Ike. It really means: Trust Ezra Benson; Trust Foster Dulles; Trust George Humphrey; Trust Charles Wilson, and it means, Trust Richard Nixon." The president just shrugged. Eisenhower's approval ratings held rock steady through the summer. Two-thirds of the American people could not be convinced to dislike Ike.

By the time the Republicans met in San Francisco for their convention, there was little mystery left in the race. Although Stassen stumped for Governor Christian Herter of Massachusetts to replace Nixon, Herter was uncomfortable being a divisive figure within the party. And yet Ike himself, just days before the convention, remained halfheartedly committed to his vice president. As late as August 19, he was jotting names of those Republicans whom he would consider acceptable replacements: Brownell as well as Dewey, Governor Goodwin Knight of California, or even the California senator Bill Knowland, who so annoyed Ike as a legislative leader but who could help carry California if Nixon were not on the ticket. Nixon's name appeared on that list, too, but as one of many, not as Eisenhower's singular choice. As the convention drew near, Herter found a way out of the controversy: he agreed to deliver the speech nominating Nixon for the vice presidency. With that, the air rushed out of Stassen's balloon.

Eisenhower did his best to skirt that episode but involved himself much more heavily in the more mundane business of drafting the party platform. He did so partly to avoid saddling his second term with unreasonable demands or expectations but also to give vent to his frustrations over civil rights. Reading the proposed Republican platform, Eisenhower tripped over a phrase stating that the "Eisenhower Administration and the Republican Party have supported the Supreme Court" in its efforts to desegregate schools. Ike vehemently protested to Brownell that he wanted the reference to his administration deleted. The president insisted that the administration never "took a stand in the matter." That must have puzzled his attorney general, who filed a brief in support of school desegregation personally edited by Ike. But Eisenhower, who had deferred to Brownell despite his misgivings over the pace of change in civil rights, now maintained that the Justice Department's brief and argument in *Brown* did not reflect an administration view of the case; instead, Ike argued, Brownell had appeared "as a lawyer, not as a member of the Eisenhower Administration." That, of course, begged the question of whom Brownell was representing, if not the administration, but Eisenhower insisted that the cabinet had never debated the case, and thus Brownell could not have appeared on behalf of that body. Eisenhower was emphatically wrong but in no mood to compromise on the question: unless he got his way and the party agreed to drop any suggestion that the administration supported the *Brown* decision, Ike said he would refuse to attend the convention.

Why was Eisenhower so determined to distance himself from a ruling that was written by his appointee, that had strengthened America's position in the Cold War, and that had ennobled the nation's commitment to perfecting itself as a constitutional democracy? He was, Ike said, torn: he understood his duty to obey the Court on constitutional matters, but he also felt that *Brown* had so antagonized Southerners that it had set back civil rights. In San Francisco, floor managers secured a compromise, agreeing that the platform would read that the administration "concurred" in the ruling. Even that wasn't good enough for Eisenhower. He eventually signed off on language saying that the administration "accepts" *Brown*—a phrase so reserved that it suggested acquiescence rather than approval. For those who would later maintain that Eisenhower welcomed *Brown*, his role in crafting the 1956 party platform offers powerful evidence to the contrary. Far from appreciating or endorsing *Brown*, Ike, at every turn, attempted to minimize his role in fashioning it and to insulate his administration from its political ramifications. As a result, Eisenhower's record in that area reflected a triumph of leadership style over personal conviction: he trusted Brownell to lead where he himself had reservations, and though he balked occasionally, the administration made progress despite Ike's own reservations.

Once he secured the platform language he could accept, Eisenhower joined the celebration of his first term. He arrived at 6:53 p.m. on August 21 and bounded from the plane, "his face ruddy with returned strength and alight with expectation," as *Time* magazine put it. Ike exuded ease and health. Explaining why he decided to come to the convention earlier than expected, he said: "I suddenly discovered this was too interesting a place to stay away from. I just read the names of too many friends in the paper, and

I wanted to see them." Thousands lined the route from the airport to his hotel; two thousand more awaited his arrival in Union Square, where bands played "We Love the Sunshine of His Smile."

San Francisco, thrilled to be the first California city to host a Republican convention, warmed to the event in bipartisan spirit—crowds milled in Union Square in front of the St. Francis Hotel and lined the streets. Eisenhower occupied the hotel's seventh floor; Pete Jones took a room one floor above, while other members of the Gang stayed at the nearby Fairmont. The city, *Time* reported, "was like wine to Ike." The president ordered that speakers maintain a high tone of inclusiveness, urging organizers to avoid personal attacks on the Democratic ticket and to avoid "excessive partisanship." Only one speaker defied that directive. It came on the first day, when Arthur Langlie, governor of Washington and a favorite of Ike's, argued that Democrats "are now addicted to the principle that loyalty to a political party comes ahead of devotion to our beloved country." Eisenhower was sitting next to Sherman Adams at the time, and he turned crossly to his aide. "Whoever let him say that?" the president demanded.

Even at this late date, Eisenhower announced himself willing to consider any challenge to Nixon's place on the ticket. None came forward. Up at 6:00 the next morning, Eisenhower met with Stassen, and Stassen— "phlegmatically," as the *New York Times* described it—gave up his crusade to replace the vice president. Eisenhower accepted Stassen's statement and released it himself. The two were photographed smiling. Nixon pronounced himself "deeply appreciative."

Langlie's sharp critique of the Democrats at the convention's outset was soon forgotten. In general, the convention was devoted to praising its nominee, which Eisenhower could hardly help but enjoy. Charles Halleck, in his nomination speech, described Eisenhower as "the most widely beloved, the most universally respected, the most profoundly dedicated man of our times." Politics, where hyperbole is the coin of the realm, encourages such grandiosity, but Halleck's description was, in this case, refreshingly accurate. Ike ran in 1956 as a beloved incumbent as well as a revered general and champion of peace. Against such praise, squabbling over Nixon or the occasional indulgence of partisanship seemed small. Surrounded by friends and family, Ike good-naturedly allowed himself to be adored. For Nixon, as always, life was more complicated: his father fell gravely ill during the convention and died before Election Day.

When it came time for him to address the convention, Ike did so with vigor. The speech was meticulous in Ike's style: there was a careful listing of the five reasons why the Republican Party was the party of the future and an equally systematic enumeration of the "three imperatives of peace." On the topic of social justice, Eisenhower was mildly defensive, claiming a record "not [of] words and promise, but [of] accomplishment." He cited elimination of discrimination in the District of Columbia, the armed services, and government contractors as the administration's great achievements; technically true, but none of those institutions had reached anything close to racial equality. The address included the requisite acclamation of the Republican Party and its principles—it was, after all, a national convention speech. But the most enduring passages echoed the grand oratory of his "The Chance for Peace" or "Atoms for Peace" addresses, those in which he wrestled with the dominant issue of his presidency: the balance between national security and the securing of an international peace. Before a loving convention and a deeply appreciative American people, Eisenhower once again reflected on the existential challenge of the Cold War, the paradox of armed strength and terrifying vulnerability.

"No one is more aware than I that it is the young who fight the wars," Eisenhower said. "It is not enough that their elders promise 'Peace in our time'; it must be peace in their time too, and in their children's time; indeed, my friends, there is only one real peace now, and that is peace for all time."

Under Eisenhower's leadership—with Dulles in foreign affairs, Wilson in Defense, Humphrey guiding economic policy, Weeks anchoring Commerce—"our military strength has been constantly augmented," but that buildup was neither headlong nor precipitous. It was, Eisenhower reminded his audience, done "soberly and intelligently," aimed not at aggression or intimidation but as part of a conscientious devotion to collective security, one that rejected isolationism in favor of a coalition of nations in search of safety from a dangerous foe. "We live in a shrunken world, a world in which oceans are crossed in hours, a world in which a single-minded despotism menaces the scattered freedoms of scores of struggling independent nations." Victory would not be won by military might alone, he emphasized. "There can be no enduring peace for any nation while other nations suffer privation, oppression, and a sense of injustice and despair. In our modern world, it is madness to suppose that there could be an island of tranquility and prosperity in a sea of wretchedness and frustration."

All of that underlined Eisenhower's determination to create a world of alliances, to lead by aid and example, not merely to cow America's enemies within their borders. Still, he knew, too, that nuclear weapons, so essential to his New Look for American security, formed their own, independent threat, that they recalibrated the moral considerations of war itself. Once a force for freedom and liberation, America's military strength now carried the potential of human annihilation, as did its enemy's. "With such weapons," Eisenhower told the suddenly sobered audience, "war has become, not just tragic, but preposterous. With such weapons, there can be no victory for anyone. Plainly, the objective now must be to see that such a war does not occur at all."

Eisenhower's phrasing was elegant and memorable: "not just tragic, but preposterous," "a sea of wretchedness and frustration," "a single-minded despotism" menacing "scattered freedoms." But even more striking was the substance of his speech. Here was an American president able and willing to warn his people that they would not win a war for which he was asking them to arm. Only Eisenhower, the world's most revered public statesman, could sound such an alarm and yet confidently carry the warm affection of his nation. "My friends," he concluded, "in firm faith, and in the conviction that the Republican purposes and principles are 'in league' with this kind of future, the nomination that you have tendered me for the Presidency of the United States I now—humbly but confidently—accept." Sinny Weeks was among those deeply moved. It was, he thought, the best speech Ike had given as president.

His address over, the balloons released, the crowds energized, Ike then "was given a reward," as Adams put it. He and the Gang headed for one of the president's favorite courses, Cypress Point, in Pebble Beach, California, for a long weekend of golf and bridge.

Ike promised a gentler campaign and delivered it. He knew Stevenson had no way to beat him, so he campaigned mostly from the White House, shunning the exhausting regimen of train travel that had marked the 1952 effort, instead favoring a strategy more heavily reliant on advertising than personal appearances. Stevenson lashed out now and again and occasionally drew a reply—Eisenhower was particularly dismissive of Stevenson's proposal for a ban on atmospheric testing of nuclear weapons—but the president largely ignored the campaign to unseat him. The *New York Times*, which backed Ike in 1952, did so even more enthusiastically in 1956. With Election Day approaching, Ike was the heavy favorite to win.

That is not to say that he took victory for granted. In September, the Supreme Court justice Sherman Minton, a capable if undistinguished member of the Court, announced his plans to retire on October 15, when the Court resumed its fall term. Eisenhower was mildly miffed—Minton had declared his support for Stevenson, and his announcement gave Ike little time to react—but the president had his third vacancy: Warren was his first appointment, and in 1955 he had replaced the eloquent Robert

Jackson with an elegant, estimable conservative, John Marshall Harlan II, who would follow in his grandfather's footsteps as one of history's most distinguished justices.

With the 1956 election so close, Eisenhower approached this nomination with political thoughts in mind. He had few areas of weakness, but among them was his relatively mediocre standing among Catholic Democrats. Discussing the appointment with Brownell, Eisenhower specifically suggested that the attorney general look for a conservative judge, preferably a Democrat and definitely a Catholic.

Brownell delivered on a Catholic Democrat but either misjudged or misled Eisenhower on the appointee's politics. William J. Brennan Jr. was the son of an immigrant labor organizer. He grew up in New Jersey and went on to graduate from Harvard Law School. He was charming, brilliant, and impish, a distinguished member of the New Jersey Supreme Court, highly recommended by that court's chief justice. All of which inarguably qualified him for the Supreme Court. But Brennan was hardly a conservative. The *Washington Post* described him as a "moderate liberal," and others noted his party affiliation and working-class upbringing. Still, Eisenhower liked him—most men did—and announced his appointment on September 29.

Ike would come to regret Brennan's appointment as the years passed, privately expressing disappointment in him as well as in Warren. In Warren's case, Eisenhower could perhaps be forgiven for misgauging the California Republican's true political convictions. He had less of an excuse with Brennan. Eisenhower misunderstood him, and that miscalculation had lasting consequences. Brennan took his seat on October 15, 1956; he was easily confirmed the following spring, with only Senator McCarthy voting no. Brennan did not leave the Court until July 1990.

On the Edge

T he trouble began, as it would so often, in the Middle East. Its origins in some ways resembled the Iran crisis that greeted Eisenhower when he first took office. Britain found itself in escalating conflict with a charismatic statesman in a struggle involving Communism, imperialism, and access to resources and shipping. In Iran, oil was the commodity, and Mossadegh was the adversary. This time, the battleground was Egypt, the issue was the Suez Canal, and the threat to Britain's hegemony was Gamal Abdel Nasser.

Stern, brave, literally and figuratively scarred by his struggle against British imperialism, Lieutenant Colonel Nasser was a galvanizing figure in the Middle East, a uniting leader who sought for decades to ally Arab nations in a struggle against foreign domination. Even Eisenhower was grudgingly impressed by Nasser, describing him as dynamic and personable, a tip of the cap to a fellow military man who puzzled Ike but interested him, too. The son of a postal inspector raised in southern Egypt, Nasser lost his mother as a young boy; she died giving birth to his brother. His father remarried, and Nasser went to live with relatives, eventually joining the rising student movement directed against the presence of British troops on Egyptian soil. Literate, articulate, and dashing—Nasser's broad face and grin belied his ferocious will—he eventually landed a place in the Egyptian military academy (one of his classmates was Anwar Sadat). Driven to expel the British from his homeland, Nasser conferred with Italian leaders during World War II on a plan to overthrow his government and expel the British forces. The coup plans were dropped, but Nasser's ambition burned.

By the 1950s, he had orchestrated the fall of King Farouk and helped General Mohammed Naguib assume the mantle of Egyptian authority, though it was Nasser who commanded genuine power in the new government. An attempt on Nasser's life in 1954 gave him the excuse to sentence Naguib to house arrest—as well as to authorize a brutal repression of rivals and dissenters. From that point on, Nasser ruled Egypt.

His ouster of Naguib, however, left Nasser with bitter enemies inside Egypt, making his hold on power uncertain. To solidify his base, establish his leadership over the Arab world, and modernize his nation, Nasser proposed the construction of the Aswan High Dam in southern Egypt. The mammoth undertaking would, he believed, control flooding of the Nile, boost Egyptian agriculture, and raise his nation's international stature. Eisenhower supported the plan and offered American assistance, reasoning that the project would aid Egypt, and that American backing would help win friends in the region, tightening the United States' grasp on oil flowing from the Middle East.

Eisenhower had another objective as well: to foil Soviet influence. The administration insisted that in return for its loans for the dam, Nasser refuse offers of Soviet assistance. That pushy attempt to force Nasser into the Western orbit offended the Egyptian leader, steeped as he was in anti-colonialism and determined as he was to strike a neutralist position akin to that of India's Nehru. Rather than respond immediately, Nasser took the Eisenhower proposal under advisement, considering it for months while conspicuously cultivating his relationship with the Communist world. At the same time, Eisenhower faced domestic pressure, as supporters of Israel, critics of mutual aid, and growers of American cotton found common ground in questioning use of American money to subsidize an Egyptian dam that would expand the agricultural capacity of a nation whose products competed with American goods.

Nasser did not help his own case. With America's offer still on the table, he recognized China's Communist government, purchased weapons from Czechoslovakia, and fortified his military presence along the border with Israel. By July, when he decided to accept American support for the dam, he had exhausted Washington's patience, and the offer was effectively withdrawn. Nasser was furious. He publicly denounced the United States on July 24. Two days later, he seized the Suez Canal, announcing that Egypt would henceforth operate the canal and use revenue from it to help pay for the dam. He ordered canal employees to stay at work or face imprisonment.

The Suez Canal Company was an international institution, but the government of Britain and French investors were its principal owners, and trade through the canal was vital to the economic and security interests of both nations. Consequently, Nasser's action was guaranteed to infuriate leaders of both countries. Eisenhower tried to head off a confrontation that he believed would lead to profoundly uncertain consequences for the world. On July 31, he wrote to Anthony Eden and urged calm in the face of provocation. Eisenhower had received word through an intermediary that Eden was already considering a military response, and Ike pleaded with his counterpart, whom he addressed as "Anthony," to refrain. Eisenhower recommended convening an international conference to exert pressure on Egypt to insure continued, efficient operation of the canal, and he grimly warned against precipitous resort to force. "For my part," he wrote, "I cannot over-emphasize the strength of my conviction that some such method must be attempted before action such as you contemplate should be undertaken." The American people, Eisenhower warned, would balk at military action to resolve the crisis, as would those of other nations. The Western alliance would be sorely tested: "I do not want to exaggerate, but I assure you that this could grow to such an intensity as to have the most far-reaching consequences."

Those were the prudent words of a wise military leader, but Eden ignored them. Although Britain, France, and other nations—though not Egypt—agreed to attend an August conference in London, Nasser rejected the conference's recommendation for an international oversight board to supervise the workings of the canal. Dulles scrambled to negotiate a solution but succeeded mainly in alienating his allies. Angry nations now hurtled toward the confrontation that Eisenhower most feared. Israel called up troops; Britain and France became suspiciously quiet.

Then, just as the Suez conflict came to a boil, another crisis erupted. This one flared from Khrushchev's famous secret speech on the depravity of Stalin's reign. Washington had been cautiously hopeful that a thaw in relations might follow and had hoped the measured Soviet response to Polish demands suggested progress. Still, American analysts saw no prospect for fundamental change in Moscow, merely for a gentler era of confrontation.

In Hungary, nationalists had no way of knowing that the Eisenhower administration lacked any realistic plan to assist their struggle for liberation. They imagined that Khrushchev was providing an opening, that the events in Poland indicated that Moscow might now tolerate limited dissent, so long as it was within the broad ideological rubric of advancing Communism. Hungarians began to speak openly of a break with Moscow, increasingly unsettling Russia's ambassador to Hungary, Yuri Andropov. As the Suez crisis escalated, Andropov warned his superiors in Moscow that the situation had "sharply deteriorated. Hostile elements, who see Hungary as one of the weakest links among the countries of the socialist camp, have stepped up their activities, and have spoken openly against the Hungarian Workers' Party leadership." Andropov correctly sized up the threat posed by the growing popularity of Imre Nagy, a son of peasants and a dedicated Communist who was determined to lead his country to a Marxism free from Soviet domination. Nagy had already been ousted as prime minister, but students and intellectuals saw him as their best hope. Andropov's recommendation: persuade Nagy to issue a self-critical statement of his past party failings—his misunderstanding of collectivization or his unwillingness to cede ultimate authority to the Communist Party—and then reinstate him to the party and give him "some insignificant work." If Nagy refused, Andropov's chilling cable concluded, "it would be necessary to expose him in the eyes of Communists as a member of the opposition and as a dissenter." Whatever "peaceful coexistence" or candor about Stalin meant to Moscow, it clearly did not include liberation of Hungary.

Andropov's recommendations were not known to the students or their allies, much less to Nagy. In the long days of Hungary's warm summer, passions intensified. In July, the Hungarian Writers' Union openly criticized the Hungarian Workers' Party; the head of the party resigned eight days later and fled to Moscow. A group of dissidents executed in 1949 after a show trial were posthumously rehabilitated and reburied in October—100,000 people attended the funeral.

How distant those tribulations seemed to Americans in 1956, as "peace, prosperity and progress," Eisenhower's reelection slogan, dominated the national discourse. This was the year of "Howl," Allen Ginsberg's rollicking announcement of America's bohemian culture, not to mention the mounting urgency of civil rights and the incipient force of Betty Friedan and the women's movement, whose foundations Friedan laid in 1957. Still, there was a surface ease about American life that summer.

In October, exhilaration flared around the World Series, an epic contest between the Brooklyn Dodgers and the New York Yankees. The series that year lasted seven games, and Eisenhower traveled to New York to attend as a fan. In game 5, the Yankees' Don Larsen pitched his perfect game. Don Newcombe, the Dodgers' great ace, had won twenty-seven games that year, but lost two, including game 7, in the series. Eisenhower rooted for the Yankees but felt for Newcombe. "I think I know how much you wanted to win a World Series game," the president wrote upon returning to Washington. "I for one was pulling for you. But I suggest that when you think over this past season, you think of the twenty-seven games you won that were so important in bringing Brooklyn into the World Series." Newcombe, no doubt flabbergasted to receive a note from the president, touchingly replied: "I don't think you'll ever know what [your letter] has done for my confidence, which was at a very low ebb. I was very pleased to learn that you were pulling for the Dodgers and me personally, and I'm very sorry I didn't do better, and through your letter I think I understand more clearly about the bad breaks in sports."

Events in Europe moved with gathering speed. Nagy succeeded in convincing the Hungarian Workers' Party to readmit him. Three days after that, students formed the Hungarian Association of University and College Unions. In Poland, Gomulka was named first secretary of that nation's Communist Party, and one week later Hungarian protesters released the "Sixteen Points," a blueprint for the nation of their imagination. The first demand was for withdrawal of all Soviet troops; the twelfth was for "freedom of opinion, freedom of speech, a free press and radio and a new daily paper."

The Sixteen Points rallied Hungarians, and marches the following day demonstrated the depth of animus toward Soviet rule. A crowd of some 200,000 people gathered in Lajos Kossuth Square, a grand set of monuments on the banks of the Danube, named for the man who proclaimed Hungarian independence from Austria; elsewhere in Budapest, other assemblies grew and turned increasingly confrontational. That evening, Hungarian secret police fired into a crowd, estimated at twenty thousand to thirty thousand, assembled in front of a local police station. Three died. Another band of protesters knocked over a statue of Stalin (partially fulfilling one of the Sixteen Points, which called for removal of that hated artwork and replacement of it with a monument to Hungary's war of independence). Dissidents evolved into rebels, attacking government buildings and police. Authoritarians took stock. At 11:00 p.m., Khrushchev met with his inner council in Moscow. Twelve men attended; eleven favored immediate deployment of Soviet troops to restore order. The first units of the Red Army rolled into Budapest the following morning.

Washington watched, transfixed but paralyzed, as Hungarian freedom fighters confronted Soviet tanks. At first, the struggle went shockingly well for the Hungarians. Some Soviet tank commanders sympathized with Hungarian rebels who desperately argued that they, too, were Communists, fighting only to practice Communism in their own national fashion. Hungarians boarded a few of the tanks and paraded through Budapest. But

Hungarian nationalism, encouraged by the United States and other Western powers, now met the real Soviet might. Shots were fired—to this day, it is disputed who fired first—and a tense but festive face-off descended into a bloody melee. Some one hundred people were killed, another three hundred wounded. Over the next several days, Soviet and Hungarian forces wrestled for control of the capital and surrounding cities and countryside. "Within Hungary," Dulles told Eisenhower, "the revolt has become widespread."

Then, with the world's attention focused on this extraordinary challenge to Soviet power, Israel stunned that same world by pivoting away from Lebanon and attacking Egypt across the Sinai Peninsula. Overnight, Israeli forces penetrated seventy-five miles into Egypt and by daybreak were just twenty-five miles east of Suez. The day before, Eisenhower had urged the Israeli prime minister, David Ben-Gurion, to "do nothing which would endanger the peace." Now Israeli forces parachuted into position and outmaneuvered the Egyptians. Not believing that Britain was behind this assault, Eisenhower asked Britain's UN ambassador to consider UN action against Israel. "We were astonished to find that he was completely unsympathetic," Eisenhower wrote to Eden. In fact, Britain's ambassador was openly hostile, "virtually snarling," in Lodge's words.

Even that brusque dismissal was not enough to jolt Ike into realizing Britain's complicity, though the actions of both Britain and France were tellingly suspicious. The two nations urged a cease-fire and suggested that Israeli and Egyptian forces back up ten miles each, leaving a safe zone around the canal. "Anglo-French" forces would then fill in the gap and secure the peace—while, coincidentally, wresting control of the canal from Nasser, as they had been attempting to do since July. The French-British communiqué was backed by a threat: if Israel and Egypt did not agree, the joint forces would attack Suez. Israel predictably agreed—the proposed withdrawal still left its troops deep in Egyptian territory—and Nasser just as swiftly refused. Ike urged Eden and Prime Minister Guy Mollet of France to reconsider what he described as "drastic action," advising instead that the nations pursue "peaceful processes." On October 31, without so much as a warning to Eisenhower, British bombers attacked airfields in Egypt. The United Nations convened in emergency session.

Eisenhower was stunned and despondent: his most dependable allies, two nations whose destinies he had played a weighty role in shaping, double-crossed him. They had taken advantage of his preoccupations with Hungary and his reelection, then just a week away. Why the deception?

As Mollet later acknowledged to Eisenhower, "If your government was not informed . . . [it was because of] our fear that if we had consulted it, it would have prevented us from acting."

With the crises in Eastern Europe and the Middle East now overlapping and the presidential campaign suspended, Eisenhower acceded to his aides, chiefly Sherman Adams, who insisted he needed to address the nation. Preparing such a speech occupied the tense corridors of the White House on October 31, which began with a frustrated Eisenhower searching for ways to halt the fighting in the Sinai. "Let's call it a 'Bomb for Peace,' " he exploded at an emergency session that morning. "It's as simple as this: Let's send one of Curt LeMay's gang over the Middle East, carrying an atomic bomb. And let's warn *everyone*: We'll drop it—if they *all* don't cut this nonsense out." Aghast, aides let the remark pass in silence.

Having blown off that steam, Eisenhower sent Dulles off to prepare a text for the national address. Dulles did not deliver a draft until 3:15 p.m., and Eisenhower was dismayed. It was rambling and didactic, "with no force of argument," as Emmet Hughes put it. Eisenhower and Hughes shelved the Dulles draft and pounded out a new one. Hughes called for Dulles, who came to the White House, so that he could read and edit while Hughes wrote and camera operators laid cables and put up lights. The address was scheduled for 7:00 p.m. Hughes handed the last edited page to Ike at 6:56. Eisenhower enjoyed the pressure. He grinned as he took the sheets from Hughes. "Boy, this is taking it right off the stove, isn't it?"

The speech that night captured the strange duality of the week: the "dawning of a new day" in Hungary, or so it appeared; the "somber" situation in Egypt, which, while not the cause for "extravagant fear or hysteria," nevertheless did demand "our most serious concern."

The hope for Hungary and Eastern Europe reflected an astonishing set of reports from the region. That morning, Eisenhower had been startled to receive word that the Soviets appeared to be backing down from a full-scale war. In Poland, Khrushchev had allowed a new government to be seated, and the October 31 edition of *Pravda* featured a government proclamation that appeared to signal an abrupt change in the Soviet response to the unrest in Hungary. It announced a new set of relations between the Soviet Union and its satellites—"a great commonwealth of socialist nations"— emphasizing "the principles of complete equality, of respect for territorial integrity, state independence and sovereignty, and of noninterference in one another's internal affairs." As Ike addressed the American people that night, he imagined a reborn nation, wrenched from Soviet control by the force of popular will. "Today, it appears, a new Hungary is rising from this struggle," Eisenhower stated, "a Hungary which we hope from our hearts will know full and free nationhood."

A stupefied Allen Dulles tried to make sense of the news. The morning after Eisenhower's speech, Dulles briefed the National Security Council on the *Pravda* announcement, which he described as "one of the most important statements to come out of the USSR in the last decade." The force of public opinion, he said, had overpowered military might. "The impossible had happened," Dulles announced. It was, he said, "a miracle."

It was, however, a short-lived miracle. Four days later, Russian tanks and armor rolled through Budapest, this time without sympathy for the rebels. Artillery fire commenced at 4:15 a.m. on November 4. The Hungarians were denounced as fascist usurpers. Negotiators for the Hungarian government were arrested at the table where talks with the Soviets were under way. Nagy sought asylum at the Yugoslav embassy. By nightfall, the rebellion had been broken. Eisenhower, his own alliance badly strained by the events in Egypt, now watched in dismay as Soviet tanks imposed their forbidding authority on a brave and abandoned people, encouraged to rise up by his own rhetoric of liberation, now left to fight for themselves. Bodies lay strewn throughout Budapest. "I have noted with profound distress," Eisenhower wrote to Bulganin, "the reports which have reached me today from Hungary." His note almost pleaded: "I urge in the name of humanity and in the cause of peace that the Soviet Union take action to withdraw Soviet forces from Hungary immediately." Bulganin accused Eisenhower of meddling in the internal affairs of the Soviet Union, though Hungary was nominally an independent country. He baited the president, suggesting that the United States and the Soviet Union should jointly send forces to Egypt to repel British and French invaders there. The *New York Times*'s four-deck headline on Sunday, November 4, captured the complexity of the world that day: "Soviet Attacks Hungary, Seizes Nagy; U.S. Legation in Budapest Under Fire." Beneath it, the other crisis: "U.N. Assembly Backs Call to Set Up Mideast Truce Force." And beneath that: "Stevenson Holds President Lacks 'Energy' for Job."

As that last headline suggests, the final weeks of the campaign brought out the worst in Stevenson, who sacrificed grace and honor as he grew increasingly desperate. He advanced his reckless proposal to unilaterally halt American nuclear testing, picking up the unfortunate support of Bulganin—hardly a favorite ally in the fall of 1956. Then, on the campaign's final weekend, at precisely the moment when Eisenhower was most engaged in a crisis, Stevenson suggested that the president was feeble.

"The Chief Executive," Stevenson told a Democratic audience in Chicago, "has never had the inclination and now lacks the energy for full-time work." The president's "age, his health and the fact that he cannot succeed himself make it inevitable that the dominant figure in the Republican Party under a second Eisenhower term would be Richard Nixon," he added. It was easier to run against Nixon than Ike, but Stevenson's message not only offended Eisenhower; it strained credulity, especially since it appeared the same day that Ike was dealing with the dual crises in Hungary and Suez. Ike did suffer through those weeks—his blood pressure was jumpy, and aides described him as drawn and tired. But he persisted and maintained a steady command. Ike was more disappointed than angry at Stevenson's line of attack, writing off his opponent's charges as "moves of desperation by a candidate who realizes he can't win," as the president confided to Ellis Slater.

Those chaotic weeks of October and November 1956 tested Ike as few others had. By the end of the presidential race, he was fed up, convinced that Stevenson had advanced the test-ban proposal for political gain without thought to national security. Stevenson and Kefauver, he complained to his old friend Al Gruenther, "are the sorriest and weakest pair that ever aspired to the highest offices in the land." Against such opponents, Eisenhower would only be satisfied with a resounding victory. Anything less, and "I would rather not be elected."

It was, Adams recalled, the worst period Eisenhower had ever experienced in the White House other than the days following his heart attack. The campaign was distracting, the world crises real and forbidding. To Gruenther, Ike admitted the strain. "Life," he wrote, "gets more difficult by the minute." The toll on Dulles was even greater. Drawn and ashen on the night of Ike's address to the nation, he rallied to spearhead the U.S. diplomatic effort at the United Nations. Just after midnight on November 2, he awoke with severe abdominal pains; he checked into Walter Reed hospital, where doctors found cancer and performed a three-hour operation to remove part of his large intestine. Dulles did not return to work for more than two months.

Eisenhower was then, as in those crucible weeks after D-day, a strategic commander, determined and stalwart, patient and clearheaded. His friends were astounded at his calm. "Here were . . . the ten most frustrating days of his life, and yet there was no evidence at all of pressure, of indecision or of the frustration he mentioned," Slater wrote in his diary. "Actually, he seemed completely composed."

Eisenhower's objective was the long-term preservation of democracy and

American leadership; he calibrated his responses accordingly. To the amazement of the Third World, Eisenhower stood solidly behind Egypt. He demanded that his wayward allies end hostilities around Suez and pressed his case with the United Nations despite British and French fury. The administration's armistice proposal, advanced by the still-ailing Dulles, was approved by a vote of 64–5—the no votes came from Britain, France, and Israel, as well as Australia and New Zealand. When the British and French—as well as Israel—still resisted leaving, Eisenhower applied economic pressure, denying his allies oil and refusing British access to capital during a run on the pound. Eventually, Eden succumbed; he left office in near-collapse, and Britain at last withdrew along with its allies in that misadventure.

"It really was a tough one," Eisenhower said years later, "but I thought we had to stand on principle."

In Hungary, Eisenhower's options were fewer, but he resisted the temptation to escalate. Time, he was convinced, was on America's side in the long struggle against the Soviets. He had sacrificed lives before in pursuit of grand objectives. These lives were brave Hungarians, misled into believing that Ike would come to their aid and resentful that he did not. Eisenhower allowed them to suffer for believing in his rhetoric of liberation, but his nation won through peace what it could not have secured through war. Hungary today is free in no small measure because Eisenhower allowed its revolution to fail. That is a bitter truth, but such were many victories of that perilous era.

For his part, Khrushchev showed the wear of those weeks as well. At a reception in November for Gomulka, Khrushchev was bellicose, rude, and inept. "We are Bolsheviks," he boasted to Western diplomats attending the event. "About the capitalist states, it doesn't depend on you whether or not we exist. If you don't like us, don't accept our invitations, and don't invite us to come to see you. Whether you like it or not, history is on our side. We will bury you!" Khrushchev intended the remark to underscore his view of the eventual end of peaceful coexistence—that socialism was historically determined to outlive capitalism. But he had rattled his weaponry too menacingly to be taken lightly.

Dwight Eisenhower was reelected president on November 6, 1956. He won by a smashing margin, more than 9 million votes out of 61,607,208 cast, 457 electoral votes to Stevenson's 73. Nearly 60 percent of Americans cast their votes for Ike. His only weakness ran along the band of the Deep South, where *Brown* rankled and Southerners were still voting against Lincoln. And yet this most triumphal political moment must also stand as one of this nation's least climactic. It paled beneath the carefully constructed peace in Egypt, the smoldering cease-fire in Hungary. At the end of 1956, Eisenhower was president again, and the world remained, remarkably, at peace. His reelection was a point of pride; his peace a mark of statesmanship.

It had been a long year—marked by patience and care. None of it was easy. Wrote Ike with a sigh: "I really could use a good bridge game."

PART THREE

THE SECOND TERM

The Press of Change, the Price of Inaction

T he Eisenhower who took the oath of office for the second time had been forged by his own presidency. He spoke on January 21, 1957, flanked by symbols of his term: Chief Justice Earl Warren sat to his right, Vice President Richard Nixon to his left. Mamie joined them as well, dressed in a fur coat and hat. Ike was older, thinner than he had been in 1953, less exuberant, but more forceful. He had often been frustrated by the limitations of politics but also seasoned by them and masterful at divining a middle course through a divided nation.

Ike liked the speech in his hand that morning. He arrived at the White House early to announce that he had not changed a word overnight—"the most outstanding event of the past four years, from a secretary's . . . viewpoint," Ann Whitman joked.

With the nation watching on television, Eisenhower spoke of the sacrifices of the Hungarian people and the recklessness of his allies in Suez. The Soviets and the Chinese had tested his mettle, and he knew his enemy's designs. "The divisive force," he said, "is International Communism and the power that it controls." He spoke from experience as he described the nature of that force: "The designs of that power, dark in purpose, are clear in practice. It strives to seal forever the gate of those it has enslaved. It strives to break the ties that unite the free. And it strives to capture—to exploit for its own greater power—all forces of change in the world, especially the needs of the hungry and the hopes of the oppressed."

Eisenhower also drew upon Abilene and West Point, North Africa and Washington; he projected the accumulated experience of the world's most respected leader, his style and vocabulary recognizably formal, with his distinctive appreciation for pairings—"May we pursue the right, without self-righteousness. May we know unity, without conformity"—the contrast of abundance and want, peace and threat. "We live in a land of plenty," Ike reminded his nation, "but rarely has this earth known such peril."

Eisenhower's job was demanding, of course, but family troubles also nagged at him. The very morning of his inaugural, he confronted a flare-up in the life of one of his brothers. Visiting with family that week, Ike realized that his oldest sibling, Arthur, was suffering and receiving little comfort from his demanding and difficult wife. Before leaving the White House for his swearing in, Eisenhower made time to write to Big Ike to ask his help in the matter.

The senior member of the Eisenhower brethren, Ike reported to Edgar, was struggling with heart problems and was so debilitated that his White House escort feared he was near collapse and called a doctor, believing he needed to be hospitalized. But Arthur's wife, Louise, refused and angrily implied that Arthur was somehow betraying her by entertaining offers that he be sent to Walter Reed (Louise, a member of the Unity School of Christianity, was wary of certain medical treatments). Compounding Arthur's difficulties was the messy residue from a long-ago divorce; he had fallen behind on alimony payments and ended up settling up with his first wife later that year. Arthur's difficulties worried his younger brother, who fussed over the letter to Edgar even as the hour of the inauguration approached. He confessed to Edgar that there was not much to be done for Arthur, merely that his brothers should look out for him and perhaps make it a point to drop in on him in Kansas City.

In all, Ike's letter to Edgar was the tender work of a fond and worried brother—made remarkable by the fact that he wrote just hours before being sworn in as president of the United States.

Eisenhower finished his letter, delivered his speech, and walked back to the White House with the parade. It was so cold that his fingers were numb when he trundled back inside.

Eisenhower's smashing victory in the 1956 election left no doubt about the appreciation of the American people for their leader. But Ike also was the nation's first lame-duck president (the Twenty-second Amendment, limiting the president to two terms, was ratified in 1951). In addition, Ike labored under the constraints imposed by his doctors following his heart attack and seemed to strive constantly to keep his temper in check.

Nineteen fifty-seven was to bring significant additions to the American experience and even the American vocabulary. The nation's exploratory zeal and technological prowess gave Americans the word "aerospace," while the rumblings of youthful rebellion were indelibly captured by Jack Kerouac in his masterwork, *On the Road*, which introduced "beatniks." Martin Luther King Jr. founded the Southern Christian Leadership Conference. Albert Camus won the Nobel Prize in Literature; John Kennedy won a Pulitzer Prize for *Profiles in Courage*. James Reston won a Pulitzer for his look at Ike's heart attack and its effect on the government. It was a time of struggle, tension, repression, and discovery.

Eisenhower's popularity contrasted with the Republicans' marginal appeal to the American people. Notwithstanding Stevenson's defeat, Democrats knew they had leverage, and that encouraged competition over the legislative agenda. Typical was the fight over America's foreign aid budget. Since the war, Ike had argued that America's strength lay in nurturing its network of allies, and that aid was a matter of national self-interest. Yet, more than a decade after Allied forces had defeated Nazi Germany, Eisenhower again faced opposition to his proposed mutual aid budget for 1957. Through a frustrating winter and spring, Ike leaned on legislators, appealed directly to the American people, and begged his critics to reexamine mutual aid as a function of national security rather than "do-goodism," as some alleged. Eisenhower grew increasingly irascible, especially with Republicans who insisted that foreign aid was a luxury rather than a security instrument. He felt as though he'd made his case already, only to be asked to argue it over and over again. Eisenhower grumbled that he was willing to deliver an address or two, "but I am entirely unwilling to devote time to treating the whole matter as a philosophical exercise rather than as down-to-earth, sink-or-swim, survive-or-perish."

His effort was taxing and largely unsuccessful: Ike's 1957 budget asked for $4.4 billion in mutual aid. In May, he yielded to pressure and cut the request to $3.9 billion. Congress approved only $2.8 billion. Eisenhower, recalled Sherman Adams, was deeply disturbed by what he regarded as a personal rejection. He accused the Republican Alvin M. Bentley, who proposed the final round of cuts, of being "completely indifferent to any consideration of national good or party loyalty." Stymied by his own party, Eisenhower struggled to maintain his composure and his health: his spring vacation in Augusta was dampened by his spotty golf play. Ike blamed it on flabby muscles. His friends worried about him and gently conspired to help him.

On top of all that, Congress rejected Eisenhower's requests for funding the U.S. Information Agency—a whipping boy since McCarthy's heyday—and insisted that an educational funding bill be amended to limit federal support for new classrooms to those areas that would use the money only in integrated schools. There again, Eisenhower retreated to the middle ground. He regarded those who demanded fidelity to the law and those who persisted in segregating students despite it as morally equivalent. He thus disagreed "with both extremes." The country might not have been ready to hinge all federal support for school construction on integration, but Ike's reluctance to challenge that consensus perpetuated it. The bill died in the House and, with it, a program to spend $270 million on new schools for the children of every state. Eisenhower's critics blamed him for its failure—the bill fell just five votes short—while Ike complained that despite his reservations, he would have signed the legislation if the House had passed it. Failing to educate America's children, Eisenhower insisted, was a "national calamity."

What baffled Ike more than tussling with Congress was his continuing friction with the Supreme Court, even as its ranks filled with his appointees. By the summer of 1957, four justices of the Court—Warren, Harlan, Brennan, and Charles Whittaker—owed their seats to Eisenhower, but some of their decisions continued to perplex the president, especially in the area of domestic security. Although congressional witch-hunting had abated by June 1957—and McCarthy himself had died a month earlier—the practice of legislative committees, federal and state, hauling in witnesses, badgering them about their affiliations, and demanding that they implicate others remained an insidious staple of American domestic security. In the final weeks of the Court's 1957 term, the justices made it abundantly clear how they regarded that practice as well as the larger question of the presence of Communists in American life.

The first of the landmark decisions was handed down on June 3. It resolved the case of Clinton Jencks, a union president who was accused of falsifying his history when he filed paperwork stating that he had never been a Communist. Charged with lying, Jencks asked to see the reports made by witnesses testifying against him so that his lawyer could cross-examine them; the trial judge denied the request. Jencks was convicted, and his conviction was upheld by a federal appeals court. The U.S. Supreme Court agreed to hear Jencks's appeal. Its consideration turned on how much latitude defendants should be given to peruse statements by prosecution witnesses. William Brennan, one of Eisenhower's appointees, wrote for the Court's majority—which included Warren and Harlan (Whittaker did not vote). Brennan concluded that Jencks was denied the right to assess the evidence against him. Two justices, Harlan and Harold Burton, concluded only that the judge should have screened the material himself, but they joined the majority in finding that Jencks deserved a new trial. Only Tom Clark, a Truman appointee, dissented, famously writing that the nation's intelligence agencies "may as well close up shop, for the Court has opened their files to the criminal and thus afforded him a Roman holiday for rummaging through confidential information as well as vital national secrets."

That was just the beginning. On Monday, June 17—thereafter to be known as Red Monday—the justices handed down four decisions that permanently altered the nation's approach to domestic security. Warren wrote for the majority in two cases: *Watkins v. United States* and *Sweezy v. New Hampshire*. The latter involved an economics professor from the University of New Hampshire who was ordered by that state's attorney general to discuss his lectures on economics and his involvement with the Progressive Party. The professor, Paul Sweezy, denied that he was a Communist but refused to say much more. Sweezy argued that to be required to testify further would violate not his Fifth Amendment right against self-incrimination but rather his First Amendment right of free speech and association. He was charged with contempt and convicted. The conviction was upheld by the New Hampshire Supreme Court. The Warren Court took the case and overturned the state ruling. Though it declined to find New Hampshire had violated Sweezy's First Amendment rights, it came close. "Our form of government," Warren wrote, "is built on the premise that every citizen shall have the right to engage in political expression and association." Instead, the Court concluded that it was Sweezy's right to due process that had been violated.

Warren was also careful in *Watkins*, again declining to find a specific First Amendment right that protected John Watkins, a labor organizer, from answering questions put to him by the House Un-American Activities Committee. In this case, Warren and the majority concluded that Watkins was inadequately informed of the scope of the committee's inquiry and thus could not properly assert his rights in deciding whether or not to answer. That was a bit of a dodge, but its meaning was summed up in one clear sentence: "There is no congressional power to expose for the sake of exposure." With that, the Warren Court put its stamp of disapproval on McCarthy and all that he had done.

Watkins and *Sweezy* highlighted a busy day for the Court, as it also reinstated John Service, a State Department employee dismissed after repeated—and futile—investigations of his loyalty. That case, captioned *Service v. Dulles et al.*, bore a special sting for Dulles, as it carried his name and the Court was unanimous against him. Finally, in *Yates v. United States*, the Court reversed criminal convictions of a group of California Communists convicted under the Smith Act. Both *Service* and *Yates* were written by Harlan, Ike's most conservative appointment to the Supreme Court, meaning that all four opinions released that day, as well as the *Jencks* decision from earlier that month, were the work of his appointees.

The next night, Ike hosted a stag dinner. It had been a long day: the White House had been overrun with visiting 4-H guests, followed by a rapid-fire series of meetings into the late afternoon. Finally secluded with friends, Ike let down his guard. He had "never been as mad in my life" as he was to see Communists and accused Communists coddled by the Court, he said. He was "practically fed up" with Warren.

Eisenhower's remarks made it into the press, embarrassing him and forcing him to apologize to the chief justice. He did with a halfhearted note later that week, not exactly denying the remark but hoping to tamp down Warren's reaction. "I have no doubt that in private conversation someone did hear me express amazement about one decision, but I have never even hinted at a feeling such as anger," Eisenhower explained. "To do so would imply not only that I knew the law but questioned motives. Neither of these things is true. So while resolving that even in private conversations I shall be more careful of my language, I do want you to know that if any such story appeared, it was a distortion."

Warren waited until July to answer, but then dismissed Ike's note as "in no sense necessary." Warren had won seven elections in California, had campaigned for the vice presidency in 1948, had been elected governor three times. He understood reporters. At least so he said. Years later, he confronted Ike directly, asking what the president, then retired, would have done with the Communists who came before the Court. "I would kill the SOBs," Eisenhower responded. Warren, bemused, said he regarded the president's reply as "merely petulant rather than definitive."

Tellingly, Eisenhower's unhappiness with the Court was over Communists, not civil rights. There, his reluctance to grapple with the politics of segregation was lamentable but not absolute, as he had allowed his attorney general wide authority to lead. Prodded by Brownell, Eisenhower in 1957 reintroduced a modest civil rights bill intended to begin the methodical expansion of federal supervision over integration in the southern states. The specific bill was hardly revolutionary; indeed, a version of it had been rejected by Congress in 1956 over lukewarm objections from the administration. Its principal provision was to allow the attorney general to file suit in federal court in order to punish those who violated the right to vote or the right to attend integrated schools under federal court order. If at one level, it seemed almost trivial to allow the attorney general to enforce rights already guaranteed by the Constitution and resolved by the Supreme Court, it nevertheless spelled trouble for southern segregationists, who recognized that it would empower the attorney general to bring actions against those who continued to defy the courts. The bill was fiercely contested in much of the South, and it divided the Eisenhower cabinet. When Brownell first presented the bill to the cabinet, Dulles, mindful of the propaganda advantages that segregation provided America's Communist enemies, supported the legislation. Secretary of the Treasury George Humphrey opposed the measure, and others questioned aspects of it. Secretary of Defense Charlie Wilson, for instance, warned against "adding more fuel" to the already explosive issue. Eisenhower was initially tepid. He endorsed the bill but declined to support the provision expanding the power of the attorney general to file civil rights cases. Even as the final bill was prepared, Eisenhower was still urging Brownell to emphasize the administration's understanding of the complexities faced by those confronting integration.

Eisenhower's position was politically understandable—he was running for reelection in 1956—but it was offered against vivid evidence of the price of inaction. Congress's debate was haunted by Emmett Till, whose 1955 murder still energized supporters of civil rights.

Till, a fourteen-year-old black boy visting Mississippi from Chicago, was alleged to have insulted the wife of Roy Bryant at the Bryant family store. Four days later, he was abducted from his grandmother's house. He was bludgeoned and shot, his body dumped in the Tallahatchie River. Bryant and J. W. Milam were arrested and tried by a Tallahatchie County jury. On September 23, 1955, just hours before Eisenhower suffered his heart attack in Denver, the jury acquitted Milam and Bryant. The prosecution, jurors said, had failed to positively establish that the body taken from the river was that of Till. Never mind that his mother testified that it was her son or that the ring on his finger belonged to her boy. Bryant and Milam waited just one hour and five minutes for the good news. Hearing it, they lit cigars, smiled faintly, and walked free.

Absent federal jurisdiction, there was nothing the Department of Justice could do to bring a case against Milam, Bryant, or the countless other thugs who inflicted brutalities against southern blacks. Brownell's bill would, for the first time, give the Department of Justice the power to prosecute. In addition, federal judges would acquire the authority to issue injunctions and hold violators in contempt. Beyond that, the bill also sought to establish a Civil Rights Commission, to expand the Justice Department's Civil Rights Section into a full division, and to create enforcement mechanisms for protecting voting rights.

Segregationists girded for battle. Richard Russell, the Senate's wiliest negotiator, charged that the bill would transform the attorney general into a "czar" with unbounded powers. He helped beat the bill in 1956, in part because Eisenhower refused to support the provisions regarding the attorney general. Then, during the 1956 campaign, Eisenhower reversed himself on that point. So when Congress addressed the matter in 1957, it now confronted the president himself, along with the memory of Till and the growing national impatience with southern racism.

Russell waged a side campaign against the bill, hoping to amend it and thereby undermine it. Specifically, he and other southern opponents of the legislation inserted a requirement that any person charged with contempt in federal court be entitled to a jury trial. Since southern juries had already demonstrated their willingness to forgive white perpetrators, Russell knew that such an amendment would gut Brownell's proposal. Moreover, their amendment shifted the tenor of the debate: the Eisenhower administration was forced to explain why it opposed jury trials rather than why it insisted on protecting civil rights. The amendment, Eisenhower realized, was a smoke screen to obscure the real debate. But the president could hardly say that publicly—to do so would be to accuse the South of such ingrained bigotry that it could not convict even the most egregious racist felons. James Byrnes, the former governor of South Carolina, called his friend Eisenhower's bluff, writing to the president that the bill's provisions regarding jury trials would allow the Department of Justice to circumvent the law.

Ike disingenuously denied it, but he knew what he could not say: the Department of Justice did not trust southern whites to render justice in crimes against blacks.

Compounding the attempt to circumscribe the practical effect of the bill was a second amendment to curtail its reach. Rather than authorize the attorney general to prosecute all violations of civil rights—and to allow judges to hold violators in contempt—this amendment, again backed by Russell and Lyndon Johnson, would restrict the reach of the bill to violations of voting rights. That would eliminate the use of the new federal powers to force school integration, where Russell was particularly determined to hold the line. On July 2, Russell charged that the bill was "cunningly designed to vest in the Attorney General unprecedented power to bring to bear the whole matter of the Federal government, including the

Armed Forces if necessary, to force a co-mingling of white and negro children in the state-supported public schools of the South."

Eisenhower was disoriented by Russell's attack, fleeing the White House for the quiet of Gettysburg and trying to contain a foul humor. He tried to rebut Russell's charge at a news conference. At first, it looked as if he would succeed. The bill, he stressed, was intended only to prevent people "illegally from interfering with any individual's right to vote . . . and so on." Ike's "and so on" left ample room for the bill to comprehend the full range of civil rights protections. Sensing that the president was being evasive, the *New York Times*'s James Reston pressed further and asked whether Eisenhower would be willing to limit the new law to voting rights. Trapped, Ike stumbled: "Well, I would not want to answer this in detail, because I was reading part of that bill this morning, and there were certain phrases I didn't completely understand." That was hard to believe. This was legislation that had been debated for more than a year. Ike was just getting around to reading it?

Eisenhower's equivocation hurt his bargaining position, and on July 10 he met for an hour with Russell. Brownell was not present. Eisenhower again expressed his sympathy for the strain on Southerners. He stood fast on protecting voting rights but agreed to consider Russell's "clarifying amendments." The two parted on friendly terms. Separately, and also without Brownell, Eisenhower conferred with Lyndon Johnson, who warned the president that the bill would be defeated unless Eisenhower agreed to drop the provision that allowed the attorney general to defend all civil rights. Brownell regarded that as an empty threat, but Eisenhower did not.

So even as the White House geared to push the bill through, soliciting support from prominent Americans who opposed the efforts to weaken it—Jackie Robinson, for instance, cabled that he had "waited this long for bill with meaning—can wait a little longer"—Eisenhower cut a compromise that symbolized his civil rights record. He agreed to drop the provision giving the attorney general broad authority and limit him to cases involving voting rights. Brownell was disappointed but consoled himself with the bill's passage. Though less than he had hoped for, it marked the first such legislation passed by Congress since Reconstruction and established meaningful precedent in the federal enforcement of civil rights. Eisenhower's compromise was reached on August 23 and was, Brownell later reflected, "a highly practical decision."

Could Eisenhower have held out for a more meaningful bill? Perhaps. Certainly Brownell thought he could. But Ike was often inclined to trust congressional leaders to count votes better than he could; in this case, Strom

Thurmond of South Carolina had already waged the longest filibuster in Senate history, and Johnson warned that the bill might not pass.

Eisenhower's reluctance to force a confrontation also reflected his instinctive desire to move slowly and with bipartisan support, especially in this area. In any event, the bill, even as amended, placed Eisenhower's stamp on the civil rights movement and set the precedent for more ambitious legislative achievements in the following decade. As president, Johnson would more fully embrace some of the ideas he resisted when he was a senator from Texas. More immediately, however, Eisenhower's ambivalence encouraged others to test his willingness to defend a cause he did not enthusiastically champion.

That was tragically compounded by Eisenhower's comments at a news conference during the heat of the deliberations. Before the August 23 agreement was reached, Russell and other southern senators had charged that Eisenhower was preparing to use military force to integrate schools. Ike tried to put an end to that argument at a July 17 meeting with the press. The first question that day came from Merriman Smith of United Press International. Smith asked whether Eisenhower believed the bill changed his authority or merely extended existing powers that dated to Reconstruction. Eisenhower dodged, saying, as he often did, that he was not a lawyer and thus not a constitutional expert. But this time he added: "I can't imagine any set of circumstances that would ever induce me to send Federal troops into a Federal court and into any area to enforce the orders of a Federal court, because I believe the common sense of America will never require it." Again, he hoped for a middle way between forced integration and determined resistance.

It had been a trying summer. Eisenhower had embarrassingly lost his temper with the Court, and Congress had bedeviled him on international aid, school construction, and civil rights. In late August, a reporter asked him to assess Congress's work that session. Eisenhower admitted that he was "tremendously disappointed," a sentiment he reiterated even after the deal was cut on civil rights. Worse yet, he had weathered those hot Washington weeks without Mamie. She was troubled by medical problems and on August 6 was admitted to Walter Reed for a hysterectomy. The procedure lasted two hours and was gingerly covered by the same press corps that reported Ike's every bowel movement from Denver. After Mamie's operation, Ike arrived bearing a bouquet of carnations—"Mamie Pink"— and found his wife recuperating but cranky. The doctors, Eisenhower told reporters, were delighted by Mamie's progress. But, he added with a smile, "this does not mean . . . that her disposition is necessarily so good about it."

Nearly a month later, Ike reported to Sherman Adams that she was still "just plain miserable." She and her husband eagerly looked forward to a cool escape from Washington; Ike pined for the northern woods of Wisconsin, but the press of business made that impractical. Instead, he and Mamie picked the Navy base at Newport, Rhode Island. Both the president and the First Lady badly needed a break.

Even before they departed, there were warnings of trouble from the American South. As children prepared to return to school that September, resistance was hardening in some areas. Communities across the old Confederacy determined to thwart integration no matter what the law demanded.

One community that had decided to obey the Court, however, was Little Rock, Arkansas. There, the local school board had, by the standards of the day, done a reasonable job responding to *Brown v. Board of Education*. Three days after the decision was handed down, the Little Rock school board acknowledged "our responsibility to comply" and pledged to do so as soon as the Court detailed the rules. Despite community reservations, the board drafted a proposal to integrate local schools over a ten-year period. The plan was submitted to a federal judge, Ronald Davies, who approved it as consistent with the Court's edict in *Brown II* that schools desegregate "with all deliberate speed." Most Little Rock residents accepted the plan as "the best for the interests of all pupils in the District."

The Arkansas State Legislature disagreed. There, elected leaders vowed to disrupt any attempt at integration. They passed a host of bills intended to thwart integration as they stiffened their resolve. Into that growing controversy stepped Governor Orval E. Faubus. Born in Greasy Creek, Arkansas, in 1910, Orval Eugene Faubus was the son of a militant farmer with an antipathy toward capitalism; Orval's middle name honored Eugene Debs. The young Faubus taught school and labored on behalf of the poor until deciding to run for public office in 1938, and at that point he made the first of many cynical accommodations to further his career: abandoning some of his more radical views, he endorsed Roosevelt's New Deal. Military and public service bolstered Faubus's political résumé through the 1940s, and in 1954 he challenged the incumbent governor, Francis A. Cherry. They waged a spirited campaign—Cherry at one point suggested that Faubus was a Communist—but Faubus narrowly won the Democratic primary before dispatching his Republican opponent in the general election, a perfunctory second act of most southern political campaigns of that era.

If Faubus's background gave little hint at racial animus, however, it did reveal ample willingness to adjust politics to expediency. In 1957, facing reelection and worried that he was perceived as soft on segregation, Faubus took up the mantle. Under the court-sanctioned integration plan for Little Rock, nine Negro students were expected to be admitted to Central High School on September 3. Instead, Faubus mobilized the state's National Guard under the pretext of preserving public safety but in fact to prevent the black children from going to their neighborhood school. He succeeded: the children were turned away.

Such brazen defiance of a federal court carried staggering implications for the rule of law, as Eisenhower recognized. Could governors choose which federal orders they would obey? Would public opposition justify defiance? That path led to anarchy, and Eisenhower, whatever his feelings about *Brown*, was unwilling to countenance such disregard of federal authority.

As Faubus prepared to seek an extension of the desegregation order—and to head off a contempt citation for defying the existing order—Eisenhower invited him to Newport for a face-to-face meeting. The invitation was gingerly brokered by the Arkansas congressman Brooks Hays, who persuaded Faubus to accept an invitation if it were offered. Faubus agreed, and then Eisenhower, by prearrangement, extended it. Brownell advised against even that. The attorney general was convinced Faubus was playing the issue for his reelection and would never cave.

The governor arrived on Saturday morning, September 14. It was just five days since Eisenhower had signed the Civil Rights Act of 1957.

They began the meeting alone, a departure from the White House protocol. Faubus said later that their initial banter was about the war and Faubus's service in Patton's army, a topic that can only have emphasized Ike's superior authority. When it came to the conflict between them, they presented dramatically different proposals to break the impasse. Faubus requested a ten-day break—"breathing room," in his words—as well as the assistance of federal marshals in restoring order. Eisenhower, who must have been surprised at the idea of turning over federal marshals to a governor acting in defiance of a federal court order, replied that Faubus should leave the National Guard in place but amend its orders from keeping out the black students to escorting them. If Faubus would do that, the president said, the Justice Department would urge Judge Davies not to find the governor in contempt. Lest Faubus misunderstand, Ike made it clear who controlled the situation. "In any area where the federal government had assumed jurisdiction and this was upheld by the Supreme Court," the president reminded the governor, "there could be only one outcome—that is, the state would lose."

Faubus now faced a dilemma entirely of his own making. He could accede to the power of the federal government, and almost certainly lose his office as a result; or he could defy that authority, and almost certainly lose, either in court or on the ground or both. He chose to play for time.

Both men agreed to release statements following the meeting. Eisenhower's was forceful. He recognized Faubus's "inescapable responsibility . . . to preserve law and order in his state" and stressed that the governor had told him of "his intention to respect the decisions of the United States District Court." Faubus's statement implied agreement, famously acknowledging that *Brown v. Board of Education* was the law and required obedience. Nevertheless, once back in Arkansas, Faubus refused to direct the guard to protect the black students. As for his stated acknowledgment of the rules laid down by *Brown*, he explained: "Just because I said it doesn't make it so." The governor now insisted that "the changes necessitated by the Court orders cannot be accomplished overnight." Contrary to what he had promised the president, Faubus continued to resist.

"Faubus broke his word," Eisenhower exclaimed. The president, Brownell observed, reacted as though the governor were a military subordinate who had failed him in battle. Brownell was less shocked. To him, Faubus was "a small-town politician" placing the national interest beneath his own reelection. Whatever the reason, Faubus had now backed himself into a corner. Compromise failed. Force would substitute.

On September 20, the governor was scheduled to appear before Judge Davies, but he skipped the hearing. In his absence, his lawyers asked Davies to recuse himself. Davies, his right eye bloodshot from a burst blood vessel, coolly refused, finding that the Faubus team's affidavit in support of his removal was "not legally sufficient." Their motion denied, the Faubus lawyers walked out, to the astonishment of Thurgood Marshall, there on behalf of the NAACP. That was Friday. Judge Davies ordered the black students admitted to school on Monday morning and specifically ordered Faubus not to obstruct. At 6:25 p.m., Faubus ordered the troops removed.

Having stirred public anger for weeks, Faubus became suddenly quiet. He left the state for a governors' conference at Sea Island, Georgia. Increasingly furious, Eisenhower urged the people of Little Rock to demonstrate their respect for the law and their sympathy for the difficulties faced by the nine black high school students. He wanted company and summoned the Gang to join him. Ellis Slater, Bill Robinson, and George Allen all made the trip. On Sunday, they played eighteen holes at the Newport Country Club, then Ike cooked steaks for his foursome, joined by Mamie. Later, the men played three hours of bridge. Slater and the president beat Allen and Robinson by thirty-six points.

Beneath the easy atmosphere, however, Eisenhower, like the rest of the nation, braced for Monday. He had good reason to worry.

Egged on by a friend of the governor's who insinuated himself into the crowd, hundreds of white men and women—their ranks swollen by Klansmen and White Citizens' Council members—wheeled on any black person they could find. Four black reporters were among the first victims. "Kill them, kill them," one person screamed. The students themselves, neatly dressed, dignified, and frightened, were surrounded by a spitting, screaming mob. The state's National Guard, as ordered by Faubus, was gone, and the children defenseless. They made it into school, but by 11:30 a.m. the crowd outside the campus had grown increasingly violent. The police removed the children for their own safety. "I hope they bring out eight dead niggers," one leader outside snarled. In Newport that night, Ike and Mamie wrapped up their day with a movie: *Song of the South*.

Woodrow Wilson Mann, the well-meaning mayor of Little Rock, knew he could not turn to his state government for help; it was, after all, the state government that was instigating the violence. After sending the nine students home on Monday, Mann anxiously waited. When Tuesday arrived, chaos ensued. Mann cabled Eisenhower for help:

THE IMMEDIATE NEED FOR FEDERAL TROOPS IS URGENT. THE MOB IS MUCH LARGER IN NUMBERS AT 8 AM THAN AT ANY TIME YESTERDAY PEOPLE ARE CONVERGING ON THE SCENE FROM ALL DIRECTIONS MOB IS ARMED AND ENGAGING IN FISTICUFFS AND OTHER ACTS OF VIOLENCE. SITUATION IS OUT OF CONTROL AND POLICE CANNOT DISPERSE THE MOB I AM PLEADING WITH YOU AS PRESIDENT OF THE UNITED STATES IN THE INTERESTS OF HUMANITY LAW AND ORDER AND BECAUSE OF DEMOCRACY WORLDWIDE TO PROVIDE THE NECESSARY FEDERAL TROOPS WITHIN SEVERAL HOURS. ACTION BY YOU WILL RESTORE PEACE AND ORDER AND COMPLIANCE WITH YOUR PROCLAMATION.

Ike was out of choices. That morning, two years to the day after he suffered his heart attack, Eisenhower conferred with Brownell and General Maxwell Taylor. They now accepted the need to dispatch American troops to suppress a southern city, precisely the course that Eisenhower had regarded as unimaginable just two months earlier. Taylor favored the National Guard, but mobilizing those units would take time, and the Arkansas Guard was understandably confused, having just been withdrawn from the scene by Faubus. At 12:15 p.m., Eisenhower authorized the deployment of regular Army troops, drawn from the famed 101st Airborne. Seven minutes later, he signed the order. Half an hour after that, he decided to return to Washington. He left behind Mamie, who was still recuperating, but he called her through the tense evening, speaking to her twice before appearing on national television.

Eisenhower addressed the nation from his desk in the Oval Office. He wanted to speak "from the house of Lincoln, of Jackson and of Wilson." Behind him were four portraits: Benjamin Franklin, George Washington, Abraham Lincoln, and Robert E. Lee. Eisenhower was careful to frame the confrontation in terms of not his own views but those of the Constitution, the Court, and obedience to their congruent commands. He had labored over this address extensively, meticulously editing, softening its hardest edges. An early draft, for instance, described the district court as repeatedly "ordering" desegregation to commence, and Eisenhower changed that to "directing"; where that version said persons were "directed" not to interfere, he emended it to "instructed."

Eisenhower refused to blame the South or the citizens of Little Rock for the crisis. Instead, he reviewed the sequence of events that had brought about the clash—from the Court's ruling in *Brown* to the actions of the Little Rock school board to the approval of the desegregation plan by the district court in Arkansas and the judge's issuance of orders to restrain those who sought to obstruct the plan. Once those orders were issued, Eisenhower explained, there was no longer room for disobedience. "Proper and sensible observance of the law then demanded the respectful obedience which the nation has the right to expect from all the people. This, unfortunately, has not been the case at Little Rock."

Only once in his address did he seem close to anger, and it was, predictably, over the Cold War ramifications of this episode. "Our enemies," he said, "are gloating over this incident and using it to misrepresent our nation." He closed with a thinly veiled warning, presented as an enticement. "If resistance to the Federal Court order ceases at once, the further presence of Federal troops will be unnecessary," he said, "and the City of Little Rock will return to its normal habits of peace and order, and a blot upon the fair name and high honor of our nation in the world will be removed." If not? He did not say. The whole address took thirteen minutes; when it was over, he called to check on Mamie.

In Little Rock, the arrival of federal troops had precisely the intended effect. The racists who were brave enough to confront defenseless high school students shrank back in the face of the U.S. Army. Under the orderly supervision of the 101st Airborne, Little Rock's black boys and girls were escorted into school to exercise their constitutional rights. Eventually, the mob lost heart and melted away. By November, the federal troops had been withdrawn, and though the students continued to suffer brutish indignities, they persevered. On May 25, Ernest Green became the first black student ever to graduate from Central High. A young black minister sat with Green's mother: Martin Luther King Jr.

The showdown in Little Rock in 1957 did not solve the riddle of Eisenhower's views on segregation. As Ike had long feared, some southern segregationists responded to integration orders by closing schools altogether. Indeed, Faubus helped spearhead that movement, winning approval from the Arkansas State Legislature for a bill that allowed him to close schools and lease them to private groups. After the 1957 school year, he shut down Central High and reopened it the following fall as a private school for whites only. His actions alarmed some Little Rock residents—some community leaders had lobbied for respect for the law even at the height of the confrontation—but Faubus was cheered across the South as he completed his expedient transformation from socialist youth to redneck officeholder. He served four more terms as governor of Arkansas.

For Eisenhower, Little Rock was both tragic and redemptive. Even before *Brown*, Eisenhower had dreaded the South's response to court-ordered desegregation. With Little Rock, his worst fears were realized, and he deployed troops with the gravest unease. Yet Little Rock would come to stand—incorrectly, in one respect—as the high mark of Eisenhower's commitment to civil rights. For while Eisenhower did defend integration with the full force of federal authority, there is no evidence that he did so out of sympathy for civil rights. He simply could not allow a governor to defy the orders of a federal court. As Eisenhower well recognized, that would have marked the effective end of federal authority and the acceptance of nullification as a constitutional principle. Race motivated Faubus throughout the crisis, but it did not drive Eisenhower.

In fact, Eisenhower's approach to civil rights was more evident in the debate over that year's bill on the issue than it was in Little Rock. At Little Rock, Ike was forced into a confrontation he sought to avoid but was determined not to lose. In his negotiations with Congress, by contrast, he moved cautiously forward. He compromised when he felt it necessary and

achieved modest but real progress, joined by centrist elements of both parties. That was how Eisenhower imagined civilized, orderly progress.

When it was over, Brownell, the architect of so much desegregation in
the Eisenhower years—the man who recommended Warren and Brennan, who stocked the southern courts with sympathetic judges, who wrote
and lobbied for the Civil Rights Act of 1957—could take no more. He
had warned Eisenhower that he intended to leave after the first term but
had delayed his departure because of Little Rock. Now that the crisis had
subsided, it was time for him to go. He worked hard on his resignation
letter, drafting it by hand, extensively editing and refining it. He submitted it in October, and Eisenhower accepted it with regret and acknowledgment that Brownell had supplied the Department of Justice—and the
nation—with "effective leadership, steadfastness of purpose and your own
devotion to principle."

"I shall be forever thankful," the president concluded.

No sooner had Little Rock subsided than the American people were
roiled again, this time from above. It was a cool October evening in
Washington, where a weeklong series of meetings brought together scientists from the United States and the Soviet Union in a tentative Cold
War exchange of collaboration and mutual suspicion. As the participants
enjoyed a reception at the Soviet embassy, a reporter from the *New York
Times* burst into the room with a breaking story out of Moscow. Tass, he
said, was reporting that the Soviet Union had launched an earth-orbiting
satellite, a scientific achievement that American and Soviet scientists had
been pursuing for months. Richard Porter, an American who was part
of the conference, tracked down another member of the delegation and
whispered: "It's up." As word trickled through the crowd, Lloyd Berkner,
America's official representative to the international committee hosting the
conference, graciously acknowledged the work of the Soviet scientists. "I
wish to make an announcement," he called out. "I've just been informed by
the *New York Times* that a Russian satellite is in orbit at an elevation of 900
kilometers. I wish to congratulate our Soviet colleagues on their achievement." The Soviets beamed.

That was an uncommonly sanguine reaction on "*Sputnik* night." The
specter of a Soviet eye peering down from the sky sent Americans into an
orbit of their own. Though hardly a technological marvel, the 183-pound
aluminum sphere traveled at eighteen thousand miles per hour and was

able to circle the earth every ninety-five minutes. On the satellite's first passes over the United States, there were four sightings: two from Columbus, Ohio; one from Terre Haute, Indiana; and another from Whittier, California. NBC and CBS both interrupted their programming to broadcast the sounds of the ping that *Sputnik* emitted. News of the launch dwarfed all other stories—nudging aside the election of Jimmy Hoffa as president of the Teamsters and even news from Little Rock, where Faubus declared that he had acted in the tradition of Robert E. Lee in choosing loyalty to the people of his state over obligation to the federal government. *Sputnik*'s literal place above America spooked a Cold War jittery nation.

Eisenhower at first was barely troubled. He was in Gettysburg on "*Sputnik* night." He had played eighteen holes of golf that morning, then inspected his cattle and toured a neighboring pig farm in the evening. He was home by 6:30 and spent the rest of the night with family, which he did not bother to interrupt to respond to reports of the Soviet satellite. He had some good reason for nonchalance. Unbeknownst to the American people, the U.S. government was already conducting regular overflights of the Soviet Union using the U-2 spy plane. So Eisenhower knew that the United States had long been exploiting this form of military reconnaissance. Moreover, *Sputnik* in theory validated the shaky defense of the U-2, namely, that flying through the airspace of another nation did not technically violate its sovereignty. In one other sense *Sputnik* validated Ike: he had proposed "Open Skies" at the Geneva Summit in 1955, and the Soviets had rejected it. Now the two sides had secretly achieved what the Soviets had publicly disdained—common occupation of the high ground.

All that made *Sputnik* initially seem inconsequential to the White House. In fact, Adams glibly derided it as a "celestial basketball," an unfortunate phrase that mainly served to remind critics of his arrogance. For, as the White House soon learned, the public did not share its lack of concern. Within a week, an internal White House analysis concluded that the satellite had significantly altered the balance of power between the United States and the Soviet Union. In Mexico, editors of scientific journals reported that they were more inclined to seek submissions from the Soviets; in Europe, officials chided the United States for falling behind, and German politicians rethought the American tilt of their neutralism. Japanese Liberal Democrats stepped up their campaign to push U.S. forces off their soil, and Iranian officials were so chagrined that they avoided bringing up *Sputnik* with their American counterparts. Most worrisome was what might happen next. "The peculiar nature and dramatic appeal of the Sputnik, making its passes over every region of the earth, are likely to give it greatest impact among those least able to understand it," White House analysts concluded. "It will generate myth, legend and superstition of a kind particularly difficult to eradicate or modify, which the Soviet Union can exploit to its advantage, among backward, ignorant, and apolitical audiences particularly difficult to reach."

The realization that the Soviet Union could credibly claim that it had surpassed the United States in an arena of strategic consequence roused Eisenhower to action. And as he grappled with the satellite's implications, a German scientist secured from the same Reich that Ike defeated twelve years earlier seized the moment to pursue his own vision of American space exploration.

Wernher von Braun was brilliant, handsome, and manipulative. At forty-five, he had spent his entire life imagining ways to put rockets into space, an ambition he used to serve Nazi Germany, helping to engineer the terrifying rocket attacks on England, while relying on the work of thousands of slave laborers housed in filthy, disease-ravaged tunnels. When the war ended, von Braun sought out the U.S. Army, where he asked to speak directly with Eisenhower but was turned down. Instead, he was squired out of Germany and quietly relocated to the United States. The Army took him in, and von Braun brought with him a passion for rocketry that transcended national loyalties.

Through the early years of Ike's administration, von Braun could not persuade Washington to give him the funding he insisted was necessary for his Jupiter program as it vied for attention with a rival effort known as Vanguard. In September 1957, worried that a Soviet breakthrough was at hand, von Braun argued for a stepped-up American investment, proposing a national space agency with funding of $100 million a year. "I am convinced," he wrote from Huntsville, Alabama, "that, should the Russians beat us to the satellite punch, this would have all kinds of severe psychological repercussions not only among the American public, but also among our allies. It would be simply construed as visible proof the Reds are ahead of us in the rocket game."

Four weeks later, *Sputnik* sailed overhead, and von Braun quickly saw his opportunity. Neil McElroy, whom Eisenhower had just nominated to succeed Charlie Wilson at the Defense Department, happened to be visiting Huntsville that October evening. Von Braun cornered him at a cocktail party: "If you go back to Washington tomorrow, Mr. Secretary, and find that all hell has broken loose, remember this. We can get a satellite up in 60 days."

America's sense of foreboding intensified over the coming weeks. In

November, the Soviets fired a second satellite, this one carrying a small "Eskimo dog" named Laika, a flight memorably dubbed "Muttnik." And then, on December 6, a much-anticipated Vanguard launch ended with the rocket exploding just a few feet off the launchpad. That became "Flopnik." The German scientist who promised quick results offered promising possibilities.

Von Braun was already well-known as a magnetic scientist, but his profile was enhanced by Lyndon Johnson, who convened congressional hearings to explore the perceived failings of America's space efforts. Johnson's hearings were chiefly a vehicle to promote his own political ambitions, but they also provided von Braun an opportunity to make his case for vastly expanded rocketry. He was a masterful witness—urbane, polished, quotable—and he argued for a federal space agency to consolidate America's technological efforts. Just three months earlier, he was quietly lobbying for $100 million for such an agency; now he urged spending of $1.5 billion.

As Congress moved to take up that idea—and, with it, to suggest that Eisenhower had been guilty of underfunding this critical aspect of American defense—von Braun fast-tracked his own program for a satellite launch. More Vanguard failures kept international attention nervously riveted while von Braun refined his missile and its payload. Finally, at 10:48 p.m. on January 31, 1958, a Jupiter-C class rocket, specially modified to carry a small satellite, lifted off at Cape Canaveral. Von Braun tracked the launch from the Pentagon, where more than an hour passed without word on the mission's success. Finally, eight excruciating minutes after the satellite was expected to pass over the West Coast tracking stations, four analysts picked it up simultaneously. The United States was in orbit, von Braun's reputation was secure, and Eisenhower's response was vindicated. As Sherman Adams put it, "The enervating suspense was over." Told of the successful launch, Eisenhower replied: "That's wonderful."

Four days later, Eisenhower asked James Killian, the president of MIT, to head up a task force to organize the government's space and missile efforts; Killian accepted, effectively becoming the nation's first presidential science adviser. On April 2, Eisenhower sent Congress a proposal calling for the creation of the National Aeronautics and Space Administration. Congress passed the bills necessary to create NASA, and Eisenhower signed the National Aeronautics and Space Act of 1958 on July 29. The following day, he appropriated NASA its first $125 million. By year's end, NASA had initiated the Mercury project, dedicated to putting a man in space.

As 1957 drew to a close, Eisenhower was tense and drawn. On a Monday afternoon just before Thanksgiving, he had greeted the king of Morocco and was preparing for a state dinner that evening. Returning from the airport, Ike reported feeling a chill and then had trouble finding his words. His assistant, Ann Whitman, rushed to Adams with the news that something was wrong with the president. She fought back tears.

They summoned Dr. Snyder, making his third emergency visit to his presidential patient in twenty-six months. Snyder put Ike to bed and called for other medical help. Those closest to Eisenhower spent an anxious afternoon, unsure if the president was gravely ill or merely out of sorts. Would the state dinner proceed? If so, could Eisenhower attend? After conferring with the doctors, the White House released word that the president would not attend the dinner, disclosing only that he had suffered a chill. Next was the question of whether Mamie should attend anyway, and as she and Adams were discussing it, Ike walked in.

"I suppose you are dis—," he began and then got stuck, "talking about the dinner tonight." Eisenhower kept tripping over his words, his frustration mounting. "There is nothing the matter with me," he finally insisted. "I am perfectly all right." And yet it was obvious that he was not. Simple words eluded him, and though he looked healthy, he remained agitated and inarticulate. When Adams, Snyder, and Mamie urged him to give up any thought of hosting the dinner, he exploded. "If I cannot attend to my duties I am simply going to give up this job," he raged. "Now that is all there is to it." He stomped out.

Adams begged Nixon to take over, and Nixon, just as he had after the heart attack, rose to the occasion. He and Pat Nixon joined Mamie in co-hosting the event, which Mamie gamely did, worrying for her husband as he lay upstairs. "It was," the White House usher J. B. West recalled, "a ghostly white Mamie Eisenhower who descended the elevator with Vice President and Mrs. Nixon that night." Mamie rushed through her duties as quickly as protocol would allow, then hurried back upstairs. As she left, she uncharacteristically chided the staff, charging that the carnations selected for the evening were too dark, making the room dull. West understood that Mamie was not really upset with the staff. "It seemed to me," West recalled, "that the room may have seemed dull because the light of her life lay ill upstairs."

Frightening though it was, this time Ike's medical setback was mild and temporary. The White House released sketchy statements that night, assuring reporters that he had no temperature, that his pulse was normal. The following day, the White House at last disclosed the nature of Eisenhower's trouble: he had suffered a mild stroke. At the same time, the administration was also able to announce that the president was rapidly recovering. By November 27, Eisenhower was back at work, afflicted only by occasional blank moments in which he struggled for a word.

Ike's verbal acuity might be an expendable luxury, but the conflicts of that year produced more lasting and consequential changes as well. Never again would an American governor question Eisenhower's determination to enforce federal law. Spurred by von Braun, Eisenhower accelerated the nation's satellite program. And, made forcefully aware of Soviet designs on the Middle East, he articulated a new American strategy for the region and held to it despite congressional uncertainty.

Informally known as the Eisenhower Doctrine, Ike's formulation for the region was a natural outgrowth of that fall's Suez confrontation, producing an overdue recognition that much of the Cold War would be fought in the Middle East and through intermediaries. Eisenhower recognized Soviet ambitions for the Middle East could be better achieved by infiltration and destabilization than by conquest. Soviet overtures first came in the form of aid, Eisenhower argued, but then devolved into control. Once under that control, the nations struggled for liberation, to no avail. Eisenhower sought a rationale for American intervention before nations fell captive to oppression. He honed his thoughts in the closing months of 1956 and then presented his proposal to a joint session of Congress early in the New Year.

"Remember Estonia, Latvia and Lithuania!" Eisenhower told Congress. All three entered mutual-assistance pacts with the Soviet Union; all three received assurances of their continued independence; all three were "forcibly incorporated into the Soviet Union." Soviet designs on the Middle East threatened a similar fate. Ike counseled those countries to look "behind the mask" before accepting aid, and he sought congressional approval to act in those instances where Soviet adventurism was making gains, where nations felt the shadow of force descending and appealed to the United States to save them. Eisenhower wanted to give himself and future presidents authority to cooperate with Middle Eastern nations to protect their independence; to supply military aid to any nation that requested it; and to dispatch American troops to protect those countries, if requested.

"Experience shows that indirect aggression rarely if ever succeeds where there is reasonable security against direct aggression; where the government disposes of loyal security forces, and where economic conditions are such as not to make Communism seem an attractive alternative," Eisenhower said. "The program I suggest deals with all three aspects of this matter and thus with the problem of indirect aggression."

Congress had some reservations about granting the president such preemptive authority, to be exercised at his will. But he persuaded the members that he needed the agility to move quickly in a crisis, and he deflected a substitute motion by Speaker Sam Rayburn to pledge military assistance to any Middle Eastern nation whose independence was threatened. Ike blanched at that, believing it would effectively place the region under an "American protectorate." Once Rayburn's idea was defeated, along with a later suggestion by Richard Russell to prohibit funds from being spent in defense of the new doctrine, the Congress turned to Ike's original motion. It cleared the House on January 30 and the Senate on March 5. The Eisenhower Doctrine became American foreign policy with the signature of its namesake on March 9.

Nuclear Interlude

Dwight Eisenhower assumed the presidency in the middle of a war and brought it to an end without resorting to the most powerful weapons in his nation's arsenal. His objection was not that nuclear weapons were immoral or that their use was unthinkable; to the contrary, he had specifically contemplated bombing North Korea and China, first in the Korean War and later in the fighting over Quemoy and Matsu and even in the debates over Indochina. He had famously compared nuclear weapons to bullets, just tools by which to destroy an enemy. And he had long pondered war with the Soviet Union on the plains of Europe, where the imbalance of conventional forces made America's nuclear stockpile its only authentic defense.

But America's nuclear hegemony eroded even as its arsenal expanded: the Soviet Union trailed the U.S. breakthrough from fission to fusion weapons but not by much, and though Russia's arsenal was dwarfed by America's (only later would the United States realize by how much), each country soon acquired the power to inflict catastrophic damage on the other. Better than anyone, Eisenhower understood the devastating power on both sides of the Cold War. Official estimates suggested that in an exchange between the superpowers, a third to a half the American population could die; industry, government, and society itself would be crushed beyond recognition. There would be no victory, merely death for millions and gruesome survival for those unlucky not to perish in the blast. "Total war," American planners had acknowledged by the end of 1956, "could bring about such extensive destruction as to threaten the survival of both Western civilization and the Soviet system." During one meeting, when a top Eisenhower economic adviser droned on about what it would take to reconstruct the dollar in the aftermath of a nuclear war, Eisenhower interrupted: "Wait a minute, boys. We're not going to be reconstructing the dollar. We're going to be grubbing for worms." Contemplating the cost of modern war, Ike exclaimed one day: "You might as well go out and shoot everyone you see and then shoot yourself." Ann Whitman winced.

Faced with the awesome implications of the Soviet Union's ability to wage nuclear war, Eisenhower changed. The nuclear enthusiast of 1953 had become a more sober leader by 1956. "In 1953, Soviet capability was not so strong," John Eisenhower observed. "Dad changed as the capability of the Soviets changed." Ike was haunted by images of a wrecked society across Europe and America—of the Northern Hemisphere so damaged it would "virtually cease to exist." He began to question the meaning of military victory in the modern world. Even as his top advisers planned for small nuclear wars in which America would use tactical weapons to contain Communist expansion, Eisenhower veered in the opposite direction. Military leaders were often appalled by his new approach, but he had nothing to prove to them.

Most nuclear strategizing is conducted through metaphor, as planners seek to frame debate over Armageddon in rational terms. Chess is a favorite of such strategists, as is poker. They suggest gamesmanship, threat, bluff, and reason. But for American leaders in the 1950s, a particularly compelling metaphor for the protection that nuclear weapons provided was that of an "umbrella," an overarching canopy that would repel Soviet or Chinese aggression by threat of retaliation. True, the umbrella was dangerously perforated: it had not stopped China from invading South Korea; it had not prevented China from menacing Quemoy and Matsu, though it had likely protected Formosa itself. It had not shielded Hungary from Soviet tanks. Nevertheless, it symbolized to the Americans protection.

But the holes in the umbrella began to work mischief on the metaphor itself. Members of the Joint Chiefs of Staff and Dulles—as well as a number of academics and intellectuals—worried that the threat of retaliation might not be taken seriously in small conflicts: Would the United States really extend its nuclear protection to remote outposts of marginal strategic significance, or would it cede those areas to Communist provocation? In Europe, the question was posed differently but with similar ramifications. In Bonn, London, and Paris, leaders wondered whether the United States was prepared to risk its own cities to save its allies. That seemed doubtful. Many began to argue for a more flexible American strategy, specifically the development of tactical nuclear weapons and strategies that could be used in "limited" wars.

At first tentatively and then with intensifying grit, Eisenhower disagreed. In early 1956, he tangled with Admiral Arthur Radford, chairman of the Joint Chiefs of Staff, at an extraordinary session of the NSC, one that a pre-eminent scholar in the field of nuclear deterrence has described as "perhaps the richest NSC meeting on nuclear strategy during the entire Eisenhower era." The meeting began with a briefing on the Twentieth Congress of the Soviet Communist Party, concluding that day in Moscow. While Khrushchev was denouncing Stalin, the council turned to the question of how and when nuclear weapons were to be used. The linchpin of the conversation was a line that governed the authority to launch nuclear weapons: "Nuclear weapons will be used in general war and in military operations short of general war as authorized by the President." Radford proposed to amend that sentence to read: "Nuclear weapons will be used in general war and will be used in military operations short of general war when the effectiveness of the operations of the U.S. forces employed will be enhanced thereby. For such operations, the decision as to specific uses will be made by the President."

Radford's language preserved Eisenhower's ultimate authority but envisioned nuclear weapons being used to enhance a military position, a markedly lower threshold than "massive retaliation." Radford argued for that because nuclear weapons were increasingly integrated into American military operations: "Inability to use these weapons would greatly reduce both our defensive and offensive capabilities."

But Eisenhower had by now come to believe that nuclear weapons were different. While he had once encouraged commanders and the public to consider them merely one more weapon in a vast array of armaments, he now believed that was an error. Using nuclear weapons to resolve regional conflicts would carry obvious political ramifications. Allies would recoil at a nuclear blast to protect an insignificant asset; such an attack would invite the world's opprobrium. World opinion might be wrong, he conceded, but the United States could not afford to act militarily "without regard for the political repercussions of such a course of action." Imagine, he continued, if field commanders had access to nuclear weapons and permission to use them to defend themselves. A military commander whose "radar informs him that a flock of enemy bombers is on the point of attacking him" would face the ultimate decision: die or launch. "What does the field commander do in such a contingency?" Ike asked. "Does he not use every weapon at hand to defend himself and his forces?" He defends his troops, of course. But if, in doing so, he obliterated thousands or even millions of civilians, what price would America pay?

To Eisenhower, the paradox of nuclear weapons was this: as the Cold War's two principal warriors developed the capacity to destroy each other and the rest of the world along with them, the viability of limited nuclear conflict receded, replaced by a universal threat to all. As Eisenhower put it: "We must now plan to fight peripheral wars on the same basis as we would fight a general war." We must, he was saying, be prepared to destroy civilization every time local conflicts were repelled by nuclear weapons, whatever their size.

What of wars short of direct confrontation between the United States and the Soviet Union? What of future Koreas? "What would we do if the Vietminh undertook to attack South Vietnam?" John Foster Dulles asked. "Would we proceed to drop atomic bombs on Peking?" Maybe not, Ike replied, but the United States would bomb any base in China used to support the attack. That might fall short of an attack on China's capital, but the casualties would be astonishing, and the world reaction extremely volatile. A regional conflict would thus immediately constitute a general war.

Eisenhower's misgivings were evident, but once he had made his point, he did not press to make it official policy at that time. The views of Dulles and the Joint Chiefs remained codified in America's official national security policy, which still left Eisenhower with ultimate authority over nuclear weapons, even if it did officially countenance their use in limited conflicts. Still, Eisenhower's growing conviction was that flexible response—using nuclear weapons to defend American military interests in remote parts of the world—was a dangerous fallacy. As that seed of doubt took root, he devoted his energies to pursuing peace and imagined the consequences of failure.

When the NSC again took up the question of the nation's basic security in 1957, Eisenhower was prepared to argue his case more forcefully. And by 1958, he had completed his evolution regarding his most basic assumptions about the use of nuclear weapons. The crucial conversation in his conversion occurred on May 27, 1957. This time, Eisenhower employed language that would assist commanders in distinguishing between local wars and general conflict—the former calling for restraint and cautious use of force, the latter demanding the deployment of the nuclear arsenal in all its terrible might. To that end, Eisenhower argued for a national security policy that specifically recognized the dangers and imperatives that applied to local wars, those that involved U.S. interests but only small numbers of American troops. Although the resulting document left open the possibility of using nuclear weapons in such conflicts, it emphasized that in the use of force on remote battlefields, it would "be applied in a manner and on a scale best calculated to avoid hostilities from broadening into general war." Restraint, not escalation, was to be pursued. Moreover, the use of nuclear weapons—a power still reserved exclusively to the president—would be appropriate to achieve not simply "military objectives," as defense leaders sought, but only "national objectives." Dulles left the meeting early that day to keep an appointment with the chancellor of West Germany, Konrad Adenauer. Once he was gone, the revised document, with Eisenhower's language intact, was approved.

Ike's victory over his own subordinates was significant, but within weeks Bobby Cutler raised objections. It would be, Cutler argued, "extremely unwise to put all the eggs in the big weapon, unlimited force power basket." To do so would be to lock the United States into a rigid and illogical defense posture, preventing commanders from meeting a local flare-up with limited nuclear power rather than risking everything. Cutler emphasized: "We want to be able to treat a hangnail without amputating the arm." His arguments represented a powerful counterpoint to Ike's and reflected the views of many within the NSC and the cabinet, not to mention the military establishment.

Advocates of flexible response were emboldened by one of the Cold War's most influential studies. After the completion of the basic national security review in early 1957, Eisenhower convened a group of scientists and analysts to review American nuclear defenses. He asked H. Rowan Gaither Jr., a founder of the RAND Corporation and chairman of the Ford Foundation, to head the panel and asked it to examine America's ability to withstand a nuclear attack. Once the committee was assembled, Gaither expanded its mandate to a more comprehensive study of nuclear weapons, their effectiveness and utility, and the relative strengths of the United States and the Soviet Union. Fatefully, Gaither brought on board Paul Nitze, a leading proponent of flexible response, the very notion that Ike was attempting to bury.

The report, formally titled *Deterrence & Survival in the Nuclear Age* but generally referred to as the Gaither Report, sketched a terrifying future. Written largely by Nitze, it argued that the Soviets were advancing quickly and on the verge of overtaking the United States' nuclear arsenal, conceivably positioning themselves for global domination. "The evidence clearly indicates an increasing threat which may become critical in 1959 or early 1960," the panel began. The conclusion was even more stark: "The next two years seem to us critical. If we fail to act at once, the risk, in our opinion, will be unacceptable."

To avoid such a calamity, the committee proposed dramatic increases in defense spending—$4.8 billion to $11.9 billion a year for five years, with unstated increases after that—and a rapid expansion of the American missile force. The committee recommended increasing the size of the medium-range missile battery from 60 to 240 and the long-range missile supply from 80 to 600. The group recommended increases in the number of nuclear weapons based on submarines and the construction of a national system of fallout shelters, estimated to cost another $25 billion—this at a time when the entire American defense budget was approximately $38 billion. The shelter proposal was wrapped in a particularly bleak vision of a postwar America, its surviving citizens forced to live underground for an undetermined period, only to reemerge and "remake a way of life in our own country." Finally, the Gaither Committee recommended what had by now become Eisenhower's bête noire: development of a doctrine to guide "when and how nuclear weapons can contribute to limited operations."

The Gaither Report was prepared through the summer and fall of 1957. Just before it was presented to the president, the Soviets triumphantly shot off *Sputnik* and sent America into spasms of self-doubt about its technical capacities and military strength. Members of the Gaither group consequently anticipated a receptive audience from Eisenhower when they presented him with their findings on November 4, three days before the report was given to the full NSC. They were disappointed.

Although Eisenhower received leaders of the committee politely, he rejected their most basic conclusions. American strategic forces were more powerful than the Gaither Committee believed, Ike said. Later intelligence was to prove him right and the committee wrong; Gaither's group had underestimated U.S. strength and vastly overestimated Soviet nuclear armaments. Eisenhower also questioned the usefulness of a national network of shelters, an extravagantly expensive program to extend the life spans of those who would inhabit the rubble of American postwar society. The shelters were dogged by practical questions as well as financial ones: Did family shelters exist for purchase? How would air be supplied to them if power were disrupted? "It looked to the President as though a lot of questions would have to find an answer before the country was ready to commit itself to a major program," Sherman Adams wrote. And as for preparing to fight limited nuclear wars, Ike emphasized, there was only one suitable use for the most powerful weapons at his disposal. "Maximum massive retaliation," Eisenhower insisted, "remains the crux of our defense."

Three days later, when the NSC received its briefing, Ike raised several sharper points. The shelter proposal, he suggested, would require such intensive government operation that it might force the government to take control of the economy. This was only a few years after the Republicans had championed the relaxation of government controls from the Truman era. "Was the Panel proposing to impose controls on the U.S. economy now?" Eisenhower asked. He recognized that *Sputnik* had scared the American people, but he refused to flinch. It was essential, he said, "that we neither become panicked nor allow ourselves to be complacent." The session that day was cut short by scheduling demands, but as it closed, Ike wondered out loud how long this top secret material would remain so.

The Gaither panel was so dire in its warnings, so histrionic in its assessment of danger, that even Dulles refused to accept its findings. He conferred privately with Eisenhower and conceded that such expenditures could probably not be justified in light of the remote danger that preoccupied the committee: the all-out surprise attack on the American homeland by a Soviet enemy willing to court its own destruction. In the event of such a war, Eisenhower reflected later that week, both nations "would be smashed so that they could not recover for a long time," leaving "another power, probably Germany [to] emerge as the greatest in the world."

Having failed to persuade the president to adopt the recommendations of the Gaither Report, a member of the group—almost certainly Nitze—elected to pursue those objectives by leaking the document to the press. Within weeks, the *Washington Post* featured a story summarizing the report, as well as Eisenhower's brusque dismissal. Democrats seized on the imbroglio as evidence of dangerous complacency on the part of the Republican administration. They lampooned Ike as a loafer, spending his time on the links while scheming Soviets stole American secrets and surpassed American strength. That image, of a country-club Eisenhower ignoring the nation's growing vulnerability, would dominate the administration's final months, as politically damaging as it was patently false.

By 1958, Ike had faced down his top advisers again and again. Though it would have pleased his advisers and placated political critics, Eisenhower would never yield to the demand that he prepare American forces to fight small nuclear wars. Instead, he insisted that the only way to preserve the peace was to make obliteration the alternative. His generals vehemently disagreed. "I'm the only Army general to have disassociated myself from

Army thinking," Ike observed to a group of advisers in 1959. "I have been called a traitor for this more than once."

Through one uprising after another, Eisenhower stood fast on the most essential aspect of his national security policy—not through inaction but by stern resolve and forceful argument. From 1958 on, it was all or nothing, deterrence or death. As Eisenhower remarked to the NSC in 1959, American policy boiled down to this: if the Russians start a war, "we will finish it." That, the NSC minutes recorded, "was all the policy the President said he had." A major war between the Soviet Union and the United States would devastate them both. But the threat of it might just keep them both alive. It was a terrible gamble, but Ike was a terrific poker player.

Many Ways to Fight

Latin America had a special place in the Eisenhower White House. Ike's brother Milton was an expert on the region, and his trip soon after Ike's election had greatly gratified American allies in the hemisphere. By 1958, there were hopeful signs in the region: Argentina had at last disposed of Perón and elected a leader, Arturo Frondizi, with whom the administration believed it could cooperate. Similarly, Colombia had cast off Gustavo Rojas Pinilla and elected Alberto Lleras Camargo, whom Nixon regarded as "an enlightened and dedicated statesman." With so much changing in the region, Eisenhower believed a high-level visit was in order. The midterm elections were approaching, so he tapped Nixon for the duty. Nixon, though he felt he would be better used at home and feared that the two-and-a-half-week excursion would be ponderously boring, nevertheless reluctantly agreed.

Accompanied by his wife, Pat, Nixon left on April 27. At first, the trip was uneventful. The Nixon party stopped in Trinidad to refuel and was greeted warmly in Uruguay. The vice president dropped in unannounced at a university in Montevideo, where he charmed all but his most hardened critics. In Argentina, Nixon conferred with leaders, threw the switch at a new nuclear power plant, and suffered through a gaucho barbecue; he attended Frondizi's inauguration but got there late—traffic delayed him, and the ceremony started four minutes early. He then visited Paraguay, Bolivia, and Peru, where he faced an unruly, rock-throwing crowd at San Marcos University. As Nixon was returning to the hotel, a protester managed to squeeze close to the vice president and spit directly in his face. "I felt an almost uncontrollable urge to tear the face in front of me to pieces," Nixon wrote later. He maintained his composure, however, and earned Ike's praise for his "courage, patience and calmness."

After uneventful stops in Ecuador and Colombia, the entourage arrived in Caracas, Venezuela, where the government assured Nixon it could control trouble despite reports of demonstrations being planned to greet the Americans. From the moment Nixon disembarked the airplane, it was obvious that the government overestimated its abilities. Dick and Pat Nixon stood politely for the playing of the Venezuelan national anthem while, from an observation deck above them, a crowd cursed and spit on them. Pat's red suit was mottled with chewing tobacco stains. The Nixons, flanked by the Secret Service, pushed through the crowd and into two waiting cars, Dick in the first, Pat in the second. They left the airport and headed for the center of the city. Stores were shuttered and sidewalks empty, but traffic seemed heavy. Then, suddenly, the car pulled to a halt, blocked by a dump truck that created a blockade. A mob descended on Nixon's car, ripping the flags from the front bumper and hurling rocks. The driver finally pushed through, only to hit a second blockade and then a third.

"Here they come," a passenger in Nixon's car said. And with that, a crowd of several hundred descended on the two vehicles. One rock shattered Nixon's windshield, scattering glass. Demonstrators pummeled both vehicles with metal bars and sticks. Then the crowd around Nixon's car began to rock it back and forth, attempting to flip it. "For an instant, the realization passed through my mind—we might be killed," Nixon said. Members of the Secret Service reached for their guns, but just as a riot seemed inevitable, the press truck traveling in front of the Nixon cars plowed through the mob and cleared a path for Nixon's driver to follow (in all his years of sparring with the press, that may have been the most appreciative Nixon ever was for a group of reporters). Pat and Dick escaped unharmed, though deeply shaken. Nixon's experience in Caracas was one of the most frightful of his life, and he later dedicated a chapter to it in his memoir, *Six Crises*.

Two days later, the Nixons returned to Washington, where Ike and Mamie greeted them at the airport. Ike brought Nixon's two daughters, Julie and Tricia, with him to welcome their parents. When the plane landed, he let the girls rush to meet it, rather than standing on protocol. Julie never forgot the courtesy. "He had the biggest smile, the brightest blue eyes," she recalled of Eisenhower.

Eisenhower's attention in early 1958 was again drawn to the Middle East, where Nasser's personal ambition and quest for leadership over the region prompted him to strike an alliance with Syria. Under it, Egypt and Syria announced their intentions to merge into a new entity, the United Arab Republic. The move did not necessarily threaten American interests. In fact, one consequence was the outlawing of the Communist Party in Syria, and the union was widely popular among ordinary Arabs thrilled by the prospect of a unifying, postcolonial identity. Many Arab leaders, by contrast, viewed Nasser's designs with unease. Eisenhower monitored the development, sounding out friends in the region and seeking their guidance on a shift that he feared could "carry serious implications" for America's Arab allies.

Among those troubled by Nasser's efforts was Lebanon's earnest but skittish president, Camille Chamoun, whose appreciation for the Western powers helped fortify his rule but also made him suspect in the eyes of Nasser and other Arab nationalists. Chamoun's own authority was weak, as he ruled over a fractious nation, divided between its Maronite Christian community and its growing Islamic population. If Nasser was intent on expanding his base, Chamoun understood that it could come at the expense of his own.

Through late 1957, Eisenhower suspected Nasser of fomenting trouble in Lebanon. He worried that the Soviets would seek a foothold in the region and that Nasser would unify Arabs against the West and threaten its oil. On a more personal level, Eisenhower liked Chamoun and had appreciated the president's kind words after Ike's heart attack in 1955. Eisenhower even asked his doctor to give Chamoun a checkup in 1957 after Chamoun too was diagnosed with heart trouble.

With his country in a state of agitation, Chamoun in early 1958 debated whether to seek another term as president. To do so would have required an amendment to the Lebanese constitution, and the mere prospect of Chamoun maneuvering to retain power enraged his critics. Still, Chamoun held on, motivated in part by concern that leaving office without a natural successor would exacerbate his country's divisions and expose it to Nasser's designs. By June, Ike had grown deeply concerned. "Chamoun is most friendly but indecisive," he confided to Paul Hoffman. "There are, of course, wheels within wheels, conflicting reports, cross currents of personal ambition and religious prejudice, and, above all, a great internal campaign of subversion and deceit, possibly communistic in origin. Unless the United Nations can be effective in the matter, it would appear that almost any course that the United States could pursue would impose a very heavy cost upon us. The two alternatives could become intervention and non-intervention."

Those were the options that remained just weeks later, when, to the surprise of the American government, the Iraqi monarchy was overthrown and its king murdered. Suddenly the entire Middle East was inflamed. The challenge, Ike wrote, "changed from quieting a troubled situation to facing up to a crisis of formidable proportions." Chamoun could not bring stability to his own nation; Iraq had failed to protect its king. The Shah of Iran, there by Ike's hand, worried about spreading instability. Saudi Arabia's monarch feared it as well. Amid such manifest weakness, Eisenhower had to admit grudgingly: "No matter what you think of Nasser, at least he's a leader." Chamoun pleaded for American troops to maintain the order that he found impossible to impose himself, and on July 14, Ike approved a decision he would make only once during the entirety of his presidency: he ordered American troops to invade a foreign land.

The invasion of Lebanon was carried out under the principles of the Eisenhower Doctrine and in keeping with Ike's views of war: it should be conducted with overwhelming force, with an articulated mission, and with a path for victory. He recognized that no one could foresee the complexities of combat, but Eisenhower would not authorize conflict without a detailed plan and the personnel to carry it out.

Dispatching American soldiers to occupy a Middle Eastern nation was, as Eisenhower had known for months, sure to embitter Arab nationalists. Just two years earlier, the United States had impressed Arabs by breaking with Britain and France during the 1956 invasion of Egypt; now America risked being cast as a colonial aggressor, rather than as a protector of nationalist aspiration. There were, however, as Eisenhower would aptly note, profound differences between the Suez crisis and the Lebanese invasion. Lebanon's rightful leader invited in U.S. forces; Egypt's president angrily denounced the force used against his nation. Access to oil, as always, hovered in the analysis of the Middle Eastern crisis, but what specifically motivated the U.S. president were American obligations under the Eisenhower Doctrine and the recognition that Communist subversion rarely came in the form of direct combat. "Today aggression is more subtle and more difficult to detect and combat," he wrote in his diary. "Its forms include propaganda barrages, bribery, corruption, subversion, and export into the affected countries of arms, munitions, supplies and, sometimes, so-called 'volunteer' combatants. This type of aggression is carried on under the name of 'civil war,' a term that connotes domestic difficulty not directly affected by outside influences."

At 3:00 p.m. on July 15, seventeen hundred Marines splashed ashore just south of Beirut, threading their way between swimmers playing in the surf. The U.S. ambassador met up with the troops on the road from the airport and escorted them the rest of the way into the capital.

In the ensuing weeks, the Soviets played up the crisis, decrying the imperialist images of American forces in the region but confining their objections to rhetoric. American troops, meanwhile, gingerly held positions in and around Beirut, building up to a force of more than fourteen thousand soldiers. Operation Blue Bat, as it was called, had the desired effect. Elections at the end of July produced a winner in General Fuad Chehab, a Christian moderate acceptable to both sides. Chehab's victory settled Lebanon, and he amused Ike when he wrote to express his misgivings about giving up the Army for politics. "His statement," Eisenhower wryly observed, "struck a responsive chord." Chamoun stepped down that fall, and by the end of October, American forces had withdrawn from the country. Over the course of that brief occupation, only one American was killed in battle, shot by a sniper (three more died in a bus accident). The American occupying forces did not kill a single civilian. Nasser, meanwhile, was left to contemplate the fortitude of Soviet power, which, when challenged, retreated into talk.

In Lebanon, Eisenhower responded to a deteriorating situation in a country within easy reach of U.S. force, far from the heart of Communist power, and of clear strategic consequence. In that same year, however, a far more complicated struggle resumed in a familiar location. Once again, the venue was the bothersome pair of scruffy rocks within sight of the Chinese mainland: Quemoy and Matsu.

China's advance on those same islands in 1954 and 1955 had produced the defense pact between the United States and Taiwan pledging America to defend Taiwan and its "related positions and territories" without specifically committing the United States to war over Quemoy and Matsu. "I won't be pressed or pinned down," Dulles said at the time, "on whether an attack on Matsu and Quemoy would be an attack on Formosa." That studied approach—strategic clarity layered over tactical ambiguity—persuaded China to halt its aggression, but Mao went away mad and now girded for another attempt to wrench the islands from the grasp of Chiang Kai-shek, or at least to provoke an American response that would work to Mao's advantage.

Chiang warned in July and August that a buildup was under way. Chinese leaders delivered bellicose statements, and two Nationalist planes were shot down in July while on routine patrol. As the hostilities mounted,

Khrushchev paid a surprise visit to Beijing, alarming Chiang as well as CIA observers. Inside China, government-sponsored demonstrations featured angry crowds protesting Taiwan's presence on the islands, and the Chinese government moved war planes to fields within striking distance of Taiwan. The threat to the islands escalated, and Eisenhower once more had to decide whether the United States was prepared to go to war over two useless island redoubts, and if so, would it wage nuclear war?

In one scenario, Eisenhower was prepared to go all the way. If China invaded the offshore islands and then turned to Taiwan itself, America's obligations under its mutual-defense treaty would leave it no choice. "If the Chinese communists attack Taiwan," Ike said, "we have got to do what is necessary." That, he added, "would be all-out war." The Joint Chiefs, meanwhile, were preparing to wage nuclear war at a lesser threshold. If the Chinese Communists succeeded in blockading the offshore islands, the chiefs believed that alone would warrant nuclear strikes against six to eight airbases in mainland China. Gerard Smith, an assistant secretary of state, was aghast to learn of the Joint Chiefs' willingness to launch a nuclear war over such insignificant islands—indeed, merely over the blockade of those islands, not even their invasion—especially in light of Eisenhower's long insistence that no nuclear conflict could remain local once it had commenced. Smith pleaded with Dulles to urge Eisenhower to explore a military alternative that would not catapult the United States into a general war with China or its closest ally, the Soviet Union.

Finally, on August 23, after weeks of escalating tension, the Chinese bombardment began. The first fusillades brought in the steel and explosive hail of as many as thirty-five thousand rounds (that was the Nationalist estimate; American sources put the number closer to twenty thousand rounds). More than five hundred Taiwanese soldiers were killed or wounded. After the first day, the shelling tapered off but still continued. Chiang Kai-shek pleaded with Eisenhower for help. Not only was artillery blanketing the island, Chiang wrote, but enemy torpedo boats had sunk or damaged two Taiwanese vessels, and Chinese planes had strafed ground positions. Three generals were dead. In his message, Chiang, who referred to the president as "Your Excellency," asked Ike to declare emphatically that the United States would repel any attack on the islands with military force and urged Eisenhower to grant Taiwanese field commanders the latitude to respond to bombardment or invasion as they saw fit (the terms of the mutual-defense treaty prevented Taiwan from attacking mainland China without U.S. approval). Eisenhower was nonplussed, and Dulles, though bafflingly out of the office on vacation as the crisis unfolded, contacted

Herter, the acting secretary of state, and reinforced his skepticism about giving Chiang a free hand to respond to the aggression.

Ike recognized the situation for what it was: Chiang had deliberately reinforced the offshore islands in order to make his soldiers hostages to just such a crisis, and Mao was bombing those positions to bait the United States into a response that would horrify the world. (The British, in particular, were fearful that the United States would launch a nuclear war over islands of such insignificance and warned the Americans that they would not be able to support such an action.)

Eisenhower was having none of it. He refused to grant Chiang the freedom he hoped to use against Communist China, and he would not declare an attack on the islands as equivalent to an attack on Taiwan itself. In short, he refused everything that Chiang sought. The Taiwanese generalissimo, dependent on the United States for his survival, fumed that Eisenhower's directives were "inhuman" and "unfair," that they required him to acquiesce in the shelling of his army and were destructive to the morale of his nation. He was, one American observer reported, "the most violent I have seen him." Eisenhower was unmoved. Military officials in the Taiwan Strait also begged for a more forceful response, convinced that the shelling was prelude to invasion. Eisenhower refused them as well. General Nathan Twining and the Joint Chiefs lobbied for permission to attack China with "small" nuclear weapons if it proceeded to invade or escalated its bombardment. Eisenhower turned them down, too.

Instead, he pursued a diplomatic solution. Working through intermediaries in governments from Auckland to Warsaw, the administration broached a proposal sure to infuriate Chiang but intended to defuse the crisis: Taiwan would agree to demilitarize the islands if, in exchange, the Chinese would stop their shelling and renounce any possibility of invasion. Not only was such a proposal anathema to Chiang; it was fiercely resisted within the upper reaches of the U.S. military, where some officials preferred World War III to conciliation. "The argument that nothing is worth a world war," Admiral Arleigh A. Burke, chief of naval operations, stated, "was the reason why the Communists had been winning all along." Khrushchev underscored that point in a bombastic letter to Eisenhower on September 7, asserting that the Soviet Union was standing firmly with its Chinese ally. Twelve days later, he added: "Those who nurture plans for an atomic attack on [China] should not forget that not only the USA but the other side as well possesses atomic and hydrogen weapons . . . If such an attack is made on [China], the aggressor will immediately receive a proper repulse with these very means." Eisenhower did not dignify that with a response.

Beneath the bluster, however, China and the United States were talking. Negotiations began in Warsaw on September 15, and after early posturing, China suspended its bombing on October 6. Taiwan reluctantly agreed—as if it had much choice—to scale back its military presence on the islands, though not to abandon them. China responded with a move that captured the lunatic order of the period. It resumed shelling on October 25, but only on odd-numbered days. Terror devolved into farce; the threat of devastation was transformed, Ike noted, into a "Gilbert and Sullivan war." The prospect of world war receded.

Eisenhower prevailed, once again overcoming the misgivings of allies, generals, and diplomats. But China also gained; by use of force and violence, it backed down the might arrayed against it. Khrushchev took note.

Despite Eisenhower's desire to avoid a world war, he was not quiescent in the face of Communism. As had been the case since his first year in office, his national security strategy included an energetic devotion to covert action. In theory, subterfuge offered what his nuclear strategy forswore: the opportunity to roll back Communism without directly confronting the Soviet Union.

Unlike Quemoy and Matsu, outposts of psychological value at best, Indonesia was a nation of strategic consequence. The world's fourth-largest country, it controlled vast natural resources—rubber, oil, and tin were among its treasures—as well as sea-lanes between Asia and the South Pacific. A hostile Indonesia could bar ships from the Strait of Malacca, disrupt trade, hinder the defense of Singapore, and isolate Australia and New Zealand from Asia.

Indonesia had spent hundreds of years under Dutch rule until 1949, when Ahmed Sukarno and Mohammad Hatta completed a four-year campaign to win national independence. Trained as an architecture student, Sukarno was a nationalist type familiar to Washington: raised in his native culture, in his case that of Java; educated in Dutch colonial schools; and fervid in his rejection of the colonial regime. To the Eisenhower administration, Sukarno seemed a South Asian Nasser, especially when his aims were coupled with his charismatic appeal to his followers and Cold War neutralism. Like Nasser and Nehru, Sukarno refused both subservience to the United States and absorption by the Soviet Union.

Popular as the hero of his revolution, Sukarno as president held firm against the centrifugal forces of Indonesia, which featured a strong government in Java but a weak hold over the nation's archipelago. He was not a Washington favorite, but U.S. planners regarded him with concern more than hostility. They recognized that while Sukarno was not under their control, neither was he a Communist. "Although U.S. efforts have been unsuccessful in pulling Indonesia from its neutral position, they have contributed in preventing it from passing into the communist orbit," American security policy concluded in 1956.

Sukarno, however, remained stubbornly immune to Western overtures and persisted in flirting with Moscow and Beijing. His speeches included ritual denunciation of colonialism. He visited the capitals of America's enemies and practiced a politics of "guided democracy" that appeared to American leaders to be "inspired by the material accomplishments if not the ideology of Yugoslavia, the Soviet Union and Communist China." Moreover, Dulles didn't like him. He was, the secretary believed, "wholly undependable . . . dangerous and untrustworthy and by character susceptible to the Communist way of thinking." Most worryingly, Sukarno welcomed leftist representation in his government, and the nation's Communist Party, pursuing its goals through legal means, grew in strength to the point that by 1957 it had emerged as the nation's largest single party. By that year, the analysts' conflicted assessment of 1956 had given way to a far bleaker view of Sukarno's "preoccupation with the restoration of 'national unity,' " an obsession that Americans felt came at the "price of communist participation in his government," and reflected his "infatuation with 'guided democracy' as a remedy for Indonesia's political and economic instability."

Eisenhower was not prepared to watch Indonesia slide into Moscow's control. Confiding to Hoffman that summer, Ike wrote: "With Sukarno's ambitions and his leftish leanings, with his readiness to take Communist support, and his seeming preference for the radicals rather than the more conservative sectors of Moslem people, the situation could well become serious in that area of the world." The question was: How to resist? The United States could attempt to woo Sukarno, but American refusal to support his claims to West New Guinea, "an issue which is an obsession with Sukarno," weakened Eisenhower's influence. The United States could and did attempt to influence Indonesian elections, but when the CIA secretly poured $1 million into the coffers of the Islamic-oriented, anti-Communist Masjumi Party in 1955, the Communists still outpolled the U.S.-supported party. There was always the possibility of invasion, but the administration lacked any pretext for attacking a peaceful, neutral nation. Moreover, military action would harden Indonesian resentment of the United States. Ike personally rejected invasion as an option in September 1957.

Instead, the United States identified two sources of opposition to Sukarno: the nation's military leadership and the nation's incoherent but energetic rebel groups, scattered across Indonesia's outer islands. The trouble was that those two groups were implacably at odds with each other. Nevertheless, Eisenhower authorized a complex covert action built on enticement of the military to check Sukarno while simultaneously supplying "all feasible covert means to strengthen anti-Communist forces in the outer islands." It was integral to success that neither the military nor the rebels become aware of aid to the other.

Late in 1957, the CIA rolled out the plan. It tapped its accounts for $843,000, a down payment on the planned actions, and the first operatives arrived in Sumatra in early 1958, along with a shipment of weapons to arm eight thousand rebels. The U.S. Navy—an aircraft carrier, two destroyers, and a heavy cruiser—stood by offshore. By the end of February, Indonesia's civil war was under way.

Despite American support, the rebels struggled. They captured some territory, but the Indonesian military pushed back. On March 12, a dawn raid on a rebel airfield drove the rebels from the area. After they scattered, Indonesian paratroop units discovered a line of abandoned trucks. Thinking that the crates inside contained canned milk, they cracked them open for a drink and found money and food, along with twenty cases of machine guns, bazookas, and rifles, among other weapons. Some of the arms bore stamps identifying them as having been made in Michigan.

Sukarno, still courting U.S. support, chose not to make a major issue of the arms discovery. The mere fact that the weapons were made in the United States, after all, did not necessarily mean that they were wielded by Americans. In conversations with U.S. officials in Jakarta, Sukarno continued to plead that he was not a Communist. He refused, however, to negotiate with the rebels and insisted that there would only be a settlement "as soon as the rebellion is quelled."

In Washington, Eisenhower and his advisers were not yet ready to give up. The National Security Council meeting on March 20 opened with Allen Dulles briefing the members on the Indonesian civil war. Dulles said the rebellion was hampered by poor communications and inadequate aircraft. Although Eisenhower was skeptical of how aircraft could be effectively used in the Indonesian jungle, Dulles argued for supplying U.S. planes. Ike entertained the idea and, a few weeks later, even suggested that the rebels might also benefit from "a submarine or two."

The rebels did not get all they wanted, but Ike agreed to let Americans join the fight. Recognizing the risk to the covert operations if Americans should be captured, he insisted that they not be drawn from the military, but if "private persons operating on their own" should join up with Indonesian rebels, who was the U.S. government to object? Eisenhower well knew that he was approving the use of CIA agents, and the CIA wasted no time dispatching two pilots nominally working for a Taiwanese company but in fact on the agency's payroll.

From that point forward, all that had gone right in Iran and Guatemala went wrong in Indonesia. The rebels proved disorganized and unwilling to fight, even when CIA "advisers" started shooting. On April 30, the Indonesian forces captured documents that revealed foreign support in arming the rebels and even in piloting rebel aircraft. The documents showed the Sumatran rebels had received ten thousand small arms, along with bazookas, artillery, and at least five airplanes, ample evidence that "the rebels were . . . receiving actual assistance in the form of military equipment from foreign government sources." Although the Indonesian government did not specifically accuse the U.S. government of complicity, the Indonesian foreign minister warned the American ambassador the planes were being piloted by Americans and Chinese. Eisenhower continued to feign ignorance, protesting that the U.S. government could not control the actions of soldiers of fortune. The noose was closing.

Goaded by their American advisers, the rebels staged a series of strikes in early May and appeared to be making headway. But the government struck back on May 15, wiping out much of the rebel air fleet. That same day, an American CIA pilot, Allen Lawrence Pope, dropped a bomb on an Indonesian transport ship; sixteen soldiers and a member of the ship's crew were killed. A few minutes later, he attempted to bomb a military camp onshore; he instead hit an adjacent market and ice factory.

Over the next few days, Pope played an active role in the back-and-forth fighting between the government and the rebels. Then, as he was flying his B-26 on a bombing run in the city of Ambon, a government pilot shot the right wing of Pope's plane, which burst into flame. Pope bailed out, hitting the tail fin as he ejected and plummeting toward the jungle. Government forces hurried to the area and captured the operative suspended from his parachute. He was still alive.

The next afternoon in Washington, Allen Dulles learned that Pope had been missing for half a day. He listened quietly, puffing on his pipe, then called his brother. "I could not see in the long run any possibility of this being a winning course," he recalled in a memorandum later, after he'd met with the secretary of state in person that afternoon. To the agents in the room, he was more direct: "We're pulling the plug."

Unlike in Iran or Guatemala, the CIA action in Indonesia failed to topple the regime that agitated Washington. In Indonesia, however, the administration's all-but-open support for the rebel movement achieved some of what it sought indirectly. After resisting Washington's entreaties to purge his government of Communists, Sukarno eventually did shake up his administration. Though it was too slow for Washington's taste, Sukarno consolidated his own power and stayed clear of Moscow's designs. Then, in 1965, Indonesia's Communists staged an attempted putsch with coordinated attacks on the nation's leading generals. Sukarno sided with the Communists and was deposed when the coup failed. He was replaced by President Suharto, who outlawed the Communist Party once and for all and placed Sukarno under house arrest, where he remained until his death in 1970.

The covert action in Indonesia was exceptionally sloppy, but it produced what Eisenhower wanted of it: an independent Indonesia, free from Soviet control. Even Pope was ultimately repatriated: sentenced to death, he remained in prison through the end of the Eisenhower administration but was released after Kennedy took office. Sukarno's parting words: "Just go home, hide yourself, get lost, and we'll forget the whole thing."

Lebanon, Quemoy-Matsu, and Indonesia represented strikingly different threads of the Cold War: one provoked an overt, conventional military response; one brought American forces to high nuclear alert; one was waged in the shadowy realm of covert action. What they had in common was instability that gave room for Communist advance, met with forceful U.S. reply. And in each case, Eisenhower's calibrated actions preserved American lives.

It was exhausting. Ike told Ellis Slater that 1958 was the "year all hell broke loose" and described it as the worst of his life. But Eisenhower, despite his battles with his health and the crush of overlapping crises, persisted. In 1958, American troops and agents occupied a Middle Eastern nation, patrolled a knife's-edge conflict between Taiwan and Communist China, and actively worked to support a rebel movement in Indonesia—with the resulting loss of a single American life. Rarely in American history has so much ground been held at so little cost.

Loss

E isenhower's string of foreign crises in 1958 occurred against a backdrop of an American recession and the loss of family members and advisers. The year would be marked by sorrow, which arrived, in Shakespeare's words quoted by Eisenhower, "not in single spies, but in battalions."

Since his earliest days, Ike had measured himself against his brothers—Roy had died in 1942, but cantankerous, conservative Edgar and elegant, erudite Milton strengthened Ike's center, while his quieter brother, Earl, supplied memories of their modest upbringing. Periodically, the brothers would gather, their easy arguments a healthy reminder that while Ike might command armies, he was still just one of six Eisenhower boys, and not the senior one at that.

Arthur, the oldest, faded visibly in 1957, and though Louise eventually yielded to Ike's urging that her husband consult a doctor, Arthur was over seventy, and his energy declined precipitously. Ike had felt his brother slipping away all year, and now he reached his end. On January 26, 1958, Arthur died. Eisenhower and Mamie attended the funeral in Kansas City. Ike returned with a sore throat and ill temper. "He was our 'big' brother," Ike realized, "always dependable and always devoted." With Arthur dead, the mantle passed to Edgar, now Ike's oldest living sibling and forever "Big Ike" among the Eisenhower boys.

Arthur's death, and especially Louise's efforts afterward to have him interred at the Eisenhower Museum in Abilene, prompted Ike to consider his own mortality. With Louise pestering him to make room for Arthur at

Abilene, Ike grumpily suggested that he wouldn't be buried there himself. He imagined perhaps Washington or West Point, obvious signposts in his long life, or Denver, home of Mamie's family. He indulged those thoughts for a few minutes, then returned to work.

As winter turned to spring, a different threat arose, this time to a confidant. Gatekeepers make enemies, and Sherman Adams was no exception. His brusque manner irritated many White House callers and puzzled even Adams's most ardent friends. When Eisenhower painted a portrait of his aide and presented it to him, Adams looked at it and said: "Mr. President, thank you, but I think you flattered me." He then turned and walked out. Eisenhower himself remarked that he never heard Adams begin a phone call with "hello" or end one with "good-bye." Ike excused his deputy's manner—"absorbed in his work, he had no time to waste." Others were less charitable. "He was the most impolite person I ever met," recalled John Eisenhower. Conservative Republicans viewed Adams as a liberal—many worried that he undermined their champion, Nixon—and elected leaders of both parties were offended at his unwillingness to pay them the courtesies to which they considered themselves entitled. They longed for the day when Adams would get his.

In early 1958, an opportunity arose and they seized it. As a legislator and later governor of New Hampshire, Adams was well schooled in the arts of constituent service. When friends or well-connected people wrote to him asking for government benefits or services, Adams's practice was to forward the request to the relevant agency without comment and then, upon receiving an answer, to return it to the constituent who requested it. That, combined with Adams's utter lack of pretentiousness—in an administration of many wealthy men, he drove his own car and sent out bottles of maple syrup as Christmas presents—made him seem an unlikely candidate for corruption. But he had forwarded constituent requests, and that practice came to haunt him in 1958.

Adams had known Bernard Goldfine for nearly two decades, going back to when Adams served as Speaker of the New Hampshire House of Representatives and Goldfine ran a textile operation in Lebanon, New Hampshire. In those days, textile mills were fleeing New England for states with cheaper labor, but Goldfine stayed put. A Russian immigrant who came to America when he was eight years old and painstakingly built his own business, Goldfine impressed his friends with his steadfastness. "He treated his employees well, paid good wages and stayed out of labor trouble," Adams said. "I was not the only New England governor who admired Goldfine's courage and resourcefulness in holding fast while other textile men were moving out." Admiration formed the basis of friendship, and over the years the two men and their families grew close. They exchanged gifts at holidays, and Adams was particularly fond of one of Goldfine's sons, who, like Adams, attended Dartmouth. Adams intervened on the boy's behalf when he ran into trouble there, and the Adamses were guests at his wedding.

Among the gifts Goldfine had given over the years were free hotel stays for Adams and his wife, as well as an Oriental rug for the Adams home in Washington, to be returned when they resumed their New Hampshire life, and, most memorably, a vicuña coat, given to Adams's wife and valued, at least by Adams, at the $69 it cost Goldfine's mill to produce it. Adams had given Goldfine presents, too: the businessman arrived at a Congressional hearing on the matter wearing a gold watch given to him by Adams to mark the occasion of Ike's inauguration.

Editorialists were skeptical of Goldfine's good intentions and of Adams's casual acceptance of the gifts. "Mr. Adams' Bad Judgment" was the headline on the *New York Times* editorial when the revelations first surfaced. Eisenhower, by contrast, flatly refused to entertain the possibility that Adams had done anything wrong, but he recognized that his deputy was in trouble. On the day the story broke, Ike tried to console Adams, who sank into a depression that Eisenhower could not talk him out of. What's more, the president realized that political challenges such as this would only grow more intense as the administration wound down. Eisenhower, Ann Whitman noted, "does not know what to do to make Adams feel better."

On June 12, Adams appeared before a House subcommittee to defend himself against allegations of favoritism. His reply was clipped and slightly bossy. Adams acknowledged his long friendship with Goldfine. He addressed the implications of that friendship without hesitation or hand-wringing. "You are concerned, and most correctly concerned," he observed of the committee, "with how such a friendship may affect the conduct of an Assistant to the President in his relationships with men of government. And you should ask me: 'Did Bernard Goldfine benefit in any way in his relations with any branch of the federal government because he was a friend of Sherman Adams?' 'Did Sherman Adams seek to secure any favors or benefits for Bernard Goldfine because of this friendship?' " Having posed the committee's questions, Adams then replied to them: "My answer to both questions is: 'No.' "

For Ike, that settled the matter, and the next day he sought to put it to rest with what he regarded as a firm defense of his subordinate. "I believe that the presentation made by Governor Adams to the congressional committee yesterday truthfully represents the pertinent facts," Eisenhower said.

"I personally like Governor Adams. I admire his abilities. I respect him because of his personal and official integrity. I need him." Reporters had been told that the president did not want questions about Adams; they honored that request.

Eisenhower badly miscalculated the impression of his remarks. The final sentence, "I need him," struck many observers not as a stalwart defense of Adams so much as a plaintive admission of presidential weakness. Eisenhower's aides had missed that interpretation when Ike shared his remarks with them. "Not one of us caught the hollow ring of the words, 'I *need* him,' " one admitted later. "And we all just sat there—and said it sounded swell." To Eisenhower, it was a measure of Adams's abilities that the president needed his assistance, and the president had every right to rely on those he needed. To Ike's congressional critics, it looked as if a timorous president depended on an unscrupulous aide.

Adams might have survived the frenzy had Goldfine not proved to be something less than just a loyal businessman, devoted to New Hampshire and fond of his friends. Instead, he was an assiduous collector of public officials, doling out gifts to men and women of influence. "Perhaps I do give gifts to too many people, but if I do, it is only an expression of my nature," Goldfine insisted when he testified on the matter. Few were buying it. From the record, it appeared that Goldfine's gifts seemed calculated to win favorable treatment, an inference strongly bolstered when it was learned that he wrote off those gifts on his income tax returns as business expenses.

As Goldfine's reputation suffered, so did Adams. In July, Senator John Williams, a Delaware conservative and one of those who disliked Adams, met with Eisenhower to complain. The following week, Ike's friend Cliff Roberts, cofounder of the Augusta National Golf Club, suggested to the president that Adams had to go, and news of that recommendation leaked to the press, suggesting both crumbling support for the assistant and disarray within the White House. The House then cited Goldfine for contempt in August after he refused to answer further questions. The House vote, a hard-to-ignore 369–8, was tallied even as Eisenhower addressed the United Nations, gathered in emergency session to discuss the Middle East. Eisenhower proposed a six-point plan to hold the peace in that twitchy region, where American forces still patrolled a fragile standoff in Lebanon. His speech was well received, and it cheered Ike up. As he rode back to his plane that morning, Eisenhower smiled at the crowds and shook hands with security officers. "I hope it does some good," he said of his thirty-minute address to the delegates. "A fellow never knows about those speeches."

Amid the normal crush of business, Eisenhower pressed on, hoping the

Adams issue would fade. On one typical day that summer, Ike met with the chairman of the Joint Chiefs and ambassadors from NATO and Guatemala; greeted winners of national science awards; considered whether to grant a request from Martin Luther King, who was seeking a meeting (he did); investigated the question of where to purchase blight-resistant elm trees for the Gettysburg farm; and pondered his most taxing question of the day: how much to pay his grandson for working around the farm that summer. He settled on thirty cents an hour.

Nothing succeeded in diverting the campaign to get Adams. Propelled by Republican political anxieties, the effort gained in intensity. The economy was struggling, and polls showed the GOP in danger of losing seats. Within the administration, some advisers urged Eisenhower to take dramatic action, particularly to show economic results. Some argued for ramping up the highway program, but it was an unwieldy tool for short-term stimulus, as it depended on states accelerating their share of the work. Others made the political and economic case for a tax cut, which Ike had approved in 1954 as part of a broader stimulus package. This time, however, Eisenhower resisted, influenced in part by Gabriel Hauge, the president's special assistant for domestic and international affairs. "I thought the timing was wrong," Hauge explained, adding that the tax proposals under consideration made more sense politically than economically; rather than encouraging investment, they would simply "lop taxpayers off the rolls." Ike refused, disappointing Republican stalwarts deprived of yet another issue to run on.

Democrats remembered Eisenhower's 1952 campaign and its vitriolic charges of Truman-era corruption. Now they turned that issue against the Republican incumbent as midterm elections approached. Adams had no friends on the right and a dwindling cadre of supporters in his own party. Eisenhower seemed flummoxed by an attack that he considered neither justified nor appropriate. Who were politicians to tell him whom he should employ as his top assistant? And, since no evidence of Adams having granted any favors to Goldfine had surfaced, what was the actual basis for demanding that he resign?

At last, Congress's session came to an end on August 23. Whitman captured the sense of relief and exhaustion at the White House. "Mostly all we did was pray," she wrote, "that they would fold their tents and steal away."

It was too late. Eisenhower recognized that he could not risk his party's fortunes to save his assistant; or, more to the point, he could not afford to provide his party's conservative wing with an excuse to blame him if it suffered losses at the midterms. Once Congress was out of town, Ike spent a few days weighing the issue in relative quiet and decided Adams had to go. As when he had considered dropping Nixon from the ticket in 1956, he declined to bring the matter up himself. This time, Eisenhower asked Nixon to take on the distasteful task that he had once experienced from the other side. The vice president was on vacation, but he came rushing back to Washington from White Sulphur Springs, West Virginia. By the time he arrived, Adams had gone for the day, but the two conferred the next morning. Adams fought back. He had become, at least in his own eyes, so irreplaceable that the administration would founder without him. That attitude annoyed others close to Ike—Whitman was convinced it was partly responsible for the false notion that Eisenhower was weak—but the president himself seemed untroubled. Indeed, after first concluding that Adams had to go, Eisenhower hesitated. The wait grew longer and longer and convinced some leading Republicans that Eisenhower was unwilling to do what they felt needed to be done.

They did not stop trying, however, and eventually Ike capitulated. He was particularly affected by a conversation with Winthrop Aldrich, a financier and former ambassador (Eisenhower appointed him to the Court of St. James early in his presidency) and one of the wealthy business leaders whose advice Eisenhower so often solicited. Unlike so many of those calling for Adams's resignation, Aldrich liked him. The trouble, Aldrich emphasized, was that Adams had publicly professed his great friendship for Goldfine, who now was widely regarded as a crook. That was too much: "This man [Adams] has got to go or we are done." Ike protested a bit more, emphasizing Adams's work and dedication, but he knew Aldrich was right.

So Ike sent Nixon back to Adams in the company of Meade Alcorn, chairman of the Republican National Committee. Their task was to persuade him that he had become a political liability, that Goldfine was dragging down the party and compromising its future leaders. This time, Adams heard the message. Eisenhower groused about the power of "cheap politicians" to "pillory an honorable man," but he cut his deputy loose to protect his administration. Once it was done, Ike relaxed, seemingly for the first time in weeks. He dictated a few letters, signed some pictures, and went out shopping with his old friend George Allen. They stopped at a roadside stand for a pumpkin, startling the girl at the register because she did not recognize the president. Then they dropped in at a Howard Johnson and bought everyone there an ice cream. Presumably, Allen paid; Eisenhower rarely carried money. The next day, Adams called the president and offered his resignation. Eisenhower accepted.

Adams lingered for a while, forcing Eisenhower to nudge him out of his office. But on September 22, he announced publicly that he was leaving. Adams and Eisenhower both insisted he had done nothing wrong, and Adams would stubbornly cling to that notion long after Goldfine had been convicted in the court of public opinion and tax court as well. Eisenhower presented Adams with a silver bowl, and his assistant went home to New Hampshire. The inscription on the bowl was signed by "his devoted friend, Dwight D. Eisenhower."

For Eisenhower, Adams's departure was in one sense a relief—the fight had been long and distracting. Just two days before Adams resigned, Khrushchev had threatened nuclear war over Quemoy and Matsu, and on that same day a deranged woman lunged at Martin Luther King in a Harlem store, stabbing him in the chest and barely missing his heart. It was no time for a president to be hobbled by an ineffective assistant.

To replace Adams, Eisenhower selected General Jerry Persons. Persons was amiable and easygoing where Adams was brusque, mellifluous where Adams was clipped, and one contemporary compared the transition to a move from "hard cider to mellow bourbon." Persons was an old friend—the two met back when Ike was working for MacArthur, and Persons was such an effective congressional advocate for the Army that Marshall turned down Eisenhower's request to bring him to Europe during the war. Now, as Adams's successor, he had Eisenhower's abiding appreciation, but he struggled to adjust to the new job. While Adams's stern blockade at Eisenhower's door had angered those who wanted greater access to the president, Persons's lighter touch added to Ike's burden. He complained to Whitman that "the staff seemed to descend upon him in droves and dump everything in his lap." It was, she added, much worse "than when Adams was here." Persons also sounded out staff for advice, again, a likable trait and one notably in contrast to Adams's imperiousness. But that, too, bogged people down in long meetings. Ike gently chided Persons about it.

In the shuffle of advisers, Eisenhower drew one of his most trusted intimates into the White House. John reported for duty on October 8. His father had always been tough, and it was no different now that he formally served him as his president. John avoided referring to him as "Dad," preferring instead to call him "Boss." And Ike gave him no special privilege. He would bark at his son just as he did his staff, forgive him just as readily, appreciate him just as deeply. For John, there was no escaping the call to duty. It was, he reflected, "the long arm of the White House," and it drew him "once more into the Boss's orbit." Cinching the bond, John moved his wife and children into a converted schoolhouse in Gettysburg, just down the road from Ike and Mamie.

Adams had been sacrificed to solidify the Republican showing in the midterm elections. Come Election Day, however, it fell well short of its goal. Ike did his part. He traveled, delivered speeches, raised money even for Bill Knowland, who was running for governor of California. (Knowland lost and never regained a position in politics. In 1974, he shot and killed himself.) But southern Democrats railed against Little Rock. Northern Democrats turned to organized labor for financial and political support. In contrast, the Republicans were divided. Democrats picked up thirteen seats in the Senate, breaking Republican strongholds in the industrial East, the mid-Atlantic region, and even the Plains states. It was, the *New York Times* reported, "a national triumph." It was not all bad news for Eisenhower: the Democratic tide also swept out remnants of the Republican old guard, the die-hard supporters of McCarthy and Knowland, the isolationists of the Taft and MacArthur era. Still, it was a trouncing, and largely one of the GOP's own doing. "The faults of the Republican Party are many," Eisenhower acknowledged to Harold Macmillan in a letter a few days after the votes were in. "If I could devote myself exclusively to a political job, I'd like to take on the one of reorganizing and revitalizing the Party."

The congressional defeats were dispiriting, but sadder still was the loss of one of Ike's oldest friends. Beginning in early 1957, Swede Hazlett had faced a series of ailments. He had high blood pressure and headaches. Treated at Bethesda—he was a Navy man—he underwent tests and responded initially to treatment. But in April 1958, he had a lung removed, and he faded to the point that he was a "virtual shut-in." Ike sent flowers, flattered him with briefings on world affairs, visited him in the hospital. Hazlett struggled to correspond with his old friend, but the labor of writing was too much. When he died in November, he left an unfinished note to Ike among his things.

Swede's passing took from Ike his most faithful friend, a tie to his youth, and a stalwart admirer to whom Eisenhower had unburdened himself for decades. "I can never quite tell you what Swede meant to me," the president wrote to Hazlett's widow. "While I am glad for his sake that he suffers no longer, his passing leaves a permanent void in my life."

It was then, shortly after Adams's farewell and Hazlett's death, that Khrushchev decided to test Eisenhower's firmness. Khrushchev had watched as Eisenhower cut a deal with China to avoid a nuclear war in Asia. Was that a reflection of a new American weakness? A fear of growing Soviet nuclear power? If the United States was moving to accommodating

Communism rather than confronting it, maybe it was time for Khrushchev to act.

Near the end of 1958, he decided to challenge Western strength not at the margins of the Cold War but rather in the heart of Europe, in the city most riven by the divisions of the era. On November 10, 1958, Khrushchev announced that the time had come to end the occupation of Berlin. And on November 27, Thanksgiving, he followed that up with an ultimatum, delivered orally to Western journalists in Moscow and in writing to Ike: vacate West Berlin in six months or have it pass into the control of East Germany. Eisenhower understood that if he walked away from Berlin, as he told John, "no one in the world could have any confidence in any pledge we make."

American policy with respect to Berlin was honed by previous conflict over that Western outpost, precariously isolated deep inside East Germany. Truman had rescued Berlin by airlift in 1948 and 1949. The Soviets eventually withdrew their blockade, but a decade later Berlin remained just as vulnerable and just as vital to Western prestige. It was, as Khrushchev alternately complained, a "thorn," a "cancer," and a "bone in my throat." In 1958, just as in 1948, the United States was prepared to wage war to protect Berlin—"all-out war," as James Forrestal, Truman's secretary of defense, had once described it; "general war," as Eisenhower now imagined it. In the intervening years, little had changed in Berlin, but much had changed inside the Soviet Union. Now that he was armed with nuclear weapons—how many, the United States did not know—Khrushchev's ultimatum threatened not just war in Europe but the destruction of mankind. The Soviet premier taunted Eisenhower. "Only madmen can go the length of unleashing another world war over the preservation of privileges of occupiers in West Berlin," he warned in a note to the American ambassador in Moscow. "If such madmen should really appear, there is no doubt that straitjackets could be found for them."

Khrushchev's long deadline allowed for negotiations and forced the Eisenhower administration again to confront the question of whether the United States was prepared to wage a nuclear war in defense of an ally. Nuclear weapons, if they were used in defense of Berlin, would be released in a mass attack that would not just drive the Soviets from Berlin or Europe but also destroy every vestige of their government and society. "Our whole stack is in this play," Eisenhower emphasized to his aides. In the event of a Soviet attack on Berlin, America's response would be simple: "Hit the Russians as hard as we could."

Yet even as Ike girded for war, he and John Foster Dulles furiously explored diplomatic alternatives. Dulles worked to cement Western unity—

no small feat given that the American strategy in the event of a war almost certainly relied upon atomizing much of Europe. Eisenhower's military and civilian aides urged him to adopt a firm response if Khrushchev turned Berlin over to East Germany. As with Quemoy-Matsu, however, Eisenhower refused to be pinned down. He insisted he was prepared for general war and yet steadfastly declined to treat Khrushchev's ultimatum as an imminent danger. Berlin was, Eisenhower complained, an "illogical" military position, but it was a political necessity and as such required American defense. Some of Ike's aides argued for a quick military probe to test the seriousness of the Soviet threat. Eisenhower refused. He would not lurch into an error.

Eisenhower's effort was both complicated and simplified by his adversary: Khrushchev was adamantly reckless and also shockingly easy to appease. He unveiled his Berlin ultimatum without even cursory consultation with the Kremlin leadership, and he escalated the crisis without any clear strategy. He was prepared to accept Western capitulation and imagined that negotiations along the lines that resolved Quemoy and Matsu might yield some advantage to the Soviet Union. He wanted to force a summit—that much seemed evident—and he coveted an invitation to visit the United States. Beyond those, the Soviet leader seemed to have few specific objectives as he bumbled toward a superpower confrontation.

Eisenhower, by contrast, was clear on his strategic objectives and flexible in tactical response. He refused to abandon Berlin and gambled that Khrushchev would not actually risk war to press his claims against the city. All through the winter of 1958 and 1959, intelligence reports confirmed that basic premise: Khrushchev, the Americans believed, would make demands and accept concessions but would not risk annihilation.

Eisenhower knew that part of Khrushchev's plan was to force a summit, and he therefore resisted the idea. The British, by contrast, favored such a gathering, and, as in 1955, Eisenhower reluctantly agreed to consider it. On March 20, with the Soviet deadline growing nearer, the president entertained Harold Macmillan at Gettysburg, and the two capped their official conversations with a long ride around the Eisenhower farm. When they returned after dusk, Macmillan was darkly troubled. As they contemplated the risk before them, an "exceedingly emotional" Macmillan pleaded with Eisenhower to agree to a summit, begging him to recognize that an attack on England with just "eight bombs," a phrase he used repeatedly, could wipe out twenty to thirty million of his countrymen. If a nuclear war seemed imminent, Macmillan asked for time to evacuate Britons to Canada and Australia.

Taken aback by Macmillan's plea, Eisenhower reminded the prime minister that estimates of American casualties in a global war exceeded sixty-seven million and that, even so, he refused to "escape war by surrendering on the installment plan." Eisenhower would not be "dragooned to a summit," but did allow that he would consider attending if the foreign ministers would meet first and produce some evidence that a high-level conference would result in progress. Even slight progress, Eisenhower said, might be enough to justify the summit that Khrushchev desired and that Macmillan believed was the way out of the crisis. Macmillan was an old man at the end of a long career. This, he said, was "a duty he owed his people" and stood likely to be "the most fateful decision he would ever have to take." With that, the two men joined their aides for dinner. They capped the evening with a Western. Macmillan remembered it as "The Great Country or some such name"—it was, undoubtedly, *The Big Country*. "It lasted three hours!" he exclaimed to his diary. "It was inconceivably banal."

Macmillan's appeal supplied the breakthrough that both sides sought. Six days later, the United States formally proposed a foreign ministers' meeting, to be followed by a summit if progress warranted it. The Berlin crisis, triggered by Khrushchev's impetuous dare, began to recede. Berlin would remain a hostage to the Cold War for decades, but the imminent threat to its survival had passed by the middle of 1959, allowing the city to resume its place as a locus of tension rather than a flash point of war.

Before the crisis could be resolved entirely, the stress of those dangerous years would claim another victim close to Ike. Ever since 1956, John Foster Dulles had battled cancer. His first operation, just after the Suez crisis, removed a tumor but did not get everything. Dulles worked on. Early in 1959, however, his illness overcame his stoicism. He complained of discomfort and warned one old ally, Adenauer, that he was going to need surgery to repair a hernia. A few days later, he checked into Walter Reed hospital. Once doctors opened him up, they realized his cancer had returned. General Snyder, Eisenhower's personal physician, monitored the operation and immediately reported that the results were "not good."

Eisenhower and Dulles had stood shoulder to shoulder for six years, from Dulles's uncomfortable wait for the appointment he believed his for the asking to Walter Reed's Ward 8. Together, they had fended off McCarthy, repelled Mao, overthrown Mossadegh and Arbenz, fenced with Khrushchev and occasionally each other. Dulles was not the dominant member of the pair, as some critics of the administration maintained. Eisenhower had watched him closely from the start, and Dulles had been forced to yield on occasion to Ike's disagreement, most notably in the administration's evolving nuclear policy. Eisenhower increasingly worried about the prospect of a war, while Dulles worried ever more deeply about the implications of being afraid to fight one. But no two Americans had done more to fashion peace within the context of the Cold War, a peace without precedent, created by their imagination and will. They had forged it as a team, in daily contact no matter where their schedules took them.

As their collaboration grew to a close, Dulles summoned up his energy and piety, lecturing as he was prone to do, when Macmillan and Ike came to visit him. A day before Eisenhower and Macmillan left for Gettysburg, the three men met in Ward 8, accompanied by Britain's foreign secretary. Eisenhower sat on a sofa, Macmillan and his deputy in armchairs, Dulles in a higher, harder seat. Dulles counseled defiance. "He was *against* almost everything," Macmillan recalled—against a summit, against a foreign ministers' meeting, against any hint of retreat from Berlin. "He thought we could 'stick it out' in Berlin, and that the Russians would not dare to interfere with us." Macmillan was moved but worried. "It was a splendid exhibition of courage and devotion. But I felt that his illness had made his mind more rigid . . . I felt also sorry for the President."

Macmillan saw in Dulles the passing of a tough negotiator and an architect of a brutal peace. Eisenhower saw a dying friend. "I have rarely seen him shaken by . . . death," Ann Whitman wrote. "But this morning he did talk a little bit about it."

On Monday, April 13, Eisenhower visited Dulles in the hospital and told him he was prepared to accept his resignation. Dulles agreed. Two days later, Eisenhower announced the news from the Colonial Room of the Richmond Hotel in Augusta. "I personally believe he has filled his office with greater distinction and greater ability than any other man our country has known," Eisenhower told reporters, his grief evident. The press, sensing his mood, was uncharacteristically gentle, asking just a few brief questions. "I can't tell you how much regret I feel about this," the president concluded. "I am quite sure that the United States will share that feeling." Dulles's letter, drafted by the White House for his convenience and then shared with him for editing, was finalized the next morning; Dulles did not change a word. He called Ann Whitman to thank her for their long association. She listened gratefully and then burst into tears.

Dulles died on May 24. Three days later, the day Khrushchev set as the deadline for Western withdrawal from Berlin, Dulles was buried at Arlington National Cemetery. The foreign ministers interrupted their meeting in Geneva to attend.

The Final Months

Nineteen fifty-nine opened with two crashing events, one foreign and one domestic: on New Year's Day, Fidel Castro swept down from the mountains to drive Fulgencio Batista off the Cuban island; later that month, the new U.S. Senate, with sixty-two Democratic members, took up the nomination of Lewis Strauss to become secretary of commerce.

Castro's triumph was initially a source of bewilderment. He had toppled a regime that deserved toppling. Still, American intelligence was unsure what to make of him, as was the American press. Even the administration's initial response was bungled: Eisenhower ordered the Navy to send ships to stand offshore, but to do so quietly, so as not to inflame the situation. Instead, the Navy announced the move and said it was ordered by the State Department. Still, the predominant mood within the Eisenhower administration was one of cautious hope. Allen Dulles did not brief the NSC on Cuba's revolution until three weeks after Castro had taken power, adding it almost as an afterthought to and update on events in the Soviet Union, Italy, Iran, and Yemen. In his briefing, Dulles anticipated future relations with Castro and alerted the council that the United States should be prepared to return refugees to Cuba if they were covered by extradition agreements with that country. Ike even went so far as to compliment Castro, remarking that the Cuban leader had learned one of the essential lessons of Ike's military hero, Clausewitz. He had focused on defeating not Batista's capacity to fight but rather his will to do so.

With that, Castro slipped toward the back of the administration's concerns. The NSC did not take up Cuba again until late March. By then, events were clearly souring for American interests. Just ninety miles from the Florida coast, Castro was consolidating power, whipping up crowds, and jeering at the United States. He accepted an invitation to address American newspaper editors, infuriating Ike, who suggested that the United States deny him a visa. Allen Dulles described himself as worried by the developments but warned against any precipitous action. There was, he said, opposition to Castro within Cuba, and the United States must take care not to undermine those forces by playing into Castro's hand.

Dulles's indecision reflected a larger uncertainty about how to regard Castro. During his early months, Castro was sympathetically portrayed in the American press, notably in the *New York Times.* In August 1959, the *Saturday Evening Post* headlined its profile of the Cuban leader "Can Castro Save Cuba?" Even Castro's murders of Batista loyalists were forgiven. "Castro's executions of Batista henchmen shocked the world," the *Post* reported, "but most Cubans considered them as just retribution."

The tension about how to respond to it froze Ike's initial response to the Cuban dictator through much of 1959. Over those months, Castro grew stronger and more belligerent. He courted Moscow, picked his brother to head the Cuban military, imprisoned critics, then feinted toward neutralism. Washington could not decide whether, or how, to react.

The Strauss nomination, by contrast, appeared simple. The Senate had never rejected an Eisenhower appointment to his own cabinet, believing in those days that wide deference was due presidents' appointments. Moreover, Strauss was experienced—he was the longest-serving head of the Atomic Energy Commission, a position for which the Senate had confirmed him—and indisputably intelligent.

He was also arrogant and rigid, prone to overstatement and defensiveness. And he had accumulated influential enemies, particularly within the party that now dominated his future. The Senate reaction when it received Strauss's nomination in January was portentous: it delayed hearings until March. Strauss at that point made his opening remarks and picked up a few endorsements, only to have the chairman then recess the session again until after Easter. It was not until April 21 that Strauss was finally exposed to the full wrath of his critics.

Estes Kefauver dredged up Strauss's marginal role in the Dixon-Yates controversy, a tussle over private-versus-public electrical power that had generated a scandal some years earlier. Strauss denied any wrongdoing and pronounced himself satisfied with the resolution of that issue. Then a panel of scientists criticized Strauss for his emphasis on secrecy in the development of American nuclear capacity. That hinted at the real reason for the controversy around the nominee. Strauss had championed a particular vision for America's nuclear strength. He ardently supported the development of bigger and more destructive weapons, and he believed that the government needed to protect those projects with utmost secrecy. He pursued those objectives with ruthless intensity and had driven his chief nemesis out of government. Thanks to Strauss, Robert Oppenheimer, the architect of America's atomic bomb, was a private citizen in 1959. Strauss had prevailed in that fight, but Oppenheimer's allies now got a second bite of the apple.

Led by Senator Clinton Anderson, who had long distrusted Strauss, senators challenged his integrity, and Strauss supplied them with enough misleading—in some cases, false—answers to justify their attacks. Strauss brought a confidential document with him one day and, when confronted, denied first that it was labeled "Top Secret," then that he had brought anything at all, a falsehood. He fenced with senators about his record and a previous finding that he had demonstrated "willful duplicity" in his dealings with Congress. "Strauss," a sympathetic biographer writes, "proved himself to be vain, arrogant, and self-righteous in defense of his record, but did these traits disqualify him?"

Eisenhower stood firmly behind Strauss. Asked at a news conference in early May whether the rancor against Strauss would make it impossible for him to serve, Eisenhower said no: "I have told you again and again that I think here is a man who is not only a valuable public servant, but who is a man of the utmost integrity and competence in administration. And if we've got to the point where a man, because of some personal antagonisms, cannot be confirmed for office in this Government, then I must say we're getting to a pretty bad situation." Two weeks later, by a vote of 9–8, the Interstate Commerce Committee recommended that Strauss be confirmed.

Eisenhower continued to push for Strauss, leaning on senators for their support. Indeed, he pressed so hard that some accused him of overreaching. He refused to be deterred. "When my conscience tells me [my recommendations to Congress] are right, I'm going to use every single influence that I can from the executive department to get the Congress to see the light," he said just days before the final vote. "If that's lobbying, I'm guilty."

The Eisenhower of 1959, faced with a Democratic Senate and his impending departure from office, did not have the clout he possessed when he was a candidate for reelection. The Senate gathered for its vote on Strauss and, by the narrowest of margins, defied the president. The final vote was 49–46. "I am losing a truly valuable associate in the business of government," Eisenhower lamented. "More than this—if the Nation is to be denied the right to have as public servants in responsible positions men of his proven character, ability and integrity, then indeed it is the American people who are the losers through this sad episode."

Eisenhower had always been prone to temper—this was still the boy who beat his fists against a tree when he was denied the chance to go trick-or-treating—but his reaction to Strauss's defeat was in a class by itself. Publicly, Ike accepted Strauss's gracious resignation: "I salute you for the calm and even generous attitude in which you have accepted what will surely go down in history as one of the most erroneous and unfortunate verdicts of our time." Privately, he was beside himself. "He thought it was a disgrace," Jim Hagerty recalled. "It completely disgusted him." He vented to friends and aides, brought it up in meeting after meeting. For the rest of his days as president, the Senate's handling of the Strauss nomination would enrage Eisenhower.

Ike approached the final chapter of his presidency with an acute sense of time running out. Adams and Dulles were gone, replaced by Persons in the White House and Christian Herter—a gentle and dignified former Massachusetts governor who amassed a long career of public service despite hobbling pain from arthritis—in the State Department. Frederick Mueller filled in at Commerce after the Senate rejected Strauss. George Humphrey and Herb Brownell also had departed, their posts filled by Robert Anderson and William Rogers at Treasury and Justice, respectively. All capable men, but in no case did they match the ability or stature of the ones they replaced. The Republican losses in the 1958 elections insured that Eisenhower would never again govern with a cooperative Congress (not that he ever really had), and the race to succeed him would inject politics into every major decision of the final years. The rejection of Strauss proved the limits of Ike's power to get his way.

Also in 1959, the United States grew—not just metaphorically, but physically as the nation absorbed two new states. Eisenhower had been skeptical of Alaska statehood. The area was so vast, so uninhabited, so removed from the rest of the nation that it hardly seemed to warrant consideration in his view. Hawaii, with its larger population and strategic significance, struck him as a sounder case. There were, moreover, political considerations: it was generally assumed in Washington that Alaska would tilt Democratic and Hawaii would vote Republican.

In the end, most of those assumptions proved wrong: Alaska's oil and proximity to the Soviet Union made it the more strategic addition, and it gradually drifted into the Republican column, while Hawaii became a solidly Democratic state. They were admitted under separate pieces of legislation, both of which Eisenhower signed, and the new states joined the Union in 1959. That meant redesigning the flag with fifty stars for fifty states. The final design was not the one Ike preferred: he liked a staggered arrangement of stars, but when he learned that a flag company was pushing that design, he reversed himself, feeling that the nation's flag should not reflect a commercial interest. The nation got its new flag in August.

Eisenhower was more limited in the twilight of his administration. He guarded his health, as did his staff. Most days featured a long midday break; aides brought bad news to him gingerly. Yet Ike saw a chance for peace in his final months, and he determined to pursue it. In August 1959, he extended an invitation to his Soviet counterpart to visit and tour the United States. Khrushchev, astonished to receive the invitation he had so wanted, reacted "with immense satisfaction, even . . . with a sense of joy," and with vindication that his pressure on Berlin had yielded newfound American appreciation for the Soviet Union.

The invitation was, in fact, clumsily delivered. Eisenhower complained later that he had only meant to extend it in the event that the foreign ministers made progress in their talks, a complaint that is, frankly, hard to accept and suggests that he was merely giving himself room to excuse his capitulation regarding the visit and a summit. Once the invitation was announced, Ike was, Ann Whitman remarked, "happy as a lad." And as events would have it, Khrushchev's visit would constitute the second act in this late-Eisenhower Cold War drama. The first occurred in July and starred Richard Nixon.

The vice president arrived in Moscow on July 23. Khrushchev immediately lit into him. The United States at the time was observing Captive Nations Week, and Khrushchev welcomed Nixon to the land of "captive people." "Would that the Vice President who has just landed come and see these captive people who are present here," Khrushchev said. Nixon at first tried to be polite: he praised Khrushchev's eloquence and remarked that he would have made a good lawyer. Khrushchev refused to be pacified. He kept up his harangue about the Captive Nations resolution, while Nixon fenced, first pointing out that it was Congress, not the president, that had passed the resolution and then gamely noting that it expressed "substantial views of the people in our country." Khrushchev grew more irritable, called Congress "stupid," cursed, and apologized for his "peasant language." After two hours, they had had enough and set out for Sokolniki Park, where an exhibition of American life awaited them.

Again, this time with reporters and others present, Khrushchev went first. Complaining about restrictions on the export of U.S. goods to the Soviet Union, he gibed that "you don't trade the way you used to." Nixon retorted: "You need to have goods to trade." And thus it went. Khrushchev bragged and bullied, Nixon deflected and rebutted. As they stood before the display of an American kitchen, featuring an automatic washing machine, Nixon commented that Americans were inventing such devices to make life easier on American women. Khrushchev said he and his colleagues did not appreciate "the capitalistic attitude toward women." Nixon explained the economics of American living, pointing out that the model house would cost about $14,000, within the reach of a steelworker. "We have steel workers and we have peasants who also can afford to spend $14,000 for a house," Khrushchev replied. Nixon showed off other appliances; Khrushchev wondered whether America had invented something "that puts food into your mouth and pushes it down." At times, Nixon seemed to enjoy himself, tossing asides to the English-speaking press, while Khrushchev was defensive and surly, accusing Nixon of threatening him. On only one thing did they conspicuously agree. "I don't like jazz music," Nixon said. "I don't like it either," Khrushchev replied.

Although the so-called Kitchen Debate became a classic of Cold War theater, Eisenhower did not immediately recognize it as such. When the reports came out, Jim Hagerty briefed Eisenhower. The president declined comment.

Nixon's visit left the Soviet premier in a surly mood but heightened anticipation for his American summer holiday. No Soviet leader had ever toured the United States, and Khrushchev's famous belligerence made him an unpredictable guest. In addition, European allies worried about being cut out of a superpower arrangement, while American conservatives imagined appeasement with an immoral foe. Nixon, fresh from his own encounter with Khrushchev and ratcheting up his campaign to succeed Ike in the White House, took the lead in allaying those fears. Some critics, he acknowledged, "suggest that Khrushchev may outwit, outsmart or trap the President and his associates." Such fears were unfounded, he insisted. Ike was well aware of the evil of Communism and the duplicity of the Soviet leaders; talk was essential, but it did not imply agreement or naïveté.

"Those who believe that this conference is going to result in appeasement, surrender, defensiveness and softness toward communism," Nixon added, "simply do not know the President of the United States."

Some approved. Martin Luther King, Eleanor Roosevelt, and Adlai Stevenson, among others, took out full-page ads complimenting Eisenhower on the invitation. Others were unconvinced. One member of Congress posted a sign on his door reading, "Khrushchev not welcome here." In New York, Cardinal Spellman initially refrained from discussing the invitation but then appeared in the pulpit at St. Patrick's Cathedral and warned against "complacently weakening our defenses, permitting the enemy's promises of peaceful negotiations to blind us to the long and well known fact that the Communist program is in the conquest of the whole free world."

When Khrushchev's entourage was announced—it included a hundred people, among them his family, his foreign minister, and various staff—the *Los Angeles Times* led its story with the wry comment that "a small Russian army" was set to "invade the United States."

Eisenhower prepared for the Soviets by touring Europe on a mission of reassurance, conferring at each stop with allies in order to assure them he would not cut a deal without them. He departed on August 26—just five days after unfurling his nation's fifty-star flag. He stopped first in Bonn, and as he made his way through the European capitals, his reception supplied ample proof that he retained a special place in the hearts of those whose armies he once commanded—and even those whom he defeated. In Germany, eager, anxious crowds waved banners and beseeched the president for protection, the latest Berlin crisis still fresh in the national consciousness; in London, the throngs were happy and spontaneous; in France, they lined the route of his motorcade beneath paper streamers imprinted with the American flag. Adenauer and de Gaulle, two of the continent's most austere political figures, beamed in Eisenhower's presence; Macmillan received Ike as an old friend. Even the traveling press corps was impressed. "We are all completely flabbergasted at the hold he has on people," one reporter reflected. "The man has it."

Ike wrapped up his European meetings on September 4. Work complete, he bedded down at Culzean Castle, which reserved for him a suite of rooms for life, and called for the Gang. Bill Robinson rounded up Pete Jones, finding him at 2:00 a.m. in Lake Placid, New York. They rushed to Europe to entertain their friend and commander in chief, meeting him at the Turnberry golf course on a gorgeous Scottish day, joined by the American ambassador, Ike's wartime friend James Gault, his son John, and a few others, including two pros from the club. Ike shot an embarrassing 89—

embarrassing, especially, because the press learned of it—then retreated to the castle for the evening.

Upon returning to the United States, Ike completed final preparations for Khrushchev's arrival. The president waited in person at Andrews Air Force Base for the premier to land. He was an hour late. Khrushchev bounded out of his Soviet-made Tu-114, a mammoth turboprop aircraft designed by captured German scientists at the end of World War II and freshly minted for the trip. Ike greeted him with a handshake and said: "Welcome to the United States, Mr. Khrushchev." Strangely, Khrushchev, who had met Eisenhower in Geneva, responded by saying he was "very pleased to meet you." Eisenhower urged Khrushchev to enjoy the American people and appreciate their commitment to peace, their disinterest in world domination. "I assure you that they have no ill will toward any other people, that they covet no territory, no additional power. Nor do they seek to interfere in the internal affairs of any other nation," the president said. "I most sincerely hope that as you come to see and believe these truths about our people there will develop an improved basis on which we can together consider the problems that divide us."

In his remarks, Khrushchev was gracious and impish, boastful and solicitous. "We have come to you," he said, "with an open heart and good intentions. The Soviet people want to live in peace and friendship with the American people." Having said that, he crowed of the Soviets' recent launch of a nuclear-powered icebreaker, and he reminded the president that the Soviets had succeeded in shooting a national emblem to the moon. Even then, he remembered to mollify his host. "We do not doubt that the splendid scientists, engineers and workers of the United States who are working to conquer outer space will likewise deliver their emblem to the moon," he said. "The Soviet emblem, as an old resident of the moon, will welcome your emblem, and they will live in peace and friendship."

So it would go over the next twelve days. A large crowd lined Khrushchev's route from the airport into Washington but watched quietly until Eisenhower dropped Khrushchev at Blair House. Once the president had shed his guest, those outside roared their approval for Eisenhower. That afternoon, the two leaders met at the White House for a brief talk, mostly about arrangements for the trip. After giving Eisenhower a model of the Soviet moon-shot projectile (Ike was "annoyed" but gritted his teeth and accepted the gift graciously), Khrushchev stressed that the world expected progress from the visit and agreed with the president that they should find time to discuss Berlin, Laos, and other points of contention.

After a night in Washington, Khrushchev hit the road. He was accompanied by Henry Cabot Lodge, whom Ike gave the unpleasant duty of escorting the Soviet leader around the country; Lodge performed admirably under trying circumstances, including Khrushchev's persistent needling. They debated the merits of a free press, the relationship between the states and the federal government, the importance of elections. ("You say you don't like violence," Khrushchev teased Lodge at one point, nudging him in the ribs for emphasis. "Did George Washington have an election in order to win the American Revolution?") Khrushchev met with industrialists in New York and delivered a startling, if transparently hyperbolic, speech to the United Nations in which he called for universal disarmament of conventional as well as nuclear weapons. He chided labor leaders in San Francisco; visited an IBM plant in San Jose; met with farmers and civic leaders in Des Moines; visited steelworkers and machinists in Pittsburgh. He sparred with reporters throughout. He could be eloquent—"May the two words, peace and friendship, be inscribed on the banners of each of our nations and may they guide the conscience and actions of our governments," he declared in Des Moines—and arrogant: "The fact that you ask such questions and the fact that some gentlemen are laughing before hearing my reply show how little they know of the substance of the matter," he told a magazine editor in New York.

The theatrical low point of the tour came in Los Angeles, where Khrushchev locked horns with one of American politics' lesser lights. At a dinner honoring the Soviet leader, he was introduced by Mayor Norris Poulson, who used his moment in the international spotlight to remind the Russian of his infamous pledge, made in the immediate aftermath of Suez and Hungary: "We will bury you." Not so fast, Poulson now countered. "We do not agree with your widely quoted phrase, 'We will bury you.' You shall not bury us, and we shall not bury you," the mayor lectured. "We are happy with our way of life. We recognize its shortcomings and are always trying to improve it, but if challenged, we shall fight to the death to preserve it."

It had been a long day. Khrushchev began the morning in New York and then flew to Los Angeles, arriving on a sweltering afternoon. He'd been condescended to at Hollywood's Fox Studios, where the mogul Spyros Skouras wagged a finger in defense of capitalism and recounted his own ascent from a poor childhood to his position of fame and wealth. (Presumably, Khrushchev was less bored by the Hollywood stars who gathered for his visit, notably Marilyn Monroe, who put on the "tightest, sexiest" dress in her wardrobe and attended without her husband, Arthur Miller. She later told her maid, "Khrushchev liked me." No wonder.) To cap off his long day, Khrushchev was denied his chance to visit Disneyland because police worried about security; instead, he was given a long, aimless car tour. Even the deputy mayor who greeted Khrushchev at the airport irritated him; the deputy's background led Khrushchev to conclude that his father had been a wealthy Jewish merchant, one of those "the Red Army had failed to take care of during the Revolution."

To make matters worse, dinner that night ran late and included an openly skeptical crowd, a "furred and bejeweled audience of capitalists," as the *Los Angeles Times* put it. Khrushchev nevertheless delivered his pleasant prepared remarks, lauding the "Golden State" and drawing similarities between its development and that of the Soviet Union. When he concluded his speech, however, he could not resist replying to Poulson. "Why do you bring that back?" he asked. "I already have dealt with it during my trip. [Khrushchev had been asked about the remark at his first American press conference and had taken umbrage there as well.] I trust even mayors read the press." Loosening up, Khrushchev continued to flail Poulson, though with an argument he might well have heeded himself. "We hold positions of too much responsibility to play upon words. The consequences of playing upon words can be too sad for our people." Then he threatened to take his ball and go home. "It took us only 12 hours to fly here," he said. "Perhaps it would take less time to get back."

Still livid, Khrushchev retired to his hotel room, where he hectored Andrei Gromyko and ordered the foreign minister to report his threats to Lodge. Gromyko did, delivering the news to a haggard Lodge after midnight. Lodge fired off a warning to the White House, and Ike's press secretary the next day rebuked Poulson, without naming him, for trying to score points off the Soviet visit. "Hagerty Asks More Courtesy to Khrushchev," the headline read. Khrushchev traveled on.

The trip improved after that. Khrushchev enjoyed the train ride up the West Coast and was charmed by San Francisco. As he traveled across country, he seemed to settle in, exhibiting more humor and less vitriol. Crowds were more curious, less hostile.

He returned to Washington on a sultry September afternoon, the air close and still. Khrushchev arrived at the White House late in the day, and Ike quickly spirited him into a helicopter, bound for Camp David—relinquishing his front seat to his guest. Over the next two days, the two leaders and a small handful of top aides ensconced themselves in the Aspen Lodge, a rustic, four-bedroom cottage that housed Eisenhower, Herter, Khrushchev, and Gromyko.

The first night was uneventful. Eisenhower was battling a cold and recognized that his guests were tired, too. So the principals and the rest of their entourages—housed in other cottages throughout the camp—retired at 11:45 p.m. By breakfast the next morning, Khrushchev was regaling Eisenhower with stories of World War II from the Soviet side and salty tales of Stalin's rule. As the meeting turned to substance, the two men talked past each other and made each other angry. They argued over Berlin. Eisenhower rejected Khrushchev's demands for progress on that city's status and explained that he would never agree to a timetable for withdrawal; the American people, Ike stressed, would never accept abandonment of Berlin, and if he agreed to it, he would be forced to resign. Khrushchev complained that the United States was "high-handed" in its dealings with the Soviets. Ike tried to defuse the tension with a visit to the camp's bowling alley after the morning meeting, but Khrushchev's anger seemed to mount through lunch. The Soviet leader snapped at Nixon and even at Gromyko. Ike excused himself for a nap but woke to find Khrushchev pacing and nervous. Sensing the need to break the mood, Eisenhower invited Khrushchev to join him on a quick trip to Gettysburg. They jumped in the helicopter at 4:28 p.m., accompanied by a few close aides, including John Eisenhower, and were on the ground in Gettysburg fifteen minutes later.

The stroll around the Eisenhower farm did Khrushchev good. He charmed Ike's grandchildren, calling them by their Russian names (save Susan, whose name has no precise Russian equivalent) and inviting them to join their grandfather on his expected visit to the Soviet Union. The children jumped at the chance. Khrushchev presented each with a red star pin (on the way home that afternoon, Barbara threw them out the window of the car). Eisenhower showed off his herd of Black Angus cattle and impulsively offered one to Khrushchev as a gift. "This seemed to please him," Eisenhower recalled, adding that once Khrushchev was removed from Camp David, he became a "benign and entertaining guest." Once again at ease, the two leaders returned to Camp David, arriving at Aspen Lodge at 6:06 p.m., just in time for cocktails.

Meetings the following morning, Sunday, were delayed while Eisenhower provocatively left Camp David to attend church while his nominally atheistic counterpart waited for his return. Once the talks resumed, Khrushchev's petulance returned. He belittled American technology. All the cars on the highways, he said, were evidence not of prosperity but of instability: "Your people do not seem to like the place where they live and always want to be on the move going someplace else." Ike, bemused, did not reply.

Finally, however, the outlines of a deal were agreed upon. The Soviet

Union would withdraw its deadlines for Western departure from West Berlin; Eisenhower would commit to attending a four-power summit and would agree that the West, too, regarded a divided Berlin as temporary, though how temporary he would not say. In short, Khrushchev agreed to back down from his threat, and Eisenhower agreed to give Khrushchev some of what the threat was intended to produce. That was hardly a resounding recalibration of international relations, but it represented a genuine attempt by both sides to defuse the crisis. Then, just when the deal seemed done, Khrushchev took a step back, refusing to allow a joint communiqué of the meeting to mention his concession on Berlin. Eisenhower exploded. "This ends the whole affair," he steamed, "and I will go neither to a summit nor to Russia."

Now it was no longer Khrushchev digging in his heels but Eisenhower, and the expectations of a deal to conclude the celebrated American tour stood at risk. Khrushchev, having dawdled and argued and fumed for days, suddenly became conciliatory. It was not, he insisted, that he was unwilling to withdraw his threat against Berlin in exchange for Eisenhower's promises; rather, it was that he could not issue such a public statement without first briefing his colleagues in Moscow. Eisenhower agreed to wait forty-eight hours after the summit concluded to make the Berlin statement public; at that point, Khrushchev said, he would publicly acknowledge it.

Business complete, Khrushchev presented the group with a box of chocolates. As they were passed around, he politely complimented the quality of American chocolate. His ambassador interjected that Russian chocolate was superior, but Khrushchev, now in a generous mood, directed his interpreter not to translate the remark. Eisenhower and Khrushchev finished their candy and rode together back to Washington by car, accompanied only by a translator. They admired the scenery and reflected on the events of the past two weeks. Khrushchev left the country that night, and both men looked forward to a summit in the coming year, followed by Eisenhower's reciprocal visit to Moscow in the fall of 1960.

Bumps in the trip notwithstanding, the pictures of a Soviet leader on Hollywood movie sets and in Iowa cornfields and Pittsburgh steel mills suggested an easing of relations that counterbalanced threats of retaliation, destruction, and conquest. On the American side, that sense of shifting emphasis—from conflict to conversation—gave rise to an imagined emergence of a "new" Eisenhower. This Eisenhower, the speculation ran, was unburdened of the twin restraints of Adams and Dulles and was freer, looser, more comfortable. That made for an appealing, though inaccurate, story line—the comeback of America's great general. The notion that Eisenhower had been down and now was suddenly back up was captured by a question from a reporter in August, who remarked on the president's busy schedule and asked "if you could explain to us whether this apparent new departure for you is due to perhaps a new concept in your own mind of the Presidency, or whether you are just feeling much better physically, or why all of this activity?" Eisenhower answered directly. "The only thing here," he said, "is that I am trying to end the stalemate and to bring people together more ready to talk."

Eisenhower rebounded politically to some degree in 1959, but not because of Dulles's death or Adams's resignation. The low point of his popularity came around the Republican defeats in 1958, when Ike was not on the ballot. Since then, the recession had abated, and the public's affection for him had returned. By the summer of 1959, 60 percent of Americans approved of his presidential performance, compared with one in four who disapproved. That strengthened his political hand and freed him to be decisive, knowing that he had the support of the electorate. Reporters contrasted that sure-footedness with what seemed a stumbling White House a year earlier and deduced that Ike was finally free to be himself, now that his powerful deputies were gone.

Within the White House, those reports were considered a joke. Ann Whitman wrote: "The newspaper people suddenly find they have been wrong in riding the President, that he is not an 'old and sick and feeble' man, with no powers because of the fact that he cannot run again." The Ike of 1959, after all, was only older than the Ike of 1958 and just as much a lame duck. Whitman acknowledged that Adams's and Dulles's departures did have consequences, just not the one that reporters believed. Herter and Persons, she observed, "are more inclined to remain in the background" than their predecessors, so the president commanded more of the foreground and seemed to outsiders more active when in reality he always had been.

Meanwhile, presidential jockeying irritated Eisenhower, and periodically the ambitions of those who would succeed him interfered with his work. In early August, Ike insulted Lyndon Johnson when he discussed potential Democratic nominees at a stag dinner for reporters and inadvertently neglected to mention Johnson as a possibility. A few days later, Johnson sulked through a session with the president and refused to speak other than to answer direct questions. Afterward, he showed White House aides some of the clips retelling Ike's alleged slight. "I have had about all I can have of this," Johnson complained. Eisenhower's staff urged him to apologize. He refused.

Similarly, when Nixon's secretary called frantically to complain that Nelson Rockefeller was quietly criticizing the Khrushchev invitation—and, presumably, seeking to take political advantage by distancing himself from the White House on that score—Whitman passed the message on to Eisenhower with a note indicating her surprise: "I said it just didn't sound like Nelson at all."

Nixon was no better. He confounded even those who liked him. In December, he dropped by science adviser George Kistiakowsky's office, ostensibly to discuss the scientist's views on nuclear weapons, but Kistiakowsky left the meeting frustrated that Nixon had held forth more than he had listened. He noted in his diary: "We were duly photographed together. This will clearly establish the fact that the Vice President is in close touch with the Special Assistant to the President for Science and Technology." The following week, the two had dinner in California, where Kistiakowsky continued to wrestle with his mixed feelings about the vice president, in part because Nixon suddenly began addressing him by his first name. "He leaves one with a strange impression," Kistiakowsky again confided to his diary. "So far I haven't heard him once make a statement which was wrong from my point of view, and most of the time he makes very sound observations, but I have a feeling that the motivation for these remarks is very strongly political and he openly admits so at times."

In a White House where disdain for personal ambition was regarded as a virtue, Nixon would always be a puzzle.

Khrushchev left Washington in a blaze of optimism. The world's two greatest antagonists—in the words of the Soviet press "a Russian worker, a revolutionary, a convinced Communist" and "a professional general, a pious man who believed in the capitalist system and who was entrusted by his country's ruling class to guard the interests of that system"—had conferred in relative harmony and professed appreciation for each other. Khrushchev had toured America; Ike was scheduled to tour Russia; the world's most powerful leaders had pledged to convene a grand summit to help insure the peace. Americans solidly voiced their approval of the trip.

Domestically, Americans were less confident. Steelworkers were on strike. The economy was just barely emerging from a sharp, short recession. There was an environmental health scare that fall and contentious debates with Congress, as Eisenhower used his remaining political leverage to press for government austerity, restrained defense spending, and balanced budgets even as congressional Democrats tried to accelerate spending, particularly on defense, in order to advance their political prospects.

And there was the matter of Cuba. Castro's victory had been cautiously regarded by Washington in 1959. Eisenhower had little sympathy with the indisputably corrupt Batista: even an appeal from the dictator's eleven-year-old son did not persuade Eisenhower to grant him asylum. Within a year, however, Ike had abandoned any hope of a working relationship with the Cuban leader, and Washington turned its sights from cooperation to destabilization. Castro was seizing private property as part of a national land reform; Cuban diplomats were seeking out allies among America's enemies, including the nations of the Eastern bloc and Egypt's Nasser, who hosted the emergent Che Guevara. "Castro and his advisers are moving very skillfully on the road toward the introduction of outright Communist Government in Cuba and are doing it in such a way as to not create by a rash act justification for intervention," Kistiakowsky reported after attending the NSC meeting of January 14, 1960. Kistiakowsky would not even write about the plans in his diary, saying they were of such "extreme sensitivity" that he hesitated to put them on paper. The NSC notes offer a clue: it might be necessary, Eisenhower remarked, to blockade Cuba.

As the administration pondered its response, Eisenhower faced a related problem he was reluctant to admit. His director of Central Intelligence, in the estimation of several of Ike's closest advisers, was woefully inept. As Castro strengthened his hold, Allen Dulles vacillated. Sometimes he urged caution and suggested that anti-Castro elements inside Cuba would topple the dictator; other times he portrayed Castro in almost demonic terms, joining with Nixon in late 1959 to compare the Cuban leader to Hitler. In July and August 1959, the United States began developing plans to "replace Castro," only to back off in response to American interests on the island who said they thought they were making headway. That promise evaporated, but U.S. hopes were raised in October, and policy turned toward supporting elements in Cuba who opposed Castro and hoping they would bring him down without America's efforts being exposed.

The confused policy was the outgrowth of poor intelligence, for which Ike's advisers blamed Dulles. Kistiakowsky, the science adviser, complained that Dulles would misreport essential details of intelligence matters (he once got the range of Soviet missiles wrong) and "knows absolutely nothing about what goes on in CIA." Bryce Harlow, a long-serving deputy to the president, considered Dulles ill informed and said he misunderstood the basic responsibilities of his job. John Eisenhower regarded the director of Central Intelligence as a "bum."

Ike never admitted that he lacked confidence in Dulles, but others wondered why he kept the enigmatic spy chief. Perhaps it was residual loyalty to the memory of John Foster Dulles. Or confidence that Ike had other sources of intelligence—the NSC, Bedell Smith, Bobby Cutler. In mid-1960, John Eisenhower suggested that Dulles be dismissed. "Dad took my head off," he said. "When you get that angry," John added, "sometimes it's because you know you're wrong."

Ike would not act against Dulles, even as the crisis in Cuba grew more alarming. Castro shut down newspapers, jailed opponents, accused the United States of practicing for an invasion. (The United States did not need any practice to invade Cuba, Ike said drily.) By March, officials in Washington were laying contingency plans in the event that Castro massacred the Americans still on the island. Invasion and military blockade of the island were among the options before the NSC. But Castro craftily deprived the United States of a pretext to invade. At Eisenhower's direction, the emphasis in 1960 moved from the prospect of war to the promise of regime change. As they had before in Guatemala, Iran, and Indonesia, covert operatives took the lead.

The steel strike had preoccupied Eisenhower since July 15, 1959, when the United Steelworkers of America walked out after deadlocking with employers over wage hikes and factory work rules. Eisenhower initially stayed out of it. He had consistently refused to invoke the government's authority to settle strikes and was justifiably proud of the peaceful labor relations that characterized most of his presidency (measured by workdays lost to strikes, his years as president included six of the seven best since World War II). When the steel strike was more than a month old, Eisenhower still resisted calls for him to intervene, insisting that "these people must solve their own problems."

But the strike dragged on, and its effects spread across the economy: in addition to 500,000 steelworkers out of work, another 200,000 workers in related industries either lost jobs or saw their hours cut. The strike even had international repercussions, as it became a source of embarrassment during Khrushchev's visit. In August, the administration grappled with possible solutions, anxious to avoid a settlement that would result in a quick price hike, adding to the country's economic troubles and injuring the competitive advantage of American steel in foreign markets. By late September, Eisenhower's frustration was beginning to show as he released a tartly worded statement announcing that he was "sick and tired of the apparent impasse" and warning that the "intolerable situation" would not "be allowed to continue." Finally, on October 9, he invoked his authority under the Taft-Hartley Act and convened a board of inquiry with the responsibility of analyzing the strike and reporting back to the president. Ten days later, he sought an injunction to force workers to return to their jobs, a "sad day for the nation" but an action that Ike felt necessary to protect the economy from further damage. The injunction was challenged but upheld by the U.S. Supreme Court; steel production resumed while talks did as well. Finally, under the leadership of Nixon, the administration brokered a deal: workers received pay and benefits increases of forty-one cents an hour, and management withdrew its attempt to gain greater control of work rules. Eisenhower was not thrilled by the terms, but he was pleased that the end of the strike helped the economy to rebound from recession.

The weeks after Khrushchev's visit seemed to create an emotional letdown in the White House. Ike caught a cold in October. He tried to shake it by getting out of town and enjoying a few days of golf at Augusta, but he was grouchy and blue and then felled with sad news: on October 16, after a long illness, General George Marshall died.

Marshall's death was a mournful occasion for the nation. His legacy included the great Allied victory, and his name was indelibly attached to Europe's recovery. Marshall's service had crossed from military to diplomatic, as he served as chief of staff of the Army, secretary of state, and secretary of defense. More than any man, he helped ready America for war after Pearl Harbor; and more than almost any other, he constructively imagined the recovery afterward. He was a general and the winner of a Nobel Peace Prize. He had been subjected to withering and unjustified criticism from Senator McCarthy and his allies, and Eisenhower was aware that he had done too little to defend his old boss during the 1952 campaign.

Marshall was a great man, and he also was an uncommonly good one. He had provided Eisenhower with a steadfast example, a counterpoint to the theatrics of MacArthur, and a study in self-effacement. It was Marshall who, upon being disappointed not to receive the command of the European invasion, nevertheless secured FDR's handwritten order and saw that Eisenhower received it as a memento. For Eisenhower, Marshall's death summoned a welter of deep emotion. Publicly, he ordered flags to be lowered to half-staff and released an eloquent encomium to his mentor: "His courage, fortitude and vision, his selflessness and stern standards of conduct and character were an inspiration, not only within the Army, but throughout the Nation and among our allies. For his unswerving devotion to the safeguarding of the security and freedom of our Nation, for his wise counsel and action and driving determination in times of grave danger, we are lastingly in his debt." To Marshall's widow, Ike was more personally reflective. "I cannot possibly describe to you the sense of loss I feel in the knowledge that George has passed to the Great Beyond," wrote the president. "I looked to him for guidance, direction and counsel ever since I first had the great privilege of meeting him late in 1941."

In just a year, Eisenhower had lost his oldest brother, his closest aide, and his most important mentor; little wonder that Augusta failed to cheer him up. But Ike was a resilient man, too responsible to be self-indulgent. He regained his equilibrium. A physical revealed him to be in sound health, and he managed to put the tragedies of recent months behind him.

The presidency permitted nothing less. The next crisis arrived just before Thanksgiving and arose from an unlikely source: the nation's cranberry industry. As long as there have been cranberries grown by humans, there have been farmers who complained of weeds. The berries grow in bogs, thick pools of water unusually susceptible to clogging and choking by invasive plants. In the mid-1950s, growers seemed to have found an answer: the U.S. Department of Agriculture approved the use of aminotriazole (ATZ) as an herbicide. Recognizing that ATZ posed some danger if ingested by humans, the Food and Drug Administration resisted granting blanket approval, and the Agriculture Department advised farmers that its use was restricted to clearing bogs at the end of the growing season, reasoning that it could then kill weeds but be rinsed clear by the time a new crop was planted. For whatever reason—growers who ignored the restrictions or the resilient presence of ATZ on the ground—the government's attempts to keep ATZ out of the food supply failed. On November 9, Arthur Flemming, secretary of the Department of Health, Education, and Welfare, announced that ATZ, which caused cancer in rats, had been detected in the nation's cranberries. The government, he added, was recommending suspension of the sale of cranberries grown in Washington and Oregon "until the cranberry industry has submitted a workable plan to separate the contaminated berries from those that are not contaminated."

It was, *Life* magazine reported, "a deed as awful as denouncing motherhood on the eve of Mother's Day." Growers charged Flemming with being "ill informed, ill advised and irresponsible." Ezra Benson, Eisenhower's long-serving secretary of agriculture, sided with farmers against his fellow cabinet member. Nixon, campaigning in Wisconsin, another leading cranberry state, publicly ate four helpings of cranberry sauce, "just like the kind mother used to make." Not to be outdone, John Kennedy drank a glass of cranberry juice.

The public was not so confident. Sales of cranberry sauce plummeted; Ike himself quietly removed it from the White House menu that Thanksgiving. And though a method of testing cranberries was ultimately developed, the scare that autumn foreshadowed a new public consciousness about the prevalence of chemicals in the nation's food supply. Three years later, Rachel Carson's *Silent Spring* was written with the cranberry crisis in mind. "For the first time in the history of the world," she wrote, "every human being is now subjected to contact with dangerous chemicals from the moment of conception until death."

In the meantime, once dangerous cranberries could be separated from safe ones, Ike gingerly asked Kistiakowsky whether it was okay to serve cranberry sauce at Christmas. "I urged him to do so," Kistiakowsky noted. "He did."

Near the end of the year, Eisenhower embarked on an eleven-nation tour that effectively served as his presidential valedictory. Accompanied by a party of twenty-one people—though not Mamie, who felt the trip was too grueling for her—Eisenhower left Andrews Air Force Base on December 3 and arrived in Italy at noon the next day. He then commenced a whirlwind trip of little substance but abundant goodwill.

Thousands greeted him in Rome, and Pope John XXIII received him that Sunday, charming John Eisenhower by remarking that they shared the same name. Tens of thousands lined the streets and squares of New Delhi, straining for a look at the president. Thousands more turned out in Washington when he returned home, even though it was nearly midnight and the weather was frigid. Many carried sparklers, twinkling in the night outside the White House.

Inside, Eisenhower barged in on Al Gruenther, Bill Robinson, George Allen, and Ellis Slater playing bridge. "Hi," Gruenther said, not bothering to get up and barely turning to face Eisenhower. "What's new?" Allen asked.

Ike pulled up a chair and sat down: "Now let's see how the experts do it."

The Khrushchev visit that fall and the abating of the Berlin crisis left two significant, unfinished pieces of business for Ike to complete in his remaining months as president: the four-power summit and his reciprocal visit to the Soviet Union. By agreement, the summit was scheduled to go first and was set for May in Paris. Plans for it dominated the administration that spring, as aides recognized that it represented the culmination of a presidency devoted to striking some sort of lasting peace with the Soviet Union.

Business in Washington posed all the usual difficulties for a president whose power was beginning to wane. Castro had become intolerable; President Rhee of South Korea, after trying to steal his reelection, instead succumbed to pressure and departed—ostensibly with Eisenhower's good wishes but in fact to his great relief. There were the usual visitors: Prime Minister Kishi of Japan came in January; Adenauer and Macmillan visited in March, de Gaulle in April. In between, Eisenhower took a grueling trip through South America, stopping in San Juan, Rio, the newly constructed city of Brasília, Buenos Aires, San Carlos, Santiago, Montevideo, and back home through Puerto Rico again. In Latin America, the mission, though mostly goodwill, also included a bit of fact-finding, as Ike sounded out his counterparts on their reactions to Castro.

Congress, meanwhile, tried again to fashion a civil rights bill as escalating civil disobedience in the South highlighted the persistence of Jim Crow. Eisenhower sidestepped the issue. Asked in March whether restaurants that denied blacks service were violating their constitutional rights, he answered: "So far as I know, this matter of types of segregation in the South has been brought time and again before the Supreme Court. Now, I certainly am not lawyer enough or wise enough in this area to know when a matter is such as actually to violate the constitutional rights of the Negroes." That was barely credible, but Ike still refused to be drawn into a debate that he believed would be resolved by "the conscience of America," and only "eventually."

Yet even as he equivocated, Eisenhower continued to mark steady, incremental progress on civil rights. On May 6, he signed another bill in that area, still just the second to clear Congress since the Civil War. As with the first, it did not go as far as he had asked, but it criminalized obstruction of a federal court order, gave the FBI authority to investigate alleged civil rights violations, and required local jurisdictions to retain voting records—all steps to enlarge and defend the rights of American blacks, particularly the right to vote.

Eisenhower also waged a last attempt to control federal spending. He opposed a housing bill that was estimated to cost $1 billion. He favored a proposal to expand health care for the elderly, but he refused to back one version that would have made health insurance compulsory and subsidized by the federal government. On the revenue side, Eisenhower declined to endorse a tax cut, despite the benefits it might have had for Nixon's political future. It was, Ike said, too likely to throw the federal budget out of balance. His refusal to yield to party conservatives on taxes hamstrung Nixon and infuriated other leading Republicans, but Ike benefited from a steadily improving American economy: by April, 66.2 million Americans were at work, and the nation's gross national product was on pace to top $500 billion for the first time in its history.

That left Eisenhower free to focus on the upcoming Paris Summit. He conferred with de Gaulle and Macmillan in the weeks leading up to the event, with Macmillan crafting the proposal for a nuclear test ban. Writing to Khrushchev on March 12, Eisenhower urged the Soviets to join with the West in suspending all such tests indefinitely. "Surely," Eisenhower suggested, "it is in the interests of our two countries and of the whole world to conclude now an agreement." That prompted an exchange of letters between the two leaders in which there appeared to be progress. There were difficulties, concentrated mainly around the issue of inspections, but by early April, Eisenhower had come to regard Khrushchev's suggestion on how to frame a test ban treaty as a "very significant and welcome development."

Secretly, Ike also prepared for the summit by gathering intelligence on the Soviets. Since June 20, 1956, high-altitude U-2 reconnaissance planes equipped with the most advanced cameras of their time had overflown the Soviet Union's satellite nations in Eastern Europe. Eisenhower granted his approval the following day for flights to penetrate the Soviet Union itself. Within weeks, he was presented with detailed aerial photographs of Leningrad and a Moscow airframe plant. Briefed about the flights, he regarded the program as "very interesting, very positive."

U-2s crisscrossed Soviet territory for four years, their flights a nuisance to Soviet radar operators, who could track the planes but not bring them down because they were out of reach of the nation's defenses. The Soviets routinely protested those intrusions on their airspace but did not publicize them for fear of what it said about the weakness of Soviet technology—this, at a time when they were boasting of scientific superiority. The result: Eisenhower knew much about Soviet military readiness, and Khrushchev knew that he knew. The essence of the U-2 program was a secret from the Soviet and American people but not from their governments. Nevertheless, Eisenhower understood how provocative the program was: it routinely violated Soviet airspace as part of a vast program of espionage. Understanding the risks, he insisted on approving every flight.

It was with special trepidation that he considered the request of Richard Bissell, the CIA's director of plans, for one more overflight in the spring of 1960. Code-named Operation Grand Slam, it was slated to cross the western Soviet Union from south to north. It was originally scheduled for early April but had been delayed by bad weather. Bissell kept returning for permission. On April 25, security adviser Andy Goodpaster informed Bissell that the president had given his okay for one last flight, on one condition: it could not be made after May 1. After that, Eisenhower was worried that it could endanger the Paris Summit, scheduled to begin on May 16.

Armed with the president's permission, the CIA selected the program's most experienced pilot, Francis Gary Powers. He was ready to go on April 28, but the flight was again scrapped because of bad weather. For the next two mornings, he prepared to take off, only to be called back, again for weather. Finally, with the president's deadline upon them, CIA officials cleared the flight. Powers took off thirty minutes late. He headed toward Afghanistan and sent one brief signal when he approached Soviet airspace at sixty-six thousand feet. Then, as with all U-2 flights, he went silent.

In Washington, there was no reason to pay particular attention to Powers's flight. Although a matter of serious national security, the U-2 program had been under way for years without serious incident. Powers's flight was more ambitious than most: rather than entering the Soviet Union and then returning the way he came, Powers was entering in the south and exiting near Scandinavia. Nevertheless, the planes had proven their invulnerability, flying beyond the reach of Soviet surface-to-air missiles and interceptor planes. Powers settled in for a long but presumably uneventful flight.

The first inklings of trouble came a few hours later when CIA officials in Washington were told that the Soviets had stopped tracking the U-2 with radar. Hours went by, and Powers did not arrive as scheduled. Concern deepened to gloom, but Bissell and his CIA colleagues were convinced that neither the pilot nor the fragile plane could survive a crash from nearly seventy thousand feet. Powers might be dead, but the chances of the mission being exposed seemed small.

At the White House, the downing of Powers's U-2 caught the president flat-footed. The administration was conducting a civil defense test that day, and members of the NSC were being judged by how quickly they could relocate to High Point, a secure location in Virginia intended for use in the event of an attack on the United States. When Jim Hagerty received news that the U-2 had disappeared, he urgently relayed word to Goodpaster, but Goodpaster, preoccupied with the NSC scramble, did not tell Ike for more than an hour, infuriating Hagerty. When Ike finally heard that the plane was missing, he was asked to authorize the release of a prearranged cover story—that a U.S. weather plane lost contact and perhaps drifted off course. "You had better wait," Eisenhower suggested. But the aide insisted: the point was to release a statement before the Soviets did. Ike didn't like it, but he agreed: "Go ahead."

Pursuant to the cover story Ike had approved in 1956, NASA released a terse statement that a weather plane on a mission in Turkey had disappeared. Before it had lost contact, the pilot, according to the statement, "reported over the emergency frequency that he was experiencing oxygen difficulties." That way, if wreckage were discovered inside the Soviet Union, the announcement would suggest that the pilot had blacked out and the plane had drifted across the border as it fell to earth.

None of that would have fooled the Soviets, of course, but since they had been complaining about these flights for years without drawing attention to what they revealed about Soviet capabilities, American authorities believed they were safe. Safe, that is, so long as the pilot and the plane were destroyed—the scenario that CIA officials regarded as "best case." Unfortunately, as the CIA's study of the U-2 program later noted, "May Day turned out to be a bad time to overfly the Soviet Union." Because it was a national holiday, much of the country's military traffic was grounded; that allowed radar operators to focus more intently on Powers's plane, which also mistakenly carried him over a missile battery that American planners did not know of. A little over four hours into his flight, a missile exploded close to Powers's U-2 (a Soviet MiG dispatched to intercept Powers was hit by a second missile). He ejected from the plane, having failed to detonate it, and then parachuted to earth, where he was captured. His film was recovered.

Americans knew none of this and assumed that the cover story about a weather aircraft would hold. Khrushchev waited, letting the U.S. government further commit to a story. It was, he relished, a magnificent opportunity to retaliate for "all the years of humiliation."

As he laid his trap, Khrushchev proceeded in the conviction that his new friend Eisenhower could not possibly have authorized the flights. Perhaps revealing something of his own relationship to his intelligence services, he imagined that the CIA or the Pentagon was conducting the espionage without the president's knowledge; the Soviet premier's gambit, then, was to expose the espionage, embarrass the United States, and still leave himself room to negotiate with Ike. Acting on those assumptions, Khrushchev played his hand for all it was worth. He delivered a long speech on May 5 to the Supreme Soviet. Well into the address, he revealed that the Soviet Union had shot down an American plane, thwarting an "aggressive act" and a clumsy attempt to put pressure on the Soviet state.

That goaded the United States into denying Khrushchev's account. After the first statement announcing that the U-2 was a weather plane, NASA elaborated with "details." It showed reporters another U-2, hastily adorned with NASA markings and a fictitious serial number. The plane shot down by the Soviets, NASA suggested, was similar to this one, assigned to perform high-altitude weather research. The Americans had now committed to a spurious version of events; they had lied and embellished in support of that lie—all on the assumption that Powers was dead and his plane destroyed.

On May 7, Khrushchev sprang. Speaking to the Supreme Soviet for the second time in three days, he began by extensively reviewing the story spun by the Eisenhower administration. Then, as captured in William Taubman's memorable biography of the Soviet premier, Khrushchev allowed himself a chuckle. "Comrades," he said, "I must tell you a secret . . . I deliberately did not say that the pilot was alive and in good health and that we have parts of the airplane." The jig was up, and Khrushchev savored his moment. He revealed that the Soviets had recovered the film from the spy plane, then boasted that Soviet cameras were superior. He also informed his audience that Powers had carried cyanide and lambasted America for the "barbarism" of demanding its pilots commit suicide. Finally, he lampooned the weather plane story by asserting that Powers carried money and jewelry. "What did he need all this for in the upper layers of the atmosphere?"

If this was a treasured moment for the Soviet leader, it also was a stupid one. Even as Khrushchev baited the United States, he trapped Eisenhower into a position that was distinctly to the Soviet's disadvantage. Imagining that Ike would disavow the U-2 and blame it on rogue elements of the Pentagon or the CIA was a fantasy; to have done so would have amounted to an acknowledgment that Eisenhower did not control his own administration. That said, the CIA had let him down, as Ike surely knew. The agency had pressed for these flights, confident that the U-2 was beyond striking distance of Soviet defenses. Allen Dulles was prepared to make it easy on Eisenhower. He offered to take responsibility and resign.

However tempted he might have been, Eisenhower could not afford to accept. It would have obliterated much of his legacy to suggest that America's most sensitive operations were conducted without his knowledge or approval. Eisenhower understood that he had to take responsibility for this or sacrifice even more. "I would like to resign," he muttered to Ann Whitman.

At the same time, Eisenhower saw no reason to apologize to Khrushchev. Since 1953, he had been urging the opening of the skies above the United States and the Soviet Union on the theory that observation would provide stability and reinforce peace. He knew that the Soviets had long been aware of the U-2, and they had, after all, launched *Sputnik*, further recognition that each country imagined itself free to gaze down on the other.

Eisenhower sized up his options. Having ruled out blaming others, he came clean. The State Department announced that despite its previous denials, the mission had been intended to spy on the Soviet Union, whose refusal to cooperate with proposed inspections such as Open Skies made such flights necessary. "The government of the United States," the statement read, "would be derelict . . . if it did not . . . take such measures as are possible unilaterally to lessen and to overcome this danger of surprise attack." In order to protect against that danger, the president, while not approving specific missions, had authorized flights, the statement added. Pointedly left unsaid was the future of the program. Khrushchev was crestfallen. This was, he told his son, a "betrayal by General Eisenhower, a man who had referred to him as a friend."

Two days later, Eisenhower twisted the knife, opening his news conference with a personal defense of the U-2, blaming the Soviet "fetish of secrecy and concealment" for the need to engage in aerial espionage, and describing such work as "a distasteful but vital necessity." If ever Khrushchev had harbored an illusion of friendship with Eisenhower, he did no more.

Although the U-2 episode badly strained U.S.-Soviet relations and embarrassed Eisenhower, American officials had every reason to think that its ramifications would be limited. Khrushchev was trumpeting the incident as evidence of American duplicity, but as Eisenhower knew, the premier had been aware of the flights for years and had continued to pursue normal diplomacy with the United States. The U-2 program had not so much as been mentioned during their talks at Camp David, when Khrushchev complained about all manner of American mistreatment. The summit, moreover, was more avidly desired by Khrushchev than by Eisenhower. So, as the U-2 crisis bubbled along, Ike continued to make plans to depart for Europe. Asked by Republican senators over breakfast whether the U-2 incident might jeopardize plans for the gathering, Eisenhower responded that Khrushchev was "much too smart" to think that this was the first such U-2 incursion and was unlikely to overreact to it.

But just as domestic considerations had prevented Eisenhower from shifting blame for the U-2 to subordinates, so, too, was Khrushchev driven now by his nation's internal dynamics. His theatrics over the U-2 had alarmed members of the Soviet military, and he had counted on Eisenhower to rescue him by disavowing the flights. When Ike took responsibility, it left Khrushchev dangling. Suddenly it was he being asked to swallow his pride and join Ike at the summit despite having made public theater of Powers and the U-2. As Khrushchev and the Soviet delegation pushed off for Paris, the premier made up his mind: Ike would have to apologize for the flights and agree to halt them, or the Soviets would boycott an event largely of their own making.

Eisenhower arrived in Paris on May 15, accompanied by twenty-five aides and greeted by more. After a brief respite at the American embassy, he met with de Gaulle and heard the French president's report on his discussion with Khrushchev. It was grim, if not entirely unexpected. Khrushchev demanded his apology and insisted that the flights be halted. The latter concession Eisenhower was willing to offer since the utility of the program was "at an end" anyway. Ike was not, however, going to concede error or publicly discontinue the U-2 in response to a threat, so even as the summit prepared to open, the allies debated whether to walk out or let Khrushchev take the initiative.

Having come all this way, the allies decided to sit tight and see what Khrushchev would do. Meeting with Khrushchev, de Gaulle made sure the Soviet leader would not be misled about allied unity in that event. As one of Ike's aides reported it to him, de Gaulle had been emphatic: "If this matter were to come to war, he wanted Mr. Khrushchev to know that France as an ally would stand with the United States."

On Monday morning, the summit opened. Khrushchev, closely surrounded by his delegation, his hands shaking with nerves, read a vitriolic denunciation of Eisenhower and the U-2 and refused to proceed with the summit unless he could be assured that the flights had been discontinued and those responsible punished. That was, as he knew, impossible: Was Ike to punish himself? With that, Khrushchev stormed out of the conference. "No matter what happens," de Gaulle reiterated to Eisenhower, "France as your ally will stand with you all the way." For Eisenhower, who had spent so many years sowing the alliance, sometimes in the face of French recalcitrance, those were heartwarming words.

Eisenhower, de Gaulle, and Macmillan all waited in the conference hall for two hours, while Khrushchev five times demanded an apology for the U-2. Without it, he refused to enter the conference. Eisenhower would not give in, so Khrushchev barnstormed around Paris and into the countryside. It was, the *New York Herald Tribune* reported, a "wildly chaotic day which would have driven Alice in Wonderland to a psychiatrist." Their patience finally exhausted, the Western leaders left the conference room.

The mood was gloomy afterward as the American delegation, suddenly deprived of a mission, straggled back to the embassy. There, the ambassador's wife had readied the patio for Ike to barbecue. He let off steam by grilling steaks.

Khrushchev's antics wrecked the summit and ruined a last chance for a major peace agreement in the Eisenhower years. Ike knew he was partly to blame. Though Khrushchev's domestic pressures drove him to sabotage the affair, the U-2 had supplied him with a pretext. Eisenhower was defensive about the lost opportunity. Weeks later, when an aide suggested that the United States work to "regain our leadership" in the aftermath of the U-2 and failed summit, Eisenhower exploded. The United States, he insisted, had not lost its leadership and therefore did not need to regain it. Never again, Ike demanded, did he want to hear anyone from his administration argue otherwise.

It was clear that the collapse of the summit weighed on the president. It is also true, however, that Khrushchev hurt himself with his handling of the affair. Internally, he gave ammunition to his critics who saw him as irresponsible; his eventual downfall was, in large measure, traceable to his actions in those weeks. He antagonized Eisenhower and cemented the common purpose of the West. Indeed, one lasting effect was to reinforce the ties that bound Eisenhower and de Gaulle, two such very different men—one garrulous and popular, the other austere and formal. De Gaulle could irritate Ike—he irritated just about everyone who knew him—but he stood with America when it counted. As he prepared to leave Paris, Eisenhower wrote to his old friend to thank him:

> I leave Paris with, of course, a measure of disappointment because our hopes for taking even a small step toward peace have been dashed by the intransigence and arrogance of one individual. But in another respect I leave Paris with the warmth and strength of your friendship, so amply demonstrated and renewed under the stress of the last four days, an even more valued possession than ever before. You and I have shared great experiences in war and in peace, and from those experiences has come, for my part at least, a respect and admiration for you that I have for few men.

Rejection

O f all the many emotions that Richard Nixon elicited from the American people, pity was surely one of those least frequently directed his way. And yet it is hard not to feel for him as he embarked on his campaign for president. Nixon was positioned as heir to one of the most popular men in America, but he launched his effort just as the administration stumbled through its least impressive months. As a candidate, he had to harness himself to Eisenhower's popularity and at the same time distance himself from what was widely perceived as the administration's dwindling effectiveness. He struggled at both, succeeded at neither.

Eisenhower did not know quite what to make of Nixon's candidacy. The vice president had grown on him since their early days, when Ike left Nixon painfully exposed during the Slush Fund controversy. Nixon had performed well in two of Eisenhower's health crises, running the cabinet after Ike's 1955 heart attack and quickly stepping forward after his alarming stroke in 1957. Nixon had successfully resisted when Eisenhower tried to push him off the ticket in 1956 and had been a model of loyalty, fencing well with Khrushchev at the Kitchen Debate and easing Adams from office with minimum fallout. Yet Ike could never regard Nixon as an equal and was flummoxed by Nixon's most primal political instincts.

In June 1959, as Nixon began to maneuver for the race to succeed Eisenhower, the two had breakfast together, and Ike left shaking his head. "It is terrible when people get politically ambitious," he confided to his secretary. "They have so many problems."

What's more, Eisenhower, perhaps forgetting how long it had taken him to warm to Nixon, seemed baffled that others showed reservations about him. Reports cascaded into Ike's office from those who were leery of Nixon's candidacy. Conservatives blamed Nixon for civil rights; blacks did not give him credit. Southerners were suspicious of him. Many Californians felt burned by him. Jews never supported him; so grim were reports of Jewish antipathy toward Nixon that Eisenhower actually pulled his vice president aside at one point to ask him why the antagonism ran so deep.

Even in the early months of the campaign when Nelson Rockefeller—once Ike's aide, now governor of New York—began to ratchet up his efforts to run, Eisenhower did his best to stump for Nixon. At Ike's direction, Malcolm Moos, then the president's chief speechwriter, researched whether Nixon and Rockefeller each could pledge to serve a single term if elected, thereby clearing the way for the other to serve as well. Nearly a hundred years earlier, Rutherford Hayes had done precisely that and had won tremendous support for his selfless renunciation of political ambition. Ike thought Nixon, identified in the public mind—and in Eisenhower's—as a victim of his crippling ambition, would potentially benefit from a similar move. Moos compiled a list of excuses that Nixon could offer (he had been in public life for eighteen years, he wanted to see more of his family once his presidency was concluded, and so on) and of reasons why Rockefeller might then benefit as well by agreeing not to challenge Nixon in return for a clear path at the nomination in four years (he would remain governor of New York and be a leading presidential contender in 1964). Neither Nixon nor Rockefeller took to the idea; they continued to pursue the presidency against each other.

Ike was eager to help, but he would not compromise on matters of consequence in order to help his vice president. Under pressure yet again from Republicans to cut taxes—this time to stimulate Nixon's chances—Eisenhower refused. He had come to office determined to erase the $8.2 billion budget deficit he had inherited from Truman. Steady resistance to federal spending, along with the expansion of the economy through the mid-1950s, had allowed Eisenhower to deliver surpluses in 1956 and 1957, only to have those dry up during the 1958 recession. But that recession had passed quickly, and the 1960 budget offered Ike his final opportunity to deliver the economy into safe hands. He held fast on spending and taxes, and left office with a $500 million surplus. Not until 1999 would another American president produce a budget in the black.

Meanwhile, on the Democratic side of the 1960 race, Lyndon Johnson pivoted from his position as a spearhead of southern influence to a national candidate, a move that Eisenhower and his aides viewed with skepticism. By 1960, Eisenhower had become accustomed to regarding Johnson as a cynical obstructionist to the administration's modest civil rights efforts in Congress. It was Johnson who had persuaded Ike to drop the most ambitious sections of his civil rights bill in 1957, but when the matter returned to the administration two years later, Johnson offered to carry a bill. Remembering their last round, Ike's aides warned the president against taking Johnson's word; he was, they said, "completely untrustworthy." Eisenhower replied that he liked Johnson personally but, more to the point, had no choice but to live with him. When Eisenhower reported that Senator Richard Russell, Johnson's mentor, regarded Attorney General Bill Rogers as a "hydra headed monster," Rogers responded that that was nothing compared to how Johnson described Ike.

So it was hard for Eisenhower to root for Johnson's candidacy. Nor was he enthusiastic about Johnson's most prominent rivals. Hubert Humphrey was too liberal, Stuart Symington too close to Truman, Stevenson was old news—Ike was responsible for that—and Governor Pat Brown of California too inexperienced in international affairs. That left John Kennedy, who seemed to Ike to be too young, too inexperienced, too ambitious—and, quite possibly, too Catholic—to win the presidency and occupy the office whose tribulations Eisenhower understood.

On the issue of Kennedy's Catholicism, there is no evidence that Ike engaged in the commonplace bigotry of the era, the sloppy assumption that a Catholic president would take orders from Rome, or at least that his public policy decisions would be dominated by his religious faith. Eisenhower put no stock in such casual prejudice; he had appointed Brennan to the U.S. Supreme Court in 1956 and had even considered running with a Catholic Democrat as his vice president. But Ike did grasp the political consequences of such widespread assumptions. He noted with interest, for example, a 1960 statement by the Vatican insisting that the doctrines and hierarchy of the Church guide adherents in their public as well as their private lives. Though that admonition was directed at Italian public officials, it carried implications for Kennedy's candidacy as well.

Kennedy announced his candidacy on January 2, 1960, and contested it with sharp-witted acumen, aided by his tough younger brother Robert. He campaigned in seven state primaries, accumulating delegates but at first not impressing the party hierarchy, which viewed his early successes primarily as evidence of Catholic loyalty (his strong showing in Wisconsin, for instance, was largely attributed to that state's substantial Catholic vote). Only after West Virginia, where he and his family heavily invested, could

Kennedy claim victory in a state without a substantial Catholic population. From that point on, he was a genuine contender, and he rolled into the Democratic convention with a solid lead in delegates but with doubts about whether he could win.

Democrats descended on Los Angeles over the weekend of July 9, 1960, welcomed to the city by its Republican newspaper and eager to contest an election in which Eisenhower would not be their opponent. Governor Pat Brown refused to endorse any candidate. The party's elder statesman, Harry Truman, was still waffling on whether to attend. Kyle Palmer, the *Los Angeles Times*'s lead political correspondent known more for his Republican leanings than his acumen, reported that Jack Kennedy had "dropped his hope of winning on the first ballot" and instead was resigned to winning, if at all, on the third or fourth tally. Johnson, even bolder, predicted Kennedy would lose after two rounds.

Kennedy was nominated on Wednesday night and won on the first ballot. Palmer now predicted that Kennedy would run as an "ultra liberal," the second of his inaccurate predictions that week. When, the following day, he wrote that Kennedy's selection for vice president, Johnson, was "unexpected," readers must have wondered as much about Palmer's abilities as about the new Democratic pairing. The Democratic ticket of rivals was chosen for political advantage, and it achieved it. Johnson buried his pride and brought Texas to the party's column, along with other wavering states of the South and near South.

Nixon, meanwhile, wrapped up his nomination more tidily, though not without incident. Campaigning as the heir to the Eisenhower era's peace and prosperity, he beat down Rockefeller's challenge and held off a threat from his right in the form of the Arizona senator Barry Goldwater, who appealed to the conservative elements of the party who never fully embraced Eisenhower. Eager to repair divisions caused by the Rockefeller-Nixon split, those around Eisenhower urged him to broker a combined ticket. But neither Nixon nor Rockefeller was amenable, so Ike directed his influence toward Lodge as Nixon's vice president.

Having secured the nomination he had so long dreamed of, Nixon began to stumble. Eisenhower sent him a private telegram congratulating him on becoming the Republican nominee and wishing him success against Kennedy: "To your hands I pray that I shall pass the responsibilities of the office of the Presidency and will be glad to do so." At the same time, Ike asked that Nixon treat the note in confidence, undoubtedly because he included some thoughts on Nixon's vice president; Colorado Republicans, Eisenhower confided based on reports from his friend Aksel

Nielsen, favored Lodge, with Robert Anderson, then Ike's secretary of the treasury, as their second choice (curious, in that those recommendations precisely mirrored Ike's own preferences). Nixon promptly violated Eisenhower's confidence by releasing the telegram to the press. That benefited Nixon; it helped dispel the persistent sense that Ike lacked confidence in him, but it embarrassed Eisenhower, who woke to read his telegram in the morning papers and thus was caught lending support to two potential vice presidents over the rest of the possible field. Rose Woods, Nixon's secretary, took the blame and apologized profusely. Lodge got the job, but it was not an auspicious start.

Modeling one aspect of his campaign on Eisenhower's 1952 effort, Nixon vowed to compete across the country. In Ike's case, that meant a promise to venture into the South; in Nixon's, he explicitly promised to campaign in all fifty states. That was a mistake, but by the time Nixon realized it, he was committed. The result was much wasted travel and energy in a race that both sides knew would be close.

The travel also took a physical toll on Nixon. In late August, he bumped his knee on a car door while campaigning in North Carolina. The injury became infected. Nixon limped along in pain.

That was nothing compared to the damage Eisenhower did to Nixon in late August. It was the end of a long press conference, and Eisenhower was irritable. Reporters had been needling him about the campaign, probing about his reaction to Francis Gary Powers's conviction and sentence after a Soviet show trial, and suggesting that the government's acknowledgment that Powers was on a spy mission might have hindered his defense. More annoyingly, the White House press corps, which would never quite accept Ike's praise for Nixon at face value, kept demanding some evidence that Nixon had played the role he was campaigning on—that of Ike's senior, trusted decision maker.

"Will you tell us some of the big decisions that Mr. Nixon has participated in since you have been in the White House?" asked Sarah McClendon of the *El Paso Times*.

"I don't see why people can't understand this," Eisenhower groused. "No one can make a decision except me if it is in the national executive area. I have all sorts of advisers, and one of the principal ones is Mr. Nixon."

The president thought that would settle the matter. But reporters kept dogging him. *Time* magazine's Charles Mohr asked whether, in light of Eisenhower's earlier answer about decision making resting solely with the president, it would be fair to characterize Nixon as more of an "observer" than a "participant" in the Eisenhower White House.

Ike smelled the trap and tried to wriggle free, but Mohr pressed again. "We understand that the power of decision is entirely yours, Mr. President," Mohr continued. "I just wondered if you could give us an example of a major idea of his that you had adopted in that role, as the decider and final—"

Eisenhower cut him off: "If you give me a week, I might think of one. I don't remember."

Ike delivered that with a smile and insisted afterward that he'd been joshing, not that he had delivered the withering insult that it appeared. But there it was: Nixon argued that he deserved to be elected because he had the seasoning necessary to guide a nation through a troubled world, that John Kennedy was too young and removed from real power to understand the perils of the office. Nixon's claim was based on eight years at the side of America's war-hero president, the builder of a complex and balanced peace. Yet when asked to supply a single example of Nixon having contributed to that peace, the president confessed that he could not name one. Ike wished he could take it back, but it was too late.

The following week, Nixon succumbed to his throbbing knee and checked into Walter Reed hospital. Ike visited him there on August 30, arriving late in the afternoon to find Nixon on the mend from a quite serious staph infection—one that Eisenhower might have sympathized with, given his boyhood experience with an infection that nearly took his leg. Ike found his vice president nursing a much deeper wound, to his ego and his political fortunes. Nixon had led in the polls since the national conventions, but Eisenhower's careless remark had hurt him just as the campaign entered its pivotal period, from Labor Day through the election. The two men took pictures at the hospital to advertise their mutual affection, but that was for political purposes. Once they were left to talk, there was, Ike recognized, "some lack of warmth" on Nixon's side. What was worse, the man seemed alone, isolated. It struck Ike then, as it had before, that his vice president, for all his loyalty, was a man of few friends. Ike had men he could turn to, men whose friendship offered him respite and comfort that professional associates could not. He understood the value of those men. And yet here was Nixon in the hospital, all by himself.

Nixon's isolation baffled Eisenhower. Others understood the difference between the two men more clearly. Eisenhower, observed Ann Whitman, "is a man of integrity and sincere in every action, be it possibly wrong. He radiates this, everybody knows it, everybody trusts and loves him." Whitman respected Nixon, too, but she grasped that he was no Eisenhower, and she summed it up with a remark as penetrating as any ever offered on the long-suffering Nixon. "The Vice President," she wrote, "sometimes seems like a man who is acting like a nice man rather than being one."

Nixon retreated into his hard, lonely shell, and rejected sound advice. Eisenhower, among others, advised him to refuse Kennedy's debate challenge. It would, many people warned him, elevate the junior senator from Massachusetts to share a stage with the vice president. And it would undermine a fundamental premise of the Republican campaign to have them spar as equals. But Nixon liked to debate. He had won in college by dint of hard work, and he had held his own against Khrushchev. He was sure he could handle Kennedy. Conversely, when Len Hall, former chairman of the Republican National Committee, pleaded with Nixon to court the support of newspaper editorial boards, Nixon refused. "What for?" he asked. "They're all against me anyway."

The world does not wait on American politics. The stirrings of liberation, cynically incited by Moscow in its colonial designs, insured that 1960 would produce its share of crises. Even as Kennedy and Nixon girded for their historic encounter, Laotian peasants rose up against their king, and the Congolese rebelled against the colonial rule of Belgium.

In the summer and fall of 1960, tiny, mountainous Laos disintegrated into factions, with North Vietnam and the Soviet Union sniffing at the possibilities. In August, Eisenhower was warned that "the situation remains so confused that anarchy is likely to develop." It deteriorated from there, and American sources reported on December 11 that howitzers were being unloaded from Soviet aircraft at a Laotian airport. Within a week, fighting was under way, and the U.S. embassy was shelled. The government of Laos, struggling for survival, asked for American help, and Eisenhower, from Walter Reed hospital, where he was for a checkup, authorized the dispatch of Thai and U.S. aircraft to resupply the government. That swift response repelled the Communist forces for the moment but did not secure a victory. As the year ended, Ike pledged to defend Laos even if it meant the United States fighting unilaterally in the region.

In the Congo, meanwhile, Belgium succumbed to the pressure for independence on June 30. Unrest followed. No sooner had the Congo liberated itself than violent bands turned on the white population. Belgium deployed troops in defense of those residents, and the new government complained that the former colonial military was exercising an authority it no longer possessed (Belgium and the new government had drafted a treaty that would bar such intrusions, but it had not been ratified at the time of independence). Complicating matters further, a mineral-rich section of the Congo known as the Katanga Province declared its independence from the new nation on July 11 and invited Belgian troops to protect whites there. The splintering of the Congo was encouraged by Belgium, and Katanga was joined by rebellion in another province, the diamond-mining area of Kasai. With the new nation on the brink of disintegrating, the United States reached out to the Congo's new prime minister, the handsome, charismatic Patrice Lumumba, to attempt a settlement.

Lumumba arrived in New York on July 24, woefully unprepared to discuss his nation's future. He had no agenda for the talks; he forgot even to bring money. American officials feigned respect for him but in fact regarded him as an oddity. Ralph Bunche, the great American diplomat and civil rights leader and winner of the 1950 Nobel Peace Prize, considered Lumumba "crazy," and the Belgians charged that he was a Communist. The CIA and the administration considered him an opportunist, not a Communist, but worried that he might seek refuge under Soviet protection. Communist or not, Ike saw Lumumba as flaky and ill equipped to manage a modern nation. Ike hoped that Lumumba's government would fall while he was away. To encourage that, he proposed a three-week tour of the United States.

Lumumba's visit had its ups and downs: the prime minister was flattered by Secretary Herter's welcome but disappointed not to meet Eisenhower; the Belgian ambassador complained of the ceremony for Lumumba, which he said angered Belgians just as it would annoy the United States if Belgium were to host a state gathering for Castro. Back in the Congo, a UN force invited by the Congolese government enforced a tenuous peace, but the Soviets stoked the unrest, and Eisenhower was perturbed when Lumumba gave an interview to the Soviet news agency. "The communists," Ike warned Herter on August 1, "are trying to take control of this." Once again, Ike readied for conflict. If the Soviets tried to enter the Congo by force, he insisted, "we would all be in the fight."

The Soviets did not send troops, but Lumumba continued to duel with Belgium and the United Nations, demanding a full and immediate withdrawal of Belgian forces and an end to the Katanga Province secession. If he did not get his way, Lumumba hinted that he might turn to the Soviet Union to supply what the West could or would not. Good to his word, when the UN did not respond as quickly as Lumumba wished, he summoned Soviet help. Soon Eastern bloc equipment and advisers were streaming into the Congo. On August 18, a CIA operative there wired his superiors that embassy officials and others believed a "classic communist effort" to overthrow the government was under way. "Decisive period not far off," the operative cabled in clipped prose. "Whether or not Lumumba actually commie or just playing commie game to assist his solidifying power, anti-West forces rapidly increasing power Congo, and there may be little time left in which take action to avoid another Cuba."

One Cuba was one too many for Ike. The National Security Council met on August 18, and Eisenhower said he wanted a plan to stabilize the Congo. What he heard was not encouraging. The UN secretary-general regarded Lumumba as "an impossible person" (and possibly under the influence of "dope"), and Allen Dulles reported that Lumumba "was in Soviet pay." Eisenhower listened to those reports and firmly replied that the United States would not permit Lumumba to expel the UN forces. There was, he insisted, no indication that the Congolese people were opposed to UN peacekeeping efforts; there was only evidence that Lumumba himself was threatened. Ike adamantly refused to stand by while the UN withdrew from the Congo and was replaced by Soviet arms and equipment. That was a prospect, the note taker recorded, "too ghastly to contemplate."

What Eisenhower said—or did not say—next has been the object of inquiry by historians and investigators ever since. According to Robert Johnson, who kept the minutes of that meeting, Eisenhower indicated with words Johnson could not recall but that "came across to me as an order for the assassination of Lumumba." Johnson was shocked that the president would issue such an order and retained the memory of that moment for decades. As time went on, however, he came to doubt himself, in part because he recognized how uncharacteristic it would have been for Eisenhower to recommend the dispatch of a foreign leader before a roomful of advisers. Others at the meeting vehemently denied that Ike made any such statement, and the minutes of the meeting that Johnson prepared included no mention of it. Douglas Dillon, the acting secretary of state at that moment, recalled that Eisenhower may well have said that Lumumba was a danger to the world and should be gotten rid of but never ordered him killed. The minutes do, in fact, reflect the suggestion of Maurice Stans, Eisenhower's budget director, that the United States "throw Lumumba out by peaceful means."

Whether Ike—who a few weeks later muttered that he wished Lumumba would "fall into a river of crocodiles"—wanted him dead or merely out of the way, Allen Dulles believed he had received presidential authorization to eliminate him. A few days later, the CIA initiated its efforts to depose Lumumba, a mission in which it regarded no methods as off-limits. In September, Dulles cabled the agency's Léopoldville station chief to urge "every possible support in eliminating Lumumba from any possibility resuming governmental position." Clandestine plots were hatched and pursued; CIA cables mused darkly of rifles needed for "hunting season," while one particularly ingenious plot involved slipping Lumumba a tube of poisoned toothpaste.

Lumumba's enemies were not confined to the West. The Congo's new president dumped him from office, but Lumumba continued to agitate and muscle his way back into a position of leadership. After Lumumba was fired, both the president and the now-former prime minister turned to the army chief of staff, Mobutu Sese Seko, and ordered him to arrest the other. Instead, Mobutu seized power for himself, retained the president, and turned on Lumumba, who fled to his home province to escape arrest. Mobutu was himself a curiosity. The first reports described the chaos in his office, with children and dogs milling about as he propounded on the role of "councils of students" in running the government. But he was a curiosity the United States could live with. He expelled the Soviet advisers, and Washington breathed easier. Deposed and on the run, Lumumba no longer posed much of a threat to the United States or Belgium, but neither the CIA nor Belgian intelligence was ready to forget about him.

Richard Nixon had rejected the advice of his betters in deciding to debate John Kennedy. He rejected it on substance, believing himself the better debater, and on style: Nixon refused to pick a suit that would match the set or to wear makeup that would improve his camera appearance. He paid the price. His performance in the first televised debate, broadcast on September 26, was substantively solid but telegenically disastrous. Still recovering from the injury to his knee, the vice president perspired. Almost from the outset, his upper lip gleamed, making him look ill at ease; he wore a gray suit that blended into the set's background, and he insisted on turning toward Kennedy, while Kennedy looked steadily into the camera. From the perspective of viewers, he seemed shifty while Kennedy appeared direct. Kennedy reminded viewers that he and Nixon had come to Congress the same year, and he demonstrated by his clear answers and his superior composure that he was every bit Nixon's equal. Although many observers scored it a tie, television viewers favored Kennedy, and with seventy million Americans watching the debate on TV, that was a powerful victory, evening the race.

Eisenhower writhed as Nixon lost momentum. If Nixon's future was at stake, so, too, was Ike's legacy. Kennedy's campaign promised change—a break from an America that he characterized as spent and sputtering. Kennedy's success required Americans to join him in rejecting what Eisenhower took pride in having built. Kennedy's most memorable criticism was at best misleading and at worst deceptive: beginning in 1958 and with increasing fervor as the campaign was engaged, he charged that Eisenhower had allowed the Soviets to take a commanding lead in building the nuclear arsenal. In February 1960, Kennedy asserted that "everyone agrees now" that a "missile gap" existed between the two nations.

But once he secured his party's nomination, Kennedy was provided with estimates of Soviet and U.S. military strength. He thus knew—or at least had been told—that the United States far exceeded the Soviet Union in nuclear capacity. But ever since *Sputnik*, he and other Democrats had been lambasting the Eisenhower administration for its supposed indifference to Soviet strength. He was not about to stop now. Kennedy continued to criticize the administration's attitude toward space, missile, and technological superiority, extracting maximum political advantage from a claim he knew to be at least contested by official estimates, if not outright false.

Even Kennedy's much-admired speech on his religion and its place in his public and political life opened with a ringing critique of Eisenhower, including a challenge to the administration's military and technological record. Far more important than Kennedy's Catholicism, the candidate argued, were:

> the spread of communist influence until it now festers only 90 miles from the coast of Florida, the humiliating treatment of our president and vice president by those who no longer respect our power, the hungry children I saw in West Virginia, the old people who cannot pay their doctors' bills, the families forced to give up their farms, an America with too many slums, with too few schools, and too late to the moon and outer space. These are the real issues which should decide this campaign.

Ike rebutted Kennedy's claims of a missile gap but refused to do so in detail, in part because the estimates of Soviet and U.S. strength were based on the top secret work of the U-2 and other intelligence methods. Even Nixon seemed tacitly to accept some of Kennedy's critique: Eager to escape criticism of Eisenhower, Nixon embraced the GOP's commitment to increased defense spending. Ike watched the campaign unfold with gnawing apprehension, torn by his desire to protect his legacy, by his mounting distrust of Kennedy, and by his abiding uncertainty about Nixon's abilities.

Khrushchev, meanwhile, spent much of October reminding Americans—Eisenhower, in particular—of what an erratic menace the Soviet Union represented with him as its leader. On the first of the month, he delivered a caustic, freewheeling address to the United Nations, berating Eisenhower for the U-2 episode and rambling on about lynching and American support for Spain's Franco, among other criticisms. The U.S. ambassador to the United Nations dismissed the speech as a "spectacle," but the Soviet premier was not done yet. Eleven days later, during a debate over a Soviet resolution on colonialism, the delegate from the Philippines rose in support of the proposal but suggested broadening it to condemn Soviet domination of Eastern Europe as well. Khrushchev banged his desk in protest and demanded recognition. Receiving it, he thundered at the delegate, calling him a "jerk" and a "stooge of American imperialism." The assembly then degenerated into chaotic name-calling and demands for attention. It climaxed with Khrushchev waving his shoe in fervid protest and banging it on his desk. The president of the assembly shattered his gavel trying to restore order, then gave up and adjourned the session.

Nixon's campaign carried a slim advantage into the final weeks, leading in twenty-two states with 161 electoral votes, while Kennedy led in fourteen states with 123 votes. The big states, however, remained too close to call, and Nixon struggled. On October 14, Eisenhower called Nixon's headquarters but was told Nixon was asleep. Then Nixon called the White House looking for Attorney General Rogers, and the switchboard operator alerted Ike's secretary, Whitman, that Nixon was on the line. He was transferred to Ike's office. Once connected, Nixon got a condescending earful. Eisenhower began by admitting that he had missed the previous night's debate, then proceeded to critique Nixon's performance anyway. The president recommended slowing down, thinking over questions before blurting out answers, trying to appear more thoughtful, less glib. Nixon considered himself an effective communicator; Ike was the one notorious for garbling his syntax and was, to boot, a stroke victim who occasionally groped for the right word. Who, Nixon must have wondered, was lecturing whom? Whitman filed away the episode under "Things I shall never understand."

Hesitation and confusion were hallmarks of Nixon's 1960 campaign, and they hurt it at a crucial moment. A month before Election Day, Martin Luther King was arrested for participating in a sit-in at an Atlanta department store. While he was in custody, a judge who had months earlier fined King and given him a twelve-month suspended sentence for driving without a proper permit asked authorities to hold him so that he could determine whether King's new arrest violated the terms of his suspended sentence. Fearful for King's safety, his supporters urged federal officials to intervene, a call that went from urgent to frantic after the minister was shipped off in the middle of the night to Georgia's notorious Reidsville prison. Harris Wofford, Kennedy's earnest and beleaguered civil rights assistant, pleaded with Kennedy's inner circle to have the senator intervene. Knowing that Bobby Kennedy was wary of any move that would antagonize southern Democrats, Sargent Shriver, the brother-in-law of both men, caught the candidate when he was alone and suggested he simply call Coretta King.

"What the hell," Kennedy agreed. "That's a decent thing to do."

Coretta was relieved and grateful to hear from the Democratic nominee. Bobby, when he learned of it, was furious. He dressed down Shriver and Wofford, accused them of jeopardizing the campaign.

Responding to King's arrest was even more complicated in the Nixon camp. Aides urged Nixon to address the incident. But Nixon still imagined that he could win away southern states from his Massachusetts opponent. He declined to issue a statement or even to make a call such as Kennedy had. When questioned by reporters, he refused to comment.

The judge in the King case reversed himself a few days later (Bobby Kennedy, after lambasting his associates for arranging the call to Coretta, called the judge himself to urge that King be granted bail). The minister was freed to the wild relief of his family and supporters. So grateful was his father that he broke with fellow preachers who were backing Nixon to proclaim his support for Kennedy. "I had expected to vote against Senator Kennedy because of his religion," he said. "But now he can be my president, Catholic or whatever he is." Kennedy marveled. "Imagine Martin Luther King having a bigot for a father," he remarked. "Well, we all have fathers, don't we?"

News of the call and the statement by King's father spread rapidly through black communities across the country, encouraged by the Kennedy campaign, which skillfully exploited the episode, publishing a pamphlet contrasting Kennedy's compassion with Nixon's lack of it and circulating it in the days just before the election. Known as the "blue bomb" for the cheap blue paper on which it was printed, it was passed from hand to hand, pew to pew, in black churches and community gatherings, moving blacks while largely escaping the notice of whites. Both sides knew the election would be close. The blue bomb reflected Kennedy's guts, while Nixon's refusal to engage the issue demonstrated his caution and indecision.

Near the end of the campaign, Eisenhower at last took to the hustings to stump for his vice president. On October 28, he addressed a large crowd in

Philadelphia. On November 2, he made a round of speeches in New York, culminating in a joint appearance with Nixon at the New York Coliseum that evening. The two appeared together again as Election Day drew near, and on the night before Americans voted, Eisenhower delivered a television address. He described his long association with Nixon, his impressions gleaned from cabinet meetings and private consultations. Nixon, Ike asserted, would provide "the right kind of leadership, steeped in the philosophy of enterprise and of hope, experienced in working for an America, confident in her destiny, secure against the devastation of war, in a world moving toward peace with justice in freedom." When the morning at last arrived, Ike flew to Gettysburg and trundled over to his polling place with John. "The first four ballots cast . . . in my precinct were for Nixon and Lodge," Eisenhower cabled Nixon. "If this marks a trend, you will win in a walk."

Not quite. The election of 1960 was among the closest in American history (Kennedy received 34,220,984 votes; Nixon received 34,108,157), and its margin may be attributed to any of several factors. Kennedy's call to Coretta King may have tilted black voters into his column; their votes provided his margin of victory in at least three states—Michigan, Illinois, and South Carolina. Kennedy's debate performance erased many of the doubts about his youth; his thoughtful address on religion helped suppress anti-Catholic sentiments. And Ike's careless unwillingness to credit Nixon with any decision of consequence did not help. Finally, consigning Eisenhower to a small role in the campaign may have deprived Nixon of the substantial affection Ike still commanded among moderates of both parties. Those close to Nixon would forever wonder whether he might have edged out Kennedy had he turned earlier and more forcefully to Eisenhower. But Nixon defied Eisenhower and debated; he hesitated rather than call Coretta; he waited until the final weeks to stitch himself close to his president. And he lost.

Eisenhower was gracious—and heartbroken. He wrote consolingly to Dick and Pat Nixon: "I want to express to you both the fervent hope that the two of you will not be too greatly disappointed by yesterday's election returns. I know that whatever disappointment you do feel will not be for yourselves but for our country and for the jeopardy in which our great hopes and aims for the future have been placed." But he took Nixon's defeat personally, called it the worst of his life. To his brother Milton, Ike confided that he felt the work of the past eight years had gone "down the drain." And to George Murphy, an acquaintance who also had campaigned hard for Nixon, Ike was blunter still. He felt "like I had been hit in the solar plexus with a ball bat."

Eisenhower rebounded, but Nixon fell into a deep gloom. He sulked through November and December while the country thrilled to its president-elect, his stylish wife, and their adorable children. Near the end of the year, Ike summoned Nixon to discuss the future of the party and Eisenhower's role in it. The president imagined writing articles, quietly convening Republican leaders, perhaps for annual gatherings at Gettysburg, and fending off what he presumed would be Kennedy's attempt to co-opt the political center that he had so long defended. The conversation was constructive until the two began to reflect on the campaign. Nixon was bitter. He complained that Lodge had hurt the ticket with his promise to put a black man in the cabinet, a jolting idea that "just killed us in the South." Eisenhower agreed. The Lodge remark, he believed, cost the Republican ticket South Carolina and Texas. Eisenhower complained that the administration had championed civil rights but received too little credit from blacks. Negroes, Ike growled, "just do not give a damn."

Nixon was not ready to concede that blacks had ignored him completely. He pointed out that he had tallied slightly more votes from blacks in 1960 than Ike had in 1952. But the black vote, Nixon said acidly, was a "bought vote, and it wasn't bought by civil rights." The Kentucky senator Thruston Morton, who headed the Republican National Committee and participated in the meeting as well, echoed that conclusion. Blacks had failed to appreciate the Republican Party's work on racial equality, the senator said. As far as he was concerned, "the hell with them."

Up to that point in his career, Nixon had a fairly commendable record on civil rights and had paid some price for it among conservatives. When he resumed his quest for the presidency in 1968, he would pursue it through the so-called southern strategy. The goal was to break the Democratic Party's hold on the South by allying the Republican Party with the forces of racism. It would prove more effective than Nixon's more accommodating approach in 1960. The southern strategy might well be said to have been born that December day in Eisenhower's White House.

Nixon's funk persisted into the new year. When NBC began shooting a tribute to Eisenhower to air on the last day of his presidency, the network invited Nixon to appear. He refused. Len Hall had to remind Nixon that his absence would surely be noted. Glumly, Nixon relented. He would, Nixon agreed, do anything he was asked.

As the days counted down on Eisenhower's presidency, Ike turned to the most vexing foreign policy problem left on his agenda. Over the course of 1960, Castro had gone from meddlesome to threatening as he sought and received substantial aid from the Eastern bloc and encouraged other Latin American movements to challenge their governments. The CIA estimated that the Soviets had supplied ten thousand to twelve thousand tons of equipment to Castro's regime, including six helicopters, many machine guns, and possibly tanks. The CIA further estimated that Castro commanded 32,000 ground forces and a militia said to number 200,000.

None of that made Castro a threat to invade the United States, but it gave him a formidable fighting force and overt Soviet support. Though the United States had long armed Turkey, similarly close to the Soviet Union, neither the American people nor their president was sanguine about a Communist foothold in the Americas. Eisenhower concluded that Castro was determined to place his country on a course inimically at odds with America's best interests, and he vowed to thwart it. As Ike put it to Harold Macmillan, "We shall seek and use every possible opportunity short of outright intervention which might bring pressure to bear on Castro."

In late November, Ike convened top members of his diplomatic and covert action staffs in his office. The goal was to bring together the various anti-Castro efforts and to unite them under a single command. State assumed the lead and proposed to contact President Frondizi of Argentina, whom Nixon had visited the previous year, in order to enlist his support in containing Castro. Meanwhile, the first step of the covert operation was authorized. Leaders of the State Department and CIA merged their "overt and covert actions" into a combined effort "completely geared into each other." Just as with Guatemala in 1954, the United States was prepared to organize the effort and, when the time came, presumably would support it.

Preparations unfolded quickly. Taking advantage of a friendly government in Guatemala, the Cuban fighting force trained there, armed by the United States. But even in the jungles of Guatemala, it is not easy to hide hundreds of armed men, feverishly preparing to invade their homeland—in this case, joined by some three hundred Guatemalans as well. In January, the *New York Times* reported that Cuban forces were training, and Eisenhower again urgently gathered his Cuba group to discuss how to respond. The notes of that meeting leave no doubt about what Ike intended: "He recognized that some day we will want the force to move into Cuba." If anything, Eisenhower was impatient, suggesting that "perhaps the real point is that we had best get started with our operation."

Allen Dulles, who had waffled throughout Castro's accumulation of power, now urged restraint. The operation was not ready, he insisted, and would not be for at least several months. Ike left office without ever approving an invasion.

After so many years of contemplating retirement, Eisenhower loosened his grip on power reluctantly. As a result, his final weeks were nostalgic and slightly sad. Earlier in the year, Ann Whitman had caught him in a White House hallway, musing about where his portrait might someday hang, imagining himself no longer as a president but rather as a relic. Hagerty believed that his boss was relieved to shed the burdens of his office but also regretful not to have accomplished more and worried about becoming bored.

Mamie tried to cheer up her husband. She threw herself into their final White House Christmas, bringing in a towering tree, lavish boughs, decorations, crèches. She marshaled her grandchildren to put on a Nativity play, rehearsing them relentlessly. Each child played multiple roles, switching in and out of costumes painstakingly fashioned by the First Lady herself. "The festivities," her granddaughter recalled, "were a high point for Mamie. In her last year in the White House, the spirit of Christmas had truly been captured."

Ike warmed to the holidays. He entertained the grandchildren of friends and aides on December 23, attended Christmas pageants and parties, and kept a light schedule. And as he prepared to shed the sense of duty that had guided him since he was a cadet, Eisenhower began to glimpse a new life ahead. He wrote to friends in good humor and with a special request: the restoration of informality. "During my entire life, until I came back from World War II as something of a VIP, I was known by my contemporaries as 'Ike,'" he reminded them. "Whether or not the deep friendships I enjoy have had their beginnings in the ante or post-war period, I now demand, *as my right*, that you, starting January 21, 1961, address me by that nickname. No longer do I propose to be excluded from the privileges that other friends enjoy."

Farewell

President Eisenhower looked directly into the television camera and thanked the networks for giving him time to speak to the American people. Back straight, owlish glasses fixed firmly across his broad face, notes before him because he still did not quite trust the teleprompters, Eisenhower began his "message of leave-taking and farewell."

He had considered this moment for many months. Indeed, his whole adult life had built toward it. Ike had served his nation since 1911, when he left his mother crying in Abilene as he departed for West Point and commenced a military career sprung from the unlikely bosom of the River Brethren. In the decades since, he had borne arms for his nation and secured a victory for American liberty unlike any other in history. As president, he had presided over a perilous peace, eight years of continuous threat, of nuclear arsenals and legions of armed men, of rising aspirations and mounting fears, of unrelenting ideological contest, of galloping technological progress and yawing uncertainty about where that progress would lead.

In the years since the end of the Korean War, annihilation still loomed, yet precisely one American died in combat, killed by a sniper in Lebanon. No American president of modern times had brought to the office greater skill as a soldier, yet none had done more to preserve the peace. Eisenhower, America's warrior-president, had much upon which to reflect, and he looked forward to sharing some final thoughts with his countrymen.

As far back as 1959, with the midterm elections behind him and the end of his presidency within sight, Eisenhower had begun to think about his farewell. "I want to have something to say when I leave here," Ike told his lead speechwriter, Malcolm Moos, adding that he was not interested in making a speech that was merely headline grabbing, but rather hoped to use the occasion of his farewell to say something meaningful. He imagined giving a ten-minute "farewell address" to the Congress and the American people.

Moos began to collect thoughts from stray sources—news clippings, books, suggestions. One of those suggestions came to him in 1960 and recommended that he and Ike consider the example of George Washington, another great soldier and the American leader whom Eisenhower's career most resembled. Moos was intrigued.

With Washington's second term drawing to a close, his heirs and rivals were fixated on the question of whether he would seek the presidency a third time. Exhausted by his long service, infuriated by the intrigues of politics and the stresses of nation building, Washington resolved to retire and to leave the nation with his reflections. Initially, he was inclined to deliver a defensive statement, but he was saved by a formidable speechwriter of his own, Alexander Hamilton. Hamilton at first tried to edit Washington's draft but ultimately tossed it out and started over. Together, they produced a message that would echo across the ages and find new expression in the statement Eisenhower now set out to draft.

In Washington's Farewell Address—inaptly named, as it was never delivered orally but rather distributed as a letter to American newspapers—the former general warned of the dangers of party and imagined a day when sectionalism would yield to a unified nation. He briefly decried the threat of large standing armies, though he did not reject a permanent military force altogether. Ever balanced, ever conscious of his position as a transcendent figure in early American life, Washington (with Hamilton) wrote that wise American leaders "will avoid the necessity of those overgrown military establishments which, under any form of government, are inauspicious to liberty, and which are to be regarded as particularly hostile to republican liberty."

Washington's address is often remembered for its perceptive foreign policy prescriptions, though the larger part of his farewell was devoted to the exhortation to unify the nation across its regional and party differences, a passage so prescient it no longer seems visionary. Washington's proposal for his nation's foreign policy, by contrast, has been cited time and again as the country repeatedly confronted the issues of entanglement in European affairs:

> The great rule of conduct for us in regard to foreign nations is in
> extending our commercial relations, to have with them as little politi-

cal connection as possible. So far as we have already formed engagements, let them be fulfilled with perfect good faith. Here let us stop.
Europe has a set of primary interests which to us have none; or a very
remote relation. Hence she must be engaged in frequent controversies, the causes of which are essentially foreign to our concerns. Hence,
therefore, it must be unwise in us to implicate ourselves by artificial
ties in the ordinary vicissitudes of her politics, or the ordinary combinations and collisions of her friendships or enmities.

At first interpretation, Washington's observations seem diametrically
opposed to Eisenhower's. Washington left office embroiled in controversy
over the Jay Treaty, which posed fundamental questions about the power
of the central government and its authority to make binding deals with
foreign powers. Washington believed in the Jay Treaty but warned of
ill-considered entanglement. Eisenhower, by contrast, saw entanglement as
a virtue of modern diplomacy. As NATO commander and president, he
had painstakingly woven a web of alliances as a common defense against
the encroachment of Communism. But Washington's warning was not a
command toward isolationism but rather an argument for limited, rational
engagement in order to advance America's standing and protect it from
harm. With that, Eisenhower had no quarrel. His presidency was rooted in
Washington's example: so, too, would be his farewell.

When it came time to begin drafting his Farewell Address in the fall
of 1960, Ike was still hurt by the embarrassment of the failed summit and
despondent over John Kennedy's attack on his record as well as Richard
Nixon's failure to defend it. It was a wounded Eisenhower who prepared to
leave, just as it had been a troubled Washington who laid down the burden
of leadership.

Eisenhower's speechwriters reflected on the themes of his presidency and
the world he had helped to fashion. For eight years, he had steadfastly
fended off those to his left who would risk the nation's private economy by
ignoring deficits and spending government money at will, and those to his
right who would do the same by cutting taxes and demanding unsustain-
able defense expenditures. He held off generals eager to wage war against
China or the Soviet Union and rejected those who imagined that Khrushchev, Mao, and Castro were sincere in their embrace of a durable international peace. He believed he represented a center point between those
who demanded immediate racial equality and those determined to sus-
tain discrimination. His middle way, as much a part of his character as of
his politics, had sustained Ike in his confrontation with McCarthy, in his

restrained budgets, and in his defense programs. He was as committed to balance at the end of his presidency as he was at the beginning.

But there was more to say than merely to rehash old arguments, no matter how salient. Castro had seized power in Cuba, China and the Soviet Union eyed Laos, the Congo was riotous, American politics was restless. Troubled by those threats to order, Eisenhower's aides contemplated a paean to "constructive change," a reminder that progress is generally the result of long and sustained work, not sharp breaks or impulsive leaps. Those thoughts captured Eisenhower's deep sense of order and control.

Those were natural topics for Eisenhower, familiar themes of his presidency, and expressions of his character. So too was another gnawing concern, made fresh by recent events. From the earliest weeks of his presidency, his 1953 speech to the American Society of Newspaper Editors, Ike had warned of the grave costs of maintaining a permanent war footing. In that first speech, he enumerated the real sacrifices extracted not merely by war but even by the threat of it. One bomber, he warned in 1953, represented the forfeit of "a modern brick school in more than 30 cities" or two electric power plants or two "fine, fully equipped hospitals" or fifty miles of concrete pavement. In that address, Ike had described the future as a choice: Vast expenditures on military might were "a theft from those who hunger and are not fed, those who are cold and are not clothed." Or the world could opt for war and, with it, the end of civilization in any recognizable form.

Eisenhower could take deep satisfaction in having preserved that civilization, often against great odds and pressures, but his anxiety about a militarized nation had only deepened. He witnessed the national hysteria over *Sputnik* and the quick response of the defense industry to capitalize on it; 1960, one missile maker happily pronounced, was the "best year we've had in the missile business." And he had angrily seen the American people accept Kennedy's false charge that the Soviets had opened up a "missile gap."

Consequently, Eisenhower's advisers suggested a second theme for his farewell speech. The emergence of a "permanent arms industry" could not be helped. In a nuclear era, the United States could no longer take the time to convert peacetime industries into war production once hostilities had begun. War between the United States and the Soviet Union, should it come, would be sharp and instant, overwhelmingly devastating, and over before the makers of cars or steel or appliances could convert their factories to the production of guns and tanks and other matériel. Instead, missiles needed to be at the ready, and the companies that produced them understood that their livelihoods depended on a threat of war that was both constant and intense. Moreover, those companies depended on relationships with the government in order to secure contracts and business; fortunately for them, retiring military officers brought such knowledge and connections as they left their services for work in this "military-industrial complex." This new phenomenon, an alliance between the military and its suppliers, created new perils. "Billions of dollars in purchasing power, and the livelihood of millions of people, are directly involved."

The task of marshaling those themes fell principally to Moos, a tiny, brilliant academic who had joined the administration in 1958. He took his job on the same day that Sherman Adams finally left the White House (one of Adams's last acts had been to swear him in). Moos had not immediately impressed Eisenhower. An early speech annoyed the president, who complained to Jerry Persons that he "did not think that Dr. Moos would do." Happily, however, that impression changed as Moos became familiar with Eisenhower's style. Within a few months, he had helped infuse Ike's rhetoric with a new vigor. Indeed, some of the press appraisal of the "new" Eisenhower derived from Moos's writing, and reporters openly, if somewhat misguidedly, wondered about Moos's influence.

As they honed their collaboration, Moos grew accustomed to Eisenhower's bursts of temper—so furious that Moos "sometimes thought the varnish was going to peel off the desk." And he adapted to Ike's system for preparing a draft. The president would weigh in at the outset on broad themes, then send his writers off to draft language, usually with an admonition to keep it short. "Ten minutes, no more," he often said. "You lose an audience after 10 minutes." His two main writers, Moos and Ralph Williams, would then return with their pages, at which point Ike would "lock in like a target-acquisition radar, throwing out paragraphs, changing sentences, fiddling with words, re-writing whole pages, until by the tenth draft he'd probably put more time into it than both of us combined."

Eisenhower got his first look at the draft of his Farewell Address in the fall of 1960 and, true to form, began to work it over in excruciating detail. He wrote the opening section himself and asked Milton to edit a full draft, which his brother did extensively. Over the course of twenty-nine drafts, the essential elements remained: Eisenhower wished his successor, whom he did not name, "Godspeed." He recounted his long service, called for "balance" in national affairs—a section that expanded significantly through the drafting—warned of the "hostile ideology" that confronted the United States and its allies, and identified new dangers facing America.

His changes were significant and telling: Moos described America's obligation to "enhance liberty, dignity and integrity among nations" as the obligation of "a free and Christian people." Eisenhower smartly changed that to "a free and religious people." Failure to achieve those obligations, an early draft noted, would constitute a "grievous hurt" and could be the result of "lack of effort, comprehension or readiness to sacrifice"; Ike amplified and rewrote that sentence so that it read: "Any failure traceable to arrogance, or our lack of comprehension or readiness to sacrifice would inflict upon us grievous hurt both at home and abroad." In a section of the address devoted to the importance of international diplomacy, Eisenhower added sentences to emphasize that international relations must be based on mutual respect, a relationship of "equals." "The weakest," Ike wrote, "must come to the conference table with the same confidence as we." He moved paragraphs for emphasis, elevated language, and trimmed references to himself in the first person. The Eisenhower-edited drafts were loftier, more powerful, more nuanced, and notably more modest.

The address was initially contemplated as Eisenhower's final State of the Union speech, but as that date drew closer, he became uncomfortable with a formal talk to Congress as Kennedy prepared to take office. On December 14, Norman Cousins, editor of the *Saturday Review*, called to suggest that Ike deliver a farewell address from the Oval Office and to offer his help in putting together a draft. Eisenhower liked the idea of speaking directly to the American people but rebuffed Cousins's offer of assistance. "The idea of trying to get anyone like Norman Cousins working on it would be dreadful," Whitman wrote to Moos. "How in the world do we diplomatically thank him, but say No[?]"

Through early January, Ike continued to tinker; Moos and Williams incorporated their ideas and fine-tuned passages and language. The final speech was fuller and more balanced than the early drafts, but the essential thoughts and structure remained intact.

On January 17, 1961, with Washington braced for snow, Eisenhower sat before the camera. More than seventy million Americans tuned in at 8:30 p.m. Washington time to hear the president's parting thoughts.

He spoke for sixteen minutes. His delivery was not flawless. He stumbled over a word here and there, once saying "disarmament" rather than "battlefield" before correcting himself. He mispronounced "insidious." Much of what he said was familiar. His message of balance was hardly news as he argued one last time for a government that deferred immediate reward for long-term stability. His description of Communism—"a hostile ideology, global in scope, atheistic in character, ruthless in purpose and insidious in method"—was uncommonly direct but hardly a departure from earlier speeches. Near his conclusion, however, were two remarks that were attention grabbing, one for its candor, the other for its subtle humor. Eisenhower acknowledged that he failed in his laborious efforts to bring about a lasting peace with the Soviet Union and thus left office with a "definite sense of disappointment," a surprising admission from a departing president. On a lighter note, he summed up his long service by presuming to "trust that in that service you find some things worthy; as for the rest of it, I know you will find ways to improve performance in the future." He ended his address, as he had commenced his presidency, with a prayer:

> We pray that peoples of all faiths, all races, all nations, may have their great human needs satisfied; that those now denied opportunity shall come to enjoy it to the full; that all who yearn for freedom may experience its spiritual blessings; that those who have freedom will understand, also, its heavy responsibilities; that all who are insensitive to the needs of others will learn charity; that the scourges of poverty, disease and ignorance will be made to disappear from the earth, and that, in the goodness of time, all peoples will come to live together in a peace guaranteed by the binding force of mutual respect and love.

But the speech's most enduring and provocative passages were tucked in its center. There, Ike and Moos had honed Eisenhower's foreboding about modern militarism into a sharp warning:

> Until the latest of our world conflicts, the United States had no armaments industry. American makers of plowshares could, with time and as required, make swords as well.
> But we can no longer risk emergency improvisations of national defense; we have been compelled to create a permanent armaments industry of vast proportions. Added to this, three and a half million men and women are directly engaged in the defense establishment. We annually spend on military security alone more than the net income of all United States corporations.
> This conjunction of an immense military establishment and a large arms industry is new in the American experience. The total influence—economic, political, even spiritual—is felt in every city, every state house, every office of the federal government. We recognize the imperative need for this development. Yet we must not fail to comprehend its grave implications. Our toil, resources and livelihood are all involved; so is the very structure of our society.
> In the councils of government we must guard against the acquisition of unwarranted influence, whether sought or unsought, by the

military-industrial complex. The potential for the disastrous rise of
misplaced power exists and will persist.

We must never let the weight of this combination endanger our
liberties or democratic processes. We should take nothing for granted.
Only an alert and knowledgeable citizenry can compel the proper
meshing of the huge industrial and military machinery of defense
with our peaceful methods and goals, so that security and liberty may
prosper together.

That was, as Eisenhower later wrote, "the most challenging message I could
have left with the people of this country." But it was only one of two related
passages; the second contained an equally disturbing insight:

Today, the solitary inventor, tinkering in his shop, has been overshadowed by task forces of scientists in laboratories and testing fields.

In the same fashion, the free university, historically the fountain-
head of free ideas and scientific discovery, has experienced a revolution
in the conduct of research. Partly because of the huge costs involved,
a government contract becomes virtually a substitute for intellectual
curiosity. For every old blackboard there are now hundreds of new,
electronic computers.

The prospect of domination of the nation's scholars by federal employment, project allocations and the power of money is
ever-present—and is gravely to be regarded.

Yet in holding scientific research and discovery in respect,
as we should, we must also be alert to the equal and opposite
danger that public policy could itself become the captive of a
scientific-technological elite.

Those notions sprang from the exhaustive drafting and editing of this
speech. At one point, the writers considered fusing the two, related phe-
nomena within a single phrase, the "military-industrial-scientific complex."
But that was imprecise. The danger of military influence over public policy
was that it would drive spending and encourage fear and even war. The
peril in the area of science was in one sense the opposite: federal domination of research would tend to push out other innovation and direct
too much intellectual capacity to government needs rather than to the
breadth of human possibility. The military-industrial complex is measured
by its achievements: when it prevails, government overspends on defense.
The technological-scientific elite is judged by a negative; its danger is in
research unperformed, in the great insights or innovations undiscovered,

crowded out by government-funded projects. Smartly, Eisenhower split the two notions, giving each its singular emphasis.

A telling review of those passages came later. Moos had weighed describing the union of military interest and government power as the "military-industrial-congressional complex," a description that might have tempted Eisenhower after eight years of wrestling with his congressional colleagues. But Ike had opened his speech with his reflection on his long relationship with Congress and his satisfaction with its cooperation with his administration. To then shift and accuse Congress of being a participant in a dangerous network would have seemed jarring and accusatory. The idea was dropped, having never been included in a formal draft.

There was something tender, even grandfatherly, beneath the import of Eisenhower's warnings. He spoke nostalgically of a blackboard replaced by "new, electronic computers." And he acknowledged that the growth of an armaments industry was as inevitable as it was pernicious. His remedy for these threats was neither legislation nor specific government action but rather a call to public vigilance. In his final hours as president, as in his early days as a second lieutenant in the U.S. Army, Eisenhower maintained a deep, even naive, confidence in the good sense of the American people.

Eisenhower delivered a message of stunning prescience, but it took some time for its full weight to impress itself on the American public. Just as with Washington, some of Eisenhower's message was lost, distorted, or selectively read in ways that tell more about the interpreter than about the message.

Ike had not set out to grab headlines, but most major newspapers extensively covered the speech the next day. "Eisenhower's Farewell Sees Threat to Liberties in Vast Defense Machine," the *New York Times* headline read. "Ike Warns of Danger in Massive Defense," summarized the *Los Angeles Times*. The *Wall Street Journal* focused on Eisenhower's budget but briefly reported on his address on its front page. Many papers published the full text of the address, and the *New York Times* even reprinted Ike's closing prayer on its front page.

But the first wave of editorials hinted at the degree to which some misunderstood Ike's message or underestimated its significance. The *New York Times* declined to editorialize on the speech, opting instead for a critical reprise of his presidency and concluding on a general note of appreciation: "Dwight Eisenhower will retire from office with the respect and goodwill of his countrymen. Few Presidents in the history of the United States have had a more secure hold on the affections of the American people." The

Los Angeles Times quoted the passage on the military-industrial complex and rightly noted that it reflected a president who spent his time in office "striving for the balance that it was his chief concern to maintain." Rather than explore the implications of Eisenhower's warning, however, that editorial concluded: "Surely the people are proud of this man and proud of themselves for electing him while he was available." Overridingly, the reaction was to regard the address with nostalgia for the presidency and appreciation for the president, to wish him well, and to move on rather than to dissect the import of the threats he identified to political integrity, the nation's safety, and the future of the country's intellectual life.

That would change over time as the Kennedy administration abandoned Eisenhower's defense strategy, exchanging its heavy reliance on the threat of nuclear retaliation for a more flexible ability to confront Communism around the world, first at the Bay of Pigs and then in Vietnam. Vast American resources and many American lives were sacrificed in that struggle, and Eisenhower's military-industrial complex seemed culpable to many. Critics of the Vietnam War imagined Eisenhower's prophecy to be part of their rhetorical heritage, though they often misconstrued his deliberately chosen words. Ike had not blamed the military-industrial complex for corrupting American life, had not suggested that it should be denied all influence. The need for a permanent armaments industry, he recognized, was "imperative," even if its implications were grave. But Ike's words captured an essential element of American militarism: some interests depended on an armed and frightened nation; they would consistently urge action where prudence might have suggested otherwise.

Meanwhile, Eisenhower's equally incisive critique of the power of government to direct research went largely unremarked, perhaps because the "scientific-technological elite" seemed less dangerous, less frightening. And yet just as Eisenhower was right to warn of unwarranted influence by those who depended upon war and the threat of war, so, too, was he correct to wonder at the substitution of government research for individual innovation. We can witness the new technologies unveiled in the service of defense or oil exploration; we can only wonder at the breakthroughs undiscovered. Universities, heavily dependent on government contracts, produced what they did in the late twentieth century; we can never know what they did not.

By the twenty-first century, few could doubt the enduring place of the military-industrial complex in American life. The defense establishment came to absorb private industry increasingly into its own ranks. Support

services for American troops in Ike's day were the province of the Pentagon; Eisenhower's invasion force was fed, clothed, and supplied with fuel by
military men and women.

In the Iraq wars, food, communications, and even security for American
troops and civilians were largely the province of contractors. Those contractors depended on government payments, and they sought influence over the
government at all levels. Boeing, Blackwater, Halliburton—these became
the point of the spear of the military-industrial complex, the recipients of
government largesse, and the suppliers of American logistics and power.
In 2001, after a closely divided American election, George Bush became
president. Seated beside him was Vice President Dick Cheney, the former
chief executive officer of Halliburton. The military-industrial complex now
had an elected representative in the White House. On March 19, 2003,
America went to war for a second time in Iraq, a conflict initially estimated
to cost the American people $50 billion. (When one White House aide
suggested it could reach $100 to $200 billion, Secretary of Defense Donald Rumsfeld called it "baloney." The official who argued otherwise was
fired.) Instead, Iraq ballooned into a war longer and costlier than World
War II; by the time the last combat brigade had departed Iraq in 2010,
the war had killed more than forty-four hundred soldiers and drained the
national treasury of more than $750 billion, much of it spent on private
contractors—one Halliburton division alone, KBR, was paid more than
$11 billion for its work from 2002 to 2004; overall, private contractors
received as much government money as the initial estimates for fighting
the entire war. Against such facts, Ike's warnings seemed profoundly true.

Moreover, the corrupting and interlocking relationship that Eisenhower
described in 1961 would find expression in other walks of American life.
Pharmaceutical companies and prison guards, public employee unions
and major construction concerns, automakers, energy firms, and agricultural enterprises all were among the interests that had come to depend
on government support—in the form of either contracts or regulatory
consideration—leading them to cultivate influence in Washington. The
result was a culture of lobbying, campaign contributions, and corporate
influence that amplified Eisenhower's original warning and sapped public
confidence in the integrity of government. That sobering trend reached its
apotheosis in 2010, when the U.S. Supreme Court ruled that corporations
possess free-speech rights that entitle them to full participation in politics. With that, the military-industrial complex and its many descendants
secured not just power but constitutional protection.

Those were the proof of Eisenhower's prescience. But they were generations away when he delivered his warnings. In the meantime, Ike quietly concluded his presidency and prepared to retire to the edge of the Gettysburg battlefield, to end his days as a philosopher-farmer in the tradition of Washington himself. On the morning after his speech, Ike awoke to the appreciative reflections on his presidency. He sparred with reporters at a friendly, final news conference and then met with Nixon. In the afternoon, he presented medals to a few of his most trusted aides, their families proudly looking on. Half a world away, Patrice Lumumba paid the heavier price in the struggle for power in the Congo. Captured by his rivals, bound, and badly beaten, Lumumba and other government foes were lined up before a tree and shot at almost precisely the moment that Eisenhower delivered his farewell. Lumumba was thirty-five years old.

Promptly at 9:00 a.m. on January 19, Kennedy arrived with his senior cabinet designees; he and Ike met privately for a few minutes, then with Christian Herter and Dean Rusk, the outgoing and incoming secretaries of state; Thomas Gates and Robert McNamara, the outgoing and incoming secretaries of defense; and Bob Anderson, the departing secretary of the Treasury, and his designated successor, Douglas Dillon, one of the few Ike aides whom Kennedy retained. Jerry Persons and Clark Clifford, personal aides to the two presidents, attended as well.

Kennedy began by asking about Laos, and Eisenhower warned him of the complexities there. The loss of that country to Communism, he said, would open the "cork in the bottle," and the rest of the Far East might collapse. Kennedy had been elected on a promise to act, had campaigned on the argument that Eisenhower had been too willing to allow Communism to gain ground. He probed his predecessor for some way to halt another loss of territory, in this case to keep the Chinese at bay. Ike offered little. It was, he said, like playing poker with tough stakes. His commitment to massive retaliation—and his refusal to countenance the use of nuclear weapons to decide limited wars—persisted to his final moments in office.

Many members of Ike's staff, trapped by the snow overnight in Washington, spent a final night at the White House, bunked in meeting rooms. Bleary the next day, they bade Eisenhower farewell, many with tears in their eyes. Eisenhower shook their hands, praised their service, acknowledged their devotion. Then he joined Kennedy on the Capitol steps to complete the transfer of power that has been an essential symbol of American democracy since Washington handed authority to John Adams. Eisenhower listened as Kennedy delivered an address that was stirring, youthful, and poetic—and unmistakably laced with rejection of his predecessor. "Let the word go forth from this time and place," Kennedy proclaimed, a sour-faced Eisenhower behind him, "to friend and foe alike, that the torch has been passed to a new generation of Americans—born in this century, tempered by war, disciplined by a hard and bitter peace, proud of our ancient heritage—and unwilling to witness or permit the slow undoing of those human rights to which this nation has always been committed, and to which we are committed today at home and around the world."

The passage that signaled a more profound reassessment of America's role in the world was not found in the speech's triumphalism. Nor was it found in Kennedy's historic call to service: "Ask not what your country can do for you; ask what you can do for your country." Rather, it was in Kennedy's pledge to all the countries of the world. "Let every nation know," he said, "whether it wishes us well or ill, that we shall pay any price, bear any burden, meet any hardship, support any friend, oppose any foe, to assure the survival and the success of liberty."

For eight years, Eisenhower had fought such grandiosity, had specifically hedged America's promises and insisted that balance was the linchpin of liberty. Now Kennedy reimagined America as limitlessly in pursuit of that ambition. Henceforth, he argued, the nation would "bear any burden" in defense of American values. Soon enough, Kennedy would learn the full measure of that burden.

Once Kennedy was sworn in, Ike and Mamie attended a lunch in their honor, then quietly slipped away. John was at the wheel. As they approached Gettysburg, students from two nearby schools—the same ones whose youngsters had welcomed him home after his heart attack in 1955—lined the road to wave. The Eisenhowers arrived at the gate, and the Secret Service escort turned around and headed back to Washington. Ike and Mamie dined that night with John and Barbara and their children at the schoolhouse on the edge of the Gettysburg farm. As they sat, John raised his glass in a toast to his father. "I suppose that tonight we welcome back a member of this clan who has done us proud," he said. Ike was too choked up to speak, joining only as his family sounded "hear, hear."

After forty-six years of service, President Eisenhower was again Ike. He was a private citizen at last.

Dwight and Mamie retired to Gettysburg, to the home they had rebuilt and the life they had long postponed. They were accompanied by John and Delores Moaney, a congenial black couple who worked as valet and cook. Ike painted and golfed; Mamie enjoyed her soap operas and the sunroom of the Gettysburg porch. Friends arranged for them to have a second place in Palm Desert, California, and thereafter they split their year.

Ike had always enjoyed play—he bounded from his car at Augusta to get to the links—but now that he had time for leisure, he missed work. "Dad was not a happy ex-president," John recalled. He felt rejected by Nixon's defeat, and his concern for the direction of the country was exacerbated by Kennedy's deliberate and sustained repudiation of his presidency. The old had given way to the new, and Eisenhower understood where that placed him.

Nixon's bitter loss, combined with the party's exasperating inability to produce a quality leadership core, left the GOP once again without an identifiable leader, so that mantle fell back on Ike. "Damn, they've had me busy," he grumbled to his son after one particularly eventful stretch. "I had more time in the White House to paint than I do now."

It was mostly time spent in the wilderness, shunned by Kennedy and his new generation of leadership. Maxwell Taylor, whose *Uncertain Trumpet* was devoted to rebutting Eisenhower's defense strategy in favor of "flexible response," was much admired by Kennedy, and Taylor's return to influence underscored the sharp rejection of Eisenhower's most considered strategic wisdom. More stinging was Kennedy's deliberate use of Eisenhower's leadership as a foil; just as he had during the campaign, Kennedy positioned himself as an emblem of energy and change, devoted to invigorating a Washington that had grown stale under Ike's aging, inattentive reign. Eisenhower understood the strategy—to friends, he compared it to FDR's vilification of Hoover—but he was not immune to it. Even the administration's belated acknowledgment that there was, in fact, no "missile gap" was admitted without apology to Eisenhower.

Eisenhower was wounded, naturally. His views of the "Washington scene," he confided to an old friend in 1961, "are not particularly flattering." Kennedy, he said to another, surrounded himself with "men who confuse 'smartness' with wisdom." (In that same note, Eisenhower hinted at his deeper contempt, referring to his successor as "young President Kennedy.") Still, he remained dutifully at the president's call, and Kennedy reciprocated with courtesies. When friends of Eisenhower's secured a bill to restore his rank as a general—a position that gave him back the title he had spent most of his life pursuing and allowed him to maintain a military aide—Kennedy was puzzled but happy to go along. He signed the legislation. Thereafter, President Eisenhower was addressed as "General."

More substantively, Kennedy sought out Ike in the aftermath of the administration's first significant blunder, the catastrophe at the Bay of Pigs. The invasion, of course, had long been contemplated by Eisenhower, who had authorized planning for it more than a year earlier. When Kennedy approved the assault, however, he botched the execution: the first strike on the Cuban air force was unsuccessful, and a second was called off when Kennedy feared American involvement would be detected; the landing spot was ill chosen; and the entire enterprise depended on an intelligence assumption that proved false, namely, that the Cuban people would greet the invasion force as liberators and turn against Castro. Instead, the four-teen hundred invaders were easily repelled, all but a few killed or captured. Chagrined, Kennedy sought out Eisenhower. He sent a helicopter to Get-tysburg, which picked up Ike and shuttled him to Camp David.

"No one knows how tough this job is until after he has been in it a few months," Kennedy lamented to Eisenhower.

"Mr. President," Ike responded, "if you'll forgive me, I think I mentioned that to you three months ago."

"I certainly have learned a lot since," Kennedy conceded.

Kennedy reviewed the planning and execution of the invasion, and Eisen-hower gently corrected the flaws in his approach. They parted respectfully, some of the campaign and early administration rancor behind them, but wary of each other still.

Mindful that his legacy was under attack in Washington, Eisenhower devoted substantial energy in retirement to construction of his own place in history. The mainstay of that effort was his memoirs—two volumes devoted to the presidency, with each roughly tracking his terms. Unlike the hell-bent effort that produced *Crusade in Europe* in just a few months, *Mandate for Change* and *Waging Peace* were constructed more methodically, and Ike's participation was more supervisory, as he delegated most of the writing to Bill Ewald, who researched domestic issues, and his son, John, who handled national security and international relations. The work began immediately after Ike left office—John and Ewald set up an office at Get-tysburg the Monday after Kennedy's inauguration—and stretched over years.

Although Ewald and John Eisenhower played the dominant role in those works, both had mastered Ike's writing style, and the books capture both his tone and his approach: dignified and painstaking, if somewhat guarded and occasionally defensive. They admit few errors—never a strong suit for presidential memoirs—but diligently and accurately record Eisenhower's active management of his own administration, and thus form a persuasive counterweight to the misimpression fostered by Kennedy that Ike was disengaged from his presidency.

At the same time, Eisenhower quietly worked to burnish his reputation in other ways. He rationed interviews, granting them only to those writers in whom he and John saw the promise of careful and favorable treatment. When, for instance, the Associated Press reporter Pat Morin contacted Ike about the possibility of writing a biography, John screened Morin's work and found it worthy. "I feel sure that the book will be friendly," he wrote to his father, "since it is being done in the same vein as the Associated Press book on Churchill." Morin was given access to Eisenhower's papers and allowed to interview the former president on several occasions.

In addition, Milton urged his brother to organize and quickly make available his presidential papers, which, like his memoirs, would record his active role in his presidency. Milton put the idea to Ike in March 1962. Once he had his brother's approval, the ten-year project was launched, and a conservative curator, Alfred DuPont Chandler Jr., was hired to manage it. He in turn brought a promising young historian, Stephen Ambrose, to assist. Although Ambrose would later wildly exaggerate his access to Eisenhower, Ike used the historian effectively, dispatching him to contest work critical of his war and presidential records.

Despite their differences, Eisenhower and Kennedy kept up courtesies. In August 1963, Ike and Mamie wrote to express their "profound sympathy" when Patrick Kennedy, born on August 7, died two days later. President Kennedy wrote back for himself and his wife. "Your message," he said, "was a comfort to me and my family."

Eisenhower was in New York on November 22, when he was pulled from a meeting that afternoon and told that Kennedy had been shot. He returned to his room at the Waldorf Astoria and headed home to Gettysburg that night.

In the national mourning that followed, Eisenhower was affected, of course. He and Mamie felt for young Jackie and her children. Eisenhower expressed his "sense of shock and dismay" at the "despicable act" and urged Americans to "join as one man in expressing not only their grief but indignation at this act." And yet Eisenhower also was a bit mystified at the grief that followed President Kennedy's death. Ike had sent many men to die. He understood sacrifice, demanded it of others, offered it himself. The convulsions that gripped America in those weeks seemed extravagant to a man so deeply imbued with duty to country. He was, his son reflected decades later, "a little bit bewildered as to why all the fuss."

Johnson was far more solicitous of Ike, and the general now found more enemies within his own party. Barry Goldwater, Arizona's cantankerous conservative senator, claimed the spiritual leadership of Ike's party in the aftermath of Nixon's defeat. Goldwater's candidacy was explicitly a rejection of Eisenhower's moderation. Ike spent eight years fending off the forces of extremism. To Goldwater, extremism was no vice.

Ike tried to head off Goldwater during the Republican primaries in 1964, then tepidly supported him once he was the Republican nominee. But he made little secret of his unhappiness. Privately, he was astounded. Goldwater, he confided to his grandson, "is just plain dumb."

Eisenhower was seventy-four when Johnson won his election, and Ike's health began to ebb. Visiting Augusta in November 1965, he had his second heart attack, then a third two days later. From that point on, Eisenhower's retreat from public life accelerated. Still, he stayed active enough to be afraid for his country. Johnson's halfhearted approach to the war in Vietnam frustrated Eisenhower, who argued that if the United States were to wage a war, it should do so with overwhelming force. Torn by his affection for Johnson and his displeasure over the dominant national security issue of the Johnson years, Ike became cranky and fulminated about "kooks" and "hippies."

Even Eisenhower's fabled Farewell Address, by this point claiming the attention it deserved, conflicted its author, especially as it was invoked to denigrate the American war in Vietnam. To former military and business friends, Ike downplayed the significance of the speech, offering that perhaps he had overstated his case or that it would have been more appropriate from another source; to others, he continued to profess pride in his prescient warning.

One exchange in particular captures Eisenhower's mixed feelings about the most quoted words of his presidency. In 1966, Stanley Karson, a representative of a group called the American Veterans Committee, wrote to Eisenhower to solicit a letter from him on the fifth anniversary of the speech. Ike drafted one in response, thanking Karson for his interest in the speech and describing weapons expenditures as "in essence, futile, costly and deadening so far as constructive progress is concerned." Before sending the reply, however, Eisenhower shared it with Bryce Harlow, his former aide then working for Procter & Gamble. Harlow warned that the group was "way out" and cautioned against giving aid to its cause. Ike deleted the revealing sentence.

By 1968, Eisenhower had known Richard Nixon for sixteen years, since they formed the Republican ticket in Ike's first campaign for public office.

They had been through travails and misunderstandings. Eisenhower would never quite understand why Nixon had so much trouble connecting with those around him or impressing voters, but he appreciated him. Moreover, Ike saw growth. "He is now even more mature and well-informed than when he was Vice President," Eisenhower wrote to George Humphrey in 1967.

Now, as Eisenhower faded, Nixon returned, both to the apex of American politics and to Ike's personal fold. Over Thanksgiving weekend of 1967, David Eisenhower and Julie Nixon announced to their families that they intended to marry (David, afraid that Ike would disapprove of his marrying so young, avoided telling him directly). Eisenhower was delighted at his grandson's good fortune, and he adored Julie Nixon. But he had vowed to stay out of the Republican presidential campaign in 1968. He was close to Johnson and shadowed by the ugly Goldwater campaign of 1964. Now, as his grandson and Nixon's daughter prepared to unite their families, Ike recognized that it would be especially difficult on Nixon if he remained neutral in this race. As he weighed whether to violate his self-prohibition on endorsing in the Republican primaries, Ike's health intervened again.

On April 29, after a labored round of golf in Palm Springs, Eisenhower suffered another heart attack. He recuperated for a time in California and then was transferred to Walter Reed to take up his familiar suite. To the amazement of his doctors, he rebounded. "He is a man of great courage," one said. "He is a man of great fortitude. He has a fine physical constitution. And he is a religious man."

As he recuperated, Mamie urged him to make a statement for Nixon, as did John. Friends of both men lobbied, while Nixon himself held back, unwilling to be seen as seeking special treatment on the basis of their soon-to-be family connection. Finally, on July 18, Ike issued the endorsement that Nixon wanted but could not bring himself to solicit. Ike cited Nixon's "intellect, acuity, decisiveness, warmth and above all his integrity . . . I feel that the security, prosperity and solvency of the United States and the cause of world peace will best be served by placing Dick Nixon in the White House in January 1969."

Ike's open support helped push Nixon through the final obstacles in the way of his nomination—talk of a Rockefeller-Reagan ticket was squelched—and Eisenhower, again from his hospital room, addressed the Republican National Convention, meeting that year in Miami Beach. On the evening of August 5, a gaunt Eisenhower was beamed into the convention, and he gave a short talk to the delegates. The following morning, he suffered yet another heart attack. Nixon accepted his party's nomination later that week. "I say," Nixon urged the delegates, "let's win this one for Ike."

Nixon's victory delighted Eisenhower, and the president-elect did his old boss the courtesy of soliciting his views on forming a cabinet and a government. Barbara Anne was married in November, but Ike could not attend, nor was he able to leave the hospital for David and Julie's wedding in December. He now was on a steeply downward slope. He still managed to flirt with the nurses, over whom Mamie kept a careful eye. ("He was an old man, but after all he'd survived, you never knew," she remarked later.) But he tired of Walter Reed and sank further into quiet. An abdominal operation in March weakened him, and by month's end he was despairing, the famous optimism slipping away.

Ike's wife, son, and grandson were at his side on the morning of March 28 when Ike barked out an order: "Lower the shades!" He then commanded his doctor and his son, "Pull me up." They lifted him partway, and he grumbled, "Two big men. Higher," he added. They did.

Sitting as he wanted, Eisenhower turned to John and spoke softly. "I want to go," he said. "God take me." The doctor administered a sedative, and Ike fell back asleep. He never spoke again. Three hours later, at 12:35 p.m. on March 28, 1969, Dwight Eisenhower died.

Epilogue

The 1950s sit nestled between two much-examined decades—the 1940s, with its great war, and the 1960s, with its cultural upheaval. One result has been to overlook the complexity of those deceptively eventful, tumultuous years, as well as that of the man who governed through them. Far from an era of consensus, the 1950s featured the rise and fall of McCarthyism and the early struggles for civil rights, sexual liberation, and feminism. The decade had bobby socks and backyard barbecues, but it also gave Americans *The Old Man and the Sea*, *The Catcher in the Rye*, *Invisible Man*, "Howl," *On the Waterfront*, and *Rebel Without a Cause*. It was jazz and Elvis, *Playboy* magazine and the Pill. Marilyn Monroe blossomed in the 1950s and barely outlived them; Julius and Ethel Rosenberg were executed as the nation fought through subversion, real and imagined, and the unsettling struggle of the Korean War. It was an age of the Red Scare, and also Castro, Che Guevara, C. Wright Mills, and Martin Luther King. And it was an epoch of perpetual danger, as two superpowers wrestled with the sudden acquisition of unimaginably destructive power, intent on burying each other but uncertain of how to win without dying.

President Eisenhower was determined that Americans should enjoy the fruits of their freedom, and he set out to wean the nation from its addiction to crisis. Americans, he believed, would only fully secure the blessings of their liberty if allowed to pursue it with tranquility. More than any man of his era, Ike gave Americans that chance. He won the future of the West on the battlefields of Europe and then nurtured it as president, patiently marking progress, steadfastly confronting the great menace of his era—Soviet Communism—without resort to global confrontation.

Eisenhower was the first American president to have access to atomic weapons and not use them. He refrained when they might have ended the Korean War, when they might have saved the French garrison at Dien Bien Phu, when they might have repelled Chinese aggression against Taiwan or Soviet threats to Berlin. He refused when his advisers begged him to use those weapons and when they urged him to develop plans for fighting smaller nuclear wars in remote areas of the world. We can only wonder how humanity's course might have been different had Eisenhower acceded to those who believed America would have been best served by use of the weapons under his control.

He was a good man, one of integrity and decency. But he was not always right. He was too enamored of covert action, and he did not fully apprehend the moral imperatives of civil rights, where his belief in measured progress, the middle way, impeded his sympathy for those who demanded their constitutional rights immediately. There, however, his record was better than his instincts. Guided by a style of leadership gleaned from his long military career—from emulation of Fox Conner and George Marshall and from rejection of Douglas MacArthur—Eisenhower knew that capable subordinates required the support of their boss. In this case, President Eisenhower relied on the leadership of Herbert Brownell and, because of it, registered the nation's most significant progress toward racial equality since the end of the Civil War. Brownell picked judges and justices, advanced programs and policies; Eisenhower, despite his limitations, knew well enough that progress required him to go along. If Earl Warren and the Supreme Court sometimes baffled or annoyed him, Eisenhower nevertheless followed their commands. And when the South threatened to defy the Court, Ike restored order and supremacy by force, as only he could.

Eisenhower was a conservative man, raised to believe in industry and thrift. He did not believe that government could or should substitute for individual initiative, and he adhered to Republican notions of private enterprise. He was, however, refreshingly unbound by partisanship. He won approval of the Civil Rights Act of 1957 with Democratic and Republican support; he championed the St. Lawrence Seaway and the Interstate Highway System even when his brother grumbled about his tolerance for socialism. When President Eisenhower was frustrated by Congress, it was more often McCarthy or Knowland who bedeviled him than liberal Democrats.

His legacy at the U.S. Supreme Court suggests Ike's lack of concern for ideological or partisan orthodoxy. Of his five appointees, one, Charles

Whittaker, can be regarded as unsuited to the position, and he did not last long. Of the others, Potter Stewart and John Harlan were conservative Republicans, Warren was a liberal Republican, and William Brennan was a liberal Democrat. Few presidents can point to a broader or more consequential range of appointees to that bench. They unanimously advanced the cause of social justice, and they did so because Ike put them there to do it.

Ike's patient pursuit of progress, his faith in his subordinates, and his rejection of doctrinaire partisanship combined to produce an American triumph in the two great challenges of his epoch: black Americans secured the right to join the society that once enslaved them, and all Americans outlasted Soviet Communism without a war of annihilation to defeat it. As Ike understood better than those around him, peace gave America time. In the fullness of that time, America fulfilled the destiny its founders imagined for it.

Dwight Eisenhower left his nation freer, more prosperous, and more fair. Peace was not given to him; he won it.

ACKNOWLEDGMENTS

Before this book was mine, it belonged to my editor, whose foresight imagined these pages and whose insight enriched them. Phyllis Grann, as all who know her know well, is far more than an editor. She is a reader of the first order, a sharp-eyed cultural critic, a shrewd businesswoman, a discerning gourmand, and, I'm happy to report, my friend. I am grateful to her for bringing me to this project and for sharing it with me.

Equally instrumental has been my extraordinary agent, Tina Bennett. Tina is responsible for my life as a book writer, and I am so deeply in her debt, so lastingly grateful for her guidance, acumen, and wisdom that I have long ago lost the ability to thank her properly. This must suffice.

Though I owe special debts to Phyllis and Tina—and their capable and cheerful assistants, Jackie Montalvo, Daniel Meyer, and Svetlana Katz—they head a long list. One who deserves special note is Ingrid Sterner, who copyedited the manuscript with deftness and care, reminding me of my lifelong debt to copy editors whose exacting labors are the unsung strength of both daily journalism and the work of making books.

The staff of the Dwight D. Eisenhower Presidential Library and Museum has supplied more knowledge and answered more questions than anyone should ever be asked to do on behalf of a writer. Several people there are worthy of special note: Tim Rives, deputy director, shared his insights into Ike's life and presidency; my appreciation for Tim is enhanced further by his kind willingness to read the manuscript and spot errors and omissions. Valoise Armstrong shepherded me through more than a dozen weeklong visits to Abilene, Kansas, guiding me to valuable material and making my trips there as pleasant as they were productive. In the reading room,

Chalsea Millner and Catherine Cain were good-natured, professional, and patient with my endless requests for help and my thousands of trips to the copy machine. Kathy Fruss helped identify and select appropriate images from the library's vast collection. Finally, Karl Weissenbach, who oversees this exemplary enterprise, was a gracious host who introduced me to members of the interlocking Eisenhower-Nixon family. Karl's institution is a credit to his leadership.

The bulk of this book is built on the holdings of the Eisenhower Library, but is supplemented by materials elsewhere, and thus owes its existence to the wisdom of librarians at Dartmouth College's Rauner Library; the Manuscript Division of the Library of Congress; the California State Archives in Sacramento; the Truman, Kennedy, and Johnson presidential libraries; and the Hoover Institution at Stanford University. To each, I am beholden. Thanks, too, to the University of California, Los Angeles, which honored me with a teaching position and a senior fellowship, allowing me to conduct much research in UCLA's astonishing libraries. Visits to those libraries meant absences from my day job at the *Los Angeles Times,* where my colleagues perform noble, sometimes heroic, work under difficult circumstances. I appreciate the paper's willingness to tolerate my double life, and am especially indebted to my assistant, Linda Hall, for maintaining that complicated balance.

I owe thanks not just to those who contributed directly to the research and writing but also to those whose thoughts enriched it, whose welcomes I overstayed, and whose friendships I treasure. Steve Stroud and Carol Stogsdill are grand souls who fortify our lives; they have given our family our summers for a decade, and many are the passages of this book that have taken shape on their Wisconsin dock or in the quiet woods beyond. Brad Hall and Julia Louis-Dreyfus bring warmth and fellowship into our family beyond measure, and they, too, have hosted us more times than I can recall—the descriptions of the Eisenhower administration's attempt to destabilize the Sukarno government were incongruously drafted at their Santa Barbara home, as far as one can imagine from Indonesia and covert action. Chris and Sarah Capel have enveloped us with their faith and grace, not to mention our annual respite with them and Sarah's mother, the magnificent Virginia Beeton Brown; there, too, is a link to these pages, as the descriptions of Ike's Farewell Address were written in their guesthouse on the banks of the Chesapeake Bay. Kelly Baker and Whitney Ellerman have put me up on many a visit to Washington, including a hasty trip that sealed the research on this book; their welcome is matched by their cheer and overwhelming goodness. And then there are Paul and Victoria Barrosse, without whom no holiday in our home is complete; Paul and Victoria radiate a spirited love of history that infects this book and makes me forever appreciative of their good company. Finally, I take this opportunity to thank those closest to me for longest: my parents, Jim and Barbara Newton, and my brother, John Newton. I owe my Newtons, well, everything.

Several others deserve special mention. JR Moehringer, my dear friend since our clerk days at the *New York Times* and the best writer I know, talked me through many crises. Henry Weinstein was, as he always has been, a font of wisdom and courage. And Bill McIntyre, whom I first relied upon in high school and who ever since has been there with kindness and wit, is among those I most admire on earth. Finally, my friend and colleague Tim Rutten offered boundless intelligence about the Eisenhower years and did me the extraordinary favor of reading the manuscript.

This is a book built largely on documents, but it also involved a number of interviews, two of which were essential. Colonel Clinton Ancker III, introduced to me by our mutual friend Will Gates, gave up a morning to educate me on military history and Eisenhower's abilities as a general. Those were invaluable insights that helped focus the book's early chapters. And most significant of all was John Eisenhower, who set aside his reluctance to tutor yet another writer on the life and accomplishments of his father and allowed me to visit with him on those subjects. John is a shrewd and thoughtful analyst, as well as a captivating writer with a practiced eye for detail and story. As a result, our time together and the exchanges of countless messages brought Ike to life for me.

In acknowledging those to whom I owed debts after my first book, I recounted the mentors and colleagues who have left deep impressions on me. I will not repeat those encomiums here, except to say that James Reston, Bill Kovach, Sonny Rawls, and John Carroll remain, individually and collectively, the bearers of a standard to which I aspire.

One further note is in order, as it regards those men and their work. Immersion in the history of the 1950s entails deep study of the many currents of life in that period. Thankfully, the story of those years was painstakingly and memorably captured in the journalism of the era. Week after week, the *New York Times* of the 1950s devoted acres of newsprint to publish transcripts of the McCarthy hearings, the debates of the United Nations, and the public addresses of Eisenhower and Stevenson; Dulles, Nixon, and Kennedy; and other leading figures of the day. When Scotty Reston broke the news of the Oppenheimer security board inquiry, the next day's paper carried not just his scoop but also the full text of the letters exchanged between Oppenheimer and the AEC. That is a tribute to

Reston, of course, but also to publishers who understood service. Devotion to chronicling society in all its serious complexity was an article of faith for American newspapers in their heyday—not just at the *Times* but also at the *New York Herald Tribune*, the *Washington Post*, and, late to the enterprise, the *Los Angeles Times*. The stewards of American journalism at its apex understood that it was expensive and difficult, that it was a job for serious, seasoned people, not amateurs, poseurs, or profiteers. They spent lavishly and constructed a vital business as well as a sustaining culture. It is a lesson that no engaged citizen should forget but that, sadly, many have.

Finally, as always, there are two people whose love overarches all these pages and transcends the normal expressions of gratitude: my wife, Karlene Goller, and my son, Jack Newton.

Karlene's gifts to me are innumerable. They start with wisdom and counsel and thankfully include much patience. Karlene read and reread these pages as they piled up, formed and re-formed. She prodded me toward a fuller, more human rendering of Ike: when my impulses tugged me toward the *Congressional Record*, she gently countered by wondering about Mamie. When we traveled together, I angled for the files at the Library of Congress; she took me to West Point and Gettysburg. The result: every draft improved with her suggestions, and the book became, I hope, one centered not on the presidency so much as on the president. For Karlene, that was no small sacrifice. She invested time and patience despite her crucial duties as the *Los Angeles Times*'s newsroom counsel, and to the exclusion of reading for fun for years on end. As a journalist, I am awestruck by her commitment to excellence; as her husband, I am ecstatically grateful for her goodness. Our marriage is the sustaining force of my life. I wake to it in wonder every morning.

When I began the business of writing books, Jack Newton was four years old. As this book goes to press, he is fourteen. Once a spirited little boy, he is now a captivating young man, complete with his own style, music, culture, and intelligence. He is, to my astonishment and thrill, a study in independence. And yet he has happily grown up with Earl Warren and Dwight D. Eisenhower. That has given me much pleasure and many opportunities to celebrate. To cite just one: when Jack was in eighth grade, as I was nearing the end of this book, he chose as a topic for a class project *Brown v. Board of Education*, which he dissected with aplomb, fresh insight, and arresting imagery. Such are the epiphanies of our overlapping lives. Having always loved my son, I now have the great joy of admiring him as well.

My life is dedicated to Karlene and Jack. So is this book.

NOTES

INTRODUCTION

1 *in twelve years: New York Times*, May 2, 1958.

1 *one meeting of consequence:* May 1, 1960, Presidential Appointment Books, DDEPL.

1 *through a mild recession:* Polling data courtesy of the APP, at http://www .presidency.ucsb.edu/data/popularity.php?pres=34&sort=time&direct=DESC& Submit=DISPLAY.

2 *"by the device of wishful thinking":* Editorial, *New York Times*, May 2, 1958.

2 *"He is moved by forces":* Childs, *Captive Hero*, p. 47.

2 *"as a weak president":* Ibid., p. 292.

3 *"to resist a Soviet attack":* 364th NSC Meeting, May 1, 1958, box 10, NSC Series, Whitman File.

3 *"urgent for us to develop":* Ibid.

3 *"In short, the United States":* Ibid.

5 *he called it a day:* May 1, 1958, Presidential Appointment Books.

CHAPTER 1: THE LESSONS OF FAMILY

9 *decamped for Kansas and college:* DDE, *At Ease*, p. 78.

10 *a confrontation with the ex-partner:* Ibid., pp. 31–32. Edgar Eisenhower, who went on to become a lawyer, said his mother used to joke that he was drawn to the law because she had been reading so many law books while she was pregnant with him.

10 *her third son:* DDE Personal folder, Name Series, Whitman File.

10 *serious to the point of being glum:* John Eisenhower, *Strictly Personal*, p. 16.

10 *"I have seldom seen":* McCallum, *Six Roads from Abilene*, p. 42. Although McCallum is the author of *Six Roads*, it is, in effect, an extended and authorized inter-

view with Ike's brother Edgar and thus constitutes Edgar's recollections of their childhood.

10   *six hundred followers in the area:* For a brief history of the River Brethren, see http://www.reformedreader.org/riverbrethren.htm.

10   *as the name suggests, to biblical study:* McCallum, *Six Roads from Abilene*, p. 86. Although the Bible Students would migrate into the Jehovah's Witnesses and both David and Ida would become Witnesses, the Eisenhower brothers never joined and took pains to suppress their parents' connection to the religion; David also eventually rejected the Witnesses. The Witnesses were intensely controversial in the early twentieth century, refusing to acknowledge the legitimacy of the American government and declining to salute the flag, as well as predicting the imminent end of days. None of that made it appealing for Ike to discuss his parents' affiliation with the Witnesses as he assumed an ever more prominent place in American life.

10   *to control a brooding temper:* Ibid., p. 30.

10   *"He was not one to be trifled with":* DDE to Edgar, June 30, 1953, Edgar Eisenhower 1953 (1) folder, Name Series, Whitman File.

11   *"a very capable and interesting boy":* Minnie Stewart to DDE, Feb. 10, 1946, I. Stewart–W. Stewart (Misc.) folder, box 105, Principal File, Pre-presidential Papers, DDEPL.

11   *"Baseball, football, boxing":* DDE, interview with Pat Morin, Aug. 5, 1965, AP-1 Pat Morin folder, box 2, 1965 Principal File, Post-presidential Papers, DDEPL.

11   *trick-or-treat with his older brothers:* DDE, *At Ease*, p. 51.

12   *"Which son do you mean?":* "The Eisenhowers of Kansas," Reynolds–R. Reynolds folder, box 95, Principal File, Pre-presidential Papers.

12   *"would philosophize":* DDE, interview with Morin, Aug. 5, 1965, p. 3.

12   *leg and the boy were saved:* Ibid., p. 5.

12   *"martyr to duty":* Gravestone in Abilene graveyard.

12   *devotion to Westerns:* John Eisenhower, exchange with author, Sept. 27, 2010.

13   *"Never . . . negotiate with an adversary":* DDE, *At Ease*, p. 30.

13   *"quiet, orderly movement":* Ibid., p. 82.

13   *to work in a local doctor's office:* Ibid., p. 36.

13   *"hot-tempered and quarrelsome":* Ibid., p. 34.

14   *prospect of a free education:* DDE, interview with Morin, Aug. 5, 1965.

14   *entrance examination for Annapolis:* Ibid.

14   *too old to be admitted:* DDE, *At Ease*, p. 105.

14   *heard his mother cry:* Susan Eisenhower, *Mrs. Ike*, p. 30.

14   *"clear blue eyes":* Ibid., p. 34.

15   *about ten days later:* Morin to Mamie, note, and her reply, Nov. 4, 1965, Memoranda (for the Record of Files) (1), box 2, 1965 Principal File, Post-presidential Papers.

15   *a 1912 football game against Tufts:* Ann Whitman, April 5, 1960, entry, April 1960 (2) folder, box 11, ACW Diary Series, Whitman File; also DDE to C. B.

Sawyer, July 23, 1953, 1-A 1952–53 (3) folder, box 2, Central Files, President's Personal Files, DDEPL.

15 *bored with his studies, lethargic:* John Eisenhower, exchange with author, Sept. 2010.

15 *"The fellows that used to call me":* DDE to Ruby Norman, Nov. 22, 1913, Correspondence from Dwight D. Eisenhower, box 1, Ruby Norman Lucier Papers, DDEPL.

15 *friends convinced him to stay:* Slater, *The Ike I Knew,* p. 207.

15 *importance of a tidy barracks:* DDE, interview with Morin, Aug. 5, 1965, p. 9.

15 *unimpressive 125th in terms of conduct:* Transcripts courtesy of DDEPL.

15 *treated to Ike's gag:* Butcher, *Three Years with Eisenhower,* p. xiii.

16 *"the handsomest man in the Corps":* Howitzer, Class of 1915, West Point.

16 *second lieutenant in the U.S. Army:* Copy of commission, U.S. Army Commissions, box 163, 1916–52 Principal File, Pre-presidential Papers.

16 *"never gives me a thought":* DDE to Harding, n.d., labeled "#2, Summer of 1915" in file, Early Letters from DDE (2), Brooks Papers.

16 *she sighed to her diary:* Harding, June 15–Aug. 31, 1915, entries, 1915 Diary (folders 1 and 2), Brooks Papers.

16 *to be able to afford one:* Susan Eisenhower, *Mrs. Ike,* p. 12.

17 *for the warmer winter:* Ibid., pp. 10–12.

17 *recall the price of a tamale:* DDE, *At Ease,* p. 113.

17 *to whom he was not yet engaged:* Susan Eisenhower, *Mrs. Ike,* p. 36. See also, Wickman/Burg oral history interview with Mamie Eisenhower, p. 5.

17 *it melted:* Morin to Mamie, note, and her reply, Nov. 4, 1965.

17 *met Ike's family for the first time:* Ibid.

17 *He was charmed:* Susan Eisenhower, *Mrs. Ike,* p. 42.

18 *"Well, young lady":* Susan Eisenhower, *Mrs. Ike,* p. 45.

18 *with pride the rest of her life:* Ibid., p. 290.

18 *"Ike never had the slightest notion":* David Eisenhower, *Going Home,* p. 23.

18 *"I was inclined to display":* DDE, *At Ease,* p. 180. In *At Ease,* Eisenhower spelled his son's nickname "Icky." Others recall that it was rendered as "Ikky." Since it was merely a nickname, there is no accepted spelling.

19 *in his father's embrace:* This account is drawn largely from Susan Eisenhower, *Mrs. Ike,* which in turn relies on the memory of Mamie.

19 *Icky loved yellow:* Ibid., p. 73.

19 *"the greatest disappointment and disaster":* DDE, *At Ease,* pp. 181–82.

20 *her husband and his driver:* Mamie's letters from the period did not survive, but she saved Ike's half of the correspondence, and those letters are preserved at DDEPL, as well as in a collection of the letters published by their son, John.

20 *"There are also a couple of WAACS":* DDE to Mamie, Feb. 3, 1943, in *Letters to Mamie,* p. 93.

20 *"go bothering your pretty head":* DDE to Mamie, Feb. 26, 1943, in ibid., p. 97.

20 *"Your letters often give me":* DDE to Mamie, June 11, 1943, in ibid., pp. 127–28.

21 *Kay was a welcome companion:* David Eisenhower, *Going Home,* p. 24.

21 *first dance at the end of the war:* Clip of AP report is attached to Mamie to her family, date unclear, but apparently Aug. 1945, Family Letters 1945, box 4, Barbara Eisenhower Papers.

21 *"When you have some spare time":* Summersby to DDE, May 31, 1948, Kay Summersby folder, box 112, Principal File, Pre-presidential Papers.

21 *"I can scarcely estimate":* DDE to Summersby, June 1, 1948, Kay Summersby folder, box 112, Principal File, Pre-presidential Papers.

22 *"Americans are funny":* John Eisenhower, interview with author, Oct. 7, 2010.

22 *glamorized the relationship:* Ibid.

CHAPTER 2: THE MENTORING OF SOLDIERS

23 *reborn soldier from ancient times:* Martin Blumenson, *Patton*, p. 29.

23 *"Beatrice Ayer was polished":* Ibid., p. 38.

24 *"I was afraid to bring the subject up":* DDE, *At Ease*, p. 171.

24 *"speedy, reliable and efficient":* D'Este, *Patton*, pp. 296–97.

24 *"They are destined for a separate existence":* Ibid., p. 297.

24 *risk court-martial:* D'Este, *Eisenhower*, p. 152. See also Korda, *Ike*, p. 152.

25 *"Club Eisenhower":* Korda, *Ike*, p. 153.

25 *Patton's invitation to dinner:* Charles H. Brown and John Ray Skates, "Fox Conner," *Journal of Mississippi History* (Aug. 1987).

25 *Patton's answer: leadership:* Patton to DDE, July 9, 1926, George S. Patton Jr. (6) folder, box 91, Principal File, Pre-presidential Papers, DDEPL.

25 *graciously credited Patton:* Ibid.

25 *angling for something more significant:* DDE to Patton, Sept. 17, 1940, Patton (6) folder, box 91, Principal File, Pre-presidential Papers.

26 *"My advice is":* DDE to Patton, Feb. 4, 1943, Patton (4) folder, box 91, Principal File, Pre-presidential Papers.

27 *rolled out of the tent:* Perrin H. Long to the Surgeon NATOUSA, memo, Aug. 16, 1943, Patton (4) folder, box 91, Principal File, Pre-presidential Papers.

27 *"The deleterious effects":* Ibid.

27 *"I am attaching a report":* DDE to Patton, Aug. 17, 1943, Patton (4) folder, box 91, Principal File, Pre-presidential Papers.

28 *"those unfortunate personal traits":* DDE to Marshall, Aug. 24, 1943, George C. Marshall (9) folder, box 80, Principal File, Pre-presidential Papers.

28 *"I believe that he is cured":* Ibid.

28 *apologized to those involved:* Patton feigned contrition but did not mean it. Writing home to his "Darling B," he expressed anger toward Pearson for reporting the slapping but offered no remorse for his own actions. Similarly, in a letter to Henry Stimson, secretary of war, Patton admitted that "my method was too forthright" and explained that Eisenhower had "very rightly" called his attention to the negative effect of his actions on public opinion. In that same letter, however, Patton described the man he slapped as a "cur" who was "skulking" and "by his cowardice . . . forcing other loyal and brave men to do his duty" (diaries for Nov. 1943, letters of Nov. 25 and 27, 1943, box 11, Patton Papers).

28 *Patton's latent anti-Semitism:* Patton in his diary referred to Jews as "lower than

animals" (Diary entry for Sept. 15, 1945, p. 751) and as having "no sense of human relationships" (entry for Sept. 16, 1945, p. 754). And, when criticized in the press in 1945 after comparing the Nazi party to Republicans or Democrats, he observed in his diary that "there is a very apparent Semitic influence in the press" (Blumenson, *Patton*, pp. 281 and 287, as well as Diary entry for Sept. 22, 1945, p. 766).

28 *"a report from you":* DDE to Patton, telegram, Sept. 25, 1945, Patton (1) folder, box 91, Principal File, Pre-presidential Papers.

28 *"Now the horrors of peace":* Blumenson, *Patton*, p. 280.

29 *"I have lost":* DDE to Bea Patton, cable, Dec. 21, 1945, Patton (1) folder, box 91, Principal File, Pre-presidential Papers.

29 *"It might be advisable":* Conner to DDE, Oct. 6 (no year in original), Fox Conner folder, box 27, Principal File, Pre-presidential Papers.

29 *the crisis passed:* D'Este, *Eisenhower*, pp. 161–64.

29 *those that Conner had created:* Brown and Skates, "Fox Conner."

29 *"Complete victory":* Ibid.

30 *Mamie hated bats:* DDE, *At Ease*, p. 184. See also oral history interview with Mamie, p. 19.

30 *far away and homesick:* Mamie to her parents, Dec. 16, 1922, Family Letters 1922, box 1, Barbara Eisenhower Papers.

30 *"not the best introduction":* DDE, *At Ease*, p. 184.

30 *"you have to start the ignition":* Susan Eisenhower, *Mrs. Ike*, p. 80.

31 *attempt to hold on to her:* Ibid., p. 83.

31 *"Am finally getting Ike housebroken again":* Mamie to her parents, n.d., marked "Thursday," box 3, Barbara Eisenhower Papers.

31 *"He gave the appearance of being leisurely":* Brown and Skates, "Fox Conner."

31 *"Clausewitz all the way":* John Eisenhower, exchange with author, Sept. 27, 2010.

32 *would test Europe before long:* DDE, interview with Pat Morin, Aug. 5, 1965, AP-1 Pat Morin folder, box 2, 1965 Principal File, Post-presidential Papers, DDEPL.

32 *"Dealing with the enemy":* Brown and Skates, "Fox Conner."

32 *"More and more in the last few days":* DDE to Conner, July 4, 1942, Conner folder, box 27, Principal File, Pre-presidential Papers.

32 *"I still long for opportunities":* DDE to Virginia Conner, Dec. 26, 1943, Cond–Connol (Misc.) folder, box 18, Principal File, Pre-presidential Papers.

32 *"no one influenced me as much":* DDE, oral history interview with Forrest C. Pogue, OH 10, p. 6, DDEPL.

33 *wherever they were located, bear his name:* DDE, *At Ease*, p. 214.

33 *move on ragged marchers:* DDE, interview with Morin, Aug. 5, 1965.

33 *"Get him away":* DDE, oral history interview with Henle, OH 106, p. 3.

34 *"That mob was a very angry looking one":* *Washington Post*, July 29, 1932.

34 *just lost the 1932 election:* Lisio, *President and Protest*, p. xiii.

34 *for waiting so long:* Clippings from Bonus March folder, Principal File, Pre-presidential Papers.

34 *Reluctantly, he went:* DDE, *At Ease*, p. 219.

35 *unexpected effects on their mission:* DDE, *Diaries*, p. 18.

35 *"He is tickled pink"*: Ibid., p. 21.

35 *"Oh hell"*: Ibid., p. 22.

35 *"He had an obsession"*: DDE, oral history interview with James, OH 501, p. 5.

35 *"The best leadership"*: DDE to John, July 29, 1952, Eisenhower Writings 1952 (1), box 2, Personal Papers of Whitman.

36 *"Best clerk I ever had"*: William Manchester, *American Caesar*, p. 182. See also Korda, *Ike*, p. 227.

36 *just across the border*: Mamie to her family, Dec. 4, 1941, Family Letters (3), box 3, Barbara Eisenhower Papers.

36 *"I'll give you one name"*: Atkinson, *Army at Dawn*, p. 43.

36 *"The Chief"*: DDE, oral history interview with Pogue, OH 10, p. 3.

36 *made vegetable soup*: John Eisenhower, exchange with author, Sept. 30, 2010.

36 *hunt for a place to live*: Mamie to her family, Dec. 20, 1941, Family Letters (3), box 3, Barbara Eisenhower Papers.

37 *"spoiled rotten"*: Mamie to her family, July 15, 1929, Family Letters 1929 (2), box 1, Barbara Eisenhower Papers.

37 *excellence in a promising officer*: DDE, interview with Morin, Aug. 5, 1965.

37 *"Yes, sir"*: Ibid.

38 *"I'm sorry, too"*: Marshall to Lieutenant General Jacob L. Devers, April 22, 1944, George Marshall Papers, quoted in Perry, *Partners in Command*, p. 19.

38 *"our general line of action"*: DDE, *Crusade in Europe*, p. 18.

38 *"Of course," Marshall replied*: DDE, interview with Morin, Aug. 5, 1965, p. 21.

38 *"I have never pondered"*: Ibid.

38 *"They may excuse failure"*: DDE, *Crusade in Europe*, p. 22.

39 *"seemingly hopeless"*: DDE, interview with Morin, Aug. 5, 1965, p. 21.

39 *"I agree with you"*: Ibid.

39 *"Here's the man who can fight"*: DDE, oral history interview with Pogue, OH 10, p. 5.

39 *open to improvisation*: DDE, interview with Morin, Aug. 5, 1965.

39 *"marked ability and conspicuous success"*: Pearson is quoted in D'Este, *Eisenhower*, p. 279; the formal recognition comes from U.S. Decorations and Certificates, box 163, Principal File, Pre-presidential Papers.

39 *"Father died this morning"*: DDE, entry for March 10, 1942, in *Diaries*, p. 50.

39 *"My only regret"*: Ibid., entry for March 12, 1942, p. 51.

39 *rejecting the importuning of others*: DDE, *Crusade in Europe*, p. 34.

40 *permitted Eisenhower's cheerier disposition*: Smith's role is thoughtfully—and exhaustively—chronicled in Crosswell's *Beetle*.

40 *more direct strike on Europe*: Office of the Chief of Military History, *Command Decisions*, p. 129.

40 *"I am to be that . . . commander"*: DDE, July 26, 1942, entry, in *Diaries*, p. 74.

40 *"We are standing"*: DDE to Marshall, Nov. 7, 1942, Marshall (11) folder, box 80, Principal File, Pre-presidential Papers.

40 *"I have operational command"*: DDE, Nov. 9, 1942, entry, in *Diaries*, p. 81.

41 *"Deficient of experience"*: Atkinson, *Army at Dawn*, p. 285.

41 *"I find myself"*: DDE to Marshall, Nov. 9, 1942, Marshall (11) folder, box 80, Principal File, Pre-presidential Papers.

41 *"many commanders but no leaders"*: Patton to Bea, Dec. 5, 1942, Diary, Dec. 1942, box 10; Patton to Bea, Jan. 11, 1943, Jan. 1943 folder, Patton Papers.

41 *lit up anyway:* Atkinson, *Day of Battle*, p. 51.

42 *French ports and facilities:* Draft agreement, Dec. 2 or 3, 1942, Jean Darlan folder, box 33, Principal File, Pre-presidential Papers.

42 *"I am pleased that you"*: DDE to Marshall, Nov. 17, 1942, Marshall (11) folder, box 80, Principal File, Pre-presidential Papers.

42 *Giraud took his place:* On Christmas Day, Ike wrote a note of sympathy to Darlan's widow. In it, he described Darlan as "a most valuable ally and a competent supporter." But one can hardly infer Ike's true appraisal from this note. The letter is in Darlan folder, box 33, Principal File, Pre-presidential Papers.

42 *"At the moment there seems nothing"*: Marshall to DDE, May 6, 1943, Marshall (10) folder, box 80, Principal File, Pre-presidential Papers.

43 *"quite a great man"*: Patton to Bea, Feb. 19, 1943, Diary, Feb. 1943, box 10, Patton Papers.

43 *"I didn't feel I could sleep"*: Kennedy, *Freedom from Fear*, p. 687.

43 *"my most cherished mementos"*: DDE, *Crusade in Europe*, p. 208.

43 *"You will enter the continent"*: Ibid., p. 225.

44 *"We'll take care of this"*: DDE, interview with Morin, Aug. 5, 1965.

44 *"No one can stop it now"*: Morgan, *Past Forgetting*, p. 191.

44 *"Our landings in the Cherbourg-Havre"*: June 5, 1944, original note is at DDEPL.

45 *"Under the command of General Eisenhower"*: Korda, *Ike*, p. 479.

45 *"the beginning of the end of the war"*: Morgan, *Past Forgetting*, p. 193.

45 *"He would sit there and smoke"*: Ibid., p. 194.

45 *complete his infantry training:* DDE, *At Ease*, p. 287.

45 *"was just one big grin"*: Morgan, *Past Forgetting*, p. 195.

45 *"there isn't an officer"*: John Eisenhower, *Strictly Personal*, p. 63.

45 *throughout John's growing up:* John Eisenhower, exchange with author, Sept. 2010.

45 *"No matter how sharply"*: Morgan, *Past Forgetting*, p. 197.

46 *"Dad told him to go ahead"*: John Eisenhower, *Strictly Personal*, p. 217.

46 *focused charge toward Berlin:* Roland G. Ruppenthal, "Logistics and the Broad-Front Strategy," in Office of the Chief of Military History, *Command Decisions*, p. 325.

46 *energies on strategic victory:* I am indebted to Colonel Clint Ancker for his insights into Eisenhower's strategic gifts as a commander. Author interview, March 5, 2010.

46 *"only man who could have made things work"*: Atkinson, *Day of Battle*, p. 49.

47 *"slightly hair-brained"*: DDE letter to "Pug" Ismay, Dec. 3, 1960, DDE Dictation Dec. 1960, box 55, DDE Diary Series, Whitman File.

47 *for fear he would be overcome:* DDE to Marshall, April 15, 1945, Marshall (6) folder, box 80, Principal File, Pre-presidential Papers.

47 *"Then suppose we get rid of that sign"*: William Opper letter, Feb. 12, 1953, and

Robert L. Schulz reply, March 2, 1953, Personal Data Concerning the President, 1952–53 (2), box 1, Central Files, President's Personal File, DDEPL.

47   *"You will, officially and personally":* DDE, *Crusade in Europe*, p. 426. Jodl was tried at Nuremberg, found guilty of war crimes, and hanged. Friedeburg killed himself two weeks after the surrender.

48   *"You have completed your mission":* Marshall to DDE, cable, May 7, 1945, Marshall (6) folder, box 80, Principal File, Pre-presidential Papers.

48   *the greatest general of all:* DDE, oral history interview with James, OH 501, p. 6.

CHAPTER 3: LEARNING POLITICS

49   *whisked to NATO headquarters:* Brownell, *Advising Ike*, p. 93.

49   *"that fell like a lead balloon":* Ibid., p. 101.

50   *taught himself bridge: Time*, Feb. 6, 1956.

50   *up to serving as his partner:* John Eisenhower, *Strictly Personal*, p. 210.

50   *picked an emissary to reel in the general:* Brownell, *Advising Ike*, p. 91.

51   *"the most highly respected man":* Brownell, oral history interview, OH 362, p. 45, DDEPL.

51   *manuscript on Friday, March 26:* Douglas Black, memo, April 1, 1948, Eisenhower (Personal) 1948 folder, box 1, Robinson Papers.

51   *was published that fall:* DDE, *At Ease*, pp. 325–29.

51   *as one reviewer put it: Saturday Review of Literature*, from jacket copy.

51   *hundreds of thousands of dollars:* Ewald, *Eisenhower the President*, p. 57.

52   *at least a month of bed rest:* See, for instance, Lasby, *Eisenhower's Heart Attack*, p. 47.

52   *"Don't think about it":* DDE, oral history interview with Adams, pp. 30–31.

52   *"Father would have liked this":* McCallum, *Six Roads from Abilene*, p. 123.

52   *shiny blue vehicle:* Dec. 30, 1948, letter, Robert Schulz, aide to Eisenhower, to A. J. Aherns (and accompanying news coverage), AH-AK folder, box 1, Principal File, Pre-presidential Papers, DDEPL.

52   *even though it would have cost less:* DDE, *At Ease*, p. 360.

53   *Churchill supplied an example:* John Eisenhower, interview with author, Oct. 7, 2010.

53   *"weird and wonderful to behold":* DDE, *At Ease*, p. 340.

53   *would form the basis of NATO:* Even before drafting him for that assignment, Truman tried to lure Eisenhower to public life another way. In Aug. 1949, he asked George Allen, a mutual friend, to relay to Eisenhower the message that Truman could insure him Democratic support for a seat in the U.S. Senate. Eisenhower replied that he "would not consider it" (special note for Aug. 29, 1949, Eisenhower [Personal] 1949 folder, box 1, Robinson Papers).

53   *"an unassailable position":* Clay to DDE, April 13, 1951, Lucius D. Clay (6) folder, box 24, Principal File, Pre-presidential Papers, DDEPL.

53   *B for Brownell:* Clay to DDE, May 18, 1951, Clay (6) folder, box 24, Principal File, Pre-presidential Papers.

53   *being unable to follow it:* DDE to Clay, Sept. 27, 1951, Clay (5) folder, box 24, Principal File, Pre-presidential Papers.

54 *thousands chanted and sang: New York Times*, Feb. 9, 1952. Others have estimated the crowd as much larger, in the neighborhood of thirty-three thousand. That seems unlikely, given the Garden's capacity in those years.

54 *where he practiced his fly casting:* Slater, *The Ike I Knew*, p. 13.

54 *"the symbol of that longing and hope":* DDE to Swede, Feb. 12, 1952, Swede Hazlett 1952, Jan.-May folder, Name Series, box 17, Whitman File.

54 *"I've not been so upset":* DDE, Feb. 12, 1952, entry, in *Diaries*, p. 214.

54 *tears ran down his cheeks:* Cochran, oral history interview, p. 25.

54 *to seek their party's nomination:* Feb. 22 letter, Drafting Eisenhower as a Candidate, box 4, Adams Papers.

55 *"They want you to come home":* Ibid.

55 *"My attitude":* DDE, *Mandate for Change*, p. 21.

55 *"the first big test":* Time, Feb. 11, 1952.

55 *bigger impression on him:* DDE, interview with Relman "Pat" Morin, Jan. 3, 1967, p. 20, box 53, 1967 Principal File, Post-presidential Papers, DDEPL.

55 *"Ike" scrawled across them:* Adams, oral history interview, p. 15.

55 *"assure you of a warm welcome":* Brownell, *Advising Ike*, p. 355.

55 *"That definitely and specifically includes":* DDE, *Crusade in Europe*, p. 444. See also DDE, interview with Morin, Jan. 3, 1967, p. 16.

55 *whether they could carry the electorate:* Brownell, *Advising Ike*, p. 97.

56 *"would not lead the charge":* Ibid., p. 99.

56 *"an important turning point":* Ibid.

CHAPTER 4: FROM CANDIDATE TO PRESIDENT

59 *"America must be spiritually":* DDE, *Mandate for Change*, p. 33.

59 *"I think I have no quarrel":* Lodge to DDE, May 16, 1952, and DDE to Lodge, May 20, 1952, Henry Cabot Lodge folder, box 72, Principal File, Pre-presidential Papers, DDEPL.

60 *"the almost evangelical loyalty":* Bain and Parris, *Convention Decisions and Voting Records*, p. 279.

60 *distant corners of the hall:* Warren, *Memoirs*, p. 218.

61 *was denied entrance, too:* Brownell, *Advising Ike*, p. 115.

61 *"stolen" delegates and party secrecy: New York Times*, July 3, 1952.

61 *"I'm going to roar out":* Ibid.

62 *they found space:* Brownell, *Advising Ike*, p. 108.

62 *"We conclude this series": New York Times*, July 3, 1952.

62 *divided up the balance: New York Times*, July 6, 1952.

63 *hardly conveyed confidence: New York Times*, July 5, 1952.

63 *collected $1 from an aide: New York Times*, July 7, 1952.

63 *"I go everyplace I can with him":* Ibid.

64 *"a stirring oration":* Ibid.

64 *"It looks like my candidate": New York Times*, July 10, 1952.

64 *many of them fighting tears:* Hagerty, oral history interview, p. 40.

65 *the next eight years:* Ibid., p. 3.

65 *"He expressed surprise":* Brownell, *Advising Ike*, p. 120.

65 *California senator Richard Nixon:* Brownell and Eisenhower recalled this exchange slightly differently. In Ike's memory, he had carried this list with him for some time, though only Brownell knew who was on it. Brownell remembered that Ike wrote out the list over a dinner during the convention when Brownell asked him for names. Since Eisenhower acknowledged some failings of memory during that period, I have relied more heavily on Brownell's version of events.

66 *"we have a traitor":* Undated memorandum titled "Republican National Convention, July 1952, Chicago, Ill.," Political Parties, Republican Party folder, box 3, HI. The memo is signed by the author, but access to it is conditioned on protecting the name, so I have omitted it here.

66 *"There comes a time":* Mazo, *Richard Nixon*, p. 88.

66 *happy to have him on the ticket:* Brownell to Sherman Adams, Dec. 23, 1958, A (1) folder, box 66, Brownell Papers.

66 *"Nixon fills all the requirements":* Mazo, *Richard Nixon*, p. 89.

67 *"Its potential for good or evil":* Full text at http://www.rockymountainnews.com/ news/1952/jul/26/transcript-adlai-stevensons-acceptance-speech-1952/.

67 *"impressed by his speaking style":* DDE, *Mandate for Change*, p. 50.

67 *"He's too accomplished":* Ibid.

67 *the teleprompter was scrapped:* Sherman Adams, unpublished MS, pp. 122–25, Adams Papers.

67 *"Thirty-five pages":* Hagerty, oral history interview, p. 44.

68 *they would be "entirely briefed":* Truman to DDE, telegram, Aug. 12, 1952, Harry Truman folder (1), box 33, Name Series, Whitman File.

68 *"It is my duty":* DDE to Truman, Aug. 14, 1952, Truman folder (1), box 33, Name Series, Whitman File.

68 *"I am extremely sorry":* Truman to DDE, Aug. 16, 1952, Truman folder (1), box 33, Name Series, Whitman File.

68 *some by Smith himself:* John L. Helgerson, *Getting to Know the President: CIA Briefings of Presidential Candidates, 1952–1992* (Washington, D.C.: Center for the Study of Intelligence, Central Intelligence Agency, 1996).

69 *"In the certainty that the whole affair":* DDE to Nixon, draft, Sept. 19, 1952, box 1, Cutler Papers.

69 *until Nixon could explain himself:* Sherman Adams to Brownell, Feb. 12, 1959, and Brownell reply, Feb. 25, 1959, A (1) folder, box 66, Brownell Papers.

69 *well short of an endorsement:* "Notes on Campaign Speeches, 1952," undated memo, 1952 Campaign folder, Whitman File.

69 *"But there comes a time":* Nixon memorandum of telephone conversation, Sept. 20, 1952, Fund File, Richard Nixon Library and Birthplace.

70 *"If the impression got around":* Ibid.

70 *"I want to tell you my side of the case":* Full text of the speech at http://www .historyplace.com/speeches/nixon-checkers.htm.

71 *Nixon laid down that challenge:* Ewald, *Eisenhower the President*, p. 55.

71 *"If you don't unqualifiedly endorse":* Edgar to DDE, cable, Sept. 25, 1952, Edgar Eisenhower 1953 (3) folder, box 11, Name Series, Whitman File.

71 *"This apparently settles the Nixon fund affair"*: "Notes on Campaign Speeches, 1952."

71 *that dated to Lincoln*: Adams, unpublished MS, p. 109.

71 *"bungled us perilously close"*: "Notes on Campaign Speeches, 1952."

72 *"us forward in the broad middle way"*: Ibid.

73 *"here in my hand"*: *Major Speeches and Debates of Senator Joe McCarthy*, beginning at p. 5. Full text also at http://historymatters.gmu.edu/d/6456.

73 *"certified to the Secretary"*: Ibid.

73 *"the most weird and traitorous"*: Ibid., pp. 190–92.

73 *"part of a conspiracy on a scale"*: McCarthy address to the U.S. Senate, June 14, 1951, *Congressional Record*, 82nd Cong., 1st sess., vol. 97, pt. 5, in *Major Speeches*, p. 305.

74 *McCarthy glowered afterward*: Adams, unpublished MS, p. 139.

74 *focused on other topics*: Here is the entire passage, as scheduled to be delivered: "George Marshall is one of the patriots of this country, and anyone who has lived with him, has worked with him as I have, knows that he is a man of real selflessness—a man who has suffered with ill health. Maybe he has made mistakes. I do not know about that, but from the time I met him on December 14, 1942, until the war was over, if he was not a perfect example of patriotism and a loyal servant of the United States, I never saw one. If I could say any more, I would say it, but I have no patience with anyone who can find in his record of service for this country anything to criticize."

74 *"high-minded and zealous"*: Adams, unpublished MS, p. 20a.

74 *"Take it out"*: Ibid., p. 140.

74 *attacks on Marshall were overstated*: DDE to Stassen, Oct. 5, 1952, Harold Stassen folder, box 35, Whitman File.

75 *"sick at heart"*: Adams, unpublished MS, p. 140. Marshall himself shrugged off the incident, at least in discussing it with others. "Eisenhower was forced into a compromise, that's all it was," he confided to his goddaughter. "There is no more independence in politics than there is in jail" (Rose Page Wilson, *General Marshall Remembered*, p. 371; quoted in Cray, *General of the Army*, p. 728).

75 *"as bad a moment"*: Hauge, oral history interview, p. 17.

75 *"terrible mistake"*: John Eisenhower, interview with author, Oct. 7, 2010.

75 *Marshall's name does not appear*: "Notes on Campaign Speeches, 1952."

75 *"straight isolationist line"*: *New York Times*, Oct. 23, 1952.

75 *"I shall go to Korea"*: *New York Times*, Oct. 25, 1952.

76 *"If you win"*: Hazlett to DDE, Nov. 3, 1952, Swede Hazlett (June–Dec. 1952) folder, box 17, Whitman File.

76 *Brownell accepted that evening*: Brownell, *Advising Ike*, pp. 132–33.

76 *any previous Republican candidate*: "The 1952 Elections: A Statistical Analysis," 138 A Elections and Voting (1) folder, box 698, Official File, White House Central Files, DDEPL.

76 *Mamie wept*: Slater, *The Ike I Knew*, p. 27.

CHAPTER 5: CHANGING AMERICA'S COURSE

77 *under the cover of darkness*: Hagerty letter to Marge Hagerty, Nov. 29, 1952, p. 3, Korea Trip 1952–53 (5), box 11, Hagerty Papers.

77 *"if you still desire to go to Korea"*: Truman to DDE, cable, Nov. 5, 1952, Harry S. Truman, Aug. 1, 1952–Jan. 1, 1953 (1) folder, box 33, Name Series, Whitman File.

77 *ended their relationship:* DDE to Truman, cable, Nov. 5, 1952, Truman Aug. 1, 1952–Jan. 1, 1953 (1) folder, box 33, Name Series, Whitman File. See also John Eisenhower, *Strictly Personal*, p. 158.

78 *"Secrecy of movement":* Lovett to DDE, Nov. 11, 1952, Robert A. Lovett folder, box 25, Administration Series, Whitman File.

78 *thirteen hundred escorted him along the way: Stars and Stripes*, Dec. 6, 1952, p. 15.

78 *boarded his plane:* Hagerty letter to Marge, Nov. 29, 1952, p. 5, Korea Trip 1952–53 (4), box 11, Hagerty Papers.

78 *opportunity to unite their country:* Halberstam, *Coldest Winter*, p. 50.

79 *perimeter in Asia as excluding South Korea:* Jian, *China's Road*, p. 119.

79 *"if you get kicked in the teeth":* Halberstam, *Coldest Winter*, p. 50.

79 *claiming the center and east coast:* "The Korean War," in *American Military History*, p. 547.

79 *"All Korea," he warned, "is lost":* John Allison, *Ambassador from the Prairie* (Boston: Houghton Mifflin, 1973), p. 137.

79 *several moments of silence:* Notes of June 26, 1950, meeting of Truman, Acheson, and congressional leaders, George M. Elsey Papers, HSTL.

80 *daunting seawalls:* "Korean War," p. 556.

80 *"Few people":* Halberstam, *Coldest Winter*, p. 311.

80 *"no stopping MacArthur now":* Weintraub, *MacArthur's War*, p. 163 (also quoted in Halberstam, *Coldest Winter*, p. 331).

80 *"If Korea were completely occupied":* This cable is included in Mao Zedong's *Manuscripts Since the Founding of the People's Republic*. It is unclear whether Stalin received it. An alternative cable included in Russian files from the period suggests that China was reluctant to commit its forces as of that day. The difference may be explained by divisions within the Chinese leadership at that point. For a discussion of this issue, see Shen Zhihua, "The Discrepancy Between the Russian and Chinese Versions of Mao's 2 October 1950 Message to Stalin on Chinese Entry into the Korean War: A Chinese Scholar's Reply," *Cold War International History Project Bulletin* (Winter 1996–97), p. 237.

81 *MacArthur disregarded the threat:* Weintraub, *MacArthur's War*, p. 207.

81 *were stashed for the Chinese:* Ibid., p. 209.

81 *MacArthur's headquarters ignored the warning:* Ibid., p. 210.

81 *"Anything MacArthur wanted":* Ibid., p. 211.

81 *"are not coming in":* Ridgway, *Korean War*, p. 254.

82 *"MacArthur seemed at the time":* Ibid., p. 153.

82 *"I am going to maintain silence":* DDE to Clay, April 16, 1951, Lucius D. Clay (7) folder, box 24, Principal File, Pre-presidential Papers, DDEPL.

82 *by December 31 of that year:* April 23, 1951, memo for the Executive Secretary, National Security Council, NSC 114–2 (1) folder, box 8, Disaster File, White House Office, NSC Staff Papers, 1948–61, DDEPL.

83 *raised the American flag: Stars and Stripes*, Dec. 6, 1952, p. 16.

83 *so as to avoid attention:* New York Times, Dec. 6, 1952.

83 *traveled fast in the cold air:* Ibid.

83 *"Police action, hell":* Stars and Stripes, Dec. 6, 1952, p. 16.

83 *"He's the man to do it":* Don Whitehead, "The Great Deception," p. 12, The Korea Trip (1), box 11, Hagerty Papers.

83 *"before being captured":* Op-Ed, New York Times, Sept. 27, 2008. John Eisenhower also describes this understanding in his memoir, *Strictly Personal.*

84 *"It would probably become necessary":* Memorandum on Ending the Korean War, Dec. 15, 1952, Douglas MacArthur folder, box 25, Administration Series, Whitman File.

84 *"a piece of demagoguery":* Dec. 11, 1952, news conference, APP.

85 *"dog and pony act":* Adams, oral history interview, p. 16.

85 *"To the best of my recollection":* Ibid., p. 127.

86 *"Dull, Duller, Dulles":* Hughes, *Ordeal of Power,* p. 251.

86 *"the brisk nodding of the head":* Ibid., p. 51.

86 *"He is not particularly persuasive":* DDE, entry for May 14, 1953, in *Diaries,* p. 237.

86 *"because for years I thought":* SecDef Histories, www.defenselink.mil/specials/secdef_histories/bios/wilson.htm.

86 *"Mr. Wilson is prone":* DDE, entry for May 14, 1953, in *Diaries,* p. 237.

87 *"I see you part your hair":* Parmet, *Eisenhower and the American Crusades,* p. 183.

87 *decades as its president:* See M. A. Hanna Company official history. Obtained by author from company headquarters, Cleveland, Ohio.

87 *"If you're going to live":* Parmet, *Eisenhower and the American Crusades,* p. 183.

87 *"When George speaks":* Saginaw Hall of Fame entry for Humphrey.

87 *"a sound business type":* DDE, entry for May 14, 1953, in *Diaries,* p. 237.

87 *Brownell did not forget:* Time, May 30, 1957.

88 *"It would be natural to suppose":* DDE, entry for May 14, 1953, in *Diaries,* p. 239.

88 *before heading to the office:* Time, May 7, 1956.

88 *"give us men with a mandate":* Ibid.

88 *take her to the hospital:* Biographical sketch of Hobby, Fondren Library, Rice University, at http://library.rice.edu/collections/WRC/digital-archive-information/online-exhilbits/oveta-culp-hobby-and-the-women-s-army-corps-exhibit/oveta-culp-hobby-biographical-sketch.

89 *turn out the lights:* See Hagerty, oral history interview, for his background and tenure.

89 *after a short time in the White House:* DDE, *Mandate for Change,* p. 119.

89 *Ike's trip to Korea:* John L. Helgerson, *Getting to Know the President: CIA Briefings of Presidential Candidates, 1952–1992* (Washington, D.C.: Center for the Study of Intelligence, Central Intelligence Agency, 1996).

89 *"And I thought":* Ibid.

90 *longest two weeks in history:* Scripps-Howard wire story, July 6, 1956.

90 *Whitman opted to drive:* Whitman letter to "Marie," undated but marked "6/58," Eisenhower Library Documents (1), box 2, Personal Papers of Whitman.

90 *"Your companionship":* Robinson to DDE, Jan. 21, 1953, Eisenhower (Personal) 1953 folder, box 2, Robinson Papers.

91 *"This ability to segregate":* Slater, *The Ike I Knew*, p. 39.

91 *"read it not for praise":* DDE, *Mandate for Change*, p. 99.

91 *"no help":* DDE, entry for January 16, 1953, in *Diaries*, p. 225.

91 *felt it demeaned the ceremony:* Neal, *Harry and Ike*, p. 285.

91 *the balance of the ride:* DDE, *Mandate for Change*, p. 101.

92 *"The faith we hold":* DDE, Inaugural Address, APP. Video of the speech is widely available on the Internet.

92 *had ever done at an inauguration:* Holt, *Mamie Doud Eisenhower*, p. 59.

93 *holing up there for two days:* Jan. 1953, Presidential Appointment Books, DDEPL.

93 *"I guess the old gal":* DDE to Edgar, Feb. 7, 1953, Edgar Eisenhower 1953 (3) folder, box 11, Name Series, Whitman File.

93 *seamstress to convert it:* Holt, *Mamie Doud Eisenhower*, p. 63.

93 *"reach over and pat Ike":* Susan Eisenhower, *Mrs. Ike*, p. 276.

93 *middle-class affectations:* Ibid., p. 281.

94 *surrounded by photographs and papers:* Slater, *The Ike I Knew*, p. 32.

94 *concentration and memory:* Ibid., p. 57.

94 *"dressing for my husband":* Susan Eisenhower, *Mrs. Ike*, p. 294.

94 *Robert Taft "blew up":* Dulles and Hagerty, conversation, April 30, 1953, White House Telephone Conversations, Jan. to April 1953, box 10, Telephone Calls Series, Dulles Papers.

94 *"one of the worst days":* DDE, entry for May 1, 1953, in *Diaries*, p. 235.

95 *Julius fell in love:* Roberts, *Brother*, p. 40.

95 *electrical engineering in early 1939:* Ibid., p. 45.

95 *Greenglass slept in:* Ibid., p. 136.

96 *"She called our bluff":* New York Times, Sept. 11, 2008 (the quotation originally appears in Sam Roberts's mesmerizing 2001 book, *The Brother*. The *New York Times* article also was by Roberts).

96 *"I consider your crime":* Kaufman's statement appears at the conclusion of the trial record. Copies of the transcript are widely available, including at http://www.law.umkc.edu/faculty/projects/ftrials/rosenb/ROS_TRIA.HTM.

96 *freed in 1969: New York Times,* Jan. 15, 1969.

97 *"if anyone . . . believes":* Cabinet Meeting, Feb. 12, 1953, box 1, Cabinet Series, White House Office, Office of the Staff Secretary Records, 1952–61, DDEPL (handwritten notes; typed minutes contained in box 1, Cabinet Series, Whitman File).

97 *pardon, commutation, or execution:* Reaction was strongly in favor of commuting the Rosenbergs' sentences and highly critical of Eisenhower for refusing to do so. One batch of telegrams tallied on Feb. 12 showed 436 opposed to Eisenhower's action compared with 57 in favor of it. See OF 101-R, Amnesty-Pardons (1), Julius and Ethel Rosenberg folder, box 354, Official File, White House Central Files, 1953–61, DDEPL.

97 *if the executions were carried out:* Bedell Smith, Memorandum for the President, Rosenberg Case Statement, May 20, 1953, box 32, Administration Series, Whitman File.

97 *jeopardized lives and national security:* The historian Stephen Ambrose maintains

that there was dissent within his cabinet over the Rosenberg case and that Ike was deeply conflicted at the prospect of allowing Ethel to be put to death. At page 182 of *Ike's Spies*, for instance, Ambrose writes: "Some of Ike's most trusted advisers told him he would have to grant a stay of execution because the nation simply could not put to death the mother of small children. Many in the Cabinet recommended clemency." As the scholar Lori Clune has revealed, Ambrose's statement is unsupported by cabinet records or any other documents—indeed, those documents all point in the opposite direction—and was contradicted by Brownell in a later oral history interview. Ambrose's analysis may charitably be regarded as a mistake. At worst, it represents a fabrication.

97   *"It is the woman who is {the} strong"*: DDE to John Eisenhower, June 16, 1953, DDE Diary, Dec. 1952–July 1953 (2), box 3, DDE Diary Series, Whitman File.

97   *"As Commander-in-Chief of the European theatre"*: Ethel Rosenberg to DDE, June 16, 1953, OF 101-R, Amnesty-Pardons (1), Rosenberg folder (1), box 354, Official File, White House Central Files, 1953–61, DDEPL.

98   *"hell of a mess"*: June 17, 1953, call with Allen Dulles, Telephone Memoranda (excepting to or from the White House) May–June 1953 (1), box 1, Telephone Calls Series, Dulles Papers.

98   *"No, I have no names"*: Roberts, *Brother*, p. 19.

98   *had begun at 8:13 p.m.*: Ibid., pp. 18–20.

98   *quiet, private dinner:* June 19, 1953, call, Telephone Memoranda (excepting to or from the White House) May–June 1953 (1), box 1, Telephone Calls Series, Dulles Papers.

98   *about their guilt:* Brownell, *Advising Ike*, p. 245.

99   *"strong possibility"*: Clark to Joint Chiefs, telegram, Feb. 9, 1953, Matthews Files, Lot 33, D 413, in *FRUS Korea, 1952–54*, vol. 15, p. 758.

99   *should nuclear weapons be deployed?:* 131st NSC meeting, Feb. 11, 1953, box 4, NSC Series, Whitman File.

99   *"in a special category"*: Ibid.

99   *drive out the Communist forces:* Ibid.

99   *effectiveness against military targets:* Cutler to Wilson, memo, March 21, 1953, in *FRUS 1952–54*, vol. 15, p. 815, C. D. Jackson Papers.

99   *in the Korean terrain:* Memorandum of Substance of Discussion at a Department of State–Joint Chiefs of Staff Meeting, March 27, 1953, State-JCS Meeting, Lot 61, D 413, in *FRUS Korea, 1952–54*, vol. 15, p. 817.

100   *to the West's strategic advantage:* Special Meeting of NSC, March 31, 1953, box 4, NSC Series, Whitman File.

100   *willing to fight on:* Rhee to DDE, April 9, 1953, in *FRUS 1952–54*, vol. 15, pp. 902–3, Whitman File.

100   *"we have to ask"*: Ibid.

100   *"deeply disturbed" by Rhee's threat:* DDE to Rhee, April 23, 1953, in *FRUS Korea, 1952–54*, vol. 15, p. 929, Whitman File.

100   *"Unless you are prepared"*: DDE, *Mandate for Change*, p. 186.

100   *"I guess Syngman Rhee"*: Ibid., p. 186n.

101   *"Danger of an atomic war"*: Sherman Adams, unpublished MS, p. 286, Adams

Papers. See also June 5, 1953, Cabinet Meeting notes, Cabinet Series, DDEPL; and DDE, interview with Relman "Pat" Morin, Jan. 3, 1967, pp. 23–24, box 53, 1967 Principal File, Post-presidential Papers, DDEPL.

101 *full-scale offensive along the Bukhan River:* Ridgway, *Korean War*, p. 223.

101 *"We have won":* DDE, Address to the American People, April 26, 1953, APP.

101 *"It was almost joy enough":* Ridgway, *Korean War*, p. 225.

101 *since World War II:* Adams, unpublished MS, p. 300.

CHAPTER 6: CONSEQUENCES

102 *he so fulsomely enumerated:* Henderson, oral history interview, p. 6.

102 *"suddenly looking old and pathetic":* Acheson, *Present at the Creation*, p. 504.

103 *only to faint dead away:* Homa Katouzian, "Mosaddeq's Government in Iranian History," in Gasiorowski and Byrne, *Mohammad Mosaddeq and the 1953 Coup in Iran*, p. 4. See also Ambassador to State Department, Feb. 28, 1953, in *FRUS Iran, 1952–54*, vol. 10, p. 688.

103 *Mossadegh was elected prime minister:* Acheson, *Present at the Creation*, p. 503.

103 *its facility in Abadan:* Kinzer, *All the Shah's Men*, p. 108.

104 *its oil production revenue:* Mary Ann Heiss, "International Boycott of Iranian Oil," in Gasiorowski and Byrne, *Mohammad Mosaddeq and the 1953 Coup in Iran*, p. 185.

104 *"where they will start trouble":* Truman's conversations with Elsey, June 26, 1950, George M. Elsey Papers, HSTL.

104 *"Back came a reply":* Acheson, *Present at the Creation*, p. 680.

104 *only be solved by deposing him:* Fakhreddin Azimi, "Unseating Mosaddeq," in Gasiorowski and Byrne, *Mohammad Mosaddeq and the 1953 Coup in Iran*, p. 81.

105 *"Not wishing to be accused":* Woodhouse, *Something Ventured*, p. 117.

105 *"rapidly . . . approaching deadlock":* Ambassador to Secretary of State, Jan. 28, 1953, in *FRUS Iran, 1952–54*, vol. 10, p. 654.

105 *"If I had $500 million":* 135th NSC Meeting, March 4, 1953, box 4, NSC Series, Whitman File.

105 *"that it was not in American interests":* CIA Report, "Overthrow of Premier Mossadeq of Iran," p. 13.

105 *"the United States government had done everything":* DDE, *Mandate for Change*, p. 164.

105 *bribe members of the Iranian Majlis:* CIA Report, "Overthrow of Premier Mossadeq of Iran," p. 28.

106 *"It was cleared directly":* July 24, 1953, calls, Telephone Conversations File, Dulles Papers; also in *FRUS Iran, 1952–54*, vol. 10, p. 737.

106 *one of the participants, Kermit Roosevelt:* The deceptions of Roosevelt's book begin with its title, *Countercoup*, intended to demonstrate that American actions were only taken in retaliation against a coup by Mossadegh. That is flatly false.

106 *he needed a vacation:* Ambassador to State Department, Feb. 25, 1953, in *FRUS Iran, 1952–54*, vol. 10, p. 682.

106 *a vacation out of his country:* Ambassador to State Department, May 30, 1953, in ibid., p. 731.

106   *but it sufficed:* CIA Report, "Overthrow of Premier Mossadeq of Iran," p. 36.

106   *threats to bomb homes:* Ibid., p. 37.

107   *"After you, Your Majesty":* Weiner, *Legacy of Ashes*, p. 90. See also Iraq Ambassador to State Department, Aug. 17, 1953, in *FRUS Iran, 1952–54*, vol. 10, pp. 746–47.

107   *"The move failed":* Smith to DDE, Aug. 18, 1953, in *FRUS Iran, 1952–54*, vol. 10, p. 748.

107   *"It was a day that":* CIA Report, "Overthrow of Premier Mossadeq of Iran," pp. 55–58. See also Ambassador to State Department, Aug. 20, 1953, in *FRUS Iran, 1952–54*, vol. 10, pp. 752–55.

107   *departed for Denver on the presidential plane:* April 19, 1953, Presidential Appointment Books, DDEPL.

107   *"I offer you my sincere felicitations":* DDE to Shah, Aug. 24, 1953, in *FRUS Iran, 1952–54*, vol. 10, p. 766.

108   *"The things we did were 'covert' ":* DDE, Oct. 8, 1953, diary entry. Released to the author. Portions of this diary were released in 1981; the entire entry, including the account of Mossadegh's overthrow, was declassified in 2009 and formally released on May 10, 2010.

108   *"When we realize that in the first hours":* Ibid.

108   *died before the ambulance could arrive:* James St. Clair and Linda Gugin, *Chief Justice Fred M. Vinson of Kentucky* (Lexington: University Press of Kentucky, 2002), p. 336.

109   *graduate school cases: Sipuel v. Board of Regents of the University of Oklahoma*, 332 U.S. 631 (1948); *Sweatt v. Painter*, 329 U.S. 629 (1950); *McLaurin v. Oklahoma State Regents*, 339 U.S. 637 (1950).

109   Plessy v. Ferguson *ruling: Plessy v. Ferguson*, 163 U.S. 537 (1896).

109   *"We cannot conclude that the education": Sweatt*, 329 U.S. 629.

109   *"impair and inhibit his ability": McLaurin*, 339 U.S. 637.

109   *The Court avoided them: Sweatt*, 329 U.S. 629.

110   *"We have deemed it more costly": Dennis v. United States*, 341 U.S. 494 (1951).

111   *in the pursuit of social change:* Jeffrey D. Hockett, *New Deal Justice* (Lanham, Md.: Rowman and Littlefield, 1996), p. 143.

111   *first solid evidence of the existence of God:* See, among other citations, Joseph L. Rauh, *New Republic*, Aug. 9, 1982, p. 31.

111   *"The very purpose of a Bill of Rights": West Virginia State Board of Education v. Barnette*, 319 U.S. 624 (1943).

112   *both sides went away bruised:* Roger Newman, *Hugo Black*, pp. 336–37.

112   *until Frankfurter finished expounding on a case:* Newton, *Justice for All*, p. 267.

112   *"efficiency, dignity and integrity":* St. Clair and Gugin, *Chief Justice Fred M. Vinson of Kentucky*, p. 336.

113   *"advice was on the mark":* Brownell, *Advising Ike*, p. 164.

113   *in a coded cable from Europe:* Ibid., p. 165.

114   *more interested in continuing in his "present post":* DDE, *Mandate for Change*, p. 227.

114   *never mentioned that offer to his attorney general:* Brownell, *Advising Ike*, p. 166.

114 *"It was kind of a hideout"*: "Conversations with Earl Warren on California Government," oral history with Warren, p. 285.

114 *"First vacancy"*: Earl Warren Jr., interview with author, Nov. 25, 2003.

114 *boasted to a friend that the job was his:* Brownell, *Advising Ike*, p. 167; and Warren, interview with Bartley Cavanaugh, p. 34, Earl Warren Oral History Project.

114 *"From the very beginning"*: Sept. 30, 1953, news conference, APP.

115 *as Warren was administered the oath:* Oct. 5, 1953, entry, President's Daily Appointments, DDEPL.

115 *"To my mind, he is a statesman"*: DDE to Edgar, Oct. 1, 1953, DDE Diary October 1953 (4), box 3, DDE Diary Series, Whitman File.

115 *"one of the finest public servants"*: *New York Times*, Feb. 21, 1954.

115 *miss a Court reception for Justice Burton:* May 5, 1954, entry, Phone Calls Jan.–May 1954 (1), box 5, DDE Diary Series. Also Nov. 3, 1953, entry, DDE Diary July–Dec. 1953, Whitman File.

115 *"No greater honor"*: Warren to DDE, note (handwritten and typed), March 19, 1954, DDE Diary March 1954 (2), box 6, DDE Diary Series, Whitman File.

116 *"my great friend"*: DDE, entry for July 24, 1953, in *Diaries*, p. 246.

116 *"Improvement in race relations"*: Ibid.

116 *"I believe that federal law"*: Ibid., pp. 246–47.

117 *he hoped they could put it off until the next administration:* DDE and Brownell, conversation, Jan. 25, 1954, Phone Calls Jan.–May 1954 (3), box 5, DDE Diary Series, Whitman File.

117 *"Anything that affects"*: DDE to Bradford Chynoweth, July 13, 1954, Brigadier General Chynoweth folder, box 5, Name Series, Whitman File.

117 *a meeting of a president's cabinet:* Max Rabb to DDE, note, Aug. 16, 1954, box 3, ACW Diary Series, Whitman File.

118 *"My dad was not a social reformer"*: John Eisenhower, interview with author, Oct. 7, 2010.

119 *"Iran was quiet—and still free"*: DDE, *Mandate for Change*, pp. 164 and 166.

CHAPTER 7: SECURITY

120 *"If I could have foreseen"*: DDE, *Mandate for Change*, p. 318.

121 *and headed home:* Lattimore, *Ordeal by Slander*, pp. 2–27.

121 *"placed too much stress"*: Ibid., p. 68.

121 *"To break the grip of fear"*: Ibid., p. 253.

121 *it supplied grist for McCarthy:* Owen Lattimore, Sept. 8, 1949, FBI File 100–1630 (FOIA).

122 *vote of confidence in "our crusade"*: DDE to McCarthy, Nov. 12, 1952, Joseph McCarthy folder, box 22, Name Series, Whitman File.

122 *"wanted all the help"*: Dulles and McCarthy, conversation, Jan. 28, 1953, Telephone Memoranda (excluding to or from the White House), Jan.–April 1953 (4), box 1, Telephone Calls Series, Dulles Papers.

122 *during Dulles's brief Senate tenure:* Sokolsky to Dulles, Sept. 14, 1949, John Foster Dulles folder, box 45, Sokolsky Papers. See also Sokolsky's testimony to

the Special Subcommittee on Investigations of the Committee on Government Operations, April 23, 1954.

122 *refused to employ them:* Dulles to Norman Thomas, Sept. 8, 1953, White House Correspondence (2), box 1, White House Memoranda Series, Dulles Papers.

122 *"it would be a serious blow":* Adams, *Firsthand Report,* p. 94.

123 *the would-be ambassador:* Dulles and Adams, conversation, March 13, 1953, White House Telephone Conversations, Jan.–April 1953, box 10, Telephone Calls Series, Dulles Papers.

123 *"not the slightest intention of withdrawing":* Dulles and DDE, conversation and accompanying memo, March 16, 1953, White House Telephone Conversations, Jan.–April 1953, box 10, Telephone Calls Series, Dulles Papers.

123 *"part of the Acheson betrayal team":* McCarthy speech to Senate, March 25, 1953, Security Matters—McLeod, Scott (Security Admin.)—Bohlen (2) folder, box 8, White House Memoranda Series, Dulles Papers.

123 *"Senator McCarthy is . . . so anxious":* DDE, *Diaries,* pp. 233–34.

123 *"a pimple on the path of progress":* DDE and Leonard Hall, phone conversation, March 8, 1954, referred to in fn. 2, doc. 762, HP.

123 *"I despise them":* DDE to Paul Helms, March 9, 1954, DDE Diary March 1954 (4), box 6, Diary Series, Whitman File.

124 *"embarrassment for the administration":* DDE to Virgil Pinkley, March 11, 1954, doc. 772, HP.

124 *American libraries abroad:* Wicker, *Shooting Star,* p. 130.

124 *"I think you are wrong about that":* Memorandum for the Archives, June 15, 1953, Richard Morin Papers, Rauner Library, Dartmouth College.

124 *"if you have anything to say":* Proskauer to John Dickey, Oct. 30, 1967, Morin Papers. Proskauer's precise quotation is rendered slightly differently in various accounts. The language here comes from his letter to Dickey.

124 *"Don't join the book burners":* Dartmouth College transcript, Rauner Library.

125 *"You have double thanks":* Memorandum for the Archives, June 15, 1953, Morin Papers.

125 *"since he entered public life":* Reprinted in the *Dartmouth Alumni Magazine,* July 1953.

125 *"but to the general proposition":* Memorandum of Conversation with the President, June 15, 1953, White House Correspondence (3), box 1, White House Memoranda Series, Dulles Papers.

125 *"buy or handle books":* Ibid.

125 *discuss a public statement:* DDE, *Mandate for Change,* pp. 143–44; see also 135th NSC Meeting, March 4, 1953, box 4, NSC Series, Whitman File.

125 *directly to the Soviet people:* 135th NSC Meeting.

126 *"It was certainly a gamble":* Ibid.

126 *"They {the Russian people} are the children":* Statement by the President Concerning the Illness of Joseph Stalin, March 4, 1953, APP.

126 *"Ever since 1946":* Hughes, *Ordeal of Power,* p. 101.

126 *"We have no reliable inside intelligence":* Haines and Leggett, *CIA's Analysis of the Soviet Union*, p. 35.

127 *"as though the hour of decision":* 163rd NSC Meeting, Sept. 24, 1953, box 4, NSC Series, Whitman File.

127 *"Global war as a defense":* Handwritten note, July 16, 1953, DDE Diary Dec. 1952–July 1953 (1), box 3, DDE Diary Series, Whitman File.

127 *"to determine our own course":* 163rd NSC Meeting.

127 *"not only in saving our money":* Ibid.

128 *National War College:* Dockrill, *Eisenhower's New-Look National Security Policy*, p. 33.

128 *"The only way to end the cold war is to win it":* Undated memo (Task Force C report begins at p. 24), Project Solarium (2) folder, box 39, Disaster File, White House Office, NSC Staff Papers, 1948–61, DDEPL.

128 *"They would undoubtedly oppose":* Ibid.

128 *"a true American Crusade":* Project Solarium, (2 folder), box 9, Subject Subseries, NSC Staff Papers, 1952–61, DDEPL.

130 *"Here is what I would like to say":* Hughes, *Ordeal*, p. 103.

130 *"I know how he feels":* These comments and the description of the speech's drafting come from Hughes, *Ordeal of Power*, pp. 107–15.

130 *"Those sitting close to him":* Childs, *Captive Hero*, p. 197.

132 *"What is the Soviet Union ready to do?":* DDE, "The Chance for Peace," April 16, 1953, APP.

132 *"a remarkable effort of will":* Childs, *Captive Hero*, p. 197.

132 *"cannot in the least contribute":* Dockrill, *Eisenhower's New-Look National Security Policy*, p. 132.

133 *"wider public discussion":* Medhurst, Ivie, Wander, and Scott, *Cold War Rhetoric*, p. 30.

133 *"the rate and impact of atomic production":* Bird and Sherwin, *American Prometheus*, p. 451.

133 *"slowly dying":* Chernus, *Eisenhower's Atoms for Peace*, p. 68.

133 *he and Oppenheimer were at odds:* Aug. 4, 1953, diary entry, box 68, C. D. Jackson Papers.

133 *from Operation Candor to Operation Wheaties:* Dockrill, *Eisenhower's New-Look National Security Policy*, p. 132. See also Nov. 27, 1953, diary entry, box 68, C. D. Jackson Papers.

133 *scheduled to speak in early December:* Nov. 17, 1953, diary entry, box 68, C. D. Jackson Papers.

134 *"twenty-one years of treason":* Eisenhower was particularly infuriated by the implication that internal subversion was tolerated by his administration. The following summer, while castigating Nixon for being excessively partisan in criticizing Democrats, he described McCarthy's remark, which he then quoted as "twenty years of treason," as "an indefensible statement" (June 29, 1954, entry, Eisenhower Library Documents [2], box 2, Personal Papers of Whitman).

134 *renewed commitment to deliver it:* Nov. 30 and Dec. 1, 1953, diary entries, box 68,

C. D. Jackson Papers. So bleak was the debate on Nov. 30 that Jackson entitled that day's diary entry "Black Monday."

134 *"President changed clothes":* Dec. 4, 5, 6, 7, 8, 1953, diary entries, box 68, C. D. Jackson Papers. See also Hagerty, oral history interview.

135 *threat of nuclear war:* DDE, "Atoms for Peace," Dec. 8, 1953, APP.

136 *"Some of his accusers":* DDE, note to Dec. 2, 1953, entry, dated Dec. 3, DDE 136 Oct.–Dec. 1953, box 4, DDE Diary Series, Whitman File.

137 *"It would not be a case":* DDE, Dec. 3, 1953, entry, DDE Diary Oct.–Dec. 1953, box 4, DDE Diary Series, Whitman File.

137 *under the new Congress:* Barton J. Bernstein, "The Oppenheimer Loyalty-Security Case Reconsidered," *Stanford Law Review* 42, no. 6 (1990), p. 1383.

137 *"based upon years of study":* Borden to J. Edgar Hoover, Nov. 7, 1953, doc. 100–17828–548, FBI (FOIA).

138 *available to Borden:* Bird and Sherwin, *American Prometheus,* p. 473.

138 *preserve his own line of attack:* Ibid., p. 471.

138 *his home in Princeton:* Branigan to Belmont, memo, June 2, 1954, FBI (FOIA).

139 *when the FBI suggested removing them:* Ibid.

139 *"they consist of nothing more":* DDE, Dec. 3, 1953, entry, DDE Diary Oct.–Dec. 1953, box 4, DDE Diary Series, Whitman File.

139 *"to place a blank wall":* DDE to Brownell, Dec. 3, 1953, doc. 583, HP.

139 *public as well as private humiliation:* Bird and Sherwin, *American Prometheus,* pp. 482–83.

139 *collapsed on the floor of his lawyer's bathroom:* Ibid., p. 484.

139 *"moments of real satisfaction":* DDE to Hazlett, Dec. 24, 1953, Swede Hazlett 1953 (1) folder, box 18, Name Series, Whitman File.

139 *"there is a clear prospect":* DDE to Bryce Harlow, Dec. 3, 1953, doc. 586, HP.

140 *"In view of the number of people":* DDE to Gruenther, Dec. 25, 1953, doc. 633, HP.

CHAPTER 8: "MCCARTHYWASM"

141 *enacted by separate legislation:* Senate Joint Resolution 1, 83rd Cong., *Congressional Record.*

142 *"Just how silly can you get?":* Edgar to DDE, March 27, 1953, Edgar Eisenhower 1953 (2) folder, box 11, Name Series, Whitman File.

142 *"I think that someone":* Edgar to DDE, March 31, 1953, Edgar Eisenhower 1953 (2) folder, box 11, Name Series, Whitman File.

142 *"You seem to fear":* DDE to Edgar, April 1, 1953, Edgar Eisenhower 1953 (2) folder, box 11, Name Series, Whitman File.

142 *"a communication which contains":* DDE to Edgar, Jan. 27, 1954, Edgar Eisenhower 1954 (3) folder, box 11, Name Series, Whitman File.

143 *"Never have I in my life":* DDE to Edgar, Feb. 3, 1954, Edgar Eisenhower 1954 (1) folder, box 11, Name Series, Whitman File.

143 *resurfaced as a serious notion:* DDE, *Mandate for Change,* p. 285.

143 *"I'm sorry you are upset":* DDE to Edgar, March 12, 1954, Edgar Eisenhower 1954 (1) folder, box 11, Name Series, Whitman File.

144   *"hush the whole matter up and forget it"*: *Wall Street Journal*, Nov. 23, 1953.

144   *"The raw, harsh, unpleasant fact"*: *Wall Street Journal*, Nov. 25, 1953.

144   *"Anyone with the brains"*: Wicker, *Shooting Star*, p. 139.

144   *"removed from any command"*: U.S. Senate, *Executive Sessions of the Senate Permanent Subcommittee on Investigations of the Committee on Government Operations, Congressional Record*, p. 16.

144   *if he weren't so fond of Stevens*: Testimony of George Sokolsky, April 23, 1954, in ibid., p. 216.

144   *had made concessions*: There are many accounts, press and otherwise, of this lunch and its aftermath. One particularly illuminating source is found at DDE and Lucius Clay, conversation, Feb. 25, 1954, Phone Calls Jan.–May 1954 (2), box 5, Diary Series, Whitman File.

145   *"What Secretary Stevens agreed to"*: *New York Times*, Feb. 25, 1954.

145   *"in a state of shock"*: DDE and Clay, conversation, Feb. 25, 1954.

145   *"blew the lid off the teakettle"*: Adams, unpublished MS, p. 430.

145   *and then resign*: Hagerty, Feb. 24, 1954, entry in *Diary*, p. 19.

145   *its way into the* Times: *New York Times*, Feb. 26, 1954.

145   *"Don't think you can lock horns"*: DDE and Clay, conversation, Feb. 25, 1954.

145   *some legal advice*: Brownell was out of the office when Eisenhower called, so the president spoke with William Rogers, Brownell's deputy.

145   *"Suppose I made up my mind"*: DDE and Rogers, conversation, March 2, 1954, Phone Calls Jan.–May 1954 (2), box 5, Diary Series, Whitman File.

145   *keep a lid on McCarthy*: DDE and Knowland, conversation, March 20, 1954, Phone Calls Jan.–May 1954 (2), box 5, Diary Series, Whitman File.

145   *chairman of the board of General Electric*: DDE to Philip Reed, June 17, 1953, DDE Diary Dec. 1952–July 1953 (2), box 3, DDE Diary Series, Whitman File.

145   *tangling with him publicly*: DDE to Robinson, March 12, 1954, William E. Robinson 1952–55 (2) folder, box 29, Name Series, Whitman File.

145   *"He's the last guy"*: Hagerty, Feb. 26, 1954, entry in *Diary*, p. 20.

146   *"We just did something to please him"*: Lucille Ball Security Matter, Investigation of Communist Activities in the Los Angeles Area, Sept. 4, 1953, FBI File 100–41702 (FOIA).

146   *"the top television comedienne"*: Sanders and Gilbert, *Desilu*, p. 78.

146   *"my favorite redhead"*: Ibid., p. 81.

146   *"God Bless America!"*: Arnaz, *Book*, p. 306.

146   *"Sooner or later"*: Hoffman to DDE, March 25, 1954, Diary March 1954 (1), box 6, DDE Diary Series, Whitman File.

147   *protections to give subordinates*: Willis to Adams, memo, March 9, 1954, The President [1954] (4) folder, box 54, Brownell Papers.

147   *defense to review*: Bird and Sherwin, *American Prometheus*, p. 498.

148   *his formal reply*: *New York Times*, April 13, 1954.

148   *"I think it only fair"*: U.S. Atomic Energy Commission, *In the Matter of J. Robert Oppenheimer*, p. 53.

148   *"May I correct that"*: Ibid.

148   *"This fellow Oppenheimer"*: James Reston, *Deadline*, p. 224.

149 *"New and special rules"*: New York Times, April 23, 1954.

150 *influenced the general's testimony*: Ibid.

150 *"close to disgusting"*: DDE to Hazlett, April 27, 1954, Swede Hazlett 1954 (2) folder, box 18, Name Series, Whitman File.

150 *"a pixie is a close relative of a fairy"*: Wicker, *Shooting Star*, pp. 152–53.

151 *ended for the week*: New York Times, May 15, 1954.

151 *"We know we value the right"*: Ibid. See also Eisenhower Daily Schedule for details of dinner, Whitman File.

151 *"Because it is essential to efficient"*: DDE to Stevens, May 17, 1954, McCarthy Letters, box 25, Administration Series, Whitman File.

151 *"Any man who testifies"*: Hagerty, May 17, 1954, entry in *Diary*, p. 53.

151 *blocked further inquiry*: New York Times, May 18, 1954.

151 *"By his statement of yesterday"*: Ibid.

152 *"implication of disloyalty"*: New York Times, April 14, 1954.

152 *"four experienced and able commissioners"*: Editorial reaction from around the nation is excerpted and can be found at Robert Oppenheimer folder, box 7, White House Central Files, Hagerty Papers.

152 *"Many . . . intelligent men"*: Reston, *Deadline*, p. 226.

153 *"communist-front" organization*: See Welch comments at hearing, as well as Hagerty, April 2, 1954, entry in *Diary*, p. 40. Although Welch did not disclose it at the hearing, Fisher also, according to Hagerty, organized a guild chapter in Massachusetts with the help of a Communist organizer.

154 *"Mr. McCarthy, I will not discuss this further"*: The exchange between McCarthy and Welch is presented on videotape at www.americanrhetoric.com/speeches/welch-mccarthy.html. Transcripts also appeared in the *New York Times* and elsewhere.

155 *"It's no longer McCarthyism"*: Minnich memo to Adams, June 21, 1955, ML-8, McCarthy Controversy—High Points, Adams Papers.

155 *servicemen huddled below*: See http://nuclearweaponarchive.org/Usa/Tests/Castle.html.

155 *United States and Japan for months*: Within the administration, there lurked a suspicion that the fishing boat was in the area spying for the Soviet Union. Lewis Strauss in particular advanced that theory, on evidence so thin as to appear ludicrous (Strauss, for instance, was suspicious that the captain of the vessel was so young). See Hagerty, April 2, 1954, entry in *Diary*, pp. 40–42.

156 *cloakroom and collapsed*: This reconstruction draws on many sources, principally the coverage from the *New York Times*, March 2, 1954.

156 *"These people just shoot wildly"*: DDE and Martin, conversation, March 1, 1954, Phone Calls, Jan.–May 1954 (2), box 5, DDE Diary Series, Whitman File.

157 *"his destiny, his responsibility"*: Embassy in the Republic of China to State Department, dispatch, April 3, 1958, in *FRUS, China*, vol. 19, p. 13.

157 *even if fired upon*: Dockrill, *Eisenhower's New-Look National Security Policy*, pp. 103–4.

157 *defeat the North Vietnamese by the end of 1955*: DDE, *Mandate for Change*, p. 338.

158 *they ignored him*: Ibid., p. 339.

158 *"Reds would win that part"*: Hagerty, March 26, 1954, entry in *Diary*, p. 35. Cabinet Meeting, March 26, 1954.

158 *"Air power might be temporarily beneficial"*: DDE, *Mandate for Change*, p. 341.

158 *"suffered reverses"*: DDE letter to Hazlett, April 27, 1954, Hazlett 1954 (2) folder, box 18, Name Series, Whitman File.

158 *Dien Bien Phu fell:* In his telling of this episode, Stephen Ambrose writes that Eisenhower reacted to the suggestion that nuclear weapons might be useful in Indochina with revulsion. "You boys must be crazy," Ambrose quotes Eisenhower telling the NSC staff adviser Bobby Cutler. "We can't use those awful things against Asians for the second time in less than ten years. My God" (Ambrose, *Eisenhower, the President*, p. 184). That statement is attributed to an undated interview with Eisenhower and must be regarded with skepticism. Eisenhower had specifically contemplated the use of nuclear weapons in Korea just one year earlier, and though he decided against it, he expressed no horror or revulsion at the thought of using "those awful things" against Asians in that conflict. As with many aspects of Ambrose's work, the absence of notes and discrepancies regarding dates make it difficult to say whether this quotation is merely inaccurate or fabricated, but it should not be regarded seriously.

158 *"Congress would be asked immediately to declare"*: Robert Cutler to Dulles, memo, June 2, 1954, summarizing meeting of same day (full meeting notes filed as well), Indochina 1954 folder, box 11, Briefing Notes Subseries, NSC Series, Office of the Special Assistant for National Security Affairs and Records, 1952–61, DDEPL.

159 *"American boys to fight in Indochina"*: Hagerty, *Diary*, p. 96.

159 *"I couldn't possibly be prouder"*: DDE to John and Barbara Eisenhower, June 11, 1954, doc. 921, HP.

159 *"by the time they are eight"*: DDE to Edgar Eisenhower, July 6, 1954, doc. 962, HP.

159 *by her side: New York Times*, July 11, 1954.

160 *"When I refer to the Middle Way"*: DDE to Chynoweth, July 13, 1954, Brigadier General Chynoweth folder, box 5, Name Series, Whitman File.

161 *"a magnificent symbol"*: D'Arcy Jenish, "Inland Superhighway," *Canadian Geographic*, July/Aug. 2009, p. 38, at http://www.greatlakes-seaway.com/en/pdf/resources_article1.pdf.

161 *rescue missions in the South China Sea:* Sherman Adams, unpublished MS, p. 603, Adams Papers.

161 *"Eisenhower had spells of depression that summer"*: Ibid., p. 604.

CHAPTER 9: REVOLUTIONS

162 *"Coup d'etat in Guatemala"*: Project Solarium, Report to the Office of the Special Assistant for National Security Affairs, NSC by Task Force C [1953] (7), p. 263, box 9, Subject Subseries, NSC Series, White House Office, Records, 1952–61, DDEPL. More specifically, the report recommended using "third forces in bringing about a supplanting of the pro-Kremlin government in Guatemala, with one of anti-Kremlin, pro-U.S. orientation" (see p. 211).

163   *"If the Guatemalans want to handle":* Cullather, *Secret History*, p. 16.

163   *the president's NSC Planning Board:* For Cutler's relationship to United Fruit, see May 26, 1954, memo, White House Telephone Memos, Jan. 1, 1954–June 30, 1954 (1), box 10, Telephone Calls Series, Dulles Papers.

163   *pay back the government over time:* Cullather, *Secret History*, p. 22.

164   *a bill for $15,854,849:* Immerman, *CIA in Guatemala*, p. 81.

164   *"As long as President Arbenz":* "Probable Developments in Guatemala," NIE 84, quoted in Cullather, *Secret History*, p. 34.

164   *evidence of such connections:* Cullather, *Secret History*, p. 26.

164   *"not as many":* Immerman, *CIA in Guatemala*, p. 183.

165   *"It was meant to be":* DDE, *Mandate for Change*, p. 423.

165   *"How could they invent an umbrella":* New York Times, March 2, 1954.

165   *"number one priority":* Chief of Western Hemisphere to Director of Plans, CIA, memo, Aug. 27, 1953, folder 3, box 73, CIA Job 79–01025A, in *FRUS 1952–54, Guatemala*, p. 92.

165   *based in Miami:* Cullather, *Secret History*, p. 75.

166   *total came to $2.735 million:* Budget Summary, folder 2, box 76, CIA Job 79–01025A, in *FRUS 1952–54, Guatemala*, p. 109.

166   *$3 million three months later:* Dulles to Wisner, memo, Dec. 9, 1953, folder 6, box 167, CIA Job 79–01025A, in ibid., p. 155.

166   *succumbed to Communist influence:* Cullather, *Secret History*, p. 56.

166   *"The Guatemalan regime has been frequently accused":* New York Times, May 18, 1954.

167   *vessels bound for Guatemala:* Immerman, *CIA in Guatemala*, pp. 158–59.

167   *"Should this ammo ship arrive":* CIA Guatemala Station to Operation PBSUCCESS Headquarters, telegram, May 21, 1954, folder 6, box 8, CIA Job 79–01025A, in *FRUS 1952–54, Guatemala*, p. 295.

167   *Eisenhower did not respond:* Cullather, *Secret History*, p. 83.

167   *imagined him to lead:* CIA Guatemala Station to Operation PBSUCCESS Headquarters, telegram, June 8, 1954, folder 3, box 11, CIA Job 79–01025A, in *FRUS 1952–54, Guatemala*, p. 316.

167   *"Even before H-hour":* Cullather, *Secret History*, p. 88.

167   *without attempting to defeat his army:* Memo Prepared in CIA (apparently by Richard Bissell, for Allen Dulles), June 20, 1954, folder 1, box 154, CIA Job 79–01025A, in *FRUS 1952–54, Guatemala*, p. 359.

168   *killed or captured:* Cullather, *Secret History*, p. 90.

168   *Eisenhower at the White House:* Cullather's CIA history places this meeting on June 23, but the president's schedule shows it at 2:30 p.m. on June 22. The official history also neglects to mention Foster Dulles's presence at the meeting; again, the schedule indicates otherwise.

168   *"cowering in their barracks":* Cullather, *Secret History*, p. 97. See also CIA Guatemala Station to Operation PBSUCCESS Headquarters, telegram, June 23, 1954, folder 5, box 11, CIA Job 79–01025A, in *FRUS 1952–54, Guatemala*, p. 374.

168   *bombs were exploding:* Cullather, *Secret History*, pp. 99–101.

168   *"Our first victory has been won":* CIA Guatemala Station to CIA Headquarters,

telegram, June 28, 1954, folder 5, box 11, CIA Job 79–01025A, in *FRUS 1952–54, Guatemala*, p. 396.

168 *a great triumph for American diplomacy:* Hagerty, June 28, 1954, entry in *Diary*, p. 79.

169 *cost precisely $3 million:* Memorandum Prepared in the CIA, May 12, 1975, folder 3, box 153, CIA Job 79–01025A, in *FRUS 1952–54, Guatemala*, p. 450.

169 *"Guatemala right now is the most interesting":* Anderson, *Che*, p. 134.

169 *failure to "arm the people":* Ibid., p. 151.

169 *"Politically, things aren't going so well":* Ibid., p. 133.

169 *"I have for announcement":* Newton, *Justice for All*, p. 324.

170 *acknowledged the next day:* Correspondence from Oct. 1 and Oct. 2, 1953, DDE Diary, October 1953 (4), box 3, DDE Diary Series, Whitman File.

170 *"The new Chief Justice":* Black to Hugo and Sterling Black, Oct. 15, 1953, Hugo Black Jr. file, 1953–54, Black Family Papers, MD, LOC.

170 *the constitutionality of Jim Crow:* Legal file, Supreme Court, Oct. term 1953; Conference notes, Dec. 12, 1953, Segregation Case File, Robert Jackson Papers. Also "Memorandum for the File in re Segregation Cases," pt. 2, May 17, 1954, William O. Douglas Papers, MD, LOC.

171 *"basic premise":* The description of the Dec. 12, 1953, conference relies on the conference notes of various justices, including Jackson, Douglas, and Burton. All are available at MD, LOC. Burton's are contained in his diary, Douglas's in a file labeled "Segregation Case File."

172 *were in the minority:* "Memorandum for the File in re Segregation Cases," pt. 2.

172 *from whether to strike down segregation to how to do it:* Jan. 15, 1954, entry, 1954 Diaries, Burton Papers.

172 *likely in the spring:* DDE and Brownell, conversation, Jan. 25, 1954, Phone Calls Jan.–May 1954 (3), box 5, DDE Diary Series, Whitman File.

173 *representing the state of South Carolina:* Warren, *Memoirs*, p. 291.

173 *"These are not bad people":* Ibid.

173 *"the war hero who had destroyed":* Nichols, *Matter of Justice*, pp. 103–9.

173 *not that Warren made up the exchange:* Brownell, *Advising Ike*, p. 174.

174 *"When the word 'unanimously' ":* Warren, *Memoirs*, p. 3.

174 *"The Supreme Court has spoken":* *New York Times*, May 20, 1954.

174 *those who sought equality and those who denied it:* See, for instance, DDE to Graham, March 30, 1956, Billy Graham folder, box 16, Name Series, Whitman File.

174 *"followed the President's formula":* Brownell and DDE, conversation, May 31, 1955, Phone Calls Jan.–July 1955 (1), box 9, DDE Diary Series, Whitman File.

174 *supported the Court's ruling in Brown:* Ann Whitman, Aug. 19, 1956, entry, Aug. 1956 (1) folder, box 8, ACW Diary Series, Whitman File.

175 *international appreciation vis-à-vis the Soviets:* Dudziak, *Cold War Civil Rights*, pp. 109–10.

175 *"I'm afraid we'll have plenty of trouble":* Hazlett to DDE, Oct. 14, 1954, Swede Hazlett 1954 (1) folder, box 18, Name Series, Whitman File.

175 *relaxing with the Gang:* Sept. 12, 1954, Presidential Appointment Books, DDEPL.

175 *condemnation of the world:* 214th NSC Meeting, Sept. 12, 1954, box 6, NSC Series, Whitman File.

176 *strike the Soviet Union itself:* Ibid.

176 *"The hard way":* DDE, *Mandate for Change*, p. 465.

176 *"armed attack in the West Pacific":* A copy of the treaty may be found at http://avalon.law.yale.edu/20th_century/chin001.asp.

176 *"In any combat where":* March 16, 1955, news conference, APP.

177 *"I am afraid":* Exchange of letters from June 29 and July 2, 1954, Arthur Eisenhower (3) folder, box 11, Name Series, Whitman File.

177 *"I know so many things":* Whitman, Nov. 24, 1954, entry, which includes Knowland conversation, Nov. 1954 (1) folder, box 3, ACW Diary Series, Whitman File.

177 *"No man on earth":* Ibid., which includes meeting with Montgomery.

178 *general's testimony earlier that year: Time*, Oct. 4, 1954.

178 *attacking Watkins as a coward:* See http://www.senate.gov/artandhistory/history/common/censure_cases/133Joseph_McCarthy.htm.

178 *against McCarthy's censure, annoying Eisenhower: New York Times*, Dec. 3, 1954.

178 *"done a very splendid job": New York Times*, Dec. 5, 1953.

178 *"I thought the stories":* Hagerty, Dec. 6, 1954, entry in *Diary*, p. 127.

178 *"Why it was called such":* DDE, *Mandate for Change*, p. 330.

179 *the U-2 program was launched:* Pedlow and Welzenbach, *CIA and the U-2 Program*, p. 37.

179 *most of his day for Clay:* Nov. 18, 1954, Presidential Appointment Books.

179 *"once he got on to the real purpose":* DDE, entry for Nov. 20, 1954, in *Diaries*, p. 288.

180 *"in some position of great responsibility":* DDE to Hazlett, Dec. 8, 1954, Hazlett 1954 (1) folder, box 18, Name Series, Whitman File.

CHAPTER 10: HEARTACHE

182 *"I still remember":* DDE to Churchill, March 22, 1955, doc. 1355, HP.

183 *"there seems to be no final answer":* DDE, Jan. 10, 1955, entry in *Diaries*, p. 291.

183 *"growing up and getting tougher":* Hagerty, Jan. 18, 1955, entry in *Diary*, p. 164.

183 *"the ability to blow hell":* Dec. 13, 1954, entry in ibid., p. 133.

184 *"I felt I was being called upon":* See Arlington National Cemetery synopsis of Ridgway's career, at http://www.arlingtoncemetery.net/ridgway.htm.

184 *"carry their dissents":* DDE and Dulles, conversation, Jan. 25, 1955, Phone Calls Jan.–July 1955 (3), box 9, DDE Diary Series, Whitman File.

184 *"A division of soldiers":* DDE and Radford, conversation, Feb. 1, 1955, Phone Calls Jan.–July 1955 (2), box 9, DDE Diary Series, Whitman File.

184 *"I said I did not think":* March 6, 1955, meeting, Meetings with the President 1955 (7) folder, box 3, White House Memoranda Series, Dulles Papers.

184 *"I said that this would require":* Ibid.

184 *invade Quemoy and Matsu by April 15:* Ann Whitman, April 2, 1955, entry, April 1955 (6) folder, box 5, ACW Diary Series, Whitman File.

184 *"By God, this has got to stop":* Hagerty, March 28, 1954, entry in *Diary*, p. 218.

185 *watch his tongue:* Memorandum for Files, March 12, 1955, doc. 1342, HP.

185 *"seems to have no comprehension":* DDE, March 12, 1955, entry in *Diaries*, p. 296.

185 *"Not by me":* March 30, 1955, news conference, APP.

185 *"I want to make clear":* Ibid.

185 *"Foster and I live":* Adams, unpublished manuscript, p. 618.

185 *"I felt an almost physical reaction":* Hughes, *Ordeal of Power*, p. 208.

186 *"I do hope you will be willing":* Eden to DDE, cable, received on May 6, 1955, John Foster Dulles May 1955 folder, box 5, Dulles-Herter Series, Whitman File.

186 *before Eden's formal note: New York Times*, May 5, 1955.

186 *open to a summit under the right conditions:* DDE to Eden, cable, May 6, 1955, Dulles May 1955 folder, box 5, Dulles-Herter Series, Whitman File.

186 *"Believe that the time has now come":* Acting Secretary to DDE, cable, transmitting from Dulles, May 9, 1955, Dulles May 1955 folder, box 5, Dulles-Herter Series, Whitman File.

186 *"This business of trying to reach":* May 11, 1955, news conference, APP.

187 *Molotov seemed flexible:* Dulles to DDE, telegram, May 14, 1955, Dulles May 1955 folder, box 5, Dulles-Herter Series, Whitman File.

187 *"is regarded as beginning":* Approval ratings courtesy of the APP; other survey data from Geneva Conference folder, box 29, Confidential File 1953–61, White House Central Files, Records of the President, DDEPL.

188 *"amateurish"* and *"dangerous":* Aug. 8, 1955, entry, Telephone Conversations General May 2, 1955–Aug. 31, 1955 (3), box 4, Telephone Calls Series, Dulles Papers.

188 *"He's got them down at Quantico":* Adams, *Firsthand Report*, p. 91.

188 *a transfer to Defense:* Whitman, May 25, 1955, entry, May 1955 (2) folder, box 5, ACW Diary Series, Whitman File.

188 *"the position of the Soviet Union":* Memorandum of Conversation, June 23, 1955, Dulles June 1955 folder, box 5, Dulles-Herter Series, Whitman File.

189 *heading for Augusta:* DDE to Hobby, Nov. 24, 1953, Oveta Culp Hobby folder (6), box 19, Administration Series, Whitman File.

189 *"nearing the end of her rope":* Whitman note to file, Feb. 24, 1954, Hobby folder (3), box 19, Administration Series, Whitman File.

189 *vaccines soon resumed:* Statement by Surgeon General Leonard A. Scheele, May 8, 1955, Hobby (1) folder, box 19, Administration Series, Whitman File.

189 *"personal reasons":* Hobby to DDE, July 13, 1955, Hobby (1) folder, box 19, Administration Series, Whitman File.

190 *"All who knew you as a dedicated":* DDE to Hobby, July 13, 1955, Hobby (1) folder, box 19, Administration Series, Whitman File.

190 *"best man in the Cabinet": Time*, July 25, 1955.

190 *"would be a mighty force":* DDE, Radio and Television Address, July 15, 1955, APP.

190 *hope that surrounded Geneva:* DDE, *Mandate for Change*, p. 512. Also John Eisen-

hower's memo of Geneva trip contained in Geneva Notes—Maj. Andy Goodpaster, Whitman File.

190 *twelve hundred feet above sea level:* These observations are from John Eisenhower's
memo of the trip.

191 *"we could hardly refuse":* Time, July 18, 1955.

191 *seating chart for the discussions:* July 17, 1955, memo, Geneva Conference, July
18–23, 1955 (4), box 2, International Meetings Series, Whitman File.

191 *an old friend, Sir James Gault:* Whitman, July 17, 1955, entry, July 1955 (3)
folder, box 6, ACW Diary Series, Whitman File.

191 *retired to dinner alone:* John Eisenhower, memo.

191 *"I trust that we are not here":* Opening statement at the Geneva Conference,
July 18, 1955, APP.

191 *by prearrangement, slipped out:* Whitman, July 18, 1955, entry, July 1955 (3) folder,
box 6, ACW Diary Series, Whitman File. Also John Eisenhower's memo.

192 *"They were jumpy as hell":* John Eisenhower, interview with author, Oct. 7, 2010.

192 *"Even Gromyko managed":* John Eisenhower, memo.

193 *"a meeting between them":* Ibid.

193 *"You can make all the pictures":* Transcript of summit meeting, July 22, 1955,
folder (13), box 29, Confidential File, 1953–61, White House Central Files,
Records of President, DDEPL.

194 *"A sound peace":* Ibid.

194 *"I didn't know I would":* John Eisenhower, memo.

194 *"I wish the people of the world":* Adams, *Firsthand Report*, p. 178.

194 *"I thought we had the makings of a breakthrough":* John Eisenhower, memo.

194 *"there was no smile in his voice":* DDE, *Mandate for Change*, p. 521.

194 *"From that moment until the final adjournment":* Ibid.

195 *confirmed Dulles's skepticism:* Adams, *Firsthand Report*, p. 177.

195 *"does not want peace":* DDE, *Mandate for Change*, p. 522.

196 *seven trout:* Details of these summer weeks are culled mainly from the Presidential Appointment Books for that period.

196 *eastern slope of the Rockies to Denver:* Draft of DDE's Heart Attack, Sept. 1955,
box 11, Howard Snyder Papers, 1881–1976, DDEPL.

196 *doctor Howard Snyder recalled:* Ibid.

197 *arriving at 3:11 a.m.:* Ibid.

197 *Ike fell into shock, according to Snyder:* Ibid.

197 *slipped out of his bed:* In addition to questions about the veracity of Snyder's
records, there are issues with their precision, as the alleged bedside notes do not
always conform to his later recollections. In this instance, his manuscript indicates that Mamie got into bed at 4:05 a.m., while his notes say the time was
4:30 a.m. Where there are discrepancies, I have opted to rely on the bedside
notes.

197 *dress in civilian clothes:* DDE Medical Records, 1955, box 3, Snyder Papers.

198 *"there has been no period of shock":* Lasby, *Eisenhower's Heart Attack*, p. 107.

198 *saving Eisenhower's life:* Robinson to various recipients, Oct. 18, 1955, Eisenhower Oct. 1955 folder, box 3, Robinson Papers.

199   *"It may have been":* Jan. 19, 1956, news conference, APP.

199   *heart attack on Icky's birthday:* Susan Eisenhower, *Mrs. Ike*, p. 288.

199   *leaving Ike's seat vacant:* See Sept. 29, 1955, Presidential Appointment Books, DDEPL, as well as Adams, *Firsthand Report*, p. 186.

199   *shocking the dour Adams:* Hagerty, oral history interview.

200   *"He is a darn good young man":* Whitman, Oct. 10, 1955, entry, Oct. 1955 (6) folder, box 7, ACW Diary Series, Whitman File.

200   *"He has not quite reached":* Ibid.

200   *"If I didn't think you knew":* Draft of DDE's Heart Attack.

200   *over the breast pocket:* John Eisenhower, *Strictly Personal*, p. 183.

200   *played on a phonograph in his room:* John Eisenhower, interview with author, Oct. 7, 2010.

201   *"a wonderful patient":* Memo of Nov. 2, 1955, trip to Denver, Aide-Mémoire folder, box 1, Cutler Papers.

201   *"I was tired and annoyed":* DDE, *Mandate for Change*, p. 544.

201   *"Every one of us took a deep breath":* Sherman Adams, unpublished MS, p. 711, Adams Papers.

201   *"more than any other possible development":* Robinson to Snyder, Oct. 18, 1955, Eisenhower Oct. 1955 folder, box 3, Robinson Papers.

201   *"it may henceforth be a place":* Susan Eisenhower, *Mrs. Ike*, p. 290.

202   *lost weight and color:* Adams, unpublished MS, p. 712.

202   *"I am to avoid all situations":* DDE to Hazlett, Jan. 23, 1956, Swede Hazlett Jan. 1956–Nov. 1958 (2) folder, box 18, Name Series, Whitman File.

202   *Blake arrested Parks:* Taylor Branch, *Parting the Waters*, pp. 128–29.

203   *built up his workday:* Presidential schedules for Dec. 1955, DDEPL.

203   *city's notorious newspaper:* Phone Calls Jan.–July 1955, Feb. 8, 1955, conversation between Eisenhower and Len Hall, box 9, DDE Diary Series, Whitman File.

203   *badly split the party:* Hagerty, Dec. 13, 1955, entry in *Diary*, p. 241.

203   *better suited to the Court:* Dec. 14, 1955, entry in ibid., p. 245.

203   *"On the whole, he felt":* Adams, unpublished MS, p. 751.

203   *convinced that Nixon was unelectable:* John Eisenhower, exchange with author, Sept. 2010.

204   *New Year's Eve:* Jan. 29–31, 1955, Presidential Appointment Books.

CHAPTER 11: CRISIS AND REVIVAL

205   *"idleness would be fatal":* Susan Eisenhower, *Mrs. Ike*, p. 294.

205   *"After a close brush with death":* Adams, *Firsthand Report*, p. 222.

205   *progress was evident:* Remarks on the State of the Union Message, Jan. 5, 1956, APP.

205   *"the full duties of the presidency":* Jan. 8, 1956, news conference in Key West, APP.

205   *preparing the place cards himself:* Susan Eisenhower, *Mrs. Ike*, p. 295.

206   *second-floor sitting room:* Memorandum of Conversation, Jan. 13, 1956, Very Private Memos of Conversations with the President and Vice President 1956–58, box 1, White House Memoranda Series, Dulles Papers.

206   *"As I saw the situation":* Ibid.

206 *"you ought to make up your mind":* Hagerty, oral history interview, p. 310.

206 *urged his brother to retire:* Sherman Adams, unpublished MS, p. 748, Adams Papers.

206 *"fearful of the strain":* Milton Eisenhower, oral history interview, p. 35.

207 *The others followed:* Hagerty, oral history interview, p. 310.

207 *"in order that I may reach":* Jan. 19, 1956, news conference, APP.

207 *implications for the rest of his administration:* John Eisenhower points out that even the selection of guests for the Jan. 13 meeting suggested which way his father was leaning. "What else would he expect from the 'fine group of subordinates' themselves," he asked of their advice (*Strictly Personal*, p. 185).

207 *they had yet to discuss it:* Jan. 25, 1956, news conference, APP.

207 *bipartisan ticket for 1956:* Ewald, *Eisenhower the President*, p. 184.

207 *"If we can count on me":* Ann Whitman, Feb. 9, 1956, entry, Feb. 1956 folder, box 8, ACW Diary Series, Whitman File.

207 *whatever Eisenhower asked him to:* Ibid.

208 *"very, very gentle":* Ibid.

208 *"radiant spirits":* Whitman, Feb. 13, 1956, entry, Feb. 1956 folder, box 8, ACW Diary Series, Whitman File.

208 *he would vote for him:* DDE, *Mandate for Change*, p. 572.

208 *"a normal risk to accept":* Dulles to file, memo, Feb. 29, 1956 (although filed on Feb. 29, the memo records a meeting of Feb. 27), Very Private Memos of Conversations with the President and Vice President 1956–58, box 1, White House Memoranda Series, Dulles Papers.

208 *"was leaving the room":* Ibid.

208 *"My next announcement":* Feb. 29, 1956, news conference, APP.

209 *"I will say nothing more":* Ibid.

209 *"If we are ever to solve":* DDE, State of the Union Address, Jan. 5, 1956, APP.

210 *the Clay Committee's recommendations:* Whitman, Jan. 11, 1955, entry, Jan. 1955 folder (4), box 4, ACW Diary Series, Whitman File.

210 *state and territory of the United States:* Weeks testimony of July 11, 1956, Highway Program 1956 folder, box 37, Weeks Papers.

210 *"six sidewalks to the moon":* DDE, *Mandate for Change*, p. 548.

210 *"I wanted the job done":* Ibid., pp. 548–49.

210 *at Walter Reed for a checkup:* Highway Program 1956 folder, box 37, Weeks Papers.

211 *started just weeks later:* Ibid.

211 *launched projects in anticipation of it:* Statement by Weeks, released with president's signature of bill, Highway Program 1956 folder, box 37, Weeks Papers.

211 *"More than any single action":* DDE, *Mandate for Change*, pp. 548–49.

211 *"He has his own way to make":* Whitman, March 13, 1956, entry, March 1956 folder (2), box 8, ACW Diary Series, Whitman File.

212 *they were uniformly opposed:* Whitman, March 19, 1956, entry, March 1956 folder, box 8, ACW Diary Series, Whitman File.

212 *"Well, he hasn't reported back":* April 25, 1956, news conference, APP.

212 *"delighted to hear":* Adams, *Firsthand Report*, p. 234.

212 *"For increasing millions of Americans":* DDE, *Mandate for Change*, p. 550.

213 *was not pictured:* Taubman, *Khrushchev*, p. 270.

213 *"a grave abuse of power":* Copies of the speech are widely available, though often abridged. A copy of the full text may be found at http://www.guardian.co.uk/ theguardian/2007/apr/26/greatspeeches1.

214 *an internal analysis prepared in 1956 and not released until 1999:* "The 20th CPSU Congress in Retrospect," June 1956, CIA/SRS-1, in Haines and Leggett, *CIA's Analysis of the Soviet Union*, p. 54.

214 *"many communists throughout the world":* Ibid., pp. 57 and 59.

214 *disapproved of his performance as president:* Poll data courtesy of APP.

214 *"I never have thought":* Edgar to DDE, April 30, 1956, Edgar Eisenhower 1956 (2) folder, box 11, Whitman File.

215 *"You cannot return":* DDE to Edgar, May 2, 1956, Edgar Eisenhower 1956 (2) folder, box 11, Whitman File.

215 *"everyone and his uncle" attended:* June 7, 1956, entry, Diary for 1956, box 59, Weeks Papers.

215 *received the news as routine:* June 8, 1956, entry, Diary for 1956, box 59, Weeks Papers.

215 *ambulance to Walter Reed:* Whitman, June 9–11, 1956, entries, June 1956 folder, box 8, ACW Diary Series, Whitman File. See also Draft of DDE's Ileitis Operation, June 1956, Howard Snyder Papers, 1881–1976, DDEPL.

216 *wheeled into the operating room at 2:07 a.m.:* Snyder notes, DDE Medical Records 1956 (2), box 3, Snyder papers.

216 *"Well," he said, "let's go":* Whitman, June 9–11, 1956, entries, June 1956 folder, box 8, ACW Diary Series, Whitman File.

216 *"I doubted seriously":* DDE to Paul Hoy Helms, June 15, 1956, doc. 1894, HP.

216 *"slowly but steadily":* DDE to Milton, July 9, 1956, doc. 1905, HP.

216 *the president was well:* Whitman, Aug. 15, 1956, entry, Aug. 1956 folder (1), box 8, ACW Diary Series, Whitman File.

216 *Ike listened in silence:* Whitman, July 20, 1956, entry, July 1956 folder, box 8, ACW Diary Series, Whitman File.

216 *Stassen went on leave:* Hagerty, oral history interview, pp. 513–14.

217 *"The Republican campaign":* New York Times, Nov. 4, 1956.

217 *not as Eisenhower's singular choice:* Whitman, Aug. 19, 1956, entry, Aug. 1956 (1) folder, box 8, ACW Diary Series, Whitman File.

217 *"took a stand in the matter":* Ibid.

218 *"as a lawyer":* Ibid.

218 *refuse to attend the convention:* Ibid.

218 *"his face ruddy":* Time, Sept. 3, 1956. See also *New York Times*, Aug. 22, 1956.

218 *"I suddenly discovered":* Time, Sept. 3, 1956.

219 *"We Love the Sunshine of His Smile":* New York Times, Aug. 21, 1956.

219 *the Gang stayed at the nearby Fairmont:* Slater, *The Ike I Knew*, p. 133.

219 *"are now addicted":* New York Times, Aug. 21, 1956.

219 *"Whoever let him say that?":* Adams, *Firsthand Report*, p. 244.

219 *released it himself:* Ibid., p. 243.

219 *"deeply appreciative"*: New York Times, Aug. 23, 1956.

219 *"the most widely beloved"*: Ibid.

219 *died before Election Day:* Sept. 5, 1956, entry, Sept. 1956 folder, box 14, Chronological File, Dulles Papers.

220 *"No one is more aware"*: DDE, Address at the Cow Palace on Accepting the Nomination of the Republican National Convention, Aug. 23, 1956, APP.

221 *"in firm faith"*: Ibid.

221 *best speech Ike had given as president:* Aug. 23, 1956, entry, Diary for 1956, box 59, Weeks Papers.

221 *long weekend of golf and bridge:* Adams, *Firsthand Report*, p. 244.

221 *gave Ike little time to react:* Whitman, Sept. 7, 1956, entry, Sept. 1956 folder, box 8, ACW Diary Series, Whitman File.

222 *preferably a Democrat and definitely a Catholic:* Ibid.

222 *party affiliation and working-class upbringing:* Seth Stern and Stephen Wermeil, *Justice Brennan*, pp. 85–86.

CHAPTER 12: ON THE EDGE

223 *Gamal Abdel Nasser:* The Suez crisis is marvelously reconstructed in David Nichols's *Eisenhower 1956: The President's Year of Crisis: Suez and the Brink of War.*

224 *oil flowing from the Middle East:* Adams, *Firsthand Report*, p. 247.

224 *offer was effectively withdrawn:* DDE, Aug. 8, 1956, entry, in *Diaries*, p. 329. Also found at doc. 1946, HP.

224 *help pay for the dam:* DDE, *Waging Peace*, p. 33.

225 *"I do not want to exaggerate"*: DDE to Eden, July 31, 1956, doc. 1935, HP.

226 *"sharply deteriorated"*: Report from Ambassador Yuri Andropov on Deteriorating Conditions in Hungary, Aug. 29, 1956, in Bekes, Byrne, and Rainer, *1956 Hungarian Revolution*, pp. 159–67.

226 *"it would be necessary to expose him"*: Ibid.

227 *"I don't think you'll ever know"*: Exchange of letters on Oct. 11 and Oct. 12, 1956, Don Newcombe folder, box 23, Name Series, Whitman File.

227 *"freedom of opinion"*: "The 'Sixteen Points,' Prepared by Hungarian Students, Oct. 22–23, 1956," in Bekes, Byrne, and Rainer, *1956 Hungarian Revolution*, pp. 188–89.

227 *Three died:* Bekes, Byrne, and Rainer, *1956 Hungarian Revolution*, timeline at p. xxxvii.

227 *Soviet troops to restore order:* "Working Notes from the Session of the CPSU CC Presidium, Oct. 23, 1956," in Bekes, Byrne, and Rainer, *1956 Hungarian Revolution*, p. 217.

228 *"the revolt has become widespread"*: DDE, *Waging Peace*, p. 69.

228 *"virtually snarling"*: Dulles Papers (quoted in Oct. 30, 1956, doc. 2051, fn. 6, HP).

228 *"peaceful processes"*: DDE to Mollet and Eden, Oct. 30, 1956, doc. 2054, HP.

229 *"If your government was not informed"*: DDE, *Waging Peace*, p. 77.

229 *remark pass in silence:* Hughes, *Ordeal of Power*, p. 218.

229 *"with no force of argument"*: Ibid., p. 219.

229 *"Boy, this is taking it":* Ibid., p. 221.

229 *"our most serious concern":* DDE, Radio and Television Report to the American People, Oct. 31, 1956, APP.

229 *"the principles of complete equality":* "Declaration by the Government of the USSR on the Principles of Development and Further Strengthening of Friendship and Cooperation Between the Soviet Union and Other Socialist States, Oct. 30, 1956," in Bekes, Byrne, and Rainer, *1956 Hungarian Revolution*, pp. 300–302.

230 *"Today, it appears, a new Hungary":* DDE, Radio and Television Report to the American People, Oct. 31, 1956, APP.

230 *"a miracle":* 302nd NSC Meeting, Nov. 1, 1956, box 8, NSC Series, Whitman File.

230 *"I have noted with profound distress":* DDE to Bulganin, Nov. 4, 1956, doc. 2067, HP.

230 *"Stevenson Holds President Lacks 'Energy' for Job":* New York Times, Nov. 4, 1956.

231 *"The Chief Executive":* Ibid.

231 *"moves of desperation":* Slater, *The Ike I Knew*, pp. 140–41.

231 *"are the sorriest and weakest pair":* DDE to Gruenther, Nov. 2, 1956, doc. 2064, HP.

231 *"gets more difficult by the minute":* Ibid.

231 *remove part of his large intestine:* New York Times, Nov. 4, 1956.

231 *work for more than two months:* Hoopes, *Devil and John Foster Dulles*, pp. 380–81.

231 *"Here were . . . the ten most frustrating days":* Slater, *The Ike I Knew*, p. 143.

232 *"It really was a tough one":* DDE, interview with Relman "Pat" Morin, Jan. 3, 1967, p. 16, box 53, 1967 Principal File, Post-presidential Papers, DDEPL.

232 *"We are Bolsheviks":* Time, Nov. 26, 1956.

233 *"I really could use a good bridge game":* DDE to Gruenther, Nov. 2, 1956, doc. 2064, HP.

CHAPTER 13: THE PRESS OF CHANGE, THE PRICE OF INACTION

237 *"the most outstanding event":* Ann Whitman, Jan. 21, 1957, entry, Jan. 1957 (1) folder, box 8, ACW Diary Series, Whitman File.

237 *"The divisive force":* Eisenhower's 1957 Inaugural Address, APP.

238 *"We live in a land of plenty":* Ibid.

238 *before being sworn in:* DDE to Edgar, Jan. 21, 1957, Edgar Eisenhower 1957–58 (2) folder, box 11, Name Series, Whitman File.

238 *when he trundled back inside:* Whitman, Jan. 21, 1957, entry, Jan. 1957 (1) folder, box 8, ACW Diary Series, Whitman File.

239 *"but I am entirely unwilling":* DDE to C. D. Jackson, April 30, 1957, doc. 138, HP.

239 *regarded as a personal rejection:* Sherman Adams, unpublished MS, p. 1077, Adams Papers.

239 *"completely indifferent":* DDE, *Waging Peace*, p. 145.

239 *blamed it on flabby muscles:* DDE to Edgar, May 6, 1957, doc. 144, HP.

239 *gently conspired to help him:* Slater, *The Ike I Knew*, p. 151.

240 *"with both extremes"*: DDE, *Waging Peace*, p. 139.

240 *"national calamity"*: July 31, 1957, news conference, APP.

241 *"may as well close up shop"*: *Jencks v. United States*, 363 U.S. 657 (1957).

241 *due process that had been violated*: *Sweezy v. New Hampshire*, 354 U.S. 234 (1957).

241 *"There is no congressional power"*: *Watkins v. United States*, 354 U.S. 178 (1957).

241 *the Court was unanimous against him*: *Service v. Dulles et al.*, 354 U.S. 363 (1957).

242 *Communists convicted under the Smith Act*: *Yates v. United States*, 354 U.S. 298 (1957).

242 *meetings into the late afternoon*: June 18, 1956, Presidential Appointment Books, DDEPL.

242 *"practically fed up"*: Ruth Montgomery, International News Service, quoted in Katcher, *Earl Warren*, p. 364.

242 *"I have no doubt that in private conversation"*: DDE to Warren, June 21, 1957, doc. 211, HP.

242 *"in no sense necessary"*: Warren to DDE, July 15, 1957, Personal File, Presidents' Correspondence, 1953–63, MD, LOC.

242 *"merely petulant rather than definitive"*: Warren, *Memoirs*, pp. 5–6.

243 *already explosive issue*: Brownell, *Advising Ike*, p. 219. See also Cabinet minutes, Dec. 2, 1955, and March 23, 1956, Whitman File.

243 *faced by those confronting integration*: Cabinet minutes, March 9, 1956, Whitman File.

243 *smiled faintly, and walked free*: *New York Times*, Sept. 24, 1955.

244 *"czar" with unbounded powers*: Brownell, *Advising Ike*, p. 202.

244 *obscure the real debate*: Cabinet minutes, Aug. 2, 1957, Whitman File.

244 *circumvent the law*: DDE to James Byrnes, July 23, 1957, footnote quotes Byrnes's letter to DDE of July 17, doc. 253, HP.

244 *justice in crimes against blacks*: Ibid.

244 *"cunningly designed"*: Warren Olney to Gerald Morgan, memo, July 12, 1957, Justice Department Civil Rights folder, Adams Papers.

245 *the quiet of Gettysburg*: Whitman, July 3, 1957, entry, July 1957 (2) folder, box 9, ACW Diary Series, Whitman File.

245 *"illegally from interfering"*: July 3, 1957, news conference, APP.

245 *"Well, I would not want to answer"*: Ibid.

245 *parted on friendly terms*: Whitman, July 10, 1957, entry, July 1957 (2) folder, box 9, ACW Diary Series, Whitman File. For Brownell not being told, see *Advising Ike*, p. 224. Whitman herself was frustrated by the debate over the Civil Rights Bill. As she noted in the above diary entry: "It seems so ridiculous to me, when it has been in the Constitution for so many years and here at last we get around to believing it might be possible for some of our citizens really to have that right."

245 *"waited this long for bill"*: Hagerty, press release, Aug. 19, 1957, Justice Department Civil Rights folder, box 8, Adams Papers.

245 *"a highly practical decision"*: Brownell, *Advising Ike*, p. 225.

246 *"I can't imagine"*: July 17, 1957, news conference, APP.

246 *"this does not mean"*: Ibid. See also *Time*, Aug. 19, 1957.

247   *"just plain miserable":* DDE to Adams, note, Sept. 3, 1957, doc. 320, HP.

247   *as soon as the Court detailed the rules:* Cooper v. Aaron, 358 U.S. 1 (1958).

247   *"with all deliberate speed":* Ibid.

247   *"the best for the interests of all pupils in the District":* Ibid.

247   *southern political campaigns of that era:* For a concise summary of Faubus's rise
      to political power, see *The Encyclopedia of Arkansas History and Culture,* at
      http://www.encyclopediaofarkansas.net/encyclopedia/entry-detail.aspx
      ?entryID=102.

248   *would never cave:* Brownell, *Advising Ike,* p. 209.

248   *"breathing room":* Ibid.

248   *not to find the governor in contempt:* Oct. 8, 1957, entry memorializing meeting of
      Sept. 14, 1957, Little Rock (2) folder, box 23, Administration Series, Whitman
      File.

248   *"In any area where the federal government":* Ibid.

249   *"Just because I said it":* Reed, *Faubus,* p. 219.

249   *Faubus continued to resist:* Statements by Eisenhower and Faubus, Sept. 14, 1957,
      Civil Rights (2) folder, box 6, Gerald Morgan Records, Whitman File.

249   *subordinate who had failed him in battle:* Brownell, *Advising Ike,* p. 210.

249   *"a small-town politician":* Oral history with Brownell.

249   *"not legally sufficient":* New York Times, Sept. 21, 1954. Some accounts of this
      episode suggest that Faubus attended the hearing. The *Times* and other con-
      temporary descriptions make clear that he did not.

249   *a governors' conference at Sea Island, Georgia:* Reed, *Faubus,* p. 222.

250   *played three hours of bridge:* Sept. 22, 1957, Presidential Appointment Books.

250   *beat Allen and Robinson by thirty-six points:* Slater, *The Ike I Knew,* p. 160.

250   *"I hope they bring out":* Reed, *Faubus,* p. 225.

250   Song of the South: Sept. 23, 1957, Presidential Appointment Books.

251   *withdrawn from the scene by Faubus:* Calls of Sept. 24, 1957, Sept. 1957 Telephone
      Calls, box 27, DDE Diary Series, Whitman File.

251   *he signed the order:* New York Times, Sept. 25, 1957.

251   *before appearing on national television:* Calls of Sept. 25, 1957, Sept. 1957 Tele-
      phone Calls, box 27, DDE Diary Series, Whitman File. There is some confusion
      about the dates in the White House records, which suggest that Eisenhower
      traveled to Washington on Sept. 25; in fact, he returned on the twenty-fourth
      and spoke to the nation that evening.

251   *he emended it to "instructed":* Undated draft of speech, copy courtesy of
      DDEPL, at http://www.eisenhower.archives.gov/Research/Digital_Documents/
      LittleRock/New%20PDFs/Little_Rock_speech_draft.pdf.

251   *"If resistance to the Federal Court order":* Transcript of the address courtesy of
      DDEPL, at http://www.eisenhower.archives.gov/Research/Digital_Documents/
      LittleRock/New%20PDFs/Press_release_92457.pdf.

251   *he called to check on Mamie:* Calls of Sept. 25, 1957, Sept. 1957 Telephone Calls,
      box 27, DDE Diary Series, Whitman File.

252   *Martin Luther King Jr.:* Reed, *Faubus,* p. 235.

252 *at the height of the confrontation:* See, for instance, DDE to William M. Shepherd, telegram, Oct. 3, 1957, doc. 367, HP.

253 *"I shall be forever thankful":* Resignation letter, Oct. 23, 1957, The President—Resignation Letter folder, box 55, Brownell Papers.

253 *collaboration and mutual suspicion:* The description of this reception is drawn largely from Launius, "Sputnik and the Origins of the Space Age."

253 *"I've just been informed":* Ibid., at http://history.nasa.gov/sputnik/sputorig.html.

253 *The Soviets beamed:* New York Times, Oct. 5, 1957.

254 *circle the earth every ninety-five minutes:* Technical specifications come from *Pravda*, Oct. 5, 1957, reprinted at NASA History Division, NASA Headquarters.

254 *over obligation to the federal government:* New York Times, Oct. 5, 1957.

254 *to respond to reports of the Soviet satellite:* Oct. 4, 1956, Presidential Appointment Books.

254 *remind critics of his arrogance:* Hauge, oral history interview, p. 125.

254 *"The peculiar nature":* Undated memo but written one week after *Sputnik* launch, Special Projects: Sputnik, Missiles, and Related Matters, box 35, White House Office of the Staff Research Group, DDEPL.

255 *filthy, disease-ravaged tunnels:* Neufeld, *Von Braun*, pp. 159–60.

255 *speak directly with Eisenhower but was turned down:* Ibid., p. 203.

255 *"I am convinced":* Ibid., p. 310.

255 *"If you go back to Washington":* Ibid., p. 311.

256 *"Muttnik":* New York Times, Nov. 4, 1957.

256 *"Flopnik":* Launius, "Sputnik and the Origins of the Space Race."

256 *"The enervating suspense was over":* Adams, unpublished MS, p. 1146.

256 *"That's wonderful":* New York Times, Feb. 1, 1958.

256 *dedicated to putting a man in space:* Dates from NASA timeline, at http://www .hq.nasa.gov/office/pao/History/Timeline/1958.html.

257 *fought back tears:* Adams, unpublished MS, p. 1173.

257 *He stomped out:* Ibid., p. 1176.

257 *"the light of her life lay ill upstairs":* Susan Eisenhower, *Mrs. Ike*, pp. 296–97.

258 *he struggled for a word:* Whitman, Nov. 25–27, 1957, entries, Present Illness of the President, box 9, ACW Diary Series, Whitman File.

258 *dispatch American troops:* DDE, Message to Congress, Jan. 5, 1957, APP.

258 *"Experience shows":* Ibid.

259 *"American protectorate":* DDE, *Waging Peace*, p. 181.

CHAPTER 14: NUCLEAR INTERLUDE

260 *"Total war":* Estimate of the Situation, p. 22, annex to NSC 5602/1—Basic National Security Policy, box 17, Policy Papers Subseries, NSC Series, White House Office, Office of the Special Assistant for National Security Affairs, DDEPL.

261 *"Wait a minute, boys":* John Eisenhower, interview with author, Oct. 7, 2010.

261 *"You might as well go out":* Ann Whitman, March 5, 1959, entry, March 1959 (2) folder, box 10, ACW Diary Series, Whitman File.

261 *"In 1953, Soviet capability"*: John Eisenhower, interview with author, Oct. 7, 2010.

261 *"virtually cease to exist"*: Slater, *The Ike I Knew*, p. 126.

262 *"perhaps the richest"*: Craig, *Destroying the Village*, p. 56.

262 *"Inability to use these weapons"*: 277th NSC Meeting, Feb. 27, 1956, box 7, NSC Series, Whitman File.

263 *immediately constitute a general war:* The preceding references to the discussion of the NSC are drawn from ibid.

264 *Eisenhower's language intact, was approved:* 325th NSC Meeting, May 27, 1957, box 8, NSC Series, Whitman File.

264 *"We want to be able to treat"*: Cutler to DDE, memo, Aug. 7, 1957, Limited War folder, box 3, Subject Subseries, OCB Series, White House Office, Office of the Special Assistant for National Security Affairs.

264 *"The evidence clearly indicates"*: A copy of the full report is available at: http://www.gwu.edu/~nsarchiv/NSAEBB/NSAEBB139/nitze02.pdf.

265 *"remake a way of life in our own country"*: Ibid.

265 *"when and how nuclear weapons"*: Ibid.

265 *"It looked to the President"*: Sherman Adams, unpublished MS, p. 1162, Adams Papers.

266 *"Maximum massive retaliation"*: Memorandum of Conference with the President, Nov. 4, 1957, in *FRUS*, vol. 19, p. 621.

266 *"Was the Panel proposing"*: 343rd NSC Meeting, Nov. 7, 1957, in ibid., p. 632.

266 *willing to court its own destruction:* Memorandum of Conversation between the President and the Secretary of State, Nov. 7, 1957, in ibid., p. 638.

266 *"would be smashed"*: Whitman, Nov. 9, 1957, entry, Nov. 1957 folder, box 9, ACW Diary Series, Whitman File.

266 *almost certainly Nitze:* Asked years later by a collaborator on his memoir how the report ended up in the hands of the *Washington Post*, Nitze at first declined to answer, then added that he assumed the reporter must have gotten it "from several sources." See Thompson, *The Hawk and the Dove*, p. 166.

266 *"I'm the only Army general"*: Nov. 16, 1959, entry, Transcript of Diary, 1959–60, Nov. 1959 folder, Kistiakowsky Papers.

267 *"we will finish it"*: 394th NSC Meeting, Jan. 22, 1959, box 11, NSC Series, Whitman File.

267 *"was all the policy the President said he had"*: Ibid.

267 *Ike was a terrific poker player:* John Eisenhower, exchange with author, Sept. 2010.

CHAPTER 15: MANY WAYS TO FIGHT

268 *"an enlightened and dedicated statesman"*: Nixon, *Six Crises*, p. 185.

268 *nevertheless reluctantly agreed:* Ibid., p. 184.

268 *the ceremony started four minutes early: New York Times*, May 2, 1958.

268 *"I felt an almost uncontrollable urge"*: Nixon, *Six Crises*, p. 204.

269 *"courage, patience and calmness"*: DDE, Message to the Vice President After the Demonstration in Peru, May 9, 1958, APP.

269 *"For an instant"*: Nixon, *Six Crises*, p. 219.

269 *"He had the biggest smile":* Julie Nixon, responding to a question at DDEPL, Oct. 14, 2010.

270 *viewed Nasser's designs with unease:* DDE, *Waging Peace*, p. 263.

270 *"carry serious implications":* DDE to Saud ibn Abd Al-Aziz, Feb. 1, 1958, doc. 561, HP.

270 *was diagnosed with heart trouble:* DDE, *Waging Peace*, p. 265.

270 *"Chamoun is most friendly but indecisive":* DDE to Hoffman, June 23, 1958, doc. 753, HP.

271 *"changed from quieting":* DDE, *Waging Peace*, p. 269.

271 *"No matter what you think":* Ann Whitman, June 15, 1958, entry, June 1958 (2) folder, box 10, ACW Diary Series, Whitman File.

271 *"Today aggression is more subtle":* DDE, July 15, 1958, diary entry, doc. 771, HP.

272 *more than fourteen thousand soldiers:* In *Waging Peace*, Eisenhower described the force as consisting of 114,357 men, but that is a typographical error. It never reached anywhere near that number.

272 *"struck a responsive chord":* DDE, *Waging Peace*, p. 286.

272 *did not kill a single civilian:* Wade, "Rapid Deployment Logistics" (no page numbers included in document at http://www.cgsc.edu/carl/resources/csi/Wade/wade.asp#72).

272 *"I won't be pressed":* The administration's options, including the possible use of nuclear weapons, are detailed in the Top Secret "U.S. and Allied Capabilities for Limited Operations to 1 July 1961," appendix on hypothetical conflict over Quemoy and Matsu begins at C-1, NSC 5724 folder, box 22, Policy Papers Subseries, NSC Series, White House Office, Office of the Special Assistant for National Security Affairs, DDEPL.

273 *within striking distance of Taiwan:* Embassy in the Republic of China to State Department, telegram, July 30, 1958, in *FRUS, China*, vol. 19, p. 33. See also 375th NSC Meeting, Aug. 7, 1958, in *FRUS* as well as box 10, NSC Series, Whitman File.

273 *"If the Chinese communists":* Memorandum for the Record, Aug. 14, 1958, in *FRUS, China*, vol. 19, p. 55.

273 *airbases in mainland China:* Acting Secretary of State Herter to Secretary of State Dulles, memo, Aug. 15, 1958, in ibid., p. 56.

273 *its closest ally, the Soviet Union:* Assistant Secretary of State for Policy Planning (Smith) to Secretary of State Dulles, memo, Aug. 15, 1958, in ibid., pp. 57–59.

273 *five hundred Taiwanese soldiers were killed or wounded:* Embassy in the Republic of China to State Department, telegram, Aug. 24, 1958, in ibid., p. 70.

273 *prevented Taiwan from attacking mainland China:* Embassy in the Republic of China to State Department, telegram, Aug. 27, 1958, in ibid., p. 83.

274 *would not be able to support such an action:* See, for instance, Memorandum of Conversation, Aug. 30, 1958, in ibid., p. 102.

274 *"the most violent I have seen him":* Embassy in the Republic of China to State Department, telegram, Aug. 31, 1958, in ibid., p. 107.

274 *"The argument that nothing":* Memorandum of Conversation, Sept. 2, 1958, in ibid., p. 119.

274 *"Those who nurture plans"*: Embassy in the Soviet Union to State Department, telegram, Sept. 19, 1958, in ibid., p. 236.

275 *"Gilbert and Sullivan war"*: DDE, *Waging Peace*, p. 304.

275 *seemed a South Asian Nasser*: Also like Nasser, Sukarno collaborated with America's World War II enemies in order to strengthen his hand against a Western colonial power. Nasser had allied himself with Italy against the British; Sukarno received Japanese support for his war against the Dutch.

276 *"Although U.S. efforts"*: NSC 5518 Policy on Indonesia (2), Oct. 10, 1956, box 16, Policy Papers Subseries, NSC Series, White House Office, Office of the Special Assistant for National Security Affairs.

276 *"inspired by the material accomplishments"*: Assistant Secretary of State for Far Eastern Affairs (Robertson) to Secretary of State Dulles, memo, Jan. 2, 1958, in *FRUS Indonesia, 1958–60*, vol. 17, p. 1.

276 *"wholly undependable"*: Memorandum of Conversation, Jan. 2, 1958, in ibid., p. 5.

276 *"preoccupation with the restoration"*: NSC 5518, Policy on Indonesia, Oct. 9, 1957, box 16, Records 1952–61, Policy Papers Subseries, NSC Series, White House Office, Office of the Special Assistant for National Security Affairs.

276 *"With Sukarno's ambitions"*: DDE to Hoffman, June 23, 1958, doc. 753, HP.

276 *Communists still outpolled*: Conboy and Morrison, *Feet to the Fire*, p. 13.

276 *rejected invasion as an option*: 337th NSC Meeting, Sept. 22, 1957, box 9, NSC Series, Whitman File.

277 *"all feasible covert means"*: Robertson to Dulles, memo, Jan. 2, 1958, p. 2.

277 *to arm eight thousand rebels*: Conboy and Morrison, *Feet to the Fire*, pp. 30–33.

277 *stood by offshore*: Brichoux and Gerner, "The United States and the 1958 Rebellion in Indonesia," p. 6.

277 *having been made in Michigan*: Embassy in Indonesia to State Department, telegram, March 15, 1958, in *FRUS Indonesia, 1958–60*, vol. 17, p. 70.

277 *"as soon as the rebellion is quelled"*: Embassy in Indonesia to State Department, telegram, March 19, 1958, in ibid., p. 79.

277 *poor communications and inadequate aircraft*: 359th NSC Meeting, March 20, 1958, box 9, NSC Series, Whitman File.

277 *"a submarine or two"*: 362nd NSC Meeting, April 14, 1958, box 10, NSC Series, Whitman File.

278 *"private persons operating on their own"*: Memorandum of Conversation with President Eisenhower, April 15, 1958, in *FRUS Indonesia, 1958–60*, vol. 17, p. 109.

278 *being piloted by Americans and Chinese*: Embassy in Indonesia to State Department, telegram, April 30, 1958, in ibid., p. 126.

278 *sixteen soldiers and a member of the ship's crew were killed*: Conboy and Morrison, *Feet to the Fire*, p. 128.

278 *He was still alive*: Ibid., pp. 138–42.

278 *met with the secretary of state*: Memorandum of Conversation, May 18, 1958, Conversations with Allen W. Dulles (All Intelligence Material) (3), box 8, White House Memoranda Series, Dulles Papers.

278 *"We're pulling the plug"*: Conboy and Morrison, *Feet to the Fire*, p. 143.

279 *through the end of the Eisenhower administration*: In Dec. 1960, Eisenhower con-

sidered a request from Pope's wife to intercede with Sukarno on her husband's behalf. Christian Herter, then secretary of state, advised against such an overture, and Eisenhower thus did not pursue it. See Dec. 21, 1960, memo, Christian Herter Dec. 1960 folder, box 13, Dulles-Herter Series, Whitman File.

279 *"Just go home"*: Conboy and Morrison, *Feet to the Fire*, p. 165.

279 *the worst of his life*: Slater, *The Ike I Knew*, p. 180.

CHAPTER 16: LOSS

280 *"not in single spies, but in battalions"*: DDE, *Waging Peace*, p. 305.

280 *sore throat and ill temper*: Ann Whitman, Feb. 5, 1958, entry, Feb. 1958 folder, box 9, ACW Diary Series, Whitman File.

280 *"He was our 'big' brother"*: DDE to Arthur Summerfield, Jan. 30, 1958, doc. 558, HP.

280 *forever "Big Ike" among the Eisenhower boys*: DDE to Louise Sondra Grieb Eisenhower, June 12, 1958, doc. 742, HP.

281 *then returned to work*: Whitman, June 24, 1958, entry, June 1958 (1) folder, box 10, ACW Diary Series, Whitman File.

281 *then turned and walked out*: Slater, *The Ike I Knew*, p. 187.

281 *"He was the most impolite"*: John Eisenhower, interview with author, Oct. 7, 2010.

281 *when Adams would get his*: DDE, *Waging Peace*, p. 311.

281 *"He treated his employees well"*: Adams, *Firsthand Report*, p. 440.

282 *"Mr. Adams' Bad Judgment"*: New York Times, June 12, 1958.

282 *"does not know what to do"*: Whitman, June 12, 1958, entry, June 1958 (2) folder, box 10, ACW Diary Series, Whitman File.

282 *"I believe that the presentation"*: June 18, 1958, news conference, APP.

283 *"Not one of us caught"*: Hughes, *Ordeal of Power*, p. 267.

283 *Few were buying it*: Time, July 14, 1958.

283 *met with Eisenhower to complain*: Whitman, July 7, 1958, entry, July 1958 (2) folder, box 10, ACW Diary Series, Whitman File.

283 *disarray within the White House*: Whitman, July 14, 1958, entry, July 1958 (2) folder, box 10, ACW Diary Series, Whitman File.

283 *"I hope it does some good"*: New York Times, Aug. 14, 1958.

284 *thirty cents an hour*: Whitman, June 16, 1958, entry, June 1958 (1) folder, box 10, ACW Diary Series, Whitman File. See also David Eisenhower, *Going Home*, p. 21.

284 *"I thought the timing was wrong"*: Hauge, oral history interview, p. 84.

284 *"Mostly all we did was pray"*: Whitman, Aug. 23, 1958, entry, Aug. 1958 (2) folder, box 10, ACW Diary Series, Whitman File.

285 *Eisenhower hesitated*: Whitman, Sept. 4, telephone call logged in Diary entry, Sept. 1958 folder, box 10, ACW Diary Series, Whitman File.

285 *"This man {Adams} has got to go or we are done"*: Whitman, Sept. 4, 1958, entry, Sept. 1958 folder, box 10, ACW Diary Series, Whitman File.

285 *bought everyone there an ice cream*: Whitman, Sept. 17, 1958, entry, Sept. 1958 folder, box 10, ACW Diary Series, Whitman File.

286 *"his devoted friend, Dwight D. Eisenhower"*: Hughes, *Ordeal of Power*, p. 269.

286 *barely missing his heart:* New York Times, Sept. 21, 1958.

286 *"hard cider to mellow bourbon":* Time, Oct. 6, 1958.

286 *chided Persons about it:* Whitman, Feb. 2, 1959, entry, Feb. 1959 (2) folder, box 10, ACW Diary Series, Whitman File.

286 *"once more into the Boss's orbit":* John Eisenhower, Strictly Personal, p. 202.

287 *"a national triumph":* New York Times, Nov. 6, 1958.

287 *"The faults of the Republican Party":* DDE to Macmillan, Nov. 11, 1958, doc. 926, HP.

287 *visited him in the hospital:* DDE to Hazlett, Feb. 20, 1957, doc. 41; Nov. 18, 1957, doc. 457; March 25, 1958, doc. 622; April 8, 1945, doc. 645, HP.

287 *"I can never quite tell you":* DDE to Elizabeth Hazlett, Nov. 3, 1958, doc. 920, HP.

288 *"no one in the world":* Taubman, Khrushchev, p. 397.

288 *"bone in my throat":* Ibid., p. 407.

288 *as Eisenhower now imagined it:* Twenty-fourth Meeting of the NSC, July 28, 1948, Truman Library, at http://www.trumanlibrary.org/whistlestop/study _collections/berlin_airlift/large/documents/index.php?documentdate=1948 -07-28&documentid=6-1&studycollectionid=&pagenumber=1.

288 *"Only madmen can go":* Craig, Destroying the Village, p. 92.

288 *"Hit the Russians":* Ibid., pp. 93–94.

289 *lurch into an error:* Memorandum of Conversation with President Eisenhower and Secretary Dulles, Nov. 30, 1958, in FRUS, vol. 8, Berlin Crisis, 1958–1960, p. 142.

289 *would not risk annihilation:* See, among others, George A. Morgan of the Policy Planning Staff to the Assistant Secretary of State for Policy Planning (Smith), memo, Dec. 8, 1958, in FRUS 1958–60, vol. 8, Berlin Crisis, 1958–59, p. 158.

289 *evacuate Britons to Canada and Australia:* See, among other sources, John Eisenhower's Strictly Personal, p. 229.

290 *joined their aides for dinner:* Memorandum of Conversation, March 20, 1959, in FRUS 1958–60, vol. 8, Berlin Crisis, 1958–59, pp. 520–21.

290 *"It lasted three hours!":* Macmillan, Riding the Storm, p. 645.

290 *surgery to repair a hernia:* Conversation with Adenauer, Feb. 8, 1959, Memos of Conversation—General A Through D, box 1, General Correspondence and Memoranda Series, Dulles Papers.

290 *"not good":* Whitman, Feb. 13, 1959, entry, Feb. 1959 (2) folder, box 10, ACW Diary Series, Whitman File.

291 *"He was* against *almost everything":* Macmillan, Riding the Storm, p. 644. Also see Hoopes, Devil and John Foster Dulles, p. 478.

291 *"I have rarely seen him shaken":* Whitman, Feb. 14, 1959, entry, Feb. 1959 (1) folder, box 10, ACW Diary Series, Whitman File.

291 *burst into tears:* Whitman, April 15 and 16, 1959, entries, April 1959 folder, box 10, ACW Diary Series, Whitman File.

CHAPTER 17: THE FINAL MONTHS

292 *ordered by the State Department:* Ann Whitman, Jan. 3, 1959, entry, Jan. 1959 (2) folder, box 10, ACW Diary Series, Whitman File.

292 *rather his will to do so:* 394th NSC Meeting, Jan. 22, 1959, box 11, NSC Series, Whitman File.

293 *playing into Castro's hand:* 400th NSC Meeting, March 26, 1959, box 11, NSC Series, Whitman File.

293 *"Can Castro Save Cuba?":* Saturday Evening Post, Aug. 1, 1959.

293 *"Castro's executions of Batista henchmen":* Ibid.

294 *"proved himself to be vain":* Pfau, *No Sacrifice Too Great,* p. 234.

294 *"I have told you again and again":* May 5, 1959, news conference, APP.

294 *"When my conscience tells me":* June 17, 1959, news conference, APP.

294 *"I am losing a truly valuable associate":* Statement by the President, June 19, 1959, APP.

295 *"I salute you for the calm":* DDE to Strauss, June 27, 1959, doc. 1215, HP.

295 *"He thought it was a disgrace":* Hagerty, oral history interview, pp. 521–22.

296 *feeling that the nation's flag:* Whitman, Jan. 3, 1959, entry, Jan. 1959 (2) folder, box 10, ACW Diary Series, Whitman File.

296 *"with immense satisfaction":* Taubman, *Khrushchev,* p. 416.

296 *"happy as a lad":* Whitman, Aug. 3, 1959, entry, Aug. 1959 (2) folder, box 11, ACW Diary Series, Whitman File.

296 *"Would that the Vice President":* New York Times, July 24, 1959.

296 *"substantial views of the people in our country":* Memorandum of Conversation, July 24, 1959, Central Files 033.1100-NI/7–2459, State Department, in *FRUS Eastern Europe Region, Soviet Union, Cyprus, 1958–60,* vol. 10, p. 338.

297 *an exhibition of American life awaited them:* Ibid., pp. 342–45.

297 *"You need to have goods to trade":* New York Times, July 25, 1959.

297 *"I don't like it either":* Ibid.

297 *president declined comment:* Ibid.

297 *"suggest that Khrushchev may outwit":* Los Angeles Times, Sept. 1, 1959.

298 *initially refrained from discussing the invitation:* Whitman, Aug. 3, 1959, entry, Aug. 1959 (2) folder, box 11, ACW Diary Series, Whitman File.

298 *"complacently weakening our defenses":* UPI, Sept. 6, 1959.

298 *"a small Russian army":* Los Angeles Times, Sept. 2, 1959.

298 *unfurling his nation's fifty-star flag:* Aug. 26, 1959, Presidential Appointment Books, DDEPL. See also President's Remarks, Aug. 21, 1959, APP.

298 *"We are all completely flabbergasted":* Los Angeles Times, Sept. 6, 1959.

298 *two pros from the club:* USA 1, April 1962 (newspaper clip is in DDEPL files).

299 *retreated to the castle for the evening:* For Ike's golf score, and his reaction to it, see DDE to Macmillan, Sept. 5, 1959, doc. 1305, HP.

299 *"I assure you":* President's welcoming remarks, Sept. 15, 1959, APP.

299 *"We have come to you":* Nikita Khrushchev, *Khrushchev in America,* pp. 14–15.

299 *roared their approval for Eisenhower:* Whitman, Sept. 15, 1959, entry, Sept. 1959 folder, box 11, ACW Diary Series, Whitman File.

299 *other points of contention:* Memorandum of Conversation, Sept. 15, 1959, Lot 64 D 560, CF 1472, Conference Files, State Department, in *FRUS Eastern Europe Region, Soviet Union, Cyprus, 1958–60,* vol. 10, pp. 392–402. Also see Kistiakowsky, *Scientist at the White House,* p. 86.

300 *"You say you don't like violence":* Memorandum of Conversation, Sept. 18, 1959, Lot 64 D 560, CF 1473, Conference Files, State Department, in *FRUS Eastern Europe Region, Soviet Union, Cyprus, 1958–60*, vol. 10, p. 418.

300 *"The fact that you ask such questions":* Khrushchev, *Khrushchev Speaks*, pp. 63 and 161. For a thorough summary of the trip from the perspective of the American ambassador to the Soviet Union, see *FRUS Eastern Europe Region, Soviet Union, Cyprus, 1958–60*, vol. 10, pp. 485–92.

300 *"We do not agree": Los Angeles Times*, Sept. 20, 1959.

300 *"Khrushchev liked me":* Taubman, *Khrushchev*, p. 430.

301 *"the Red Army had failed":* Memorandum of Conversation, Sept. 20, 1959, Lot 64 D 560, CF 1474, Conference Files, State Department, in *FRUS Eastern Europe Region, Soviet Union, Cyprus, 1958–60*, vol. 10, p. 433.

301 *"Perhaps it would take less time to get back": Los Angeles Times*, Sept. 20, 1959.

301 *haggard Lodge after midnight:* Lodge to State Department, telegram, Sept. 20, 1959, 1:03 a.m., 033.61111/9–2059, Central Files, State Department, in *FRUS Eastern Europe Region, Soviet Union, Cyprus, 1958–60*, vol. 10, pp. 428–31.

301 *"Hagerty Asks More Courtesy to Khrushchev": Los Angeles Times*, Sept. 22, 1959.

302 *retired at 11:45 p.m.:* Sept. 25, 1959, Presidential Appointment Books.

302 *forced to resign:* Memorandum of Conversation, Sept. 26, 1959, 1:00 p.m., Lot 64 D 560, CF 1475, Conference Files, State Department, in *FRUS Eastern Europe Region, Soviet Union, Cyprus, 1958–60*, vol. 10, p. 466.

302 *even at Gromyko:* Sept. 26, 1959, entry, Transcript of Diary, 1959–60, box 1, Kistiakowsky Papers.

302 *quick trip to Gettysburg:* Ibid.

302 *in Gettysburg fifteen minutes later:* Sept. 26, 1959, Presidential Appointment Books.

302 *out the window of the car:* Barbara Eisenhower, oral history interview, p. 6.

302 *"benign and entertaining guest":* DDE, *Waging Peace*, p. 444.

302 *waited for his return:* Sept. 26, 1959, Presidential Appointment Books.

302 *did not reply:* DDE, *Waging Peace*, p. 446.

303 *"This ends the whole affair":* Ibid., p. 447.

303 *would publicly acknowledge it:* Addendum to Sept. 26, 1959, entry, Transcript of Diary, 1959–60, box 1, Kistiakowsky Papers.

303 *not to translate the remark:* Memorandum of Conversation, Sept. 27, 1959, Lot 64 D 560, CF 1475, Conference Files, State Department, in *FRUS Eastern Europe Region, Soviet Union, Cyprus, 1958–60*, vol. 10, p. 483.

304 *"if you could explain to us":* Aug. 12, 1959, news conference, APP.

304 *one in four who disapproved:* Presidential Job Approval, APP, at http://www .presidency.ucsb.edu/data/popularity.php.

304 *in reality he always had been:* Whitman, special entry for week of Aug. 7–15, 1959, Aug. 1959 (2) folder, box 11, ACW Diary Series, Whitman File.

305 *"I said it just didn't sound":* Whitman to DDE, note, Aug. 14, 1959, Aug. 1959 (1) folder, box 11, ACW Diary Series, Whitman File.

305 *"He leaves one with a strange impression":* Dec. 4 and 7–10, 1959, entries, Transcript of Diary, 1959–60, box 1, Kistiakowsky Papers.

305 *"a Russian worker":* Kharlamov and Vadeyev, *Face to Face with America*, p. 385.

305 *voiced their approval of the trip:* Gallup poll, Sept. 27, 1959.

306 *to grant him asylum:* 414th NSC Meeting, July 23, 1959, box 11, NSC Series, Whitman File.

306 *emergent Che Guevara:* 432nd NSC Meeting, Jan. 14, 1960, box 12, NSC Series, Whitman File.

306 *blockade Cuba:* Ibid.

306 *compare the Cuban leader to Hitler:* 429th NSC Meeting, Dec. 16, 1959, box 12, NSC Series, Whitman File.

306 *without America's efforts being exposed:* Ibid.

306 *"knows absolutely nothing":* July 30, 1959, and Feb. 10, 1960, entries, Transcript of Diary, 1959–60, box 1, Kistiakowsky Papers.

306 *misunderstood the basic responsibilities of his job:* March 16, 1960, entry, Transcript of Diary, 1959–60, box 1, Kistiakowsky Papers.

307 *as a "bum":* John Eisenhower, interview with author, Oct. 7, 2010.

307 *"When you get that angry":* Ibid.

307 *The United States did not need any practice:* 436th NSC Meeting, March 10, 1960, box 12, NSC Series, Whitman File.

307 *options before the NSC:* March 10, 1960, entry, Transcript of Diary, 1959–60, box 1, Kistiakowsky Papers.

307 *six of the seven best since World War II:* DDE, *Waging Peace*, p. 455.

307 *"these people must solve their own problems":* Aug. 25, 1959, news conference, APP.

308 *steel in foreign markets:* Memorandum on the Steel Strike, Aug. 6, 1959, Steel Strike 1959 folder, box 35, Administration Series, Whitman File.

308 *"sick and tired":* Sept. 28, 1959, news conference, APP.

308 *reporting back to the president:* Executive Order 10843.

308 *from further damage:* Statement by the President, Oct. 19, 1959, APP.

309 *"I cannot possibly describe":* DDE to Katherine Boyce Tupper Marshall, Oct. 16, 1959, doc. 1346, HP.

309 *"until the cranberry industry":* Introduction to *Cranberry Scare of 1959*, by Barbara Constable, DDEPL.

309 *"a deed as awful":* *Life*, Nov. 23, 1959.

309 *"ill informed, ill advised and irresponsible":* Ibid.

310 *drank a glass of cranberry juice:* Kistiakowsky, *Scientist at the White House*, p. 209.

310 *"For the first time in the history of the world":* Rachel Carson, *Silent Spring*, p. 15.

310 *"I urged him to do so":* Kistiakowsky, *Scientist at the White* House, p. 210.

310 *at noon the next day:* Dec. 3 and 4, 1959, Presidential Appointment Books.

310 *they shared the same name:* John Eisenhower, *Strictly Personal*, p. 269.

310 *"What's new?":* DDE, *Waging Peace*, p. 512.

310 *"Now let's see how the experts do it":* Slater, *The Ike I Knew*, p. 214.

311 *"So far as I know":* March 16, 1960, news conference, APP.

311 *only "eventually":* March 30, 1960, news conference, APP. The issue of blacks being denied service was brought embarrassingly to Ike's attention a few months later when Michel Gallin-Douathe, newly appointed ambassador from the Central African Republic, left a meeting with the president and headed

back for New York. He stopped at a restaurant near Baltimore and was refused service. Eisenhower wrote him a consoling letter and pledged that the government would continue its efforts to eradicate such discrimination. See DDE to Gallin-Douathe, Nov. 14, 1960, doc. 1705, HP.

312   *subsidized by the federal government:* Whitman, March 22, 1960, entry, March 1960 (1) folder, box 11, ACW Diary Series, Whitman File.

312   *"it is in the interests":* DDE to Khrushchev, March 12, 1960, doc. 1454, HP.

312   *"very significant and welcome development":* DDE to Khrushchev, April 1, 1960, doc. 1493, HP.

312   *"very interesting, very positive":* Pedlow and Welzenbach, *CIA and the U-2 Program*, p. 101.

313   *could endanger the Paris Summit:* Ibid., p. 172.

313   *he went silent:* Ibid., p. 176.

314   *infuriating Hagerty:* Whitman, May 5, 1960, entry, May 1960 folder, box 11, ACW Diary Series, Whitman File.

314   *"Go ahead":* DDE, interview with Relman "Pat" Morin, Jan. 3, 1967, p. 27, box 53, 1967 Principal File, Post-presidential Papers, DDEPL.

314   *fell to earth:* Pedlow and Welzenbach, *CIA and the U-2 Program,* p. 178.

314   *regarded as "best case":* Ibid., p. 179.

314   *"May Day turned out to be":* Ibid., p. 176.

314   *His film was recovered:* For many years, American officials harbored doubts about Powers's actions. Some initially believed that he had defected and landed the plane intact (see, for instance, Kistiakowsky, *Scientist at the White House*, p. 324). So grave were the suspicions regarding his conduct that a special panel was convened after his eventual return to the United States to examine whether he was entitled to his back pay for his time in Soviet captivity. Powers was eventually vindicated and awarded his pay. He retired from the CIA and went to work for a Los Angeles radio station flying its traffic plane and later worked as a helicopter pilot for KNBC, also in Los Angeles. On Aug. 1, 1977, he crashed and died. He is buried at Arlington National Cemetery.

314   *"all the years of humiliation":* Taubman, *Khrushchev*, p. 446.

315   *pressure on the Soviet state:* Editorial note, in *FRUS 1958–60*, vol. 10, p. 510.

315   *high-altitude weather research:* NASA files, at http://www.dfrc.nasa.gov/gallery/photo/U-2/HTML/E-5442.html.

315   *"I must tell you a secret":* Taubman, *Khrushchev*, p. 457.

315   *"What did he need all this for":* Ibid.

315   *take responsibility and resign:* Pedlow and Welzenbach, *CIA and the U-2 Program*, p. 180.

316   *"I would like to resign":* Whitman, May 9, 1960, entry, May 1960 folder, box 11, ACW Diary Series, Whitman File.

316   *authorized flights, the statement added:* State Department's May 9, 1960, press release, May 11, 1960, folder, box 67, Pre–Press Conference Material, Staff Files, Hagerty Papers.

316   *"betrayal by General Eisenhower":* Taubman, *Khrushchev*, p. 458.

316   *"a distasteful but vital necessity":* State Department's May 9, 1960, press release.

316 *unlikely to overreact to it:* Memo from Ed McCabe to Whitman on senators' breakfast, May 11, 1960, Staff Notes, May 1960 (2), box 50, DDE Diary Series, Whitman File.

317 *"at an end":* Memorandum of Conference with the President, May 15, 1960, 4:30 p.m., Staff Notes, May 1960 (1), box 50, DDE Diary Series, Whitman File.

317 *"If this matter":* Ibid.

317 *heartwarming words:* Ibid.

318 *"wildly chaotic day":* New York Herald Tribune, European ed., May 18, 1960.

318 *grilling steaks:* John Eisenhower, exchange with author, Sept. 30, 2010.

318 *anyone from his administration argue otherwise:* Kistiakowsky, *Scientist at the White House,* pp. 335–36.

318 *"I leave Paris with":* DDE to de Gaulle, May 18, 1960, doc. 1538, HP.

CHAPTER 18: REJECTION

319 *"It is terrible":* Ann Whitman, June 11, 1959, entry, June 1959 (2) folder, box 10, ACW Diary Series, Whitman File.

320 *why the antagonism ran so deep:* Whitman, March 25, 1960, entry, March 1960 (1) folder, box 11, ACW Diary Series, Whitman File.

320 *pursue the presidency against each other:* Moos to DDE, memo, April 14, 1960, Staff Notes April 1960 (2) folder, box 49, DDE Diary Series, Whitman File.

321 *"completely untrustworthy":* Whitman, Feb. 3, 1959, entry, Feb. 1959 (2) folder, box 10, ACW Diary Series, Whitman File.

321 *compared to how Johnson described Ike:* Ibid.

321 *Kennedy's candidacy as well:* Memorandum of Conversation with the President, May 18, 1960, Staff Notes May 1960 (1) folder, box 50, DDE Diary Series, Whitman File.

322 *third or fourth tally:* Los Angeles Times, July 10, 1960.

322 *his inaccurate predictions that week:* Los Angeles Times, July 14, 1960.

322 *as about the new Democratic pairing:* Los Angeles Times, July 15, 1960.

322 *"To your hands I pray":* DDE to Nixon, telegram, July 27, 1960, July 1960 folder, box 11, ACW Diary Series, Whitman File.

323 *mirrored Ike's own preferences:* Ibid. Stephen Ambrose records that Eisenhower was disappointed with the selection of Lodge, having hoped "up to the end" that either Anderson or Gruenther would receive the nomination (*Eisenhower, the President,* p. 598). He supplies no citation for that claim, which is undermined by the telegram and other evidence in the Eisenhower Papers, as well as by Nixon's memoir, *Six Crises,* in which he states that Ike favored Lodge (pp. 317–18).

323 *apologized profusely:* Whitman, July 31, 1960, entry, July 1960 folder, box 11, ACW Diary Series, Whitman File.

324 *"If you give me a week":* This exchange comes from the president's news conference of Aug. 24, 1960, APP.

324 *it was too late:* Hagerty, oral history interview, p. 521.

325 *"The Vice President":* Whitman, Aug. 30, 1960, entry, Aug. 1960 (1) folder, box 11, ACW Diary Series, Whitman File.

325   *"What for?"*: Hughes, *Ordeal of Power*, p. 318.

325   *"the situation remains so confused"*: DDE, Aug. 16, 1960, entry, DDE Diary, Whitman File, in *FRUS South and Southeast Asia, 1958–60*, vol. 16, p. 802.

325   *at a Laotian airport*: Ibid., pp. 1003–4.

325   *resupply the government*: Memorandum for the Record of a Telephone Conversation Between the President and the President's Staff Assistant, Dec. 14, 1960, DDE Diary, Whitman File, in ibid., pp. 1008–9.

325   *fighting unilaterally in the region*: Memorandum of a Conference with the President, Dec. 31, 1960, DDE Diary, Whitman File, in ibid., pp. 1024–29.

326   *invited Belgian troops to protect whites there*: 453rd NSC Meeting, July 25, 1960, box 12, NSC Series, Whitman File.

326   *forgot even to bring money*: UN Mission to State Department, memo, July 25, 1960, in *FRUS 1958–60*, vol. 14, *Africa*, p. 351. See also: 453rd NSC Meeting.

326   *under Soviet protection*: Bureau of Intelligence and Research to Secretary of State, memo, July 25, 1960, in ibid., p. 355.

326   *proposed a three-week tour of the United States*: 453rd NSC Meeting.

326   *"are trying to take control of this"*: Memorandum of Conference with the President, Aug. 1, 1960, in *FRUS 1958–60*, vol. 14, *Africa*, p. 377.

326   *"we would all be in the fight"*: 454th NSC Meeting, Aug. 1, 1960, box 12, NSC Series, Whitman File.

327   *"Decisive period not far off"*: Untitled CIA cable, Aug. 18, 1960, available through CIA Lumumba FOIA files.

327   *"was in Soviet pay"*: 456th NSC Meeting, Aug. 18, 1960, box 13, NSC Series, Whitman File.

327   *"too ghastly to contemplate"*: Ibid.

327   *"came across to me"*: "Alleged Assassination Plots Involving Foreign Leaders," *An Interim Report of the Select Committee to Study Governmental Operations with Respect to Intelligence Activities*, known generally as the Church Committee, p. 55.

327   *"throw Lumumba out by peaceful means"*: 456th NSC Meeting.

327   *"fall into a river of crocodiles"*: DDE, Sept. 19, 1960, entry, DDE Diary Series, Whitman File, in *FRUS 1958–60*, vol. 14, *Africa*, p. 495.

327   *no methods as off-limits*: Church Committee, p. 61.

328   *running the government*: Congo Embassy to State Department, telegram, Sept. 18, 1960, in *FRUS 1958–60*, vol. 14, *Africa*, p. 494.

329   *U.S. military strength*: CIA briefings of Kennedy and Johnson, July 23 and 28, 1960. Details in Allen Dulles memorandum of Aug. 3, contained in Dulles Papers and available online at http://www.thespacereview.com/archive/523.pdf.

329   *contested by official estimates, if not outright false*: For a particularly comprehensive study of Kennedy's statements regarding the missile gap, see Christopher A. Preble, "Who Ever Believed in the 'Missile Gap'?" *Presidential Studies Quarterly* 33, no. 4 (Dec. 2003).

329   *"the spread of communist influence"*: Kennedy speech in Houston, Sept. 2, 1960.

330   *the Soviet premier was not done yet*: *Los Angeles Times*, Oct. 2, 1960.

330   *gave up and adjourned the session*: *Los Angeles Times*, Oct. 13, 1960.

330 *led in fourteen states with 123 votes:* Associated Press survey, Oct. 2, 1960.

330 *more thoughtful, less glib:* Whitman, Oct. 14, 1960, entry, Oct. 1960 (1) folder, box 11, ACW Diary Series, Whitman File.

330 *"Things I shall never understand":* Ibid.

331 *have the senator intervene:* Taylor Branch, *Parting the Waters,* p. 361.

331 *dressed down Shriver and Wofford:* Ibid., pp. 364–68.

331 *"Imagine Martin Luther King":* Ibid., p. 370.

332 *"the right kind of leadership":* Pre-election Address, Nov. 7, 1960, box 38, Speech Series, Whitman File.

332 *"The first four ballots cast":* DDE to Nixon, cable, Nov. 8, 1960, doc. 1695, HP.

332 *"I want to express to you both":* DDE to Nixon, Nov. 9, 1960, doc. 1699, HP.

332 *worst of his life:* Slater, *The Ike I Knew,* p. 230.

332 *"down the drain":* Whitman, Nov. 10, 1960, entry, Nov. 1960 folder, box 11, ACW Diary Series, Whitman File. This file was inexplicably missing from the DDEPL archives in early 2011.

333 *"like I had been hit":* DDE to Murphy, Nov. 20, 1960, doc. 1711, HP.

333 *cost the Republican ticket:* Slater, *The Ike I Knew,* p. 230.

333 *"just do not give a damn":* Memorandum for the Record, Dec. 28, 1960, Staff Notes Dec. 1960 folder, box 55, DDE Diary Series, Whitman File.

333 *"the hell with them":* Ibid.

333 *do anything he was asked:* Whitman, Dec. 29, 1960, entry, Dec. 1960 folder, box 11, ACW Diary Series, Whitman File.

334 *machine guns, and possibly tanks:* Briefings Dec. 1960, box 55, DDE Diary Series, Whitman File. Although the quoted document is undated, it was filed with briefing materials from Dec. 1960, so it appears to be an analysis presented late in the year. It is titled "Military Buildup in Cuba—CIA Rpt."

334 *"We shall seek and use":* DDE to Macmillan, Aug. 8, 1960, doc. 1606, HP.

334 *presumably would support it:* Herter to DDE, memo, Dec. 2, 1960, Christian Herter Dec. 1960 folder, box 13, Dulles-Herter Series, Whitman File.

334 *"He recognized that some day":* Jan. 12, 1961, entry, Staff Notes Jan. 1961 folder, box 55, DDE Diary Series, Whitman File.

334 *"perhaps the real point":* Ibid.

335 *for at least several months:* Ibid.

335 *rather as a relic:* Whitman, Aug. 19, 1960, entry, Aug. 1960 (1) folder, box 11, ACW Diary Series, Whitman File.

335 *worried about becoming bored:* Hagerty, oral history interview, pp. 548–49.

335 *"The festivities":* Susan Eisenhower, *Mrs. Ike,* p. 301.

335 *kept a light schedule:* Dec. 23–26, 1960, Presidential Appointment Books, DDEPL.

335 *"During my entire life":* DDE to Alfred Gruenther, Dec. 26, 1960, doc. 1743, HP. Because Eisenhower sent the letter to a number of friends, copies of it appear in various places; the citation here merely refers to one of the most easily accessed.

CHAPTER 19: FAREWELL

336 *"message of leave-taking and farewell":* Eisenhower's Farewell Address is widely available in transcript and audio and video formats. Unless otherwise noted,

quotations in this chapter are taken from the reading copy on file with DDEPL, as checked against the videotaped version of the speech as delivered.

337 *say something meaningful:* Malcolm Moos, oral history interview, p. 33.

337 *Congress and the American people:* Moos memo for the record, May 20, 1959, Farewell Address (1) folder, box 16, Arthur Larson and Malcolm C. Moos Records, DDEPL.

337 *the American leader whom Eisenhower's career most resembled:* H. P. Harding to Andy Goodpaster, April 6, 1960, Farewell Address (1) folder, box 16, Larson and Moos Records.

337 *it no longer seems visionary:* Ellis, *His Excellency: George Washington,* pp. 230–37.

337 *"The great rule of conduct":* Text of Washington's Farewell Address courtesy of the Avalon Project of Yale Law School, at http://avalon.law.yale.edu/18th _century/washing.asp.

339 *not sharp breaks or impulsive leaps:* Memorandum for File, Ideas for 1961 State of the Union, Oct. 31, 1960, Chronological (1) folder, Williams Papers.

339 *"best year we've had in the missile business":* Bernard A. Schriever, interview, *U.S. News & World Report,* Jan. 23, 1961.

340 *"Billions of dollars":* Undated draft, styled at "Commencement," Farewell Address (2) folder, box 16, Larson and Moos Records. See also Oct. 31, 1960, Chronological (1) folder, Williams Papers.

340 *had been to swear him in:* Moos, oral history interview, p. 9.

340 *"did not think that Dr. Moos":* Ann Whitman, Sept. 30, 1958, entry, Sept. 1958 folder, box 10, ACW Diary Series, Whitman File.

340 *wondered about Moos's influence:* Schlesinger, *White House Ghosts,* p. 96. As Moos himself noted of the influence of presidential aides: "I don't think you push a President in the direction of the way he does not want to move" (oral history, p. 28).

340 *"sometimes thought the varnish":* Moos, oral history interview, p. 18.

340 *"You lose an audience after 10 minutes":* Ibid., p. 25. Moos recalled that Ike seemed especially concerned with keeping remarks short after his stroke.

340 *"lock in like a target-acquisition radar":* Williams to Martin Teasley, Oct. 28, 1986, Letters 1985–88, Williams Papers.

340 *which his brother did extensively:* Undated drafts along with notes from Whitman to Moos, Farewell Address (9) folder, box 16, Larson and Moos Records.

341 *notably more modest:* These and other changes are recorded in the extensive files at DDEPL pertaining to the address. Those files were invaluably supplemented in 2010 by the discovery of a host of heretofore missing drafts and notes, recovered by Moos's son and daughter from the family boathouse in Minnesota. I reported that discovery for the *New Yorker* in Dec. 2010.

341 *"The idea of trying to get anyone":* Whitman to DDE and Moos, notes, Dec. 14, 1960, Farewell Address (1) folder, box 16, Larson and Moos Records.

343 *"the most challenging message":* DDE, *Waging Peace,* p. 616.

343 *scientific-technological elite:* These passages are from audio and video tapes of the speech as delivered. They depart slightly from transcripts of the address, including the one used by Eisenhower in *Waging Peace.*

344 *idea was dropped:* Although not privy to the newly discovered materials, Schlesinger deftly described the process of writing and editing the speech in *White House Ghosts*, pp. 97–100.

344 *"Dwight Eisenhower will retire":* New York Times, Jan. 20, 1961.

345 *"Surely the people are proud":* Los Angeles Times, Jan. 19, 1961.

346 *initial estimates for fighting the entire war:* Center for Public Integrity, "Special Report: Windfalls of War," at http://projects.publicintegrity.org/wow/.

346 *seemed profoundly true:* Other costs, including the long-term health care of those wounded, as well as the lost productivity of the dead and those unable to work again, pushed some estimates of American expense in Iraq to more than $3 trillion (see, for instance, Linda J. Bilmes and Joseph E. Stiglitz, *Washington Post*, March 9, 2008).

346 *full participation in politics: Citizens United v. Federal Election Commission*, 558 U.S. 50 (2010).

347 *lined up before a tree and shot:* De Witte, *Assassination of Lumumba*, pp. 120–21.

347 *aides to the two presidents, attended as well:* Memorandum for Record, Jan. 19, 1961, John F. Kennedy 1960–61 (2) folder, box 2, Augusta–Walter Reed Series, Post-presidential Papers, DDEPL.

347 *his final moments in office:* Ibid.

348 *"Let every nation know":* Kennedy Inaugural Address, Jan. 20, 1961, APP.

348 *"hear, hear":* David Eisenhower, *Going Home*, p. 6. Susan Eisenhower describes the return home differently in her book, *Mrs. Ike*, and it is no surprise that two siblings, still young at the time, would recall the evening differently. I have relied on David's account because John Eisenhower, their father, says it conforms to his memory as well.

349 *"Dad was not a happy ex-president":* John Eisenhower, interview with author, Oct. 7, 2010.

349 *"Damn, they've had me busy":* Ibid.

349 *but he was not immune to it:* Slater, *The Ike I Knew*, p. 240.

349 *"are not particularly flattering":* DDE to Anderson, Sept. 6, 1961, President Eisenhower 1957–62 (3) folder, box 287, Anderson Papers.

349 *"men who confuse":* DDE to McCone, Feb. 13, 1968, John McCone 1968 folder, box 12, Name Series, Post-presidential Papers.

350 *"I certainly have learned a lot since":* There are various renderings of this exchange. This comes from a Nov. 8, 1966, interview of DDE by Malcolm Moos in Kennedy folder, box 2, Augusta–Walter Reed Series, Post-presidential Papers.

350 *and stretched over years:* Rives, "Ambrose and Eisenhower," at http://hnn.us/articles/126705.html.

351 *"I feel sure that the book":* John Eisenhower to DDE, July 20, 1965, AP-1 Pat Morin folder, box 2, Post-presidential Papers.

351 *critical of his war and presidential records:* Rives, "Ambrose and Eisenhower."

351 *"was a comfort to me and my family":* Exchange of letters of Aug. 10 and 15, 1963, Kennedy 1962–67 (1) folder, box 2, Augusta–Walter Reed Series, Post-presidential Papers.

351 *"join as one man":* David Eisenhower, *Going Home*, p. 121.

351 *"a little bit bewildered":* John Eisenhower, interview with author, Oct. 7, 2010.

352 *"is just plain dumb":* David Eisenhower, *Going Home*, p. 149.

352 *fulminated about "kooks" and "hippies":* Craig Allen, *Eisenhower and the Mass Media*, p. 197.

352 *"in essence, futile":* DDE to Karson, draft, Feb. 3, 1966, K (3) folder, box 36, 1966 Principal File, Post-presidential Papers.

352 *deleted the revealing sentence:* DDE to Harlow, Feb. 7, 1966, K (3) folder, box 36, 1966 Principal File, Post-presidential Papers.

353 *"He is now even more mature":* DDE to Humphrey, July 21, 1967, Politics 1967–68 folder, box 2, Augusta–Walter Reed Series, Post-presidential Papers.

353 *"He is a man of great courage":* Morin article submitted for Eisenhower review, Sept. 30, 1968, PU-3 Written About the General (1) folder, box 27, 1968 Principal File, Post-presidential Papers.

353 *make a statement for Nixon, as did John:* John Eisenhower, interview with author, Oct. 7, 2010.

353 *soon-to-be family connection:* David Eisenhower, *Going Home*, p. 256.

353 *"in the White House in January 1969":* New York Times, July 19, 1968.

354 *"let's win this one for Ike":* Nixon address accepting the nomination, Aug. 8, 1968, APP.

354 *"He was an old man":* David Eisenhower, *Going Home*, p. 269.

354 *on March 28, 1969, Dwight Eisenhower died:* John Eisenhower, *Strictly Personal*, pp. 336–37.

BIBLIOGRAPHY

ABBREVIATIONS AND SHORTHAND DESCRIPTIONS

APP: The American Presidency Project. Online reproductions of public presidential material, including transcripts of news conferences, some correspondence, and public statements. The project, housed at the University of California, Santa Barbara, is accessible online at http://www.presidency.ucsb.edu.

CSL: California State Library, Sacramento

DDEPL: Dwight D. Eisenhower Presidential Library, Abilene, Kans.

FRUS: *Foreign Relations of the United States* (references to this material specify the title and volume; in many instances, documents in *FRUS* and those from various libraries are duplicative; citations in the text refer to where I located them)

HI: Hoover Institution, Stanford, Calif.

HP: Hopkins Papers. This shorthand refers to the Johns Hopkins collection of Eisenhower's presidential papers (a subset of the Eisenhower Library's holdings devoted mostly to Eisenhower's correspondence). The Hopkins collection is available online at http://www.eisenhowermemorial.org/presidential-papers/index.htm.

HSTL: Harry S. Truman Library, Independence, Mo.

MD, LOC: Manuscript Division, Library of Congress, Washington, D.C.

Whitman File: This is common shorthand for reference to Dwight D. Eisenhower, Papers as President, Main White House File, DDEPL. (Note: Within the Whitman file are two notable diary series. The DDE Diary Series contains official documents, correspondence, and details of Eisenhower's schedule. The ACW Diary Series is a collection of Whitman's notes and observations of Eisenhower as president.)

SELECTED BOOKS

Abraham, Henry J. *Justices and Presidents: A Political History of Appointments to the Supreme Court.* 3rd ed. New York: Oxford University Press, 1992.

Acheson, Dean. *Present at the Creation: My Years in the State Department.* New York: W. W. Norton, 1969.

Adams, Sherman. *Firsthand Report: The Story of the Eisenhower Administration.* New York: Harper and Brothers, 1961.

Albertson, Dean. *Eisenhower as President.* New York: Hill and Wang, 1963.

Allen, Craig. *Eisenhower and the Mass Media: Peace, Prosperity, and Prime-Time TV.* Chapel Hill: University of North Carolina Press, 1993.

Allen, George E. *Presidents Who Have Known Me.* New York: Simon and Schuster, 1960.

Alsop, Joseph, and Turner Catledge. *The 168 Days.* New York: Doubleday, 1938.

Ambrose, Stephen E. *Eisenhower, the President.* New York: Simon and Schuster, 1984.

———. *Eisenhower, Soldier and President.* New York: Simon and Schuster, 1990.

———. *Ike's Spies: Eisenhower and the Espionage Establishment.* Jackson: University Press of Mississippi, 1999.

Anderson, Jon Lee. *Che: A Revolutionary Life.* New York: Grove Press, 1997.

Angelo, Bonnie. *First Mothers: The Women Who Shaped the Presidents.* New York: Perennial, 2001.

Arnaz, Desi. *A Book.* New York: Warner Books, 1976.

Atkinson, Rick. *An Army at Dawn: The War in North Africa, 1942–1943.* New York: Henry Holt, 2003.

———. *The Day of Battle: The War in Sicily and Italy, 1943–1944.* New York: Henry Holt, 2007.

Axelrod, Alan. *Patton: A Biography.* New York: Palgrave Macmillan, 2006.

Bain, Richard C., and Judith H. Parris. *Convention Decisions and Voting Records.* 2nd ed. Washington, D.C.: Brookings Institution, 1973.

Bekes, Csaba, Malcolm Byrne, and Janos M. Rainer, eds. *The 1956 Hungarian Revolution: A History in Documents.* Budapest: Central European University Press, 2002.

Beschloss, Michael R. *Eisenhower: A Centennial Life.* New York: HarperCollins, 1990.

Bill, James A., and William Roger Louis, eds. *Musaddiq, Iranian Nationalism, and Oil.* London: Tauris, 1988.

Bird, Kai, and Martin J. Sherwin. *American Prometheus: The Triumph and Tragedy of J. Robert Oppenheimer.* New York: Vintage Books, 2005.

Black, Hugo L., and Elizabeth Black. *Mr. Justice and Mrs. Black: The Memoirs of Hugo L. Black and Elizabeth Black.* New York: Random House, 1986.

Blumenson, Martin. *Patton: The Man Behind the Legend, 1885–1945.* New York: William Morrow and Company, 1985.

Blumenson, Martin, ed. *The Patton Papers, 1940–1945.* Boston: Houghton Mifflin Company, 1957.

Botti, Timothy J. *Ace in the Hole: Why the United States Did Not Use Nuclear Weapons in the Cold War, 1945 to 1965.* Westport, Conn.: Greenwood Press, 1996.

Boyle, Peter G. *Eisenhower: Profiles in Power.* Harlow, U.K.: Pearson Education, 2005.

Branch, Taylor. *Parting the Waters: America in the King Years, 1954–63.* New York: Simon and Schuster, 1988.

Branyan, Robert L., and Lawrence H. Larsen. *The Eisenhower Administration, 1953–1961: A Documentary History.* New York: Random House, 1971.

Brownell, Herbert. *Advising Ike: The Memoirs of Attorney General Herbert Brownell.* Lawrence: University Press of Kansas, 1993.

Butcher, Harry C. *Three Years with Eisenhower: The Personal Diary of Captain Harry C. Butcher, USNR, Naval Aide to General Eisenhower, 1942 to 1945.* London: Heinemann, 1946.

Carson, Rachel. *Silent Spring.* New York: Houghton Mifflin, 1962.

Chernus, Ira. *Eisenhower's Atoms for Peace.* College Station: Texas A&M University Press, 2002.

Childs, Marquis. *Eisenhower: Captive Hero: A Critical Study of the General and the President.* New York: Harcourt, Brace, 1958.

Conboy, Kenneth, and James Morrison. *Feet to the Fire: CIA Covert Operations in Indonesia, 1957–1958.* Annapolis, Md.: Naval Institute Press, 1999.

Craig, Campbell. *Destroying the Village: Eisenhower and Thermonuclear War.* New York: Columbia University Press, 1998.

Craig, Campbell, and Fredrik Logevall. *America's Cold War: The Politics of Insecurity.* Cambridge, Mass.: Belknap Press of Harvard University Press, 2009.

Cray, Ed. *General of the Army: George C. Marshall, Soldier and Statesman.* New York: Cooper Square Press, 2000.

Crosswell, D. K. R. *Beetle: The Life of General Walter Bedell Smith.* Lexington: University Press of Kentucky, 2010.

Cullather, Nick. *Secret History: The CIA's Classified Account of Its Operations in Guatemala, 1952–1954.* Stanford, Calif.: Stanford University Press, 1999.

DeGregorio, William A. *The Complete Book of U.S. Presidents.* Fort Lee, N.J.: Barricade Books, 2005.

D'Este, Carlo. *Eisenhower: A Soldier's Life.* New York: Henry Holt, 2002.

———. *Patton: A Genius for War.* New York: HarperCollins, 1995.

De Witte, Ludo. *The Assassination of Lumumba.* Translated by Ann Wright and Renee Fenby. New York: Verso, 2001.

Dobbs, Michael. *One Minute to Midnight: Kennedy, Khrushchev, and Castro on the Brink of Nuclear War.* New York: Alfred A. Knopf, 2008.

Dockrill, Saki. *Eisenhower's New-Look National Security Policy, 1953–61.* London: Macmillan, 1996.

Douglas, William O. *The Autobiography of William O. Douglas: The Court Years, 1939–1975.* New York: Random House, 1980.

Dudziak, Mary L. *Cold War Civil Rights: Race and the Image of American Democracy.* Princeton, N.J.: Princeton University Press, 2000.

Eisenhower, David. *Going Home to Glory: A Memoir of Life with Dwight D. Eisenhower, 1961–1969.* With Julie Nixon Eisenhower. New York: Simon and Schuster, 2010.

Eisenhower, Dwight D. *At Ease: Stories I Tell to Friends.* Garden City, N.Y.: Doubleday, 1967.

———. *Crusade in Europe.* New York: Doubleday, 1948; Baltimore: Johns Hopkins University Press, 1997.

———. *The Eisenhower Diaries.* Edited by Robert H. Ferrell. New York: W. W. Norton, 1981.

―――――. *Letters to Mamie.* Edited and with commentary by John S. D. Eisenhower. Garden City, N.Y.: Doubleday, 1977.

―――――. *Mandate for Change: The White House Years, 1953–56.* New York: Doubleday, 1963.

―――――. *Waging Peace: The White House Years, 1956–1961.* New York: Doubleday, 1965.

Eisenhower, John S. D. *General Ike: A Personal Reminiscence.* New York: Free Press, 2003.

―――――. *Strictly Personal: A Memoir.* Garden City, N.Y.: Doubleday, 1974.

Eisenhower, Susan. *Mrs. Ike: Memories and Reflections on the Life of Mamie Eisenhower.* New York: Farrar, Straus and Giroux, 1996.

Ellis, Joseph. *His Excellency: George Washington.* New York: Random House, 2004.

Evans, M. Stanton. *Blacklisted by History: The Untold Story of Senator Joe McCarthy and His Fight Against America's Enemies.* New York: Crown Forum, 2007.

Ewald, William Bragg, Jr. *Eisenhower the President: Crucial Days, 1951–1960.* Englewood Cliffs, N.J.: Prentice-Hall, 1981.

Farago, Ladislas. *The Last Days of Patton.* New York: McGraw-Hill Book Company, 1981.

Feldman, Glenn, ed. *Before Brown: Civil Rights and White Backlash in the Modern South.* Tuscaloosa: University of Alabama Press, 2004.

Friedan, Betty. *The Feminine Mystique.* New York: W. W. Norton, 1962.

Friedman, Joel William. *Champion of Civil Rights: Judge John Minor Wisdom.* Baton Rouge: Louisiana State University Press, 2009.

Gaddis, John Lewis. *The Cold War: A New History.* New York: Penguin Press, 2005.

Gasiorowski, Mark J., and Malcolm Byrne, eds. *Mohammad Mosaddeq and the 1953 Coup in Iran.* Syracuse, N.Y.: Syracuse University Press, 2004.

Greenstein, Fred I. *The Hidden-Hand Presidency: Eisenhower as Leader.* Baltimore: Johns Hopkins University Press, 1994.

Hagerty, James C. *The Diary of James C. Hagerty: Eisenhower in Mid-Course, 1954–1955.* Bloomington: Indiana University Press, 1983.

Halberstam, David. *The Coldest Winter: America and the Korean War.* New York: Hyperion, 2007.

―――――. *The Fifties.* New York: Villard, 1993.

Hemingway, Ernest. *The Old Man and The Sea.* New York: Charles Scribner's Sons, 1952.

Herman, Arthur. *Joseph McCarthy: Reexamining the Life and Legacy of America's Most Hated Senator.* New York: Free Press, 2000.

Holbo, Paul S., and Robert W. Sellen. *The Eisenhower Era: The Age of Consensus.* Hinsdale, Ill.: Dryden Press, 1974.

Holt, Marilyn Irvin. *Mamie Doud Eisenhower: The General's First Lady.* Lawrence: University Press of Kansas, 2007.

Hoopes, Townsend. *The Devil and John Foster Dulles.* Boston: Little, Brown, 1973.

Hughes, Emmet John. *The Ordeal of Power: A Political Memoir of the Eisenhower Years.* New York: Atheneum, 1975.

Immerman, Richard H. *The CIA in Guatemala: The Foreign Policy of Intervention.* Austin: University of Texas Press, 1982.

Jervis, Robert. *The Meaning of the Nuclear Revolution: Statecraft and the Prospect of Armageddon*. Ithaca, N.Y.: Cornell University Press, 1989.

Jian, Chen. *China's Road to the Korean War: The Making of the Sino-American Confrontation*. New York: Columbia University Press, 1994.

Karnow, Stanley. *Vietnam: A History*. New York: Viking, 1983.

Katcher, Leo. *Earl Warren: A Political Biography*. New York: McGraw-Hill, 1967.

Kennedy, David M. *Freedom from Fear: The American People in Depression and War, 1929–1945*. New York: Oxford University Press, 1999.

Kharlamov, M., and O. Vadeyev, eds. *Face to Face with America: The Story of Nikita S. Khrushchev's Visit to the USA*. Honolulu: University Press of the Pacific, 2003.

Khrushchev, Nikita. *Khrushchev in America*. New York: Crosscurrents Press, 1960.

Kinzer, Stephen. *All the Shah's Men: An American Coup and the Roots of Middle East Terror*. Hoboken, N.J.: John Wiley and Sons, 2008.

Kistiakowsky, George B. *A Scientist at the White House: The Private Diary of President Eisenhower's Special Assistant for Science and Technology*. Cambridge, Mass.: Harvard University Press, 1976.

Kluger, Richard. *Simple Justice*. New York: Alfred A. Knopf, 1976.

Korda, Michael. *Ike: An American Hero*. New York: HarperCollins, 2007.

Lasby, Clarence G. *Eisenhower's Heart Attack: How Ike Beat Heart Disease and Held on to the Presidency*. Lawrence: University Press of Kansas, 1997.

Lattimore, Owen. *Ordeal by Slander*. New York: Carroll and Graf, 2004.

Leckie, Robert. *Conflict: The History of the Korean War*. New York: G. P. Putnam's Sons, 1962.

Lilienthal, David E. *The Journals of David E. Lilienthal*. Vols. 2–4. New York: Harper and Row, 1964–69.

Lisio, Donald J. *The President and Protest: Hoover, MacArthur, and the Bonus Riot*. New York: Fordham University Press, 1994.

Macmillan, Harold. *Riding the Storm, 1956–1959*. London: Macmillan, 1971.

Manchester, William. *American Caesar: Douglas MacArthur, 1880–1964*. Boston: Little, Brown, 1978.

Mao Zedong. *Manuscripts Since the Founding of the People's Republic*. Beijing: Central Press of Historical Documents, 1987.

Mazo, Earl. *Richard Nixon: A Political and Personal Portrait*. New York: Harper and Brothers, 1959.

McCallum, John. *Six Roads from Abilene: Some Personal Recollections of Edgar Eisenhower*. Seattle: Wood and Reber, 1960.

McCarthy, Joseph. *Major Speeches and Debates of Senator Joe McCarthy, Delivered in the United States Senate, 1950–1951* (reprinted from the *Congressional Record*). New York: Gordon Press, 1975.

Medhurst, Martin J., Robert L. Ivie, Philip Wander, and Robert L. Scott. *Cold War Rhetoric: Strategy, Metaphor, and Ideology*. East Lansing: Michigan State University Press, 1997.

Morgan, Kay Summersby. *Past Forgetting: My Love Affair with Dwight D. Eisenhower*. New York: Simon and Schuster, 1975.

Morris, Roger. *Richard Milhous Nixon: The Rise of an American Politician*. New York: Henry Holt, 1991.

Neal, Steve. *Harry and Ike: The Partnership That Remade the Postwar World*. New York: Scribner, 2001.

Neufeld, Michael J. *Von Braun: Dreamer of Space, Engineer of War*. New York: Alfred A. Knopf, 2007.

Newman, Roger. *Hugo Black: A Biography*. New York: Pantheon Books, 1994.

Newton, Jim. *Justice for All: Earl Warren and the Nation He Made*. New York: Riverhead, 2006.

Nichols, David A. *A Matter of Justice: Eisenhower and the Beginning of the Civil Rights Revolution*. New York: Simon and Schuster, 2007.

————. *Eisenhower 1956: The President's Year of Crisis, Suez and the Brink of War*. New York: Simon and Schuster, 2011.

Nixon, Richard. *Six Crises*. Garden City, N.Y.: Doubleday, 1962.

Oren, Michael B. *Power, Faith, and Fantasy*. New York: W. W. Norton, 2007.

Pach, Chester J., and Elmo Richardson. *The Presidency of Dwight D. Eisenhower*. Rev. ed. Lawrence: University Press of Kansas, 1991.

Parmet, Herbert S. *Eisenhower and the American Crusades*. New York: Macmillan, 1972.

Patterson, James T. *Grand Expectations: The United States, 1945–1974*. New York: Oxford University Press, 1996.

Pearson, Drew. *Diaries, 1949–1959*. Edited by Tyler Abell. New York: Holt, Rinehart and Winston, 1974.

Perret, Geoffrey. *Eisenhower*. New York: Random House, 1999.

Perry, Mark. *Partners in Command: George Marshall and Dwight Eisenhower in War and Peace*. New York: Penguin Books, 2007.

Pfau, Richard. *No Sacrifice Too Great: The Life of Lewis L. Strauss*. Charlottesville: University Press of Virginia, 1984.

Pinkley, Virgil, and James F. Scheer. *Eisenhower Declassified*. Old Tappan, N.J.: Fleming H. Revell, 1979.

Powe, Lucas A., Jr. *The Warren Court and American Politics*. Cambridge, Mass.: Belknap Press of Harvard University Press, 2000.

Preble, Christopher A. *John F. Kennedy and the Missile Gap*. DeKalb: Northern Illinois University Press, 2004.

Reed, Roy. *Faubus: The Life and Times of an American Prodigal*. Fayetteville: University of Arkansas Press, 1997.

Reeves, Richard. *President Kennedy: Profile of Power*. New York: Simon and Schuster, 1993.

Reston, James. *Deadline: A Memoir*. New York: Random House, 1991.

Richardson, Elmo. *The Presidency of Dwight D. Eisenhower*. Lawrence: Regents Press of Kansas, 1979.

Ridgway, Matthew B. *The Korean War: How We Met the Challenge, How All-Out Asian War Was Averted, Why MacArthur Was Dismissed, Why Today's War Objectives Must Be Limited*. Garden City, N.Y.: Doubleday, 1967.

Roberts, Sam. *The Brother: The Untold Story of Atomic Spy David Greenglass and How He Sent His Sister, Ethel Rosenberg, to the Electric Chair*. New York: Random House, 2001.

Roosevelt, Kermit. *Countercoup: The Struggle for the Control of Iran.* New York: McGraw-Hill, 1979.

Salinger, J. D. *The Catcher in the Rye.* New York: Little, Brown, 1951.

Sanders, Coyne Steven, and Tom Gilbert. *Desilu: The Story of Lucille Ball and Desi Arnaz.* New York: HarperEntertainment, 2001.

Schlesinger, Robert. *White House Ghosts: Presidents and Their Speechwriters from FDR to George W. Bush.* New York: Simon and Schuster, 2008.

Sixsmith, E. K. G. *Eisenhower as Military Commander.* New York: Stein and Day, 1972.

Slater, Ellis D. *The Ike I Knew.* Ellis D. Slater Trust, 1980.

Snead, David L. *The Gaither Committee, Eisenhower, and the Cold War.* Columbus: Ohio State University Press, 1999.

Socolofsky, Homer E., and Huber Self. *Historical Atlas of Kansas.* 2nd ed. Norman: University of Oklahoma Press, 1988.

Stern, Seth, and Stephen Wermeil. *Justice Brennan: Liberal Champion.* New York: Houghton Mifflin Harcourt, 2010.

Stone, I. F. *The Haunted Fifties.* London: Merlin Press, 1963.

Summersby, Kay. *Eisenhower Was My Boss.* New York: Dell, 1948.

Taubman, William. *Khrushchev: The Man and His Era.* New York: W. W. Norton, 2003.

Taylor, Maxwell. *The Uncertain Trumpet.* New York: Harper and Brothers, 1959.

Terzian, Philip. *Architects of Power: Roosevelt, Eisenhower, and the American Century.* New York: Encounter Books, 2010.

Thompson, Nicholas. *The Hawk and the Dove: Paul Nitze, George Kennan, and the History of the Cold War.* New York: Henry Holt, 2009.

Warren, Earl. *The Memoirs of Chief Justice Earl Warren.* Lanham, Md.: Madison Books, 1977.

Weiner, Tim. *Legacy of Ashes: The History of the CIA.* New York: Doubleday, 2007.

Weintraub, Stanley. *MacArthur's War: Korea and the Undoing of an American Hero.* New York: Free Press, 2000.

Weir, William. *Guerrilla Warfare: Irregular Warfare in the Twentieth Century.* Mechanicsburg, Pa.: Stackpole Books, 2008.

Wicker, Tom. *Shooting Star: The Brief Arc of Joe McCarthy.* Orlando, Fla.: Harcourt, 2006.

Wilber, Donald N. *Regime Change in Iran: Overthrow of Premier Mossadeq of Iran, November 1952–August 1953.* Nottingham, U.K.: Spokesman, 2006.

Wilson, Sloan. *The Man in the Gray Flannel Suit.* New York: Simon and Schuster, 1955.

Woodhouse, C. M. *Something Ventured.* London: Granada, 1982.

Zeilig, Leo. *Patrice Lumumba: Africa's Lost Leader.* London: Haus, 2008.

Zelizer, Julian E. *Arsenal of Democracy: The Politics of National Security—from World War II to the War on Terrorism.* New York: Basic Books, 2010.

PAPERS

Sherman Adams Papers, Rauner Library, Dartmouth College (Adams's papers include the unpublished and unedited version of his memoir)

George E. Allen Papers, DDEPL

Robert Anderson Papers, DDEPL

William J. Brennan Jr. Papers, MD, LOC

Gladys Harding Brooks Papers, DDEPL

Herbert Brownell Jr. Papers, DDEPL

Harold H. Burton Papers, MD, LOC

Robert Cutler Papers, DDEPL

John Foster Dulles Papers, 1951–59, DDEPL

Barbara Eisenhower Papers, DDEPL

Dwight D. Eisenhower, Papers as President, Main White House File, DDEPL

Dwight D. Eisenhower, Post-presidential Papers, DDEPL

Dwight D. Eisenhower, Pre-presidential Papers, DDEPL

Felix Frankfurter Papers, MD, LOC

Alfred M. Gruenther Papers, DDEPL

James Hagerty Papers, DDEPL

Edward E. "Swede" Hazlett Papers, DDEPL

C. D. Jackson Papers, 1931–67, DDEPL

Robert Jackson Papers, MD, LOC

George Kistiakowsky Papers, DDEPL

Henry Cabot Lodge Papers, DDEPL

Douglas MacArthur Papers, DDEPL

Malcolm Moos Papers, DDEPL

Richard Nixon Papers, Nixon Presidential Library and Museum, Yorba Linda, Calif.

Robert Oppenheimer Papers, MD, LOC

George Patton Papers, MD, LOC

Wilton B. Persons Papers, DDEPL

William E. Robinson Papers, DDEPL

Walter Bedell Smith Papers, DDEPL

George Sokolsky Papers, HI

Thomas E. Stephens Records, DDEPL

Earl Warren Papers, MD, LOC (Most of Warren's relationship with Eisenhower is captured in these papers. Some details relating to his appointment as chief justice are kept with his gubernatorial papers at the California State Archives in Sacramento.)

Sinclair Weeks Papers, Rauner Library, Dartmouth College

Personal Papers of Ann Whitman, DDEPL (these are Whitman's personal papers, as distinct from her official file)

Ralph E. Williams Papers, DDEPL

Howard Young Papers, DDEPL

Boston Globe

Bulletin of the Atomic Scientists

Chicago Tribune

Cleveland Plain Dealer

Cold War International History Project Bulletin

Commentary

Dartmouth College Alumni Magazine

Harper's Magazine

Indianapolis News
Journal of Cold War Studies
Kansas City Star
Kansas History: A Journal of the Central Plains
Los Angeles Times
MHQ: The Quarterly Journal of Military History
Minneapolis Star-Tribune
Nation
National Review
New Leader
Newsweek
New York Herald (and *Herald Tribune*)
New York Times
Petaluma News
Playboy
Pravda
Progressive
Reviews in American History
Santa Cruz Sentinel
Saturday Evening Post
Stars and Stripes
St. Paul Pioneer Press
Time
Washington Post
Washington Times

NOTABLE ARTICLES

Brichoux, David, and Deborah J. Gerner. "The United States and the 1958 Rebellion in Indonesia." Institute for the Study of Diplomacy, 2002.

Chernus, Ira. "Ambrose on Eisenhower: The Impact of a Single Faulty Quotation." *History News Network*, May 17, 2010.

Clune, Lori. "Stephen Ambrose's Falsifications of the Rosenberg Execution." *History News Network*, May 17, 2010.

Launius, Roger D. "Sputnik and the Origins of the Space Age." NASA History, article is undated but site updated as of Feb. 2, 2005.

Prados, John. "The Perfect Failure." *Quarterly Journal of Military History* 19, no. 3 (2007).

Rives, Timothy D. "Ambrose and Eisenhower: A View from the Stacks in Abilene." *History News Network*, May 17, 2010.

Schlesinger, Arthur, Jr. "The Ike Age Revisited." *Reviews in American History* 11, no. 1 (March 1983).

Spiller, Roger J. "Not War but Like War: The American Intervention in Lebanon." Combat Studies Institute, U.S. Army Command and General Staff College, Fort Leavenworth, Kans., Jan. 1981.

Wade, Gary H. "Rapid Deployment Logistics: Lebanon 1958." Combat Studies Institute, U.S. Army Command and General Staff College, Fort Leavenworth, Kans., Oct. 1984.

Weiss, Leonard. "Atoms for Peace." *Bulletin of the Atomic Scientists* 59, no. 6 (Nov. 1, 2003).

GOVERNMENT DOCUMENTS

American Military History. Army Historical Series. Washington, D.C.: Office of the Chief of Military History, U.S. Army, 1988.

Greenfield, Kent Roberts (general editor). *Command Decisions.* Prepared by the Office of the Chief of Military History, Department of the Army. New York: Harcourt, Brace and Company, 1959.

Haines, Gerald K., and Robert E. Leggett, eds. *CIA's Analysis of the Soviet Union.* Washington, D.C.: Government Reprints Press, 2001.

Pedlow, Gregory W., and Donald E. Welzenbach. *The CIA and the U-2 Program, 1954–1974.* Washington, D.C.: CIA, Center for the Study of Intelligence, 1998.

Republican National Committee. "The 1952 Elections: A Statistical Analysis." Oct. 1953.

Security Resources Panel of the Science Advisory Committee. *Deterrence & Survival in the Nuclear Age.* Washington, D.C., Nov. 7, 1957 (copy obtained from National Security Council Files 5724 [2], box 22, Policy Papers Subseries, NSC Series, White House Office, Office of the Special Assistant for National Security Affairs, DDEPL).

U.S. Atomic Energy Commission. *In the Matter of J. Robert Oppenheimer: Transcript of Hearing Before Personnel Security Board, Washington, D.C., April 12, 1954, Through May 6, 1954.* Washington, D.C.: Government Printing Office, 1954.

U.S. Department of State. Committee on Atomic Energy. *A Report on the International Control of Atomic Energy.* Washington, D.C.: Government Printing Office, 1946.

U.S. Senate. *Executive Sessions of the Senate Permanent Subcommittee on Investigations of the Committee on Government Operations. Congressional Record.* 83rd Cong., 1st and 2nd sess., 1953–54. Made public in 2003.

U.S. Senate. Committee on Foreign Relations. *The United States and the Korean Problem: Documents, 1943–1953.* Washington, D.C.: Government Printing Office, 1953.

ORAL HISTORIES

Adams, Sherman, by Ed Edwin, Oral History Research Office, Columbia University (obtained through DDEPL), 1972.

Briggs, Ellis, Oral History Research Office, Columbia University (obtained through DDEPL), 1973.

Brownell, Herbert, Feb. 24, 1977, DDEPL. Also Earl Warren Oral History Project, University of California, Berkeley.

Eisenhower, Barbara, by Carol Hegeman and Lawrence Eckert, Aug. 20 and Sept. 12, 1983, DDEPL.

Eisenhower, Dwight D., by D. Clayton James, Aug. 26, 1967, DDEPL.

Eisenhower, Dwight D., by Raymond Henle, July 13, 1967, DDEPL.

Eisenhower, Dwight D., by Philip Crowl, July 28, 1964, DDEPL.

Eisenhower, Dwight D., by Ed Edwin, July 20, 1967, DDEPL.

Eisenhower, Dwight D., by Forrest C. Pogue, July 28, 1962, DDEPL.

Eisenhower, Dwight D., interviews by Pat Morin, 1965–67 (although these are not formal oral histories, Morin preserved transcripts, which are housed at DDEPL and filed with the Post-presidential Papers).

Eisenhower, Mamie, by Maclyn Burg and John Whitman, July 20, 1972, DDEPL.

Eisenhower, Milton, by John Luter, Oral History Research Office, Columbia University (obtained through DDEPL), 1967.

Hagerty, James, Eisenhower Administration, by Ed Edwin, Oral History Research Office, Columbia University (obtained through DDEPL), 1968.

Hauge, Gabriel, Eisenhower Administration, by Ed Edwin, Oral History Research Office, Columbia University (obtained through DDEPL), 1972.

Henderson, Loy, Eisenhower Administration, Oral History Research Office, Columbia University (obtained through DDEPL), 1972.

Moos, Malcolm, by T. H. Baker, Oral History Research Office, Columbia University (obtained through DDEPL), 1972.

O'Connor, Roderic, Eisenhower Administration, Oral History Research Office, Columbia University (obtained through DDEPL), 1973.

Warren, Earl, Earl Warren Oral History Project, University of California, Berkeley.

Williams, Ralph, by James Leyerzapf, DDEPL, 1988.

INDEX